Essential
Revision Notes
for MRCP
Third Edition

Dedicated to your success

JAYPEE BROTHERS MEDICAL PUBLISHERS (P) LTD

Kolkata • St Louis (USA) • Panama City (Panama) • New Delhi • Ahmedabad
Bengaluru • Chennai • Hyderabad • Kochi • Lucknow • Mumbai • Nagpur

D1333597

Dedication

To my wife, Marian, and children, Michael, Gabriella and Alicia, who will always inspire

Essential
Revision Notes
for MRCP
Third Edition

edited by

Philip A Kalra MA MB BChir FRCP MD
Consultant Nephrologist and Honorary Reader Hope Hospital,
Salford Royal Hospitals Trust and The University of Manchester

Dedicated to your success

JAYPEE BROTHERS MEDICAL PUBLISHERS (P) LTD

Kolkata • St Louis (USA) • Panama City (Panama) • New Delhi • Ahmedabad
Bengaluru • Chennai • Hyderabad • Kochi • Lucknow • Mumbai • Nagpur

FIRST INDIAN EDITION 2010

Published by
Jitendar P Vij
Jaypee Brothers Medical Publishers (P) Ltd

Corporate Office
4838/24 Ansari Road, Daryaganj, **New Delhi** - 110002, India
Phone: +91-11-43574357, Fax: +91-11-43574314

Registered Office
B-3 EMCA House, 23/23B Ansari Road, Daryaganj, **New Delhi** - 110 002, India
Phones: +91-11-23272143, +91-11-23272703, +91-11-23282021
+91-11-23245672, Rel: +91-11-32558559, Fax: +91-11-23276490, +91-11-23245683
e-mail: jaypee@jaypeebrothers.com, Website: www.jaypeebrothers.com

Offices in India
- **Ahmedabad**, Phone: Rel: +91-79-32988717, e-mail: ahmedabad@jaypeebrothers.com
- **Bengaluru**, Phone: Rel: +91-80-32714073, e-mail: bangalore@jaypeebrothers.com
- **Chennai**, Phone: Rel: +91-44-32972089, e-mail: chennai@jaypeebrothers.com
- **Hyderabad**, Phone: Rel:+91-40-32940929, e-mail: hyderabad@jaypeebrothers.com
- **Kochi**, Phone: +91-484-2395740, e-mail: kochi@jaypeebrothers.com
- **Kolkata**, Phone: +91-33-22276415, e-mail: kolkata@jaypeebrothers.com
- **Lucknow**, Phone: +91-522-3040554, e-mail: lucknow@jaypeebrothers.com
- **Mumbai**, Phone: Rel: +91-22-32926896, e-mail: mumbai@jaypeebrothers.com
- **Nagpur**, Phone: Rel: +91-712-3245220, e-mail: nagpur@jaypeebrothers.com

ISBN 978-81-8448-871-5

Printed by
Rajkamal Electric Press

Contents

Contents

Contributors to Third Edition

Emma Burkitt Wright MBCh MPhil MRCP(UK)
Academic Clinical Fellow, Medical Genetics Research Group and University of Manchester, St Mary's Hospital, Manchester *Genetics*

Louise Byrd MRCOG
Specialist Registrar in Obstetrics and Gynaecology, North West Region *Maternal Medicine*

Colin M Dayan MA MBBS FRCP PhD
Consultant Senior Lecturer in Medicine, Head of Clinical Research, URCN, Henry Wellcome Laboratories for Integrative Neuroscience and Endocrinology, University of Bristol *Endocrinology*

Ben Goorney MBChB FRCP
Consultant Genito-Urinary Physician, Department of Genito-Urinary Medicine, Hope Hospital, Salford *Genito-urinary Medicine and AIDS*

Philip A Kalra MA MB BChir FRCP MD
Consultant Nephrologist and Honorary Reader, Hope Hospital, Salford *Nephrology*

Mike McMahon BSc MBChB FRCP
Consultant Physician and Rheumatologist, Department of Rheumatology, Dumfries and Galloway Royal Infirmary, Dumfries *Immunology & Rheumatology*

John Paisey DM MRCP
Consultant Cardiac Electrophysiologist, Royal Bournemouth Hospital, Bournemouth *Cardiology*

Keith Patterson FRCP FRCPath
Consultant Haematologist, Department of Haematology, University College London Hospitals, London *Haematology*

Jaypal Ramesh MRCP(UK)
Consultant Gastroenterologist, University Hospital of South Manchester, NHS Foundation Trust, Manchester *Gastroenterology*

Geraint Rees BA BMBCh MRCP PhD
Wellcome Senior Clinical Fellow, Institute of Cognitive Neuroscience, University College London *Neurology*

Helen Robertshaw BSc(Hons) MBBS MRCP
Specialist Registrar in Dermatology, Southampton University Hospitals Trust, Southampton
Dermatology

Liz Sampson MBChB MRCPsych MD
Lecturer in Old Age Psychiatry, Royal Free and University College Medical School, University College
London *Psychiatry*

Kirk W Siddals BSc PhD
Research Fellow, Vascular Research, Salford Royal Hospital, Stott Lane, Salford *Molecular Medicine*

Smeeta Sinha MBChB MRCP
Specialist Registrar Nephrology, Salford Royal NHS Foundation Trust, Salford, Manchester
Metabolic Diseases

Katherine Smyth MBChB MRCP FRCOpth
Consultant Opthalmologist, Royal Bolton Hosptial, Bolton *Ophthalmology*

Clare L van Halsema MBChB MRCP DTM&H
Specialist Registrar in Infectious Diseases, Monsall Unit, Department of Infectious Diseases and
Tropical Medicine, North Manchester General Hospital, Manchester *Infectious Diseases*

Angie Wade MSc PhD CStat ILTM
Senior Lecturer in Medical Statistics, Institute of Child Health and Great Ormond Street Hospital,
London *Statistics*

Deborah A Wales MBChB MRCP FRCA
Consultant Respiratory Physician, Nevill Hall Hospital, Brecon Road, Abergavenny, Monmouthshire
Respiratory Medicine

Gary Whitlock BHB MBChB MPH(Hons) PhDFAFPHM
Clinical Research Fellow, Clinical Trial Service Unit, University of Oxford *Epidemiology*

Stephen Waring MRCP(UK)
Consultant Physician in Acute Medicine and Toxicology, The Royal Infirmary of Edinburgh *Clinical
Pharmacology*

Contributors to Second Edition

Professor Philip Baker BMed Sci BM BS DMR FRCOG
Maternity and Fetal Research Director, St Mary's Hospital, Whitworth Park, Manchester *Maternal Medicine*

Louise Byrd MRCOG
Specialist Registrar in Obstetrics and Gynaecology, North West Region *Maternal Medicine*

Colin M Dayan MA MBBS FRCP PhD
Consultant Senior Lecturer in Medicine, Head of Clinical Research, URCN, Henry Wellcome Laboratories for Integrative Neuroscience and Endocrinology, University of Bristol *Endocrinology*

Ben Goorney MBChB FRCP
Consultant Genito-Urinary Physician, Department of Genito-Urinary Medicine, Hope Hospital, Salford *Genito-urinary Medicine and AIDS*

Philip A Kalra MA MB BChir FRCP MD
Consultant Nephrologist, Department of Renal Medicine, Hope Hospital, Salford *Nephrology*

Mike McMahon BSc MBChB FRCP
Consultant Physician and Rheumatologist, Department of Rheumatology, Dumfries and Galloway Royal Infirmary, Dumfries *Immunology & Rheumatology*

Donal J O'Donoghue BSc MBChB FRCP
Consultant Renal Physician, Department of Renal Medicine, Hope Hospital, Salford *Metabolic Diseases*

John Paisey BM MRCP
Specialist Registrar, Cardiology, Wessex Region *Cardiology*

Keith Patterson FRCP FRCPath
Consultant Haematologist, Department of Haematology, University College London Hospitals, London *Haematology*

Geraint Rees BA BMBCh MRCP PhD
Wellcome Senior Clinical Fellow, Institute of Cognitive Neuroscience, University College London *Neurology*

Helen Robertshaw BSc(Hons) MBBS MRCP
Specialist Registrar in Dermatology, Southampton University Hospitals Trust, Southampton
Dermatology

Andrew Robinson MA BM BcH FRCP PhD
Consultant Gastroenterologist, Honorary Clinical Lecturer, Hope Hospital, Salford *Gastroenterology*

Liz Sampson MBChB MRCPsych MD
Lecturer in Old Age Psychiatry, Royal Free and University College Medical School, University College
London *Psychiatry*

Kevin Talbot MBBS MRCP DPhil
MRC-GlaxoSmithKline Clinical Scientist Fellow/Honary Consultant Neurologist, University of Oxford
Molecular Medicine

Angie Wade MSc PhD CStat ILTM
Senior Lecturer in Medical Statistics, Institute of Child Health and Great Ormond Street Hospital,
London *Statistics*

Deborah A Wales MBChB MRCP FRCA
Consultant Respiratory Physician, Nevill Hall Hospital, Brecon Road, Abergavenny, Monmouthshire
Respiratory Medicine

Gary Whitlock BHB MBChB MPH(Hons) PhDFAFPHM
Clinical Research Fellow, Clinical Trial Service Unit, University of Oxford *Epidemiology*

Louise C Wilson BSc MBChB MRCP
Consultant in Clinical Genetics, Clinical and Molecular Genetics Unit, Institute of Child Health,
London *Genetics*

Louise Kenny MBChB Hons, PhD, MRCOG
Clinical Lecturer in Maternal and Fetal Health, Tommy's The Baby Charity funded Maternal and Fetal
Health Research Centre, St Mary's Hospital, Manchester *Maternal Medicine*

Katherine Smyth MBChB MRCP FRCOpth
Consultant Opthalmologist, Royal Bolton Hosptial, Bolton *Ophthalmology*

Stephen Waring MRCP(UK)
Consultant Physician in Acute Medicine and Toxicology, The Royal Infirmary of Edinburgh *Clinical
Pharmacology*

Preface to the Third Edition

The aim of 'Essential Revision Notes for MRCP' is to provide the practising physician with accessible, concise and up-to-date core knowledge across all of the subspecialties of medicine. For candidates who are preparing for the MRCP, it fills the void between those large detailed textbooks and those smaller texts which concentrate specifically on how to pass the examinations. However, this is an invaluable career-long companion many physicians can continue to use as a concise source of reference long after they have successfully collected their exam certificates.

In this 3rd edition the successful style of the Essential Revision Notes series has been maintained placing emphasis upon 'user-friendliness' with succinct text, bullet points and tables. The new double-column format is a further development which enhances readability and revision. Every chapter has been thoroughly revised and updated by experts in the subject.

I would like to thank our skilled team of contributing authors for their outstanding efforts which have ensured that this new edition maintains the standard set by previous editions and allowed publication in timely fashion. Thanks especially go to Cathy Dickens (again) for co-ordinating the book production process at PasTest.

Philip A Kalra
Consultant Nephrologist and Honorary Reader
Salford Royal Hospital and University of Manchester

Chapter 1
Cardiology

CONTENTS

Cardiology

1.1 CLINICAL EXAMINATION

1.1.1 Jugular venous pulse (JVP)

This reflects the right atrial pressure (normal to 3 cm above the clavicle with the subject at 45°). This should fall with inspiration, which increases venous return by a suction effect of the lungs, and with expansion of the pulmonary beds. However, if the neck veins are distended by inspiration this implies that the right heart chambers cannot increase in size due to restriction by fluid or pericardium: **Kussmaul's sign**. Non-pulsatile JVP elevation occurs with superior vena caval obstruction.

Normal waves in the JVP

a wave
Due to atrial contraction – active push up superior vena cava (SVC) and into the right ventricle (may cause an audible S4).

c wave
An invisible flicker in the x descent due to closure of the tricuspid valve, before the start of ventricular systole.

x descent
Downward movement of the heart causes atrial stretch and a drop in pressure.

v wave
Due to passive filling of blood into the atrium against a closed tricuspid valve.

y descent
Opening of the tricuspid valve with passive movement of blood from the right atrium to the right ventricle (causing an S3 when audible).

Pathological waves in the JVP

a waves
Lost in atrial fibrillation, giant in tricuspid stenosis or in pulmonary hypertension with sinus rhythm (atrial septal defect (ASD) will exaggerate the natural a and v waves in sinus rhythm).

Giant v(s) waves
Merging of the a and v waves into a large wave (with a rapid y descent) as pressure continues to increase due to ventricular systole in patients with tricuspid regurgitation.

Steep x descents
Occur in states where there is atrial filling only due to ventricular systole and downward movement of the base of the heart, ie compressed atrial states with tamponade or constrictive pericarditis.

Rapid y descent
Occurs in states where high flow occurs with tricuspid valve opening (eg tricuspid regurgitation (high atrial load) or constrictive pericarditis) – vacuum effect. A slow y descent indicates tricuspid stenosis.

Cannon a waves
Atrial contractions against a closed tricuspid valve due to a nodal rhythm, a ventricular tachycardia, ventricular-paced rhythm (regular), complete heart block or ventricular extrasystoles (irregular). They occur regularly but not consistently in type 1 second-degree heart block.

1.1.2 Arterial pulse associations

- **Collapsing**: aortic regurgitation, arteriovenous fistula, patent ductus arteriosus or other large extra-cardiac shunt
- **Slow rising**: aortic stenosis (delayed percussion wave)
- **Bisferiens**: a double shudder due to mixed aortic valve disease with significant regurgitation (tidal wave second impulse)
- **Jerky**: hypertrophic obstructive cardiomyopathy
- **Alternans**: severe left ventricular failure

- **Paradoxical (pulsus paradoxus)**: an excessive reduction in the pulse with inspiration (drop in systolic BP >10 mmHg) occurs with left ventricular compression, tamponade, constrictive pericarditis or severe asthma as venous return is compromised

---

Causes of an absent radial pulse

- Dissection of the aorta with subclavian involvement
- Iatrogenic: post-catheterisation
- Peripheral arterial embolus
- Takayasu's arteritis
- Trauma

1.1.3 Cardiac apex

An absent apical impulse

The apex may be impalpable in the following situations:

- Obesity/emphysema
- Right pneumonectomy with displacement
- Pericardial effusion or constriction
- Dextrocardia (palpable on right side of chest)

Apex associations

Palpation of the apex beat (reflecting counter-clockwise ventricular movement striking the chest wall during isovolumic contractions) can detect the following pathological states:

- **Heaving**: left ventricular hypertrophy (LVH) (and all its causes), sometimes associated with palpable fourth heart sound
- **Thrusting/hyperdynamic**: high left ventricular volume (eg in mitral regurgitation, aortic regurgitation, patent ductus arteriosus (PDA), ventricular septal defect)
- **Tapping**: palpable first heart sound in mitral stenosis
- **Displaced and diffuse/dyskinetic**: left ventricular impairment and dilatation (eg dilated cardiomyopathy, myocardial infarction (MI))
- **Double impulse**: with dyskinesia is due to left ventricular aneurysm; without dyskinesia in hypertrophic cardiomyopathy (HCM)
- **Pericardial knock**: constrictive pericarditis
- **Parasternal heave**: due to right ventricular hypertrophy (eg ASD, pulmonary hypertension, chronic obstructive pulmonary disease (COPD), pulmonary stenosis)
- **Palpable third heart sound**: due to heart failure and severe mitral regurgitation

1.1.4 Heart sounds

Abnormalities of first heart sounds are given in Table 1.1 and of second heart sounds are given in Table 1.2.

Table 1.1. Abnormalities of the first heart sound (S1): closure of mitral and tricuspid valves

Loud	Soft	Split	Variable
Mobile mitral stenosis	Immobile mitral stenosis	RBBB	Atrial fibrillation
Hyperdynamic states	Hypodynamic states	LBBB	Complete heart block
Tachycardic states	Mitral regurgitation	VT	
Left-to-right shunts	Poor ventricular function	Inspiration	
Short PR interval	Long PR interval	Ebstein's anomaly	

LBBB, left bundle branch block; RBBB, right bundle branch block; VT, ventricular tachycardia

Table 1.2. Abnormalities of the second heart sound (S2): closure of aortic then pulmonary valves (<0.05 s apart)

Intensity	Splitting	
Loud:	**Fixed:**	**Single S2:**
Systemic hypertension (loud A2)	ASD	Severe pulmonary stenosis/aortic stenosis
Pulmonary hypertension (loud P2)		Hypertension
Tachycardic states	**Widely split:**	Large VSD
ASD (loud P2)	RBBB	Tetralogy of Fallot
	Pulmonary stenosis	Eisenmenger syndrome
Soft or absent:	Deep inspiration	Pulmonary atresia
Severe aortic stenosis	Mitral regurgitation	Elderly
		Reversed split S2:
		LBBB
		Right ventricular pacing
		PDA
		Aortic stenosis

A2, aortic second sound; ASD, atrial septal defect; LBBB, left bundle branch block; P2, pulmonary second sound; PDA, patent ductus arteriosus; RBBB, right bundle branch block; VSD, ventricular septal defect

Third heart sound (S3)

Due to the passive filling of the ventricles on opening of the AV valves, audible in normal children and young adults. Pathological in cases of rapid left ventricular filling (eg mitral regurgitation, ventricular septal defect (VSD), congestive cardiac failure and constrictive pericarditis).

Fourth heart sound (S4)

Due to the atrial contraction that fills a stiff left ventricle, such as in LVH, amyloid, HCM and left ventricular ischaemia. It is absent in atrial fibrillation.

Causes of valvular clicks

- **Aortic ejection**: aortic stenosis, bicuspid aortic valve
- **Pulmonary ejection**: pulmonary stenosis
- **Mid-systolic**: mitral valve prolapse

Opening snap (OS)

In mitral stenosis an OS can be present and occurs after S2 in early diastole. The closer it is to S2 the greater the severity of mitral stenosis. It is absent when the mitral cusps become immobile due to calcification, as in very severe mitral stenosis.

1.2   CARDIAC INVESTIGATIONS

1.2.1   Electrocardiography (ECG)

Both the axis and sizes of QRS vectors give important information. Axes are defined:

- $-30°$ to $+90°$: normal
- $-30°$ to $-90°$: left axis
- $+90°$ to $+180°$: right axis
- $-90°$ to $-180°$: indeterminate

Tip – if the QRS is positive in leads 1 and aVF the axis is normal.

The causes of common abnormalities are given in the box on p. 7. ECG strips illustrating typical changes in common disease states are shown in Figure 1.1.

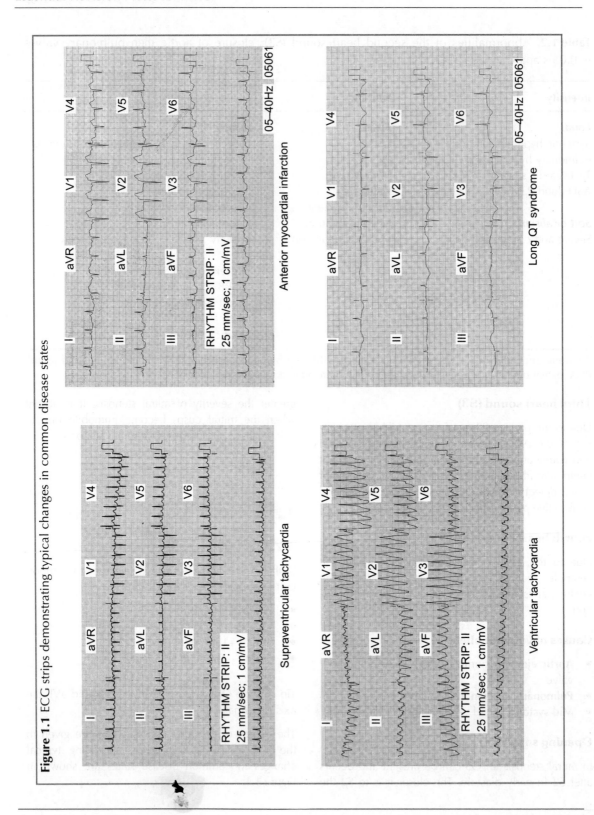

Figure 1.1 ECG strips demonstrating typical changes in common disease states

Causes of common abnormalities in the ECG

- **Causes of left axis deviation**
  - Left bundle branch block (LBBB)
  - Left anterior hemi-block (LAHB)
  - LVH
  - Primum ASD
  - Cardiomyopathies
  - Tricuspid atresia
- **Low-voltage ECG**
  - Pulmonary emphysema
  - Pericardial effusion
  - Myxoedema
  - Severe obesity
  - Incorrect calibration
  - Cardiomyopathies
  - Global ischaemia
  - Amyloid
- **Causes of right axis deviation**
  - Infancy
  - Right bundle branch block (RBBB)
  - Right ventricular hypertrophy (eg lung disease, pulmonary embolism, large secundum ASD, severe pulmonary stenosis, tetralogy of Fallot)
- **Abnormalities of ECGs in athletes**
  - Sinus arrhythmia
  - Sinus bradycardia
  - First-degree heart block
  - Wenckebach phenomenon
  - Junctional rhythm

Clinical diagnoses which can be made from the ECG of an asymptomatic patient

- Atrial fibrillation
- Complete heart block
- HCM
- ASDs (with RBBB)
- Long QT and Brugada syndromes
- Wolff–Parkinson–White (WPW) syndrome (delta waves)
- Arrhythmogenic right ventricular dysplasia (cardiomyopathy)

Short PR interval

This is rarely less than 0.12 s; the most common causes are those of pre-excitation involving accessory pathways or of tracts bypassing the slow region of the atrioventricular (AV) node; other causes do exist.

- **Pre-excitation**
  - WPW syndrome
  - Lown–Ganong–Levine syndrome (short PR syndrome)
- **Other**
  - Ventricular extrasystole falling after P wave
  - AV junctional rhythm (but P wave will usually be negative)
  - Low atrial rhythm
  - Coronary sinus escape rhythm
  - Normal variant (especially in the young)

Causes of tall R waves in V1

It is easy to spot tall R waves in V1. This lead largely faces the posterior wall of the left ventricle (LV) and the mass of the right ventricle. As the overall vector is predominantly towards the bulkier LV in normal situations, the QRS is usually negative in V1. This balance can be reversed in the following situations:

- Right ventricular hypertrophy (myriad causes)
- RBBB
- Posterior infarction
- Dextrocardia
- WPW syndrome with left ventricular pathway insertion (often referred to as type A)
- HCM (septal mass greater than posterior wall)

Bundle branch block and ST-segment abnormalities

Complete bundle branch block is a failure or delay of impulse conduction to one ventricle from the AV node, requiring conduction via the other bundle, and then transmission within the ventricular myocardium; this results in abnormal prolongation of QRS duration ($\geqslant$120 ms) and abnormalities of the normally isoelectric ST segment. In contrast to RBBB, LBBB is always pathological.

- **Causes of LBBB**
  - Ischaemic heart disease (recent or old MI)
  - Hypertension
  - LVH
  - Aortic valve disease
  - Cardiomyopathy
  - Myocarditis
  - Post-valve replacement
  - Right ventricular pacemaker
  - Tachycardia with aberrancy or concealed conduction
  - Ventricular ectopy
- **Causes of RBBB**
  - Normal in the young
  - Right ventricular strain (eg pulmonary embolus)
  - ASD
  - Ischaemic heart disease
  - Myocarditis
  - Idiopathic
  - Tachycardia with aberrancy or concealed conduction
  - Ventricular ectopy
- **Causes of ST elevation**
  - Early repolarisation
  - Acute MI
  - Pericarditis (saddle-shaped)
  - Ventricular aneurysm
  - Coronary artery spasm
  - During angioplasty
  - Non-standard ECG acquisition settings (eg on monitor)
- **Other ST-T wave changes (not elevation)**
  - Ischaemia: ST depression, T inversion and peaking
  - Digoxin therapy: downsloping ST depression
  - Hypertrophy: ST depression, T inversion
  - Post-tachycardia: ST depression, T inversion

- Hyperventilation: ST depression, T inversion and peaking
- Oesophageal/upper abdominal irritation: ST depression, T inversion
- Cardiac contusion: ST depression, T inversion
- Mitral valve prolapse: T wave inversion
- Acute cerebral event (eg subarachnoid haemorrhage):   ST depression, T inversion
- Electrolyte abnormalities

Q waves can be permanent (reflecting myocardial necrosis) or transient (suggesting failure of myocardial function, but not necrosis).

- **Permanent Q waves**
  - Transmural infarction
  - LBBB
  - WPW syndrome
  - HCM
  - Idiopathic cardiomyopathy
  - Amyloid heart disease
  - Neoplastic infiltration
  - Friedreich's ataxia
  - Dextrocardia
  - Sarcoidosis
  - Progressive muscular dystrophy
  - Myocarditis (may resolve)
- **Transient Q waves**
  - Coronary spasm
  - Hypoxia
  - Hyperkalaemia
  - Cardiac contusion
  - Hypothermia

Potassium and ECG changes

There is a reasonable correlation between plasma potassium and ECG changes.

- **Hyperkalaemia**
  - Tall T waves
  - Prolonged PR interval
  - Flattened/absent P waves
- **Very severe hyperkalaemia**
  - Wide QRS
  - Sine wave pattern
  - Ventricular tachycardia/ventricular fibrillation/asystole
- **Hypokalaemia**
  - Flat T waves, occasionally inverted
  - Prolonged PR interval
  - ST depression
  - Tall U waves

ECG changes following coronary artery bypass surgery

- U waves (hypothermia)
- Saddle-shaped ST elevation (pericarditis)
- PR-segment depression (pericarditis)
- Low-voltage ECG in chest leads (pericardial effusion)
- Changing electrical alternans (alternating ECG axis – cardiac tamponade)
- S1Q3T3 (pulmonary embolus)
- Atrial fibrillation
- Q waves
- ST-segment and T-wave changes

Electrocardiographic techniques for prolonged monitoring

- **Holter monitoring**: the ECG is monitored in one or more leads for 24–72 h. The patient is encouraged to keep a diary in order to correlate symptoms with ECG changes
- **External recorders**: the patient keeps a monitor with them for a period of days or weeks. At the onset of symptoms the monitor is placed to the chest and this records the ECG
- **Wearable loop recorders**: the patient wears a monitor for several days or weeks. The device records the ECG constantly on a self-erasing loop. At the time of symptoms, the patient activates the recorder and a trace spanning some several seconds before a period of symptoms to several minutes afterwards is stored
- **Implantable loop recorders**: a loop recorder is implanted subcutaneously in the pre-pectoral region. The recorder is activated by the patient or according to pre-programmed parameters. Again the ECG data from several seconds before symptoms to several minutes after are stored; data are uploaded by telemetry. The battery life of the implantable loop recorder is approximately 18 months

1.2.2 Echocardiography

Principles of the technique

Sound waves emitted by a transducer are reflected back differentially by tissues of variable acoustic properties. Moving structures (including fluid structures) reflect sound back as a function of their own velocity. The signal-to-noise ratio is improved by minimising the distance and number of acoustic structures between the transducer and the object being recorded.

A longitudinal beam differentiating structures by reflectivity plotted against time gives an M-mode image. *Allows accurate measurement of dimensions, eg LA size, end-diastolic dimension.*

A longitudinal beam measuring velocities gives a Doppler velocity – a continuous wave picks up the greatest velocity along the line, a pulsed wave focuses on a specific point and tissue Doppler on a fixed point of myocardium. Velocities can be used to calculate pressure gradients. *Used to measure valve gradients and wall motion parameters.*

A broad beam gives a two-dimensional moving image that can be processed into a three-dimensional image with appropriate echo probe and processing software. *The standard windows permit imaging of the cardiac chambers to assess structural abnormalities and function.*

Sampling multiple velocities within a two-dimensional image and assigning colours to the positive and negative velocities gives a visual image of colour flow mapping. *Ideal for assessing valvular regurgitation.*

Diagnostic uses of echocardiography

Conventional echocardiography is used in the diagnosis of:

- Pericardial effusion and tamponade
- Valvular disease (including large vegetations)
- HCM, dilated cardiomyopathy, LV mass and function
- Cardiac tumours and intracardiac thrombus
- Congenital heart disease (eg PDA; coarctation of the aorta)
- Right ventricular function and pressure

Stress echo is used in the diagnosis of myocardial viability and ischaemia.

Standard contrast echo is used in the diagnosis of right-to-left shunts, especially ASD/VSD.

Transpulmonary contrast echo is used to improve discrimination between the blood pool and the endocardium to improve definition in those subjects whose characteristics lead to poor image quality. It is also used to diagnose LV thrombus and other specific conditions (eg the congenital failure of muscle fibre alignment (known as non-compaction) and apical hypertrophy).

Tissue Doppler imaging is used to improve the accuracy of LV wall motion assessments.

Three-dimensional echo is used to investigate congenital heart disease and in valve studies; it also has research applications.

Transoesophageal echocardiography (TOE) is indicated in the diagnosis of aortic dissection, suspected atrial thrombus, the assessment of vegetations or abscesses in endocarditis, prosthetic valve dysfunction or leakage, intraoperative assessment of LV function, and where there is a technically suboptimal transthoracic echocardiogram.

Intravascular ultrasound gives high-resolution images of coronary arteries; it is useful in assessing plaque size and in stent deployment.

Intracardiac ultrasound images the heart chambers from within; it is used mainly in those with congenital heart disease and in electrophysiological procedures.

Classic M-mode patterns

Due to improvements in real-time image quality M-mode imaging is now used less in clinical practice; it does, however, allow interpretable traces to be printed as still images, and these still occasionally feature in exams. Particular M-mode patterns that have been used in past MRCP exams include:

- **Aortic regurgitation:** fluttering of the anterior mitral leaflet is seen
- **HCM:** systolic anterior motion (SAM) of the mitral valve leaflets and asymmetrical septal hypertrophy (see Figure 1.2)
- **Mitral valve prolapse:** one or both leaflets prolapse during systole
- **Mitral stenosis:** the opening profile of the cusps is flat and multiple echoes are seen when there is calcification of the cusps

1.2.3 Nuclear cardiology: myocardial perfusion imaging (MPI)

Perfusion tracers such as thallium or technetium can be used to gauge myocardial blood flow, both at rest and during exercise- or drug-induced stress. Tracer uptake is detected using tomograms and displayed in a colour scale in standard views.

Lack of uptake may be:

- **Physiological:** due to lung or breast tissue absorption
- **Pathological:** reflecting ischaemia, infarction or other conditions in which perfusion abnormalities also occur (eg HCM or amyloidosis)

Pathological perfusion defects are categorised as fixed (scar) and reversible (viable but ischaemic tissue).

Figure 1.2 Classic valvular disease patterns seen with M-mode echocardiography

AR: Aortic regurgitation
HCM: Hypertrophic cardiomyopathy
MVP: Mitral valve prolapse
MS: Mitral stenosis

MPI can be used to:

- Detect infarction
- Investigate atypical chest pains
- Assess ventricular function
- Determine prognosis and detect myocardium that may be 're-awakened' from hibernation with an improved blood supply (eg after coronary artery bypass grafting (CABG))

1.2.4   Cardiac catheterisation

Coronary and ventricular angiography

Direct injection of radio-opaque contrast into the coronary arteries allows high-resolution assessment of restrictive lesions and demonstrates any anomalies. Left ventriculography provides a measure of ventricular systolic function.

Aortography in cardiac diagnoses

Improved availability and resolution of cross-sectional imaging techniques have greatly reduced the need for diagnostic aortography.

The following can be identified with an aortogram:

- AR
- Coarctation of the aorta
- Aortic dissection

- PDA
- Aberrant subclavian arteries
- Aortic root abscess
- Coronary artery anomalies
- Paraprosthetic AR
- Bypass grafts
- Aortic root dilatation (eg Marfan syndrome)

Right heart catheterisation

Catheterisation of the right heart chambers and pulmonary artery (PA) can be undertaken as a ward investigation using a Swan–Ganz flotation catheter or as part of an X-ray-fluoroscopy-guided cathlab study.

It allows right ventricular and PA angiography, and direct pressure and saturation measurements of the right atrium (RA), right ventricle (RV) and PA. Wedging the catheter in small arteries prevents forward pressure from being transmitted, so the transducer measures the pressure of the pulmonary capillary bed, which is equal to pulmonary venous pressure.

In the cathlab initial manoeuvres such as simultaneous LV catheterisation and contrast injection add to the diagnostic value of the procedure: a gradient between pulmonary wedge (PV) pressure and left ventricular end-diastolic pressure (LVEDP) quantifies mitral stenosis (usually previously diagnosed by echocardiography) and direct pulmonary angiography can be performed. Direct pulmonary angiography has now been largely replaced by CT angiography.

Complications of cardiac catheterisation

Complications are uncommon (approximately 5%, including minor complications); these include contrast allergy, local haemorrhage from puncture sites with subsequent occurrence of thrombosis, false aneurysm or arteriovenous (AV) malformation. Vasovagal reactions are common. Other complications are:

- Coronary dissection (particularly the right coronary artery in women) and aortic dissection or ventricular perforation
- Air or atheroma embolism: in the coronary or other arterial circulations, with consequent ischaemia or strokes
- Ventricular dysrhythmias: can even cause death in the setting of left main stem disease
- Mistaken cannulation and contrast injection into the conus branch of the right coronary artery can cause ventricular fibrillation
- Overall mortality rates are quoted at <1/1000 cases

1.2.5   Exercise stress testing

This is used in the investigation of coronary artery disease, in exertion-induced arrhythmias, and in the assessment of cardiac workload and conduction abnormalities. Exercise tests also give diagnostic and prognostic information post-infarction, and generate patient confidence in rehabilitation after MI. Diagnostic sensitivity is improved if the test is conducted with the patient having discontinued antianginal (especially rate-limiting) medication.

The main contraindications to exercise testing include those conditions where fatal ischaemia or arrhythmias may be provoked, or where exertion may severely and acutely impair cardiac function.

These include the following:

- Severe aortic stenosis or HCM with marked outflow obstruction
- Acute myocarditis or pericarditis
- Pyrexial or coryzal illness
- Severe left main stem disease
- Untreated congestive cardiac failure
- Unstable angina
- Dissecting aneurysm
- Ongoing tachy- or bradyarrhythmias
- Untreated severe hypertension

Indicators of a positive exercise test result

The presence of each factor is additive in the overall positive prediction of coronary artery disease:

- Development of anginal symptoms
- A fall in BP of >15 mmHg or failure to increase BP with exercise
- Arrhythmia development (particularly ventricular)
- Poor workload capacity (may indicate poor left ventricular function)
- Failure to achieve target heart rate (allowing for β-blockers)
- >1 mm down-sloping or planar ST-segment depression, 80 ms after the J point
- ST-segment elevation
- Failure to achieve 9 min of the Bruce protocol due to any of the points listed

Exercise tests have **low specificity** in the following situations (often as a result of resting ST-segment abnormalities):

- Ischaemia in young women with atypical chest pains
- Atrial fibrillation
- LBBB
- WPW syndrome
- LVH
- Digoxin or β-blocker therapy
- Anaemia
- Hyperventilation
- Biochemical abnormalities such as hypokalaemia

1.2.6 24-hour ambulatory blood pressure monitoring

The limited availability and relative expense of ambulatory blood pressure monitoring prevents its use in all hypertensive patients. Specific areas of usefulness include the following situations:

- Assessing for 'white coat' hypertension
- Borderline hypertensive cases that may not need treatment
- Evaluation of hypotensive symptoms
- Identifying episodic hypertension (eg in phaeochromocytoma)
- Assessing drug compliance and effects (particularly in resistant cases)
- Nocturnal blood pressure dipper status (non-dippers are at higher risk)

1.2.7 Computed tomography (CT)

CT has theoretical capability in both anatomical (coronary arteries, chamber dimension, pericardium) and functional (contractility, ischaemia, viability) assessments of the heart. It is the gold standard investigation for:

- Pulmonary thromboembolic disease
- Anatomical assessment of the pericardium (eg in suspected constriction)
- Anomalous coronary artery origins (reliable imaging of the proximal third of major coronary arteries)
- Extramyocardial mediastinal masses

Other indications include assessment of:

- Chamber dimensions
- Myocardial function, perfusion and ischaemia

1.2.8 Magnetic resonance imaging (MRI)

Cardiac MRI is the gold standard technique for assessment of myocardial function, ischaemia, perfusion and viability, cardiac chamber anatomy and imaging of the great vessels. It has a useful adjunctive role in pericardial/mediastinal imaging. Major drawbacks are its contraindication in patients with certain implanted devices (eg pacemakers) and time (consequently also cost), as a full functional study can take about 45 minutes. The contrast used (gadolinium), while not directly nephrotoxic, is subject to increased risk of metabolic toxicity in renally impaired individuals.

Chief indications of cardiac MRI:

- Myocardial ischaemia and viability assessment
- Differential diagnosis of structural heart disease (congenital and acquired)
- Chamber anatomy definition
- Initial diagnosis and serial follow-up of great vessel pathology (especially aortopathy)
- Pericardial and mediastinal structural assessment

1.3 VALVULAR DISEASE AND ENDOCARDITIS

1.3.1 Murmurs

Benign flow murmurs: soft, short systolic murmurs heard along the left sternal edge to the pulmonary area, without any other cardiac auscultatory, ECG or chest X-ray abnormalities. Thirty per cent of children may have an innocent flow murmur.

Cervical venous hum: continuous when upright and is reduced by lying; occurs with a hyperdynamic circulation or with jugular vein compression.

Large AV fistula of the arm: may cause a harsh flow murmur across the upper mediastinum.

Effect of posture on murmurs: standing significantly increases the murmurs of mitral valve prolapse and HCM only. Squatting and passive leg raising increase cardiac afterload and therefore decrease the murmur of HCM and mitral valve prolapse, whilst increasing most other murmurs such as ventricular septal defect, aortic, mitral and pulmonary regurgitation, and aortic stenosis.

Effect of respiration on murmurs: inspiration accentuates right-sided murmurs by increasing venous return, whereas held expiration accentuates left-sided murmurs. The strain phase of a Valsalva manoeuvre reduces venous return, stroke volume and arterial pressure, decreasing all valvular murmurs but increasing the murmur of HCM and mitral valve prolapse.

Classification of murmurs

- **Mid-/late systolic murmurs**
  - Innocent murmur
  - Aortic stenosis or sclerosis
  - Coarctation of the aorta
  - Pulmonary stenosis
  - HCM
  - Papillary muscle dysfunction
  - ASD (due to high pulmonary flow)
  - Mitral valve prolapse
- **Mid-diastolic murmurs**
  - Mitral stenosis or 'Austin Flint' due to aortic regurgitant jet
  - Carey Coombs (rheumatic fever)
  - High AV flow states (ASD, VSD, PDA, anaemia, mitral regurgitation, tricuspid regurgitation)
  - Atrial tumours (particularly if causing AV flow disturbance)
- **Continuous murmurs**
  - PDA
  - Ruptured sinus of Valsalva aneurysm
  - ASD
  - Large AV fistula
  - Anomalous left coronary artery
  - Intercostal AV fistula
  - ASD with mitral stenosis
  - Bronchial collaterals

1.3.2 Mitral stenosis

Two-thirds of patients presenting with this are women. The most common cause remains chronic rheumatic heart disease; rarer causes include congenital disease, carcinoid, systemic lupus erythematosus (SLE) and mucopolysaccharidoses (glycoprotein deposits on cusps). Stenosis may occur at the cusp, commissure or chordal level.

- Anticoagulation for atrial fibrillation protects from 17× increased risk of thromboembolism

Features of severe mitral stenosis

- **Symptoms**
  - Dyspnoea with minimal activity
  - Haemoptysis
  - Dysphagia (due to left atrium enlargement)
  - Palpitations due to atrial fibrillation
- **Chest X-ray**
  - Left atrial or right ventricular enlargement
  - Splaying of subcarinal angle (>90°)
  - Pulmonary congestion or hypertension
  - Pulmonary haemosiderosis
- **Echo**
  - Doming of leaflets
  - Heavily calcified cusps
  - Direct orifice area <1.0 cm^2
- **Signs**
  - Low pulse pressure
  - Soft first heart sound
  - Long diastolic murmur and apical thrill (rare)
  - Very early opening snap, ie closer to S2 (lost if valves immobile)
  - Right ventricular heave or loud P2
  - Pulmonary regurgitation (Graham Steell murmur)
  - Tricuspid regurgitation
- **Cardiac catheterisation**
  - Pulmonary capillary wedge end diastole to left ventricular end-diastolic pressure (LVEDP) gradient >15 mmHg
  - Left atrium (LA) pressures >25 mmHg
  - Elevated RV and PA pressures
  - High pulmonary vascular resistance
  - Cardiac output <2.5 l min^{-1} m^{-2} with exercise

Mitral balloon valvuloplasty

Valvuloplasty using an Inoue balloon requires either a trans-septal or a retrograde approach and is used only in suitable cases where echo shows that:

- The mitral leaflet tips and valvular chordae are not heavily thickened, distorted or calcified
- The mitral cusps are mobile at the base
- There is minimal or no mitral regurgitation
- There is no left atrial thrombus seen on TOE

1.3.3 Mitral regurgitation (MR)

The full structure of the mitral valve includes the annulus, cusps, chordae and papillary musculature, and abnormalities of any of these can cause regurgitation. The presence of symptoms and increasing left ventricular dilatation are indicators for surgery in the chronic setting. Operative mortalities are 2%–7% for valvular replacements in patients with NYHA grade II–III symptoms. Various techniques have revolutionised mitral valve surgery, transforming outcomes from being no better than medical therapy with replacement to almost normal with repair. In skilled surgical hands the repair is tailored to the precise anatomical abnormality.

Functional MR is a term used to describe MR that is due to stretching of the annulus secondary to ventricular dilatation.

Main causes of MR

- Myxomatous degeneration
- Functional, secondary to ventricular dilatation
- Mitral valve prolapse
- Ischaemic papillary muscle rupture
- Congenital heart diseases
- Collagen disorders
- Rheumatic heart disease
- Endocarditis

Indicators of the severity of MR

- Small-volume pulse

- Left ventricular enlargement due to overload
- Presence of S3
- Atrial fibrillation
- Mid-diastolic flow murmur
- Precordial thrill, signs of pulmonary hypertension or congestion (cardiac failure)

Signs of predominant MR in mixed mitral valve disease

- Soft S1; S3 present
- Displaced and hyperdynamic apex (left ventricular enlargement)
- ECG showing LVH and left axis deviation

Mitral valve prolapse

This condition occurs in 5% of the population and is commonly over-diagnosed (depending on the echocardiography criteria applied). The patients are usually female and may present with chest pains, palpitations or fatigue, although it is often detected incidentally in asymptomatic patients. Squatting increases the click and standing increases the murmur, but the condition may be diagnosed in the absence of the murmur by echo. Often there is myxomatous degeneration and redundant valve tissue due to deposition of acid mucopolysaccharide material. Antibiotic prophylaxis before dental or surgical interventions should be recommended for those with a murmur. Mitral valve prolapse is usually eminently suitable for mitral valve repair although this should only be undertaken if the severity of the regurgitation associated with the condition justifies it (see above). Several conditions are associated with mitral valve prolapse (see overleaf), and patients with the condition are prone to certain sequelae.

Sequelae of mitral valve prolapse:

- Embolic phenomena
- Rupture of mitral valve chordae
- Dysrhythmias with QT prolongation
- Sudden death
- Cardiac neurosis

Conditions associated with mitral valve prolapse

- Coronary artery disease
- Polycystic kidney disease
- Cardiomyopathy – dilated cardiomyopathy/HCM
- Secundum ASD
- WPW syndrome
- PDA
- Marfan syndrome
- Pseudoxanthoma elasticum
- Osteogenesis imperfecta
- Myocarditis
- SLE; polyarteritis nodosa
- Muscular dystrophy
- Left atrial myxoma

1.3.4 Aortic regurgitation (AR)

Patients with severe chronic aortic regurgitation (AR) have the largest end-diastolic volumes of those with any form of heart disease and also have a greater number of non-cardiac signs. AR may occur acutely (as in dissection or endocarditis) or chronically when the left ventricle has time to accommodate.

Causes of AR

- **Valve inflammation**
  - Chronic rheumatic
  - Infective endocarditis
  - Rheumatoid arthritis; SLE
  - Hurler syndrome
- **Aortitis**
  - Syphilis
  - Ankylosing spondylitis
  - Reiter syndrome
  - Psoriatic arthropathy

- Aortic dissection/trauma
- Hypertension
- Bicuspid aortic valve
- Ruptured sinus of Valsalva aneurysm
- VSD with prolapse of (R) coronary cusp
- Disorders of collagen
  - Marfan syndrome (aortic aneurysm)
  - Hurler syndrome
  - Pseudoxanthoma elasticum

Eponymous signs associated with AR

- Quincke's sign – nail-bed fluctuation of capillary flow
- Corrigan's pulse – (waterhammer); collapsing radial pulse
- Corrigan's sign – visible carotid pulsation
- De Musset's sign – head nodding with each systole
- Duroziez's sign – audible femoral bruits with diastolic flow (indicating moderate severity)
- Traube's sign – 'pistol shots' (systolic auscultatory finding of the femoral arteries)
- Austin Flint murmur – functional mitral diastolic flow murmur
- Argyll Robertson pupils – aetiological connection with syphilitic aortitis
- Müller's sign – pulsation of the uvula

Indications for surgery

Acute severe AR will not be tolerated for long by a normal ventricle and therefore requires prompt surgery, except in the case of infection, where delay for antibiotic therapy is preferable (if haemodynamic stability allows). At 10 years, 50% of patients with moderate chronic AR are alive, but once symptoms occur deterioration is rapid.

Features of AR indicative of the need for surgery

- **Symptoms of dyspnoea/left ventricular failure**
  - Reducing exercise tolerance
- **Rupture of sinus of Valsalva aneurysm**
- **Infective endocarditis not responsive to medical treatment**
- **Enlarging aortic root diameter in Marfan syndrome with AR**
- **Enlarging heart**
  - End-systolic diameter >55 mm at echo
  - Pulse pressure >100 mmHg
  - Diastolic pressure <40 mmHg
  - Lengthening diastolic murmur
  - ECG: lateral lead T-wave inversion

1.3.5 Aortic stenosis (AS)

Patients often present with the classic triad of symptoms: angina, dyspnoea and syncope. Echo and cardiac catheterisation gradients of >60 mmHg are considered severe and are associated with a valve area <0.5 cm². The gradient may be reduced in the presence of deteriorating left ventricular function or mitral stenosis, or significant AR.

- **Causes of AS**: may be congenital bicuspid valve, degenerative calcification (common in the elderly) and post-rheumatic disease
- **Subvalvular**: causes of aortic gradients include HCM and subaortic membranous stenosis, while **supravalvular** stenosis is due to aortic coarctation, or Williams syndrome (with elfin facies, mental retardation, hypercalcaemia)
- **Sudden death**: may occur in AS or in subvalvular stenosis due to ventricular tachycardia. The vulnerability to ventricular tachycardia is due to LVH
- **Complete heart block**: may be due to calcification involving the upper ventricular septal tissue housing the conducting tissue. This can also occur post-operatively (after valve replacement) due to trauma

- **Calcified emboli**: can arise in severe calcific AS.
- All symptomatic patients should be considered for surgery: operative mortality for AS is predominantly related to the absence (2%–8%) or presence (10%–25%) of left ventricular failure

Indicators of severe AS

- Symptoms of syncope or left ventricular failure
- Signs of left ventricular failure
- Absent A2
- Paradoxically split A2
- Presence of precordial thrill
- S4
- Slow-rising pulse with narrow pulse pressure
- Late peaking of long murmur
- Valve area <0.5 cm² on echocardiography

1.3.6 Tricuspid regurgitation (TR)

Causes of severe TR include the following:

- Functional, due to right ventricular dilatation (commonly co-exists with significant MR)
- Infection. The tricuspid valve is vulnerable to infection introduced by venous cannulation (iatrogenic or through intravenous drug abuse)
- Carcinoid (nodular hepatomegaly and telangiectasia)
- Post-rheumatic
- Ebstein's anomaly: tricuspid valve dysplasia with a more apical position to the valve. Patients have cyanosis and there is an association with pulmonary atresia or ASD and, less commonly, congenitally corrected transposition

1.3.7 Prosthetic valves

Valve prostheses may be metal or tissue (bioprosthetic). Mechanical valves are more durable but tissue valves do not require full lifelong anticoagulation. All prostheses must be covered with antibiotic therapy for dental and surgical procedures; they have a residual transvalvular gradient across them.

Mechanical valves

- **Starr–Edwards**: ball and cage – ejection systolic murmur (ESM) in the aortic area and an opening sound in the mitral position are normal
- **Bjork–Shiley**: single tilt disc – audible clicks without stethoscope
- **St Jude (Carbomedics)**: double tilting discs with clicks

Tissue valves

- **Allografts**: porcine or bovine three-cusp valve – 3 months' anticoagulation sometimes recommended until tissue endothelialisation. No need for long-term anticoagulation if patient is in sinus rhythm
- **Homografts**: usually cadaveric and, again, need no long-term anticoagulation

Infection of prosthetic valves

- Mortality is still as high as 60% depending on the organism
- Within 6 months of implantation, it is usually due to colonisation by *Staphylococcus epidermidis*
- Septal abscesses may cause PR-interval lengthening
- Valvular sounds may be muffled by vegetations; new murmurs may occur
- Mild haemolysis can occur, and is detected by the presence of urobilinogen in the urine
- Dehiscence is an ominous feature requiring urgent intervention

Anticoagulation in pregnancy

Warfarin may cause fetal haemorrhage and has a teratogenicity risk of 5%–30%. This risk is dose-dependent and abnormalities include chondrodysplasia, mental impairment, optic atrophy and nasal

hypoplasia. The risk of spontaneous abortion may be increased. There is no agreed consensus on the ideal strategy: warfarin, unfractionated heparin and low-molecular-weight heparin all have advocates and detractors.

1.3.8 Infective endocarditis

Clinical presentation

Commonly presents with non-specific symptoms of malaise, tiredness and infective-type symptoms. Heart failure secondary to valvular regurgitation or heart block may also occur as may an incidental presentation in the context of another primary infection.

Signs of infective endocarditis

As well as cardiac murmurs detected at auscultation, there are several other characteristic features of infective endocarditis:

- **Systemic signs of fever and arthropathy**
- **Hands and feet**: splinter haemorrhages, Osler nodes (painful), Janeway lesions (painless) and clubbing (late); needle-track signs may occur in arm or groin
- **Retinopathy**: Roth spots
- **Hepatosplenomegaly**
- **Signs of arterial embolisation** (eg stroke or digital ischaemia)
- Vasculitic rash
- *Streptococcus viridans* (α-haemolytic group) are still the most common organisms, occurring in 50% of cases
- Marantic (metastatic-related) and SLE-related (Libman–Sacks) endocarditis are causes of non-infective endocarditis
- Almost any pathogenic organism may be implicated, particularly in the immunocompromised patient

See also Section 1.3.7 on 'Prosthetic valves' and Table 1.3.

Table 1.3. Infective endocarditis

Groups affected by endocarditis	% of all cases of endocarditis
Chronic rheumatic disease	30
No previous valve disease	40
Intravenous drug abuse	10
Congenital defects	10
Prosthetic	10

Management of infective endocarditis

The aim of treatment is to sterilise the valve medically (usually 4–6 weeks of IV antibiotics) then assess whether the valvular damage sustained (eg degree of incompetance) or the risk of recurrence (eg if prosthetic valves) mandates surgical replacement. Earlier operations are only undertaken if clincally necessary as outcomes are poorer.

- **Poor prognostic factors in endocarditis**
  - Prosthetic valve
  - *Staphylococcus aureus* infection
  - Culture-negative endocarditis
  - Depletion of complement levels
- **Indications for surgery**
  - Cardiac failure or haemodynamic compromise
  - Extensive valve incompetence
  - Large vegetations
  - Septic emboli
  - Septal abscess
  - Fungal infection
  - Antibiotic-resistant endocarditis
  - Failure to respond to medical therapy

Antibiotic prophylaxis

The conditions listed in the next box are associated with an increased risk of endocarditis.

- Acquired valvular heart disease with stenosis or regurgitation
- Valve replacement
- Structural congenital heart disease, including surgically corrected or palliated structural conditions, **but excluding isolated ASD, fully repaired VSD or fully repaired PDA, and closure devices that are judged to be endothelialised**
- Previous infective endocarditis
- HCM

Antibiotic and chlorhexidine mouthwash prophylaxis is no longer recommended for dental procedures, endoscopies or obstetric procedures.

Patients should be made aware of non-medical risk-prone activities (eg IV drug use, piercings) and the symptoms of possible endocarditis.

1.4   CONGENITAL HEART DISEASE

Causes of congenital acyanotic heart disease*

- **With shunts**
  - Aortic coarctation (with VSD or PDA)
  - VSD
  - ASD
  - PDA
  - Partial anomalous venous drainage (with ASD)
- **Without shunts**
  - Congenital AS
  - Aortic coarctation

*Associated shunts

Causes of cyanotic heart disease

- **With shunts**
  - Tetralogy of Fallot (VSD)
  - Severe Ebstein's anomaly (ASD)
  - Complete transposition of great vessels (ASD ± VSD/PDA)
- **Without shunts**
  - Tricuspid atresia
  - Severe pulmonary stenosis
  - Pulmonary atresia
  - Hypoplastic left heart

1.4.1 Atrial septal defect (ASD)

ASDs are the most common congenital defects found in adulthood. Rarely, they may present as stroke in young people, due to paradoxical embolus that originated in the venous system and reached the cerebral circulation via right-to-left shunting. Fixed splitting of the second heart sound is the hallmark of an uncorrected ASD. There may be a left parasternal heave and a pulmonary ESM due to increased blood flow. There are three main sub-types:

- **Secundum (70%)**: central fossa ovalis defects often associated with mitral valve prolapse (10%–20% of cases). ECG shows incomplete or complete RBBB with *right* axis deviation. Note that a **patent foramen ovale** (slit-like deficiency in the fossa ovalis) occurs in up to 25% of the population, but this does not allow equalisation of atrial pressures, unlike ASD
- **Primum (15%)**: sited above the AV valves, often associated with varying degrees of mitral and tricuspid regurgitation and occasionally a VSD, and thus usually picked up earlier in childhood. ECG shows RBBB, *left* axis deviation, first-degree heart block. Associated with Down syndrome, Klinefelter syndrome and Noonan syndrome
- **Sinus venosus (15%)**: defect in the upper septum, often associated with anomalous

pulmonary venous drainage directly into the right atrium

Operative closure is recommended with pulmonary-to-systolic flow ratios above 1.5:1. Closure of secundum defects may be performed via cardiac catheterisation.

Holt–Oram syndrome: (triphalangeal thumb with ASD) is a rare syndrome (autosomal dominant with incomplete penetration). It is associated with absence (or reduction anomalies) of the upper arm.

Lutembacher syndrome: a rare combination of an ASD with mitral stenosis (the latter is probably rheumatic in origin).

Investigations for ASDs

Right atrial and right ventricular dilatation may be seen on any imaging technique as may pulmonary artery conus enlargement. Other characteristic features are:

- **Chest X-ray**: pulmonary plethora
- **Echo**: paradoxical septal motion, septal defect and right-to-left flow of contrast during venous injection with Valsalva manoeuvre
- **Catheterisation**: pulmonary hypertension – raised right ventricular pressures and step-up in oxygen saturation between various parts of the right circulation (eg SVC to high right atrium)

Treatment of ASD

There is no specific medical therapy for ASDs; they are managed by either closure (percutaneous or surgical) or clinical and echocardiographic follow-up.

Indications for closure:

- Symptoms (dyspnoea)
- Systemic embolism
- Chamber dilatation
- Elevated right heart pressures
- Significant left-to-right shunt

1.4.2 Ventricular septal defect (VSD)

VSDs are the most common isolated congenital defect (2/1000 births; around 30% of all congenital defects); spontaneous closure occurs in 30%–50% of cases (usually muscular or membranous types). As with ASDs, closure may be performed via cardiotomy or percutaneously.

Indications for closure

- Significant left-to-right shunt
- Associated with other defect requiring cardiotomy
- Elevated right heart pressure
- Endocarditis

- Irreversible pulmonary changes may occur from 1 year of age, with vascular hypertrophy and pulmonary arteriolar thrombosis, leading to Eisenmenger syndrome
- Parasternal thrill and pansystolic murmur are present. The murmur may be ejection systolic in very small or very large defects. With large defects the aortic component of the second sound is obscured, or even a single/palpable S2 is heard; a mitral diastolic murmur may occur. The apex beat is typically hyperdynamic

Once the Eisenmenger complex develops, the thrill and left sternal edge (LSE) murmur abate and signs are of pulmonary hypertension ± regurgitation and right ventricular failure. Surgery should occur earlier to avoid this situation; otherwise a combined heart/lung transplant would be required.

- **Other cardiac associations of VSD**
  - PDA (10%)
  - AR (5%)
  - Pulmonary stenosis
  - ASD
  - Tetralogy of Fallot
  - Coarctation of the aorta

- **Types of VSD**
  - Muscular
  - Membranous
  - AV defect
  - Infundibular
  - Into the right atrium (Gerbode defect)

1.4.3 Patent ductus arteriosus (PDA)

PDA is common in premature babies, particularly female infants born at high altitude; also if maternal rubella occurs in the first trimester. The connection occurs between the pulmonary trunk and the descending aorta, usually just distal to the origin of the left subclavian artery. PDA often occurs with other abnormalities.

Key features of PDA

- A characteristic left subclavicular thrill
- Enlarged left heart and apical heave
- Continuous 'machinery' murmur
- Wide pulse pressure and bounding pulse

Signs of pulmonary hypertension and Eisenmenger syndrome develop in about 5% of cases. Indometacin closes the duct in about 90% of babies while intravenous prostaglandin E_1 may reverse the natural closure (useful when PDA is associated with coarctation, hypoplastic left heart syndrome and in complete transposition of the great vessels, as it will help to maintain flow between the systemic and pulmonary circulations). The PDA may also be closed thoracoscopically or percutaneously.

1.4.4 Coarctation of the aorta

Coarctation can present in infancy with heart failure or in adulthood (third decade) with hypertension, exertional breathlessness or leg weakness. This 'shelf-like' obstruction of the aortic arch, usually distal to the left subclavian artery, is 2–5 times more common in males and is responsible for about 7% of congenital heart defects.

Treatment is by surgical resection, preferably with end-to-end aortic anastomosis, or by balloon angioplasty for recurrence after surgery (which occurs in 5%–10% of cases). Complications may occur despite resection/repair and these include hypertension, heart failure, berry aneurysm rupture, premature coronary artery disease and aortic dissection (in the third or fourth decade of life).

Associations of coarctation

- **Cardiac**
  - Bicuspid aortic valve (and thus AS ± AR) in 10%–20%
  - PDA
  - VSD
  - Mitral valve disease
- **Non-cardiac**
  - Berry aneurysms (circle of Willis)
  - Turner syndrome
  - Renal abnormalities
- **Signs of coarctation**
  - Hypertension
  - Radio–femoral delay of arterial pulse
  - Absent femoral pulses
  - Mid-systolic or continuous murmur (infraclavicular)
  - Subscapular bruits
  - Rib notching on chest X-ray
  - Post-stenotic aortic dilatation on chest X-ray

1.4.5   Eisenmenger syndrome

Reversal of left-to-right shunt, due to massive irreversible pulmonary hypertension (usually due to congenital cardiovascular malformations), leads to Eisenmenger syndrome. Signs of development include:

- Decrease of original pansystolic (left-to-right) murmur
- Decreasing intensity of tricuspid/pulmonary flow murmurs
- Single S2 with louder intensity, palpable P2; right ventricular heave
- Appearance of Graham Steell murmur due to pulmonary regurgitation

- PSM and 'v' waves due to tricuspid regurgitation (TR)
- Clubbing and central cyanosis

Eisenmenger syndrome

- **Causes**
  - VSD (the Eisenmenger complex)
  - ASD
  - PDA
- **Complications of Eisenmenger syndrome**
  - Right ventricular failure
  - Massive haemoptysis
  - Cerebral embolism/abscess
  - Infective endocarditis (rare)

1.4.6   Tetralogy of Fallot

The most common cause of cyanotic congenital heart disease (10%), usually presenting after age 6 months (as the condition may worsen after birth).

Key features

- Pulmonary stenosis (causes the systolic murmur)
- Right ventricular hypertrophy
- VSD
- Overriding of the aorta
- Right-sided aortic knuckle (25%)

Clinical features

- Cyanotic attacks (pulmonary infundibular spasm)
- Clubbing
- Parasternal heave
- Systolic thrill
- Palpable A2
- Soft ejection systolic murmur (inversely related to pulmonary gradient)
- Single S2 (inaudible pulmonary closure)
- ECG features of right ventricular hypertrophy

Possible complications of Fallot's

- Endocarditis
- Polycythaemia
- Coagulopathy
- Paradoxical embolism
- Cerebral abscess
- Ventricular arrhythmias

- Cyanotic attacks worsen with catecholamines, hypoxia and acidosis. The murmur lessens or disappears as the right ventricular outflow gradient increases
- Squatting reduces the right-to-left shunt by increasing systemic vascular resistance; it also reduces venous return of acidotic blood from lower extremities, and hence reduces infundibular spasm
- The presence of a systolic thrill and an intense pulmonary murmur differentiates the condition from Eisenmenger syndrome
- A Blalock shunt operation results in weaker pulses in the arm from which the subclavian artery is diverted to the pulmonary artery

1.4.7 Important post-surgical circulations

Systemic right ventricle

Transposition of the great vessels and similar conditions in which the right ventricle supplies the aorta and the left ventricle supplies the pulmonary artery are now treated by arterial switch. Effectively this is a complete correction.

Prior to the development of the arterial switch procedure, treatment was by 'venous redirection' – the vena cavae redirected via the atria to the left ventricle and the pulmonary veins to the right ventricle via the atria, with the morphological right ventricle then pumping oxygenated blood into the aorta. However, there was a high risk of ventricular dysfunction, valve regurgitation and ventricular arrhythmias in these patients and decompensation would be provoked by development of atrial arrhythmias.

Single ventricular circulation

Individuals born with only one functional ventricle are treated by redirecting the vena cavae directly into the pulmonary arteries (total cavopulmonary correction) and now do very well. Early versions of this operation (the classic Fontan) used the right atrium between the vena cavae, but this often led to atrial dilatation and then fibrillation with a risk of decompensation.

Common congenital circulations

Common congenital circulations are summarised in Table 1.4 overleaf.

1.5 ARRHYTHMIAS AND PACING

Atrial fibrillation (AF) remains the most common cardiac arrhythmia, with incidence increasing with age (Framingham data indicate a prevalence of 76/1000 males and 63/1000 females aged 85–94 years). Atrial flutter frequently co-exists with atrial fibrillation, and although it has a different immediate causal mechanism it is a reflection of the same underlying disease. These arrhythmias assume particular significance because of the stroke risk associated with them.

'SVT' is the term usually used to indicate a presumed re-entry tachycardia involving the AV node or an accessory pathway.

Ventricular tachycardia and ventricular fibrillation are life-threatening conditions, but there is a clear evidence base for the use of implantable cardioverter defibrillators in both primary and secondary prevention (see Appendix II). Anti-arrhythmic drugs or catheter ablation may be useful adjuncts to treatment or, in some cases, they can be used as alternatives to defibrillators.

1.5.1 Bradyarrhythmias

Any heart rate below 60 beats per minute is a bradycardia. A bradyarrhythmia is a pathological bradycardia. Bradyarrhythmias are considered according to their prognostic significance and sympto-

Table 1.4. Common congenital circulations

	Cardinal features	Pulmonary hypertension	Ventricular dysfunction	Ventricular arrhythmias	Endocarditis	Cyanosis	Atrial arrhythmias	Systemic embolism	Treatment of choice
VSD	Pansystolic murmur	May develop	Late feature	If ventricle dilates	High risk in restrictive defects	Only after shunt reverses			Percutaneous or surgical closure for significant shunt or endocarditis
ASD	Fixed split second sound	May develop			Low risk	Only after shunt reverses	Atrial fibrillation, typical and atypical flutter	Associated with paradoxical emboli	Percutaneous or surgical closure for significant shunt or emboli
PDA	Continuous murmur	May develop			High risk	Only after shunt reverses			Percutaneous closure
Transposition of the great vessels	Cyanosis	In some anatomical variants	If right ventricle used for systemic circulation	If ventricle dilates		Early feature			Arterial switch
Single functioning ventricle	Cyanosis, heart failure					Early feature			Total cavopulmonary connection
Systemic right ventricle	Post-surgical or congenital, corrected transposition		Late feature	After ventricular dilatation			Especially post-surgical types of anatomy		Medical management of heart failure and arrhythmias

matic impact. High-grade AV block (Mobitz 2 or complete) is associated with sudden death and patients should be paced urgently even if asymptomatic. Permanent pacing is very effective in reducing symptoms in most bradyarrhythmias; the exception is neurocardiogenic syncope where the results are disappointing.

Common bradyarrhythmias and associated conditions

Neurocardiogenic symptoms

An exaggerated vasodepressor (hypotension), cardioinhibitory (bradycardic) or mixed reflex may cause syncope or presyncope. Various drugs have been tried as treatment, with limited success. In patients with a predominant cardioinhibitory component, dual chamber pacing may reduce the severity and frequency of syncopal episodes but results are often disappointing.

Sinus node disease

Sinus bradycardia and sinus pauses can cause syncope, presyncope or non-specific symptoms. Thyroid function and electrolytes should be checked on presentation and corrected prior to considering pacemaker therapy. Pacing is only indicated in significantly symptomatic cases (as there is no prognostic benefit of pacing in sinus node disease).

First-degree AV block

A PR interval of >200 ms is abnormal but usually requires no treatment. The combinations of first-degree AV block with (1) LBBB, (2) RBBB with axis deviation or (3) with alternating LBBB and RBBB is interpreted as trifascicular block (more accurately block in two fascicles and delay in the third). If associated with syncope, trifascicular block represents an indication for pacing on both prognostic and symptomatic grounds.

Second-degree Mobitz 1 (Wenckebach) AV block

Progressive prolongation and then block of the PR interval is categorised as Mobitz 1. It may be normal during sleep and in young, physically fit individuals (who have high vagal tone). If it occurs when the patient is awake and is associated with symptoms in older people, pacing may be indicated on symptomatic grounds.

High-grade AV block (second-degree Mobitz 2 block and third-degree complete heart block)

Bradycardias with more than one P wave per QRS complex (second-degree Mobitz 2) or with AV dissociation are grouped together as high-grade AV block. Untreated, they are associated with mortality that may exceed 50% at 1 year, particularly in patients aged over 80 years and in those with non-rheumatic structural heart disease. Pacing is indicated on prognostic grounds even in the asymptomatic.

- Complete heart block is the most common reason for permanent pacing
- When related to an infarction, high-grade AV block occurs mostly with right coronary artery occlusion, as the AV nodal branch is usually one of the distal branches of the right coronary artery
- In patients with an anterior infarct, high-grade AV block is a poor prognostic feature, indicating extensive ischaemia
- Congenital cases may be related to connective tissue diseases; however, in patients with normal exercise capacities, recent studies show that the prognosis is not as benign as was previously thought and pacing is therefore recommended in a wide range of circumstances (see ESC guidelines by Vardas et al. *Eur Heart J*, 2007; **28**:2256–95)

Tachyarrhythmias

Tachyarrhythmias are caused by **re-entry**, **triggered activity** or **automaticity**:

- Re-entry – the arrhythmia is anatomically dependent and usually the primary problem as opposed to sequelae of another reversible state
- Automaticity – arrhythmia is often secondary to a systemic cause (eg electrolyte imbalance, sepsis, adrenergic drive) and is multifocal

- Triggered activity – shares features of both mechanisms and is seen in both primary arrhythmias and in drug toxicity

1.5.2 Supraventricular tachycardias

There are two major groups of re-entrant tachycardias often described as SVT:

- **AV nodal re-entry tachycardia (AVNRT)**: involves a re-entry circuit in and around the AV node
- **AV re-entry tachycardia (AVRT)**: this involves an accessory pathway between the atria and ventricles some distance from the AV node (eg WPW syndrome and related conditions)

AV nodal re-entry tachycardia

Differential conduction in tissue around the AV node allows a micro re-entry circuit to be maintained, resulting in a regular tachycardia.

Accessory pathways

An accessory pathway that connects the atrium and ventricle mediates the tachycardia by enabling retrograde conduction from ventricle to atrium. More seriously, the accessory pathway may predispose to unrestricted conduction of AF from atria to ventricles as a result of anterograde conduction through the pathway. This may lead to ventricular fibrillation.

WPW is said to be present when a delta wave (partial pathway-mediated pre-excitation) is present on the resting ECG. Associations with WPW include: Ebstein's anomaly (may have multiple pathways), HCM, mitral valve prolapse and thyrotoxicosis; it is more common in men.

Some accessory pathways are not manifest by a delta wave on the resting ECG but are still able to participate in a tachycardia circuit.

Atrial tachycardias, including flutter, AF, sinus tachycardia and fascicular ventricular tachycardia may all be mistaken for SVT.

1.5.3 Atrial arrhythmias

Atrial flutter

The atrial rate is usually between 250 and 350 beats/min and is often seen with a ventricular response of 150 beats/min (2:1 block). The block may vary between a 1:1 ratio and a 1:4 or even a 1:5 ratio. Isolated atrial flutter (without atrial fibrillation) has a lower association with thromboembolism; however, recommendations for anticoagulation are the same as for AF.

- The ventricular response may be slowed by increasing the vagal block of the AV node (eg carotid sinus massage) or by adenosine, which 'uncovers' the flutter waves on ECG
- This is the most likely arrhythmia to respond to DC cardioversion with low energies (eg 25 volts)
- Amiodarone and sotalol may chemically cardiovert, slow the ventricular response or act as prophylactic agents
- Radiofrequency ablation is curative in up to 95% of cases

Atrial flutter is described as typical when associated with a sawtooth atrial pattern in the inferior leads and positive flutter waves in V1. Atypical flutters tend to occur in congenital heart disease or after surgery or prior ablation.

Atrial fibrillation (AF)

This arrhythmia is due to multiple wavelet propagation in different directions. The source of the arrhythmia may be myocardial tissue in the openings of the four pulmonary veins, which enter into the posterior aspect of the left atrium, and this is particularly the case in younger patients with paroxysmal AF. AF may be paroxysmal, persistent (but 'cardiovertable') or permanent, and in all three states is a risk factor for strokes. Treatment is aimed at ventricular rate control, cardioversion, recurrence prevention and anticoagulation. Catheter ablation is indicated in symptomatic individuals who are resistant to, or intolerant of, medical therapy.

With AF a major decision is whether to control rate

or alter the rhythm:

- Surprisingly, rhythm control does not reduce the risk of stroke (indeed paroxysmal AF carries the same stroke risk as chronic AF) and therefore does not affect the indications for anticoagulation
- Cardioversions, multiple drugs and ablations are all used to alter rhythm
- In asymptomatic individuals rate control is recommended

Associations with atrial fibrillation

- Ischaemic heart disease
- Pericarditis
- Mitral valve disease
- Pulmonary embolus
- Hypertension
- Atrial myxomas
- Thyroid disease
- LVH
- Acute alcohol excess/chronic alcoholic cardiomyopathy
- ASD
- Post-coronary artery bypass graft (CABG)
- Caffeine excess
- Dilated left atrium (>4.5 cm)
- Pneumonia
- WPW syndrome
- Bronchial malignancy

The overall risk of systemic emboli is 5%–7% annually (higher with rheumatic valve disease); this falls to 1.6% with anticoagulation. **Transoesophageal echocardiography** (TOE) may exclude atrial appendage thrombus but cannot predict the development of a thrombus in the early stages post-cardioversion; anticoagulation is therefore always recommended post-cardioversion.

- **Risk factors for stroke with non-valvular AF**
  - Previous history of cerebrovascular accident or transient ischaemic attack (risk ×22.5)
  - Diabetes (×1.7)
  - Hypertension (×1.6)
  - Heart failure
- **Risk factors for recurrence of AF after cardioversion**
  - Long duration (>1–3 years)
  - Rheumatic mitral valve disease
  - Left atrium size >5.5 cm
  - Older age (>75 years)
  - Left ventricular impairment

The CHADS 2 score can be used for stratifying thromboembolic risk in AF:

- 1 point is awarded for each of: **c**ongestive heart failure, **h**ypertension, **a**ge over 75, **d**iabetes
- 2 points are awarded for **s**ystemic emboli
- A score of 3 indicates a high risk of thrombus formation and is a strong indication for anticoagulation
- Scores of 1 and 2 are intermediate values (anticoagulation is given at the discretion of the physician)
- The score has the virtue of simplicity but is quite conservative, probably underestimating the risk associated with prior stroke/transient ischaemic attack

1.5.4 Ventricular arrhythmias and channelopathies

Ventricular tachycardia (monomorphic)

Ventricular tachycardia (VT) has a poor prognosis when left ventricular function is impaired. After the exclusion of reversible causes such patients may need implantable defibrillators and anti-arrhythmic therapy.

- Ventricular rate is usually 120–260 beats/min
- Patients should be DC cardioverted when there is haemodynamic compromise; overdrive pacing may also terminate VT
- Amiodarone, sotalol, flecainide and lidocaine may be therapeutic adjuncts or prophylactic agents; magnesium may also be useful

Associations of ventricular tachycardia

- Myocardial ischaemia
- Hypokalaemia or severe hyperkalaemia
- Long QT syndrome (see below)
- Digoxin toxicity (VT may arise from either ventricle, especially with associated hypokalaemia)
- Cardiomyopathies
- Congenital abnormalities of the right ventricular outflow tract (VT with LBBB and right axis deviation pattern)

Features favouring ventricular tachycardia in broad-complex tachycardia

It is often difficult to distinguish VT from SVT with aberration (disordered ventricular propagation of a supraventricular impulse); VT remains the most common cause of a broad-complex tachycardia, especially with a previous history of MI. The following ECG observations favour VT:

- Capture beats: intermittent SA node complexes transmitted to ventricle
- Fusion beats: combination QRS from SA node and VT focus meeting and fusing (causes cannon waves)
- RBBB with left axis deviation
- Very wide QRS >140 ms

- Altered QRS compared to sinus rhythm
- V lead concordance with all QRS vectors, positive or negative
- Dissociated P waves: marching through the VT
- History of ischaemic heart disease: very good predictor
- Variable S1
- Heart rate <170 beats/min with no effect of carotid sinus massage

Note: none of the above has as high a positive predictive value for VT diagnosis as a history of structural heart disease (especially MI).

Ventricular tachycardia (polymorphic) – torsades de pointes

Anti-arrhythmic agents (particularly class III) may predispose to torsades as the arrhythmia is often initiated during bradycardia. The VT is polymorphic (QRS complexes of different amplitudes twist around the isoelectric line), with QT prolongation when the patient is in sinus rhythm.

- Intravenous magnesium and K^+ channel openers may control the arrhythmia, whereas isoprenaline and temporary pacing may prevent bradycardia and hence the predisposition to VT
- May be due to QT prolongation of any cause (see later)

Proarrhythmic channelopathies

Abnormally prolonged QT intervals may be familial or acquired, and are associated with syncope and sudden death, due to ventricular tachycardia (especially torsades de pointes). Mortality in the untreated symptomatic patient with a congenital abnormality is high but some patients may reach the age of 50–60 years despite repeated attacks. Causes and associations are shown below.

Proarrhythmic causes of abnormal repolarisation (ST-T changes)

- **Familial**
  - Long QT syndromes 1–5
  - Brugada syndrome
  - Short QT syndrome
  - Arrhythmogenic right ventricular dysplasia
- **Drugs**
  - Quinidine
  - Erythromycin
  - Amiodarone
  - Tricyclic antidepressants
  - Phenothiazines
  - Probucol
  - Non-sedating antihistamines (eg terfenadine)
- **Ischaemic heart disease**
- **Metabolic**
  - Hypocalcaemia
  - Hypothyroidism
  - Hypothermia
  - Hypokalaemia
- **Rheumatic carditis**

Long QT syndromes: The corrected QT is >540 ms (normal = 380–460 ms). Ninety per cent are familial, with chromosome 11 defects being common (Romano–Ward syndrome has autosomal dominant inheritance; Jervell–Lange-Nielsen syndrome is autosomal recessive and associated with congenital deafness). Arrhythmias may be reduced by a combination of β-blockers and pacing.

Cardiac causes of electromechanical dissociation

When faced with a cardiac arrest situation it is important to appreciate the list of causes of electromechanical dissociation (EMD):

- Hypoxia
- Hypovolaemia
- Hypokalaemia/hyperkalaemia
- Hypothermia
- Tension pneumothorax
- Tamponade
- Toxic/therapeutic disturbance
- Thromboembolic/mechanical obstruction

1.5.5   Pacing and ablation procedures

Temporary pacing

The ECG will show LBBB morphology (unless there is septal perforation, when it is RBBB). Pacing may be ventricular (right ventricle apex) or AV (atrial appendage and right ventricle apex) for optimised cardiac output.

Complications include:

- Crossing the tricuspid valve during insertion, which causes ventricular ectopics, as does irritating the outflow tract
- Atrial or right ventricular perforation and pericardial effusion
- **Pneumothorax:** internal jugular route is preferable to the subclavian one, as it minimises this risk and also allows control after inadvertent arterial punctures

Permanent pacing

More complex permanent pacing systems include rate-responsive models, which use movement sensors or physiological triggers (respiratory rate or QT interval) to increase heart rates. Although more expensive they avoid causing pacemaker syndrome and they act more physiologically for optimal left ventricular function.

- **Indications for temporary pacing**
  - Asystole
  - Haemodynamically compromised bradycardia
  - Prophylaxis of MI complicated by second-degree or complete heart block
  - Prior to high-risk cardiac interventions or pacemaker replacement
  - Prevention of some tachyarrhythmias (eg torsades)
  - Overdrive termination of various arrhythmias (eg atrial flutter, VT)
- **Indications for permanent pacing**
  - Chronic AV block
  - Sick sinus syndrome with symptoms (including chronotropic incompetence – the inability to appropriately increase the heart rate with activity)
  - Post-AV nodal ablation for arrhythmias (elective or inadvertent)
  - Neurocardiogenic syncope
  - HCM
  - Dilated cardiomyopathy (may pace more than two chambers)
  - Long QT syndrome
  - Prevention of atrial fibrillation
  - Post-cardiac transplantation

Pacing in heart failure

There are several synonymous terms for pacing in patients with cardiac failure. These include 'cardiac resynchronisation therapy', 'biventricular pacing' and 'multisite pacing'. In heart failure pacing is indicated when all of the following are present:

- NYHA III–IV heart failure
- QRS duration >130 ms or other clear evidence of dyssynchrony
- Left ventricular ejection fraction <35% with dilated ventricle and patient on optimal medical therapy (diuretics, angiotensin-converting enzyme (ACE) inhibitors and β-blockers)

The atria and right ventricle are paced in the usual fashion and in addition to this a pacing electrode is placed in a tributary of the coronary sinus on the lateral aspect of the left ventricle. The two ventricles are paced simultaneously or near-simultaneously with a short AV delay. The aim is to optimise AV delay and reduce inter- and intraventricular asynchrony. This therapy is known to reduce mortality, to improve exercise capacity, to improve quality of life and to reduce hospital admissions.

Implantable cardioverter defibrillators (ICD)

ICDs are devices that are able to detect life-threatening tachyarrhythmias and to terminate them by overdrive pacing or a counter-shock. They are implanted in a similar manner to permanent pacemakers. Current evidence supports their use in both secondary prevention of cardiac arrest and also as targeted primary prevention (eg for individuals with left ventricular impairment and those with familial syndromes such as arrhythmogenic right ventricular dysplasia, Brugada syndrome, long QT variants).

Radiofrequency ablation

Radiofrequency ablation is resistive, heat-mediated (65°C) protein membrane disruption causing cell lysis. Using cardiac catheterisation (with electrodes in right- or left-sided chambers) it interrupts electrical pathways in cardiac structures. Excellent results are obtained in the treatment of accessory pathways and atrial flutter, and with complete AV nodal ablation or AV node modification. Ventricular tachycardia is technically more difficult to treat (ventricular myocardium is much thicker than atrial myocardium).

Isolation of the pulmonary veins by ablation therapy is now an established technique to treat atrial fibrillation. Current cure rates are around 85%, but more than one procedure is required in half the cases. Complete heart block and pericardial effusions are rare complications of radiofrequency ablation.

Indications to refer to an electrophysiologist

Indications for referral to an electrophysiologist are given in Table 1.5.

Table 1.5. Indications for referral to an electrophysiologist

Condition	When to refer	Potential treatment
SVT	More than one episode	Radiofrequency ablation
Atrial flutter	More than one episode	Radiofrequency ablation
Atrial fibrillation	Highly symptomatic, refractory to or intolerant of drug therapy	Radiofrequency ablation
Ventricular fibrillation	Unless there is an obvious reversible cause, eg ST-segment elevation MI (STEMI)	ICD
Ventricular tachycardia	Unless obvious reversible cause	Radiofrequency ablation or ICD
Ischaemic cardiomyopathy	Ejection fraction <30% on optimal medical therapy	Primary prevention ICD
NYHA class III–IV heart failure, QRS >130 ms, ejection fraction <35%	On optimal medical therapy	Heart failure pacing

1.6 ISCHAEMIC HEART DISEASE

In 1990 coronary artery disease became the leading worldwide cause of death, currently claiming 7.2 million lives per year.

Risk factors for coronary artery disease

- **Primary**
  - Hypercholesterolaemia (LDL*)
  - Hypertension
  - Smoking
- **Unclear**
  - Low fibre intake
  - Hard water
  - High plasma fibrinogen levels
  - Raised Lp(a) levels
  - Raised factor VII levels
- **Protective factors**
  - Exercise
  - Moderate amounts of alcohol
  - Low cholesterol diet
  - Increased HDL:LDL**
- **Secondary**
  - Reduced HDL cholesterol
  - Obesity
  - Insulin-dependent diabetes mellitus
  - Non-insulin-dependent diabetes
  - Family history of coronary artery disease
  - Physical inactivity
  - Stress and personality type
  - Gout and hyperuricaemia
  - Race (Asians)
  - Low weight at 1 year of age
  - Male sex
  - Chronic renal failure
  - Increasing age
  - Low social class
  - Increased homocystine levels and homocystinuria

*Low-density lipoprotein
**Ratio of high-density lipoprotein to LDL

Smoking and its relationship to cardiovascular disease

Smokers have an increased incidence of the following cardiovascular complications:

- Coronary artery disease
- Malignant hypertension
- Ischaemic stroke
- Morbidity from peripheral vascular disease
- Sudden death
- Subarachnoid haemorrhage
- Mortality due to aortic aneurysm
- Thromboembolism in patients taking oral contraceptives

Both active and passive smoking increase the risk of coronary atherosclerosis by a number of mechanisms. These include:

- Increased platelet adhesion/aggregation and whole-blood viscosity
- Increased heart rate; increased catecholamine sensitivity/release
- Increased carboxyhaemoglobin level and, as a result, increased haematocrit
- Decreased HDL cholesterol and vascular compliance
- Decreased threshold for ventricular fibrillation

1.6.1 Angina

Other than the usual forms of stable and unstable angina, those worthy of specific mention include:

- **Decubitus**: usually on lying down – due to an increase in LVEDP or associated with dreaming, cold sheets, or coronary spasm during rapid eye movement (REM) sleep
- **Variant (Prinzmetal)**: unpredictable, at rest, with transient ST elevation on ECG. Due to coronary spasm, with or without underlying arteriosclerotic lesions
- **Syndrome X**: this refers to a heterogeneous group of patients who have ST-segment depression on exercise testing but angiographically normal coronary arteries. The patients may have very-small-vessel disease and/or abnormal ventricular function. It is

commonly described in middle-aged females and oestrogen deficiency has been suggested to be an aetiological factor

- **Vincent angina**: nothing to do with cardiology; infection of the pharyngeal and tonsillar space!

Causes of non-anginal chest pains

- **Pericardial pain**
- **Aortic dissection**
- **Mediastinitis**
  - Associated with trauma, pneumothorax or diving
- **Pleural**
  - Usually with breathlessness in pleurisy, pneumonia, pneumothorax or a large peripheral pulmonary embolus
- **Musculoskeletal**
- **Gastrointestinal**
  - Including oesophageal, gastric, gallbladder, pancreatic
- **Hyperventilation/anxiety**
  - Reproduction of sharp inframammary pains on forced hyperventilation is a reliable test
- **Mitral valve prolapse**
  - May be spontaneous, sharp, superficial, short-lived pain

Symptomatic assessment of angina

The Canadian cardiovascular assessment of chest pain is useful for grading the severity of angina:

- **Grade I**: angina only on strenuous or prolonged exertion
- **Grade II**: angina climbing two flights of stairs
- **Grade III**: angina walking one block on the level (indication for intervention)
- **Grade IV**: angina at rest (indication for urgent intervention)

1.6.2 Myocardial infarction

Conservative estimates suggest there are 113 000 myocardial infarctions per year in the UK with significant pre-hospital mortality, and 5%–6% in-hospital mortality and 6%–7% 30-day mortality for those surviving to hospital admission. Overall 19% of UK deaths are directly attributable to coronary disease.

Diagnosis of MI

Acute, evolving or recent MI

Either one of the following criteria satisfies the diagnosis for an acute, evolving or recent MI:

- Typical rise and gradual fall (troponin) or more rapid rise and fall (CK-MB) of biochemical markers of myocardial necrosis with at least one of the following:
  - Ischaemic symptoms
  - Development of pathological Q waves on the ECG
  - ECG changes indicative of ischaemia (ST-segment elevation or depression)
- Pathological finding of an acute MI (eg at postmortem)

Established MI

Any one of the following criteria satisfies the diagnosis of an established MI:

- Development of new pathological Q waves on serial ECGs. The patient may or may not remember previous symptoms. Biochemical markers of myocardial necrosis may have normalised, depending on the length of time that has passed since the infarct developed
- Pathological finding of a healed or healing MI
- Previous MI is also suggested when coronary artery disease and a regional ventricular wall motion abnormality are seen, or characteristic myocardial scars are observed with MRI

Distinction between ST-segment elevation MI (STEMI) and non-STEMI (NSTEMI)

An acute MI should be classified as **STEMI** when there is:

- ST-segment elevation (2 mm in two or more chest leads, or 1 mm in two or more limb leads)
- A chronic MI with Q-wave formation
- Pathological or imaging evidence of a full-thickness scar

Other MIs that do not meet these criteria should be classified as **NSTEMI**.

Cardiac enzymes

The widespread use of troponin assays has both simplified and lowered the bar for the diagnosis of MI. A number of markers of cardiac damage are now available. Table 1.6 is a guide to the timing of the initial rise, peak and return to normality.

Troponin assays in patients with renal failure

The troponin level may be elevated simply because a patient has renal failure. In patients with renal failure who present with chest pain it is helpful to assess the troponin level at baseline as well as at 12 h after the onset of symptoms, and sometimes at later time points. In these circumstances only a rising troponin level would be suggestive of ischaemic myocardial damage.

Complications of MI

Since the advent of thrombolysis, complication rates have been reduced (eg halved for pericarditis, conduction defects, ventricular thrombus, fever, Dressler syndrome). All complications may be seen with any type of infarction, but the following are the most common associations.

- **Complications of anterior infarctions**
  - Late VT/VF
  - Left ventricular aneurysm
  - Left ventricular thrombus and systemic embolism (usually 1–3 weeks post-MI)*
  - Complete heart block (rare)
  - Ischaemic mitral regurgitation
  - Congestive cardiac failure
  - Cardiac rupture – usually at days 4–10 with EMD
  - VSD with septal rupture
  - Pericarditis and pericardial effusion (**Dressler syndrome** with high erythrocyte sedimentation rate (ESR), fever, anaemia, pleural effusions and anti-cardiac muscle antibodies is seen occasionally)

Table 1.6. Guide to the timing of changes in cardiac enzymes

Marker	Initial rise	Peak	Return to normal	Notes
Creatine phosphokinase*	4–8 h	18 h	2–3 days	CPK-MB is main cardiac isoenzyme
Myoglobin	1–4 h	6–7 h	24 h	Low specificity from skeletal muscle damage
Troponin**	3–12 h	24 h	3–10 days	Troponins I and T are the most sensitive and specific markers of myocardial damage available
Lactate dehydrogenase (LDH)	10 h	24–48 h	14 days	Cardiac muscle mainly contains LDH

* Creatine phosphokinase has three isoenzymes, of which the CPK-MB isoenzyme is most cardiac-specific, although numerous other organs possess the enzyme in small quantities. A CPK-MB of >2.5% of the total CPK has been suggested as very specific for MI in the context of chest pain. This is inaccurate in situations of significant acute or chronic skeletal injury, where CPK levels will be high

** Troponin interpretation is specific to the assay used and local guidelines should be consulted. A level greater than the 99th centile for the assay is regarded as positive. Assays may be read only, semi-quantitative or quantitative. Positives occur in all conditions where myocardial damage occurs, including pulmonary embolus, myocarditis, extreme bradycardia or tachycardia, sepsis, renal impairment and uncontrolled diabetes mellitus

- **Complications of inferior infarctions**
  - Higher re-infarction rate
  - Inferior aneurysm – with mitral regurgitation (rare)
  - Pulmonary embolism (rare)
  - Complete heart block and other degrees of heart block
  - Papillary muscle dysfunction and mitral regurgitation
  - Right ventricular infarcts need high filling pressures (particularly if posterior extension)

*Although **warfarin** provides no general benefit, it may reduce the overall CVA rate (1.5%–3.6%) in those patients with echocardiographically demonstrable mural left ventricular thrombus after a large anterior MI, so recommended for up to 6 months after the infarction

Heart block and pacing after myocardial infarction

- Temporary pacing is indicated in anterior MI complicated by complete heart block. This presentation is associated with high mortality due to the extensive myocardial damage. The decision as whether to temporarily pace a patient with inferior infarction and complete heart block is primarily dictated by the patient's haemodynamic status. Atropine and isoprenaline can also be tried. Narrow-complex escape rhythms are more stable. An observational period of 7 days post-MI is appropriate to allow the return of sinus rhythm before considering permanent pacing
- The right coronary artery is the dominant vessel (over left circumflex) in 85% of patients. As this gives off branches to SA and AV nodes, heart

block might be observed if a dominant right coronary artery is occluded

1.6.3 Medical therapy for myocardial infarction

Thrombolysis is beneficial up to 6 h after pain onset but may be given for up to 12 hours in the context of continuing pain or deteriorating condition. Recanalisation occurs in 70% of patients after thrombolysis (compared with a 15% recanalisation rate without thrombolysis) and results in a higher, earlier creatine phosphokinase (CPK) rise (but a lower total CPK release). Reperfusion arrhythmias are common within the first 2 hours after thrombolysis.

Primary angioplasty is superior to thrombolysis for acute MI; the same ECG criteria apply to case selection.

Tissue plasminogen activator and similar recombinant agents are accompanied by a prothrombotic phase lasting about 48 hours and this period should be covered with heparin.

Contraindications to thrombolysis

Although there are numerous relative contraindications where the risk/benefit considerations are individual to the patient, there are several absolute contraindications to thrombolysis.

Contraindications to thrombolysis

- **Absolute contraindications**
  - Active internal bleeding or uncontrollable external bleeding
  - Suspected aortic dissection
  - Recent head trauma (<2 weeks)
  - Intracranial neoplasms
  - History of proved haemorrhagic stroke or cerebral infarction <2 months earlier
  - Uncontrolled high BP (>200/120 mmHg)
  - Pregnancy

- **Relative contraindications**
  - Traumatic prolonged cardiopulmonary resuscitation
  - Bleeding disorders
  - Recent surgery
  - Probable intracardiac thrombus (eg AF with mitral stenosis)
  - Active diabetic haemorrhagic retinopathy
  - Anticoagulation or INR >1.8

Groups particularly benefiting from thrombolysis (determined by the GUSTO, ISIS 2 and ISIS 3 trials) include:

- Those with large anterior infarction
- Those with pronounced ST elevation
- Elderly (>75 years)
- Those with poor left ventricular function or LBBB, or systolic BP <100 mmHg
- Those who have early administration: within 1 h of pain onset

Posterior infarction (a tall R wave in V1 with ST depression in leads V1–V3): no clear benefit of thrombolysis has been shown as few such patients have been enrolled into major trials (ECG interpretation is often difficult when the presentation is not with inferior infarct). However, the general consensus would still be to give thrombolysis. Sixty per cent of posterior MIs are due to right coronary artery disease.

NSTEMI: have not been shown to benefit from thrombolysis. They have a low in-patient but high (65%) untreated 1-year mortality (compared to 34% for STEMI infarcts) and they should be investigated early and aggressively.

There is now a good evidence base for a range of pharmacological treatments in patients presenting with acute coronary syndromes (See Table 1.7). These are aimed at dispersing clot (aspirin, clopidogrel, heparin), preventing arrhythmias (β-blockers), stabilising plaque (statins) and preventing adverse remodelling.

Table 1.7. Summary of clinical trials in patients with acute MI*

Agents used for acute MI	Mortality in treated group (%)	Mortality in control subjects (%)	Number treated to save 1 life	Trials involved
Aspirin	9.4 (at 5 weeks)	11.8	42	ISIS 2
Clopidogrel	11.4	9.3	Composite endpoint	CURE
Thrombolytics	10.7[†] (at 21 days)	13.0[†]	43[†]	GISSI 1[†], ISIS 2, TIMI II, GUSTO
β-Blockers	3.9 (at 7 days)	4.6	143	ISIS 1
ACE inhibitors	35.2[†] (after 39-month mean follow-up)	39.7[†]	22[†]	SAVE, SOLVD[†], AIRE
Lipid-lowering therapy (patients with average cholesterol)	10.2 (after 5 years)	13.2	33	CARE (note endpoints included second non-fatal MI and cardiac deaths)
Heparin with aspirin and any form of thrombolysis	8.6	9.1	200	Meta-analysis of 68 000 patients
Magnesium: contradictory data but no mortality reduction				LIMIT 1, 2, ISIS 4
Nitrates: no clear benefit				ISIS 4, GISSI 3
Warfarin: no proved benefit above aspirin after thrombolysis				

* See also Appendix II: Summary of further trials in cardiology
† Data from that particular trial

1.6.4 Coronary artery interventional procedures

Percutaneous coronary intervention (PCI)

After coronary angioplasty the recurrence or re-stenosis rate is 30% within 3 months and 40%–60% for total occlusions that are successfully dilated as treatment of acute MI. These figures have been greatly reduced, first by bare metal stents and then further by drug-eluting stents. Drug-eluting stents are covered by an antimitotic agent to prevent smooth muscle/fibrous tissue proliferation. Unfortunately, they also inhibit endothelialisation so increasing the risk of thrombosis and so dual antiplatelet therapy (aspirin and clopidogrel) is mandatory for 12 months after the intervention and lifelong single antiplatelet therapy is required thereafter.

- Lesions particularly amenable to PCI include those that are discrete, proximal, non-calcified, unoccluded, that are away from side branches and that occur in patients with a short history of angina. While there is a small acute occlusion rate, these can usually be managed successfully with intra-coronary stenting, such that the need for emergency CABG has fallen to under 1%
- More challenging lesions include those within grafts, at bifurcations, calcified or long lesions and those within small vessels. Diabetics have poorer outcomes compared with non-diabetics
- Almost any lesion can be stented including left main stem disease, three-vessel disease and even chronic total occlusions but careful evaluation and discussion with the patient are necessary, as in many situations bypass grafting has a better evidence base

Coronary artery bypass grafting (CABG)

CABG has clear benefits in specific groups of patients with chronic coronary artery disease (when compared with medical therapy alone). Analysis has previously been limited because randomised trials included small numbers and were performed several decades ago; patients studied were usually males aged <65 years. The population now receiving CABG has changed, but so has medical therapy.

- Prognostic benefits are shown for symptomatic, significant left main stem disease (Veterans' Study), symptomatic proximal three-vessel disease and in two-vessel disease which includes the proximal left anterior descending artery (CASS data)
- Patients with moderately impaired left ventricular function show greater benefit, but those with poor left ventricular function have greater operative mortality. Overall mortality is <2%, rising to between 5% and 10% for a second procedure. Eighty per cent of patients gain symptom relief
- Peri-operative graft occlusion is around 10% for vein grafts, which otherwise last 8–10 years. Arterial grafts (internal mammary, free radial, gastro-epiploic) have a higher initial patency rate but long-term outcomes are disappointing with the exception of internal mammary grafts, which are clearly superior to vein grafts
- A 'Dressler-like' syndrome may occur up to 6 months post-surgery
- Minimally invasive CABG involves the redirection of internal mammary arteries to coronary vessels without the need for cardiac bypass and full sternotomy incisions (often termed 'off pump' coronary revascularisation). Recovery times following this procedure are shorter than for conventional surgery but the procedures are technically more challenging

Post-MI rehabilitation

After MI patients are kept in hospital for 5 days, should take 2 months off work and have 1 month's abstinence from sexual intercourse and driving (see following text). Cardiac rehabilitation is particularly important for patient confidence. Depression occurs in 30% of patients. Patients who are fully revascularised or invasively investigated and found to have no ongoing ischaemic focus may be discharged after 3 days and be rehabilitated more rapidly.

Fitness to drive

The DVLA provides extensive guidelines for coronary disease and interventions. Their website (www.dvla.gov.uk) should be consulted, especially

Table 1.8. Fitness to drive

Condition	Driving restriction	Notes
Unexplained syncope	6 months from last episode or until effective treatment is given	Clear vasovagal events that occur only when the patient is erect do not preclude driving
Cardiac catheter procedure (including angiography, percutaneous coronary intervention, electrophysiological studies/ablation)	1 week	Should be able to perform emergency stop unhindered
Myocardial infarction	1 month	
Permanent pacemaker	1 month	Only 1 week if the patient has never been syncopal
Prophylactic ICD	1 month	No clinical arrhythmia or syncope
Secondary prevention ICD	6 months	DVLA must be informed
ICD shock therapy	6 months	Unless an inappropriate shock is preventable by reprogramming or intervention, eg a change in the detection or therapy programming to avoid shocks for sinus tachycardia or atrial arrhythmias

with regard to class 2 licences (for vehicles over 3500 kg, minibuses and buses) but the essential points are given in Table 1.8.

1.7 OTHER MYOCARDIAL DISEASES

1.7.1 Cardiac failure

Cardiac failure can be defined as the pumping action of the heart being insufficient to meet the circulatory demands of the body (in the absence of mechanical obstructions). A broad echocardiographic definition is of an ejection fraction (EF) <40% (as in the SAVE trial, which enrolled patients for ACE inhibitors post-MI). Overall 5-year survival is 65% with EF <40%, compared to 95% in those with EF >50%.

The most common single cause of cardiac failure in the Western world is ischaemic heart disease (IHD).

- Hypertension is also a very frequent cause – either acting alone or in combination with IHD
- **Diastolic heart failure** is increasingly recognised although difficult to diagnose as an isolated condition. It describes impaired ventricular filling that elevates pulmonary and/or systemic venous pressure with activation of the neurohormonal system as seen in systolic heart failure
- All patients with systolic heart failure have a degree of diastolic dysfunction – some believe that isolated diastolic dysfunction may be an early step prior to development of systolic heart failure

EF is only a guide to cardiac function, which also depends on other factors including pre-load, afterload and tissue demand. However, EF is reduced in patients with systolic heart failure.

- **Pre-load**: will affect LVEDP
- **After-load**: will affect left ventricular systolic wall tension

Other echocardiographic features of LV dysfunction include reduced fractional shortening, LV enlargement and paradoxical septal motion.

The New York Heart Association (NYHA) classification is a helpful indication of severity (Table 1.9).

Drug therapy for cardiac failure

After diagnosis and during investigation for a cause of cardiac failure, drug therapy is commenced:

- If oedema is present a loop diuretic is used – if no peripheral oedema is present care must be taken to avoid hypovolaemia
- Vasodilators such as nitrates and hydralazine also give symptomatic benefit (the vasodilating actions of ACE inhibitors and β-blockers are significant)
- ACE inhibitors are commenced early and titrated up rapidly to the maximum tolerated dose
- Once the patient is stable and well diuresed β-blockers are cautiously introduced; the lowest dose is commenced and uptitrated at minimum intervals of 2 weeks, once more aiming for the maximum tolerated dose. (Patients should be warned that each time their β-blocker dose increases they may initially feel worse – but robust study data indicate they will benefit both symptomatically and prognostically)

- Cessation of previously stable ACE inhibitor and β-blocker therapy (eg when the patient is admitted with intercurrent infection leading to hypotension and/or acute renal impairment) is associated with an increased mortality. These drugs should be continued if at all possible, or at least re-commenced after clinical stability has been restored

Summary of therapeutic interventions in heart failure

A summary of therapeutic interventions in heart failure is given in Table 1.10.

1.7.2 Hypertrophic cardiomyopathy (HCM)

Characteristic features of HCM

- Jerky pulse with large tidal wave as outflow obstruction is overcome
- Large a waves in the JVP
- Double apical impulse (palpable atrial systole, S4, in sinus rhythm)
- LSE systolic thrill (turbulence) with harsh ESM radiating to axilla
- Often accompanied by mitral regurgitation
- Often paradoxical splitting of second heart sound
- The ejection systolic murmur (ESM) increases with a Valsalva manoeuvre and decreases with squatting

Table 1.9. NYHA classification of heart failure

NYHA class	Symptoms	One-year mortality (%)
I	Asymptomatic with ordinary activity	5–10
II	Slight limitation of physical activities	15
III	Marked limitation of physical activities	30
IV	Dyspnoeic symptoms at rest	50–60

Table 1.10. Summary of therapeutic interventions in heart failure

Intervention	Benefit	Comment
Diuretics	Symptom control	Loop diuretic or loop diuretic with thiazide
ACE inhibitors	Mortality and symptoms	Should be titrated to maximum tolerated dose
Angiotensin-receptor blockers	Mortality and symptoms	In place of or in addition to ACE inhibitors
β-Blockers	Mortality and symptoms	Bisoprolol and carvedilol have the best evidence base
Aldosterone antagonists	Symptom control	NYHA III–IV
Digoxin	Symptom control	NYHA III–IV
Vasodilators	Symptom control	
Cardiac resynchronisation therapy	Mortality and symptoms	NYHA III–IV, see Section 1.5.5
Implantable cardioverter defibrillator	Mortality	See Section 1.5.5
Anticoagulation	Stroke morbidity	In AF or if there are prior thromboemboli

Important points to remember

- Associations with Friedreich's ataxia, WPW, phaeochromocytoma, familial lentiginosis
- ESM *increases* with: glyceryl trinitrate (GTN), digoxin and standing, due to volume reduction in diastole; ESM *decreases* with: squatting, β-blockers, Valsalva release, handgrip
- Avoid digoxin (if in sinus rhythm), nitrates, atropine, inotropes, diuretics (unless in left ventricular failure)
- Cardiac catheterisation abnormalities include a 'banana' or 'spade-shaped' left ventricular cavity in systole, mitral regurgitation and 'sword fish' narrowing of the left anterior descending artery
- Autosomal dominant in half the patients, associated with chromosomes 1, 11, 14 or 15. May also result from a gene mutation that leads to myocardial disarray and varying expression of hypertrophy. Prevalence <0.2% in the general population. Life expectancy is variable with symptoms and investigations determining risk of sudden death
- **Sudden death** may be due to catecholamine-driven extreme outflow obstruction, ventricular fibrillation related to accessory pathway – transmitted AF, or massive MI. Sudden death may occur without hypertrophy. Annual mortality of 2.5% in adults and 6% in children
- Poor prognostic features include young age at diagnosis, family history of sudden death and syncopal symptoms, but there is no correlation with the left ventricular outflow tract gradient
- Pregnancy is possible, but haemorrhage, prolonged vaginal delivery effort and epidural analgesia are best avoided; antibiotic prophylaxis and counselling are advised

- Therapeutic options include β-blockers, calcium antagonists, amiodarone, dual-chamber pacing, internal defibrillators, surgical myomectomy or therapeutic septal infarction

Echocardiographic features of HCM (none is diagnostic)

- Asymmetrical septal hypertrophy: septum >30% thicker than left ventricular posterior wall
- Left ventricular outflow tract gradient ± turbulence
- Premature closure of aortic cusps
- Variable obliteration of left ventricular cavity
- Systolic anterior motion of anterior mitral valve cusp probably due to Venturi effect (see on M-mode)
- Tip thickening of anterior mitral cusp tip where it strikes the septum
- Other patterns of hypertrophy which may only be apical

1.7.3 Dilated cardiomyopathy (DCM)

DCM is a syndrome of global ventricular dysfunction and dilatation, usually with macroscopically normal coronary arteries (if causes of ischaemic cardiomyopathy are excluded). The aetiology is often undetermined and the condition is more common in males and Afro-Caribbeans (this association is possibly because of undiagnosed hypertensive cardiomyopathy). There is often LBBB or poor R wave progression on ECG and anticoagulation may be warranted as the incidence of AF and ventricular thrombus is high.

Causes of DCM

- Alcohol
- Undiagnosed hypertension
- Autoimmune disease
- Nutritional deficiency (eg thiamine and selenium)

- Muscular dystrophies
- Viral infections (eg Coxsackie and HIV)
- Peripartum
- Drugs (eg doxorubicin)
- Infiltration (eg haemochromatosis, sarcoidosis)
- Tachycardia-mediated cardiomyopathy (uncontrolled fast heart rates, eg atrial fibrillation)

1.7.4 Restrictive cardiomyopathy

This produces identical symptoms to constrictive pericarditis (*see* Section 1.8.1) but surgery is of little use in restrictive cardiomyopathy. The ventricles are excessively rigid and impede diastolic filling. AF may supervene and stagnation of blood leads to thrombus formation.

- **Myocardial causes**
  - Idiopathic
  - Scleroderma
  - Amyloid (see below)
  - Sarcoid
  - Haemochromatosis
  - Glycogen storage disorders
  - Gaucher's disease
- **Endomyocardial causes**
  - Endomyocardial fibrosis
  - Hypereosinophilic syndromes (including Löffler's)
  - Carcinoid
  - Malignancy or radiotherapy
  - Toxin-related

Cardiac amyloidosis

Cardiac amyloidosis behaves like restrictive cardiomyopathy but it may also be accompanied by pericardial thickening (due to nodular deposition), pericardial effusion and, rarely, tamponade. It is important to avoid digoxin in amyloid cardiac disease because of the risk of heart block and asystole.

1.7.5 Myocarditis

Myocarditis may be due to many different aetiological factors (eg viral, bacterial, fungal, protozoal, autoimmune, allergic and drugs). It may be difficult to differentiate from DCM, but the following features may help:

- Usually a young patient
- Acute history
- Prodrome of fever, arthralgia, respiratory tract infection, myalgia
- Neutrophilia
- Slight cardiomegaly on chest X-ray
- Episodes of VT, transient AV block and ST/T-wave changes
- Elevated viral titres
- Cardiac enzymes raised (with normal coronary arteries)

Rheumatic fever

This follows a group A streptococcal infection; pancarditis usually occurs and valvular defects are long-term sequelae. The cardiac histological marker is the Aschoff nodule. Patients are treated with penicillin and salicylates or steroids.

Criteria for diagnosis include the need for evidence of preceding α-haemolytic streptococcal infection (raised antistreptolysin O titre (ASOT), positive throat swab or history of scarlet fever), together with two major (or one major and two minor) Duckett–Jones criteria (see below).

> **Rheumatic fever (Duckett–Jones diagnostic criteria)**
>
> - **Major criteria**
>   - Carditis
>   - Polyarthritis
>   - Chorea
>   - Erythema marginatum
>   - Subcutaneous nodules

> - **Minor criteria**
>   - Fever
>   - Arthralgia
>   - Previous rheumatic heart disease
>   - High ESR and C-reactive protein (CRP)
>   - Prolonged PR interval on ECG

1.7.6 Cardiac tumours

Myxomas are the most common cardiac tumours, comprising 50% of most pathological series.

Atrial myxomas

- **Autopsy incidence** of <0.3%; more common in females (2:1) and in the left atrium (75% of myxomas); usually benign and occasionally familial
- **Signs**: fever and weight loss occur in 25%, and this may be due to release of interleukin-6 (IL-6). There may be transient mitral stenosis, early diastolic 'plop', clubbing, Raynaud's phenomenon (rare), pulmonary hypertension. Usually the rhythm is sinus. Atrial myxomas may present with the classic triad of systemic embolism, intra-cardiac obstruction and systemic symptoms
- **Investigations**: white cell count high, platelets low, haemolytic anaemia or polycythaemia, raised immunoglobulins, raised ESR in 60% (thought to be due to secretion of IL-6)
- Avoid left ventricular catheterisation; use TOE to diagnose. They occur most commonly on the inter-atrial septum
- Atrial myxomas grow rapidly with a risk of embolisation and sudden death, so they should be resected surgically without delay

Other primary cardiac tumours

These include papillomas, fibromas, lipomas, angiosarcomas, rhabdomyosarcomas and mesotheliomas, which are all rare lesions.

1.7.7 Alcohol and the heart

Acute alcoholic intoxication is the most common cause of paroxysmal AF amongst younger individuals. Chronic excessive intake over 10 years is responsible for a third of the cases of DCM in Western populations; alcohol is also aetiologically related to hypertension, cerebrovascular accident (CVA), arrhythmias and sudden death. AF may be the first presenting feature (usually between the ages of 30 and 35 years).

Pathological mechanisms

- Direct myocardial toxic effect of alcohol and its metabolites
- Toxic effect of additives (eg cobalt)
- Secondary effect of associated nutritional deficiencies (eg thiamine)
- Effect of hypertension

Treatment includes nutritional correction and – most importantly – complete abstinence from alcohol, without which 50% will die within 5 years. Abstinence can lead to a marked recovery of resting cardiac function.

Beneficial mechanisms of modest amounts of alcohol

- Favourable effects on lipids (50% of this benefit is due to raised HDL levels)
- Antithrombotic effects (perhaps by raising natural levels of tissue plasminogen activator)
- Antiplatelet effects (changes in prostacyclin:thromboxane ratios)
- Increase in insulin sensitivity
- Antioxidant effects of red wine (flavonoids and polyphenols)

1.7.8 Cardiac transplantation

Six UK centres currently conduct heart transplants with 150–200 operations carried out per year, most often for intractable coronary disease and cardiomyopathy (44%); survival rates have been estimated at 80% at 1 year, 75% at 3 years and 40%–50% at 10 years. Myocarditis is yet another indication; transplantation during the acute phase does not worsen prognosis, but myocarditis may recur in the donor heart.

The major complications encountered after transplantation include accelerated coronary atheroma, lymphoma, skin cancer (and other tumours) and chronic kidney disease (CKD; due to ciclosporin A or tacrolimus toxicity).

1.8 PERICARDIAL DISEASE

1.8.1 Constrictive pericarditis

Rare in clinical practice, it presents in a similar way to restrictive cardiomyopathy, ie with signs of right-sided heart failure (cachexia, hepatomegaly, raised JVP, ascites and oedema) due to restriction of diastolic filling of both ventricles. It is treated by pericardial resection.

Other specific features include:

- A diastolic pericardial knock occurs after the third heart sound, at the time of the y descent of the JVP and this reflects the sudden reduction of ventricular filling – 'the ventricle slaps against the rigid pericardium'
- Soft heart sounds and impalpable apex beat
- Severe pulsus paradoxus occurs rarely and indicates the presence of a co-existent tense effusion
- Thickened, bright pericardium on echocardiography

Causes of constrictive pericarditis

- Tuberculosis (usually post-pericardial effusion)
- Mediastinal radiotherapy
- Pericardial malignancy
- Drugs (eg hydralazine, associated with a lupus-like syndrome)
- Post-viral (especially haemorrhagic) or bacterial pericarditis
- Following severe uraemic pericarditis
- Trauma/post-cardiac surgery
- Connective tissue disease
- Recurrent pericarditis

Signs common to constrictive pericarditis and restrictive cardiomyopathy

- Raised JVP with prominent x + y descents
- AF
- Non-pulsatile hepatomegaly
- Normal systolic function

Some key features distinguish constrictive pericarditis from restrictive cardiomyopathy:

- Absence of LVH in constrictive pericarditis
- Absent calcification on chest X-ray, prominent apical impulse and conduction abnormalities on ECG, which are features of restrictive cardiomyopathy

However, a combination of investigations, including cardiac CT, MRI and cardiac biopsy, may be necessary to differentiate between the two conditions.

1.8.2 Pericardial effusion

A slowly developing effusion of 2 litres can be accommodated by pericardial stretching and without raising the intrapericardial pressure. The classic symptoms of chest discomfort, dysphagia, hoarseness or dyspnoea (due to compression) may be absent. A large effusion can lead to muffled heart sounds, loss of apical impulse, occasional pericar-

dial rub, small ECG complexes and eventually electromechanical dissociation.

Other key features are:

- **Pulsus alternans**: variable left ventricular output and right ventricular filling
- **Pulsus paradoxus**: exaggerated inspiratory fall in systolic BP (mechanism described in Section 1.1.2)
- **Electrical alternans on ECG**: 'swinging QRS axis'
- **Globular cardiac enlargement on chest X-ray**

Causes of pericardial effusion

- All causes as listed for constrictive pericarditis
- Aortic dissection
- Iatrogenic due to pacing or cardiac catheterisation
- Ischaemic heart disease with ventricular rupture
- Anticoagulation associated with acute pericarditis

1.8.3 Cardiac tamponade

In contrast, if a small amount of intrapericardial fluid (eg <200 ml) accumulates rapidly, it can significantly limit ventricular filling, reduce cardiac output and elevate intracardiac pressures (particularly right-sided initially). Thus the y descent due to right ventricular filling with tricuspid valve opening is lost as right ventricular pressures are high, and the x descent of right atrium filling due to right ventricular contraction is prominent. The right atrium collapses in diastole as a result of impaired filling and high intrapericardial pressures. In early diastole even the right ventricle may collapse.

Occasionally the stretched pericardium may compress the lingular lobe of the left lung, causing bronchial breathing at the left base (Ewart's sign). The QRS axis of the ECG may also be altered (electrical alternans).

Common signs of cardiac tamponade

- Elevated jugular venous pressure
- Kussmaul's sign
- Tachypnoea
- Systolic hypotension
- Pulsus paradoxus
- Tachycardia
- Diminished heart sounds
- Impalpable apex beat

Treatment is by urgent drainage – usually under echocardiographic control. Surgical 'pericardial' windows may be necessary for chronic (eg malignant) effusions.

1.9 DISORDERS OF MAJOR VESSELS

1.9.1 Pulmonary hypertension

It is important to determine whether pulmonary hypertension is secondary to an underlying condition as this may be treatable. The most common cause of secondary pulmonary hypertension is chronic obstructive pulmonary disease (COPD).

Causes of pulmonary hypertension

- **Primary pulmonary hypertension**
- **Secondary causes**
  - Mitral valve disease
  - DCM/IHD
  - Chronic parenchymal lung disease (eg COPD)
  - Chronic pulmonary thromboembolism
  - Left-to-right shunt (eg ASD, VSD)
  - Chronic hypoxia (high altitude, polio, myasthenia)
  - HCM
  - Cor triatrium
  - Constrictive pericarditis and restrictive cardiomyopathy
  - Left atrial myxoma

Primary pulmonary hypertension (PPH)

PPH is a rare disease with an incidence of 2 per million per year; it is a disease of children and young adults, with a ratio of females:males of 2:1. PPH constitutes less than 1% of all cases of pulmonary hypertension and is characterised by a mean pulmonary artery pressure of >25 mmHg at rest, in the absence of another demonstrable cause. One in ten cases is familial. PPH is associated with connective tissue disease, vasculitis, HIV infection and also the use of appetite suppressants (eg fenfluramine). The pulmonary arteries become dilated and abnormally thickened; there is dilatation of the proximal pulmonary vessels with thick-walled, obstructed 'pruned' peripheral vessels. As a consequence of the high pulmonary pressure the right ventricle undergoes marked hypertrophy.

Three types of PPH are recognised:

- Primary plexogenic pulmonary arteriopathy
- Thrombotic pulmonary arteriopathy
- Pulmonary veno-occlusive arteriopathy

Patients present with gradually worsening exertional dyspnoea and, in the later stages, angina of effort and syncope occur. Fatigue is common and haemoptysis may occur.

- Signs include: cyanosis, right ventricular heave, loud P2, tricuspid regurgitation, peripheral oedema and ascites
- Untreated, the median survival is approximately 3 years

Treatment of primary pulmonary hypertension

This would usually be undertaken at a specialist centre. The chief aspects involve:

- Advise avoidance of strenuous exercise and recommend contraception, as pregnancy is harmful
- Anticoagulation to avoid thrombus formation in situ in the pulmonary arteries and also pulmonary embolism
- Prostacyclin (PGI_2), a potent pulmonary and systemic vasodilator, is used, particularly to

bridge patients to transplantation. The drug has an extremely short half-life and has to be given by continuous intravenous infusion, usually through a tunnelled central venous catheter. It is also very expensive

- Endothelin-receptor blockade (eg bosentan)
- Calcium-channel antagonists have been used to lower pulmonary (and systemic) pressure
- Diuretics are helpful in the management of right heart failure
- Continuous ambulatory inhaled nitric oxide is being developed, and this would provide good pulmonary vasodilatation, but without systemic effect

The chief therapeutic option is transplantation, as other treatments are of limited benefit, or are difficult to administer.

Summary of available treatments for pulmonary hypertension

- **General**
  - Address secondary causes where possible
  - Digoxin, even in patients with sinus rhythm
  - Diuretics for symptoms
  - Ambulatory supplemental oxygen for some
  - Anticoagulation
- **Vasodilator therapy (only helps some subjects)**
  - Endothelin-receptor blockers (eg bosentan)
  - PGI_2 or PGE (chronic infusion)
  - Adenosine infusions or boluses
  - Nitric oxide inhalation, nitrates (chronic infusion)
  - Calcium-channel blockers
- **Surgical options (in selected cases)**
  - Heart-lung or single/double lung transplant
  - Atrial septostomy (only if no resting hypoxia)

1.9.2 Venous thrombosis and pulmonary embolism

The true incidence of pulmonary embolism (PE) is unknown but PE probably accounts for 1% of all admissions. Predisposing factors are discussed in Chapter 9, Haematology.

One or more predisposing risk factors are found in 80%–90% of cases. The oral contraceptive increases the risk of deep vein thrombosis (DVT)/PE two to four times. However, thromboembolism is rare in women taking oestrogens without other risk factors.

Clinical features

Nearly all patients have one or more of the following symptoms: dyspnoea, tachypnoea or pleuritic chest pain. With a large PE patients may present with collapse. Hypoxaemia may be present with moderate or large pulmonary emboli.

Investigations

- **Chest X-ray**
  - May be normal; pleural-based, wedge-shaped defects described classically are rare and areas of oligaemia may be difficult to detect
- **D-dimer**
  - Will be raised in PE but the test is non-specific
- **Helical CT scanning**
  - Will demonstrate pulmonary emboli in the large pulmonary arteries but may not show small peripheral emboli
- **ECG**
  - May show sinus tachycardia and, in massive PE, features of acute right heart strain; non-specific ST-segment and T-wave changes occur
- **Arterial blood gases**
  - Shows a low or normal pCO_2 and may show a degree of hypoxaemia
- **Ventilation/perfusion (*V/Q*) scanning**
  - Shows one or more areas of *V/Q* mismatching

- **Pulmonary angiography**
  - Remains the 'gold standard', but this is underused

In each case a clinical assessment of the probability of PE should be made. As demonstrated in the PIOPED study:

- Cases of high clinical probability combined with a high-probability *V/Q* scan are virtually diagnostic of PE
- Similarly, cases of low clinical suspicion combined with low-probability or normal *V/Q* scans make the diagnosis of PE very unlikely
- All other combinations of clinical probability and *V/Q* scan result should be investigated further
- Patients who present with collapse need urgent echocardiography, helical CT scan or pulmonary angiogram to demonstrate PE

Management

In all cases of moderate or high clinical probability of PE, anticoagulation with heparin should be started immediately after baseline coagulation studies have been taken. If unfractionated heparin is used, an initial loading dose of 5000–10 000 units should be given intravenously followed by a continuous infusion of 1300 IU/h (adjusted according to the results of the activated partial thromboplastin time (APTT), which should be 1.5–2.5 times the control). Low-molecular-weight heparin, given as a once daily subcutaneous injection, is licensed for the treatment of PE; no monitoring is required. Patients should be treated with heparin for at least 5 days; during that time warfarin is introduced and the heparin is discontinued once the INR is two to three times the control.

- Warfarin is continued for 3–6 months in most cases; for PE occurring post-operatively, 6 weeks' anticoagulation is adequate. In recurrent PE, anticoagulation should be for longer periods (eg 1 year) and consideration should be given to lifelong treatment
- In cases of collapse due to massive PE, thrombolysis with streptokinase or recombinant

tissue plasminogen activator given by peripheral vein should be considered. This should be avoided when the embolic material is an infected vegetation (eg intravenous drug abusers)

- Occasionally, pulmonary embolectomy is used for those with massive PE where thrombolysis is unsuccessful or contraindicated
- Inferior vena caval filters should be considered in patients where anticoagulation is contraindicated or in those who continue to embolise despite anticoagulation

1.9.3 Systemic hypertension

Overall, 30% of the UK adult population have hypertension, with the prevalence increasing with age to 70% in the eighth decade. Guidelines for treatment continually adapt to new clinical evidence, but the British Hypertension Society (BHS) has issued guidelines (Table 1.11) to identify those in need of treatment.

Suggested treatment targets are <140/85 mmHg in general; <130/80 mmHg for high-risk patients, such as diabetics.

A suggested treatment algorithm is given in Table 1.12.

MRFIT (Multiple Risk Factor Intervention Trial)

This involved 350 000 men, aged 35–75 years, who had no previous history of cardiovascular disease. Follow-up was long (11.6 years) and the outcomes of patients with different baseline blood pressure were noted. When compared with a blood pressure of 120/80 mmHg, all strata of blood pressure above this were associated with an increased risk of cardiovascular death.

HOT (Hypertension Optimal Treatment) Study (1998)

This involved approximately 19 000 patients, aged 50–80 years, who had diastolic hypertension. They were randomised to receive treatment to achieve one of three diastolic blood pressure targets (<90,

Table 1.11. British Hypertension Society Guidelines.

Systolic pressure (mmHg)	Diastolic pressure (mmHg)	Observation	Cofactor	Recommendation
180	110	Single reading		Treat
160–179	100–109	Multiple readings		Treat
140–159	90–99	Multiple readings	DM, TOD, 10-year risk >20%	Treat
140–159	90–99	Multiple readings	None of the above	Reassess annually
<140	<90	Multiple readings		Reassess annually
130–139	80–85	Single reading		Reassess annually
>130	>80			Reassess in 5 years

DM, diabetes mellitus; TOD, target organ damage (eg any cardiovascular disease, LVH by echo or ECG, proteinuria)

Table 1.12. Treatment algorithm for hypertension

First line for those >55 years old or for black patients	Calcium blocker or thiazide
First-line treatment for others	ACE Inhibitor or angiotensin receptor blocker (ARB)
Second-line treatment	ACE Inhibitor or ARB + calcium blocker or thiazide
Third-line treatment	ACE Inhibitor or ARB + calcium blocker + thiazide
Additional possibilities	Other diuretic, α/β-blockers

<85 or <80 mmHg). The lowest cardiovascular event incidence was seen at a mean DBP of 82 mmHg. In the diabetic patients within the study, cardiovascular events were 51% less in patients randomised to the <80 mmHg group compared with the <90 mmHg DBP group.

UK PDS 38 (1998)

This included 1148 hypertensive type 2 diabetic patients who were randomised to receive treatment so as to achieve either tight or suboptimal blood pressure control. At the end of the 8-year follow-up period, the mean blood pressures achieved in each group were 144/82 mmHg versus 154/87 mmHg. A significant reduction in macrovascular and micro-vascular complications, as well as mortality, was noted in the patients with better controlled blood pressure.

SysEurTrial (2000)

This investigated the effects of treatment of sustained **systolic** blood pressure upon outcomes. Active treatment was shown to significantly reduce cardiovascular and cerebrovascular events.

Other considerations in hypertension management

- Investigation of **phaeochromocytomas**: recommend three 24-h urinary catecholamine derivatives of all drugs on a vanilla-free diet (and off all drugs). Urinary metadrenalines may also be measured

- Hypertension **increases the risk** (Framingham data) of: stroke ($\times 7$); cardiac failure ($\times 4$); coronary artery disease ($\times 3$); peripheral vascular disease ($\times 2$)
- Potassium salt should be substituted for sodium salt where possible
- **Drugs to avoid in pregnancy**: diuretics, ACE inhibitors, angiotensin II-receptor blockers. **Drugs with well-identified risks preferred in pregnancy**: β-blockers (especially labetalol), methyldopa and hydralazine
- Young black men have a poor response to ACE inhibitors and β-blockers as they are salt conservers by background, and so are resistant to renin manipulation and are particularly likely to develop the side-effect of impotence

1.9.4 Aortic dissection

Two-thirds of tears occur in the ascending aorta with about one fifth occurring in the descending aorta. Mortality is highest in the first few hours if the dissection is untreated. The differential diagnosis for ascending dissection includes MI if the vulnerable right coronary ostium is involved (giving rise to an inferior infarct pattern). This is particularly important when considering thrombolysis; aortic regurgitation provides supportive evidence of the diagnosis.

Associations with aortic dissection

- Systemic hypertension (present in 80%)
- Marfan syndrome
- Cystic medial degeneration (rare in the absence of Marfan syndrome)
- Noonan and Turner syndromes
- Trauma
- Aortic coarctation
- Congenital bicuspid aortic valve (present in 10%–15% and dissection is therefore associated with aortic stenosis)
- Giant-cell arteritis
- Pregnancy (particularly in patients with Marfan syndrome)
- Cocaine abuse

Involvement of ascending aorta may cause

- Aortic regurgitation
- Inferior MI
- Pericardial effusion (including cardiac tamponade)
- Carotid dissection
- Absent or decreased subclavian pulse

Medical therapy to be considered for

- Old, stable dissections (>2 weeks)
- Uncomplicated dissection of descending aorta
- Isolated arch dissections

Investigations for aortic dissection

- TOE, aortic MRI or contrast-enhanced spiral CT scans all have a high diagnostic sensitivity, but CT rarely identifies the site of the tear or the presence of aortic regurgitation or coronary involvement
- MRI is of the highest quality but is contraindicated in patients with pacemakers, certain vascular clips and metal valve prostheses
- TOE is probably the most widely used investigation as it is available in the acute situation and has high sensitivity and specificity
- Aortography is no longer the gold standard and coronary angiography is applicable only when deciding on the need for concomitant CABG

APPENDIX I

Normal cardiac physiological values

ECG

- PR interval 0.12–0.20 s
- QRS duration >0.10 s
- QTc (males) 380 ms, (females) 420 ms
- QRS axis –30° to + 90°

Indices of cardiac function

- Cardiac index = Cardiac output/body surface area (BSA) = $2.5-4.0 \ \mathrm{l \cdot min^{-1} \cdot m^{-2}}$
- Stroke volume index = stroke volume/ BSA = $40-70 \ \mathrm{ml \cdot m^{-2}}$
- Systemic vascular resistance (SVR) = 80 × (Ao–RA)/cardiac output = $770-1500 \ \mathrm{dyn \cdot s \cdot cm^{-5}}$, where Ao is the mean aortic pressure and RA is the mean right atrial pressure
- Ejection fraction = proportion of blood ejected from left ventricle = 50%–70%

Cardiac catheterisation pressures	mmHg	Criteria for significant oxygen saturation set up	
Mean right atrial	0–8	SVC/IVC to RA	>7% (eg ASD)
Right ventricular systolic	15–30	RA to RV	>5% (eg VSD)
End diastolic	0–8	RV to PA	>5% (eg PDA)
		Any level:	
Pulmonary artery systolic	15–30	SVC to PA	>7%
End-diastolic	3–12	Usual saturations (SaO_2)	
Mean	9–16	Venous	65%–75%
Pulmonary artery wedge		Arterial	96%–98%
A	3–15		
V	3–12		
Left atrial mean	1–10		
Left ventricular systolic	100–140		
End-diastolic	3–12		
Aortic systolic	100–140		
End-diastolic	60–90		
Mean	70–105		

APPENDIX II

Summary of further trials in cardiology

Major trials

Condition	Intervention	Trials	Main finding	References
Heart failure	β-Blockers	MERIT-HF, CIBIS II, COPERNICUS	β-Blockers reduce mortality and morbidity	*Lancet* 1999;**353**:2001–7, *Lancet* 1999;**353**:9–13, *N Engl J Med* 2001;**344**:1659–67
Heart failure	ACE inhibitors	SOLVD, ATLAS, CONCENSUS	ACE inhibitors reduce mortality and morbidity	*N Engl J Med* 1991;**325**:293–302, *Circulation* 1999;**100**:2312–18
Heart failure	Cardiac resynchronisation therapy (CRT)	MUSTIC, MIRACLE, COMPANION, CARE-HF	CRT reduces mortality and morbidity	*N Engl J Med* 2001;**344**:873–80, *N Engl J Med* 2002;**346**:1845–53, *N Engl J Med* 2004;**350**:2140–50,*N Engl J Med* 2005;**352**:1539–49
Ventricular arrhythmia	Implantable defibrillators (ICD)	AVID, MADIT II, COMPANION	ICD reduce mortality in primary and secondary prevention	*N Engl J Med* 1997;**337**:1576–83, *N Engl J Med* 2002;**346**:877–83, *N Engl J Med* 2004;**350**:2140–50
Acute MI	Aspirin	ISIS 2	Aspirin reduces mortality	*Lancet* 1988;**ii**:349–60
Acute MI	Thrombolysis	ISIS 2, ISIS 3, GUSTO, GISSI 1	Thrombolysis reduces mortality	*Lancet* 1988;**ii**:349–60, *Lancet* 1992;**339**:753–70, *New Engl J Med* 1993;**329**:673–82, *Lancet* 1986;**i**:397–401
Ischaemic heart disease	β-Blockers	ISIS, BHAT, CAPRICORN	β-blockers reduce mortality	*Lancet* 1986;**ii**:57–66, *JAMA* 1982;**247**:1707–14, *Lancet* 2001;**357**:1385–90
Ischaemic heart disease	ACE inhibitors	AIRE, SAVE, GISSI 3, TRACE	ACE inhibitors reduce mortality	*Lancet* 1993;**342**:821–8, *N Engl J Med* 1992;**327**:669–77, *Lancet* 1994;**343**:1115–22, *N Engl J Med* 1995;**333**:1670–6
Ischaemic heart disease	Statins	SSSS, WOSPCOPS, HPS	Statins are effective in primary and secondary prevention	*Lancet* 1994;**344**:1383–89, *N Engl J Med* 1995;**333**:1301–7, *Lancet* 2002;**360**:7–22

Chapter 2
Clinical Pharmacology, Toxicology and Poisoning

CONTENTS

Clinical Pharmacology, Toxicology and Poisoning

2.1 DRUG METABOLISM AND INTERACTIONS

2.1.1 Genetic polymorphisms of drug metabolism

Genetic variation may alter response to drug therapy. For example, angiotensin-converting enzyme (ACE) inhibitors may prevent the occurrence of diabetes in homozygous carriers of the 1166A variant of the angiotensin type 1 receptor gene, but not in heterozygotes and non-carriers.

Genetically determined enzyme activity may alter individual susceptibility to adverse drug reactions. For example, the slow acetylator phenotype (possessed by 50% of Caucasians) may be associated with adverse effects due to higher drug concentrations:

- Drug-induced lupus
- Isoniazid-induced peripheral neuropathy

Drug-induced lupus is associated with slow acetylation and possession of HLA DR4. In contrast to autoimmune systemic lupus erythematosus (SLE), the incidence is equal in men and women and laboratory findings include antibodies to histones and single-stranded DNA. Clinical features of drug-induced lupus include:

- Arthralgia
- Butterfly rash
- Pleurisy

Renal involvement (except with hydralazine) and neuropsychiatric manifestations are unusual.

Drugs causing a lupus erythematosus-like syndrome

- β-Blockers
- Hydralazine
- Phenytoin
- Chlorpromazine
- Isoniazid
- Procainamide
- Clonidine
- Lithium
- Sulfasalazine
- Flecainide
- Methyldopa
- Sulphonamides
- Haloperidol
- Penicillin
- Tetracyclines

Poor metabolisers of particular drugs

- **Nateglinide** is metabolised more slowly by patients with the CYP2C9*3/*3 genotype than by carriers of CYP2C9*1, so that the former patients may be at increased risk of hypoglycaemia
- **s-Mephenytoin**: 3%–5% of the UK population are poor metabolisers of this anti-epileptic agent

Rapid acetylators

Rapid acetylators may have an increased propensity to adverse drug effects due to the actions of excess drug metabolite, for example hepatitis due to a metabolite of isoniazid.

2.1.2 Liver enzyme induction

Many drugs are capable of inducing liver enzyme systems, thereby increasing the metabolism (and decreasing the effectiveness) of other drugs. Enzyme induction normally takes several days to be clinically apparent due to the time required to synthesise new enzyme. Enzyme induction may decrease the effectiveness of:

- Hydrocortisone
- Oral contraceptive pill
- Phenytoin
- Warfarin

The drugs that cause this effect can be remembered by the mnemonic **PC BRAS**:

(**P**henytoin, **C**arbamazepine, **B**arbiturates, **R**ifampicin, **A**lcohol (chronic excess), **S**ulphonylureas)

2.1.3 Liver enzyme inhibition

A number of drugs are capable of inhibiting hepatic enzyme systems, and the effect may be immediate. Enzyme inhibition can slow the metabolism of other drugs, thereby increasing their plasma concentrations and the risk of adverse effects. Enzyme inhibition can increase the effects of:

- Carbamazepine
- Ciclosporin
- Phenytoin
- Theophyllines
- Warfarin

Drugs capable of inhibiting liver enzymes may be recalled by the mnemonic **AODEVICCES**:

(**A**llopurinol, **O**meprazole, **D**isulfiram, **E**rythromycin, **V**alproate, **I**soniazid, **C**iprofloxacin, **C**imetidine, acute **E**thanol intoxication, **S**ulphonamides)

2.1.4 Failure of the combined oral contraceptive pill

Any condition that leads to impaired absorption of the components of the contraceptive pill (eg travellers' diarrhoea) can result in its failure as a contraceptive agent. In addition:

- The oestrogenic component of the oral contraceptive may be metabolised more rapidly in the presence of liver enzyme inducers (see above), leading to pill failure, but enzyme inhibitors have no clinically significant effect
- Pill failure may also result from concomitant antibiotic usage. For example, ampicillin, amoxicillin and tetracyclines may eradicate gut flora that deconjugate bile salts, thereby interrupting enterohepatic cycling of the oestrogenic component

2.2 PRESCRIBING IN PARTICULAR CLINICAL STATES

2.2.1 Drugs and breast-feeding

Infants under 1 month of age are at greatest risk from drugs in breast milk due to immature metabolism and excretion. Drugs that are excreted in breast milk and are contraindicated during breast-feeding include:

- **Amiodarone**: thyroid anomalies
- **Cytotoxics and chloramphenicol**: blood dyscrasia

Other drugs that should not be taken by breast-feeding mothers include:

- **Gold**: haematological reactions and renal impairment
- **Indometacin**: has been reported to cause seizures
- **Iodides**: thyroid disturbance
- **Lithium**: involuntary movements
- **Oestrogens**: feminisation of male infants

2.2.2 Pregnancy and drug therapies

During the first 16 weeks of pregnancy, drugs may exert teratogenic effects on the fetus leading to malformations. Particular associations are:

- **ACE inhibitors and angiotensin-receptor blockers**: oligohydramnios
- **Lithium**: cardiac abnormalities

- **Phenytoin**: facial fusion abnormalities such as cleft lip and palate
- **Sodium valproate** and **retinoids**: neural tube defects
- **Warfarin**: abnormalities of long bones and cartilage

Later in pregnancy some drugs may cross the placenta and harm the fetus:

- **Carbimazole**: neonatal goitre (which may even be large enough to obstruct labour)
- **Gentamicin**: cranial nerve VIII nerve deafness in the newborn

2.2.3 Prescribing in liver disease and liver failure

Patients with liver impairment are more prone to sedative effects of drugs, and certain drugs may induce hepatic encephalopathy, for example opioids and benzodiazepines. Thiazides and loop diuretics may worsen hypokalaemia and provoke encephalopathy. Other important aspects of drug metabolism in liver disease are listed below:

- Drugs excreted via the bile, such as rifampicin, can accumulate in patients with obstructive jaundice
- Hypoalbuminaemia may reduce available protein binding, and increase the proportion of drug that is unbound ('free'), thereby increasing the risk of adverse effects (eg phenytoin)
- Reduced clotting factor synthesis may enhance the risk of bleeding associated with warfarin
- Salt and water retention and ascites may be made worse by non-steroidal anti-inflammatory drugs (NSAIDs) and corticosteroids

2.2.4 Prescribing in renal failure

In patients with established renal impairment, nephrotoxic agents may exacerbate renal damage (especially in acute renal failure). Patients with low glomerular filtration rate (GFR) will be prone to accumulation of drugs normally eliminated by the kidney, for example water-soluble drugs.

Drugs that may cause toxicity due to accumulation in patients with severe renal failure (GFR <10 ml/min) include:

- **Atenolol**: bradycardia, heart block
- **Digoxin**: cardiac arrhythmias, heart block
- **Enoxaparin**: bleeding risk
- **Erythromycin**: encephalopathy
- **Lithium**: cardiac arrhythmias and seizures
- **Penicillins** (high dose): lead to encephalopathy
- **Cephalosporins:** (high dose) encephalopathy

Nephrotoxic drugs capable of precipitating or worsening acute renal impairment should be avoided where possible. Therapeutic drug monitoring may be required in some cases, for example gentamicin or parenteral vancomycin. Examples of nephrotoxic drugs include:

- ACE inhibitors and angiotensin-receptor antagonists
- Aminoglycosides
- Amphotericin
- Diuretics (especially high doses of loop diuretics)
- NSAIDs
- Calcineurin inhibitors (ciclosporin and tacrolimus)

Other drugs may have specific nephrotoxic effects, such as gold-induced proteinuria or nephrotic syndrome, which is usually due to membranous glomerulonephritis. (*See also* Chapter 15, Nephrology.)

2.3 INDIVIDUAL DRUGS AND THOSE USED IN SPECIFIC CLINICAL CONDITIONS

2.3.1 Cardiology

Abciximab (ReoPro®)

This chimeric monoclonal antibody irreversibly binds GpIIb/IIIa glycoprotein receptors in platelets, preventing the final common pathway of platelet activation and aggregation. It is capable of preventing acute thrombosis and re-stenosis in patients with unstable angina who are undergoing coronary artery stent insertion. Risks of thrombocytopenic haemorrhage are low and may be reversed by platelet administration. Abciximab should be used only once in any individual.

Adenosine

Adenosine is a purine nucleoside with a half-life of 8–10 seconds. It acts via adenosine receptors that activate K^+ channels in sinoatrial and atrioventricular nodes. It is capable of terminating supraventricular tachycardia (SVT), and is used as a diagnostic aid to distinguish SVT from ventricular tachycardia. Its duration of action may be increased by dipyridamole.

Side-effects of adenosine
• Anxiety • Chest tightening • Bronchospasm (avoid in asthmatic patients) • Facial flushing

Aliskiren

Aliskiren is a direct renin inhibitor (inhibits conversion of angiotensinogen to angiotensin I). Its mechanisms of action are complex and not fully understood. Aliskiren is licensed for treatment of essential hypertension, and is effective alone or in combination with other antihypertensives (including optimal doses of ACE inhibitor or angiotensin-receptor antagonist). Adverse effects include renal impairment and hyperkalaemia, especially in patients receiving other medications capable of increasing serum potassium (for example, spironolactone, ACE inhibitors, angiotensin-receptor antagonists).

Amiodarone

Amiodarone may be used to control supraventricular and ventricular arrhythmias. Its main action is to prolong the refractory period, with corresponding QT prolongation on the ECG. It reduces mortality in patients with recurrent ventricular tachycardia (VT) or hypertrophic cardiomyopathy.

- It is iodine-containing and has a very long half-life (26–127 days)
- Protein binding interaction causes increased effects of digoxin and warfarin
- Given intravenously, the anti-arrhythmic action occurs within a few hours; given orally this may take 1–3 weeks
- Amiodarone is the least negatively inotropic anti-arrhythmic with the exception of digoxin
- Hyperthyroidism may result from enhanced peripheral de-iodination of thyroxine to T_3

Hypothyroidism arises from increased production of reverse T_3 in the liver.

Side-effects of amiodarone
• Arrhythmias (torsades de pointes) • Ataxia • Alveolitis • Hepatitis • Hyperthyroidism • Hypothyroidism • Metallic taste • Peripheral neuropathy • Photosensitivity • Pulmonary fibrosis • Reversible corneal microdeposits • Slate-grey discoloration of skin

Angiotensin-converting enzyme (ACE) inhibitors

ACE inhibitors reduce mortality in heart failure, prolong survival after myocardial infarction, and they are also beneficial in slowing progressive diabetic nephropathy. They are contraindicated in bilateral functional renal artery stenosis and should be used with caution in severe renal impairment.

- Dry cough occurs in around 20%, thought to be due to increased alveolar and bronchiolar concentrations of kinins
- Hypersensitivity reactions can occur, including angioedema
- Potassium may increase due to inhibition of aldosterone effects

Angiotensin-receptor blockers

Angiotensin II receptor (type AT1) antagonists do not inhibit bradykinin breakdown (unlike ACE inhibitors) and are less likely to provoke cough. They improve survival in patients with hypertension, cardiac failure and after myocardial infarction, and they are also beneficial in patients with diabetic nephropathy (*see* Nephrology, Chapter 15). They may precipitate acute renal failure in patients with reduced renal blood flow (eg bilateral renal artery stenosis, severe cardiac failure, hypovolaemia) in an identical manner to that seen with ACE inhibitors. Angioedema is also recognised, but may be less common than with ACE inhibitors.

Digoxin

Digoxin delays atrioventricular node conduction, and may slow ventricular rate in atrial fibrillation and flutter. It has a limited role as a positive inotrope but may be effective in patients with coexistent heart failure and atrial fibrillation.

- 85% is eliminated unchanged in the urine; digoxin may accumulate in renal impairment
- The steroid-like structure of digoxin has occasionally caused gynaecomastia with chronic use
- Digoxin has a narrow therapeutic index, and small increases in dose may cause toxicity

Digoxin toxicity

Any arrhythmia may occur with digoxin toxicity, including heart block and atrial fibrillation. Pulsus bigeminus is indicative of a ventricular ectopic coupled to a normal QRS complex on the ECG and this may herald digoxin toxicity.

- The 'reversed tick' (ST-segment depression in the inferior and lateral leads on the ECG) is a sign of **digoxin therapy** and not necessarily toxicity. First-degree heart block may also be seen in patients with sinus rhythm who take digoxin
- Electrolyte imbalance may predispose to digoxin toxicity: hypokalaemia, hypomagnesaemia and hypercalcaemia
- Amiodarone may displace digoxin from tissue-binding sites, leading to toxicity. Quinine and

calcium antagonists may impair renal tubular clearance of digoxin and cause toxicity

Toxic effects of digoxin

- Anorexia
- Nausea/vomiting
- Arrhythmias (eg atrial fibrillation, heart block)
- Yellow vision (xanthopsia)
- Diarrhoea

Flecainide

A class 1c agent used for treatment of ventricular arrhythmias, pre-excitation syndromes and for chemical cardioversion of acute atrial arrhythmias. The CAST trial suggests that flecainide is pro-arrhythmic after myocardial infarction; it should be avoided in left ventricular impairment. Its half-life is about 16 hours; other adverse effects are vertigo and visual disturbance.

HMG CoA reductase inhibitors

Statins inhibit the rate-limiting enzyme in cholesterol synthesis (3-hydroxy-3-methyl-glutaryl coenzyme A (HMG CoA) reductase), which is normally predominantly active during sleep (due to fasting and increased hepatic blood flow). They also cause up-regulation of low-density lipoprotein (LDL) receptors, thereby reducing LDL by 30% and increasing the clearance of cholesterol, and increasing high-density lipoprotein (HDL). Most statins have minimal effects on triglycerides. However, although atorvastatin may reduce triglycerides, mortality data are still awaited.

- Statins reduce mortality after myocardial infarction and in patients with diabetes mellitus, hypertension, or other major cardiovascular risk factors
- Statins may cause rhabdomyolysis, and this is more likely in patients with renal impairment, after high doses, or when given with a fibrate; drug-induced hepatitis may also occur

- In patients with established coronary heart disease, the Joint British Societies recommend a target total serum cholesterol of <4 mmol/l and LDL cholesterol of <2 mmol/l

Ivabradine

Ivabradine acts on the I_f channel (an inward sodium-potassium channel) found predominantly in the sinoatrial node, resulting in reduced resting and exercising heart rate. It is indicated for the treatment of angina, and may be less negatively inotropic than β-blockers and may cause fewer symptoms attributed to reduced peripheral blood flow (muscle cramps, cold peripheries). It is contraindicated in patients with resting bradycardia and sick sinus syndrome, and in patients taking a β-blocker or rate-limiting calcium-channel blocker (diltiazem, verapamil).

Nicorandil

A potassium-channel opener that induces arterial vasodilatation, it also possesses a nitrate component that promotes venous relaxation. Used as an anti-anginal agent. Side-effects are transient headache, flushing and dizziness. In large doses it may cause hypotension with a reflex tachycardia.

Thiazide diuretics

Thiazides are capable of lowering blood pressure. The mechanism is uncertain, but is independent of the modest diuretic effect provided by these agents. Maximum blood pressure reduction is achieved using low doses (eg bendroflumethiazide 2.5 mg daily). They are associated with a number of dose-dependent metabolic effects:

- Hyponatraemia, hypokalaemia and hypomagnesaemia; a hypochloraemic alkalosis
- Raised plasma urate due to reduced tubular clearance; gout may be precipitated
- Diabetic glycaemic control may worsen on thiazides due to impaired insulin release and increased insulin resistance
- Postural hypotension, photosensitivity and impotence (mechanism unclear)

Rare dose-independent side-effects of thiazide diuretics

- Agranulocytosis
- Pancreatitis
- Thrombocytopenia

Clopidogrel

Clopidogrel inhibits ADP-mediated platelet aggregation. It is used in acute coronary syndrome, and to prevent ischaemic heart disease and stroke. It is at least as effective as aspirin, and limited data indicate that its addition to aspirin may confer additional benefit. Adverse effects include neutropenia, although this is uncommon.

2.3.2 Endocrinology

Carbimazole

Carbimazole inhibits a peroxidase that catalyses all phases of thyroid hormone production from the amino acid tyrosine. It takes at least 6 weeks to reduce blood levels of thyroid hormones. Therefore, somatic symptoms of hyperthyroidism, such as tachycardia and anxiety, are best suppressed by β-blockers (eg propranolol).

- Agranulocytosis may occur within the first 16 weeks of therapy and in the event of a sore throat patients should be advised to seek medical help
- The drug crosses the placenta, and may cause neonatal goitre and hypothyroidism

Exenatide

A synthetic form of exendin-4 that potentiates the release of insulin in response to hyperglycaemia. It is licensed for use in patients with type 2 diabetes in combination with metformin or sulphonylurea or both, and in patients with inadequate glycaemic control. It requires subcutaneous administration, and its utility requires further evaluation.

Hormone replacement therapy

On average, over a third of a woman's life is in the post-menopausal phase, yet only 12% receive hormone replacement therapy (HRT); 60%–75% experience vasomotor symptoms that may be reduced by HRT.

- Without HRT, women aged 70 years have a 50% reduction in bone mass and one in two will have an osteoporosis-related fracture
- HRT may reduce the occurrence of fractures. There is uncertainty over the possible impact of HRT on heart disease and stroke risk, and HRT may be associated with an increased risk of breast cancer. *See also* Chapter 4, Endocrinology, Section 4.3.5

Nateglinide and repaglinide

These agents have a short duration of action and may be used to stimulate insulin release in patients with type 2 diabetes prior to meals. They may also be given alongside metformin. Side-effects include gastrointestinal upset and hypersensitivity reactions.

Acarbose

Acarbose inhibits intestinal α-glucosidase and thereby delays absorption of starch and sucrose. It reduces post-prandial hyperglycaemia in type 1 diabetes and is used as an adjunct to metformin or sulphonylurea therapy in type 2 diabetes. Excess flatus is a common adverse effect.

Sitagliptin

Sitagliptin is a dipeptidylpeptidase-4 (DPP-4) inhibitor that increases insulin secretion and inhibits glucagon secretion. Sitagliptin may be added to metformin or a thiazolidinedione (see below) if glycaemic control is inadequate. DPP-4 inhibitors depend on intrinsic insulin secretion and therefore are not expected to cause hypoglycaemia.

Thiazolidinediones (pioglitazone and rosiglitazone)

Thiazolidinediones reduce peripheral insulin resistance and are used in combination with metformin or sulphonylureas to treat patients in whom combined therapy with the latter two agents is inadequate or not tolerated. Thiazolidinediones may delay the requirement for insulin. Hepatic impairment is a recognised adverse effect, and hence regular monitoring of liver biochemistry is required.

2.3.3   Gastroenterology

Mesalazine and olsalazine

Mesalazine and olsalazine differ from sulfasalazine in being purely 5-amino salicylic acid (5-ASA) molecules that are split for local action in the colon. They suppress local inflammation in ulcerative colitis.

- They have some systemic side-effects, including nausea, abdominal pain, headache and sometimes worsening of colitis
- Rare side-effects of mesalazine and olsalazine include reversible pancreatitis, blood dyscrasias and interstitial nephritis (with mesalazine)

Orlistat

Orlistat inhibits the action of pancreatic lipase and may be used in obesity where the body mass index is >30 kg/m^2 and the patient has been able to lose 2.5 kg in weight over a 4-week period. It causes liquid, oily stools and may reduce the absorption of fat-soluble vitamins.

Sulfasalazine

Sulfasalazine consists of a sulphonamide molecule plus 5-ASA. It is used in the treatment of ulcerative colitis, and also as a disease-modifying antirheumatic in rheumatoid arthritis. The sulphonamide moiety frequently leads to gastrointestinal upset. Other key features are as follows:

- Oligospermia, leading to male infertility, may occur but this is usually reversible on stopping sulfasalazine
- Patients may note orange discoloration of body fluids

- Slow acetylators may experience more toxicity with sulfasalazine due to exposure to higher levels of the sulphonamide constituent
- Rare side-effects of sulfasalazine include Stevens–Johnson syndrome, blood dyscrasias (especially agranulocytosis and aplasia) and nephrotic syndrome

2.3.4 Neurology

Treatment of Parkinson's disease

Enhanced dopaminergic transmission is central to the medical management of Parkinson's disease:

- **Selegiline** is a type B monoamine oxidase inhibitor (MAO-B); inhibition of monoamine oxidase potentiates dopamine and reduces end-dose akinesia. It was thought that selegiline might also retard progression of Parkinson's disease by preserving dopaminergic neurones. This is now known to be untrue
- **Amantadine** potentiates dopamine by preventing its re-uptake into presynaptic terminals
- **Levodopa** (L-dopa) is absorbed in the proximal small bowel by active transport, but the presence of amino acids (and thus meals) may reduce absorption. It is a pro-drug which must be converted to dopamine within the nigrostriatal pathway. The drug is largely metabolised by catechol-*o*-methyl transferase. After 8 years of therapy with L-dopa, 50% of patients will have choreoathetoid dyskinesia and end-dose akinesia. By this time many patients will have deteriorated to pre-treatment levels of disability due to progression of Parkinson's disease
- **Dopamine-receptor agonists** include apomorphine, bromocriptine, cabergoline, pergolide, pramipexole and ropinirole. These agents cause less dyskinesia than L-dopa but they are associated with more neuropsychiatric adverse effects. Certain of these agents have been associated with pulmonary and retroperitoneal fibrosis (bromocriptine, cabergoline, pergolide). **Apomorphine** is a powerful dopamine agonist which needs to be

given by parenteral administration under specialist supervision. It is highly emetogenic and domperidone must therefore be given 2 days prior to the commencement of therapy

Side-effects of L-dopa

- Cardiac arrhythmias
- Involuntary movements (dyskinesia) occur commonly; seizures are rare
- Nausea and vomiting
- Postural hypotension
- Psychosis (depression or mania)
- Somnolescence (including sudden onset)

Treatment of epilepsy

Recent developments in the therapeutics of epilepsy have concentrated on agents that interact with neurotransmitters.

- **Glutamic acid** is an excitatory central nervous system neurotransmitter; lamotrigine inhibits it, so suppressing seizures. The side-effects of lamotrigine include mood changes, maculopapular rashes, influenza-like symptoms and Stevens–Johnson syndrome
- **γ-Aminobutyric acid** (GABA) is an inhibitory central nervous system neurotransmitter. Gabapentin and vigabatrin potentiate GABA and so may be used to treat seizures
- **Vigabatrin** is used for refractory epilepsy, potentiating GABA by irreversible inhibition of GABA transaminase. Side-effects of vigabatrin include mood disturbance and psychosis in 5%. Severe visual field defects may occur from 1 month to several years after initiation of therapy; regular visual field assessment is advised
- **Diazepam** also terminates seizures by indirectly interacting with GABA transmission. It stimulates the benzodiazepine receptor in the brain which in turn enhances the affinity of the neighbouring GABA receptor for its neurotransmitter
- **Carbamazepine** is a derivative of the tricyclic antidepressants and is useful for epilepsy and also neural pain (eg trigeminal or post-herpetic

neuralgia). Patients commonly experience headaches and diplopia on starting carbamazepine and 5%–15% of patients can develop a generalised morbilliform rash

- **Sodium valproate** is used in absence attacks and temporal lobe epilepsy. It inhibits liver enzymes and may potentiate other anti-epileptics such as phenytoin. It may cause alopecia, with curly regrowth after stopping the drug

Adverse effects of valproate

- Alopecia
- Hepatitis (sometimes fatal)
- Amenorrhoea
- Liver enzyme inhibition
- Ataxia
- Thrombocytopenia
- Gynaecomastia
- Weight gain

5-Hydroxytryptamine agonists (sumatriptan and rizatriptan)

5-Hydroxytryptamine (5HT) agonists are used during the acute phase of migraine. They maintain vascular tone and prevent headache associated with the vasodilator phase of migraine. They must not be given in hemiplegic migraine, or within 24 hours of ergotamine, as intense vasospasm may lead to permanent neurological damage. Sumatriptan may lead to permanent neurological damage. It may also cause angina due to coronary vasospasm.

Side-effects of sumatriptan

- Chest pain
- Flushing
- Drowsiness
- Vasospasm
- Fatigue

2.3.5 Psychiatry

Chlorpromazine

Chlorpromazine blocks many different receptors; for example, it acts as a dopamine blocker, an α-blocker, anticholinergic and antihistamine. Due to prolongation of the QT interval on the ECG, ventricular tachycardia may result (particularly when used in high dose).

Adverse effects of chlorpromazine

- Agranulocytosis
- Contact dermatitis and purple pigmentation of the skin
- Dystonias (including oculogyric crisis)
- Neuroleptic malignant syndrome
- Photosensitivity
- Tardive dyskinesia (chronic use)
- Ventricular tachycardia (prolonged QT)

Other antipsychotics

Newer, so-called 'atypical' antipsychotic agents, have a different adverse effect profile, and generally cause less sedation. Olanzapine and risperidone are associated with an increased risk of stroke in elderly patients, and should be used only with caution in this group.

Lithium

Lithium carbonate is used for prophylaxis in bipolar affective disorder, acute mania/hypomania, and in aggressive behaviour in patients with learning disabilities. It has a narrow therapeutic range (0.5–1.0 mmol/l). Toxic effects occur at levels >2.0 mmol/l.

- **Toxicity** is more likely in renal impairment or when there are imbalances of electrolytes or if lithium excretion is impaired by diuretics, ACE inhibitors or NSAIDs
- Lithium may cause **histological changes** in the kidney and it has been recommended that long-term treatment is reviewed every 2–3 years
- **Polyuria** arises due to nephrogenic diabetes insipidus; lithium prevents antidiuretic hormone

(ADH) from interacting with the collecting duct receptor, so leading to water loss. There is a compensatory increase in ADH release

Toxic effects of lithium

- **At 1–2 mmol/l**
  - Anorexia and vomiting
  - Ataxia and dysarthria
  - Blurred vision
  - Coarse tremor
  - Diarrhoea
  - Drowsiness
  - Muscle weakness
- **Severe toxicity >2 mmol/l**
  - Circulatory failure
  - Coma
  - Convulsions
  - Death
  - Hyper-reflexia
  - Oliguria
  - Toxic psychoses

Side-effects of lithium*

- **Common**
  - Fine tremor (in about 15% of patients)
  - Leucocytosis
  - Loose motions
  - Nausea
  - Oedema
  - Polydipsia
  - Polyuria
  - Weight gain
- **Rare**
  - Goitre
  - Hypothyroidism
  - Interstitial nephritis
  - Worsening of psoriasis and acne

*May arise despite therapeutic range dosing

- Antacids, theophylline and acetazolamide lead to decreased plasma lithium carbonate
- Central nervous system (CNS) toxicity has been described with selective serotonin re-uptake

inhibitors (SSRIs), carbamazepine and phenytoin, methyldopa, antipsychotics (especially haloperidol), calcium-channel blockers and sumatriptan

2.3.6 Rheumatology

Penicillamine

Penicillamine is used as a disease-modifying agent in rheumatoid arthritis and also to chelate cysteine in cystinuria and copper in Wilson's disease, respectively. In the first 6 weeks of therapy reversible loss of taste may occur. This may resolve without stopping the drug.

- After 4–18 months of therapy, proteinuria due to membranous glomerulonephritis may ensue
- Thrombocytopenia and neutropenia may result from penicillamine therapy; patients should be warned to seek medical advice if a sore throat or ready bruising develop
- Myasthenia, drug-induced lupus and Stevens–Johnson syndrome have also been reported

Agents used in the treatment of gout

Allopurinol inhibits xanthine oxidase, the enzyme which converts purines into uric acid, and so prevents gout. However, commencement of therapy will occasionally provoke an acute attack of gout. Established gouty tophi may regress with chronic use of allopurinol.

- Azathioprine, a pro-drug, is converted to 6-mercaptopurine in the body and may accumulate, causing bone marrow toxicity in patients receiving allopurinol
- The renal clearance of cyclophosphamide may also be impeded in patients receiving allopurinol and this again leads to marrow toxicity

Colchicine inhibits macrophage migration into a gouty joint but its use is limited by the frequent occurrence of diarrhoea. It has therefore been said that with colchicine 'you run before you can walk'!

Urate oxidase enzymatically degrades urate to allantoin. Intravenous administration causes a significant reduction in serum urate concentrations (by up to 95%) and is used to prevent renal impairment in tumour lysis syndrome.

2.3.7 Miscellaneous

A detailed description of the mechanism of action, important pharmacokinetics and characteristic or serious side-effects of commonly used antibacterial, antiviral and anthelmintic agents is provided in Chapter 11, Infectious Diseases.

Ciprofloxacin

This 4-quinolone inhibits DNA bacterial gyrase, an enzyme that prevents supercoiling of bacterial DNA. It is active against both Gram-positive and Gram-negative organisms. It is a liver enzyme inhibitor and may increase the effect of theophylline in particular. Ciprofloxacin is not recommended for children under 12 years of age (except in cystic fibrosis) because of the potential for causing bony anomalies.

Adverse effects of ciprofloxacin
• Anaphylaxis • Impaired motor function • Arthralgia • Photosensitivity • Crystalluria • Sedation (which may affect driving) • Diarrhoea • **Seizures** – occur because ciprofloxacin can compete with the inhibitory neurotransmitter, GABA, within the brain

Ciclosporin A

Ciclosporin A is used to reduce transplant rejection and it has significantly improved graft survival. After initiation of therapy (when doses are usually highest) it causes dose-dependent nephrotoxicity and

has a narrow therapeutic range; therapeutic drug monitoring is indicated. Unfortunately, late nephrotoxic effects do occur and are often unrelated to plasma levels (*See also* Chapter 15, Nephrology.)

Gum hyperplasia is common; it is increased in individuals with poor oral hygiene, and also those concomitantly taking dihydropyridine calcium-channel blockers. As with most immunosuppressives, there is an increased risk of skin and lymphoproliferative malignancy with long-term therapy.

Adverse effects of ciclosporin A
• Burning hands and feet (especially during first week of therapy) • Hypertension • Hypertrichosis • Fluid retention • Liver dysfunction • Gum hyperplasia • Nephrotoxicity • Hyperkalaemia • Algodystrophy (complex regional pain syndrome)

Cytotoxics

The majority of cytotoxic agents have the potential to cause marrow suppression.

Specific side-effects of cytotoxic agents

• **Bleomycin**
  • Causes dose-dependent lung fibrosis; it is one of the least myelotoxic chemotherapeutic agents
• **Capecitabine**
  • Desquamation (hand-foot syndrome)
• **Cisplatin**
  • May cause ototoxicity, nephrotoxicity (interstitial nephritis), hypomagnesaemia and peripheral neuropathy
Continues...

Continued. . .

- **Doxorubicin**
  - May cause skin irritation and cardiomyopathy; risk of cardiomyopathy is reduced by dexrazoxane (an iron-chelating agent)
- **Methotrexate**
  - May cause severe mucositis and myelosuppression, which is prevented by the use of folinic acid rescue. During chronic administration, pneumonitis and liver fibrosis may occur
- **Vincristine** and vinblastine
  - Cause a reversible peripheral neuropathy

Leukotriene antagonists

Agents such as montelukast block the effects of leukotriene in the airways. They are used as add-on therapy in mild to moderate asthma. They should not be used to attempt to relieve acute asthma. Churg–Strauss-like eosinophilic vasculitis and peripheral neuropathy have been reported with these agents.

Omalizumab

Omalizumab is a monoclonal antibody that binds to immunoglobulin E, and is licensed for use in the prophylaxis of severe allergic asthma confirmed by allergy testing. Requires subcutaneous administration, and adverse effects include hypersensitivity reactions and Churg–Strauss syndrome.

Retinoids

Oral retinoids are indicated for the treatment of severe psoriasis and acne that is resistant to other therapies. They are teratogenic, leading to neural tube defects. Like other vitamin A derivatives they may cause benign intracranial hypertension. Dryness of mucous membranes leading to intolerance of contact lenses has been noted during treatment with retinoids.

High-dose retinoids can rarely cause diffuse interstitial skeletal hyperostosis.

Adverse effects of retinoids

- Alopecia
- Photosensitivity
- Benign intracranial hypertension
- Reduced night vision
- Dry mucous membranes
- Skeletal abnormalities (with high doses)
- Hepatitis
- Hypertriglyceridaemia
- Teratogenicity
- Mood changes
- Thrombocytopenia

Strontium

Strontium ranelate is licensed for post-menopausal osteoporosis. It increases new bone formation and suppresses bone resorption. Recognised adverse effects include severe allergy, and **D**rug **R**ash with **E**osinophilia and **S**ystemic **S**ymptoms (DRESS).

2.4 SPECIFIC ADVERSE EFFECTS

2.4.1 Secondary amenorrhoea

Dopamine inhibits prolactin release and so dopamine-blocking drugs, such as chlorpromazine and cimetidine (but not ranitidine), may provoke hyperprolactinaemia and hence amenorrhoea. Sodium valproate may also cause amenorrhoea.

2.4.2 Bronchospasm

Bronchospasm may be induced by **aspirin** and **non-steroidal anti-inflammatory drugs**, particularly in patients with late-onset asthma. Sensitivity to these agents is thought to relate to pharmacological effects on prostaglandin metabolism; the effect is not immunological, and thus it is termed 'pseudo-allergic'.

- **Adenosine** should be avoided in asthma, as it may cause bronchoconstriction via stimulation of adenosine receptors found in bronchial smooth muscle

- **β-Blockers** (even cardioselective ones such as atenolol) may provoke bronchospasm
- **Sodium cromoglicate** is a mast-cell stabiliser; it is an inhaled, preventative agent in asthma. However, bronchospasm has occasionally been reported, because cromoglicate is administered as a dry powder
- **Acetylcysteine** may cause bronchospasm and anaphylactoid reactions

2.4.3 Dyskinesia and dystonia

Both dopamine agonists and antagonists can lead to movement disorders.

- Drugs with **dopamine-like effects** that are used to treat Parkinson's disease may cause dyskinesia (L-dopa, bromocriptine and pergolide)
- **Dopamine-blocking agents** such as phenothiazines (chlorpromazine) or butyrophenones (haloperidol) may also cause dyskinesias. This is a recognised complication of treatment with dopamine antagonists such as metoclopramide. It is less common with domperidone due to poorer uptake of this agent across the blood–brain barrier
- **SSRIs** may cause dystonias and rarely are associated with serotonergic syndromes

2.4.4 Gynaecomastia

Gynaecomastia can complicate treatment with drugs that are oestrogen-like in action or anti-androgens.

Oestrogen-like action

Digoxin
Spironolactone
Diethylstilbestrol

Anti-androgen action

Cimetidine
Cyproterone acetate
Luteinising hormone-releasing hormone (LHRH) analogues (eg goserelin)

2.4.5 Hypothyroidism

Impaired thyroid hormone production may result from:

- Amiodarone
- Carbimazole
- Lithium
- Propylthiouracil
- Radio-iodine

2.4.6 Drug-induced liver disease

Drug-induced liver disease may represent either dose-dependent or dose-independent effects.

- Dose-dependent liver disease includes paracetamol poisoning, fatty change due to tetracyclines and alcoholic hepatitis
- Dose-independent liver disease usually involves either **hepatitis** or **cholestasis**; it generally has an allergic basis and may on occasion be associated with liver failure

Drug-induced hepatitis occurs with

- Amiodarone
- HMG CoA reductase inhibitors
- Isoniazid metabolite
- Methyldopa
- Paracetamol
- Phenytoin
- Pyrazinamide
- Valproate (especially in patients receiving other anti-epileptics and those aged < 2 years)

Causes of drug-induced cholestasis

- Carbamazepine
- Chlorpromazine
- Co-amoxiclav (combination of amoxicillin and clavulanic acid)
- Erythromycin
- Sulphonylureas

- Liver tumours may be associated with use of androgens and oestrogens (which can also cause Budd–Chiari malformations); liver fibrosis may accompany methotrexate treatment

2.4.7 Drugs provoking myasthenia

- Aminoglycosides, certain **β-blockers** (propranolol, oxprenolol), **phenytoin**, **lidocaine**, **quinidine** and **procainamide** may all impair acetylcholine release, leading to worsening or unmasking of myasthenia
- **Penicillamine** may cause formation of antibodies against the acetylcholine receptor, and a syndrome indistinguishable from myasthenia results. This resolves in two-thirds of cases after penicillamine withdrawal
- **Lithium** may also cause myasthenia-like weakness by impairing synaptic transmission

2.4.8 Photosensitivity

Drugs causing photosensitivity

- Amiodarone
- Piroxicam
- Ciprofloxacin
- Psoralens
- Griseofulvin
- Retinoids
- Loop and thiazide diuretics
- Sulphonylureas
- Oral contraceptives
- Tetracyclines

2.4.9 Drug-induced vasculitis

Drug-induced vasculitis can affect the skin or internal organs.

Recognised drug causes of vasculitis

- Allopurinol
- Captopril
- Cimetidine
- Hydralazine

- Leukotriene antagonists
- Penicillin
- Quinidine
- Sulphonamides
- Thiazides

2.4.10 Acute pancreatitis

Acute pancreatitis is a recognised adverse effect of a number of drugs.

Drugs causing acute pancreatitis

- Antiretrovirals (ritonavir, didanosine, zalcitabine, stavudine, lamivudine)
- Azathioprine
- Corticosteroids
- Fibrates
- HMG CoA reductase inhibitors
- Omega-3 fish oils
- Thiazide diuretics

2.4.11 Syndrome of inappropriate ADH secretion (SIADH)

SIADH is characterised by hyponatraemia, concentrated urine and low plasma osmolality, all occurring in the absence of oedema, diuretic use or hypovolaemia.

Drugs causing SIADH

- Carbamazepine
- Chlorpropamide
- Cytotoxic agents
- Opiates
- Oxytocin
- Psychotropic agents
- Rifampicin

In addition there are a number of non-pharmacological causes, which include malignancy, central nervous system disorders, suppurative pulmonary disease and porphyria (*see* Chapter 4, Endocrinology, Section 4).

2.5 POISONING

2.5.1 Paracetamol overdose

Overdose with paracetamol is one of the most common means of self-poisoning. Early features are minor (nausea and vomiting) but hepatic or renal failure may occur later; and liver damage peaks at 2–3 days after ingestion. Paracetamol toxicity is thought due to excess reactive oxygen metabolites arising from hepatic oxidation that overwhelm glutathione-linked pathways of detoxification. The active free-radical metabolite binds to liver cell macromolecules and causes necrosis.

- The international normalised ratio (INR), or prothrombin ratio, is the most sensitive indicator of impaired liver function. Hypoglycaemia is a feature of advanced liver damage
- Poor prognosis is indicated by an INR >3.0, raised serum creatinine, and plasma pH <7.3 more than 24 hours after overdose
- Patients taking enzyme inducers such as phenytoin have an increased risk of hepatic necrosis after paracetamol poisoning
- Renal failure may sometimes develop and this generally occurs later than hepatic injury
- Acetylcysteine improves prognosis in paracetamol poisoning even after hepatic encephalopathy has developed

2.5.2 Tricyclic antidepressant and venlafaxine overdose

Tricyclic antidepressants and venlafaxine exert a number of toxic effects:

- **Anticholinergic effects**: pupillary dilatation, acute confusion, tachycardia, dry mouth
- **α-Blocking effects**: systemic hypotension and reduced conscious level
- **Sodium-channel blockade**: arrhythmia and seizures
- Prolongation of the QRS complex >100 ms may be associated with increased risk of arrhythmia
- Seizure threshold is reduced and status epilepticus may occur; abnormalities of thermoregulation can also occur

- Treatment is supportive, with emesis, gastric lavage and use of activated charcoal. Fluid and electrolyte balance should be maintained; diazepam is used for convulsions. Intravenous sodium bicarbonate reduces the risk of arrhythmias and seizures in high-risk patients

2.5.3 Theophylline toxicity

May cause tachyarrhythmia due to phosphodiesterase inhibition. Electrolyte abnormalities include severe acidosis and hypokalaemia (the latter partly due to intractable vomiting). Reduced conscious level, seizures and confusion may also occur.

- Treatment is with repeated doses of oral activated charcoal (which significantly enhances theophylline clearance), and correction of fluid and electrolyte depletion
- Haemodialysis or, preferably, charcoal haemoperfusion is indicated for patients with severe toxicity (plasma theophylline >60 mg/l)

2.5.4 Carbon monoxide poisoning

Carbon monoxide binds to haemoglobin with high affinity (>200 times that of oxygen), and decreases oxygen-carrying capacity, resulting in tissue hypoxia. Normal carboxyhaemoglobin levels are <3% in non-smokers and 5%–6% in smokers. Mild exposure (10%–30% carboxyhaemoglobin) may be associated with headache and mild exertional dyspnoea.

Signs of marked toxicity (carboxyhaemoglobin 30%–60%)

- Acute renal failure
- Agitation and confusion
- Bullous lesions
- ECG changes and arrhythmias
- Hyperpyrexia
- Hypertonia and hyper-reflexia
- Muscle necrosis
- Pink mucosae
- Vomiting

- Severe toxicity may be associated with coma, convulsions and cardiorespiratory arrest
- Treatment is with 100% oxygen by mask; hyperbaric oxygen (2.5 atmospheres pressure) will increase the elimination (half-life reduced from 4 hours to 0.5 hours)
- Neuropsychiatric changes may develop over several weeks after recovery from poisoning and these include intellectual deterioration, personality change, cerebral and cerebellar damage, and extrapyramidal damage

2.5.5   Quinine toxicity

Quinine poisoning may result in visual disturbance due to anticholinergic effects and direct neurotoxicity. **Blindness** typically occurs at between 6 and 24 hours after ingestion, and may be irreversible.

- **Arrhythmias**: because these drugs prolong the QT interval on the ECG
- **Hypotension**: which may occur due to α-adrenoceptor blockade
- **Tinnitus**
- **Abdominal pain**

2.5.6   Iron poisoning

The key features of iron poisoning are shown in the box below. Gastric lavage should be contemplated if the patient presents within 1 hour of ingestion. Desferrioxamine chelates iron and may improve clinical outcome when given by intravenous infusion. Desferrioxamine treatment is based on the serum iron concentration, although in severe cases it may be commenced before this is available.

Clinical features
- Abdominal pain - Diarrhoea - Haematemesis - Lower gastrointestinal blood loss - Nausea and vomiting

Severe poisoning
- Coma - Death - Delayed hepatocellular necrosis - Hypotension

2.5.7   Salicylate overdose

The adverse effects of salicylate poisoning are due to direct stimulation of the respiratory centre in the CNS (respiratory alkalosis) and to the acidic properties of the drug as well as to the accumulation of organic acids (metabolic acidosis).

Early features of poisoning
- Hypokalaemia - Respiratory centre stimulation in the CNS, and hence alkalosis - Sweating - Tinnitus

Later features of poisoning
- Acute renal failure - Hypoglycaemia - Hypoprothrombinaemia - Metabolic acidosis - Pulmonary oedema

Key aspects of management of salicylate poisoning involve:

- Activated charcoal
- Correction of electrolyte and metabolic abnormalities
- Intravenous fluids to ensure adequate hydration (forced alkaline diuresis is unsafe and is not recommended)
- Intravenous sodium bicarbonate to correct acidosis (this will reduce the extent of tissue absorption, and may enhance aspirin clearance)
- **Haemodialysis**: for very severe salicylism (eg blood salicylate >750 mg/l)

2.5.8 Ethylene glycol poisoning

Poisoning with ethylene glycol may have a similar clinical appearance to ethanol intoxication, within the first 12 hours. Initially there is a raised plasma osmolar gap due to the presence of ethylene glycol. This is then broken down, the degradation products, including oxalate, giving rise to a wide-anion-gap metabolic acidosis. Toxic effects include severe metabolic acidosis, hypocalcaemia, acute tubular necrosis, crystalluria, and cardiac failure and pulmonary oedema.

Treatment for ethylene glycol poisoning

- Sodium bicarbonate
  - To correct acidosis and enhance clearance of active metabolites
- Intravenous ethanol
  - Can inhibit ethylene glycol metabolism
- Fomepizole
  - This blocks the conversion of ethylene glycol to toxic metabolites, so that ethylene glycol may be excreted unchanged
- Calcium
  - To correct hypocalcaemia
- Haemodialysis
  - Active elimination of ethylene glycol is by haemodialysis

2.5.9 Haemodialysis for overdose or poisoning

Drugs or poisons that are poorly removed by haemodialysis are those with a large volume of distribution (eg amiodarone and paraquat) or those which are highly protein-bound (eg digoxin and phenytoin). Repeated or continuous dialysis treatment may be required for drugs which are widely distributed throughout the body (eg lithium) and a rebound increase in plasma concentrations may occur. There are limited data concerning the impact of haemodialysis on patient outcomes, and it is normally only undertaken in patients with severe poisoning.

Removal of drugs or toxins by haemodialysis/haemoperfusion

- **Haemodialysis effective**
  - Alcohol
  - Barbiturates
  - Ethylene glycol
  - Lithium
  - Methanol
  - Salicylate
- **Charcoal haemoperfusion**
  - Paracetamol metabolites
  - Theophylline

Chapter 3
Dermatology

CONTENTS

Dermatology

3.1 STRUCTURE AND FUNCTION OF SKIN AND TERMINOLOGY OF SKIN LESIONS

3.1.1 Structure

The skin consists of three distinctive layers: the epidermis, dermis and the subcutis.

- **Epidermis**: this forms the outermost layer and is the largest organ in the body. The principal cell is the keratinocyte. The epidermis has four layers, which are the basal cell layer, stratum spinosum, stratum granulosum and the stratum corneum
- **Dermis**: this lies beneath the epidermis and is a support structurally and nutritionally, and contributes 15%–20% of total body weight. The principal cell is the fibroblast, which makes collagen (giving the skin its strength), elastin (providing elasticity) and proteoglycans. It also contains adnexal structures, including hair follicles, sebaceous glands, apocrine glands and eccrine glands
- **Dermo-epidermal junction**: separates the epidermis from the dermis. Anomalies of this can give rise to some of the blistering disorders
- **Subcutis**: contains adipose tissue, loose connective tissue, blood vessels and nerves

3.1.2 Function

The skin has numerous functions, all of which are designed to protect the rest of the body.

- **Barrier properties**: the skin acts as a two-way barrier, preventing the inward or outward passage of fluid and electrolytes
- **Mechanical properties**: the skin is highly elastic and so can be stretched or compressed

- **Immunological function**: the skin provides defence against foreign agents. In the epidermis, antigen presentation is carried out by Langerhans' cells
- **Sensory function**: the skin perceives the sensations of touch, pressure, cold, warmth and pain
- **Endocrine properties**: as a result of exposure to ultraviolet B radiation, vitamin D_3 is synthesised from previtamin D_3
- **Temperature regulation**: the rich blood supply of the dermis plays an important role in thermoregulation
- **Respiration**: the skin plays a minor role in gaseous exchange with the environment

3.1.3 Terminology of skin lesions

- **Macule**: a flat lesion due to a localised colour change; when >1 cm in diameter, this is termed a 'patch'
- **Papule**: a small solid elevation of skin <1 cm diameter
- **Plaque**: a raised flat-topped lesion >1 cm diameter
- **Nodule**: a raised lesion with a rounded surface >1 cm diameter
- **Bulla**: a fluid-filled lesion (blister) >1 cm diameter
- **Vesicle**: a fluid-filled skin lesion <1 cm diameter
- **Pustule**: a pus-filled lesion
- **Wheal**: a raised compressible area of dermal oedema
- **Scale**: flakes arising from abnormal stratum corneum
- **Crust**: dried serum, pus or blood

3.2 SPECIFIC DERMATOSES AND INFECTIONS OF THE SKIN

3.2.1 Psoriasis

This is a genetically determined, inflammatory and proliferative disorder of the skin, occurring in 1%–2% of the UK population. Its aetiology is unknown but multiple genetic factors in combination with environmental factors are thought to be important. Thirty per cent of individuals with psoriasis have an affected first-degree relative and the risk of a child developing psoriasis if both parents are affected is approximately 75% (falling to 20% if one parent is affected). The risk in monozygotic twins is 2–3 times greater than in dizygotic twins. PSOR-1, located on chromosome 6, is a gene in the major histocompatibility complex that is found in up to 50% of cases of psoriasis, although there are likely to be many more genetic loci involved. Environmental factors are also important and can affect the course of disease or exacerbate the condition – see below. Psoriasis can occur at any time of life – it is more common in the second and sixth decades, with the mean age of onset being 33 years.

Pathogenesis

Psoriasis is now recognised as a T-cell-mediated disease with epidermal proliferation occurring as a result of activation of the immune system. The cause of psoriasis is unclear; however, it is postulated that an individual develops an immune response to a particular stimulus, and that this triggers a cascade of immunological events and the production of key cytokines such as tumour necrosis factor alpha (TNFα) and interferon gamma (IFNγ).

Clinical presentation

- **Chronic plaque** (90% of cases): well-defined, red, disc-like plaques covered by white scale, which classically affect elbows, knees and scalp
- **Pustular (generalised pustular)**: sheets of small, sterile yellow pustules on a red background. This presentation may be accompanied by systemic symptoms and progression to erythroderma

- **Pustular (palmo-plantar pustulosis)**: yellow/brown sterile pustules and erythema on palms or soles. Strongly associated with smoking. This is most often seen in middle-aged women
- **Guttate**: an acute eruption of drop-like lesions, often following a streptococcal sore throat
- **Erythrodermic**: confluent areas affecting most of the skin surface
- **Nail psoriasis**: onycholysis, pitting and subungal hyperkeratosis
- **Flexural**: affects axillae, submammary areas and the natal cleft. Lesions are often smooth, red and glazed in appearance

Associations with psoriasis

- **Arthropathy**: arthritis occurs in about 8% of patients with psoriasis. There are several different forms (*see* Chapter 20, Rheumatology) – distal interphalangeal joint disease, large single-joint oligoarthritis, arthritis mutilans, sacroiliitis and psoriatic spondylitis have all been described
- **Gout**: this is due to deposits of urate crystals
- **Malabsorption**: Crohn's and ulcerative colitis are associated with psoriasis
- **The metabolic syndrome**: psoriasis is associated with the metabolic syndrome and its components, such as obesity, diabetes and hypertension. It is also associated with an increased risk of cardiovascular disease independent of traditional risk factors. Obesity has been shown to be a risk factor for the development of psoriasis and an increasing body mass index (BMI) is associated with greater degrees of disease severity
- **Lymphoma**: there is a reported threefold increase in the rates of lymphoma in psoriasis patients

Factors that can exacerbate psoriasis

- **Trauma**: the Köbner phenomenon (the development of the disease in areas of trauma)
- **Infection**: eg streptococci (guttate psoriasis, as above)

- **HIV**: psoriasis is more common in patients with HIV; the severity may dwindle in the late stages of the disease
- **Endocrine**: psoriasis generally tends to improve during pregnancy and deteriorate in the post-partum period
- **Drugs**: β-blockers, lithium, antimalarials, interferon and the withdrawal of oral steroids can exacerbate psoriasis
- **Alcohol**
- **Stress**: most patients report a flare of disease with physical or psychological stress
- **Smoking**: smokers have an increased risk of psoriasis and heavy smokers have more severe disease
- **UV light**: although most patients find UV light beneficial, a small proportion find it flares their skin condition

Causes of the Köbner phenomenon

- Psoriasis
- Lichen planus
- Vitiligo
- Viral warts
- Molluscum contagiosum

Causes of erythroderma

- Psoriasis
- Eczema
- Mycosis fungoides
- Adverse drug reactions
- Underlying malignancy
- Pityriasis rubra pilaris

Management of psoriasis

A careful explanation of the disease process and the likely necessity for long-term treatment should always be given. The type and severity of psoriasis influence the choice of treatment. However, it is usual to prescribe topical agents as the first-line treatment.

Topical therapy

- **Tar preparations**: coal tar has a range of anti-inflammatory and antiproliferative properties. Tar is not usually used in flexures as it can lead to irritation at these sites. Crude coal tar is particularly useful in thick-plaque psoriasis and may be used in combination with UVB (Goeckerman regimen)
- **Dithranol**: a synthetic derivative of anthracene. It is an effective therapy, but needs to be applied accurately as it can stain and burn the surrounding normal skin. It also stains clothing
- **Vitamin D analogues**, eg calcipotriol cream or ointment or calcipotriol with betamethasone (Dovobet®, commonly used in primary care)
- **Weak topical steroids**: for face, genitalia and flexures

For widespread or severe disease, further treatment options are **ultraviolet radiation**, **systemic treatment**, or newer **biological agents**.

Ultraviolet radiation

- PUVA (oral/topical psoralen and UVA)
- UVB narrowband (311–313 nm) is now replacing broadband UVB (290–320 nm)

Systemic treatment

The benefits must be weighed against side-effects of the drugs.

Methotrexate is most commonly used; it blocks DNA synthesis by inhibiting dihydrofolate reductase. It is administered once weekly, orally or subcutaneously. The risks of nausea, anaemia and pancytopenia are reduced with folic acid supplementation. There is a risk of liver fibrosis with long-term use. A serological marker for fibrosis, amino-terminal peptide procollagen III (P3NP) is measured 3-monthly and if consistently high a liver biopsy is performed.

Ciclosporin: inhibits T-lymphocyte transcription of interleukin-2 (IL-2). Major side-effects are renal toxicity and hypertension.

Retinoids: acitretin is the retinoid of choice and is used alone or in combination with UVB or PUVA. Teratogenicity is a problem and treatment should be avoided in women of child-bearing potential. Mucocutaneous side-effects are common and elevated triglyceride levels are often observed.

Treatments used less commonly include: azathioprine, hydroxyurea, mycophenolate mofetil (MMF) and fumaric acid esters.

Biological agents

These are promising new treatments and all but alefacept are approved by NICE, but there are strict eligibility criteria, including disease severity, psychological morbidity and failure or unsuitability of conventional therapies.

- **Etanercept**: human fusion protein of the TNF receptor that acts as a TNFα inhibitor. Delivered subcutaneously twice weekly
- **Efalizumab**: this is a humanised monoclonal antibody which blocks T-cell activation/ migration. Efalizumab has been also approved for patients unresponsive to, intolerant of, or with contraindications to etanercept. Delivered subcutaneously
- **Adalimumab**: a human monoclonal antibody which binds to TNFα. Delivered subcutaneously
- **Infliximab**: a chimeric monoclonal antibody which binds to TNFα. Delivered by infusion
- **Alefacept**: a recombinant fusion protein which interferes with activation/proliferation of T cells

3.2.2 Eczema (dermatitis)

Eczema is an inflammatory skin disorder with characteristic histology and clinical features, which include itching, redness, scaling and a papulo-vesicular rash. Eczema can be divided into two broad groups, exogenous or endogenous:

- **Exogenous eczema** – irritant dermatitis, allergic contact dermatitis
- **Endogenous eczema** – atopic dermatitis, seborrhoeic dermatitis, pompholyx

Seborrhoeic dermatitis is a red, scaly rash caused by *Pityrosporum ovale*. The eruption occurs on the scalp, face and upper trunk and is more common in young adults and HIV patients.

Pompholyx is characterised by itchy vesicles occurring on the palms and soles.

Atopic dermatitis is a characteristic dermatitic eruption associated with a personal or family history of atopy. The age of onset is usually between 2 months and 6 months, with males being more affected than females. The disease is chronic but tends to improve during childhood. The flexural sites are commonly affected and features include itching, exudative papules or vesicles, dryness and lichenification. There is an increased risk of bacterial (staphylococcal or streptococcal) and viral (herpes simplex) infection.

Management of atopic eczema

Initial treatment consists of avoidance of irritants and exacerbating factors. Thereafter:

- **Topical therapy**: regular emollients, topical steroids, tar bandages, wet wraps and antibiotic ointment (for minor infections). Topical tacrolimus and pimecrolimus also have a place in treatment
- **Ultraviolet radiation**: UVB or PUVA (*see* Psoriasis, Section 3.2.1)
- **Systemic treatment**: this can be with ciclosporin, azathioprine, antihistamines, as well as antibiotics for any infective episodes. Occasionally oral prednisolone is used for severe flares

3.2.3 Acne

Acne is the commonest of the dermatological disorders and affects most people at some time during their life. Although not life-threatening, acne can have severe psychosocial consequences and may lead to poor self-esteem, social isolation and depression.

Pathogenesis

Acne is a disease of the pilosebaceous unit. There are four main factors that are important in the development of acne lesions:

- Plugging of the follicle due to epidermal hyperproliferation
- Excess sebum production
- Colonisation with *Propionibacterium acnes*
- Inflammation

The pilosebaceous unit is under androgen control and androgens stimulate sebum production; genetic factors play a role but have not been defined as yet.

Polycystic ovary syndrome, congenital adrenal hyperplasia and other endocrine disorders with excess androgens may trigger the development of acne.

Clinical features

Acne is characterised by comedones, papules, pustules, nodules, cysts and scars. It affects the areas of skin where the sebaceous follicles are most dense: the face, back and chest.

Treatment

Choice of treatment should be based on the severity of the disease and the type of acne, eg comedonal, non-inflammatory acne may only require a keratolytic agent. Most acne needs a combined approach to treat both the comedones and the inflammatory lesions.

Topical treatments

- Topical antibiotics: these are not comedolytic and are best used in combination with benzoyl peroxide or another keratolytic agent
- Topical retinoids: comedolytic and anti-inflammatory. They may be used in combination with other acne medications. They often cause skin irritation
- Benzoyl peroxide: a keratolytic that comes in many formulations

Systemic treatments

- **Antibiotics**: the tetracycline group of antibiotics is the most commonly prescribed. Improvement takes 2–3 months and maintenance treatment must be continued
- **Anti-androgens**: Dianette® consists of cyproterone acetate and oestrogen and acts as a contraceptive pill and an acne treatment
- **Isotretinoin**: a systemic retinoid that is highly effective. It is indicated if there is scarring, if the acne is resistant to multiple treatments (including long-term systemic antibiotics) or if the disease is causing severe psychological distress. Isotretinoin is a teratogen and strict guidelines for its use and prescription are now in place. Women of child-bearing age are advised to use two methods of contraception and to have monthly pregnancy testing. The most common side-effects are mucocutaneous, with severe drying of lips and skin. Mood changes and severe depression have been reported

3.2.4 Rosacea

Rosacea is an inflammatory skin disease which causes erythema, telangiectasia, inflammatory papules and pustules. In some cases it may look like acne, although the skin is not usually greasy and comedones are not present.

It may cause flushing and in severe cases causes rhinophyma (usually in men). Ocular rosacea may occur and cause blepharitis, conjunctivitis or keratitis. Trigger factors include alcohol, sunlight, exercise, high and low temperatures and spicy foods.

Treatment

Topical
Topical metronidazole or azelaic acid may help to control inflammation in mild to moderate rosacea.

Systemic
Most commonly tetracyclines or erythromycin are used. A third of patients respond to 2 months of treatment. Many patients need long-term treatment.

A β-blocker or clonidine may help flushing. In severe, resistant cases isotretinoin may be used.

3.2.5 Lichen planus

This presents as an itchy, shiny, violaceous, flat-topped, polygonal, papular rash with white lines on the surface known as Wickham's striae. Other affected sites include mucous membranes, genitalia, palms, soles, scalp and nails. Lichen planus causes a white lace-like pattern on the buccal mucosa.

Causes of white lesions in the oral mucosa

- Lichen planus
- Leukoplakia
- Chronic candidiasis
- Chemical burns

3.2.6 Erythema multiforme

This is usually a maculopapular, targetoid rash, which can occur anywhere, including the palms, soles and oral mucosa. The cause is unknown but it is thought to be associated with infections, mainly viral. Stevens–Johnson syndrome, on the other hand, is more likely to affect mucosal surfaces and is thought to be associated with drug reactions.

Causes of erythema multiforme

- **Infections**
  - Herpes simplex virus
  - *Mycoplasma*
  - Psittacosis
  - *Rickettsia*
  - HIV
  - Hepatitis B virus
  - Orf
  - Infectious mononucleosis
  - Mumps

- **Drug reactions**
  - Barbiturates
  - Penicillin
  - Sulphonamides

- **Others**
  - Lupus erythematosus
  - Polyarteritis nodosa
  - Wegener's granulomatosis
  - Underlying malignancy
  - Sarcoidosis

3.2.7 Erythema nodosum

This is a hot, tender, nodular, erythematous eruption lasting 3–6 weeks, which is more common in the third decade and in females.

Causes of erythema nodosum

- **Bacterial infection**
  - Streptococcal throat infection (commonly)
  - *Salmonella*
  - *Campylobacter*
  - Tuberculosis
  - *Mycoplasma pneumoniae*
  - *Yersinia enterocolitica*
- **Mycoses**
  - Coccidomycosis
  - Histoplasmosis
  - Blastomycosis
- **Inflammatory bowel disease**
- **Sarcoidosis**
  - Behçet syndrome
- **Drugs**
  - Penicillin
  - Tetracyclines
  - Oral contraceptive pill
  - Sulphonamides
  - Sulphonylureas
- **Malignancy**
  - Hodgkin's lymphoma
  - Acute myelocytic leukaemia
- **Pregnancy**
  - Viral infection

3.2.8 Specific skin infections

These can be subdivided into bacterial, fungal and viral infections as well as infestations.

Specific infections of the skin

- **Bacterial infections**
  - **Streptococcal**: cellulitis, erysipelas, impetigo, necrotising fasciitis, rheumatic fever (erythema marginatum), scarlet fever
  - **Staphylococcal**: folliculitis, impetigo, staphylococcal scalded-skin syndrome, toxic-shock syndrome
  - **Mycobacterial**: TB (lupus vulgaris, scrofuloderma), fish-tank granuloma, Buruli ulcer, leprosy
  - **Spirochaetal**: syphilis, Lyme disease (erythema chronicum migrans)
- **Fungal**
  - **Dermatophytes**: *Trichophyton rubrum, T. interdigitale, Epidermophyton floccosum* (tinea pedis, tinea corporis, tinea cruris, tinea unguium)
  - **Yeasts**: *Candida* (intertrigo, oral, genital or systemic); *Pityrosporum orbiculare*: pityriasis versicolor
- **Viral**
  - **Human papilloma virus**: warts
  - **Herpes virus**: varicella (chickenpox), zoster (shingles), simplex 1 (face and lips), simplex 2 (genital)
  - **Pox virus**: molluscum contagiosum, parapox virus (orf)
  - **Parvovirus B19**: erythema infectiosum (fifth disease)
  - **RNA virus**: measles, rubella
  - **Coxsackie A16**: hand, foot and mouth disease
  - **HIV/AIDS**: skin disease is common, affecting 75% of patients, who can be at any stage of HIV disease (*see* Chapter 8, Genito-urinary Medicine and AIDS)

- **Infestations**
  - ***Sarcoptes scabiei***: scabies mite infestation
  - Lice infestation (pediculosis): head lice, pubic lice

3.3 BULLOUS ERUPTIONS

This is a rare group of disorders characterised by the formation of bullae. The development of blisters can be due to congenital, immunological or other causes. The level of split within the epidermis or within the dermo-epidermal junction determines the type of bullous disorder.

Causes of bullous eruptions

- **Congenital**
  - Epidermolysis bullosa
- **Others**
  - Streptococcal infection
  - Staphylococcal scalded-skin syndrome
  - Toxic epidermal necrolysis
  - Diabetic bullae
  - Chronic renal failure
  - Haemodialysis
- **Immunological**
  - Pemphigus
  - Bullous pemphigoid
  - Cicatricial pemphigoid
  - Herpes gestationis
  - Dermatitis herpetiformis
- **Drug overdose**
  - Barbiturates

Epidermolysis bullosa is the term used for a group of genetically determined disorders characterised by blistering of the skin, palms, soles and mucosae, especially the mouth and oesophagus.

Pemphigus is a rare group of disorders characterised by blistering of the skin and mucous membranes.

Bullous pemphigoid is more common than pemphigus. It is a disorder characterised by large tense blisters found on the limbs, trunk and flexures in the elderly. Oral mucosal involvement is rare.

Cicatricial pemphigoid is a rare, chronic blistering disease of the mucous membranes and skin, which results in permanent scarring, particularly of the conjunctivae.

Dermatitis herpetiformis is an itchy, vesiculo-bullous eruption mainly occurring on the extensor areas. The majority of patients have asymptomatic gluten-sensitive enteropathy.

3.4 THE SKIN IN CONNECTIVE TISSUE DISORDERS

3.4.1 Systemic sclerosis

This is a rare, multisystem, connective tissue disease of unknown aetiology, characterised by fibrosis of the skin and visceral organs and accompanied by the presence of relatively specific antinuclear antibodies. The incidence peaks in the fifth and sixth decades and females are more affected than males (*see also* Chapter 20 Rheumatology).

Morphoea (localised scleroderma) consists of indurated plaques of sclerosis in the skin; systemic features are not found.

Skin changes in systemic sclerosis

- Facial telangiectasia
- Restricted mouth opening
- Peri-oral puckering
- Smooth shiny pigmented indurated skin
- Raynaud's phenomenon with gangrene
- Sclerodactyly
- Pulp atrophy
- Dilated nail-fold capillaries
- Ragged cuticles
- Calcinosis cutis
- Livedo reticularis
- Leg ulcers

3.4.2 Rheumatoid arthritis

Specific skin changes in rheumatoid arthritis

- Rheumatoid nodules
- Nail-fold infarcts
- Vasculitis with gangrene
- Pyoderma gangrenosum

3.4.3 Dermatomyositis

Specific skin changes in dermatomyositis

- Heliotrope rash around eyes
- Gottron's papules: red plaques on extensor surfaces of finger joints
- Gottron's sign: erythema over knees and elbows
- Dilated nail-fold capillaries and prominent, ragged cuticles
- Nail-fold infarct

3.4.4 Lupus erythematosus

Discoid lupus erythematosus is associated with scaly erythematous plaques with follicular plugging on sun-exposed sites. These tend to heal with scarring.

Systemic lupus erythematosus (**SLE**) is commonly associated with dermatological manifestations. These include malar rash, photosensitivity, vasculitis, Raynaud's phenomenon, alopecia and oropharyngeal ulceration.

3.5 THE SKIN IN OTHER SYSTEMIC DISEASES

3.5.1 Sarcoidosis

Skin lesions are found in approximately 25% of patients with systemic sarcoid and can occur in the absence of systemic disease:

- Erythema nodosum
- Scar sarcoid
- Lupus pernio
- Scarring alopecia

3.5.2 The porphyrias

- **Porphyria cutanea tarda** is the commonest of the porphyrias. Skin signs develop in sun-exposed areas. Patients have decreased levels of uroporphyrinogen decarboxylase. Eighty per cent of cases are acquired, in which case the condition is provoked by a hepatotoxic factor such as alcohol, oestrogens, hepatitis C, iron, lead and certain aromatic hydrocarbon hepatotoxins
- **Acute intermittent porphyria**: skin signs are not seen
- **Congenital erythropoietic porphyria**: patients have brown teeth which fluoresce red under Wood's light, giving the 'werewolf' appearance

The typical skin signs of the porphyrias are:

- Photosensitivity
- Blister formation
- Scarring with milia
- Hypertrichosis

3.5.3 Pyoderma gangrenosum

This is a painful ulcerating disease that typically occurs on the legs; it may occur peri-stomally in inflammatory bowel disease.

Causes of pyoderma gangrenosum
<ul><li>**Gastrointestinal**<ul><li>Ulcerative colitis</li><li>Crohn's colitis</li></ul></li><li>**Rheumatological**<ul><li>Rheumatoid arthritis</li><li>Ankylosing spondylitis</li></ul></li><li>**Liver**<ul><li>Chronic active hepatitis</li><li>Primary biliary cirrhosis</li><li>Sclerosing cholangitis</li></ul></li><li>**Haematological**<ul><li>Leukaemia</li><li>Lymphoma</li><li>Myeloproliferative disorders</li></ul></li></ul>

- **Others**
  - Diabetes mellitus
  - Thyroid disease
  - Sarcoidosis
  - Wegener's granulomatosis
- **Other malignancies**

3.5.4 Diabetes

Skin signs in diabetes mellitus

- Necrobiosis lipoidica
- Disseminated granuloma annulare
- Diabetic rubeosis
- Candidiasis and other infections
- Vitiligo
- Neuropathic foot ulcers

Diabetic rubeosis is an odd redness of the face, hands and feet thought to be due to diabetic micro-angiopathy.

3.6 GENERALISED PRURITUS

Pruritus is an important skin symptom and occurs in dermatological diseases such as atopic eczema. In the absence of localised skin disease or skin signs, patients should be fully investigated to exclude an underlying cause.

Causes of generalised pruritus
<ul><li>**Obstructive liver disease**</li><li>**Haematological**<ul><li>Iron-deficiency anaemia</li><li>Polycythaemia</li></ul></li><li>**Endocrine**<ul><li>Hyperthyroidism</li><li>Hypothyroidism</li><li>Diabetes mellitus</li></ul></li><li>**Chronic renal failure**</li><li>**Malignancy**<ul><li>Internal malignancies</li><li>Lymphoma</li></ul></li></ul>

- **Drugs**
  - Morphine
- **Other**
  - Pregnancy
  - Senility

3.7 CUTANEOUS MARKERS OF INTERNAL MALIGNANCY

There are numerous skin changes associated with internal malignancy. These can be either genetically determined syndromes with cutaneous manifestations, where there is a recognised predisposition to internal malignancy, or paraneoplastic syndromes, where the cutaneous signs are significantly associated with malignancy of various organs.

3.7.1 Genetically determined syndromes with skin manifestations

Most of these diseases have an autosomal dominant inheritance.

- **Gardner syndrome**: epidermal cysts, lipomas and fibromas are associated with colonic carcinoma
- **Peutz–Jeghers syndrome**: mucocutaneous pigmentation is associated with mainly gastrointestinal malignancy
- **Howel–Evans syndrome**: tylosis (palmo-plantar keratoderma) has been reported with oesophageal carcinoma
- **Torre–Muir syndrome**: sebaceous tumours are associated with gastrointestinal malignancy
- **Cowden disease**: tricholemmomas (facial nodules) and warty hyperplasia of the mucosal surface is associated with breast and thyroid carcinoma
- **Neurofibromatosis**: the presence of six or more café-au-lait macules, axillary freckling and neurofibromas is associated with malignant schwannomas and astrocytomas

- **Tuberous sclerosis**: angiofibromas, together with periungual fibromas, shagreen patches and ash-leaf macules are associated with sarcomas and rhabdomyomas
- **Multiple endocrine neoplasia type 2B**: mucosal neuromas are associated with medullary thyroid carcinoma and phaeochromocytoma
- **Gorlin syndrome (basal cell naevus syndrome)**: multiple basal cell carcinomata associated with medulloblastoma, meningioma, astrocytoma and ovarian tumours
- **von-Hippel–Lindau syndrome**: café-au-lait macules and haemangiomas are associated with vascular tumours of the central nervous system, phaeochromocytoma, renal and pancreatic carcinoma
- **Sturge–Weber syndrome**: port-wine stain associated with ipsilateral vascular meningeal malformation and epilepsy
- **Wiskott–Aldrich syndrome**: a sex-linked recessive disease characterised by eczema, immunodeficiency and an increased risk of lymphoma and leukaemia
- **Chediak–Higashi syndrome**: a fatal autosomal recessive disease with recurrent bacterial infections and widespread infiltration with lymphocytes suggesting a lymphoma
- **Ataxia telangiectasia**: an autosomal recessive disease characterised by mucocutaneous telangiectasia and an increased risk of lymphoma and leukaemia
- **Xeroderma pigmentosum**: an autosomal recessive group of conditions characterised by multiple melanomas and non-melanoma skin malignancies which start developing from childhood in sun-exposed skin

3.7.2 Skin signs as paraneoplastic features

Dermatological features can be seen in all types of malignant disease but some are more common in certain types of neoplasia.

Specific dermatological features and the common types of malignancy with which they are associated

- **Acanthosis nigricans:** gastrointestinal adenocarcinoma
- **Acanthosis palmaris (tripe palms):** bronchial carcinoma
- **Acanthosis palmaris with nigricans:** gastrointestinal adenocarcinoma
- **Generalised pruritus:** lymphoma
- **Dermatomyositis (in adults):** bronchial, breast and ovarian tumours
- **Erythema gyratum repens:** bronchial carcinoma
- **Acquired hypertrichosis lanuginosa:** gastrointestinal and bronchial tumours
- **Necrolytic migratory erythema:** glucagonoma
- **Migratory thrombophlebitis:** pancreatic carcinoma
- **Acquired ichthyosis:** lymphoma
- **Pyoderma gangrenosum:** myeloproliferative tumours
- **Erythroderma:** lymphoma and leukaemia
- **Clubbing:** bronchial carcinoma
- **Herpes zoster:** myeloproliferative tumours

Causes of acanthosis nigricans

- Internal malignancy
- Acromegaly
- Cushing's disease
- Obesity
- Insulin-resistant diabetes mellitus
- Oral contraceptive pill
- Familial
- Nicotinic acid
- Hypothyroidism

3.8 DISORDERS OF PIGMENTATION

The major colour determinant of the skin is melanin. This is produced by melanocytes, which are found in the basal layer of the epidermis. Pigmentary disorders usually present with either hypopigmentation or hyperpigmentation.

Causes of hypopigmentation

- **Genetic**
  - Albinism
  - Phenylketonuria
  - Tuberous sclerosis
- **Chemical**
  - Chloroquine
- **Infections**
  - Pityriasis versicolor
- **Endocrine**
  - Hypopituitarism
- **Autoimmune**
  - Vitiligo
- **Post-inflammatory**
  - Eczema
  - Psoriasis
  - Lupus erythematosus

Causes of hyperpigmentation

- **Genetic**
  - Peutz–Jeghers syndrome
  - Xeroderma pigmentosum
  - Albright syndrome
- **Metabolic**
  - Cirrhosis
  - Haemochromatosis
  - Porphyria
  - Renal failure
- **Drugs**
  - Oral contraceptive pill
  - Minocycline
  - Amiodarone
- **Endocrine**
  - Addison's disease
  - Cushing syndrome
  - Nelson syndrome
  - Pregnancy
- **Nutritional**
  - Malabsorption
  - Carcinomatosis
  - Kwashiorkor
  - Pellagra

- **Post-inflammatory**
  - Lichen planus
  - Eczema
  - Secondary syphilis
  - Cutaneous amyloid

3.9 DRUG ERUPTIONS

The incidence of drug eruptions is approximately 2%.

The most common drug eruptions are:

- **Toxic erythema**: the commonest type of eruption. It is usually characterised by a morbilliform or maculopapular eruption which may become confluent. Causes include antibiotics (including sulphonamides), carbamazepine, allopurinol, gold, thiazides and antituberculous drugs
- **Fixed drug eruption**: this occurs in a localised site each time the drug is administered (see later)
- **Toxic epidermal necrolysis**: a life-threatening eruption due to extensive skin loss. This can be associated with allopurinol, sulphonamides, penicillin, carbamazepine, phenytoin, NSAIDs, gold, salicylates and barbiturates
- **Urticaria**: (see below)
- **Photosensitivity** (*see* Chapter 2, Clinical Pharmacology, Toxicology and Poisoning)
- **Lupus erythematosus-like syndrome**: a number of drugs have been implicated as causes of this relatively rare disorder (*see* Chapter 2, Clinical Pharmacology, Toxicology and Poisoning)
- **Vasculitis** (*see* Chapter 2, Clinical Pharmacology, Toxicology and Poisoning)
- **Erythema multiforme**: this is associated with penicillins, sulphonamides, phenytoin, carbamazepine, ACE inhibitors, NSAIDs, gold, barbiturates, thiazides
- **Contact dermatitis**
- **Hyperpigmentation** (see above): associated with amiodarone, minocycline, bleomycin, chlorpromazine, antimalarials

Urticaria is a transient, itchy, erythematous rash characterised by the presence of wheals. It is thought to occur due to histamine release from mast cells, but other agents such as prostaglandins and leukotrienes have also been implicated. **Angi-oedema** is similar to urticaria, but histologically there is greater swelling of the subcutaneous tissue and mucosal sites are often affected. Ninety-five per cent of cases are idiopathic.

Drugs that cause urticaria

- Penicillin
- Salicylates
- Quinidine
- Cephalosporin
- ACE inhibitors
- Hydralazine
- Opiates

Drugs that cause a fixed drug eruption

- Tetracyclines
- Barbiturates
- Dapsone
- Chlordiazepoxide
- Sulphonamides
- Benzodiazepines
- NSAIDs
- Quinine
- Paracetamol

Diseases aggravated by sunlight

- Lupus erythematosus
- Dermatomyositis
- Xeroderma pigmentosum
- Herpes simplex infection
- Rosacea
- Porphyrias (except acute intermittent)
- Pellagra
- Carcinoid syndrome

3.10 SKIN TUMOURS

3.10.1 Malignant melanoma

This has an incidence of around 10 per 100 000 per year but the rate is doubling every decade. The prognosis is related to tumour thickness. Early lesions are often curable by surgical excision. Any changing mole (bleeding, increase in size, itching, etc) should be viewed suspiciously.

The different types of melanoma are:

- **Superficial spreading**: this is the most common. An irregularly pigmented macule or plaque which may have an irregular edge and colour variation
- **Nodular**: a pigmented nodule, often rapidly growing and aggressive
- **Lentigo maligna melanoma**: occurs in the elderly in a long-standing lentigo maligna (a slowly expanding, irregularly pigmented macule)
- **Acral lentiginous melanoma**: occurs on the palms, soles and nail beds. This is the commonest type of melanoma in Chinese and Japanese people

3.10.2 Basal cell carcinoma

These are the commonest skin cancer and are seen most commonly on the face of elderly or middle-aged patients. They only very rarely metastasise. Predisposing factors for basal cell carcinoma are:

- Prolonged sun exposure (most common)
- Radiation treatment
- Chronic scarring
- Ingestion of arsenic (tonics)
- Basal cell naevus syndrome (Gorlin syndrome)

Basal cell carcinomas are classified as:

- Nodular/cystic
- Morphoeic
- Pigmented
- Superficial

3.10.3 Squamous cell carcinoma

There are several predisposing factors for squamous cell carcinoma:

- **Actinic damage**: squamous carcinomas can also develop in just sun-damaged skin (in the absence of actinic keratosis)
- **X-irradiation**
- **Chronic scarring or inflammation**
- **Smoking (particularly lesions of the lip)**
- **Arsenic ingestion**
- **Organic hydrocarbons**
- **Immunosuppression**
- **Human papilloma virus**

3.10.4 Other skin tumours

Keratoacanthoma

A rapidly growing tumour arising in sun-exposed skin. This is normally thought of as benign but histologically it is similar to squamous cell carcinoma.

Cutaneous T-cell lymphoma (mycosis fungoides)

A lymphoma that evolves in the skin, usually over a protracted course of many years. The clinical pattern may be varied.

3.11 HAIR AND NAILS

3.11.1 Disorders of hair

The first signs of hair follicles appear in the region of the eyebrows, upper lip and chin at around 9 weeks' gestation. By 22 weeks the full complement of follicles is established. Hair abnormalities comprise either excessive hair growth or hair loss.

Excessive hair growth can be androgen-independent 'hypertrichosis' or androgen-dependent 'hirsutism'.

Causes of hypertrichosis

- **Congenital/hereditary**
  - Congenital hypertrichosis lanuginosa
  - Porphyrias
  - Epidermolysis bullosa
  - Hurler syndrome
- **Acquired**
  - Acquired hypertrichosis lanuginosa
- **Endocrine**
  - Hypothyroidism
  - Hyperthyroidism
- **Drugs**
  - Diazoxide
  - Minoxidil
  - Ciclosporin
  - Streptomycin
- **Other**
  - Malnutrition
  - Anorexia nervosa

Causes of hirsutism

- **Ovarian**
  - Polycystic ovary syndrome
  - Ovarian tumours
- **Androgen therapy**
- **Adrenal**
  - Congenital adrenal hyperplasia
  - Cushing's disease
  - Prolactinoma

Loss of hair is called alopecia and can be scarring or non-scarring. Scarring alopecia is loss of hair with destruction of the hair follicles. Non-scarring alopecia is when the hair follicles are preserved. A good example of this is the 'exclamation mark' hair seen in alopecia areata.

Causes of scarring alopecia

- **Hereditary**
  - Ichthyosis
- **Bacterial**
  - Tuberculosis
  - Syphilis
- **Physical injury**
  - Burns
  - Radiotherapy
- **Fungal**
  - Kerion
- **Others**
  - Lichen planus
  - Lupus erythematosus
  - Morphoea
  - Sarcoidosis
  - Cicatricial pemphigoid

Causes of non-scarring alopecia

- **Male pattern/androgenetic alopecia** (the most common in men and women)
- **Alopecia areata**
- **Endocrine**
  - Hypopituitary state
  - Hypothyroidism
  - Hyperthyroidism
  - Hypoparathyroidism
  - Pregnancy
- **Drugs**
  - Retinoids
  - Anticoagulants
  - Antimitotic agents
  - Oral contraceptive pill
  - Carbimazole
  - Thiouracil
  - Lithium
- **Iron deficiency**
- **Chronic illness**

Alopecia areata is associated with nail dystrophy, cataracts, vitiligo, autoimmune thyroid disease, pernicious anaemia and Addison's disease.

3.11.2   Disorders of nails

Nails are derived from keratin. This is a protein complex and gives the nail its hard property. The nail can be affected in a variety of skin and systemic disorders.

Causes of nail changes associated with skin disorders

- **Psoriasis**: nail changes include onycholysis, nail pitting, hyperkeratosis, pustule and occasional loss of nail
- **Fungal**: signs include discoloration, onycholysis and thickening of the nail
- **Bacterial**: usually due to staphylococcal infections. *Pseudomonas* infections give a green discoloration to the nail
- **Lichen planus**: nail changes occur in 10% of cases, with thinning of the nail plate and longitudinal linear depressions. Occasionally there is destruction of the nail (pterygium)
- **Alopecia areata**: pitting, thickening and ridging of the nail (sandpaper nail) is seen
- **Dermatitis**: coarse pits, cross-ridging and onycholysis may be seen

Causes of nail changes associated with systemic disease

- **Koilonychia**: the nails are thin, brittle and concave. There is an association with iron-deficiency anaemia
- **Yellow nail syndrome**: the nails are yellow and excessively curved. Associations include recurrent pleural effusions, chronic bronchitis, bronchiectasis, nephrotic syndrome and hypothyroidism
- **Nail–patella syndrome**: loss of ulnar half of the nails, usually the thumbnail, is seen. Associations include small patellae, bony spines over posterior iliac crests, renal abnormalities, over-extension of joints and laxity of the skin
- **Beau's lines**: these are transverse depressions in the nail due to temporary arrest in growth. They usually occur after a period of illness or infection
- **Half and half nails**: the proximal nail bed is white and distal, pink or brown. They are associated with chronic renal failure and rheumatoid arthritis

Causes of onycholysis (lifting of the nail plate from the nail bed)

- **Idiopathic**: excessive manicuring or wetting
- **Dermatological disease**: psoriasis, fungal infection, dermatitis
- **Systemic disease**: impaired peripheral circulation, hypothyroidism, hyperthyroidism
- **Trauma**

Chapter 4
Endocrinology

CONTENTS

Endocrinology

4.1 HORMONE ACTION

There are three main types of hormone:

- Amine
- Steroid
- Peptide

Knowing which category a particular hormone fits into makes it possible to guess much of its physiology. Thyroxine is an exception to this as shown below.

4.1.1 Types of hormone

- **Amine**: catecholamines, serotonin, **thyroxine**
- **Steroid**: cortisol, aldosterone, androgens, oestrogens and progestogens and **vitamin D**
- **Peptide**: everything else! (made up of a series of amino acids)

Thyroxine is chemically an amine but it acts like a steroid. Vitamin D has the structure of a steroid hormone and it acts like one.

Amines/peptides

- Short half-life (minutes)
- Secretion may be pulsatile
- Act on a cell surface receptor
- Often act via a second messenger

Steroids

- Longer biological half-life (hours)
- Act on an intracellular receptor
- Act on DNA to alter gene expression

This information can be used to predict hormone action. For example, aldosterone is a steroid hormone so it must have a biological half-life of several hours, bind to an intracellular receptor and affect gene transcription. Glucagon is not a steroid or an amine so it must be a polypeptide hormone which has a short circulation half-life, acts via a cell surface receptor and probably utilises a second messenger (cAMP in fact).

4.1.2 Hormones that act at the cell surface

Peptide and amine hormones act at the cell surface via specific membrane receptors. The signal is transmitted intracellularly by one of three mechanisms:

- Via cAMP
- Via a rise in intracellular Ca^{2+} levels
- Via receptor tyrosine kinases

If in doubt, assume the action of a peptide or amine hormone (excluding thyroxine) is via cAMP unless it is insulin or has the word 'growth' in its name, in which case it is likely to act via a receptor tyrosine kinase (Table 4.1).

cAMP and G-proteins

Hormone receptors linked to cAMP (eg thyroid-stimulating hormone (TSH) receptor) typically have seven transmembrane domains. The receptor does not directly generate cAMP but acts via separate 'G-proteins' on the cell surface which, in turn, interact with the cAMP-generating enzyme, adenylate cyclase, on the cell surface. (*See* Figure 14.4 in Chapter 14, Molecular Medicine.)

Hormones that raise the level of cAMP intracellularly (all hormones in this category except somatostatin) act via a stimulatory G-protein, 'G_s'. Hormones that lower the level of cAMP (somatostatin) act via an inhibitory G-protein, 'G_i'.

Table 4.1. Mechanisms of hormone action

Via cAMP	Via Ca^{2+}	Via receptor tyrosine kinases
Adrenaline (β-receptors)	GnRH	Insulin
All pituitary hormones except GH, PRL	TRH	GH, PRL
Glucagon	Adrenaline (α-receptors)	'Growth factors': IGF-1, EGF
Somatostatin		

cAMP = cyclic adenosine monophosphate; GnRH = gonadotrophin-releasing hormone; GH = growth hormone; PRL = prolactin; TRH = thyrotrophin-releasing hormone; IGF-1 = insulin-like growth factor 1; EGF = epidermal growth factor

G-proteins are important in endocrinology because mutations in G_s have been found to be associated with certain diseases:

- **Acromegaly**: 40% of patients with acromegaly have an activating somatic mutation of G_s in their pituitary tumour. As a result, the cells are always 'switched on' and continuously make GH (resulting in acromegaly)
- **McCune–Albright syndrome**: an activating mutation of G_s early in embryonic development causes hyperfunction of one or more endocrine glands with the following sequelae: precocious puberty (gonad hyperfunction), acromegaly (GH hypersecretion), Cushing's (adrenal gland hyperfunction), thyrotoxicosis or hyperparathyroidism. The syndrome is associated with café-au-lait spots and polyostotic fibrous dysplasia. Because the mutation occurs after the zygote stage, affected individuals are a mosaic and different patterns of tissue involvement may be seen between individuals
- **Pseudohypoparathyroidism**: inactivating germ-line mutations in G_s result in pseudohypoparathyroidism type 1A **if maternally inherited**, with dysmorphic features (including short 4th or 5th metacarpal) and resistance to a variety of hormones that act via cAMP (including parathyroid hormone, TSH and gonadotrophins). Spontaneously occurring or paternally inherited mutations cause the dysmorphic features alone

(**pseudopseudohypoparathyroidism**). The dysmorphic bone features are sometimes referred to as '**Albright's hereditary osteodystrophy**' and they can be present in either the maternally or paternally inherited form

Intracellular Ca^{2+}

Some hormones release intracellular Ca^{2+} as a second messenger (*see* table above for examples). The receptors for these hormones activate different G-proteins (eg G_q) which in turn activate the cytoplasmic enzyme phospholipase C (PLC). PLC releases the small molecule inositol 1,4,5-trisphosphate (IP_3) from membrane phospholipids. IP_3 in turn binds to the IP_3-sensitive receptor on the endoplasmic reticulum within the cell causing Ca^{2+} to be released from stores in the endoplasmic reticulum into the cytoplasm. The Ca^{2+} subsequently affects cell metabolism by binding to the protein calmodulin.

Receptor tyrosine kinases

The insulin, GH, prolactin and growth factor receptors do not use second messengers. The receptors themselves can act as enzymes which phosphorylate ('kinase activity') other proteins when hormone is bound at the cell surface. This is followed by a cascade of proteins phosphorylating other proteins until gene transcription in the nucleus is modulated.

4.1.3 Hormones that act intracellularly

Steroids, vitamin D and thyroxine are sufficiently lipid soluble that they do not need cell surface receptors but can diffuse directly through the cell membrane. They then bind to receptors in the cytoplasm which results in shedding of heat shock proteins that protect the empty receptor. The hormone–receptor complex migrates into the nucleus where the complex alters the transcription of a large number of genes (*see* Figure 14.6 in Chapter 14, Molecular Medicine).

4.1.4 Hormone resistance syndromes

The following are conditions of hormone resistance with the site of the defect shown.

- **Receptor defect (hormone involved)**
  - Laron dwarfism (GH)
  - Leprechaunism (Donahue syndrome, Rabson–Mendenhall syndrome (insulin))
  - Nephrogenic diabetes insipidus (antidiuretic hormone (ADH))
  - Androgen resistance (testicular feminisation syndrome (testosterone))
  - Vitamin-D-dependent rickets type 2 = hereditary vitamin D resistance rickets (vitamin D)*
- **Second messenger defect**
  - Pseudohypoparathyroidism
- **Defect unknown**
  - Type 2 diabetes

* Vitamin-D-dependent rickets type 1 is due to a failure of 1-hydroxylation of vitamin D

4.2 SPECIFIC HORMONE PHYSIOLOGY

4.2.1 Hormones in illness

During illness/stress, the body closes all unnecessary systems down 'from the top', eg the thyroid axis closes down by a fall in TRH, TSH and L-thyroxine/L-thyronine (T_4/T_3). It is orchestrated by the hypothalamus, not by the end organs. Hormones involved in the stress response may rise.

Hormones which fall

- TSH, T_4/T_3*
- LH, FSH
- Testosterone, oestrogen
- Insulin (starvation)

May rise (stress hormones)

- GH (though IGF-1 falls)
- ACTH, glucocorticoids
- Adrenaline
- Glucagon (starvation)
- Prolactin

* In this case conversion of T_4 to T_3 is inhibited so T_3 falls more than T_4

TSH = Thyroid-stimulating hormone; GH = growth hormone; IGF-1 = insulin-like growth factor 1; LH = luteinising hormone; FSH = follicle-stimulating hormone; ACTH = adrenocorticotrophic hormone; T_3 = L-thyronine; T_4 = L-thyroxine

In starvation alone, without illness, all hormones fall except glucagon. In anorexia nervosa there is also stress: all hormones fall except glucagon, GH and glucocorticoids.

4.2.2 Hormone changes in obesity and the physiology of leptin

In the absence of other diseases (eg type 2 diabetes) which might develop in obese patients, the following changes are seen in obesity:

- Hyperinsulinaemia
- Increased cortisol turnover but not hypercortisolism
- Increased androgen levels in women
- Reduced GH
- Conversion of androgens to oestrogens

- All bad lipid changes (low high-density lipoprotein (HDL), high low-density lipoprotein (LDL) and triglyceride)

Leptin, adipokines and other hormones involved with appetite and weight

Leptin was identified as a product of the *ob* gene in 1994. *Ob/ob* mice make no leptin owing to a homozygous *ob* gene mutation and are grossly obese.

- Leptin is a polypeptide hormone, released from fat cells, that acts on specific receptors in the hypothalamus to reduce appetite
- Circulating leptin levels are directly proportional to fat mass, and so they tell the brain how fat an individual is
- Leptin appears to have stimulatory effects on metabolic rate and levels fall in starvation (appropriate change for weight homeostasis)
- Adequate leptin levels are required for the onset of puberty
- Persistently obese individuals appear relatively resistant to leptin
- Hereditary leptin deficiency (very rare) results in grossly obese children due to a voracious appetite

Several other hormones have recently been shown to affect appetite and weight:

- **Ghrelin**: this was first identified as a growth hormone-releasing hormone. It is released from the stomach when subjects are fasting and triggers hunger. Ghrelin levels fall after gastric bypass surgery which may help weight loss (by reducing appetite)
- **Peptide YY** (a member of the neuropeptide Y family): released from L cells in the small and large bowel. Levels rise after meals and reduce appetite. This may be the main regulator of day-to-day appetite
- **Glucagon-like peptide-1** (GLP-1): also released from L cells of the intestine after meals and powerfully promotes insulin secretion in response to raised glucose ('incretin effect') as well as possibly reducing appetite. Inactivated by the enzyme dipeptidyl peptidase IV (DPP IV).

Derived from tissue-specific cleavage of proglucagon

- **Oxyntomodulin**: also released from L cells and derived from proglucagon; appears to act on the same receptor as GLP-1 but with less incretin and has more of an appetite-suppressing effect
- In the hypothalamus itself, neuropeptide Y (NPY) and Agouti-related protein (AgRP) increase appetite while α-melanocyte-stimulating hormone (α-MSH; a melanocortin) reduces appetite

In addition to leptin a number of other hormones have recently been identified as being released from fat cells. These 'adipokines' include **adiponectin**, which reduces insulin resistance, and **resistin** and **acylation-stimulating protein (ASP)**, which both increase insulin resistance. **Visfatin** (also known as nicotinamide phosphoribosyltransferase (NAMPT) and pre-B cell colony-enhancing factor) is released predominantly from visceral fat and has insulin-like actions. The role of these adipokines in the association between obesity and insulin resistance remains uncertain.

4.2.3 Hormones in pregnancy

As a general rule, most hormone levels rise in pregnancy. Insulin resistance develops, causing a rise in circulating insulin levels. Insulin requirements are highest in the last trimester but fall slightly in the last four weeks of pregnancy.

Other key features of hormone metabolism in pregnancy are as follows:

- **Prolactin** levels rise steadily throughout pregnancy and in combination with oestrogen prepare the breast for lactation. Post-partum surges of prolactin and oxytocin are generated by the nipple stimulation of breast-feeding. However, after several weeks prolactin levels fall almost to normal even if breast-feeding continues
- **LH/FSH** from the pituitary are no longer necessary after conception for continued pregnancy (although the pituitary does double in size) – the placenta takes over

- **Thyroid axis**. Thyroid-binding globulin (TBG) levels rise in the first trimester, causing a rise in total T_4 and total T_3. However, human chorionic gonadotrophin (hCG) from the placenta shares its alpha subunit with TSH and very high levels in the first trimester can cause true mild thyrotoxicosis (not just a binding protein rise), especially associated with hyperemesis gravidarum. Note that T_4 and T_3 do not cross the placenta very efficiently but sufficient T_4 does cross to prevent a fetus with congenital hypothyroidism becoming hypothyroid until after birth

4.2.4 Investigations in endocrinology

The plasma level of almost all hormones varies through the day (because of pulsatile secretion, environmental stress or circadian rhythms) and is influenced by the prevailing values of the substrates they control. This makes it hard to define a 'normal range'. For example, insulin values depend on the glucose level, GH levels depend on whether a pulse of GH has just been released or the blood sample is taken in the trough between pulses.

Dynamic testing is therefore frequently used, ie suppression or stimulation tests. The principle is, 'If you think a hormone level may be high, suppress it; if you think it may be low, stimulate it.'

- **Suppression tests** are used to test for hormone EXCESS – eg dexamethasone suppression for Cushing syndrome, glucose tolerance for GH in acromegaly
- **Stimulation tests** are used to test for hormone DEFICIENCY – eg Synacthen® tests for hypoadrenalism, insulin-induced hypoglycaemia for GH deficiency and/or hypoadrenalism

4.2.5 Growth hormone

This is secreted in pulses lasting 30–45 minutes separated by periods when secretion is undetectable. The majority of GH pulses occur at night ('children grow at night'). In response to GH pulses, the liver makes insulin-like growth factor-1 (IGF-1, previously called somatomedin C), the plasma level of which is constant and which mediates almost all the actions of GH, ie GH does not act directly. The effective levels of IGF-1 are influenced by changes in the level of its six binding proteins (IGF-BP 1–6).

4.2.6 Prolactin

Prolactin causes galactorrhoea but not gynaecomastia (oestrogen does this). Raised prolactin levels are essentially the only cause of galactorrhoea, although occasionally prolactin levels in the normal range can cause milk production in a sensitised breast. Raised prolactin levels also 'shut down' the gonadal axis 'from the top' (hypothalamic level) resulting in low GnRH, LH and oestrogen/testosterone levels. Surprisingly, prolactin is a stress hormone and levels rise after an epileptic fit.

Prolactin release from the pituitary is under **negative** control by dopamine from the hypothalamus. Oestrogens (the pill, pregnancy) and nipple stimulation raise prolactin.

Prolactin is raised by

- Phenothiazines, haloperidol (*not* tricyclics)*
- Anti-emetics (eg metoclopramide)
- Damage to hypothalamus (eg radiation)
- Pregnancy
- Nipple stimulation
- Damage to pituitary stalk (eg pressure from a pituitary tumour)
- Oestrogens
- Polycystic ovary syndrome

Prolactin is suppressed by

- **Dopamine agonist drugs** (eg bromocriptine, cabergoline)

* Female psychiatric patients may complain of galactorrhoea – doctors often do not believe them but the patients are right and it is due to the doctor's treatment!

Gynaecomastia

This is due to a decreased androgen:oestrogen ratio in men. Gynaecomastia is unrelated to galactorrhoea (which is always due to prolactin). Breast enlargement is not necessary to make milk.

Causes of gynaecomastia:

- Pubertal (normal)
- Obesity – not true gynaecomastia
- Hypogonadism (eg Klinefelter syndrome, testicular failure)
- Cirrhosis, alcohol
- Hyperthyroidism
- Drugs: including spironolactone, digoxin, oestrogens, cimetidine, anabolic steroids, marijuana
- Tumours, including adrenal or testicular making oestrogen; lung, pancreatic, gastric making hCG; hepatomas converting androgens to oestrogens

4.2.7 Adrenal steroids

These act intracellularly to alter the transcription of DNA to mRNA (*see* Section 4.1, Hormone action). Surprisingly, the mineralocorticoid (aldosterone) and glucocorticoid receptors have an equal affinity for cortisol. However, the cellular enzyme **11-β-hydroxysteroid dehydrogenase** 'protects' the mineralocorticoid receptor by chemically modifying any cortisol that comes near the receptor to an inactive form while having no effect on aldosterone itself. Inactivating mutations of this enzyme or inhibition of it by liquorice causes 'apparent mineralocorticoid excess' since cortisol (which circulates at much higher concentrations than aldosterone) is able to stimulate the mineralocorticoid receptor. The effects of adrenal steroids and their duration of action are given in Table 4.2.

4.2.8 Thyroid hormone metabolism

More than 95% of thyroid hormones are bound to plasma proteins in the circulation, predominantly TBG and thyroid-binding pre-albumin (TBPA). T_4 (L-thyroxine, four iodine atoms per molecule) has a half-life of 7 days (so if a patient is in a confused state it is possible to administer his/her total weekly dose of thyroxine once a week). It is converted partly in the thyroid and partly in the circulation to T_3 (L-thyronine, three iodine atoms per molecule), which is the active form and has a half-life of 1 day.

There are three deiodinase enzymes that act on thyroid hormones (D_1–D_3). D_1 and D_2 promote the generation of active hormone (T_3) by converting T_4 to T_3 (see Figure 4.1). D_3 opposes this by promoting conversion of T_4 to rT_3 and destroying T_3 by conver-

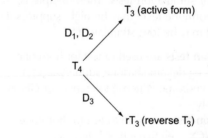

Figure 4.1 Metabolism of thyroid hormones, D1–D3 – different deiodinase enzymes that act on thyroid hormone

Table 4.2. Adrenal steroids

	Relative glucocorticoid effect	Relative mineralocorticoid effect	Duration of action
Cortisol = hydrocortisone	1	+	Short
Prednisolone	4	±	Medium
Dexamethasone	30	–	Long
Fludrocortisone	10	+++	

sion to T_2 (inactive). The D_1 and D_2 enzymes are inhibited by illness, propranolol, propylthiouracil, amiodarone and ipodate (formerly used as X-ray contrast medium for study of gallbladder disease). This reduces the level of active hormone, T_3, with little change or a rise in T_4. rT_3 levels rise (T_4 spontaneously converts to rT_3 if the monodeiodinase is not available) but rT_3 is *not* detected in laboratory tests of T_3 levels.

It is said that you should, 'Never measure thyroid function tests on ITU as you will not be able to interpret them.' In illness, TSH and free T_3 levels fall ('sick euthyroidism'). The only interpretable finding in sick patients is a raised free T_3 – this would almost definitely indicate thyrotoxicosis.

4.2.9 Renin–angiotensin–aldosterone

Aldosterone secretion is controlled almost completely by the renin–angiotensin system, not by ACTH. The initial letters of the zones of the adrenal cortex from outside inwards spell 'GFR', like glomerular filtration rate: glomerularis, fasciculata, reticularis. Aldosterone is the 'outsider hormone' and is made on the 'outside' (zona glomerulosa).

Renin is released from the JGA (juxtaglomerular apparatus) of the kidney in response to low Na^+ delivery or reduced renal perfusion. Renin is an enzyme that converts angiotensinogen to angiotensin I (10 amino acids). ACE (angiotensin-converting enzyme) in the lung converts angiotensin I to angiotensin II, which is the active form. ACE also breaks down bradykinin: ACE inhibitors (eg captopril) are believed to cause cough by causing a build-up of bradykinin in the lung. The renin–angiotensin system is designed to restore circulating volume. It is therefore activated by hypovolaemia (see Figure 4.2) and its end product, angiotensin II, has three actions which restore volume:

- Releasing aldosterone from the adrenal (retains Na^+, excretes K^+ in the distal tubule)
- Vasoconstriction (powerful)
- Induction of thirst (powerful)

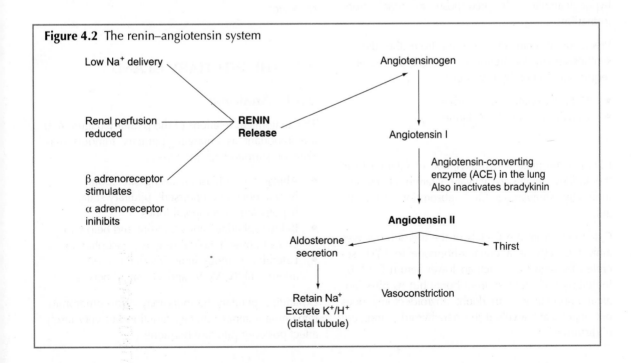

Figure 4.2 The renin–angiotensin system

4.2.10   Calcium, PTH and vitamin D

(*See also* Chapter 13, Metabolic Diseases.)

Plasma calcium is tightly regulated by parathyroid hormone (PTH) and vitamin D, acting on the kidney (PTH), bone (PTH) and the gut (vitamin D).

PTH controls Ca^{2+} levels minute to minute by mobilising Ca^{2+} from bone and inhibiting Ca^{2+} excretion from the kidney. Vitamin D has a more long-term role, predominantly by promoting Ca^{2+} absorption from the gut. Its actions on the kidney and bone are of lesser importance. Ca^{2+} levels are sensed by a specific calcium-sensing receptor on the parathyroid glands. Mutations that reduce the activity of this receptor result in a resetting of calcium and PTH to higher levels (**familial hypocalciuric hypercalcaemia, FHH**). Activating mutations can also occur which result in a picture almost indistinguishable from hypoparathyroidism, with a low Ca^{2+} (**autosomal dominant hypocalcaemia with hypercalciuria**). It is important to identify these conditions as they run a benign course and only attempted treatment causes problems (eg raising the serum Ca^{2+} in autosomal dominant hypocalcaemia will predispose to renal stone formation).

Precursor vitamin D, obtained from the diet or synthesised by the action of sunlight on the skin, requires activation by two steps:

*   25-Hydroxylation in the liver
*   1-Hydroxylation in the kidney

PTH can promote 1-hydroxylation of vitamin D in the kidney, ie it can activate vitamin D, thereby indirectly stimulating Ca^{2+} absorption from the gut.

Calcitonin (from the C-cells of the thyroid) behaves almost exactly as a counter-hormone to PTH (secreted by high Ca^{2+}, acts to lower serum Ca^{2+} by inhibiting Ca^{2+} release from bone) but its physiological importance is in doubt (thyroidectomy does not affect Ca^{2+} levels if the parathyroid glands are undisturbed).

4.2.11   Atrial natriuretic peptide (ANP)

ANP physiology can be predicted from its name.

*   **Atrial**: it is synthesised by the myocytes of the right atrium and ventricle
*   **Natriuretic**: it causes a natriuresis (urinary excretion of sodium). It thereby *reduces* circulating volume (opposite of renin–angiotensin). As you would predict therefore, it is secreted in conditions of *hyper*volaemia – via stretch of the right atrial and ventricular walls. It also antagonises the other actions of angiotensin-II by causing vasodilatation and reduced thirst/salt craving
*   **Peptide**: it is a peptide hormone (which acts via cAMP)

There are two other natriuretic peptides, B-type and C-type natriuretic peptides (BNP and CNP). BNP is similar to ANP, and is produced from the heart especially in heart failure. Serum levels are more stable than those of ANP, and BNP is proving to be a useful test of heart failure. CNP is produced by the vascular endothelium rather than by cardiac myocytes.

4.3   THE PITUITARY GLAND

4.3.1   Anatomy

The anatomical relations of the pituitary (Figure 4.3) are important as enlarging pituitary tumours may press on surrounding structures.

*   **Above**: optic chiasm (causing bitemporal hemianopia if compressed), pituitary stalk, hypothalamus, temporal lobes
*   **Below**: sphenoid sinus (in front and below to allow trans-sphenoidal surgery), nasopharynx
*   **Lateral**: cavernous sinus, internal carotid arteries, III, IV, V_1, V_2 and VI cranial nerves

Expanding pituitary tumours may also compromise remaining anterior pituitary function but very rarely affect posterior pituitary hormones.

Figure 4.3 Schematic sagittal section through the pituitary to show its relation to surrounding structures

4.3.2 Pituitary tumours

A microadenoma is a pituitary tumour less than 1 cm in size. The size and frequency of pituitary tumours are related.

Pituitary tumours

- Large – non-secreting (typically chromophobe): 50% of all tumours
- Large – prolactinomas in men: 25% of all tumours
- Medium – acromegaly (typically 'acidophil', 70% are >1 cm): 12% of all tumours
- Small – Cushing's disease (often undetectable on CT/MRI, typically basophil: 5%–10% of all tumours
- Small – TSH-secreting: 1% (very rare)

The commonest tumours are small, non-functioning microadenomas, which have been reported to occur in up to 20% of people at post-mortem. Note that **prolactinomas** in women are usually picked up at the microadenoma size due to their effects upon menstrual disturbance. Note also that pituitary tumours may also form part of the MEN-1 syndrome (*see* p. 114).

Nelson syndrome arises after adrenalectomy for pituitary-dependent Cushing syndrome (Cushing's disease). The small tumour is no longer suppressed by high steroid levels and can become very invasive. Local tumour effects and hyperpigmentation result.

Pituitary apoplexy is sudden enlargement of the pituitary by haemorrhage into a tumour, typically causing the combination of headache, neck stiffness and sudden blindness associated with cardio-vascular collapse due to hypopituitarism. Treatment is with steroid replacement and urgent surgery for visual loss (to decompress the optic chiasm). In **pituitary failure** the only two hormones that **must** be replaced for survival are thyroxine and hydrocortisone.

Forty per cent of cases of **acromegaly** (GH tumours) arise because of a G-protein mutation (*see* Section 4.1.2).

Craniopharyngiomas are benign tumours that arise from remnants of Rathke's pouch. Two-thirds arise in the hypothalamus itself (suprasellar), one-third in the sella. They are usually cystic, frequently calcify, often recur after aspiration and, although they represent an embryonic remnant, they not infrequently present in adulthood.

4.3.3 Diabetes insipidus

Antidiuretic hormone (ADH, also called vasopressin or arginine-vasopressin, AVP) is synthesised in the hypothalamus and transported to the posterior pituitary, along with oxytocin, for storage and release. Diabetes insipidus (DI) is caused either by a failure to secrete vasopressin from the posterior pituitary (**central or cranial DI**) or resistance to the action of vasopressin in the kidney (**nephrogenic DI**). To cause **cranial DI**, the hypothalamic nuclei (supraoptic and paraventricular) need to be damaged – it is not sufficient simply to compress the posterior pituitary as vasopressin can be secreted directly from the hypothalamus itself. Pituitary tumours therefore rarely cause DI.

Major causes of cranial diabetes insipidus
• Idiopathic • Craniopharyngiomas • Infiltrative processes of the hypothalamus (eg sarcoid, histiocytosis X) • Trauma • Pituitary surgery • Lymphocytic hypophysitis • Dysgerminomas

Causes of nephrogenic diabetes insipidus
Reduced action of ADH on the kidney can have several causes: • **Primary** • Childhood onset: X-linked/dominant abnormality in tubular ADH receptor • **Secondary (common)** • Hypercalcaemia • Hypokalaemia • Renal disease (particularly if it involves the medullary interstitium) • Lithium • Demeclocycline

Water deprivation test

A water deprivation test (Table 4.3) is used to identify the cause of polydipsia and/or polyuria. Major metabolic causes should first be excluded (eg hyperglycaemia (diabetes mellitus), hypercalcaemia, hypokalaemia, chronic renal failure). The patient is then deprived of water (from the night before if polyuria is not excessive) and hourly urine and plasma osmolality are measured until 3% of the body weight is lost. The patient is then given an injection of DDAVP® (a synthetic analogue of ADH).

Interpretation of the water deprivation test

• **Primary polydipsia (compulsive water drinking)**: in this condition the patient is not dehydrated

Table 4.3. Interpretation of the water deprivation test

	Initial plasma osmolality	Final urine osmolality (mosmol/kg)	Urine osmolality post-DDAVP® (mosmol/kg)	Final plasma ADH
Normal	Normal	>600	>600	High
Cranial DI	High	<300	>600	Low
Nephrogenic DI	High	<300	<300	High
Primary polydipsia	Low	300–400 (approx.)	400 (approx.)	Moderate
Partial cranial DI	High	300–400	400–600	Relatively low

but water-overloaded in the resting state (Na$^+$ <140 mmol/l). Chronic polydipsia in this condition can result in washout of the renal medullary concentrating gradient so that even if the patient does become dehydrated, with a rise in ADH, urine cannot be concentrated

- **Partial cranial DI**: in this condition there is weak ADH production. There is a similar effect upon the renal medullary concentrating gradient to that seen in primary polydipsia, and so the two conditions can not be differentiated unless a post-hydration serum ADH level is obtained

4.3.4 Acromegaly

The common features of acromegaly are well known (hand and foot enlargement, coarse facial features, overbite of the lower jaw, splaying of the teeth) but the following also occur (*see* Box):

Features of acromegaly
<ul><li>Diabetes</li><li>Arthropathy – often pseudogout</li><li>Sleep apnoea</li><li>Carpal tunnel syndrome</li><li>Multinodular goitre</li><li>Increase in malignancies, especially colonic polyps</li><li>Hypertension</li><li>Twofold increase in death from cardiovascular disease</li><li>Cardiomyopathy</li><li>Left ventricular hypertrophy</li><li>Enlarged testes</li><li>Renal stones (hypercalciuria)</li><li>Raised phosphate</li><li>Raised prolactin, galactorrhoea, menstrual change</li><li>Raised triglycerides</li></ul>

Acromegaly is almost always due to a GH-secreting pituitary tumour. Rarely the condition is due to ectopic GH-releasing hormone (GHRH) secretion from a tumour (typically carcinoid) which stimulates the normal pituitary (no discrete tumour seen on

MRI scan). Acromegaly is diagnosed by failure of GH to suppress to less than 2 mU/l at any time in a standard 75 g glucose tolerance test (GTT). This may produce a double diagnosis as the GTT may diagnose acromegaly-induced diabetes at the same time.

First-line treatment is **trans-sphenoidal surgery** to the pituitary tumour (or transcranial surgery if there is a large suprasellar extension of tumour). The cure rate (40%–70%) depends on the initial tumour size. Alternative therapies are **octreotide** (long-acting analogue of somatostatin), **pituitary radiotherapy** (may take years to take effect and result in hypopituitarism), **pegvisomont** (GH antagonist derived from the GH receptor) or **bromocriptine** (effective in less than 20% of cases). After successful treatment of acromegaly (GH <5 mU/l, IGF-1 in the normal range), most physical features do not regress. Features of active disease are increased sweating and oedema of the hands and feet which can regress after therapy.

4.3.5 Hypopituitarism and growth hormone deficiency in adults

Hypopituitarism

Panhypopituitarism can be caused by enlarging pituitary tumours, cranial irradiation (including specific pituitary radiotherapy), pituitary apoplexy, Sheehan syndrome (infarction following post-partum haemorrhage), and then by any of the conditions which can cause cranial diabetes insipidus (*see* Box on p. 102).

Patients present with a soft, smooth 'baby' skin, 'crows' feet' lines around the eyes and possibly features of other specific hormone loss (eg hypotension associated with hypoadrenalism, hypothyroidism)

Diagnosis

Growth hormone production (tested with insulin-hypoglycaemia stress test or GHRH-arginine stimulation) and gonadal function (test for low testosterone/oestrogen combined with low or inappropriately normal LH, FSH; or GnRH stimulation test) are lost early. Free T$_4$ (FT$_4$) alone is sufficient to test for hypothyroidism (TSH is misleading) and cortisol production can be assessed by either a short Synacthen test (in long-standing hypopituitarism) or an insulin-hypoglycaemia stress test.

- Only replacement therapy with steroids and thyroxine is essential for life
- In suspected hypopituitarism, the steroids should be given first and certainly before thyroid replacement therapy. This is because correction of hypothyroidism will accelerate cortisol metabolism and would precipitate a hypoadrenal crisis (if thyroxine is given before exogenous steroids)
- If the pituitary is damaged, GH production is lost early so that most patients are growth hormone-deficient (see below)
- Despite conventional hormone replacement therapy (thyroxine, glucocorticoid and sex steroids), mortality rates are increased in hypopituitarism owing to either an increase in cardiovascular events or malignancy. The potential for GH therapy to reverse this trend is currently being researched

GH is required for growth in children. It was thought to have little function in adults but recently the following have been ascribed to **adult GH deficiency**:

- Reduced muscle, increased fat
- Low mood (some patients improve markedly with GH therapy)
- Raised lipids
- Reduced left ventricular function
- Osteoporosis
- Impaired endothelial function

Treatment of adult GH deficiency with daily GH injections is now recommended in patients whose quality of life is shown to improve significantly after a 3-month trial of GH therapy.

4.4 HYPONATRAEMIA AND SIADH

Antidiuretic hormone (ADH or vasopressin) is synthesised in magnocellular neurones in the supraoptic and paraventricular nuclei of the hypothalamus and stored in the posterior pituitary. ADH is released in response to rising plasma osmolality and acts on the distal tubule and renal collecting ducts to increase water permeability. Water is reabsorbed and the urine becomes more concentrated. When the ADH system is working normally, 'the urine should reflect the blood', that is, concentrated urine should occur when the plasma osmolality is high and vice versa.

However, hypovolaemia is also a strong signal for ADH release and in the presence of hypovolaemia ADH will be secreted even if the osmolality is low. This explains the hyponatraemia seen in renal, cardiac and liver failure as well as following excessive sodium loss (eg diarrhoea). Other stimuli can also commonly override control of ADH secretion by osmolarity (*see* SIADH below).

Syndrome of inappropriate ADH secretion (SIADH)

Many common stimuli override the control of osmolality and cause inappropriate amounts of ADH to be secreted, causing hyponatraemia. Sodium concentration should be high in the urine (excluding hypovolaemia), renal, adrenal and thyroid function should be normal and diuretic therapy needs to be excluded before SIADH is diagnosed. Treatment is by fluid restriction or, if necessary, oral demeclocycline.

Table 4.4. Causes of hyponatraemia

Urine sodium (mmol/l)	Hypovolaemia present	Eu/Hypervolaemia ± oedema
>20	Diuretics	SIADH
	Hypoadrenalism	Hypothyroidism
	Salt-losing nephropathy	Renal failure
<10	Vomiting, diarrhoea	Congestive cardiac failure, cirrhosis, nephrotic syndrome
	Loss of other fluid	

Causes of inappropriate secretion of ADH include

- Nausea
- Pain
- Fits
- Pneumonia
- Other CNS/lung insults
- Smoking
- Chlorpropamide
- Carbamazepine
- Head injury
- Cerebrovascular accidents (CVAs)
- Tumours making ectopic ADH (eg bronchus)

If a tumour is the cause, it is usually obvious: a search for malignancy beyond a chest X-ray is not required in SIADH. Smoking makes you pass less urine (releases ADH); drinking (alcohol) makes you pass more (inhibits ADH secretion).

Causes of hyponatraemia

Hyponatraemia can be divided into three categories:

- 'Real' (low serum osmolality)
- Pseudohyponatraemia: high triglycerides, high protein (eg myeloma) (normal serum osmolality)

- Dilutional: high glucose, ethanol, mannitol (serum osmolality may be raised)

If hyponatraemia is confirmed to be 'real' (low plasma osmolality, glucose not raised and no suggestion of ethanol or mannitol in blood) then the following clinical and laboratory pointers must be considered:

- Careful history for drug use (especially diuretics) and of fluid loss (eg diarrhoea)
- Examination for circulatory volume status (oedema, postural hypotension and skin turgor)
- Measurement of urinary sodium concentration (*see* Table 4.4)

Hypoadrenalism is the most important diagnosis not to be missed, since untreated it can result in death.

4.5 THE THYROID GLAND

4.5.1 Hyperthyroidism and hypothyroidism

The common features of hyperthyroidism (eg weight loss, tremor, palpitations) and hypothyroidism (eg weight gain, dry skin, slowing up) are well known but questions are often asked on the more unusual features. 'Recognised' features of the two major thyroid syndromes are summarised in Table 4.5.

Table 4.5. Features of hyper- and hypothyroidism

Features	Hyperthyroidism	Hypothyroidism
General	Weight gain (rarely) Gynaecomastia Occult in elderly Hair loss	Weight gain Serous effusions (pleural, pericardial, ascites, joint) Hair loss
Gynae	Amenorrhoea Raised sex hormone-binding globulin (SHBG)	Menorrhagia Infertility
GI	Diarrhoea Raised alkaline phosphatase (derived from liver and bone) Vomiting	Constipation
Muscle	Proximal myopathy Periodic paralysis (especially Chinese)	Raised creatine kinase Chest pain (muscular) Muscle cramps
CVS	Dyspnoea Atrial fibrillation with high stroke rate High-output cardiac failure	Hypercholesterolaemia Ischaemic heart disease
Bone	Osteoporosis Hypercalcaemia	
Neuro	'Apathetic thyrotoxicosis'	Deafness Ataxia, confusion, coma
Eyes	Eye signs (*see* Section 4.5.5)	Periorbital oedema
Blood	Leucopenia Microcytic anaemia	Macrocytic anaemia Microcytic if menorrhagia
Skin	Urticaria	Dry, orange (caroteinaemia)

Features of hyper- and hypothyroidism

Amenorrhoea is predictable in hyperthyroidism because of associated weight loss. In hypothyroidism, everything slows down except the periods! The menorrhagia can cause a microcytic anaemia in contrast to the more usual macrocytosis. In both conditions there may be subfertility. In the GI tract, the symptoms of hyperthyroidism are almost indistinguishable from those of anxiety. The diarrhoea is actually more like the increased bowel frequency before an examination.

- Both hyperthyroidism (if Graves' disease) and hypothyroidism can cause periorbital oedema. (*See* note in Section 4.5.5 on eye signs in thyrotoxicosis)
- The leucopenia of thyrotoxicosis can be misdiagnosed: thionamide drugs (eg carbimazole) used as treatment also commonly cause a lymphopenia. Both of these are separate from the agranulocytosis that rarely occurs with thionamide drugs
- In hyperthyroidism the urticaria due to the disease itself can cause confusion with the maculopapular rash which develops in 10% of patients treated with thionamide drugs

Side-effects of anti-thyroid drugs (carbimazole, propylthiouracil)

- **Common**
  - Rash
  - Leucopenia
- **Rare**
  - Agranulocytosis
  - Aplastic anaemia
  - Hepatitis
  - Fever
  - Arthralgia
  - Vasculitis (propylthiouracil)

(*See also* Chapter 2, Clinical Pharmacology, Toxicology and Poisoning)

4.5.2 Causes of thyrotoxicosis

The three common causes of thyrotoxicosis are:

- Graves' disease
- Toxic multinodular goitre
- Toxic (hot) nodule

In all these conditions all or part of the gland is overactive and the gland takes up a normal or increased amount of radioiodine.

In the following conditions, there is thyrotoxicosis without increased production of new hormone by the thyroid gland itself, ie radio-iodine uptake is suppressed:

- Excess thyroxine ingestion
- Thyroiditis: post-viral (de Quervain's), post-partum or silent thyroiditis
- Ectopic thyroid tissue, eg lingual thyroid or ovary (struma ovarii)
- Iodine administration: gland is actually still active but cold iodine competes with radio-iodine during scanning

4.5.3 Thyroid cancer and nodules

Only 5%–10% of thyroid nodules are malignant (the rest are adenomas). Thyroid cancer virtually never causes hyperthyroidism so 'hot nodules' can usually be presumed to be benign. In order of increasing malignancy and decreasing frequency the thyroid epithelial cancers are:

- Papillary
- Follicular
- Anaplastic

Lymphomas occur in Hashimoto's disease. Medullary thyroid cancer is from the C-cells (calcitonin), not from the thyroid epithelium. Serum calcitonin is a tumour marker for this cancer which often occurs in families, sometimes as part of the multiple endocrine neoplasia type 2 syndrome (*see* Section 4.7).

4.5.4 Drugs and the thyroid

- **Lithium**
  - Inhibits T_4 release from the gland causing hypothyroidism
- **Oestrogens**
  - Raised thyroid-binding globulin (TBG) and hence 'total' T_4/T_3
- **Amiodarone**
  - Inhibits T_4 to T_3 conversion, increasing reverse T_3
  - High iodine content can cause hyper*- or hypothyroidism
- **Iron** – if taken at the same time as thyroxine can reduce its absorption
- **Interferon**
  - Induces antithyroid autoantibodies and hypothyroidism (usually transient)

*Note on amiodarone-induced hyperthyroidism. This may be due to drug-induced damage (thyroiditis) or to the excess iodine in amiodarone and can be very resistant to treatment

4.5.5 Autoimmunity and eye signs in thyroid disease

In areas such as the UK where there is relatively little iodine deficiency, more than 90% of spontaneous hypothyroidism is due to autoimmunity. Antithyroglobulin autoantibodies are present in 60% of cases and antimicrosomal antibodies (now identified as anti-thyroid peroxidase antibodies) are present in up to 90%. Antibodies that block the TSH receptor may also be present. Similar antibodies are present in Graves' disease but the anti-TSH receptor antibodies are stimulatory, causing the thyrotoxicosis. The term LATS (long-acting thyroid stimulator) referring to this stimulatory antibody is no longer used.

The eye signs in thyroid disease are shown in the box below (*see also* Chapter 17, Ophthalmology). Retro-orbital inflammation and swelling of the extra-ocular muscles are only seen in Graves' dis-

ease. Note that each of the features listed can occur separately in thyroid eye disease (eg diplopia without exophthalmos) and, surprisingly, disease of the two eyes is usually asymmetrical. The target of the antibody or T-cell reaction causing this inflammation is not known for certain and eye disease activity can occur in the absence of thyrotoxicosis and even with hypothyroidism.

Thyrotoxicosis from any cause

- Lid retraction
- Lid lag

Graves' disease only

- Soft tissue signs: periorbital oedema, conjunctival injection, chemosis
- Proptosis/exophthalmos
- Diplopia/ophthalmoplegia
- Optic nerve compression causing visual failure

4.5.6 Thyroid function tests

TSH is the most sensitive measure of thyroid status in patients with an intact pituitary. T_4 and T_3 are over 95% protein-bound, predominantly to TBG. The following alter TBG levels and hence total but not free hormone levels.

Conditions which alter thyroid-binding globulin (TBG)

Raised TBG	Low TBG
Pregnancy	Nephrotic syndrome
Oestrogen	Congenital TBG
Hepatitis	abnormality
Congenital TBG abnormality	

Table 4.6. Thyroid function tests

	TSH		
	Low	**Normal**	**Raised**
Raised FT$_4$/FT$_3$	Thyrotoxicosis	*Rare:* (applies to both normal and raised) • TSH-secreting pituitary tumour • Thyroid hormone resistance (receptor defect) • Hypoadrenalism • Acute psychiatric illness • Intermittent T$_4$ therapy (poor compliance) • T$_4$ acute overdose (TSH normal) • Interfering anti-T$_4$/T$_3$ antibody (TSH normal) • Familial dysalbuminaemic hyperthyroxinaemia (TSH normal)	
Normal FT$_4$/FT$_3$	Subclinical thyrotoxicosis: • Excess thyroxine • Steroid therapy • Non-thyroidal illness • Dopamine infusion	**Normal**	Subclinical hypothyroidism: • Poor compliance with T$_4$ therapy • Interfering (heterophile) antibody • Recovery from non-thyroidal illness • Hypoadrenalism
Low FT$_4$/FT$_3$	Non-thyroidal illness: (applies to both low and normal) • Pituitary failure • Recent (excessive) treatment for hyperthyroidism		**Hypothyroidism**

Interpretation of thyroid function tests

This is generally straightforward in ambulant out-patients if the causes of different patterns of thyroid function tests (TFTs) are known (see Table 4.6). Special care in interpretation should be taken in the following circumstances:

• Known or suspected pituitary disease (TSH is misleading and should NOT be used as a test)
• Acutely ill patients (eg in intensive care) – TSH often low with low free T$_3$ (FT$_3$)

4.6 ADRENAL DISEASE AND HIRSUTISM

4.6.1 Cushing syndrome

Cushing syndrome refers to the sustained over-production of cortisol (hypercortisolism) which causes:

• Centripetal obesity with moon face
• 'Buffalo hump'
• Hirsutism
• Recurrent infections

- Osteoporosis
- Oligomenorrhoea
- Hypokalaemia
- Striae
- Acne
- Proximal muscle weakness
- Hyperglycaemia
- Psychiatric disturbances
- Hypertension

If untreated, death is usually due to infection. Other than due to steroid treatment, Cushing syndrome is rare. In the first instance, it needs to be distinguished from simple obesity. Once Cushing syndrome is confirmed, the cause needs to be identified.

The diagnosis is made in two phases.

Tests to confirm hypercortisolism (Cushing syndrome)

- Loss of diurnal variation (midnight cortisol not lower than morning cortisol)
- Overnight dexamethasone suppression test (1 mg at midnight then 9 am cortisol)
- Low-dose dexamethasone suppression test (0.5 mg qds for 48 hours)
- Urinary free cortisol (24-hour collection)

If one or more of these are positive then one can proceed to localisation. NB: Depression or alcoholism can both cause cortisol over-production ('pseudo-Cushing's'). If these conditions are present, further investigation is very difficult.

Tests to localise the cause of Cushing syndrome

Possible causes of Cushing syndrome are:

- Adrenal tumour
- Pituitary tumour (Cushing's disease)
- Ectopic production of ACTH – either from cancer (eg small-cell cancer of lung) or from a bronchial adenoma (often very small)
- Ectopic production of corticotrophin-releasing hormone (CRH) (very rare)

MRI scanning of the adrenal or pituitary alone cannot be relied on to localise the cause. Firstly, the tumours of the pituitary causing Cushing's disease are often too small to see and, secondly, incidental tumours of both the pituitary and adrenal are common and may not be functional. Tests used to identify the causes of Cushing syndrome are shown in Table 4.7.

- With modern assays, an undetectable ACTH level with confirmed hypercortisolism is usually sufficient for a diagnosis of an adrenal source

Nelson syndrome: bilateral adrenalectomy will cure the hypercortisolism of pituitary-dependent Cushing syndrome but loss of suppression (provided by the previously high cortisol levels) may allow a pre-existing pituitary adenoma to grow very rapidly, years later, causing local damage and generalised pigmentation.

Endocrine causes of obesity

- Steroid excess (Cushing syndrome)
- Hypothyroidism
- Hypothalamic tumours (hyperphagia)
- Prader–Willi syndrome
- GH deficiency

4.6.2 Primary hyperaldosteronism

Primary hyperaldosteronism comprises hypertension, hypokalaemia (80% of cases), hypomagnesaemia and metabolic alkalosis. Patients can, however, have a serum potassium within the normal range. Primary hyperaldosteronism is now thought to account for 1%–3% of all cases of hypertension.

- **Symptoms (if present) relate to hypokalaemia**: weakness, muscle cramps, paraesthesiae, polyuria and polydipsia. Patients rarely develop peripheral oedema ('sodium escape' mechanism)
- **Causes**: aldosterone-secreting adenoma (**Conn syndrome** is almost never caused by a malignancy), idiopathic bilateral adrenal hyperplasia, unilateral hyperplasia (rare)
- **Investigations** (not standardised): the **renin : aldosterone ratio** should be assessed to

Table 4.7. Tests used to identify causes of Cushing syndrome

	Adrenal	Pituitary	Ectopic
ACTH	Suppressed	Mid-range	High
High-dose dexamethasone suppression	No change in cortisol	Suppression of cortisol*	No change
CRH stimulation test	No change	Rise in ACTH and cortisol*	No change
Metyrapone	Rise in 11-deoxycortisol <220-fold	Rise in 11-deoxycortisol >220-fold*	Rise in 11-deoxycortisol <220-fold
Petrosal sinus ACTH**	Equals peripheral level	Higher than peripheral level	Equals peripheral level

* 'Under pressure' (ie at high doses), pituitary adenomas behave like a normal pituitary in dynamic endocrine testing, whereas adrenal or ectopic sources do not. A positive response to high-dose suppression (2 mg qds for 48 hours) is >10% suppression of plasma cortisol or 24-hour-urine free cortisol

** In a petrosal sinus sampling a catheter is placed in the draining sinus of the pituitary gland, via a femoral or jugular venous approach. The ACTH level is compared with that in the peripheral blood before and after CRH injection

confirm high aldosterone levels in the presence of low renin. Ideally, the ratio should be assessed after the patient has ceased antihypertensive drugs (β-blockers lower renin and aldosterone levels; spironolactone, diuretics and vasodilators raise renin and aldosterone levels; whereas ACE inhibitors and calcium-channel blockers raise renin but lower aldosterone levels, so they may all lead to a false-negative result). Alpha-blockers (eg doxazosin) have the least effect. However, discontinuing antihypertensive therapy for 2–6 weeks is often impractical and measurement of the ratio after the patient has been upright (sitting or standing) for 2 hours (to stimulate renin levels) is now considered to be a useful screening test for primary hyperaldosteronism, even in the presence of one or two drugs. If hyperaldosteronism is confirmed, a CT or MRI scan of the abdomen may identify a unilateral adrenal adenoma. However, the tumours are usually <2 cm in diameter and so if imaging is negative, adrenal vein sampling may be required in order to distinguish unilateral hypoplasia or a tiny adenoma from idiopathic bilateral hyperplasia

- **Treatment**: spironolactone and amiloride are often successful treatments when the cause is bilateral hyperplasia. Eplerenone is a selective aldosterone antagonist that can be used in patients who develop gynaecomastia or breast soreness with spironolactone. An adenoma or unilateral adrenal hyperplasia may be surgically removed; hypertension may persist if this was previously long-standing

(*See* Chapter 1, Cardiology, Section 1.9.3 Systemic hypertension. *See also* Chapter 15, Nephrology, Section 15.3.4 for differential diagnoses of hypokalaemia.)

4.6.3 Congenital adrenal hyperplasia (CAH)

Two enzyme defects account for 95% of all CAH:

- 21-Hydroxylase (90%)
- 11-Hydroxylase (5%)

The block caused by these enzyme defects leads to reduced production of cortisol, but increased production of other intermediates in steroid metabolism, including androgenic steroids. 17-Hydroxylase, 3-β-hydroxysteroid dehydrogenase and cholesterol side-chain cleavage enzyme defects are very rare causes of CAH and have differing effects (see the following box).

Features of congenital adrenal hyperplasia

- Autosomal recessive
- Both gene deletions and point mutations can occur
- Plasma ACTH is high (renin is high if salt-losing)
- Can cause male precocious puberty (not 17-hydroxylase or side-chain enzyme); can cause ambiguous genitalia in females (not 17-hydroxylase or side-chain enzyme)
- Treat with glucocorticoids ± mineralocorticoids at night
- Can have a minor, late-onset form resembling polycystic ovary syndrome
- Surgery may be required to correct ambiguous genitalia/cliteromegaly
- Antenatal steroid therapy to the mother has been used

It is possible to distinguish between the different enzyme defects in CAH (see Table 4.8).

4.6.4   Hypoadrenalism

In the UK, spontaneous hypoadrenalism is most commonly due to autoimmune destruction of the adrenal glands (Addison's disease – adrenal auto-antibodies present in 70% of cases). Vitiligo is present in 10%–20% of cases. Other causes include TB, HIV or haemorrhage into the adrenal glands and anterior pituitary disease (secondary hypoadrenalism). Hypoadrenalism after withdrawal of long-standing steroid therapy is similar to secondary hypoadrenalism.

The following are 'recognised' features of hypoadrenalism:

- **Biochemical**: raised urea, hypoglycaemia, hyponatraemia, hyperkalaemia, raised TSH, hypercalcaemia
- **Haematological**: eosinophilia, lymphocytosis, normocytic anaemia
- **Clinical features**: weight loss, abdominal pain, psychosis, loss of pubic hair in women, hypotension, auricular cartilage calcification, increased pigmentation

Hyperkalaemia and increased pigmentation are absent in secondary hypoadrenalism since there are low levels of circulating ACTH and mineralocorti-

Table 4.8. Differentiating features in congenital adrenal hyperplasia

	21-Hydroxylase	**11-Hydroxylase**	**17-Hydroxylase/side-chain enzyme**
Frequency	90% cases	5% cases	Very rare
Presentation in females	Virilising, intersex 70% salt-losing*	Virilising, hypertension, low K+	Non-virilising (intersex in boys)
Biochemistry	Raised 17-hydroxylase, progesterone	Raised 11-dehydroxycortisol	

* Salt-losing individuals can have addisonian crises soon after birth

coid continues to be secreted via the renin–angio-tensin–aldosterone system. Hypoadrenalism is diagnosed by failure of plasma cortisol to rise above 550 nmol/l at 30 or 60 minutes following IM or IV injection of 250 µg of synthetic ACTH (short Synacthen® test)

Acute adrenal failure (addisonian crisis)

Addisonian crisis presents with hypovolaemia, hyponatraemia, hyperkalaemia (if primary adrenal failure), hypoglycaemia and cardiovascular collapse, which can be fatal. A mildly raised TSH may also be seen even in the absence of thyroid disease. Urgent treatment is necessary and this includes intravenous fluid and electrolyte replacement as well as steroid replacement.

4.6.5 Polycystic ovary syndrome (PCOS) and hirsutism

Hirsutism (Table 4.9) is the increased growth of terminal (dark) hairs in androgen-dependent areas. Virilisation is temporal hair recession (male pattern), breast atrophy, voice change, male physique and (most important) cliteromegaly. Hirsutism and acne are invariably also present.

A serum testosterone >4.5 nmol/l (normal <1.8), recent onset of hirsutism and signs of virilisation in women should prompt a search for other causes (eg a tumour). Dehydroepiandrostenedione (DHEA) is a weak androgen produced in the adrenal only.

- Measure the 17-hydroxyprogesterone level after stimulation with ACTH to check for late-onset 21-hydroxylase deficiency (partial enzyme deficiency)
- Other than androgens, the drugs listed strictly cause hypertrichosis, an increase in vellus hair, rather than an increase in androgen-sensitive terminal hairs (*see* Chapter 3, Dermatology)

Polycystic ovary syndrome

There is no widely recognised definition and up to 20% of women have a degree of hirsutism. In practice, the three main presenting complaints in PCOS are **hirsutism/acne**, **oligo/amenorrhoea** and **subfertility**. The following are recognised associations of PCOS:

- **Clinical features**: obesity, acanthosis nigricans, oligomenorrhoea, polycystic ovaries, subfertility, hypertension, premature balding in male relatives, hirsutism
- **Biochemical**: insulin resistance and hyperinsulinaemia, raised testosterone, raised LH/FSH ratio, raised prolactin, low HDL

Treatment: metformin will lower insulin resistance and it has been shown to promote ovulation, improve conception rates and reduce hirsutism. Weight loss may also be beneficial. Separate specific treatments are available for hirsutism (eg flutamide, cyproterone, finasteride) and infertility (ovulation induction)

Table 4.9. Causes of hirsutism

Ovarian	Adrenal	Drugs
PCOS (>90% of cases)	CAH (may be late-onset)	Minoxidil
Virilising tumour	Cushing's/adrenal carcinoma	Phenytoin Diazoxide Ciclosporin Androgens

4.7 PHAEOCHROMOCYTOMA AND MULTIPLE ENDOCRINE NEOPLASIA (MEN) SYNDROMES

Phaeochromocytomas are rare tumours of the adrenal medulla or ganglia of the sympathetic nervous system. They are the 'tumour of 10%':

- 10% are outside the adrenal glands – paragangliomas (including organ of Zuckerkandl)
- 10% are multiple (eg bilateral)
- 10% are malignant
- 10% are familial

The most sensitive and specific test for the diagnosis of phaeochromocytoma is the measurement of plasma or urinary fractionated metanephrines. This is not available in all centres and measurement of urinary catecholamines is an alternative (measurement of urinary catecholamine metabolites – 3-methoxy-4-hydroxymandelic acid (VMAs) – has now been superseded). As is the case with most endocrine tumours, the histology is not a reliable guide to the malignant potential in phaeochromocytomas. The diagnosis of malignancy is made by the presence of metastases.

Familial phaeochromocytomas occur in

- Multiple endocrine neoplasia type 2 (see below)
- Spontaneously in some families (not associated with a syndrome)
- von Hippel–Lindau syndrome (retinal and cerebral haemangioblastomas and renal cystic carcinomas)
- von Recklinghausen's disease (neurofibromatosis) – 1%–2%
- Carney's triad: gastric leiomyosarcoma, pulmonary chondroma, Leydig testicular tumour
- Paraganglioma syndromes (PGL types 1–4): associated with head and neck paragangliomas and phaeochromocytomas. Mutations in one of the four succinate dehydrogenase subunits (SDH), especially SDHD (PGL1) and SDHB (PGL 4)

Important features of phaeochromocytomas

- 70% have persistent rather than episodic hypertension
- The triad of headache, sweating and palpitations is said to be >90% predictive
- Extra-adrenal tumours do not make adrenaline (they secrete noradrenaline/dopamine)
- Hypotension or postural hypotension may occur, particularly if adrenaline is produced
- They give characteristically a 'bright' (white) signal on T_2-weighted MRI scan
- MIBG (meta-iodobenzylguanidine) scanning may help localisation
- Phaeochromocytomas may produce chromogranin A
- Preoperative preparation is with α-adrenergic blockade (eg phenoxybenzamine) *before* β-blockade

---

Causes of episodic sweating and/or flushing

- Oestrogen/testosterone deficiency (eg menopause, castration)
- Carcinoid syndrome (flushing, diarrhoea, wheeze)
- Phaeochromocytoma (sweat but do not flush)
- Hypoglycaemia (in diabetes)
- Thyrotoxicosis (not usually episodic)
- Systemic mastocytosis (histamine release)
- Allergy

Multiple endocrine neoplasia (MEN) syndromes are syndromes with multiple benign or malignant endocrine neoplasms (Table 4.10). They should not be confused with polyglandular autoimmune syndromes which relate to autoimmune endocrine diseases.

- MEN-1 was formerly known as Werner syndrome. MEN-2A was known as Sipple syndrome. All MEN syndromes are autosomal dominant. Genetic (DNA-based) screening is available for both MEN-1 and MEN-2. The MEN-2 mutation in *ret* activates the protein.

Table 4.10. Classification of multiple endocrine neoplasia

	MEN-1	MEN-2A	MEN-2B
Genetics	*menin* gene Chromosome 11	*ret* gene Chromosome 10	*ret* gene Chromosome 10
Tumours	Parathyroid Pituitary Pancreas (Carcinoid) (Adrenal adenomas)	Parathyroid Phaeochromocytoma Medullary thyroid cancer	Parathyroid Phaeochromocytoma Medullary thyroid cancer Marfanoid Mucosal neuromas

Inactivating mutations of *ret* are seen in Hirschsprung's disease
- All MEN syndromes can be associated with hypercalcaemia. This is usually due to hyperplasia of all four parathyroids, not a single parathyroid adenoma as with sporadic hyperparathyroidism. Hypercalcaemia is often the first manifestation in MEN-1
- Gastrinomas and insulinomas are the most common pancreatic tumours in MEN-1. Of the pituitary tumours, prolactinomas are the most common, followed by acromegaly and Cushing's disease

Medullary thyroid cancer (MTC) is always malignant, secretes calcitonin and is preceded by C-cell hyperplasia. Prophylactic thyroidectomy in patients with genetically confirmed MEN-2 should be performed to prevent this most serious manifestation. The exact site of the *ret gene* determines the age at which thyroidectomy should be performed, in many cases under the age of 2 years.

4.8 PUBERTY/GROWTH/INTERSEX

4.8.1 Normal puberty

In 95% of children, puberty begins between the ages of 8 and 13 years in females and between 9 and 14 years in males. The mean age of menarche is 12.8 years. The events of puberty occur in a particular order, although the later stages overlap with the earlier ones.

> **Order of events in normal puberty (earliest events listed first)**
>
> - Male
>   - Scrotal thickening (age 9–14)
>   - Testicular enlargement (>2 ml)
>   - Pubic hair
>   - Phallus growth
>   - Growth spurt (age 10–16) + increasing bone age
> - Female
>   - Breast development (age 8–13)
>   - Growth spurt
>   - Pubic hair
>   - Menstruation (age 10–16) + increasing bone age

4.8.2 Precocious puberty

True precocious puberty is rare. It is diagnosed if multiple signs of puberty develop before age 8 in females and age 9 in males, accompanied by increased growth rate, accelerated bone age and raised sex steroid levels. Isolated premature breast development (thelarche) or the appearance of pubic hair alone (from adrenal androgens – adrenarche) are both benign conditions if no other stages of puberty are entered.

Causes of precocious puberty

- True 'central' gonadotrophin-dependent precocious puberty
  - Idiopathic
  - Other CNS disease (eg hydrocephalus, encephalitis, trauma)
  - CNS hamartoma (eg pineal)
- Other causes (gonadotrophin-independent)
  - Adrenal, ovarian tumour
  - CAH (males)
  - Testotoxicosis (males)
  - Exogenous oestrogen (females)
  - McCune–Albright syndrome
  - Follicular cysts (females)
  - Profound hypothyroidism

McCune–Albright syndrome is more common in girls (*see* Section 4.1.2 on activating G-protein mutations).

4.8.3 Delayed puberty/short stature

Short stature in children is often due to delayed puberty and hence the two problems are usually grouped together. Three per cent of children are 'statistically delayed', ie for girls no breast development by age 13 or menses by age 15 and for boys no testicular enlargement by age 14. The majority will have 'constitutional delay' and will later enter puberty spontaneously. However, there is no endocrine test that can reliably distinguish constitutional delay from other organic causes of delayed puberty.

In investigation, systemic diseases or syndromes that can cause delayed puberty should be excluded before considering pituitary testing. A karyotype (for Turner syndrome) should always be requested in girls (see following text).

Causes of delayed puberty/short stature

- **General causes**
  - Overt systemic disease
  - Social deprivation
  - Anorexia, excess exercise
  - Chemotherapy/gonadal irradiation
  - Cranial irradiation
- **Syndromes causing delayed puberty/short stature**
  - Turner syndrome (XO)
  - Noonan syndrome ('male Turner')
  - Prader–Willi
- **Occult systemic disease**
  - Renal failure/renal tubular acidosis
  - Crohn's/coeliac disease
  - Hypothyroidism
  - Asthma
  - Anterior pituitary disease
  - Hyperprolactinaemia
  - Isolated GH deficiency
- **Syndromes causing delayed puberty but normal stature**
  - Androgen insensitivity (testicular feminisation – XY female)
  - Polycystic ovary syndrome (delayed menarche only)
  - Kallman's (XY), anosmia
  - Klinefelter syndrome (XXY) – males

In Turner syndrome, Noonan syndrome, androgen insensitivity and Klinefelter syndrome, raised LH and FSH are present. **Kallman syndrome** is due to failure of GnRH-secreting neurones to migrate to the hypothalamus. LH and FSH levels, as well as sex steroids, are low and patients typically have associated anosmia. Mutations in at least five genes can cause the syndrome, the best recognised being the classic X-linked locus (*KAL-1* also known as *anosmin-1* – the syndrome associated with anosmia) and the autosomal loci fibroblast growth factor receptor 1 (*FGFR1*, a syndrome associated with orofacial clefting and hypodontia). However, gene mutations only account for around 40% of cases of **idiopathic hypogonadotrophic hypogonadism**. There is no biochemical test that can currently distinguish Kallman syndrome from constitutional delay of puberty, and therefore a clinical diagnosis is made when delayed puberty is associated with anosmia.

Turner syndrome (XO) (*see* Chapter 7, Genetics) occurs in 1 in 2500 live births. The typical features (abnormal nails, neonatal lymphoedema, web neck, widely spaced nipples, wide carrying angle) may be absent. A karyotype should always be requested in girls with short stature/delayed puberty because the final height can be increased by early treatment with high doses of growth hormone. Other important complications which may occur in Turner syndrome include aortic root dilatation (often the cause of death) or coarctation, renal abnormalities, abnormal liver function tests and deafness. Women with Turner syndrome are generally infertile but in some cases will have relatively minor X deletions and/or chimaerism with cells of a normal karyotype, both menstruation and pregnancy can occur.

Klinefelter syndrome (XXY) (*see* Chapter 7, Genetics) occurs in 1 in 1000 live births (by meiotic nondisjunction) but is usually undiagnosed until adulthood. Testosterone production is around 50% of normal, but is sufficient to allow secondary sexual characteristics and normal height to develop. Patients usually come to attention because of small testes, gynaecomastia or infertility.

4.8.4   Intersex

(*See also* Chapter 7, Genetics.) Ambiguous genitalia at birth require urgent diagnosis with steroid profile and karyotype to assign the appropriate sex of rearing and identify the risk of a salt-losing crisis (CAH). Causes can be grouped as follows:

Causes of intersex

- **Virilised female (XX)**
  - CAH (21-OH or 11-OH)
  - Maternal androgen ingestion
- **Non-masculinised male (XY)**
  - Unusual CAH (17-OH/side-chain/3-β-OH)
  - Androgen resistance:
    - Receptor defect ('testicular feminisation')
    - 5-α-reductase deficiency

Mothers who have a virilised daughter with CAH can be treated antenatally with steroids in subsequent pregnancies in order to suppress androgen production by the fetus. Steroids are continued until the sex of the baby can be established by chorionic villus sampling.

4.9   DIABETES MELLITUS

Diabetes may be defined as chronic hyperglycaemia at levels sufficient to cause microvascular complications:

- 85% of cases are due to insulin resistance of unknown origin (type 2, maturity-onset, non-insulin-dependent)
- 10% of cases are due to autoimmune destruction of the pancreatic islets causing insulin deficiency (type 1, juvenile-onset, insulin-dependent)
- Around 5% of cases are due to miscellaneous secondary causes (*see* Section 4.9.3)

4.9.1 Risk factors and clinical features of type 1 and type 2 diabetes mellitus

Table 4.11 summarises the differences between type 1 and type 2 diabetes mellitus. Note that type 2 diabetes mellitus is more common in non-Caucasian races and that despite being 'late onset', it is more strongly inherited than the juvenile-onset form.

In addition to insulin resistance, there is relative failure of the β cells in type 2 diabetes: they are unable to maintain the very high insulin levels required.

Rule of 10s (approximate)

- Incidence of type 1: 0.01%
- Prevalence of type 1 = incidence of type 2: 0.1%
- Prevalence of type 2 (10 times type 1): 1% (actually closer to 2%–3%)

Table 4.11. Comparison between type 1 and type 2 diabetes mellitus

	Type 1	Type 2
Genetics	Both parents affected: 10%–20% risk for child	Both parents affected: 70%–100% risk for child
	Identical twins: 50% concordance	Identical twins: up to 90% concordance
	Caucasians	Asian, black, Pima Indians, other indigenous peoples
	Increased risk: HLA DR3/4, DQ8, insulin gene, (minor loci: *CTLA-4, PTPN22, CD25*) Protective: HLA-DR2, DQasp57	No HLA association At least 10 loci identified by genome-wide association studies affecting insulin resistance and pancreatic development
Autoantibodies	60%–90% islet cell Ab (ICA) positive at diagnosis	No association with antibodies
	70%–90% positive for anti GAD and/or anti-IA2 antibodies*	
	35% risk of diabetes in 5 years if ICA-positive	
	3% of siblings ICA-positive	
Other risk factors		Impaired glucose tolerance
		Gestational diabetes (50% diabetic in 10 years)

(continued)

Table 4.11. *(continued)*

	Type 1	Type 2
Incidence	Approx. 1/10 000 per year (rising especially in under-5s)	Approx. 1–2/1000 per year
Prevalence	Approx. 1/1000	Approx. 3/100
Clinical features (at diagnosis) and pathology	Age <40	Age usually >20 at diagnosis and often asymptomatic (except MODY – see below) but paediatric cases now reported
		often asymptomatic
	Weight loss	Overweight
	Ketosis-prone	Ketone negative
	Insulin-deficient	Insulin resistant
	Autoimmune aetiology (associated with other autoimmune disorders)	Acanthosis nigricans
		Associated with 'syndrome X': hypertension, IHD, hyperinsulinaemia, glucose intolerance
		Amyloid deposition in islets

*GAD = glutamic acid decarboxylase; IA2 = islet-associated antigen 2 (a protein tyrophosphatase). These are both proteins largely confined to the islet

Maturity-onset diabetes of the young (MODY) is the term used to describe type 2 diabetes occurring in patients under the age of 25 with a strong family history. Single gene defects with an autosomal-dominant mode of inheritance have been found in the majority of cases (see Table 4.12).

Table 4.12. Classification of MODY disorders

Gene	% of MODY cases	Classification
Glucokinase	20	MODY 2 – 'mild'; complications are rare
HNF-1α	60	MODY 3 – diagnosed later (around 35 years of age) Progressive beta cell failure but very sensitive to sulphonylureas
HNF-4α	1	MODY 1
HNF-1β	1	MODY 5 – associated renal development abnormalities or cysts
IPF-1	1	MODY 4
Unknown	15	'MODY X'
SUR1, Kir6.2	<1%	Hyperinsulinism in infancy and β cell failure in adulthood

NB: mitochondrial DNA abnormalities can be associated with diabetes and deafness and the MELAS syndrome (**m**itochondrial **e**ncephalopathy, **l**actic **a**cidosis, **s**troke-like episodes). *See* Chapter 7, Genetics, Section 7.5 Mitochondrial disorders.

4.9.2 Diagnostic criteria for diabetes

This remains a controversial area. The key criterion is a plasma glucose of >11.1 mmol/l 2 hours after 75 g of glucose, but this is an inconvenient test to perform in routine practice. The original 1985 WHO definition equated this to a fasting level of

>7.8 mmol/l; but this was later improved to 7.0 mmol/l, a fasting figure that was used to replace the glucose tolerance test (GTT) in the new American Diabetes Association (ADA) 1997 criteria. However, some individuals can have fasting glucose levels as low as 5.8 mmol/l and yet are diabetic as their 2-hour GTT level is >11.1 mmol/l.

Two overlapping syndromes of '**pre-diabetes**' are recognised:

- Impaired glucose defined by 2-hour GTT levels
- Impaired fasting glucose (in the absence of GTT testing) – see below

Note that if typical symptoms are absent, the test should be performed on two separate occasions to confirm sustained hyperglycaemia.

ADA 2005 and WHO 2006 diagnoses of diabetes and pre-diabetes*

*Values are based on venous plasma. Glucose values are lower with capillary samples or whole blood.

- **With symptoms**: fasting glucose >7.0 mmol/l or random glucose >11.1 mmol/l or a glucose of >11.1 mmol/l 2 hours after 75 g GTT (GTT to be performed when fasting glucose is >6 mmol/l and, if diabetes is suspected, when random blood glucose is <11.1 mmol/l)
- **Without symptoms**: either fasting glucose >7 mmol/l or random glucose >11.1 mmol/l, present on two occasions
- **Impaired glucose tolerance**: 2-hour GTT glucose 7.8–11.1 mmol/l (WHO 2006)
- **Impaired fasting glucose**: fasting glucose >5.6 but <7.0 mmol/l (approximately equivalent to impaired glucose tolerance, above) (ADA 2005). WHO do not recognise this category and suggest GTT testing where fasting glucose is >6.0 mmol/l

In impaired glucose tolerance (IGT) glucose levels are insufficient to cause microvascular complications but there is still an increased macrovascular

risk (see Section 4.9.8). Twenty per cent or more of individuals with IGT will progress to type 2 diabetes within 5 years although some will return to normo-glycaemia.

Note that most people with normal glucose tolerance will have fasting glucose <5.6 mmol/l.

4.9.3 Prevention of type 2 diabetes mellitus

Progression from impaired glucose tolerance ('pre-diabetes') to diabetes can be slowed by a programme of diet and exercise (58% reduction in cases), weight loss from any cause and also by drugs, including metformin, acarbose and thiazolidinediones (eg rosiglitazone, proglitazone).

4.9.4 Secondary diabetes

A variety of conditions can lead secondarily to chronic hyperglycaemia fulfilling the criteria of diabetes either by reducing insulin secretion (type-1-like) or by increasing insulin resistance (type-2-like). A pigmented rash in the axillae, neck and groin (acanthosis nigricans) is seen in many conditions associated with insulin resistance.

Causes of secondary diabetes

- **Insulin deficiency**
  - Pancreatitis
  - Haemochromatosis
  - Pancreatic cancer/surgery
  - Cystic fibrosis
  - Somatostatin
- **Insulin resistance**
  - Polycystic ovary syndrome
  - Cushing's, steroid use
  - Acromegaly
  - Glucagonoma
  - Phaeochromocytoma
  - Insulin-receptor (see Section 4.1.4) or signalling defect
  - Anti-insulin receptor antibodies
  - Partial lipodystrophy (*LMNA* mutation)

4.9.5 Treatment of type 1 diabetes mellitus

Insulin replacement is essential in type 1 diabetes. This is usually achieved by two to four injections of subcutaneous insulin daily using a combination of short-acting (soluble or intermediate (isophane)) insulin combined with regular capillary glucose monitoring and adjustment of doses to match increased carbohydrate intake (more insulin) and exercise (less insulin). Recent developments include insulin analogues (see below), the delivery of insulin by continuous subcutaneous insulin infusion (CSII, pump therapy), and islet and whole pancreas transplantation. In the UK, CSII is approved for patients with type 1 diabetes who cannot achieve target HbA1c values due to recurrent hypoglycaemia.

In addition, aggressive cardiovascular risk factor management is indicated as in type 2 diabetes (especially cholesterol lowering and treatment of hypertension).

4.9.6 Treatment of type 2 diabetes mellitus

Seven categories of drug are available to lower glucose levels in type 2 diabetes mellitus (Table 4.13). A gradual decline in insulin reserve leads to an increasing requirement for medication over time and around 30% of type 2 diabetes patients ultimately require insulin therapy to achieve satisfactory glycaemic targets. **Weight loss** (via diet and exercise, weight loss drugs or bariatric surgery), **antihypertensive agents** and drugs to **reduce cardiovascular risk** (aspirin, statins and other lipid-lowering drugs) are also equally important in the management of type 2 diabetes mellitus. Currently available weight loss agents that have proved value in diabetes include orlistat (intestinal lipase inhibitor) and sibutramine (centrally acting stimulant).

Table 4.13. Drugs used in glucose control of type 2 diabetes mellitus

Drug	Action/comments
Sulphonylureas	Increase insulin secretion; weight gain, risk of hypoglycaemia *2nd line*
Biguanides (eg metformin)	Reduce insulin resistance (less hepatic glucose production). GI side-effects. Do not cause hypoglycaemia but risk of lactic acidosis (rare) *1st line.*
Alpha-glucosidase inhibitor (acarbose)	Slows carbohydrate absorption, not complicated by hypoglycaemia, but flatus ++
Thiazolidinediones (eg rosiglitazone and pioglitazone)	Activate intracellular peroxisome proliferator-activated receptors (PPAR-γ) so reducing insulin resistance. Increased weight; fluid retention with increased risk of heart failure; increased fractures and risk of myocardial ischaemia
Insulin	Often used in combination with other drugs (eg metformin); leads to weight gain
Glucagon-like peptide 1 agonists (eg exenatide)	Increase secretion of endogenous insulin, suppress glucagon, reduce appetite and promote weight loss. Given by injection
Dipeptidyl peptidase IV inhibitors (eg sitagliptin, vildagliptin)	Increase secretion of endogenous insulin. No weight loss. Taken orally

HbA1c >58 → consider insulin.

Insulin analogues

These have now been introduced for the treatment of both type 1 and type 2 diabetes mellitus. Examples are insulin lispro (a lysine to proline substitution) and insulin aspart (an asparagine substitution) both of which are designed to replace soluble (regular) insulin. They have an ultra-fast absorption and elimination, so reducing late hypoglycaemia. Newer intermediate-acting insulin analogues have also been developed with a smoother 24-hour profile ('peakless') and these include insulin glargine (which is soluble in the vial at pH 4 but precipitates under the skin at pH 7) and insulin detemir (whose action is prolonged by binding to albumin due to a fatty acid side chain). These analogues also reduce the likelihood of hypoglycaemia.

4.9.7 Glycated haemoglobin (HbA1, HbA1c)

Red cell haemoglobin is non-enzymically glycated at a low rate according to the prevailing level of glucose. The percentage of glycated haemoglobin provides an accurate estimate of mean glucose levels over the preceding 6 weeks and correlates well with the risk of microvascular complications. HbA1c is a more specific fraction of glycosylated haemoglobin than HbA1 and values are 1%–2% lower. Optimal control equates to an HbA1c of 7% in most assays. Modern assays for glycated haemoglobin are rarely misleading but the following conditions should be considered if the results do not correlate with home glucose monitoring results:

Abnormally low HbA1c

- Haemolysis
- Increased red cell turnover
- Blood loss
- HbS or HbC

Abnormally high HbA1c

- Persistent HbF (fetal haemoglobin)
- Thalassaemia
- Uraemia (carbamylated haemoglobin)

4.9.8 Microvascular and macrovascular complications of diabetes

Long-term diabetic complications are due to vascular damage. Damage to the microvasculature and its consequences (see box opposite) correlate well with levels of glycaemic control and can be delayed or prevented by maintaining near-normal glucose levels. Microvascular complications take a minimum of 5 years to develop, even with poor glycaemic control. However, they may be apparently present 'at diagnosis' in type 2 diabetes as hyperglycaemia has often been present for many years prior to diagnosis. Neuropathy (70%–90%) and retinopathy (90%) occur in virtually all patients if control is not perfect and diabetes is present for long enough. Thirty to forty per cent of patients will develop diabetic nephropathy, usually within 20 years of onset of the diabetes (see Chapter 15, Nephrology, Section 15.12.4).

The incidence of microvascular complications was reduced by around 50% in the Diabetes Control and Complications Trial (DCCT) by tight glycaemic control.

In contrast, macrovascular disease, which is responsible for most of the increased mortality in diabetes, does not appear to be so closely related to the level of glycaemic control. However, the increased risk of macrovascular disease in diabetes is at least partly explained by a combination of higher blood pressure, lower HDL and higher triglyceride levels, although absolute cholesterol levels are not raised. Macrovascular complications are markedly reduced

HbA1c 48mmol.

BP target <140/80.
<130/80 if end organ
demage.
ACE 1st line.

by hypertension treatment (which also reduces the risk of retinopathy and nephropathy especially with ACE inhibitors) and aggressive lipid lowering with statins. Multiple risk factor management appears particularly effective.

- Note that chest pain due to angina is often absent or atypical in diabetes and easily missed
- **Proteinuria** is a strong risk factor for ischaemic heart disease in diabetes, presumably as it is a marker for endothelial dysfunction. Individuals with microalbuminuria or proteinuria should be treated to lower blood pressure levels (eg 125/75 mmHg) to protect renal function
- Peripheral neuropathy predisposes to foot ulceration (occurs in around 10% of patients) and, particularly in combination with peripheral vascular disease, increases the risk of amputation (occurs in 1%–2% of patients). Rarely, patients with peripheral neuropathy develop Charcot osteoarthropathy with collapse of the bones of the midfoot and development of deformity

Micro- and macrovascular complications of diabetes

- **Microvascular**
  - Retinopathy (90%)*
  - Neuropathy (70%–90%)*
  - Nephropathy (30%–40%)*
  - HbA1c-dependent
- **Macrovascular**
  - Ischaemic heart disease (accounts for up to 70% of deaths in diabetes)
  - Peripheral vascular disease
  - CVA, hypertension
  - Less HbA1c-dependent
  - (Also present in IGT)

* Approximate percentages of diabetics who will have this complication to some degree during their lifetime (data from retrospective studies)

4.9.9 Autonomic neuropathy

Autonomic complications of diabetes mellitus occur in very long-standing disease and include the following:

Manifestations of diabetic autonomic neuropathy

- Postural hypotension
- Gastroparesis, vomiting
- Gustatory sweating
- Generalised sweating
- Cardiac arrhythmia ('dead in bed')
- Diarrhoea, constipation
- Reduced appreciation of cardiac pain

4.10 HYPOGLYCAEMIA

4.10.1 Hypoglycaemia in diabetes mellitus

Hypoglycaemia can occur in diabetic patients taking either insulin or sulphonylurea drugs. Autonomic symptoms (sweating, tremor) appear when the blood glucose is <3.5 mmol/l and cerebral function becomes progressively impaired at glucose levels <2.5 mmol/l. In patients on insulin, failure of the normal counter-regulatory responses (sympathetic nervous system activation, adrenaline and glucagon release) may develop in long-standing insulin-treated diabetes, particularly in the presence of frequent hypoglycaemic episodes. This results in **hypoglycaemia unawareness**. The patient has no warning of impending neurological impairment and cannot take appropriate action (glucose ingestion). More frequent hypoglycaemic episodes result, exacerbating the problem – 'hypos beget hypos'. Hypoglycaemia awareness can be restored by relaxing control to allow a prolonged (3-month) hypoglycaemia-free period. There is no proof that hypoglycaemia unawareness is more common with human compared with animal insulin.

4.10.2 Hypoglycaemia unrelated to diabetes

True hypoglycaemic episodes unrelated to diabetes therapy are rare. A blood sugar of 2.5 mmol/l or less should be documented, associated with appropriate symptoms which resolve after treatment (eg food – 'Whipples' triad'). A supervised 72-hour fast can be used to precipitate and document an episode, particularly to diagnose an insulinoma.

Causes of hypoglycaemia

- **Fasting**
  - Insulinoma*
  - Tumour (IGF-2)
  - Hypoadrenalism
  - Alcohol
  - Severe liver failure
  - Factitious (insulin or sulphonylurea)*
  - Drugs (pentamidine, quinidine)
  - Anti-insulin antibodies (delayed post-prandial release of insulins)*
- **Post-prandial**
  - Post-gastrectomy
  - Idiopathic (rare)

* Associated with detectable insulin levels and low β-hydroxybutyrate levels at the time of hypoglycaemia

---

Chapter 5
Epidemiology

CONTENTS

Epidemiology

5.1 COMPARING DISEASE RATES

In clinical textbooks, the term 'epidemiology' is commonly used to describe which groups of people are most likely to present with a specific disease. More particularly, epidemiology involves the comparison of disease rates between different groups of people. As well as providing a general guide to clinical practice, comparing disease rates between different groups of people can:

- Suggest **causes** of a disease (the usual goal of observational epidemiological studies, such as cohort studies and case–control studies)
- Identify effective **treatments** of a disease (the usual goal of experimental epidemiological studies, ie randomised trials)

A fundamental strategy of epidemiological research is to investigate **associations** between **variables** in large populations, while taking proper account of extraneous factors.

5.1.1 Variables

Five key types of variable are important in comparing disease rates between different groups of people (Figure 5.1):

- Exposure variables (**exposures**)
- Outcome variables (**outcomes**)
- Confounding variables (**confounders**)
- Intermediate variables (**intermediate factors**)
- Risk-modifying variables (**effect modifiers**)

Exposure

An exposure is the variable that is used to define the comparison groups. It is often a risk factor for, or a cause or a treatment of, the outcome. For example, in an observational study of the causes of high blood pressure, possible exposures of interest could include salt intake or physical activity; whilst in a randomised trial of blood pressure lowering, the exposure would be the intervention intended to lower blood pressure.

Outcome

The outcome is the disease (or other health-related endpoint) under investigation. Assuming all else is equal, if the exposure causes the outcome then outcome occurrence can be expected to vary between exposure groups. Measures of outcome occurrence include:

- **Incidence rate**: the number of new cases divided by the total person-years at risk of becoming a case (where the person-years is the number of people multiplied by the average number of years of follow-up)

Figure 5.1 Relationships between key types of epidemiological variable

- **Incidence proportion** (or **'average risk'**): the proportion of people who became new cases during a specified period of follow-up
- **Survival time**: for each person, the length of time from the start of follow-up until the person became a case or, if they did not become a case, until the end of follow-up
- **Prevalence**: the proportion of people in a given population, at a given point in time, who had the disease. (Prevalence can provide useful information for clinical practice and public health planning, but it is less useful for indicating the effects of an exposure, as it is determined not only by the incidence of new cases, but also by how long people have the disease before they either die or recover)

Confounders

A confounder is an extraneous variable whose own effects on the outcome are mixed in with those of the exposure. To be a confounder, a variable must be related independently to both the exposure and the outcome, while not being an intermediate factor that causally links the two. For example, any attempt to estimate the relationship between alcohol intake (as an exposure) and lung cancer (as an outcome) will be susceptible to confounding by smoking, because smoking is related both to alcohol intake (smoking and heavier drinking tend to go together) and – causally, as it happens – to lung cancer, while not being an intermediate factor that somehow causally links alcohol intake with lung cancer.

Intermediate factors

As with confounders, intermediate factors are related to both the exposure and the outcome, but, in contrast to confounders, they are simultaneously effects of the exposure *and* causes of the outcome. To take a common example, higher blood pressure is an intermediate factor in the relationship between obesity and coronary heart disease.

Effect modifiers

An effect modifier is a variable that can be used to define two or more categories in which the strength of the relationship between the exposure and the outcome differs. The presence of effect modification is sometimes called 'statistical interaction'. For example, if the relationship between the exposure and the outcome is stronger at one age than another, then the relationship is said to be modified by age, or that there is an interaction between age and the exposure. Quite commonly, **relative risks** are stronger in middle age than old age. This is, for example, true for blood pressure and total plasma cholesterol in relation to coronary heart disease and stroke – but in the elderly, the **absolute risks** may actually be greater.

5.1.2 Associations

Investigating associations (termed 'relationships' above) between exposures and outcomes is a cornerstone of epidemiology. An exposure is said to be associated with the outcome if the outcome occurs more frequently in one exposure group than in another, and the difference is greater than would reasonably be expected by the play of chance alone. Associations often need to be controlled for **confounding** (otherwise the effects of extraneous variables might remain mixed in with the estimated effects of the exposure), but they should not be controlled for intermediate factors (otherwise some or all of the effects of the exposure will be masked).

Measures of association compare outcome occurrence in different exposure groups. These measures fall into two categories: relative risks (which are ratios) and absolute risks (which are differences).

Relative risks

Commonly used measures of relative risk include:

- **Incidence rate ratio**: the ratio of incidence rates in different exposure groups; this ratio is often considered the basic building block of aetiological epidemiology

- **Risk ratio**: the ratio of the average risk (incidence proportion) in different exposure groups; this ratio is nearly always a good approximation to the incidence rate ratio
- **Hazard ratio**: the usual measure of relative risk in a study with information on survival time; this ratio is potentially even more informative than the incidence rate ratio
- **Odds ratio**: the ratio of the odds of exposure in the cases to the odds of exposure in the controls; in a case–control study, this is usually a reasonable approximation to the incidence rate ratio if the control selection was appropriate. (The odds of an event is the ratio of its probability to one minus its probability: eg if the probability is 0.20, then the odds will be 0.25)

Relative risks provide a better measure of the 'aetiological force' of an exposure than do absolute risks; they therefore also tend to be more generalisable between populations.

Example

During a specified period of time, people with a body mass index (BMI) of 30 kg/m² or more are on average twice as likely to develop coronary heart disease as people with a BMI of 20–24 kg/m²: the relative risk of coronary heart disease in the more obese group, compared with the leaner group, is therefore about 2. If obesity were a weaker cause of coronary heart disease, then the relative risk would tend to be less extreme, and if it were not a cause at all, then the real relative risk would be 1.

Absolute risks

The main measures of absolute risk are:

- **Rate difference**: the difference between the incidence rates in different exposure groups
- **Risk difference**: the difference between the average risks (incidence proportions) in different exposure groups

Absolute risks generally give a better estimate of the public health and clinical burden of disease associated with an exposure than do relative risks.

Example

Again comparing people with a BMI of 30 kg/m² or more with people with a BMI of 20–24 kg/m², if in a western European population the annual incidence rate of coronary heart disease was 100 per 10 000 people in the more obese group and 50 per 10 000 people in the leaner group, while in an eastern Asian population it was 10 and 5 per 10 000 people in these two groups, respectively, then while the relative risk would still be 2 in both populations, the annual absolute risk would be 50 per 10 000 people in the European population but only 5 per 10 000 people in the Asian population. Thus, while obesity would be as strong a *cause* of coronary heart disease in the two populations (as indicated by the relative risks), the importance of the association to *population health* would be much greater in the European population (as indicated by the absolute risks).

5.1.3 Causation

The existence of an association between an exposure and an outcome does not imply that the exposure necessarily caused the outcome. Other mechanisms that can account for an observed association include:

- **Chance**: even if the association is greater than 'would reasonably be expected by the play of chance alone', chance can occasionally be unreasonable
- **Bias**: measurement error or misclassification (of exposures, outcomes or confounders) – note that random errors in exposure measurement tend to attenuate associations (this is sometimes called regression dilution bias, eg blood pressure in relation to vascular risk – *see* Section 5.2.2 on cohort studies); selection biases (eg inappropriate control selection in a case–control study, or losses to follow-up in a cohort study); and confounding
- **Statistical artefact**: these may result from violation of assumptions involved in statistical modelling (eg if in a multiple linear regression model, the level of the outcome does not vary linearly with the level of the exposure)

- **Reverse causation**: the outcome causing the exposure (eg in a study of the association between BMI and ovarian cancer, an inverse association might be accounted for by the tendency of ovarian cancer itself to cause weight loss)

Factors that lend support to the interpretation that an exposure caused the outcome are:

- **Random allocation** to the exposure (ie the study is a randomised trial)
- A **stronger association** (ie a more extreme relative risk)
- A **dose–response association** (ie outcome occurrence either only increases, or only decreases, as exposure levels increase; this might be indicated by a *p*-value for trend)
- **Low plausibility** of competing explanations: chance (this is less likely if there are: a larger number of outcome events, tighter confidence intervals and lower *p*-values), bias (eg confounding is well controlled, and there is little exposure or outcome measurement error), statistical artefact (eg modelling assumptions are not violated) and reverse causation (eg in a cohort study, people with the outcome at the start of the study are excluded from the analysis)
- **High plausibility** of possible biological mechanisms
- **Consistency** of the total body of epidemiological, clinical and biomedical evidence

Example
The evidence that smoking causes lung cancer does not include direct evidence from randomised trials in humans (long-term trials of smoking in humans would clearly be unethical), but the other strands of evidence together make the case conclusive:

- Studies sufficiently large to rule out the play of chance have consistently reported that the association between smoking and lung cancer is strong, with relative risks of 10–20 when comparing long-term smokers with lifelong non-smokers

- The association is stronger among heavy smokers than light smokers
- No known bias or statistical error could plausibly account for associations of such strength
- Additionally, tobacco smoke contains a large number of known carcinogens, and observational studies have shown that smoking cessation is associated with lower lung cancer risk

5.1.4 Attributable fractions

Attributable fractions estimate both the proportion of cases attributable to the exposure and the proportion of cases that could theoretically be avoided if the exposure were eliminated. The two most commonly used measures of attributable fraction, which each assume that the exposure caused the outcome, are the **aetiological** and **population-attributable fractions**.

- **Aetiological fraction**: the proportion of exposed cases that is attributable to the exposure
- **Population-attributable fraction**: the proportion of cases in a particular population that is attributable to the exposure

Example
If the relative risk of lung cancer in smokers compared with lifelong never-smokers is 15, then 14 out of every 15 lung cancer cases that occur among *smokers* in that population would be attributable to smoking (ie the aetiological fraction would be 14/15ths, or about 93%). If the prevalence of smoking was 25% in this population, then 78% of *all* lung cancer cases in that population would be attributable to smoking; or, if the prevalence was 50%, then the population-attributable fraction would instead be 88%. (The formulae for attributable fractions can be found in epidemiological textbooks.)

5.1.5 Generalisability

If an association is similar in a wide range of populations, then it is said to be generalisable. Purely descriptive associations (eg the prevalence of smoking in various communities) tend not to be generalisable, whereas aetiological associations tend to be so (eg smoking is about as likely to cause lung cancer in doctors, or in bricklayers, as in the general population). Being representative of the general population is therefore usually more important for descriptive studies than for aetiological studies.

5.2 STUDY DESIGNS

There are several study designs that allow direct or indirect comparisons of disease rates between different exposure groups (Figure 5.2). The most important are:

- Randomised trials
- Cohort studies (which can be prospective or retrospective)
- Case–control studies
- Cross-sectional studies
- Ecological studies

The value of the evidence from an epidemiological study depends not only on the characteristics of the study itself, but on the nature of the question being asked. For example, if a study is trying to determine whether a treatment is effective, and the real effect is not large, then anything other than a large randomised trial (or perhaps a meta-analysis of smaller ones) is unlikely to provide a clear and reliable answer. If, however, the question is whether smoking causes pancreatic cancer, a randomised trial would certainly be unethical (a cohort study or a case–control study would be indicated); alternatively, if the question is what proportion of people in a given country regularly eat fish, then a randomised trial would probably be unhelpful (a representative cross-sectional study would be better).

5.2.1 Randomised trials

The hallmark of a randomised trial is random allocation of participants to exposures. Usually, each participant is randomly allocated to either the treatment under investigation or an established alternative (or possibly, if there is no such alternative, to a placebo). Participants are then followed up for a certain period of time and at the end of follow-up the disease rates (often called event rates) in the different treatment groups are compared.

A large, well-designed and appropriately analysed randomised trial can provide the highest standard of epidemiological evidence possible. Proper randomisation blocks confounding by preventing associations from forming between the treatment and factors related to prognosis. *Non*-randomised studies of treatments are generally susceptible to confounding (eg by age) because those with a poorer prognosis (eg older people) often are more – or less – likely to be allocated the treatment.

- Randomised trials avoid this possibility because all levels of the prognostic factor (eg age) are, by design, equally likely to be allocated the treatment
- Randomised trials consequently provide a reliable way to identify treatment effects. Indeed, if the real effects are only small or moderate, large randomised trials (or, potentially, meta-analyses of smaller ones) are the only reliable way to identify them

The features of a randomised trial that can influence the trustworthiness of its findings include the:

- Quality of randomisation
- Number of outcome events
- Compliance with treatment allocation
- Losses to follow-up
- Presence of participant or investigative blinding
- Use of appropriate analyses

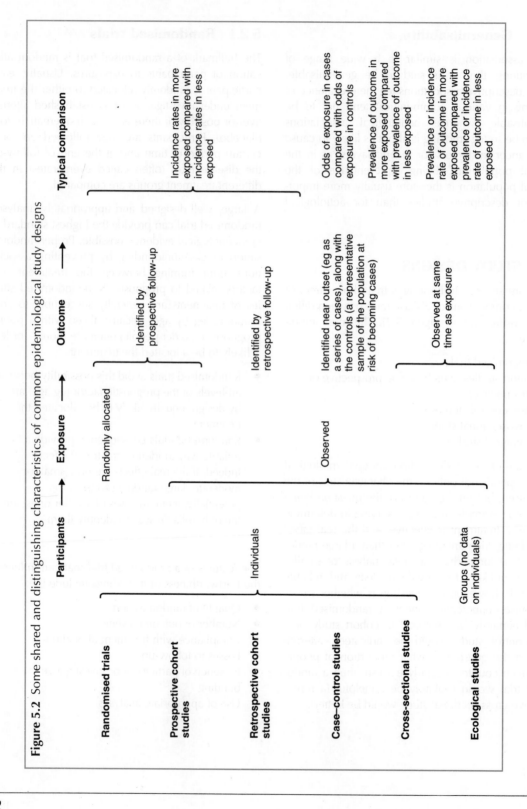

Figure 5.2 Some shared and distinguishing characteristics of common epidemiological study designs

Randomised trials

Major advantages

Greatly reduced potential for bias, particularly:

- Confounding
- Observer or investigator recall bias (if there is blinding)

Major disadvantages

- Expensive
- For some exposures/treatments, randomisation is not feasible
- Special ethical issues (cf the **uncertainty principle**: a patient should be randomised only if there is substantial uncertainty about which trial treatment is appropriate for that patient)

The quality of randomisation

Even slight deviations from true randomisation potentially create cracks through which confounding can leak in. Proper randomisation requires that foreknowledge of a participant's treatment allocation must be impossible, and that once the allocation has been made, it is irreversible. Any scheme which allows an investigator or participant to know, or guess, the next allocation – for example, by holding an envelope up to the light – can influence the treatment allocation, whether consciously or subconsciously, according to factors that might be related to prognosis.

The number of outcome events

The smaller the real effect, the larger the number of events needed to reliably detect the effect's existence. Additionally, a study with a small number of events typically cannot rule out the existence of a potentially important real effect. Insufficient events are more likely if a study has too few participants, they are followed up too briefly, or they are at low risk of the outcome. Randomised trials (and other epidemiological studies) need to be sufficiently large to have a reasonably high probability (eg 80%) of detecting an association, or treatment

effect, if one really exists. This probability is called a study's **statistical power**. Methods are available for estimating a planned study's statistical power based on the expected effect size, the expected number of events, and a specified level of 'statistical significance' (often <0.05, ie $p<0.05$).

Compliance with treatment allocation

Compliance with (or equivalently, adherence to) treatment allocation is the extent to which participants keep to their allocated treatment during the follow-up period. Non-compliance occurs when participants allocated the treatment stop taking it ('treatment drop-out'), or when participants not allocated the treatment start taking it ('treatment drop-in'). Non-compliance generally makes estimated treatment effects smaller, and therefore harder to detect, but it can also mimic or exaggerate real effects, particularly if the non-compliance is substantial or unevenly balanced between treatment groups.

Losses to follow-up

If a participant's health (or vital status) is not determined up to the end of the follow-up period, then the participant is lost to follow-up. As with non-compliance, losses to follow-up generally attenuate estimated treatment effects, but they can also mimic or exaggerate real effects, especially if the losses are substantial or unequal between treatment groups.

Presence of participant or investigator blinding

In a double-blind study, neither the investigators nor participants know any of the individual treatment allocations, while in a single-blind study, one of these parties (usually the investigators) does. Blinding adds further protection against biases, such as the tendency for participants or investigators to misreport or misrecord data if they have prior beliefs about what to expect with any given treatment.

Use of appropriate analyses

Potential pitfalls in the analysis of randomised trials include inadequate emphasis on **intention-to-treat**

analyses, and undue emphasis on analyses of sub-groups.

- **Intention-to-treat analyses** compare the event rates in different treatment groups by analysing each participant in their originally allocated group, regardless of any dropping in or out from that allocation, or of any losses to follow-up, during the course of the study. This approach provides the greatest assurance that deviations from true randomisation (and therefore potential for confounding) are minimised
- Alternative approaches, such as so-called **on-treatment analyses**, can be appropriate for investigating adverse effects
- **Subgroup analyses** are particularly susceptible to the play of chance because they necessarily involve smaller numbers of events. As a consequence they often suggest differences between subgroups (ie effect modification) that tend to be refuted by larger (and therefore generally more reliable) studies. The results of subgroup analyses are less likely to be misleading if the study has a larger total number of events, and if subgroup analyses were specified at the time that the study was designed, rather than, for example, after the study data had been collected and explored

The usual ethical principle guiding modern randomised trials is the **uncertainty principle**, in which a person is regarded as eligible for randomisation if there is substantial uncertainty about which trial treatment is more appropriate for that individual (ie none of the possible treatment allocations is definitely indicated or contraindicated in that person).

Variants of the basic randomised trial design include:

- **Factorial trials**: trials in which participants are randomly allocated to each of two active treatments, or to their respective comparison treatments
- **Crossover trials**: trials in which participants are switched to another treatment part-way through the study

Randomised trials have contributed enormously to the armoury of effective treatments now available to physicians for combatting cancer, communicable diseases and vascular diseases. For example, the **Heart Protection Study** (2002) randomised about 20 000 patients to either 40 mg simvastatin daily or a matching placebo, and showed that treatment with the statin substantially lowered risks of coronary heart disease and stroke at all ages, and in both sexes, irrespective of initial blood cholesterol concentration.

5.2.2 Cohort studies

A **prospective** cohort study can be thought of as a randomised trial in which the exposure is merely observed at the start of the study ('baseline') rather than randomly allocated. As in a randomised trial, participants are then followed up, and at the end of follow-up, disease rates in the different exposure groups are compared. **Retrospective** cohort studies differ from prospective cohort studies in that follow-up had already ended when the investigators started the study (ie the follow-up was retrospective rather than prospective).

Prospective cohort studies

Major advantages

- Less susceptible to reverse causation or exposure recall bias
- Can investigate multiple outcomes

Major disadvantages

- Relatively expensive (might involve a large number of participants followed up for many years)
- Potential bias due to losses to follow-up
- Might be more difficult to obtain rigorous outcome data

Cohort studies are most often used to identify causes of, or risk factors for, disease. Prospective cohort studies are often considered to provide the best observational (ie non-randomised) epidemiological evidence possible. The key factors that can affect the quality of the findings from a cohort study are the:

- **Kind of follow-up**: studies with prospective follow-up are generally less susceptible to reverse causation than studies in which the follow-up is retrospective (in a prospective study it is easier to determine disease status at the start of follow-up, and therefore to exclude participants with known disease at baseline)
- **Number of outcome events (and quality of ascertainment)**: as for randomised trials above. Cohort studies vary greatly in the rigour with which they ascertain the outcome. Some actively follow up participants using regular health examinations and intensive scrutiny of personal health records, while others passively follow up participants by screening routinely collected data in national mortality or morbidity databases. The appropriateness of the method used will depend on the outcome in question. For instance, national mortality and morbidity databases might be adequate for investigating associations with total stroke, but less so for investigating associations with particular stroke subtypes
- **Exposure measurement error**: snapshot assessment of exposure levels at the start of a study can provide a good estimate of usual exposure levels throughout the follow-up period if the exposure is more or less fixed (eg gender) or otherwise stable (eg height). But if the exposure fluctuates considerably (eg blood pressure), or tends to systematically increase (or, alternatively, to systematically decrease) with time, then steps need to be taken to ensure that the estimated associations are not biased. The best strategy is usually to estimate the direction and extent of change in the exposure levels by measuring exposure levels at least once after baseline. For example, repeat measurements of blood pressure several months or years apart enable associations with *usual* blood pressure to be estimated; because of regression dilution bias, these associations are typically 50% to 100% stronger than associations with blood pressure if blood pressure is measured at a

single survey only. Retrospective studies are usually more susceptible to exposure measurement error as they often have to estimate exposure levels many years previously
- **Losses to follow-up**: as for randomised trials above
- **Use of appropriate analyses**: because the exposure is not randomised, the exposure is often associated with extraneous variables that are themselves risk factors for the disease. Control for confounding – for example, by restricting the analysis to one level of the potential confounder, or by statistical adjustment – is therefore usually essential. For example, a cohort study of the association between parity and risk of breast cancer which fails to control for confounding by age could be heavily confounded by that variable, as both the exposure (parity) and the outcome (breast cancer) will be strongly associated with age. The potential hazards of subgroup analyses are the same for cohort studies as for randomised trials

Example

Among the most well-known British cohort studies is the **British Doctors' Study**, which recruited and surveyed about 34 000 male British doctors in 1951, and then followed them up for the next 50 years using periodic resurveys and regular monitoring of national mortality records. The 50-year follow-up results showed that prolonged cigarette smoking tripled overall mortality rates (on average resulting in death 10 years earlier than lifelong non-smoking), but that cessation at age 50 halved this hazard, and that cessation at age 30 avoided nearly all of it.

5.2.3 Case–control studies

As the name might suggest, a case–control study recruits two types of participant: cases and controls. Exposure status is assessed in each participant, then the ratio of the odds of exposure in the cases to the odds of exposure in the controls (the odds ratio) is estimated.

- In a case–control study, incidence rates in exposed and unexposed participants cannot be estimated directly because, in the absence of any follow-up, data on person-years at risk are unavailable

Case–control studies

Major advantages

- Relatively inexpensive
- Can investigate rare outcomes

Major disadvantages

More susceptible to:

- Selection biases (eg if the controls are not representative of the population at risk of becoming cases)
- Exposure recall bias (eg cases might tend to overestimate their exposure levels if they are aware of the study hypothesis)

As with cohort studies, case–control studies are most often used to investigate causes of, and risk factors for, disease. But because case–control studies recruit cases directly (rather than waiting for them to arise during follow-up), and merely a sample of the population at risk (rather than an entire population at risk), they are usually much more cost-efficient than prospective cohort studies.

A good case–control study can provide evidence that is as reliable as that from a good prospective cohort study, but it is easier for a case–control study to go wrong. The major points to check in a case–control study are:

- **The quality of control selection**: the purpose of the controls is to provide an estimate of the exposure distribution in the population at risk of becoming cases (eg in a case–control study of asbestos in relation to laryngeal cancer, the controls should give a reliable estimate of asbestos exposure in the source population from which the laryngeal cancer cases arose); therefore, it is essential that the probability of control selection is not itself related to exposure

status (eg if people who were exposed to asbestos were more likely to agree to take part in the study – as controls – then the distribution of asbestos exposure in the population at risk would be overestimated, and the odds ratio biased). Biases introduced by poor control selection can invalidate the results of a case–control study
- **The number of cases**: as for randomised trials and cohort studies above
- **The potential for recall bias**: cases and controls are usually asked to recall their exposure experience during some earlier, aetiologically relevant period. In some situations, cases might be more likely than controls to over-report (or to under-report) exposure levels, particularly if they are aware of the hypothesised association. Such recall biases can be minimised by: ensuring that information is elicited from cases and controls in an identical manner; ensuring that no information about specific hypotheses is needlessly disclosed; and, if possible, by gathering corroborating objective data about early exposure levels
- **The use of appropriate analyses**: as for cohort studies above

Two notable case–control studies published in 1950 – one British (a precursor to the British Doctors' Study mentioned above) and one American – provided the first strong evidence that smoking is associated with lung cancer. In both studies, the proportion of smokers was much higher among people who had lung cancer than among those who did not.

5.2.4 Cross-sectional studies

Cross-sectional studies assess both the exposure and the outcome at one point in time. The prevalence of the outcome can then be compared between different exposure groups. Cross-sectional studies can suggest possible causes of, or risk factors for, disease, but they are generally more useful for describing the distributions of disease, or of risk factors, in specific populations. When investigating aetiological hypotheses, the chief limitation of cross-sectional studies is the difficulty of ruling out the possibility that outcome status somehow influenced the measured exposure levels (whether by reverse causation, or as a result of recall bias).

Example

The World Health Organisation's MONICA project monitored trends in vascular risk factors, such as blood pressure, blood lipids and BMI, through regular cross-sectional surveys of risk factor levels in representative samples of the adult populations in several different countries.

5.2.5 Ecological studies

In each of the above study designs, investigators gather data for each individual participant. Ecological studies differ in that they involve no data on individuals – merely average values for one or more groups of people. Data of this kind sometimes permit the average incidence rate or prevalence of a given disease to be compared between different populations (eg comparing bowel cancer mortality rates between countries), or within a given population over time (eg bowel cancer mortality rates in a country over a period of decades). While potentially providing clues about causes of disease, ecological studies are not themselves adequate for testing aetiological hypotheses, primarily because the absence of data on confounders in individuals greatly hampers the ability to control for confounding.

Example

International ecological studies of dietary fat and salt intake were among the first to suggest that a high intake of saturated fat is associated with increased risk of coronary heart disease, and that high salt intake is associated with high blood pressure.

5.2.6 Meta-analyses

Epidemiological evidence can be most trusted when biases are small and the number of participants (or, more particularly, the number of cases) is large. Meta-analysis can help achieve this second criterion by quantitatively combining data from two or more relevant studies.

Meta-analysis has at least three potential goals

- To identify important gaps in existing knowledge
- To obtain overall precise estimates of associations ('lumping')
- To identify possible sources of heterogeneity in associations ('splitting')

If there are substantial differences in the relative risks obtained in different studies, then it makes more sense to explore the sources of this heterogeneity than to obtain some overall pooled estimate. But if there is only slight or modest heterogeneity, an overall pooled estimate can potentially be informative. Pooled estimates are likely to be biased if (i) the studies utilised are a biased sample of all of the available studies (it is therefore essential to try to include *all* relevant studies), or (ii) if the available studies misrepresent reality, for example because the studies themselves were biased, or because of the dual tendency for studies with more striking findings to be published even if the findings are spurious, and for studies with statistically non-significant findings to remain unpublished even if the findings are real (two aspects of publication bias).

- **Publication bias** can be explored using a funnel plot, in which an estimate of effect size is plotted against a measure of study size

(deviation from a symmetrical funnel shape sometimes indicates publication bias)

- Meta-analyses that merely combine the published results of studies (literature-based meta-analyses) are much less able to control for confounding than are meta-analyses that combine data on all the individuals decided in several studies (individual participant data meta-analyses)

Example

Until the late 1980s, the net benefits and risks of streptokinase in the treatment of acute myocardial infarction were controversial. The many small randomised trials to have investigated this question had produced inconsistent results; however, when the data were combined in meta-analyses, a moderate but clear net benefit (which was subsequently confirmed by large randomised trials) became evident.

5.3   INTEGRATING THE EVIDENCE

The results of a single randomised trial or observational study are seldom definitive. It is therefore essential for anyone wanting a good understanding of the evidence about a particular question to weigh the evidence from all relevant studies (or to consult a source that has already done this), rather than to focus on the results of a single study, or of just a few selected studies. In weighing the evidence from all sources, more weight should be assigned to studies that are likely to have tackled chance and bias more effectively. Thus, more weight should generally be assigned:

- To **studies that are bigger**, especially if they involve more cases or events, as these studies will generally be less susceptible to the play of chance
- To **randomised trials** than to observational studies,
- To **prospective studies** than to retrospective studies, and
- To **studies that use individual participant data** than to studies that use aggregated data (as the first type of study in each of these pairs is usually less vulnerable to bias)
- To studies with fewer evident flaws in their conduct or analysis, as these studies may generally also be less susceptible to bias

However, these criteria should not be viewed as prescriptive: how much weight to assign to the evidence from a particular study will inevitably involve a degree of judgement. On occasion, the findings from a large case–control study, for example, will be more important than those from a small randomised trial; yet on other occasions, the opposite may be true. The value of the evidence obtained from any given study will often depend less on the above criteria than on the nature of the question being asked.

Chapter 6
Gastroenterology

CONTENTS

Gastroenterology

6.1 ANATOMY AND PHYSIOLOGY OF THE GI TRACT

6.1.1 Oesophagus

The oesophagus is 25 cm long, and is composed of outer longitudinal and inner circular muscle layers. In the upper part these are both striated muscle and in the lower part both are smooth muscle, with the myenteric plexus lying between the two layers. The mucosa is lined with squamous epithelium.

The oesophagus is protected from acid damage by a number of defences, including the lower oesophageal sphincter pressure (10–30 mmHg), salivary bicarbonate, oesophageal *bicarbonate* secretion, gravity and the 'pinchcock' effect of the diaphragmatic crura.

6.1.2 Stomach

At the gastro-oesophageal junction the squamous epithelium of the oesophagus changes to columnar epithelium. Secretions total approximately 3 litres per day. In gastric pits there are chief cells producing pepsin, and parietal cells (fuelled by H^+ $K^+ATPase$) producing hydrochloric acid and intrinsic factor. Mucus and bicarbonate are secreted by surface cells.

Innervation is both parasympathetic via the vagus (motor and secretory supply) and sympathetic via Meissner's and Auerbach's plexuses. Blood supply is derived from the coeliac trunk.

The control of gastric acid secretion is summarised in Figure 6.1 (GIP = gastric inhibitory peptide).

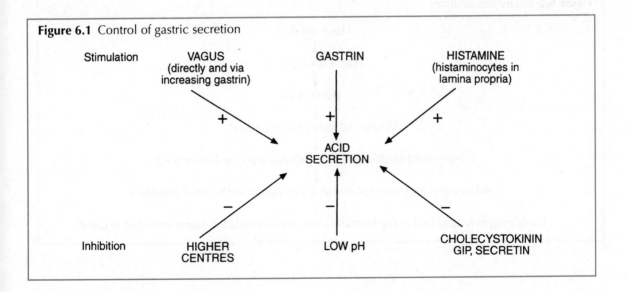

Figure 6.1 Control of gastric secretion

Stimulation

VAGUS (directly and via increasing gastrin)

GASTRIN

HISTAMINE (histaminocytes in lamina propria)

+ + +

ACID SECRETION

− − −

Inhibition

HIGHER CENTRES

LOW pH

CHOLECYSTOKININ GIP, SECRETIN

6.1.3 Pancreas

Between 1200 ml and 1500 ml of alkaline fluid, containing proteins and electrolytes, is secreted daily. Ninety-eight per cent of the pancreatic mass consists of exocrine acini of epithelial cells; the islets of Langerhans from which endocrine secretion occurs make up the remaining 2%. Innervation is via the coeliac plexus.

Pancreatic secretions

- **Exocrine (from acini of epithelial cells)**
  - Trypsinogen
  - Chymotrypsinogen
  - Pancreatic amylase
  - Lipase
- **Endocrine (from islets of Langerhans)**
  - Glucagon from α cells
  - Insulin from β cells
  - Somatostatin from δ cells
  - Pancreatic polypeptide

6.1.4 Liver

Blood supply is from the hepatic artery and portal vein (bringing blood from the gut and spleen); drainage is via the hepatic vein into the inferior vena cava. Between 250 ml and 1000 ml of bile is produced daily; stimulation of release from the gallbladder is by cholecystokinin. A schema of biliary metabolism is shown in Figure 6.2.

6.1.5 Small intestine

This is 2–3 metres in length, with the villi and enterocytes providing a huge surface area that allows the absorption of up to 6 litres daily. The main function of the small intestine is absorption, with most taking place in the duodenum and jejunum. However, it also has an important immune role, with lymphoid aggregates throughout, especially in the form of Peyer's patches in the ileum.

There is secretion of approximately 2 litres of alkaline fluid with mucus and digestive enzymes daily from the enterocytes of the villi, Paneth cells at the

Figure 6.2 Biliary metabolism

Haemoglobin
↓
Haem (and globin)
↓
Biliverdin
↓
Bilirubin (albumin-bound→liver)
↓
Conjugated bilirubin (soluble, secreted into the biliary tract)
↓
Urobilinogen and stercobilinogen (by oxidation in the small intestine)
↓
Urobilinogen reabsorbed in the terminal ileum for recirculation (some excreted in urine)

bases of the crypts of Lieberkühn and Brunner's glands.

Blood supply from the mid-duodenum onwards is derived from the superior mesenteric artery.

6.1.6 Colon

This is 90–125 cm in length and its main function is the absorption of water, sodium and chloride. Typically 1–1.5 litres is absorbed daily but in some circumstances this can rise to 5 litres per day. Secretion of mucus, potassium and bicarbonate also takes place.

The blood supply is derived from the superior mesenteric artery up to the distal transverse colon; the inferior mesenteric artery supplies the remainder.

6.1.7 Gut hormones

The response to a meal is regulated by complex hormonal and neural mechanisms (Table 6.1). Secretion of most hormones is determined by the composition of the intestinal contents.

Table 6.1. Major gut hormones

Hormone	Source	Stimulus	Action
Gastrin	G cells in antrum	Gastric distension Amino acids in antrum	Secretion of pepsin, gastric acid and intrinsic factor
Cholecystokinin-pancreozymin (CCK-PZ)	Duodenum and jejunum	Fat, amino acids and peptides in small bowel	Pancreatic secretion Gallbladder contraction Delays gastric emptying
Secretin	Duodenum and jejunum	Acid in small bowel	Pancreatic bicarbonate secretion Delays gastric emptying
Motilin	Duodenum and jejunum	Acid in small bowel	Increases motility
Vasoactive intestinal peptide (VIP)	Small intestine	Neural stimulation	Inhibits gastric acid and pepsin secretion Stimulates secretion by intestine and pancreas
Gastric inhibitory peptide (GIP)	Duodenum and jejunum	Glucose, fats and amino acids	Inhibits gastric acid secretion Stimulates insulin secretion Reduces motility
Somatostatin	D cells in pancreas	Vagal and β-adrenergic stimulation	Inhibits gastric and pancreatic secretion
Pancreatic polypeptide	PP cells in pancreas	Protein-rich meal	Inhibition of pancreatic and biliary secretion

6.1.8 Metabolism of haematinics

Iron

Total body iron is between 4 g and 5 g, with iron content being maintained by control of absorption in the upper small intestine. Most iron intake is in the Fe^{3+} form and approximately 5%–10% of that consumed is absorbed. Iron is better absorbed from foods of animal than of plant origin.

Factors which affect iron absorption

- **Increased absorption**
  - Increased erythropoiesis (eg pregnancy)
  - Decreased body iron (eg GI blood loss)
  - Vitamin C*
  - Gastric acid*
- **Decreased absorption**
  - Partial/total gastrectomy
  - Achlorhydria
  - Disease of the small intestine (eg Crohn's disease, coeliac disease)
  - Drugs (eg desferrioxamine)

*Gastric acid and vitamin C promote reduction of Fe^{3+} to Fe^{2+} which is more easily absorbed

---

For a more detailed account of iron metabolism *see* Chapter 9, Haematology.

Folate

The usual requirement for this nutrient is approximately 50–200 µg/day. It is present in green vegetables. Absorption takes place in the duodenum and jejunum, so deficiency may occur with coeliac disease, Crohn's disease or any other small-bowel pathology. Dietary folate is converted into 5-methyltetrahydrofolate, which enters the portal blood. Deficiency may also develop if the demands of the body increase, for example in haemolysis, pregnancy and in patients being treated with antimetabolites such as methotrexate. Clinical deficiency results in a macrocytic anaemia, and in pregnancy this can be associated with neural tube defects in the fetus.

Vitamin B_{12}

Adults require 1–2 µg of dietary vitamin B_{12} daily. This is predominantly obtained from foods of animal origin. It is tightly protein-bound and is released by peptic digestion. Oral B_{12} binds to intrinsic factor in the stomach and is then absorbed in the terminal ileum. Deficiency can therefore occur for several reasons:

- Dietary deficiency in vegetarians or vegans
- Post-gastrectomy (lack of intrinsic factor)
- Atrophic gastritis (pernicious anaemia)
- Terminal ileal disease
- Blind loops

The Schilling test

The **Schilling test** determines whether deficiency is due to malabsorption in the terminal ileum or to lack of intrinsic factor (eg post-gastrectomy, pernicious anaemia)

1. Administer orally labelled B_{12}
2. Administer intramuscular unlabelled B_{12} to saturate body binding sites
3. Assay amount of labelled B_{12} excreted in urine (>10% in normal subjects)
4. Repeat above with concurrent administration of intrinsic factor: the amount excreted will rise if B_{12} deficiency was due to lack of intrinsic factor which is now corrected

---

In pernicious anaemia, autoantibodies to gastric parietal cells result in B_{12} deficiency, atrophic gastritis and achlorhydria. Approximately 1% of the population aged over 50 years is affected, with a female preponderance and a familial tendency.

Autoantibodies to gastric parietal cells are present in 90%, and autoantibodies to intrinsic factor are present in 50%. Pancytopenia may occur and other autoimmune disease may be present. The risk of gastric cancer is increased threefold.

6.2 DISORDERS OF THE MOUTH, TONGUE AND SALIVARY GLANDS

6.2.1 Mouth ulcers (aphthous ulcers)

Aphthous ulcers can been minor aphthae, major aphthae or herpetiform ulcerations. Minor aphthae are small, cause minimal symptoms, heal within 7–10 days and leave no scar. Major aphthae are larger, heal slowly over a month, occur more frequently and can leave a scar. Herpetiform ulceration is common in elderly females, can be very painful, recurrent, and begins with vesicles and progresses to ulceration.

Causes of mouth ulcers

- Inflammatory bowel disease
- HIV
- Drugs
- Malignancy
- Nutritional deficiency (B$_{12}$, folate, iron)
- Behçet's disease
- Coeliac disease
- Sweet's syndrome

6.2.2 Oral manifestations of systemic and dermatological disorders

The following can cause oral lesions:

- Systemic lupus erythematosus
- Sjögren syndrome
- Inflammatory bowel disease
- Gastro-oesophageal reflux disease
- Sarcoidosis
- Amyloidosis
- HIV
- Drugs
- Infections
- Stevens–Johnson syndrome
- Pemphigus vulgaris
- Pemphigoid
- Epidermolysis bullosa
- Acanthosis nigricans
- Lichen planus

6.3 DISORDERS OF THE OESOPHAGUS

6.3.1 Achalasia

Achalasia is a condition of unknown aetiology resulting in abnormal peristalsis and lack of relaxation of the lower oesophageal sphincter. There is a concentric thickening of the muscularis propria layer of the oesophagus. The incidence is approximately 1/100 000 per year, occurring at any age (usually 3rd to 5th decade) but rarely in children.

It is demonstrable on manometry, endoscopy or barium studies, where it is characterised by oesophageal dilatation with a smooth distal 'bird's beak' stricture. Chest X-ray may show an air/fluid level behind the heart. Presentation is usually with dysphagia which, unlike other types of stricture, may affect solids and liquids from the outset.

Regurgitation, pain and weight loss may occur. There is a risk of recurrent aspiration. Squamous carcinoma is a late and rare complication.

Treatment is with endoscopic dilation or surgical myotomy. In some cases, injection of botulinum toxin to the lower oesophageal sphincter may be effective.

6.3.2 Reflux oesophagitis

Reflux oesophagitis is an endoscopic diagnosis. Symptoms of acid reflux are extremely common – *approximately 40% of Western populations experience 'heartburn' at least once per month*. The development of reflux oesophagitis depends on a number of factors.

Factors predisposing to reflux oesophagitis

- **GI factors**
  - Acid/bile content of refluxate
  - Mucosal defences in oesophagus
  - Gastric/oesophageal motility
  - Hiatus hernia

- **Other factors**
  - Obesity
  - Smoking
  - Alcohol and coffee intake
  - Large meals (especially late at night)
  - Drugs (most commonly theophyllines, nitrates, calcium antagonists and anticholinergics)

The correlation between symptoms and endoscopic appearances is poor; severe symptoms are compatible with a normal gastroscopy. The gold standard for diagnosis is 24-hour oesophageal pH monitoring.

- The main symptom is heartburn but other symptoms include chest pain, odynophagia (painful swallowing) and dysphagia due to oesophageal dysmotility
- Complications include strictures, haemorrhage, Barrett's oesophagus and carcinoma of the oesophagus (independent of Barrett's)

Treatment of reflux oesophagitis

Treatment is with lifestyle modifications (not evidence-based), antacids, H_2 antagonists or proton-pump inhibitors, with the addition of a pro-motility agent (metoclopramide or domperidone) for large-volume reflux. Surgery is indicated for patients failing medical therapy, those with large-volume reflux, bile reflux and those preferring to avoid long-term medical therapy. Most fundoplication procedures are now performed laparoscopically and endoscopic anti-reflux procedures are under evaluation.

Complications of gastro-oesophageal reflux

- Barrett's oesophagus
- Benign oesophageal stricture
- Dental erosions
- Nocturnal asthma
- Laryngitis

6.3.3　Other causes of oesophagitis

Candidal oesophagitis may occur in patients who are immunosuppressed, on antibiotics or steroids (especially inhaled corticosteroids), or suffering from diabetes mellitus. Barium swallow shows irregular filling defects in the oesophagus and white patches can be seen on endoscopy – biopsy will confirm the diagnosis.

Chemical oesophagitis may be caused by drugs such as non-steroidal anti-inflammatory drugs (NSAIDs), tetracycline and potassium chloride tablets.

Eosinophilic oesophagitis is an increasingly recognised entity, presenting as dysphagia or with food bolus obstruction. Treatment is with oral steroids.

Herpes simplex virus (HSV) may cause oesophagitis in the immunocompromised.

6.3.4　Barrett's oesophagus

This is found in 10%–20% of patients with long-standing acid reflux. It consists of extension of the columnar gastric epithelium into the oesophagus to replace the normal squamous epithelium. It is usually caused by chronic acid exposure, and it is premalignant, although estimates of the rate of transformation to adenocarcinoma vary widely from 30 to 100 times greater than in the normal population. Treatment is of the underlying reflux disease; the benefits of regular endoscopic surveillance and biopsy to detect dysplastic change are controversial although most centres undertake periodic endoscopy with multiple biopsies to detect evidence of dysplastic change. Photodynamic therapy, argon-beam ablation and endoscopic mucosal resection are being assessed as potential cures. Patients need to receive long-term acid suppression therapy.

Hiatus hernia occurs when part of the upper stomach herniates through the diaphragm into the chest and is extremely common, especially with increasing age and obesity. The majority are asymptomatic and found incidentally during investigations. There are two types:

- Sliding, 80% – may cause aspiration and acid reflux
- Rolling, 20% – may obstruct or strangulate

Hiatus hernia can be diagnosed at endoscopy, by CT scan or with barium studies and may be seen on a plain chest X-ray. Treatment is symptomatic with acid suppression where necessary. Surgical correction may sometimes be warranted.

6.3.5 Oesophageal carcinoma

Oesophageal carcinomas can be squamous or adenocarcinoma. The incidence of the latter is rising rapidly, and adenocarcinomas might soon be the most common oesophageal malignancies. It also increases with advancing age. The squamous tumours arise in the mid-thoracic portion of the oesophagus, while adenocarcinomas arise in the lower oesophagus or on a background of Barrett's mucosal changes.

Risk factors for and clinical features of oesophageal carcinoma

- **Risk factors**
  - Smoking
  - High alcohol intake
  - Plummer–Vinson syndrome
  - Achalasia
  - Barrett's oesophagus
  - Chronic reflux (independent of Barrett's oesophagus)
  - Chinese or Russian ethnicity
  - Obesity (for adenocarcinoma)
  - Tylosis (autosomal dominant palmar and plantar keratosis – very high risk)
- **Clinical features**
  - Pain and dyspepsia
  - Progressive dysphagia for liquids then solids
  - Weight loss
  - Vomiting

Oesophageal carcinoma is often asymptomatic until a late stage, resulting in poor survival figures. Diagnosis is usually by endoscopy, allowing biopsy and histological confirmation. Barium swallow typically shows a stricture with irregular shouldering, unlike the smooth outline of a benign peptic stricture. CT scanning is used for staging, particularly for detection of distant metastases, although the accuracy is very poor, especially for lymph node spread; laparoscopy may be useful. Endoscopic ultrasound is especially useful for assessing the locoregional (T and N) staging but is not yet generally available.

Treatment of oesophageal carcinoma

- **Surgery**
  - Radical, high operative mortality (up to 10%)
  - Only a third of lesions are suitable for resection at presentation
  - Improves 5-year survival to approximately 10%
- **Oesophageal stenting**
- **Radical radiotherapy***
- **Chemotherapy* (eg epirubicin, cisplatin, 5-fluorouracil)**

*Used alone or in combination with surgery

Over 50% of patients have local or distant spread such that palliation is the only option. The overall 5-year survival is less than 10%, but survival is age-related. Those diagnosed at an early stage may be cured by surgery.

6.4. DISORDERS OF THE STOMACH

6.4.1 Peptic ulcer disease

Most epidemiological data are from studies predating the rediscovery and treatment of *Helicobacter pylori*. The incidence rates of peptic ulcer are 0.1%–0.3%; the ratio of duodenal to gastric ulceration is 4:1 and males are more susceptible than females. Incidence increases with age and peaks at approximately 60 years of age. Most patients are treated medically with acid suppression and *H. pylori* eradication, and surgery is limited to those with complications unresponsive to medical or endoscopic therapy.

Recent NICE guidelines recommend a 'test and treat' strategy for the management of dyspepsia. This will heal underlying lesions and avoid the necessity for endoscopy in many cases. Patients with 'sinister' symptoms (weight loss, iron deficiency, dysphagia, haematemesis/melaena or an abdominal mass) require urgent endoscopy to exclude gastric and oesophageal malignancy.

Peptic ulcer disease

- **Risk factors**
  - *H. pylori* colonisation
  - High alcohol intake
  - NSAID use
  - Severe stress
  - High-dose steroids*
  - Male sex
  - Smoking (increases acid, decreases protective prostaglandins)
  - Zollinger–Ellison syndrome

* When combined with NSAIDs

- **Clinical symptoms**
  - Epigastric pain (sometimes radiating to the back if a posterior duodenal ulcer)
  - Vomiting
  - Symptoms often relapsing/remitting
  - Weight loss
  - Iron-deficiency anaemia
  - Acute haemorrhage**

** Duodenal ulcers are the most common cause of upper GI haemorrhage

- **Treatment**
  - Remove precipitating factors
  - Proton-pump inhibitors
  - Eradication of *H. pylori*
  - Biopsies of gastric ulcers should be obtained to rule out malignancy
  - Surgery if perforation, pyloric stenosis, or resistant haemorrhage

Causes of upper gastrointestinal haemorrhage

- **Common**
  - Duodenal ulcer – 35%
  - Gastric ulcer – 20%
  - Gastric erosions – 18%
  - Mallory–Weiss tear – 10%
- **5% or less**
  - Duodenitis
  - Oesophageal varices
  - Oesophagitis
  - Upper GI neoplasia
- **Rare (1% or less)**
  - Angiodysplasia
  - Hereditary haemorrhagic telangiectasia
  - Portal hypertensive gastropathy
  - Aorto-duodenal fistula

Management of severe upper gastrointestinal haemorrhage

- Urgent initial attention to airway, breathing and circulation
- Two large-bore cannulae or central venous pressure (CVP) line
- Blood for full blood count, urea and electrolytes, liver function tests, clotting, group and save/cross-match
- Priority is fluid resuscitation to improve haemodynamic status
- Catheterise and monitor urine output
- Enlist ICU/HDU help
- Stop potentially offending drugs, correct coagulopathy, transfuse to keep haemoglobin near 10 g/dl
- Proton-pump inhibitors
- Terlipressin and antibiotics if variceal haemorrhage suspected.
- Aim to perform gastroscopy when the patient is haemodynamically stable

Helicobacter pylori

This Gram-negative spiral bacillus is the primary cause of most peptic ulcer disease. Infection rates increase with age – more than half of those over

50 years of age are colonised by *H. pylori* in the gastric antral mucosa. *H. pylori* has been detected in 70% of patients with gastric ulcer and over 90% of patients with duodenal ulcer compared with 50% of control subjects.

Detection of *Helicobacter pylori*

- Antral biopsy at endoscopy with haematoxylin/eosin or Giemsa stain
- Urease testing – the bacillus secretes a urease enzyme which splits urea to release ammonia. A biopsy sample is put into a jelly containing urea and a pH indicator; this will change colour if *H. pylori* is present
- ^{14}C breath testing – the patient ingests urea labelled with ^{14}C; CO_2, produced by urease, is detected in the exhaled breath. This test is best used to confirm eradication
- Serology (stays positive after treatment and NOT useful for confirming eradication)
- Stool testing – *Helicobacter* antigen can be detected by enzyme immunoassay
- In cases of recurrent *H. pylori*, culture from antral biopsies may be used to detect antibiotic sensitivities

---

H. pylori causes chronic gastritis and is associated with gastric carcinoma. All patients with peptic ulceration or gastritis found to be positive should undergo eradication therapy. Effective eradication should be assessed by either repeat biopsies or breath testing in patients with complications (perforation or haemorrhage) and those with persistent symptoms.

Relapse of peptic ulcer disease after *H. pylori* eradication is less than 5% per year, compared with more than 60% in patients without eradication therapy. Evidence to support eradication of *H. pylori* in patients with non-ulcer dyspeptic symptoms is mixed, although a recent meta-analysis suggested that the number needed to be treated to cure one patient is 20. Eradication regimes vary but usually involve triple therapy of a proton-pump inhibitor and two antibiotics (eg amoxicillin and clarithromycin); metronidazole resistance is a problem in some areas.

6.4.2 Zollinger–Ellison syndrome

This is a rare condition with an incidence of one per million population. Gastrin-secreting adenomas cause severe gastric and/or duodenal ulceration – the tumour is usually pancreatic in origin, although it may arise in the stomach, duodenum or adjacent tissues. Fifty to sixty per cent are malignant; 10% are multiple neoplasms. It may occur as part of the syndrome of multiple endocrine neoplasia type 1, in which case malignancy is more likely.

Clinical signs of Zollinger–Ellison syndrome

- **Pain and dyspepsia**
  From multiple ulcers
- **Steatorrhoea**
  From acid-related inactivation of digestive enzymes and mucosal damage in the upper small bowel
- **Diarrhoea**
  Due to copious acid secretion

Diagnosis is suggested by very high serum fasting gastrin levels, with little further increase with pentagastrin, and elevated basal gastric acid output. There is a rise in gastrin with secretin (unlike raised gastrin secondary to achlorhydria or proton-pump inhibitor (PPI) therapy). CT scanning may be useful to locate the adenoma and assess for hepatic metastases, although 40% of adenomata are smaller than 1 cm and thus difficult to detect on CT. Endoscopic ultrasonography may help in the detection of small lesions.

Treatment of Zollinger–Ellison syndrome

- **High-dose acid suppression**
  (eg omeprazole 80–120 mg od)
- **Surgical resection of adenoma**
  (May be possible)

- **Chemotherapy**
  (Although poor response) and embolisation may be used for hepatic metastases
- **Somatostatin analogues**
  To reduce gastric secretion and diarrhoea

The 5-year survival rate is 80% for a single resectable lesion but falls to 20% if hepatic metastases are present.

6.4.3 Gastric carcinoma

The incidence of gastric carcinoma is decreasing in the Western world but it remains one of the commonest causes of cancer deaths. It usually takes the form of an adenocarcinoma, most commonly in the pyloric region; however, the incidence of carcinoma occurring in the cardia is rising. There is very little early detection in the UK, unlike Japan where the extremely high incidence of the disease merits an intensive screening programme. Most patients have local spread at the time of diagnosis, making curative resection unusual.

Gastric carcinoma

- **Risk factors**
  - Japanese
  - Hypo/achlorhydria (pernicious anaemia, chronic atrophic gastritis, partial gastrectomy)
  - Male sex
  - Dietary factors (high salt, nitrites)
  - Gastric polyps (rare)
- **Clinical presentation**
  - Dyspepsia (often only symptom)
  - Epigastric pain
  - Anorexia and weight loss
  - Early satiety
  - Iron-deficiency anaemia
  - Haematemesis/melaena

Very few tumours are confined to the mucosa at diagnosis, when cure rates are above 90%. Overall survival is below 10%. Diagnosis is by endoscopy and biopsy; endoscopic ultrasound and CT scan of the abdomen and thorax are used to determine resectability. Adjuvant chemotherapy before and after surgery may improve prognosis, although patients are often too unwell post-operatively to receive the second course.

Other gastric tumours include lymphoma (about 5%), which has a good prognosis, and leiomyosarcoma (<1%), which has a 50% 5-year survival.

Gastrointestinal stromal tumours (GIST) are being increasingly identified as incidental lesions as a result of widespread use of imaging and endoscopic investigations. They are submucosal tumours with malignant potential, initially thought to be benign leiomyomas. GIST have a characteristic histological appearance and typical staining with CD 117 (C-KIT). Treatment is by resection and, if advanced, with chemotherapy.

6.4.4 Other gastric pathology

Gastroparesis

Reduced gastric motility results in vomiting, bloating and weight loss. Some cases are idiopathic; others are due to diabetes, autonomic neuropathy or follow vagotomy. Gastric distension and delayed emptying can be demonstrated using a barium meal (which is useful to exclude obstructing lesions) or isotope scintigraphy (which is more useful for quantifying the amount of delay). Treatment is with promotility agents such as metoclopramide, domperidone or erythromycin but if symptoms are severe or if aspiration pneumonia occurs a feeding jejunostomy may be required. Electrical stimulation with gastric pacemakers is currently being evaluated.

Ménétrier's disease

This is a very rare condition associated with mucus cell hypertrophy and parietal cell atrophy, mediated by epidermal growth factor. This results in gross thickening of the gastric mucosa, hypochlorhydria and protein-losing enteropathy.

Gastric polyps

Unlike colonic polyps, gastric polyps are rare and usually benign, occurring in about 2% of the population.

- Multiple hamartomatous polyps are occasionally found in Peutz–Jeghers syndrome and adenomata in polyposis coli, but over 90% are hyperplastic (usually arising from Brunner's glands)
- Adenomatous polyps should be removed in view of their pre-malignant potential

6.4.5 Complications of gastric surgery – dumping syndrome

Gastric surgery is much less common since the advent of H_2 antagonists and PPIs, but long-term complications of previous gastric surgery are frequently encountered. **Dumping syndrome** results from an inappropriate metabolic response to eating and can occur within half an hour of eating (early dumping) or between 1 and 3 hours (late dumping). It occurs in about 20% of patients following gastrectomy/vagotomy.

- Symptoms include palpitations, sweating, hypotension and light-headedness
- Early dumping is a vagally mediated response to rapid gastric emptying
- Late dumping is due to hypoglycaemia – a rebound insulin-mediated phenomenon following transient hyperglycaemia due to a heavy carbohydrate load to the duodenum
- Diagnosis is usually clinical, but may be confirmed by glucose, electrolyte or blood pressure monitoring during an attack
- Treatment is conservative, with small frequent meals with high protein and fat for early dumping and high carbohydrate for late dumping
- Anecdotal reports suggest a benefit from octreotide analogues

6.5 DISORDERS OF THE PANCREAS

6.5.1 Acute pancreatitis

Acute pancreatitis is a common and potentially fatal disease. Mortality in hospital remains at 7%–10%, usually due to multi-organ failure or peripancreatic sepsis. Scoring systems, such as the APACHE II, Ranson's criteria or the Glasgow criteria, aim to identify those patients at high risk by assessing factors such as age, urea, hypoxia and white cell count (WCC) but are unreliable within the first 48 hours. Obstruction of the pancreatic duct by gallstones accounts for over 50% of cases, most of the rest being alcohol-related. Four per cent are thought to have a viral aetiology; all other causes are rare. Oxygen-free radicals are thought to mediate tissue injury.

Acute pancreatitis

- **Causes**
  - Gallstones
  - Alcohol
  - Viral (eg mumps, Coxsackie B)
  - Trauma
  - Drugs (eg azathioprine, oral contraceptive pill, furosemide, steroids)
  - Hypercalcaemia
  - Hypertriglyceridaemia
  - Ascariasis in tropics
  - Post-surgery to bile duct/endoscopic retrograde cholangiopancreatography (ERCP)
- **Early complications**
  - Adult respiratory distress syndrome
  - Acute renal failure
  - Disseminated intravascular coagulation
  - Pleural effusions
- **Poor prognostic indicators (Glasgow criteria)**
  - Age >55 years
  - WCC >15 × 10^9/l
  - Urea >16 mmol/l
  - pO_2 <60 mmHg (<8 kPa)

Continues...

Continued...
- Calcium <2 mmol/l
- Albumin <32 g/l
- Glucose >10 mmol/l
- Lactate dehydrogenase (LDH) >600 IU/l
- Aspartate aminotransferase (AST) > 200 IU/l
- (Severe attack if more than three factors are present within 48 hours)
- **Late complications**
  - Splenic or portal vein thrombosis
  - Pseudocyst
  - Abscess

Clinical presentation is usually with severe epigastric pain, radiating to the back and vomiting with tachycardia and hypotension in more severe cases. Amylase (in blood, urine or peritoneal fluid) is raised, usually to at least four times normal values. A plain abdominal X-ray may show a sentinel loop of adynamic small bowel adjacent to the pancreas.

Treatment is supportive, with fluids and analgesia; the presence of three or more poor prognostic indicators suggests that referral to ITU should be considered. Prophylactic antibiotics reduce morbidity. In severe pancreatitis due to gallstones (where jaundice and cholangitis are present), early ERCP to achieve duct decompression is of proved value. Any patient with a biliary cause should have cholecystectomy during the same admission once the acute symptoms have settled.

6.5.2 Chronic pancreatitis

Chronic pancreatitis is an inflammatory condition characterised by irreversible damage to the exocrine and later to the endocrine tissue of the pancreas. Most cases are secondary to alcohol but it is occasionally due to cystic fibrosis. There is a male predominance, often with a long history of alcohol abuse.

Chronic pancreatitis

- **Clinical signs**
  - Malabsorption and steatorrhoea
  - Abdominal pain radiating to the back, often severe and relapsing
  - Diabetes mellitus
- **Diagnosis**
  - X-ray may show speckled calcification, present in 50%–60% of advanced cases
  - CT is the most sensitive for detection of pancreatic calcification
  - ERCP shows irregular dilatation and stricturing of the pancreatic ducts although magnetic resonance cholangiopancreatography (MRCP) is now the modality of choice for diagnostic pancreatography
  - Endoscopic ultrasonography has emerged as being sensitive and accurate for diagnosing early and late changes of chronic pancreatitis
  - Pancreolauryl and PABA (*p*-aminobenzoic acid) testing are of use to assess exocrine function – both these involve ingestion of an oral substrate which is cleaved by pancreatic enzymes and can then be assayed in the urine
  - The faecal elastase test is increasingly used for detecting exocrine insufficiency and is more acceptable to patients
  - An oral glucose tolerance test can be used to diagnose early glucose intolerance

Treatment is with abstention from alcohol, pancreatic enzyme supplementation, analgesia and insulin to treat diabetes. Antioxidants (vitamins A, C and E) are of unproved value and coeliac axis block for pain relief is now rarely performed because of poor results and surgical complications. Sixty per cent survive for 20 years – death is usually from complications of diabetes or alcohol.

6.5.3 Pancreatic carcinoma

Carcinoma of the exocrine pancreas is responsible for more than 6000 deaths per year in the UK, with an incidence of 110–120 per million, rising to 800–1000 per million over the age of 75 years. Seventy to eighty per cent arise in the head of the pancreas where there is maximal pancreatic tissue; those in the tail are often silent in the early stages and present at an advanced stage. Pancreatic carcinoma may invade the common bile duct causing obstructive jaundice and the typical 'double duct sign' at ERCP. It can also invade the duodenum, leading to small-bowel obstruction.

- The risk is increased 2–3-fold in smokers, and also possibly in those with diabetes, although it has been suggested this is an early symptom of carcinoma rather than a risk factor. Alcohol does not increase the risk
- Clinical signs include abdominal pain radiating through to the back, weight loss and obstructive jaundice in 80%–90%. The exocrine and endocrine functions are usually maintained
- Ultrasound and pancreatic protocol CT is used to detect any distant metastases
- Endoscopic ultrasound is useful for loco-regional staging and allows histological diagnosis via fine-needle aspiration
- ERCP with a view to bile duct stenting is probably of most use in relieving jaundice and pruritus

Between 10% and 20% of patients are suitable for surgery but perioperative mortality is high. Radiotherapy and chemotherapy are under evaluation but so far have been shown to confer little survival benefit. Median survival remains 2–3 months from diagnosis, with 1- and 5-year survival rates of 10% and 3%, respectively.

6.5.4 Endocrine tumours

These are very rare, with an annual incidence of 4 per million but they are incidentally detected at post-mortem. They can occur independently, or as part of multiple endocrine neoplasia (MEN 1) syndrome.

The more important lesions include:

- **Insulinoma**
- **Gastrinoma (Zollinger–Ellison syndrome,** *see* Section 6.4.2)
- **Glucagonoma**
- **VIPoma**
- **Somatostatinoma**

Insulinoma

These arise from the Islets of Langerhans and often present with unusual symptoms (visual disturbances, irritability, abnormal behaviour, confusion, amnesia, paraesthesiae and drowsiness) after an overnight fast or before meals as a result of hypoglycaemia. Patients often discover that glucose is helpful and may go for years without diagnosis.

Glucagonoma

These tumours arise from α cells of the pancreas and present clinically with a characteristic rash (migratory necrolytic erythema), weight loss, glucose intolerance or frank diabetes, and anaemia. Tumours are often very large at diagnosis and are usually malignant.

VIPoma

Excessive VIP (vasoactive intestinal polypeptide) produces an extreme secretory diarrhoea (usually >3 litres per day) resulting in hypochlorhydia and hypokalaemia.

Somatostatinoma

This rare tumour produces a syndrome of diabetes mellitus, diarrhoea, gallbladder disease, weight loss, steatorrhoea and hypochlorhydia due to inhibition of insulin and pancreatic enzymes.

6.6 SMALL-BOWEL DISORDERS

The small bowel is the main site of absorption of nutrients for the body, so small-bowel diseases such as coeliac disease or Crohn's disease often result in malabsorption and malnutrition.

Small-bowel pathology can be difficult to diagnose because of the inaccessibility of this part of the GI tract. Special investigations, such as enteroscopy or wireless capsule endoscopy may be of use in addition to more routine tests such as gastroduodenoscopy or barium studies. CT/MR enterography are increasingly being used.

6.6.1 Coeliac disease

Also known as gluten-sensitive enteropathy, this common and under-diagnosed condition is caused by an immunological reaction to the gliadin fraction of wheat and other cereals. Some 0.1%–0.2% of the population are affected and the onset may be at any age, although peaks occur in babies and in the third decade. The incidence is greatly increased in western Ireland and it has been postulated that this is due to increased reliance on potatoes rather than wheat products as a source of carbohydrate. Thus those affected with gluten intolerance continued to thrive and reproduce.

HLA B8, DRw3 is present in 90%. Pathologically, gliadin provokes an inflammatory response which results in partial or total villous atrophy in the proximal small bowel; this reverses on a gluten-free diet but recurs on re-challenge.

Coeliac disease

- **Clinical picture**
  - Diarrhoea
  - Oral aphthous ulcers
  - Weight loss
  - Growth retardation
  - General malaise
  - Neurological symptoms – ataxia, weakness and paraesthesiae
  - Abdominal pain
  - Amenorrhoea
- **Complications**
  - Anaemia – folate, B_{12} or iron deficiency
  - Increased malignancy*
  - Hyposplenism

- Dermatitis herpetiformis – itchy rash, improves with dapsone
- Osteomalacia
- Abnormal liver function tests
- **Diagnosis**
  - Anti-endomysial antibody
  - Upper GI endoscopy with duodenal/jejunal biopsy

*There is an increased risk of all GI malignancies but especially small-bowel lymphoma, occurring in approximately 6% of cases. This risk returns to almost normal with treatment of the disease

Treatment is by strict avoidance of wheat, rye and barley. The role of oats is debatable and many patients can eat oats without significant pathological or clinical effects. Patients require folate, iron and calcium supplements in the early stages of treatment. Failure to respond to treatment is usually due to non-compliance with diet (often unwittingly), but the possibility of supervening pathology, such as lymphoma, should always be excluded. A small number of patients with refractory coeliac disease may require steroids to control their symptoms.

Although 10% of first-degree relatives will develop coeliac disease routine screening is not advocated unless they have symptoms to suggest the diagnosis.

Other causes of villous atrophy:

- Whipple's disease
- Hypogammaglobulinaemia
- Lymphoma
- Giardiasis
- Cow's milk protein intolerance
- Tropical sprue: aetiology unknown, but likely to be infective as it responds to long-term tetracycline therapy

6.6.2 Carcinoid tumours

These are relatively common; it is estimated that carcinoid tumours are an incidental finding in up to 1% of post-mortems. **Carcinoid syndrome**, however, is extremely rare. Carcinoid tumours arise from the enterochromaffin cells of intestinal mucosa (neuro-endocrine cells found in the lamina propria) throughout the gut. The most common GI sites are the appendix (from which site metastasis is rare) and the ileum.

- The tumours secrete serotonin and therefore can be detected by assay of the metabolite 5-hydroxyindoleacetic acid (5-HIAA) in the urine
- Serotonin causes bronchoconstriction and increased gut motility, resulting in the symptoms documented below
- Histamine and adrenocorticotrophin may also be synthesised
- Carcinoid syndrome occurs only when secondaries in the liver release serotonin into the systemic circulation; any hormone from non-metastatic gut carcinoids will be metabolised in the liver

---

Clinical features of carcinoid syndrome

- Diarrhoea
- Bronchospasm
- Local effect of the primary (eg obstruction, intussusception)
- Flushing
- Right heart valvular stenosis (left heart may be affected in bronchial carcinoid or if an atrial septal defect (ASD) is present)
- **Treatment** depends on the site of the primary and presence of metastases. Many carcinoids are very slow growing, with patient survival of more than 20 years. With widespread metastases 5-year survival varies from zero to 25%, the better figures reflecting the less aggressive nature of appendiceal primaries

---

Treatment of carcinoid tumours and syndromes

- **Surgical resection**
  - Good prognosis if no metastases
- **Octreotide, methysergide and cyproheptadine**
  - For diarrhoea
- **Resection or embolisation**
  - Of hepatic metastases
- **Phenoxybenzamine**
  - For flushing

Carcinoid tumours may occasionally cause pellagra due to tumour uptake of tryptophan (the precursor of nicotinic acid).

6.6.3 Whipple's disease

This is an uncommon condition usually affecting middle-aged men (occasionally women and children) caused by infection with *Tropheryma whippelii*. Jejunal biopsy shows deposition of macrophages containing PAS-positive granules within villi. Clinical features include abdominal pain, weight loss, diarrhoea, and arthropathy. The central nervous system can be involved in later stages, characterised by cognitive function abnormalities, as well as oculomasticatory and oculofacioskeletal myorhythmia (rhythmic movements of masticatory and other skeletal muscles synchronised with ocular movements). Whipple's endocarditis can also occur. Whipple's disease remains poorly understood but symptoms respond to extended courses of tetracycline or penicillin.

6.6.4 Angiodysplasia

Although most commonly occurring in the caecum and ascending colon, angiodysplasia is included here because of the diagnostic challenge it may present when present in the small intestine. Angio-dysplasia can be found throughout the GI tract and its frequency in the population is unknown. It is a rare but significant cause of acute gastrointestinal haemorrhage, but presents more frequently as occult iron-deficiency anaemia.

Diagnosis of angiodysplasia

This can be difficult, but useful investigations include:

- **Gastroscopy/colonoscopy**: may detect gastric and large-bowel lesions
- **Mesenteric angiography**: only of use if currently bleeding; if so, will locate source in approximately 40%
- **Small-bowel enteroscopy**: intubation of the upper small bowel is possible using an elongated endoscope with an overtube to provide rigidity
- **Capsule enteroscopy**: this is the most effective method of detecting small-bowel angiodysplasia and other sources of small-bowel bleeding. A small (11 × 27 mm) capsule is swallowed which transmits thousands of images from the gut as it transits. Images are analysed manually and with computer assistance

Treatment of angiodysplasia

Treatment is by argon plasma photocoagulation at endoscopy or by embolisation of the bleeding point during angiography. Surgery may be indicated if the lesions are very numerous or if there is severe bleeding. Patients need to receive long-term iron supplementation. Hormonal treatment with oestrogen (± progesterone) has been tried with poor results.

6.7   NUTRITION

6.7.1   Assessment of nutritional status

The following assessments help evaluate nutritional status:

- Body mass index (BMI): weight in kilograms ÷ (height in metres)^2
- Fasting lipid profile
- Haemoglobin
- Biochemical markers: renal profile, electrolytes, albumin, C-reactive protein (CRP), glucose and HbA1c
- Dietary assessment: food diary
- Behavioural patterns to food intake

The maintenance of adequate nutrition requires three main criteria to be fulfilled:

1. **Intact GI tract**
   This may be compromised by resections resulting in a short-bowel syndrome, or by fistulae such that segments of bowel are bypassed. As different nutrients are absorbed from different parts of the gut a variety of clinical sequelae may occur depending upon the segment of bowel affected (eg B_{12} deficiency after terminal ileal resection, iron deficiency after partial gastrectomy).
2. **Ability to absorb nutrients**
   Impairment of absorptive function may be caused by mucosal damage such as occurs in Crohn's or coeliac disease, or after radiation damage. Motility problems resulting in accelerated transit times may reduce absorption.
3. **Adequate intake**
   This is dependent both on the motivation to maintain an adequate oral intake, often lacking in sick or elderly patients, and on the composition of the diet.

Inability to maintain nutrition is an indication to provide supplementation by one of the three routes listed below. The underlying disease will determine which is appropriate.

- **Oral**: obviously the most simple form but relies on a conscious patient with an intact swallowing mechanism. High-protein or carbohydrate drinks may be used to provide good nutritional intake in a small volume
- **Enteral**: useful when swallowing impaired (eg in neurological disease) or when high-volume intake is needed. May take the form of a simple nasogastric tube, or a percutaneous gastrostomy (PEG) or jejunostomy which can be inserted endoscopically, radiologically or surgically. Can be for short- or long-term supplementation
- **Parenteral**: this is intravenous feeding, either to supplement enteral nutrition or to provide total support in the case of complete intestinal failure

---

Problems with parenteral nutrition

- **Central venous access needed**
- Patient/carer must be sufficiently motivated and competent to master aseptic techniques and care for venous line
- **Electrolyte abnormalities may occur** – need for careful monitoring; also need to monitor trace elements such as zinc and selenium
- **Risk of sepsis** – central venous catheter infections, right heart endocarditis

---

Examples of specific nutritional deficiencies are covered in Chapter 13, Metabolic Diseases.

6.7.2 Diarrhoea

Diarrhoea means different things to different people but medically is defined as >200 ml of stool per day. In lay terms, diarrhoea is used to describe increased frequency and/or decreased consistency of motions. There are several causes (as illustrated below), and these result in diarrhoea by differing mechanisms.

Various classifications can be used:

- Acute or chronic
- Large bowel (often smaller amounts, may contain blood or mucus)
- Small bowel (often voluminous, pale and fatty)

Causes of diarrhoea

- **Osmotic** (osmotic agents draw water into the gut)
  - Osmotic laxatives (lactulose, polyethylene glycol)
  - Magnesium sulphate
  - Lactase deficiency* (poorly absorbed lactose acts as a laxative)
  - *Stops with fasting*
- **Secretory** (failure of active ion absorption ± active ion secretion)
  - Infection (eg *Escherichia coli*, cholera)
  - Malabsorption
  - Bile salts (↑ deposition into bowel after cholecystectomy)
  - *Continues with fasting, nocturnal, high volume (>1 l/day)*
  - *Stool electrolytes and osmotic gap can be used to differentiate between secretory and osmotic diarrhoeas*
- **Altered motility** (altered peristalsis or damage to autonomic nervous system)
  - Irritable bowel syndrome
  - Thyrotoxicosis
  - Post-vagotomy
  - Diabetic autonomic neuropathy
  - *Stops with fasting*

*Lactase deficiency may be congenital (possibly severe) or acquired, and often occurs in the setting of viral gastroenteritis or coeliac disease. Complete exclusion of lactose from the diet is usually not necessary – there is often a threshold below which symptoms are absent

Causes of bloody diarrhoea

- Ulcerative colitis
- Crohn's disease
- Colorectal cancer
- Ischaemic colitis
- Pseudomembranous colitis
- Schistosomiasis
- *Salmonella*
- *Shigella*
- Amoebiasis
- *Campylobacter*
- *Strongyloides stercoralis*
- Haemolytic uraemic syndrome (which can be caused by *E. coli* type O157, *Campylobacter*, *Shigella*, etc)

Investigations for diarrhoea

- **History and examination vital, including rectal examination**
  History may be suggestive of large- or small-bowel cause; examination per rectum to exclude overflow or rectal tumour
- **Gut hormone assay**
- **Sigmoidoscopy/colonoscopy**
  If large-bowel cause suspected
- **B_{12}, folate, and iron assay**
  If small-bowel cause suspected
- **Gastroscopy**
  With duodenal biopsy if small-bowel cause suspected
- **Biochemistry**
  Electrolyte disturbance: include thyroid function tests, albumin and calcium
- **Stool examination**
  Including examination for ova, cysts and parasites and laxative screen
- SeHCAT (^{75}selenium homotaurocholic acid retention) test for bile salt malabsorption. This is a radiolabelled isotope scan for measuring bile acid loss from enterohepatic circulation.

- **Faecal elastase:**
  If pancreatic exocrine insufficiency suspected
- **Small-bowel radiology**
  If small-bowel cause suspected
- **Urine analysis**
  Laxative screen
  5-HIAA
- **Hydrogen breath test**
  Bacterial overgrowth in the small bowel can be identified by detection of exhaled hydrogen from ingested glucose or lactulose. False positives occur with rapid small-bowel transit that results in prolonged hydrogen release
- **Serology**
  Anti-endomysial antibody

Treatment of diarrhoea

Depends on the underlying disease process, which should be treated if possible. Loperamide or codeine increase gut transit time and so may control symptoms. **Octreotide** may be useful for chronic secretory diarrhoea, short-bowel symptoms and diarrhoea secondary to endocrine tumours. Cholestyramine can be useful in bile salt malabsorption.

6.7.3   Malabsorption

Malabsorption may be defined as a failure to absorb sufficient exogenous nutrients or to reabsorb endogenous substances such as bile salts. It may be caused by several factors because normal absorption depends on gut structure, motility and secretion of hormones and enzymes. Malabsorption usually results in diarrhoea. Clinical presentation depends on the type and site of defect, and includes weight loss and general ill health, osteomalacia, or specific nutritional deficiencies such as of B_{12} and folate.

Investigation of malabsorption

Investigation is as for diarrhoea. In addition, specific tests for malabsorption include:

- **Schilling test**: see earlier

- **Xylose absorption test**: 25 g of xylose is given orally. Urinary excretion of xylose is quantified. More than 20% should appear in the urine if small-bowel absorption is normal
- **Pancreatic function testing**: see earlier
- **^{14}C breath testing**: to detect overgrowth (although the most accurate test remains quantitative bacteriological assay of jejunal aspirates)

Causes of malabsorption

- **Structural abnormalities**
  - Coeliac disease*
  - Crohn's disease*
  - Post-surgical resections*
  - Bacterial overgrowth due to blind loops or anatomical abnormalities
  - Whipple's disease
  - Tropical sprue
- **Motility abnormalities**
  - Thyrotoxicosis
  - Drugs (eg neomycin)
  - Diabetes
- **Secretory abnormalities**
  - GI tract infection (eg *Giardia*, amoebiasis)
  - Chronic pancreatitis*
  - Cystic fibrosis

*Common causes in the UK

Bacterial overgrowth of the small bowel

This is common in patients who have undergone small-bowel resections or in those with jejunal diverticulae or systemic sclerosis. These bacteria are able to metabolise vitamin B_{12} and carbohydrate but the serum folate usually remains normal or elevated. Patients usually have diarrhoea, and malabsorption may ensue. Treatment is with antibiotics such as metronidazole, tetracycline or ciprofloxacin, and recurrent courses of these antibiotics may be necessary.

6.8 LARGE-BOWEL DISORDERS

6.8.1 Crohn's disease and ulcerative colitis

Crohn's disease and ulcerative colitis are both chronic relapsing inflammatory diseases of the gastrointestinal tract.

Aetiology of inflammatory bowel disease

There is an undoubted genetic predisposition based on the identification of at least five susceptibility loci in family studies, and the recent discovery of the *NOD2/CARD15* gene on chromosome 16 which is clearly associated with the development of Crohn's disease. This gene codes for a protein which facilitates opsonisation of gut bacteria, and animal studies have conformed that colitis does not develop in animals raised in a sterile environment. Putative infectious agents including *Mycobacterium paratuberculosis* have not been confirmed, and recent speculation about the role of measles or the measles vaccination in Crohn's disease has no epidemiological basis. The use of NSAIDs and the oral contraceptive pill have also been implicated but mechanisms remain unclear.

The major similarities and differences between the two diseases are detailed in Table 6.2.

Treatment of inflammatory bowel disease

Treatment is similar for both Crohn's disease and ulcerative colitis, although the latter may be more amenable to topical drug therapy. The major treatment strategies are:

- **5-Aminosalicylic acid (5-ASA) compounds** (sulfasalazine, mesalazine, olsalazine, balsalazide): these are used to treat mild–moderate relapses of colitis and are taken long-term to maintain remission. Oral 5-ASAs are targeted to the colon using pH-dependent or bacterial cleavage systems to release active 5-ASA from carrier molecules. Side-effects are common with sulfasalazine, and these include rash, infertility, agranulocytosis, headache,

Table 6.2. Clinico-pathology of Crohn's disease and ulcerative colitis

	Crohn's disease	**Ulcerative colitis**
	Affects any part of the Gl tract from mouth to anus. Commonly terminal ileum (70%), colon (30%), anorectum (30%). May be 'skip lesions' of normal mucosa between affected areas	Always involves the rectum and extends confluently into the colon. Terminal ileum may be affected by 'backwash ileitis' but remainder of the gut unaffected
Pathology	Transmural inflammation Mucosal ulcers (in 30% only) Fissuring ulcers Lymphoid aggregates Neutrophil infiltrates	Mucosa and submucosa only involved Inflammatory cell infiltrate Crypt abscesses
Clinical	Abdominal pain prominent and frequent fever Diarrhoea ± blood per rectum Anal/perianal/oral lesions Stricturing common, resulting in obstructive symptoms	Diarrhoea, often with blood and mucus Fever Abdominal pain less prominent

Associations	Increased incidence in smokers (50%–60% smokers)
	Skin disorders:
	    Erythema nodosum (5%–10%)
	    Pyoderma gangrenosum (0.5%)
	Iritis/uveitis (3%–10%)
	Joint pain/arthritis (6%–12%)
	Cholelithiasis (common)
	Primary sclerosing cholangitis
	Clubbing
	Depression
		Decreased incidence in smokers (70%–80% non-smokers)
		Increased incidence of:
		    Primary biliary cirrhosis
		    Chronic active hepatitis
		    Sclerosing cholangitis
		Other systemic manifestations occur but less common than in Crohn's disease

Diagnosis	Barium studies:
	    Cobblestoning of mucosa
	    Rosethorn ulcers
	    Strictures
	    Skip lesions
	Endoscopy with biopsy
	Isotope leucocyte scans useful to diagnose active small-bowel disease
	CT/MR enterography can be used if small-bowel disease suspected
		Barium studies:
		    Pseudopolyps between ulcers
		    Loss of haustral pattern
		    Featureless shortened colon
		Sigmoidoscopy with biopsy may be sufficient

(*continued*)

Table 6.2. (*continued*)

	Crohn's disease	Ulcerative colitis

Complications	Fistulae:
	  Entero-enteral
	  Entero-vesical
	  Entero-vaginal
	  Perianal
	Carcinoma – slightly increased risk of colonic malignancy (see later)*
	B_{12} deficiency common (decreased absorption in terminal ileal disease)
	Iron deficiency anaemia
	Abscess formation
	Venous thromboembolism
		Fistulae do not develop
		Toxic megacolon (uncommon – usually an indication for urgent colectomy)
		Increased risk of carcinoma* (risk increases with time since diagnosis, extent of disease and early age of onset)
		Iron-deficiency anaemia
		Venous thromboembolism

*See section 'Carcinoma complicating inflammatory bowel disease'

diarrhoea and renal failure. Interstitial nephritis is a rare side-effect of all 5-ASA drugs
- **Steroids**: this is the main treatment for active disease, and is available for topical, oral and intravenous administration. Terminal ileal Crohn's disease may be treated with topically acting oral budesonide, which is metabolised in the liver and has far fewer systemic side-effects
- **Immunosuppressants**: **azathioprine** is very effective as a steroid-sparing agent and in some patients who are steroid-unresponsive. Its use is limited by gastrointestinal and systemic side-effects and close monitoring for evidence of marrow suppression and hepatotoxicity is necessary. Pancreatitis is an uncommon but potentially serious idiosyncratic side-effect. **Methotrexate** is useful in patients with Crohn's disease but does not appear to be effective in patients with ulcerative colitis. **Intravenous ciclosporin** is sometimes effective in the treatment of acute, steroid-resistant colitis, but long-term benefit has not been established
- **Metronidazole and ciprofloxacin**, used in treatment of perianal disease
- **Anti-tumour necrosis factor alpha (infliximab)**: this chimeric (mouse/human) monoclonal

antibody is very effective in the treatment of active Crohn's disease and many patients benefit from long-term maintenance therapy. The cost (up to £15 000/year) has to be balanced against the reduced costs of hospital admission, surgery, lost productivity and improved quality of life. In the UK its use is restricted to patients who are unresponsive to immunosuppressant therapy, who have severe symptoms and who are unsuitable for surgery
  - Adalumimab is a new recombinant human IgG1 monoclonal antibody against TNFα that can be administered subcutaneously
- **Nutritional support and treatment**: patients with inflammatory bowel disease are often malnourished and require nutritional supplementation (enteral or parenteral), especially if surgery is planned. An elemental diet may be as effective as steroids in inducing remission in Crohn's disease
- **Surgery**: surgical resection is very effective for symptom relief in obstructive Crohn's disease, and colectomy offers a cure to patients with ulcerative colitis. The recurrence rate for Crohn's disease after surgery is approximately 50%, although this can be reduced with post-operative azathioprine. Ileo-anal pouch surgery

restores continence to patients undergoing colectomy

Carcinoma complicating inflammatory bowel disease

The risk of carcinoma associated with inflammatory bowel disease is increased if:

- Onset occurs at less than 15 years of age
- Disease duration has been longer than 10 years
- There is widespread disease (eg total colitis)
- The disease takes an unremitting course
- Compliance with treatment and follow-up is poor

Colonoscopic follow-up

- The British Society of Gastroenterology recommends screening colonoscopy 8–10 years after the onset of colitis and regular surveillance colonoscopies after 8–10 years of pancolitis and after 15–20 years for left-sided disease
- The frequency would depend on disease extent and duration. For example, patients with pancolitis should have colonoscopies performed every 3 years in their second decade of disease, every 2 years in the third decade and yearly in the fourth decade and beyond
- Patients with co-existing primary sclerosing cholangitis should have annual colonoscopies

6.8.2 Pseudomembranous colitis

This is acute colitis due to the enterotoxin of *Clostridium difficile*, usually precipitated by broad-spectrum antibiotics (particularly clindamycin). It is common in the elderly or chronically ill, and mortality may be as high as 20%. Patient-to-patient spread in hospital is common. Diagnosis is by demonstration of the toxin in stools in most cases, but rarely by endoscopy (which shows inflamed mucosa with yellow pseudomembranes) when the stool test is negative and there is a strong suspicion.

Treatment

- Oral vancomycin or metronidazole, depending on the severity of the disease

- Close monitoring of full blood count, CRP, electrolytes and albumin is necessary
- CT scanning is used to detect toxic megacolon in severe cases, which may need colectomy
- Recurrent cases may need a tapering regime of vancomycin over a period of a few weeks

C. difficile can be detected in normal stools but is treated only when it causes diarrhoea.

6.8.3 Familial polyposis coli

This is an autosomal dominant condition, caused by mutation in the *APC* tumour suppressor gene which is located on the long arm of chromosome 5. Estimates of the incidence vary from 1 in 7000–30 000 of the population in the UK.

Multiple adenomata occur throughout the colon; if untreated, malignancy is inevitable, often when patients are aged only 30 or 40 years. Surveillance colonoscopy begins in adolescence and prophylactic colectomy usually follows at around the age of 20 years in view of the high risk of malignant change. Many patients opt for an ileo-anal pouch. Screening of family members is essential.

6.8.4 Peutz–Jeghers syndrome

This is an autosomal dominant condition in which multiple hamartomatous polyps occur throughout the GI tract (particularly in the small bowel). Patients may have mucocutaneous pigmentation and perioral freckles. Lesions may lead to GI haemorrhage and may undergo malignant change (carcinoma is increased 12-fold in patients with this condition).

6.8.5 Hereditary non-polyposis colorectal cancer (HNPCC)

This is a dominantly inherited disorder of DNA mismatch repair genes located on chromosomes 2 and 3. Malignancies such as those affecting the colon, breast, ovary and endometrium occur at a young age. Relatives of affected patients require genetic counselling and cancer screening.

6.8.6 Colorectal cancer

This is the second most common cause of cancer death in the UK, with an incidence of approximately 44/100 000. A National Bowel Cancer Screening Programme based on faecal occult blood (FOB) testing followed by colonoscopy has been introduced in the UK. Colorectal cancer is common from the sixth decade onwards and the incidence increases with advancing age. Recent studies have suggested that NSAIDs may have a protective effect.

Pathologically, it is an adenocarcinoma usually arising from tubular and villous adenomatous polyps (although in inflammatory bowel disease, malignant change arises directly from the mucosa). The commonest sites are the rectum and sigmoid colon.

Risk factors and clinical features of colorectal cancer

- **Increased incidence**
  - Male sex
  - Family history
  - Inflammatory bowel disease, especially ulcerative colitis
  - Familial polyposis coli
  - Diet low in fibre, fruit and vegetables
  - Diet high in fat and red meat
  - Cholecystectomy (bile salts 'dumped' in colon)
  - Obesity
- **Genetics**
  - Sporadic mutations may occur in the p53, Ras and APC genes. p53 regulates the cell cycle and causes apoptosis in the event of DNA damage – its loss therefore leads to uncontrolled proliferation of cells

- **Clinical signs**
  - These depend on the site of the lesion; all can cause weight loss and obstructive symptoms
  - Right-sided
    - Iron-deficiency anaemia
    - Abdominal pain
    - Abdominal mass
  - Left-sided
    - Blood per rectum
    - Altered bowel habit
    - Abdominal mass
  - Rectum
    - Blood per rectum
    - Tenesmus
    - Obstruction
- **Complications**
  - Local spread to organs and lymph nodes
  - Metastasis to liver, lung, brain and bone
  - Obstruction ± perforation

Treatment of colorectal cancer

This consists of surgery (for cure) or symptomatic relief, depending on **Duke's staging (Table 6.3)**.

Table 6.3. Duke's classification and prognosis of colorectal cancer

Stage	5-year survival
A – confined to mucosa and submucosa	80%+
B – extends through muscularis propria	60%–70%
C – regional lymph nodes involved	30%–40%
D – distant spread	0%

- **Radiotherapy** may be used as an adjuvant, particularly to reduce tumour bulk before surgery
- Adjuvant chemotherapy (eg 5-fluorouracil post-operatively) has been shown to improve prognosis for patients at Duke's stages B and C; toxicity is low so quality of life tends to be good
- Chemotherapeutic agents such as oxaliplatin and irinotecan have been used for advanced colorectal cancer
- Serial monitoring of carcinoembryonic antigen (CEA), a glycoprotein from gastrointestinal epithelia, may be of use in detecting recurrence. However, surveillance colonoscopies are indicated
- Isolated hepatic metastases to a single lobe of liver can be resected

Carcinoma complicating inflammatory bowel disease: this is discussed in Section 6.8.1, Crohn's disease and ulcerative colitis.

6.8.7 Irritable bowel syndrome (IBS)

This is a chronic, relapsing functional gut disorder with no recognisable pathological abnormality. In most cases the diagnosis is based on clinical presentation although symptoms presenting in older patients require investigation to exclude other pathologies. IBS affects up to 10% of the population with a ratio of 5:1 female dominance. Strict diagnosis is based on Rome II criteria, requiring abdominal pain provoked by eating or relieved by defecation and a change in bowel habit occurring for at least 3 months in a year.

Full blood count, erythrocyte sedimentation rate (ESR), CRP, anti-endomysial antibody, thyroid function tests (TFTs) and stool culture are useful screening investigations to exclude common diagnoses, and sigmoidoscopy provides reassurance for patients and clinicians that there is no underlying pathology.

- Bloating, borborygmi, excessive flatus, belching and mucorrhoea are common gastrointestinal symptoms

- IBS is often associated with alternating bowel habit but may also present with 'diarrhoea-dominant' or 'constipation-dominant' symptoms
- Patients with IBS often complain of other 'functional' symptoms and have a higher prevalence of fibromyalgia, non-cardiac chest pain, tension headache, sterile cystitis, dyspareunia, back pain, anxiety and depression
- There is a clear association with a history of childhood abuse
- In about a quarter of cases IBS is preceded by gastrointestinal infection, raising the possibility of damage to the neuroenteric innervation in some cases

Treatment of irritable bowel syndrome

Treatment is usually symptomatic and includes anti-spasmodics, increased dietary fibre, laxatives, constipating agents, antidepressants, hypnotherapy and psychotherapy. The latter are particularly useful for patients whose symptoms occur on a background of significant psychological morbidity.

6.9. GASTROINTESTINAL INFECTIONS

AIDS and the gut is covered in Chapter 8, Genitourinary Medicine and AIDS.

6.9.1 Gastroenteritis

Most gastrointestinal infections in the UK are viral or self-limiting bacterial infections such as *Staphylococcus aureus* or *Campylobacter*. Most patients require no treatment but antidiarrhoeals (such as loperamide) and oral rehydration therapy (ORT) may be required in patients who are at risk of dehydration. ORT utilises the capacity of the small bowel to absorb chloride, sodium and water via a glucose-dependent active transport channel that is not disrupted by infections. More intensive therapy is confined to those systemically unwell or immunosuppressed.

The following are some of the more important gastrointestinal infections. (*See also* Chapter 11, Infectious Diseases.)

Amoebiasis

- Infection is due to *Entamoeba histolytica* with faecal–oral spread
- The clinical spectrum ranges from mild diarrhoea to dysentery with profuse bloody stool; a chronic illness with irritable bowel-type symptoms may also occur. Colonic or hepatic abscesses occur, the latter commonly in the setting of a severe amoebic colitis
- Treatment is with metronidazole

Campylobacter

This is due to a Gram-negative bacillus; spread is faecal–oral.

- Gram-negative rods
- Clinically, patients are often systemically unwell with headache and malaise prior to the onset of diarrhoeal illness. Abdominal pain may be severe, mimicking an acute abdomen
- Erythromycin may be indicated if symptoms are prolonged

Cholera

- Infection is due to *Vibrio cholerae* (Gram-negative rods) which colonise the small bowel; spread is faecal–oral. A high infecting dose is needed as the bacteria are susceptible to gastric acid
- A severe toxin-mediated diarrhoea occurs with 'rice-water' stool which may exceed 20 litres per day. Dehydration is the main cause of death, especially in young or elderly, and mortality is high without rehydration treatment
- Tetracycline may reduce transmission

Giardiasis

- Infection is due to *Giardia lamblia* (a flagellate protozoan) which colonises the duodenum and jejunum; spread is faecal–oral

- Bloating and diarrhoea (not bloody) occur and may be chronic. Malabsorption may occur with small-intestinal colonisation. Asymptomatic carriage is common and duodenal biopsy may be necessary to make the diagnosis in patients with chronic diarrhoea or malabsorption symptoms
- Treatment is with metronidazole

Salmonella

- A Gram-negative bacillus with multiple serotypes divided into two main groups: those causing typhoid and paratyphoid (enteric fever), and those causing gastroenteritis. Spread is faecal–oral
- Diarrhoea (may be bloody) occurs, with or without vomiting and abdominal pain
- Rose spots tend to appear on the chest and abdomen about 2 weeks after the onset of symptoms
- Diagnosis is made by blood culture
- Treatment is supportive but occasionally ciprofloxacin or trimethoprim may be required for chronic symptoms or severe illness in the very young or elderly. Chronic asymptomatic carriage is rare (less than 1% compared with 3%–4% in typhoid/paratyphoid)

Shigella

- Gram-negative rods. Spread is faecal–oral with a very low infecting dose of organisms needed owing to its high virulence
- The clinical spectrum ranges from diarrhoeal illness to severe dysentery, depending on the infecting type: *S. sonnei, S. flexneri, S. boydi, S. dysenteriae*
- Diarrhoea (may be bloody), vomiting, abdominal pain
- Treat if severe with ampicillin or tetracycline, although there is widespread resistance

6.9.2 Gastrointestinal tuberculosis

This is common in developing countries, and causes ileocaecal TB (mimicking Crohn's disease) or occasionally spontaneous TB peritonitis. There has been a recent increase in abdominal TB, particularly in patients with AIDS. The infection may occur secondary to pulmonary TB as a result of swallowing infected sputum or by haematogenous spread.

- Clinical features are often non-specific, such as malaise, fever and weight loss, as well as diarrhoea and abdominal pain
- Ultrasound, barium studies or CT may suggest the diagnosis but biopsy, either by laparoscopy or endoscopy, is confirmative
- Treatment is with conventional antituberculous therapy

6.10. HEPATOLOGY

6.10.1 Jaundice

Jaundice is one of the most common symptoms of liver disease, caused by the accumulation of bilirubin in the tissues. Bilirubin is formed as the end product of catabolism of haem-containing compounds and is clinically detectable at a level of >40 mmol/l. The formation and excretion of bilirubin is shown in Figure 6.3.

The most common causes of jaundice in the UK are alcoholic liver disease, gallstones and tumours of the liver and pancreas.

Hyperbilirubinaemia may occur because of excess production or decreased elimination of bilirubin. Jaundice can thus be broadly divided into three categories depending on the site of the pathology.

Causes of jaundice

The following classification is used (Table 6.4):

- **Pre-hepatic**: excess production of bilirubin or failure of uptake into the liver. Bilirubin is unconjugated and insoluble, so it does not appear in the urine – acholuric jaundice
- **Hepatic**: defect is at the level of hepatocyte. There is diminished hepatocyte function, and so both conjugated and unconjugated bilirubin appear in the urine

Table 6.4. Causes of jaundice

Pre-hepatic	Haemolysis causing excess haem production Congenital hyperbilirubinaemia (eg Gilbert syndrome, Crigler–Najjar syndrome (see Table 6.5)
Hepatic	Alcoholic hepatitis Viral infection (eg hepatitis A, B, Epstein–Barr virus) Drugs (eg phenothiazines, augmentin and other antibiotics) Wilson's disease Rotor and Dubin–Johnson syndromes (see Table 6.5) Cirrhosis Multiple hepatic metastases Hepatic congestion in cardiac failure
Post-hepatic	Gallstones Carcinoma of pancreas or bile ducts Lymph nodes at porta hepatis (eg metastatic, lymphomatous) Primary biliary cirrhosis – small-bile-duct obliteration Sclerosing cholangitis Structural abnormality of the biliary tree – post-surgery, congenital (eg biliary atresia)

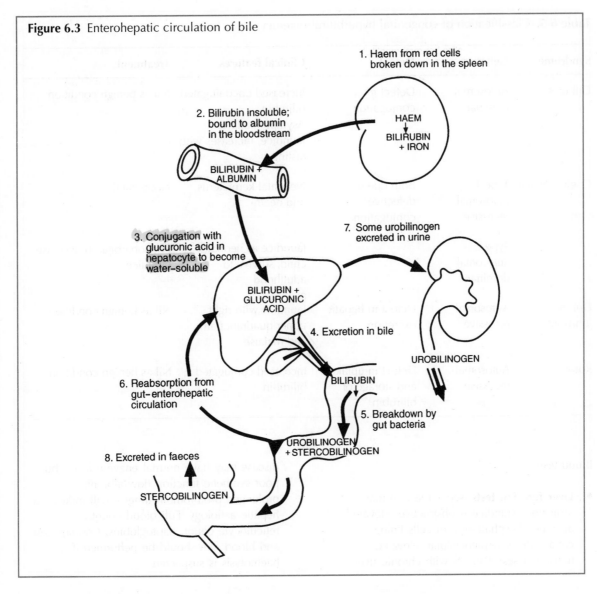

Figure 6.3 Enterohepatic circulation of bile

1. Haem from red cells broken down in the spleen

HAEM
↓
BILIRUBIN
+ IRON

2. Bilirubin insoluble; bound to albumin in the bloodstream

BILIRUBIN + ALBUMIN

3. Conjugation with glucuronic acid in hepatocyte to become water–soluble

BILIRUBIN + GLUCURONIC ACID

7. Some urobilinogen excreted in urine

UROBILINOGEN

4. Excretion in bile

BILIRUBIN

6. Reabsorption from gut–enterohepatic circulation

5. Breakdown by gut bacteria

UROBILINOGEN + STERCOBILINOGEN

8. Excreted in faeces

STERCOBILINOGEN

- **Post-hepatic**: there is impaired excretion of bile from liver into the gut. Conjugated bilirubin is therefore reabsorbed, which increases serum and urine levels and produces dark urine. The stools become pale due to lack of stercobilinogen; urobilinogen (produced in the gut – see Figure 6.3) becomes undetectable in urine

Investigation of jaundice

Overleaf is a typical systematic approach (also see Figure 6.4).

Figure 6.4 Investigation of jaundice

Biochemical screen
Viral screen
Autoimmune screen
⇓
Ultrasound scan
⇓   ⇓
Duct dilatation   No duct dilatation
⇓   ⇓
ERCP ± CT   Liver biopsy

Table 6.5. Classification of congenital hyperbilirubinaemia

Syndrome	Genetics	Defect	Clinical features	Treatment
Gilbert's	Autosomal dominant	Defect in conjugation	Increased unconjugated bilirubin Asymptomatic ± jaundice, increases with fasting	Nil as benign condition
Crigler–Najjar	Type 1 – autosomal recessive	Both due to defective conjugation	Neonatal kernicterus and death	None; fatal
	Type 2 – autosomal dominant		Jaundice as neonate/ child; survive to adulthood	Phenobarbital to decrease jaundice
Dubin–Johnson	Autosomal recessive	Defect in hepatic excretion	Jaundice with right upper quadrant pain and malaise	Nil as benign condition
Rotor	Autosomal recessive	Defect in uptake and storage of bilirubin	Increased conjugated bilirubin	Nil as benign condition

Blood tests

- **Liver function tests** (see Table 6.6) may indicate if jaundice is obstructive (elevated alkaline phosphatase from cells lining canaliculi) or hepatocellular (elevated transaminases). Patients with chronic liver disease may have normal enzyme levels but poor synthetic function (low albumin, prolonged prothrombin time) – will indicate a hepatic aetiology. Full blood count, reticulocyte count, haptoglobins, Coombs' test and blood film should be performed if haemolysis is suspected

Table 6.6. Liver function tests in jaundice

	Unconjugated bilirubin	Conjugated bilirubin	ALT/AST	Alkaline phosphatase	Gamma GT
Pre-hepatic	↑↑	Normal	Normal	Normal/↑↑	Normal/↑↑
Hepatic	Normal	↑↑	↑↑	↑	↑
Post-hepatic	Normal	↑↑	↑	↑↑	↑↑

↑ Moderately raised; ↑↑ raised

- **Viral serology** (hepatitis A, B and C), **autoantibody titres** (antimitochondrial M2 for primary biliary cirrhosis and anti-smooth muscle for chronic autoimmune hepatitis), α_1-antitrypsin, α-fetoprotein (AFP), ferritin and copper studies are essential when investigating unexplained jaundice or chronic liver disease.

Imaging and biopsy

- **Liver ultrasound**: is the single most useful radiological test and will identify obstruction, metastases, cirrhosis and hepatoma
- **CT scanning**: is frequently used to complement ultrasound images, to define lesions more clearly and to diagnose lesions not seen on ultrasound
- **ERCP**: is used to investigate obstructive jaundice and to stent obstructing tumours or remove obstructing gallstones
- **Liver biopsy**: may be helpful in non-obstructive jaundice, but is contraindicated in the presence of uncorrected coagulation disorders and is technically difficult if ascites is present

6.10.2   Gallstone disease

Gallstones are one of the commonest causes of jaundice, usually presenting with colicky upper abdominal pain and cholestatic liver function tests. Approximately 1 litre of bile is secreted by the hepatocytes each day. Half of this drains directly into the duodenum whilst the remainder is stored and concentrated in the gallbladder by removal of sodium, chloride, bicarbonate and water. Cholecystokinin (CCK) then stimulates its release.

- Stones are found in 10%–20% of the population (with a female preponderance) but are asymptomatic in the majority
- 70%–90% gallstones are a mixture of cholesterol and bile pigment and 10% are pure cholesterol. Pure pigment stones are rare except with chronic haemolysis (eg sickle cell disease, spherocytosis)

Risk factors for and clinical presentation of gallstones

- **Risk factors for stone formation**
  - Female sex
  - Increasing age
  - Drugs (eg oral contraceptive pill, clofibrate)
  - Crohn's disease (terminal ileum)
  - Short-bowel syndrome
  - Haemolysis (pigment stones)
- **Clinical presentation**
  - Acute/chronic cholecystitis
  - Biliary colic
  - Cholestatic jaundice if duct obstruction
  - Pancreatitis
  - Cholangitis
  - Gallstone ileus

NB: Stones may form in the common bile duct even after cholecystectomy

---

- **Diagnosis** in most cases may be established by ultrasound. **MRCP** has replaced ERCP as a useful, non-invasive investigation. ERCP is reserved for the therapeutic intent to deal with stones that have been confirmed by other imaging investigations
- Definitive treatment is by cholecystectomy. ERCP with sphincterotomy and balloon clearance of the common bile duct is indicated for intraduct stones. Medical treatment with ursodeoxycholic acid can be used to dissolve cholesterol stones; however, this is extremely slow and should be reserved only for patients who are unfit for other treatment

6.10.3   Ascites

Ascites is defined as the accumulation of free fluid within the peritoneal cavity. It can be subdivided into transudate or exudate (Table 6.7) depending on whether the protein content is less or greater than 30 g/l, respectively. The most common causes in the UK are cirrhosis and malignant disease.

Table 6.7. Causes of ascites

Transudate	Portal hypertension
	Nephrotic syndrome
	Malnutrition
	Cardiac failure
	Budd–Chiari syndrome
	Myxoedema
Exudate	Hepatic or peritoneal malignancy
	Intra-abdominal TB
	Pancreatitis

The **treatment** of ascites depends on the aetiology.

- **Transudates** respond to fluid restriction, low sodium intake and diuretic therapy, to promote sodium and water excretion via the kidneys. Paracentesis may be used for tense ascites or ascites that is not responding to diuretics. However, paracentesis may result in a further shift of fluid from the intravascular space into the peritoneal cavity with the risk of circulatory collapse. This can be reduced by supporting the circulation using intravenous albumin. The drain should be removed at the earliest opportunity because of the risk of introducing infection which can in turn lead to decompensation of liver disease
- **Exudates** can be safely paracentesed without protein replacement

Hepatorenal syndrome (HRS)

- Acute renal failure can complicate chronic liver disease, but it can also occur with fulminant hepatic failure:
  - Type 1 HRS occurs as a rapidly progressive renal impairment, with a very high mortality rate, all patients dying within weeks without treatment
  - In Type 2 HRS renal impairment is more stable and some hepatic reserve is preserved. Mortality is again high, but some patients survive over 6 months

- Treatment is with parenteral fluids, albumin, terlipressin and dialysis. Suitable patients should be referred to a liver unit for evaluation for transplantation

6.10.4 Viral hepatitis

The six major hepatitis viruses are described below, but further types are already postulated. Hepatitis B and C in particular are major causes of morbidity and mortality worldwide, although recent advances in treatment with interferon and other antivirals have improved the outcome in certain groups.

Hepatitis A

Spread: faecal–oral
Virus: RNA
Clinical: anorexia, jaundice, nausea, joint pains, fever
Treatment: supportive
Chronicity: no chronic state
Vaccine: yes

Hepatitis B

Spread: blood-borne (eg sexual, vertical, congenital transmission)
Virus: DNA
Clinical: acute fever, arteritis, glomerulonephritis, arthropathy
Treatment: supportive; for chronic HBV the available options include interferon and, antiviral agents lamivudine, adefovir, entecavir and telbivudine
Chronicity: 5% progress to chronic carriage (risk of cirrhosis and hepatocellular carcinoma)
Vaccine: yes

Hepatitis C

Spread: blood-borne, sexual
Virus: RNA
Clinical: acute hepatitis – less severe than A or B, fulminant failure rate
Treatment: pegylated interferon alpha (interferon bound to polyethylene glycol) for chronic HCV. This

may be more effective when used in combination with ribavirin

Chronicity: 60%–80% develop chronic hepatitis and 20% of these progress to cirrhosis (of whom a third will develop hepatocellular carcinoma). IV-drug-related hepatitis C represents a major public health problem in the UK

Vaccine: no

Hepatitis D (delta agent)

Spread: blood-borne (dependent on concurrent hepatitis B infection for replication)

Virus: incomplete

Clinical: exacerbates established hepatitis B infection and increases risk of hepatic failure and cirrhosis

Treatment: interferon of limited benefit

Chronicity: increases incidence of cirrhosis in chronic HBV

Vaccine: no

Hepatitis E

Spread: faecal–oral

Virus: RNA

Clinical: acute self-limiting illness, but there is a 25% mortality (fetal and maternal) in pregnancy, which increases in later stages of gestation

Treatment: supportive

Chronicity: no chronic state

Vaccine: no

Hepatitis G

Spread: blood-borne

Virus: RNA

Clinical: doubtful relevance; 20% of patients with chronic HCV are infected with hepatitis G

Treatment: viraemia may decline with interferon

Chronicity: unknown – may cause cirrhosis and hepatocellular carcinoma

Vaccine: no

Interferon in viral hepatitis

Interferon is predominantly of benefit in patients suffering from chronic hepatitis B and C. In hepatitis B, there is a response in 40% of chronic carriers. The response is poorer in Asian patients. The response is likely to be very poor if the patient is also infected with HIV and thus treatment is not usually indicated in this group. In hepatitis C, there is a response in 50% of chronic carriers but 50% of these will relapse despite treatment.

Hepatitis B serology

Antigens/antibodies related to viral surface (**s**), envelope (**e**) and core (**c**) are useful for determining the stages, infectivity and chronicity of hepatitis B infection:

- **HBsAg**: present in acute infection; if present longer than 6 months = chronic hepatitis
- **HBeAg**: present in acute or chronic infection; signifies high infectivity
- **HBcAg**: present in acute or chronic infection; found only in liver tissue; present for life
- **AntiHBs**: signifies immunity after vaccination or acute infection
- **AntiHBe**: signifies declining infectivity and resolving infection
- **AntiHBe IgM**: signifies recent acute infection; lasts less than 6 months
- **AntiHBc IgG**: a lifelong marker of past acute or chronic infection; does not signify immunity or previous vaccination

AntiHBC → prev. infection

6.10.5 Drug-induced hepatitis

Many drugs can cause hepatitis. Toxicity may be due to overdose (eg paracetamol), idiosyncratic (eg flucloxacillin) or may be related to dosage or duration of therapy (eg azathioprine). Three patterns of damage can occur:

- **Cholestasis**: some drugs produce a functional obstruction to bile flow by causing bile duct inflammation and interfering with excretory transport mechanisms. The commonest examples are flucloxacillin, erythromycin, chlorpromazine, oral contraceptives and anabolic steroids

- **True hepatitis**: some drugs produce direct hepatocellular damage which may be trivial or result in fulminant liver failure. Several mechanisms are responsible. Common examples include statins, antituberculous drugs, immunosuppressants, ketoconazole and halothane
- **Hepatic necrosis**: if the ability of the liver to detoxify metabolites is overwhelmed, glutathione levels fall and toxic metabolites accumulate, causing liver necrosis. This is the pattern of damage with carbon tetrachloride ingestion and paracetamol overdosage

Other causes of acute hepatitis include:

- Alcohol
- Other viruses (eg Epstein–Barr, yellow fever, CMV, rubella, herpes simplex)
- Other infections (eg malaria, toxoplasmosis, leptospirosis, brucellosis)

6.10.6 Autoimmune hepatitis

This condition occurs predominantly in female patients. Other autoimmune disease is often present and patients are usually ANF-positive. It responds to steroids and azathioprine but the majority progress to cirrhosis, although 90% are alive at 5 years and may be candidates for transplantation.

6.10.7 Cirrhosis

Cirrhosis is characterised by the irreversible destruction and fibrosis of normal liver architecture with some regeneration into nodules.

There are four stages of pathological change:

- Liver cell necrosis
- Inflammatory infiltrate
- Fibrosis
- Nodular regeneration

Regeneration may be macronodular (eg alcohol- or drug-induced), micronodular (eg viral hepatitis) or mixed, but a more useful categorisation is according to the aetiological agent.

Causes of cirrhosis

- Alcohol (most common in the UK, approximately 30% of all cases)
- Haemochromatosis
- Hepatitis B or C (most common worldwide)
- α1-antitrypsin deficiency
- Cryptogenic
- Primary biliary cirrhosis
- Wilson's disease
- Non-alcoholic steato-hepatitis (NASH)
- Autoimmune hepatitis

Evidence of chronic liver disease may or may not be present

Clinical features of cirrhosis

Clinical features are related to hepatic insufficiency:

- **Confusion/encephalopathy**: due to failure of liver to metabolise ammonium salts
- **Haemorrhage**: bruising/bleeding/petechiae secondary to deficiency in factors II, VII, IX and X, and thrombocytopenia
- **Oedema**: secondary to hypoalbuminaemia
- **Ascites**: due to portal hypertension, hypoalbuminaemia and secondary hyperaldosteronism
- **Jaundice**: failure to metabolise and/or excrete bilirubin
- **Other clinic features** include: palmar erythema, spider naevi, Dupuytren's contracture, caput medusae and splenomegaly (due to portal hypertension)
- **Gastrointestinal haemorrhage** secondary to varices (oesophageal, gastric or rectal)
- Hepatorenal syndrome

Diagnosis of cirrhosis

Cirrhosis may be suspected on ultrasound scanning but biopsy is required to confirm this and to help identify the aetiology. Ultrasound-guided biopsy is mandatory as the liver is often very small. Rarely, a transjugular biopsy is attempted, particularly if clotting is markedly deranged.

Treatment of cirrhosis

Treatment is aimed at the removal of causal factors such as alcohol. Specific treatments include interferon for viral hepatitis and ursodeoxycholic acid for primary biliary cirrhosis. Transplantation is the best hope but many patients are not suitable.

Contraindications for liver transplantation include:

- Poor cardiac reserve
- Co-morbidity such as HIV infection or severe respiratory disease
- Failure to abstain from alcohol

There is no definitive cut-off regarding age but patients over 70 years are less likely to be suitable.

Conditions which may be amenable to hepatic transplantation

- **Fulminant hepatic failure** (eg due to hepatitis C or paracetamol toxicity)
- **Primary biliary cirrhosis**
- **Wilson's disease**
- **Hepatitis B** – although there is frequent recurrence after transplant; this can be reduced with pre-transplant treatment with interferon
- **Cholangiocarcinoma** – if unresectable at presentation
- **Alcohol** – following psychological review and if abstained for more than 6 months
- **Haemochromatosis**
- **Hepatocellular carcinoma** – if not multifocal, if <5 cm and no evidence of vascular invasion

6.10.8 Portal hypertension and varices

Portal hypertension occurs as a result of increased resistance to portal venous flow. Pressure in the portal vein rises and is said to be pathological when >12 mmHg, although pressures of up to 50 mmHg may occur. The spleen enlarges and anastomoses may open between the portal and systemic circulation. Some of the collaterals, which most commonly occur at the oesophagogastric junction, umbilicus and rectum, may become very large with a risk of bleeding.

A variety of conditions may cause portal hypertension; in the UK the single most common is cirrhosis secondary to alcohol.

Causes of portal hypertension

- Cirrhosis due to any cause
- Portal vein thrombosis (congenital malformation, pancreatitis, tumour)
- Budd–Chiari syndrome (thrombosis or obstruction of hepatic vein due to tumour, haematological disease or the oral contraceptive pill)
- Intrahepatic tumours such as cholangiocarcinoma or hepatocellular carcinoma
- Constrictive pericarditis
- Right heart failure
- Splenic vein thrombosis (segmental portal hypertension)

Variceal haemorrhage

Thirty per cent of patients with varices will bleed at some point with a mortality of 50% for that episode. The majority of survivors will rebleed with a mortality of 30%. Bleeding is often catastrophic as many patients also have coagulopathy as a result of their underlying liver disease.

Primary prevention of haemorrhage

All patients with cirrhosis of the liver should have upper GI endoscopy to determine the presence or absence of varices. If there are none, or only very small varices, no treatment is required except regular endoscopic review every 2–3 years. Larger varices in patients with no history of variceal haemorrhage should be treated with prophylactic β-blockade alone or in combination with a nitrate (nitrates given alone are of no benefit). These reduce portal pressure and thus the risk of haemorrhage. Patients intolerant of propranolol and who are at high risk of bleeding may be considered for endoscopic variceal ligation.

Treatment of variceal haemorrhage

After resuscitation and correction of any coagulopathy the treatment of choice is early gastroscopy with band ligation of the varices (now shown to be superior to injection sclerotherapy). Temporary balloon tamponade (Sengstaken–Blakemore tube) may be useful if endoscopy is not immediately available or if bleeding cannot be stopped endoscopically. Vasoactive drugs, such as terlipressin (Glypressin®), are widely used but should not be viewed as a substitute for endoscopy and banding. Bleeding which does not respond to these measures may be an indication for emergency transjugular intrahepatic porto-systemic shunting (TIPSS). All patients with variceal haemorrhage should be treated with antibiotics, and blood products to correct coagulopathies and thrombocytopenia.

Secondary prevention of haemorrhage

Patients should undergo repeated band ligation until varices are eradicated. Beta-blockers should be given as this reduces the risk of rebleeding by up to 40%. Recurrent haemorrhage may be an indication for TIPSS.

Transjugular intrahepatic porto-systemic shunting (TIPSS)

This involves placement of a shunt under radiological screening which decompresses the portal venous system. As it is less invasive than surgery it may be a useful rescue procedure for patients with recurrent or resistant haemorrhage who are not fit for surgery. The major problems are that shunting may precipitate hepatic encephalopathy (this occurs in up to 24%, but seems more responsive to treatment than encephalopathy from other causes), and shunt blockage. In the latter case a second shunt may be 'piggy-backed' across the first. TIPSS may be particularly helpful as a palliative procedure in patients with recurrent haemorrhage due to malignancy.

6.10.9 Hepatic encephalopathy

Hepatic encephalopathy is a neuropsychiatric syndrome which may complicate acute or chronic liver disease from any cause. Symptoms include confusion, falling level of consciousness, vomiting, fits and hyperventilation. Renal failure may often supervene – the chance of recovery from hepatorenal failure is extremely poor. The underlying mechanisms are complex but the absorption of toxins such as ammonia from bacterial breakdown of proteins in the gut is thought to play a major part. Porto-systemic shunting of blood occurs – toxins thus bypass the liver and cross the blood–brain barrier.

The most common causes of **acute hepatic encephalopathy** are fulminant viral hepatitis and paracetamol toxicity which are potentially fully reversible. Indicators of poor prognosis are:

- Worsening acidosis
- Rising prothrombin time
- Falling Glasgow Coma Scale score

These patients should be referred to a specialist centre as they may need transplantation.

Chronic hepatic encephalopathy may supervene in chronic liver disease of any type. It is often precipitated by:

- Alcohol
- Drugs
- GI haemorrhage
- Infections
- Constipation

It is characterised by a flapping tremor, decreased consciousness level and constructional apraxia.

Treatment of hepatic encephalopathy

- Screen for and treat sepsis aggressively – if ascites is present consider bacterial peritonitis and perform a diagnostic ascitic tap. There should be a low threshold for prescribing antibiotics
- Strict fluid and electrolyte balance
- High protein diet
- Laxatives (lactulose) to clear the gut and thus reduce toxin absorption; neomycin is now rarely used

---

- Remove or treat precipitants
- Mortality is high, especially if renal failure supervenes, when the mortality exceeds 50%

6.10.10 Primary biliary cirrhosis

Primary biliary cirrhosis accounts for approximately 5% of deaths due to cirrhosis. The cause is unknown although factors point to an autoimmune aetiology, especially the strong association with other autoimmune disease such as rheumatoid arthritis, Sjögren syndrome and CREST syndrome. Histologically, progressive inflammation and destruction of small intrahepatic ducts leads to eventual cirrhosis. Ninety per cent of patients are female, often in middle age. There are four stages of primary biliary cirrhosis:

1. Destruction of interlobular ducts
2. Small-duct proliferation
3. Fibrosis
4. Cirrhosis

Primary biliary cirrhosis

- **Clinical features**
  - Cholestatic jaundice
  - Xanthelasmata due to hypercholesterolaemia
  - Skin pigmentation
  - Clubbing
  - Hepatosplenomegaly
  - Portal hypertension ± varices
  - Osteoporosis and osteomalacia
- **Diagnosis**
  - Antimitochondrial (M2) antibody present in 95%
  - Predominantly raised alkaline phosphatase – often raised in advance of symptoms/signs
  - Raised IgM
  - Liver biopsy showing the features listed above

Treatment is symptomatic; cholestyramine relieves pruritus. Ursodeoxycholic acid is widely used but it

is doubtful whether this agent either improves the prognosis or delays time to liver transplantation. Rising bilirubin levels are an indication that the disease is approaching end stage, and as liver transplantation remains the only hope of cure, patients should be assessed for this later treatment at an appropriate stage of their disease process.

6.10.11 Other causes of chronic liver disease

Haemochromatosis: this is an autosomal recessive disorder of iron metabolism leading to deposition in the liver, pancreas, pituitary and myocardium. (*See* Chapter 13, Metabolic Diseases.)

Wilson's disease: this is an autosomal recessive disorder of copper metabolism causing deposition in the liver, basal ganglia and cornea (Kayser–Fleischer ring). (*See* Chapter 13, Metabolic Diseases.)

6.10.12 Parasitic infections of the liver

Hydatid disease

This is caused by *Echinococcus granulosus* (a dog tapeworm), and is most common in areas of sheep and cattle farming. Ingestion results from eating contaminated vegetables or as a result of poor hand hygiene. The parasitic embryos hatch in the small intestine and enter the bloodstream via the portal venous circulation to the liver, but there may also be spread to lung or brain.

- Many cases are asymptomatic but right upper quadrant pain is the commonest symptom. Jaundice occurs if there is duct obstruction, and peritonitis will result from cyst rupture
- Diagnosis is confirmed using a haemagglutination test, but eosinophilia or the presence of cystic lesions on liver ultrasound in an at-risk individual is strongly suggestive of the disease
- Active infection is treated with albendazole followed by surgical resection of the intact cyst. Chronic calcified cysts can be left untreated

Schistosomiasis

This affects about 250 000 000 people worldwide. It is caused by *Schistosoma mansoni* (Africa, South America) or *Schistosoma japonicum* (Asia). Infection occurs when the parasite penetrates the skin during swimming or bathing in infected water contaminated by the intermediate host – the freshwater snail. The parasite migrates to the liver via the portal venous system where it matures, migrates back along the portal (and mesenteric) veins and produces numerous eggs which penetrate the gut wall and are excreted to continue the cycle. A chronic granulomatous reaction occurs in the liver leading to periportal fibrosis and cirrhosis.

- Early symptoms are related to the site of entry of the organism (swimmer's itch) and systemic effects, including malaise, fever, myalgia, nausea and vomiting
- Diagnosis confirmed by detecting ova in stool or liver biopsy. Liver function tests show raised alkaline phosphatase, and there is an eosinophilia
- Treatment is with praziquantel

6.10.13 Hepatic abscesses

Pyogenic abscesses most commonly occur following intra-abdominal sepsis but they can occur spontaneously. The most common organism isolated is *E. coli* but *Enterococcus, Proteus, Staphylococcus aureus* and anaerobes are recognised.

- Patients present with swinging pyrexia, weight loss, right upper quadrant pain and anorexia. Septic shock or jaundice may develop
- Diagnosis is confirmed by liver ultrasound, which is used to guide aspiration or insertion of a drain
- Broad-spectrum antibiotics are given until sensitivities are available; occasionally surgical resection is required

Amoebic abscesses are caused by *Entamoeba histolytica* which spreads from the gut (where it can cause an acute diarrhoeal illness) via the portal system to the liver. Single or multiple abscesses may

be found on ultrasound and treatment is with metronidazole.

6.10.14 Hepatobiliary tumours

There are a number of types of primary hepatic malignancy, all of which are rare. Secondary tumours, however, are common, typically metastasising from the stomach, colon, breast and lung.

Treatment of metastatic tumours is usually not indicated as the disease process is far advanced, although chemotherapy may slow progression in selected patients.

Hepatocellular carcinoma

This is rare in the UK (1–2/100 000 population) but the incidence is increased 20–30 times in Africa, Asia and Japan.

Incidence is increased by:

- Hepatitis B (commonest cause worldwide) and hepatitis C virus
- Cirrhosis from any cause, particularly hepatitis B and C and haemochromatosis
- Aflatoxin – a carcinogen from the mould *Aspergillus flavus* which may contaminate food
- Long-term oral contraceptive use

Raised serum α-fetoprotein (AFP) suggests the diagnosis and, in association with ultrasound, has been suggested as an appropriate annual screening for patients with cirrhosis. The treatment and prognosis are outlined in Table 6.8.

Cholangiocarcinoma

This is an uncommon adenocarcinoma arising from the biliary epithelium. It usually presents with obstructive jaundice.

Predisposing factors:

- Sclerosing cholangitis
- Choledochal cyst or other biliary tract abnormality
- Liver fluke infection

Table 6.8. Treatment and prognosis of hepatocellular carcinoma

Treatment	Prognosis
Resection	Only 5%–15% are suitable, with 20% operative mortality; 5-year survival <30%
Transplant	Very few patients are suitable – they should have single tumours smaller than 5 cm with no vascular or metastatic spread; 5-year survival 90%
Chemotherapy/ethanol injection into tumour/embolisation	Palliative with little survival benefit

- Caroli's disease (dilatation of the intrahepatic bile ducts predisposing to infection and stone formation)

The treatment and prognosis of cholangiocarcinoma are outlined in Table 6.9. Palliative stenting relieves jaundice and improves quality of life.

Carcinoma of the gallbladder

This adenocarcinoma occurs in the elderly but is uncommon. It has usually invaded locally or metastasised by the time of diagnosis.

Benign hepatic adenoma

The incidence of this is increased in patients who have been taking oral contraceptives for longer than 5 years and also with the use of anabolic steroids. It is usually asymptomatic but may rarely cause intraperitoneal bleeding or right upper quadrant pain.

Hepatic haemangioma

This is common, and is often an incidental finding on ultrasound. It is benign but may occasionally rupture.

Table 6.9. Treatment and prognosis of cholangiocarcinoma

Treatment	Prognosis
No treatment	Average survival 2 months
Resection	Fewer than 20% of patients are suitable; average survival approximately 3 years
Transplant	Very few patients are suitable but this gives the best prognosis

6.11. ACUTE ABDOMEN

An acute abdomen is one of the more frequent presentations to the Accident and Emergency department. Commoner causes are given in Table 6.10.

6.11.1 Investigations of acute abdomen

- Bloods: full blood count, urea and electrolytes, liver function tests, CRP, amylase, arterial blood gases, calcium
- Chest X-ray
- Abdominal X-ray
- ECG
- CT scan of abdomen
- Laparotomy

Table 6.10. Acute abdomen: causes

Bowel	Acute appendicitis
	Perforated viscus
	Inflammatory bowel disease
	Diverticular disease
	Bowel obstruction
	Mesenteric ischaemia
	Incarcerated inguinal hernia
	Incarcerated femoral hernia
	Volvulus
	Intussusception
Pelvic organs	Torsion of ovaries
	Pelvic inflammatory disease
	Endometriosis
Pancreas	Acute pancreatitis
	Acute on chronic pancreatitis
Gallbladder/ biliary system	Cholecystitis
	Cholangitis
Peritoneum	Peritonitis
Kidneys	Renal calculi
Spleen	Splenic infarcts

Chapter 7
Genetics

CONTENTS

Genetics

7.1 CHROMOSOMES

Within the nucleus of somatic cells there are 22 pairs of autosomes and one pair of sex chromosomes. Normal male and female karyotypes are 46,XY and 46,XX, respectively. The normal chromosome complement is known as **diploid**. Genomes with a single copy of each chromosome are known as **haploid**, and those with three copies of each chromosome are known as **triploid**. A karyotype with too many or too few chromosomes, in which the total is not a multiple of 23, is called **aneuploid**. Chromosomes are divided by the centromere into a short 'p' arm ('petit') and long 'q' arm. **Acrocentric** chromosomes (13, 14, 15, 21, 22) have the centromere at one end.

Lyonisation is the process whereby in a cell containing more than one X chromosome, only one is active. Selection of the active X is usually random and each inactivated X chromosome can be seen as a Barr body on microscopy.

Mitosis is diploid-to-diploid cell division (Figure 7.1). This occurs in somatic cells, resulting in two diploid daughter cells with nuclear chromosomes that are genetically identical both to each other and to the original parent cell.

Meiosis is diploid-to-haploid cell division (Figure 7.2). This occurs in the germ cells of the gonads and is also known as 'reduction division'. It results in four **haploid** daughter cells, each containing just one member (homologue) of each chromosome pair. Meiosis involves two divisions (**meiosis I and II**). The reduction in chromosome number occurs during meiosis I and is preceded by exchange of chromosome segments between homologous chro-

---

Figure 7.1 Mitosis

Chromosomes replicate forming
2 chromatids joined at the centromere,
and condense

Homologous chromosomes
align independently on the spindle

Chromatids move to opposite
poles and cell divides

2 diploid daughter cells, genetically
identical to each other and the
parent cell

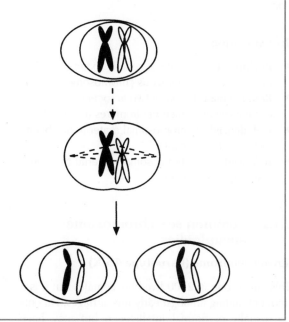

Figure 7.2 Meiosis

Chromosomes replicate, condense
and homologues pair up and cross over

Meiosis I (reduction division)
Homologous chromosomes move to opposite
poles and the cell divides

chromosomes align on
spindle in pairs

Meiosis II
Chromatids move to opposite poles
and the cells divide

chromosomes align on
spindle

4 haploid daughter
cells, all genetically
different

mosomes, called **crossing over**. All four daughter cells are genetically different, due to **recombination** from these crossovers. In males, the onset of meiosis and spermatogenesis is at puberty. In females, replication of the chromosomes and crossing over begins in fetal life, but the oocytes remain suspended prior to the first cell division until just before ovulation.

Translocations

- **Reciprocal**: exchange of genetic material between non-homologous chromosomes
- **Robertsonian**: fusion of two acrocentric chromosomes at their centromeres (eg 14;21)
- **Unbalanced**: if chromosomal material has been lost or gained overall
- **Balanced**: if no chromosomal material has been lost or gained overall

7.1.1 Common sex chromosome aneuploidies

Turner syndrome (karyotype 45,X)

This affects one in 2500 live-born females but it is a frequent finding amongst early miscarriages. Patients are usually of normal intelligence but may have

reduced visuospatial ability. They have streak ovaries which result in failure of menstruation, low oestrogen with high gonadotrophins and infertility.

Normal secondary sexual characteristics may develop spontaneously or be induced with oestrogens. Short stature throughout childhood with failure of the pubertal growth spurt is typical. Final height can be increased by early treatment with growth hormone. Other features may include the following.

Features of Turner syndrome

- Webbed or short neck
- Shield chest with widely spaced nipples
- Renal abnormalities (eg horseshoe kidney, duplicated ureters, renal aplasia) in approximately 30%
- Cubitus valgus (wide carrying angle)
- Low hairline
- Cardiovascular abnormalities, particularly aortic coarctation in 10%–15%
- Non-pitting lymphoedema in approximately 30%

When a woman with Turner syndrome is fertile, this is often due to the presence of 45,X/46,XX mosaicism. Her offspring may be at increased risk of being 45,X (or having other sex chromosome aneuploidy) or trisomy 21.

Triple X syndrome (karyotype 47,XXX)

These patients show little phenotypic abnormality but tend to be of tall stature, usually above the 80th centile. Intelligence is slightly reduced compared with siblings, by on average 10–15 IQ points, but it still usually falls within normal or low–normal limits. Speech delay is more common than in 46,XX and there is a greater likelihood of 47,XXX girls needing some help with this or other schooling needs (but they usually manage in mainstream schools). Fertility is normal, but the incidence of premature ovarian failure is increased. There is a low risk of recurrence in offspring.

Klinefelter syndrome (karyotype 47,XXY)

This affects 1 in 600 newborn males. Phenotypic abnormalities are rare pre-pubertally other than a tendency to tall stature. At puberty, spontaneous expression of secondary sexual characteristics is variable but poor growth of facial and body hair is common. The testes are small in association with azoospermia, testosterone production around 50% of normal and raised gonadotrophins. Gynaecomastia occurs in 30% and there is an increased (but still not high) risk of male breast cancer. Female distribution of fat and hair and a high-pitched voice may occur but are not typical. Intelligence is marginally reduced compared with siblings but usually falls within normal or low–normal limits. Mild developmental delay (especially speech) and behavioural problems are more common.

47,XYY males

Occurs in approximately 1 in 1000 newborn males. These males are phenotypically normal but tend to be tall. Intelligence is usually within normal limits but there is an increased incidence of behavioural abnormalities. Fertility is usually normal, with a low risk for recurrence in offspring.

7.1.2   Common autosomal chromosome aneuploidies

In general, trisomy is tolerated better by the organism than monosomy. There are no whole autosome monosomies that are compatible with life. It is no coincidence that the three autosomal aneuploidies compatible with live birth involve the three least gene-rich chromosomes.

Down syndrome (trisomy 21)

Down syndrome affects 1 in 700 live births overall and is usually secondary to meiotic non-disjunction during oogenesis, which is more common with increasing maternal age. Two per cent of patients have an underlying Robertsonian translocation, most commonly between chromosomes 14 and 21. This arises de novo in 50% and is inherited from a parent in 50%. Around 3% have detectable **mosaicism** (a mixture of trisomy 21 and karyotypically normal cells), usually resulting in a milder phenotype. Phenotypic features are listed in the following box:

Phenotypic features of Down syndrome

- Brachycephaly
- Protruding tongue
- Single palmar crease, 5th finger clinodactyly, wide sandal gaps between 1st and 2nd toes
- Upslanting palpebral fissures, epicanthic folds, Brushfield spots on the iris
- Hypotonia and moderate mental retardation

The following are more common in patients with Down syndrome (see box below).

Common features of Down syndrome

- Cardiovascular malformations in 40%, particularly atrioventricular septal defects (AVSD)

Continues...

Continued...
- Haematological abnormalities, particularly acute lymphoblastic leukaemia (ALL), acute myeloblastic leukaemia (AML) and transient leukaemias
- Gastrointestinal abnormalities in 6%, particularly duodenal atresia and Hirschsprung's disease
- Hypothyroidism
- Cataracts in 3%
- Alzheimer disease in the majority by 50 years of age

Edwards syndrome (trisomy 18)

This typically causes intrauterine growth retardation, characteristic facies, prominent occiput, overlapping fingers (2nd and 5th overlap 3rd and 4th), rockerbottom feet (vertical talus) and short dorsiflexed great toes. Malformations, particularly congenital heart disease, diaphragmatic hernias, renal abnormalities and dislocated hips, are more common. Survival beyond early infancy is rare and associated with profound mental handicap.

Patau syndrome (trisomy 13)

Affected infants usually have multiple malformations, including holoprosencephaly (abnormal formation of midline brain and facial structures) and other central nervous system (CNS) abnormalities, scalp defects, microphthalmia, cleft lip and palate, post-axial polydactyly, rockerbottom feet, renal abnormalities and congenital heart disease. Survival beyond early infancy is rare and associated with profound mental handicap.

7.1.3 Microdeletion syndromes

These are caused by chromosomal deletions that are too small to be seen microscopically but involve two or more adjacent genes. They can be detected using specific fluorescent probes (fluorescent in situ hybridisation (**FISH**)).

Examples of microdeletion syndromes are:

- **DiGeorge syndrome**: parathyroid gland hypoplasia with hypocalcaemia, thymus hypoplasia with T-lymphocyte deficiency, congenital cardiac malformations (particularly interrupted aortic arch and truncus arteriosus), cleft palate and learning disability due to microdeletions at 22q11. There is an increased incidence of psychiatric disorders, particularly within the schizophrenic spectrum
- **Williams syndrome**: supravalvular aortic stenosis, hypercalcaemia, stellate irides, mental retardation and chatty, sociable behaviour known as a 'cocktail party manner' due to microdeletions involving the elastin gene on chromosome 7

7.2 MENDELIAN INHERITANCE

7.2.1 Autosomal dominant (AD) conditions

These result from mutation of one copy (allele) of a gene carried on an autosome. All offspring of an affected person have a 50% chance of inheriting the mutation. Within a family the severity may vary (**variable expression**) and known mutation carriers may appear clinically normal (**reduced penetrance**). Some conditions, such as achondroplasia and neurofibromatosis type 1, frequently begin de novo through new mutations arising in the egg or (more commonly) in the sperm.

Examples of autosomal dominant (AD) conditions*

- Achondroplasia
- Ehlers–Danlos syndrome (most forms are AD)
- Facioscapulohumeral dystrophy
- Familial adenomatous polyposis coli

- Familial hypercholesterolaemia
- Gilbert syndrome
- Hereditary non-polyposis colorectal cancer
- Huntington's disease
- Marfan syndrome
- Neurofibromatosis types 1 and 2
- Osteogenesis imperfecta (most cases)
- Porphyrias (except congenital erythropoietic and erythropoietic protoporphyria, which are autosomal recessive)
- Tuberous sclerosis
- von Willebrand's disease

*Conditions prefixed 'hereditary' or 'familial' are usually autosomal dominant. An important exception is hereditary haemochromatosis which is autosomal recessive (see Section 7.2.2)

Noonan syndrome

This is an autosomal dominant condition, affecting about 1 in 2500 people. It is genetically heterogeneous, ie mutations at more than one gene locus can cause the Noonan phenotype. In around half of patients, the condition is caused by mutations in the *PTPN11* gene (*protein tyrosine phosphatase non-receptor type 11*) on chromosome 12. Mutations in several other genes (coding for other proteins that are members of the MAPK kinase pathway) have recently been identified in Noonan syndrome, whilst the genetic basis of the syndrome in many families remains unclear. As with other single-gene disorders, the karyotype is usually normal.

Clinical features of Noonan syndrome

- **Cardiac**
  - Pulmonary valve stenosis
  - Hypertrophic cardiomyopathy
  - Septal defects (ASD, VSD)
  - Branch pulmonary artery stenosis
- **Other features**
  - Poor feeding and hypotonia in infancy
  - Ptosis
  - Low-set and/or posteriorly rotated ears
  - Small genitalia and undescended testes in boys

- Coagulation defects in 30% (particularly factor XIc, XIIc and VIIIc deficiencies)
- von Willebrand's disease
- Juvenile myelomonocytic leukaemia (rarely)
- Thrombocytopenia
- Mild mental retardation in 30%
- **Musculoskeletal**
  - Webbed or short neck
  - Pectus excavatum or carinatum
  - Wide-spaced nipples
  - Cubitus valgus
  - Short stature in 80%

7.2.2 Autosomal recessive (AR) conditions

These result from mutations in both copies (alleles) of an autosomal gene. Where both parents are carriers, each of their offspring has a one in four (25%) risk of being affected, and a 50% chance of being a carrier. Healthy siblings of an affected individual therefore have a two-thirds chance of being a carrier.

Examples of autosomal recessive (AR) conditions

- Alkaptonuria
- Ataxia telangiectasia
- β-thalassaemia
- Congenital adrenal hyperplasia
- Crigler–Najjar syndrome (severe form)
- Cystic fibrosis
- Dubin–Johnson syndrome
- Fanconi anaemia
- Galactosaemia
- Glucose-6-phosphatase deficiency (von Gierke's disease)*
- Glycogen storage diseases
- Homocystinuria
- Haemochromatosis
- Mucopolysaccharidoses (all except Hunter syndrome)
- Oculocutaneous albinism

Continues...

Continued...
- Phenylketonuria
- Rotor syndrome (usually)
- Sickle cell anaemia
- Spinal muscular atrophy
- Wilson's disease
- Xeroderma pigmentosum

Most metabolic disorders are autosomal recessive – remember the exceptions:

- Hunter syndrome (mucopolysaccharidosis type 2)
- Glucose-6-phosphate dehydrogenase deficiency (favism)
- Childhood form of adrenoleukodystrophy

(The above three are all **X-linked recessive**)

- Ornithine transcarbamylase deficiency, a urea cycle disorder, also shows X-linked inheritance, with affected males often having a severe neonatal onset whilst carrier females may remain healthy into later life. They may, however, be at significant risk of dangerous hyperammonaemia in periods of stress or starvation

Autosomal dominant exceptions: acute intermittent porphyria, variegate porphyria, familial hypercholesterolaemia

Do not confuse with glucose-6-phosphate dehydrogenase deficiency (favism) which is X-linked recessive

Hereditary haemochromatosis

As stated previously, 'hereditary' or 'familial' conditions are usually autosomal dominant. However, hereditary haemochromatosis is autosomal recessive, due to mutation in the *HFE* gene, C282Y being much the commonest mutation. The carrier frequency for this is high (greater than 1 in 10) and so **pseudodominant** inheritance has been observed. This occurs when the partner of an affected person is, coincidentally, a carrier so that, on average, 50% of their offspring will have a genotype predisposing to clinical haemochromatosis. An apparent vertical

(dominant) transmission may therefore be observed. Only a small proportion of patients with mutations on both alleles will ever become symptomatic, and the penetrance is higher in males than females. (*See also* Chapter 6, Gastroenterology and Chapter 13, Metabolic Diseases.)

7.2.3   X-linked conditions

These result from a mutation in a gene carried on the X chromosome and most commonly affect males, because they have just one copy of each gene on the X chromosome. X-linked inheritance is characterised by the following:

- No male-to-male transmission (an affected father passes his Y chromosome to all his sons)
- All daughters of an affected male are carriers (an affected father passes his X chromosome to all his daughters)
- Sons of a female carrier have a 50% chance of being affected and daughters have a 50% chance of being carriers

Females are usually unaffected by X-linked recessive conditions, but may have mild manifestations as a result of lyonisation. Many X-linked conditions do not fit neatly into a purely recessive or dominant pattern, but have more severe expression in males than females, for example:

- X-linked **Alport syndrome**, due to mutations in *COL4A5*, causes renal failure and deafness in boyhood. Carrier females may have haematuria from early in life, but generally remain clinically well unless they develop hypertension (as happens in one third), or renal failure (up to 15%), and deafness, later in life (*see* Chapter 15, Nephrology)
- **Fragile X**, a trinucleotide repeat disorder, causes significant learning disability in affected boys, but up to half of female full mutation carriers (*see* Section 7.4.1) also have some learning or behavioural problems. These are usually, but not always, less severe than those seen in affected boys
- **Fabry disease**, in which the long-recognised, mainly cardiovascular and renal phenotype in

males is also seen in a milder form in significant numbers of female mutation carriers. These females have a reduced life expectancy compared with non-carriers as a result of the disease

X-linked recessive inheritance

- Becker's muscular dystrophy
- *Duchenne muscular dystrophy
- *Fabry disease
- Glucose-6-phosphate dehydrogenase deficiency (favism)
- Haemophilias A and B (Christmas disease)
- Hunter syndrome (MPS II)
- Lesch–Nyhan syndrome
- Ocular albinism
- Red–green colour blindness
- Androgen insensitivity syndrome
- Wiskott–Aldrich syndrome

*Recent evidence shows an increased risk of cardiac complications in female carriers of Duchenne muscular dystrophy (10% lifetime risk of overt cardiac failure) and Fabry disease. This warrants 5-yearly echocardiographic screening in asymptomatic individuals, and more frequently if symptoms are present

X-linked dominant (XLD) conditions

In these conditions, both male and female mutation carriers are affected by a mutation in a gene on the X chromosome. Females are usually less severely affected because of lyonisation, but these disorders are frequently lethal in males, because they have only a single X chromosome.

- All offspring of an affected female have a 50% chance of being affected, however if the

condition is lethal in the male embryo, as is the case in **incontinentia pigmenti**, a skewed birth ratio may be observed, ie 1 affected female: 1 unaffected female: 1 unaffected male (and an excess of miscarriages may be observed, representing affected male conceptions)

Examples of X-linked dominant conditions include:

- **Vitamin D-resistant rickets**: this results from mutations in the *PHEX* (phosphate regulating gene with homology to endopeptidases, X-linked) gene
- **Incontinentia pigmenti**: a disorder of girls causing vesicular skin lesions in infancy with variable hypodontia (small teeth), alopecia, retinal and other abnormalities. This results from mutations in the *NEMO* (NFκ-B essential modulator) gene
- **Rett syndrome**: a disorder of girls associated with developmental regression, progressive microcephaly, stereotypic hand movements and irregular breathing patterns. This results from mutations in the *MeCP2* (methyl CpG binding protein 2) gene
- **Periventricular nodular heterotopia**: this is associated with epilepsy and occasional learning disability in females and with embryonic lethality in males. It results from certain mutations in the *FLNA* (filamin A) gene

7.2.4 Genetic heterogeneity

This means that a particular phenotype can be caused by mutations in more than one gene. Examples are given in Table 7.1.

Table 7.1. The genetic heterogeneity of various conditions

Condition	Genes (modes of inheritance)
Alport syndrome	*COL4A5* (X-linked), *COL4A4 and COL4A3* (AR and ?AD)
Autosomal dominant polycystic kidney disease	*PKD1*, *PKD2* (AD)
Noonan syndrome	*PTPN11*, others (AD)
Retinitis pigmentosa	*RHO* (rhodopsin, accounts for 30% of cases, AR), 40 or more other genes (X-linked, AR and AD)
Tuberous sclerosis	*TSC1*, *TSC2* (AD)
Long QT syndrome	Genes coding for ion channel proteins (AD or AR)
Hypertrophic cardiomyopathy	Genes coding for components of the sarcomere (AD)
Hereditary motor and sensory neuropathy (Charcot–Marie–Tooth disease)	*PMP22* (AD), also several other genes (AD, AR and X-linked)
Hereditary non-polyposis colon cancer	Mismatch repair genes *MLH1*, *MSH2*, *MSH6* and others (AD, remember reduced penetrance)
Hereditary breast and ovarian cancer	*BRCA1*, *BRCA2* (AD, remember reduced penetrance)

7.3 MOLECULAR GENETICS

7.3.1 DNA (deoxyribonucleic acid)

DNA is a **double-stranded** molecule composed of purine (adenine + guanine) and pyrimidine (cytosine and thymine) bases linked by a backbone of covalently bonded **deoxyribose sugar** phosphate residues. The two anti-parallel strands are held together by hydrogen bonds, which can be disrupted by heating, and re-form on cooling.

- **Adenine (A)** pairs with **thymine (T)** by two hydrogen bonds
- **Guanine (G)** pairs with **cytosine (C)** by three hydrogen bonds

7.3.2 RNA (ribonucleic acid)

DNA is **transcribed** in the nucleus into messenger RNA (mRNA) which is **translated** by ribosomes in the cytoplasm into a polypeptide chain. RNA differs from DNA in that:

- It is single-stranded
- Thymine is replaced by **uracil**
- The sugar backbone is **ribose**

7.3.3 Polymerase chain reaction (PCR)

This is a widely used method for generating large amounts of DNA from very small samples. PCR can be adapted for use with RNA providing the RNA is first converted to DNA. For a more detailed account *see* Chapter 14, Molecular Medicine.

7.4 TRINUCLEOTIDE REPEAT DISORDERS

(*See also* Chapter 14, Molecular Medicine.) These conditions are associated with genes containing stretches of repeating units of three nucleotides.

Trinucleotide repeat disorders

- Fragile X syndrome, X-linked
- Huntington's chorea, AD
- Spinocerebellar ataxia, AD
- Myotonic dystrophy, AD
- Friedreich's ataxia, AR

In normal individuals the number of repeats varies slightly but remains below a defined threshold. Affected patients have an increased number of repeats, called an **expansion**, above the disease-causing threshold. The expansions may be unstable and enlarge further in successive generations causing increased disease severity ('**anticipation**') and earlier onset, eg **myotonic dystrophy**, particularly congenital myotonic dystrophy following transmission by an affected mother.

7.4.1 Fragile X syndrome

This causes learning disability, macro-orchidism and seizures and is often associated with a cytogenetically visible constriction on the X chromosome. The inheritance is X-linked but complex. Among controls there are between 6 and 55 stably inherited trinucleotide repeats in the *FMR1* gene. People with between 55 and 230 repeats are said to be **premutation carriers** but are unaffected by fragile X syndrome. During oogenesis in female premutation carriers, the triplet repeat is unstable and may expand into the disease-causing range (230 to >1000 repeats) known as a **full mutation**. All males and around 50% of females with the full mutation are affected by fragile X syndrome.

The effects of being a **premutation carrier** do not usually include learning disability, but premutation carrier females are at increased risk of premature ovarian failure, compared with controls or full mutation carriers. Males with premutations have about a 3% risk of developing fragile-X-associated tremor/ataxia syndrome, which includes symptoms of parkinsonism and cognitive decline, at around 50 years of age.

7.5 MITOCHONDRIAL DISORDERS

(*See also* Chapter 14, Molecular Medicine.) Mitochondria are **exclusively maternally inherited**, deriving from those present in the cytoplasm of the ovum. They contain copies of their own **circular 16.5-kilobase chromosome** carrying genes for several respiratory chain enzyme subunits and transfer RNAs. Mitochondrial genes differ from nuclear genes in having no introns and using some different amino acid codons. Within a tissue or even a cell there may be a mixed population of normal and abnormal mitochondria known as **heteroplasmy**. Different proportions of abnormal mitochondria may be required to cause disease in different tissues, known as a **threshold effect**. Disorders caused by mitochondrial gene mutations include the following:

- **MELAS** (**m**itochondrial **e**ncephalopathy, **l**actic **a**cidosis, **s**troke-like episodes)
- **MERRF** (**m**yoclonic **e**pilepsy, **r**agged **r**ed **f**ibres)
- Mitochondrially inherited diabetes mellitus and deafness
- Leber's hereditary optic neuropathy (note that other factors also contribute, resulting in higher penetrance in males)

7.6 GENOMIC IMPRINTING

For most genes both copies are expressed, but for some genes either the maternally or the paternally derived copy is preferentially used, a phenomenon known as genomic imprinting. The best-known examples are the **Prader–Willi** and **Angelman** syndromes (Table 7.2), both caused by either cytogenetic deletions of the same region of chromosome 15q or by **uniparental disomy** of chromosome 15 (where both copies of chromosome 15 are derived from one parent with no copy of chromosome 15 from the other parent).

Other well-recognised imprinting disorders include:

- Beckwith–Wiedemann syndrome
- Russell–Silver syndrome
- Albright's hereditary osteodystrophy
- Familial paraganglionoma

Albright's hereditary osteodystrophy

This results from the deactivating mutations in the *GNAS* gene (alpha subunit of the adenylyl cyclase stimulating G-protein, Gs) on chromosome 20q13. Mutations on the maternally derived *GNAS* allele

Table 7.2. Genomic imprinting: comparison between Prader–Willi and Angelman syndromes

	Prader–Willi	Angelman
Clinical	Neonatal hypotonia and poor feeding Moderate learning disability Hyperphagia + obesity in late childhood Small genitalia	'Happy puppet', unprovoked laughter/clapping Microcephaly, severe learning disability Ataxia, broad-based gait Seizures, characteristic electroencephalogram (EEG)
Genetics	70% deletion on paternal chromosome 15 30% maternal uniparental disomy 15 (ie no paternal contribution)	80% deletion on maternal chromosome 15 2%–3% paternal uniparental disomy 15 (ie no maternal contribution) Many of remainder due to mutations in *UBE3A* gene

result in an associated pseudohypoparathyroidism. The typical clinical features are:

- Short adult stature with a tendency to obesity
- Round facies
- Mild–moderate learning disabilities
- Brachydactyly: short metacarpals, particularly 4 and 5, and short distal phalanges (particularly the thumb)
- Ectopic ossifications

Beckwith–Wiedemann syndrome

This is due to abnormal imprinting of the *IGF2/H19/p57^{KIP}/KvLqQT1* gene cluster on chromosome 11p15.

The clinical features are of:

- Large birth weight
- Neonatal hyperinsulinism causing hypoglycaemia
- Omphalocele (exomphalos)
- Hemihypertrophy
- Facial naevus flammeus
- Increased risk of childhood abdominal tumours (particularly Wilms' tumour and hepatoblastoma)

Russell–Silver syndrome

- This condition has a prenatal onset with small stature and relative macrocephaly; very poor feeding is usual
- Patients also have a triangular face, asymmetry and 5th finger clinodactyly
- Maternal uniparental disomy for chromosome 7 is seen in around 10% of cases; abnormalities of other imprinted regions are also observed

Familial paraganglioma

In this condition, paragangliomas, including phaeochromocytomas and glomus jugulare tumours, occur throughout the body (most commonly in the head and neck). This is due to mutations in *SDHB*, *SDHC* and *SDHD* genes, but the mutation causes disease only when it has been inherited from the father. This is because the maternally inherited allele is imprinted (ie inactivated), and hence will not cause disease in the individual who inherits a mutation from his or her mother, see Figure 7.3.

Although the inheritance of mutations causing these conditions is autosomal dominant, such that there is a 50% chance of the disease genotype being inher-

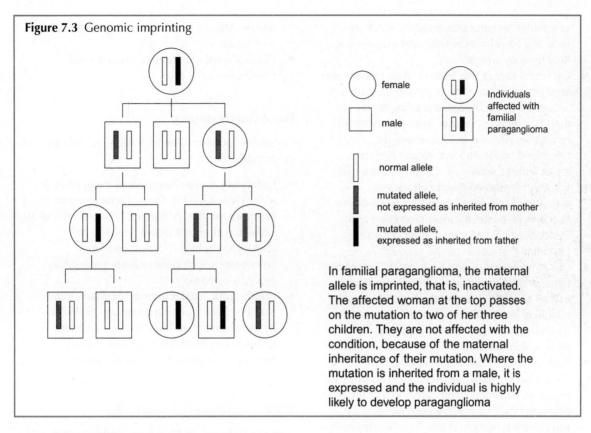

Figure 7.3 Genomic imprinting

○ female

□ male

In familial paraganglioma, the maternal allele is imprinted, that is, inactivated. The affected woman at the top passes on the mutation to two of her three children. They are not affected with the condition, because of the maternal inheritance of their mutation. Where the mutation is inherited from a male, it is expressed and the individual is highly likely to develop paraganglioma

Individuals affected with familial paraganglioma

normal allele

mutated allele, not expressed as inherited from mother

mutated allele, expressed as inherited from father

ited by each child, the expression or not of the mutant allele depends upon the parental origin of the allele, as shown in Figure 7.3.

7.7 OTHER IMPORTANT GENETICS TOPICS

This section includes short notes on conditions that form popular exam topics. See also homocystinuria (Chapter 13, Metabolic Diseases) and muscular dystrophy (Chapters 14, Molecular Medicine, and 16, Neurology).

7.7.1 Cancer genetics

Details of the increasing number of inherited cancer predisposition syndromes now defined are beyond the scope of this chapter (*see also* polyposis syndromes, Chapter 6; multiple endocrine neoplasia syndrome, Chapter 4; and Li–Fraumeni syndrome,

Chapter 14). However, general points to remember are:

- Nearly all have autosomal dominant transmission (reduced penetrance, see below)
- Young age at diagnosis or unusual combinations of cancers raise the suspicion of a heritable cancer predisposition syndrome
- Penetrance is often reduced, for example there is an 80% risk of breast cancer in female carriers of *BRCA1* or *BRCA2* mutations; colorectal cancer risk in hereditary non-polyposis colon cancer (HNPCC) is approximately 80% for males and 60% for females, with an approximately 50% risk of endometrial cancer in female *HNPCC* mutation carriers
- Even in a high-risk family, non-genetic lifestyle factors are important moderators of an individual's cancer risk; these include avoidance of smoking, diet (high intake of fresh fruit and

vegetables; in particular, resistant starch for reducing bowel cancer risk), and maintaining a healthy body weight

- For breast cancer risk, hormonal factors are also very important: late age of menarche, early age at birth of first baby, breast-feeding for more than 6 months and earlier menopause are all protective, whereas being overweight, combined oral contraceptive and hormone replacement therapy use can all increase risk

- In Gorlin syndrome (basal cell naevus syndrome), and other conditions predisposing to skin cancer, meticulous sun protection and avoidance of X-radiation if at all possible is important

- von Hippel–Lindau disease is nearly completely penetrant, ie it is unusual for a person who carries a mutation to not develop at least one feature of the condition (cerebellar or spinal haemangioblastoma, retinal angioma, phaeochromocytoma, renal cell carcinoma)

- Certain tumours are unusual enough to be almost pathognomic for a certain syndrome: for example, transitional cell carcinoma of the renal pelvis in HNPCC, or sebaceous tumours in Muir–Torre syndrome (Muir–Torre syndrome is the name for HNPCC occurring with these skin tumours)

Screening

Screening may be recommended for at-risk individuals in several cancer-predisposing conditions, including:

- HNPCC: colonoscopy every 18–24 months for proved mutation carriers and those who are at 50% risk of carrying a mutation. The recommended frequency of surveillance endoscopy for other cancer-predisposing conditions may vary

- High-risk hereditary breast and ovarian cancer: mammography, MRI breast screening where available (the benefits of ovarian screening are not proved)

- von Hippel–Lindau disease: annual renal ultrasound, urinary catecholamines, ophthalmic

review. MR scans of brain and spine every 2–3 years

- Familial renal carcinomas: annual renal ultrasound

Prophylactic surgery

Discussion of prophylactic surgery is indicated in certain conditions:

- **Colectomy** (as development of malignancy is almost inevitable) in familial adenomatous polyposis is often performed between 16 and 30 years (this does not usually need to be considered in HNPCC, as surveillance colonoscopy with polypectomy successfully prevents cancers)

- **Prophylactic mastectomy or oophorectomy** may be chosen (after appropriate counselling) by some women in high-risk breast cancer families. Oophorectomy reduces the risk of breast cancer as well as ovarian cancer

7.7.2 Ambiguous genitalia

(*See also* 'Intersex' in Chapter 4, Endocrinology.)

The 6-week embryo has undifferentiated gonads, Müllerian ducts (capable of developing into the uterus, Fallopian tubes and upper vagina), Wolffian ducts (capable of forming the epididymis, vas deferens and seminal vesicles) and undifferentiated external genitalia (Figure 7.4).

In the presence of a Y chromosome the gonads become testes, which produce testosterone and Müllerian inhibiting factor (MIF). Testosterone causes the Wolffian ducts to persist and differentiate and, after conversion to dihydrotestosterone (by 5α-reductase), masculinisation of the external genitalia. MIF causes the Müllerian ducts to regress.

In the absence of a Y chromosome the gonads become ovaries which secrete neither testosterone nor MIF. In the absence of testosterone the Wolffian ducts regress and the external genitalia feminise. In the absence of MIF, the Müllerian ducts persist and differentiate.

Figure 7.4 Outline of the normal development of the reproductive tract and external genitalia

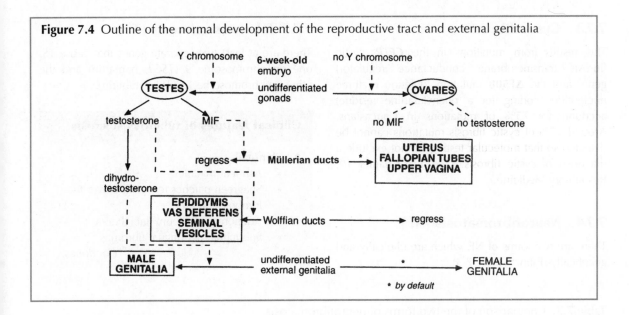

The causes of **ambiguous genitalia** divide broadly into those resulting in undermasculinisation of a male fetus, those causing masculinisation of a female fetus, and those resulting from mosaicism for a cell line containing a Y chromosome and another which does not. They are summarised in Figure 7.5.

Figure 7.5 Outline of the causes of abnormal genitalia

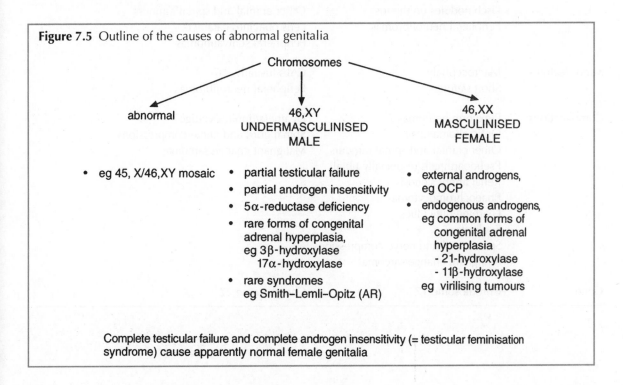

7.7.3 Cystic fibrosis

This results from mutations in the **CFTR** (cystic fibrosis transmembrane conductance regulator) gene, and the **ΔF508** mutation (deletion of three nucleotides coding for a phenylalanine residue) accounts for 75% of mutations in Caucasians. Around 15% of cystic fibrosis mutations cannot be detected so that molecular testing cannot exclude a diagnosis of cystic fibrosis. (*See also* Chapter 19, Respiratory Medicine.)

7.7.4 Neurofibromatosis (NF)

There are two forms of NF, which are clinically and genetically distinct (Table 7.3).

7.7.5 Tuberous sclerosis (TS)

There are at least two separate genes that cause TS, one on chromosome 9 (*TSC1*, hamartin) and the other on chromosome 16 (*TSC2*, tuberin).

Clinical features of tuberous sclerosis

- **Skin/nails**
  - Ash-leaf macules
  - Shagreen patches (especially over the lumbosacral area)
  - Adenoma sebaceum (facial area)
  - Subungual/periungual fibromas

Continues...

Table 7.3. Comparison of the two forms of neurofibromatosis

	NF1	NF2
Major features	≥6 café-au-lait patches (CALs) Axillary/inguinal freckling Lisch nodules on the iris Peripheral neurofibromas	Bilateral acoustic neuromas (vestibular schwannomas) Other cranial and spinal tumours Lens opacities/cataracts Peripheral schwannomas
Minor features	Macrocephaly Short stature	CALs (usually <6) Peripheral neurofibromas
Complications	Plexiform neuromas Optic glioma (2%) Other cranial and spinal tumours Pseudoarthrosis (especially tibial) Renal artery stenosis Phaeochromocytoma Learning difficulties Scoliosis Spinal cord and nerve compressions Malignant change/sarcomas	Deafness/tinnitus/vertigo Spinal cord and nerve compressions Malignant change/sarcomas
Gene	Chromosome 17	Chromosome 22

Continued...

- **Kidneys**
  - Renal cysts
- **Neuroimaging**
  - Intracranial calcification (periventricular)
  - Subependymal nodules
- **Eyes**
  - Retinal hamartomas
- **Heart**
  - Cardiac rhabdomyomas, detectable antenatally, usually regressing during childhood
- **Neurological**
  - Seizures
  - Learning disability

7.7.6 Marfan syndrome

This results from mutations in the fibrillin 1 gene on chromosome 15. Intelligence is usually normal.

Clinical features of Marfan syndrome

- **Musculoskeletal**
  - Tall stature with disproportionately long limbs (dolichostenomelia)
  - Arachnodactyly
  - Pectus carinatum or excavatum
  - Scoliosis
  - High, narrow-arched palate
  - Joint laxity
  - Pes planus

- **Heart**
  - Aortic root dilatation and dissection
  - Mitral valve prolapse
- **Eyes**
  - Lens dislocation (typically upward)
  - Myopia
- **Skin**
  - Striae
- **Pulmonary**
  - Spontaneous pneumothorax
  - Apical blebs on chest X-ray
- **Radiological**
  - Protrusio acetabulae
  - Dural ectasia on spinal MRI

The diagnosis of Marfan syndrome is based upon the Ghent criteria (which are beyond the scope of this chapter), which divide clinical features into major and minor within each body system. For a definite diagnosis of Marfan syndrome patients should have:

- A major criterion in at least two body systems and involvement of a third **or**
- A major criterion in one body system with involvement of a second system **and**
- A first-degree relative with confirmed Marfan syndrome

Chapter 8
Genito-urinary Medicine and AIDS

CONTENTS

Genito-urinary Medicine and AIDS

8.1 SEXUALLY TRANSMITTED INFECTIONS

The incidence of sexually transmitted infection (STI) has increased dramatically over the past 50 years both globally and in the UK. As well as the more 'traditional' diseases such as syphilis and gonorrhoea, a wider spectrum of diseases transmitted by sexual contact has increasingly been recognised (eg oro-anal transmission of enteric infections such as giardiasis and hepatitis A). Human immunodeficiency virus (HIV) infection arrived on the scene in the late 1970s.

8.1.1 Gonorrhoea

Transmission is primarily sexual; there is a large asymptomatic reservoir, mainly pharyngeal, rectal and cervical. *Neisseria gonorrhoea* is a capsulated organism, and it therefore resists phagocytosis. In the UK >10% of isolates show resistance to penicillin and quinolones. This has resulted in cephalosporins currently being the first-choice antibiotic in uncomplicated gonorrhoea. Treatment should be guided by the appropriate antibiotic sensitivities of the gonococcal isolates.

Disseminated (bacteraemic) infection is unusual but is more common in women. Responsible strains are nearly always highly susceptible to penicillin. Pharyngeal and rectal infection is often asymptomatic. Ophthalmia neonatorum is treated with systemic antimicrobials and appropriate eye drops.

8.1.2 Syphilis

Transmission is primarily sexual, although it may be congenital or, rarely, by blood transfusion. Penicillin is the drug of choice, with tetracycline as an alter-native option. **Concurrent HIV infection may increase the risk of neurosyphilis**, and extended courses of treatment are required. Diagnosis is by:

- **Serology**: two specific treponemal tests, enzyme immunoassay (EIA) and *Treponema pallidum* haemagglutination assay (TPHA) (would use a specific treponemal antigen), plus a quantitative non-treponemal test, ie rapid plasma reagin (RPR) or Venereal Disease Reference Laboratory (VDRL). The latter are non-specific (cardiolipin antigen) and biologically false-positive results can be obtained in other conditions
- **Dark-ground microscopy**: of **fresh** material from chancres or lesions of secondary syphilitic rash

8.1.3 *Chlamydia* infections

Non-gonococcal urethritis (NGU) due to *Chlamydia trachomatis* is the most common bacterial STI in the Western world. Serovars D to K are responsible. It is also a major cause of pelvic inflammatory disease in women (frequently silent) and prostatitis/epididymitis in men. Neonatal conjunctivitis and, more rarely, diffuse interstitial pneumonia are both complications of serovars D to K; infection is acquired by passage through an infected birth canal.

- **Trachoma** (corneal scarring) is caused by serovars A, B and C
- **Lymphogranuloma venereum (LGV)** is due to serovars L1, L2 and L3 and is an emerging cause of rectal infection and proctitis in men who have sex with men (MSM)

Both neonatal pneumonia and conjunctivitis need systemic treatment with erythromycin. Tetracycline or azithromycin is the drug of choice for adults.

8.2 BASIC EPIDEMIOLOGY AND VIROLOGY OF HIV/AIDS

8.2.1 Epidemiology

HIV/AIDS is a global disease. Of the estimated 33 million people infected with HIV, 22 million (68%) are from sub-Saharan Africa. Figures from the World Health Organisation (WHO) also indicate an emerging epidemic in the former Soviet Union and eastern Europe. In the UK there were approximately 52 000 prevalent HIV patients in 2006. In 2007 there were 6840 newly diagnosed cases, with approximately 15% presenting with advanced HIV disease (acquired immunodeficency syndrome or AIDS).

The following are the estimated routes of transmission in the current UK HIV population):

- Sexual intercourse between men (42%)
- Sexual intercourse between men and women (49%) – mainly acquired abroad
- Injecting drug abuse (2.7%)
- Blood and blood products (5%)

Risk factors facilitating sexual transmission include:

- Seroconversion and advancing stage of disease
- Concurrent STIs, particularly ulcerative disease of the genitalia
- Hepatitis C co-infection

Materno–fetal transmission occurs in 15%–20% of non-breast-fed and 33% of breast-fed infants of patients with HIV/AIDS.

The risk of transmission from mother to baby can be reduced by:

- Antiretroviral therapy (this can reduce transmission to only 1%–2% if therapy is started before the third trimester)
- Avoidance of breast-feeding
- Delivery by caesarean section

8.2.2 The virus

Human retrovirus is a member of the lentivirus family. It contains RNA that is transcribed to DNA via a reverse transcriptase enzyme. The main target sites of action of antiretroviral drugs are reverse transcriptases and proteases. There are two types of human immunodeficiency virus:

- **HIV-1**: (previously known as HTLV III) is prevalent worldwide
- **HIV-2**: is common in West Africa

Pathogenesis

The HIV virus has tropism for the following CD4 cells:

- T-helper lymphocytes
- B lymphocytes
- Macrophages
- Central nervous system (CNS) cells

HIV infection causes progressive immune dysfunction, characterised by CD4 cell depletion. Impairment of immunity is primarily cell-mediated, but as the disease progresses there is general immune dysregulation.

The following laboratory markers are associated with disease progression:

- Decreased CD4 lymphocyte count (normal $> 500/mm^3$ or $0.5 \times 10^9/l$). In the USA, a CD4 count of $<200/mm^3$ is regarded as AIDS, irrespective of the presence of clinical disease
- High HIV viral load, using HIV polymerase chain reaction (PCR) assay (note that CD4 and HIV viral load are the only markers monitored in clinical practice which help to predict progression as well as the response to treatment)

8.2.3 Seroconversion and the HIV antibody test

After inoculation the window or seroconversion period can be up to 3 months; HIV antibody may not be detectable during this time. The HIV p24 antigen becomes detectable during seroconversion. Current antibody tests detect HIV-1 and HIV-2. Approximately 30% of patients develop clinical seroconversion illnesses of variable severity, and which are often diagnosed retrospectively. HIV PCR and p24 antigen are used to diagnose HIV infection during this window period, and they are then confirmed by a positive antibody test. If the sero-conversion illness is severe then antiretroviral combination treatment should be used. Whether such early treatment improves long-term prognosis is unknown.

Seroconversion illnesses

- Fever
- Malaise
- Diarrhoea
- Meningo-encephalitis
- Rash
- Sore throat
- Lymphadenopathy
- Arthralgia

8.2.4 Centers for Disease Control and Prevention (CDC) classification of HIV/AIDS

The CDC classification is adopted in the USA and most developed countries. HIV infection is not synonymous with AIDS – the latter is a stage of severe immunodeficiency characterised by opportunistic infections and/or tumour.

CDC classification of HIV/AIDS

- **Stage 1**
  - Primary seroconversion illness
- **Stage 2**
  - Asymptomatic
- **Stage 3**
  - Persistent generalised lymphadenopathy
- **Stage 4a**
  - AIDS-related complex (ie advanced HIV disease, but having none of the features of stages 4b–d)
- **Stages 4b–d**
  - AIDS: patient may have opportunistic infection or tumours, which are termed 'AIDS indicator' illnesses

---

8.3 RESPIRATORY DISEASES ASSOCIATED WITH HIV/AIDS

8.3.1 *Pneumocystis carinii* pneumonia (PCP)

Pneumonia is the most common opportunistic infection and clinical presentation of AIDS. *Pneumocystis carinii* pneumonia (PCP) constitutes 40% of all AIDS-defining illness.

The symptoms of PCP include dry cough, dyspnoea, fever and malaise. There are remarkably few abnormal signs on chest examination.

Investigations for PCP

- **Chest X-ray**: the typical appearance of PCP is bilateral mid- and lower-zone interstitial shadowing. Atypical chest X-ray findings are found in 10% of PCP cases and include: cavitation, upper zone opacities, pneumothorax or unilateral consolidation. The chest X-ray may be normal and effusions are rare
- **Pulse oximetry**: hypoxia with low/normal pCO_2 is typically seen in moderate to severe infection. If O_2 saturation is normal then exercise-induced oxygen desaturation (O_2 saturation falling by $\geqslant 5\%$ and/or to a saturation of $\leqslant 90\%$, with exercise) will support the diagnosis of PCP
- **Identification of *Pneumocystis* cysts**: samples obtained by inducing sputum or from broncho-alveolar lavage (BAL) can be stained with silver or immunofluorescent antibody
- The combination of an HIV-positive person (usually with CD4 $<200/mm^3$) who is not taking PCP prophylaxis and who has a typical radiological appearance and hypoxia is sufficient for a confident diagnosis to be made. Empirical treatment with co-trimoxazole should be started. It is now unusual to have to resort to lung biopsy for PCP diagnosis

Poor prognostic features in PCP include poor response to treatment, co-infection, requirement for assisted ventilation and pneumothorax.

Treatment for PCP

- Treatment is with high-dose co-trimoxazole or intravenous pentamidine for severe cases. Clindamycin/primaquine, atovaquone and dapsone/trimethoprim are alternative treatments
- ·Intolerance to co-trimoxazole is common, with nausea, vomiting, rash, leucopenia and thrombocytopenia
- Steroids have been shown to improve prognosis in those with pO_2 <8 kPa (60 mmHg)

There is a 50% risk of recurrence within 12 months. **PCP prophylaxis** (co-trimoxazole, nebulised pentamidine, dapsone or atovaquone) is always given to patients with a CD4 count <200/mm³ and to those who have already had an episode of PCP. Prophylaxis is continued until the CD4 count is increased above 200/mm³ with the use of highly active antiretroviral treatment (HAART).

8.3.2 Pulmonary tuberculosis

The incidence of infection depends upon the prevalence of tuberculosis (TB) in the rest of the general population and it is therefore much more common in African patients. In some areas of the UK up to a quarter of patients with TB are HIV positive.

Atypical features include:

- Extrapulmonary involvement
- Normal or atypical appearances on chest X-ray
- Occurs at any stage of HIV disease, and at any level of CD4 count
- Atypical mycobacterial infections (when CD4 count <50/mm³) – usually *Mycobacterium avium intracellulare*. The usual presenting features are fever, anaemia, anorexia and the disease is commonly extrapulmonary

8.3.3 Other respiratory diseases in HIV/AIDS

Other causes of respiratory disease in HIV/AIDS

- **Viral**
  - Cytomegalovirus (CMV) pneumonitis
- **Fungal**
  - *Candida*
  - Histoplasmosis
  - *Cryptococcus*
  - *Nocardia*
- **Bacterial**
  - *Streptococcus pneumoniae*
  - *Staphylococcus aureus*
  - *Mycobacterium tuberculosis*
  - *Mycobacterium avium intracellulare*
- **Protozoal**
  - *Toxoplasma*
- **Tumour**
  - Kaposi's sarcoma (*see* Section 8.6.1)
  - Non-Hodgkin's lymphoma

Radiological appearance of other infections

- **Cavitation**: *M. tuberculosis*, *Nocardia*, *S. aureus*
- **Consolidation**: *S. pneumoniae*, *Toxoplasma*
- **Effusion**: TB (Kaposi's sarcoma may also cause effusion)

8.4 GASTROINTESTINAL DISEASES IN PATIENTS WITH HIV/AIDS

There are four main presentations:

- Oral/oesophageal disease
- Abdominal pain/diarrhoea
- Biliary/pancreatic disease
- Anorectal symptoms

8.4.1 Oral/oesophageal conditions

Ninety per cent of patients will develop an oral/oesophageal condition:

- Oral and oesophageal candidiasis
- Periodontal disease (including gingivitis)
- Herpes simplex
- Lymphoma
- Oral hairy leukoplakia (caused by EBV)
- Aphthous ulcers
- Kaposi's sarcoma
- Cytomegalovirus

These conditions may be asymptomatic, or patients may have dysphagia or odynophagia.

8.4.2 Diarrhoea/abdominal pain

Weight loss, diarrhoea and malnutrition are very common in patients with any stage of HIV infection, and can be due to specific infection or advanced disease. Approximately 50% of diarrhoeal illnesses are infective in origin (due to specific enteropathogens or opportunistic infections).

Enteropathogens found in HIV

- **Bacteria**
  - *Salmonella*
  - *Shigella*
- **Protozoal**
  - *Giardia lamblia*
- **Viral**
  - CMV
- **Opportunistic organisms**
  - Bacterial
    - Atypical mycobacteria (*M. avium intracellulare* with CD4 <100/mm^3)
  - Protozoal
    - *Isospora belli*
    - Cryptosporidia (intracellular protozoan)
    - Microsporidia

Clinical presentation can be with watery diffuse diarrhoea as exemplified by *Cryptosporidium*, or abdominal pain and bloody diarrhoea (eg CMV proctocolitis).

- **Cryptosporidiosis**: this is a coccidian parasite of the gastrointestinal tract which is responsible for 10%–15% of HIV-associated diarrhoeas, particularly occurring in patients with advanced HIV disease
- *Salmonella*: much more frequent in HIV-infected patients than in the general population. More likely to cause bacteraemia and recurrence is common

The investigation of infective diarrhoea includes the following:

- Identification of organisms in stool samples: microscopy and culture for pathogens, ova and parasites
- If stool specimen negative, stain with modified Ziehl–Neelsen for *Cryptosporidium*
- Sigmoidoscopy/colonoscopy with biopsy: with culture or PCR detection of the specimen for viruses, mycobacteria, bacteriology and mycology. Histological appearances are often important

Gastrointestinal tumours

These may also cause abdominal pain and diarrhoea.

- **Kaposi's sarcoma; may cause rectal bleeding**
- Intra-abdominal lymphoma (often high-grade non-Hodgkin's B-cell lymphoma)

8.4.3 Biliary and pancreatic disease

The two most common presentations are **cholangiopathy** and **pancreatitis**.

- **Cholangiopathy**: due to *Cryptosporidium*, CMV, or *Microsporidium*
- **Pancreatitis**: this can be induced by drugs used in HIV treatment (eg DDI (didanosine), or DDC (zalcitabine), which are both reverse transcriptase inhibitors), or by the biliary organisms listed previously

8.4.4 Anorectal conditions

These usually present with proctitis.

Symptoms and infective causes of anorectal conditions

- **Symptoms**
  - Anal discharge
  - Tenesmus
  - Pruritus ani
  - Rectal bleeding
  - Diarrhoea
- **Causative organisms**
  - Herpes simplex virus
  - Cytomegalovirus
  - *Neisseria gonorrhoeae* (gonorrhoea)
  - Non-specific/*Chlamydia*
  - Wart virus
  - *Treponema pallidum* (syphilis)
  - *Chlamydia* serovars 1–3, LGV

8.5 HIV/AIDS-RELATED NEUROLOGICAL DISORDERS

Neurological disease is the first presentation of AIDS in 10% of HIV patients. An acute self-limiting lymphocytic meningitis may occur at the time of seroconversion. Chronic neurological syndromes or opportunistic infections occur later in the course of HIV infection. The most common cause is the neurotropic effect of the virus itself.

Clinical presentation may be:

- **Focal**: hemiparesis, fits
- **Generalised**: drowsiness, confusion, behavioural change
- **Asymptomatic**: in early HIV disease

Patients may also develop proximal myopathy, or drug-induced neuropathy (eg didanosine) and myopathy (eg zidovudine).

8.5.1 Direct neurotropic effects of HIV

These include:

- AIDS dementia complex (see below)
- Vacuolar myelopathy
- Neuropathy (see below)

Neurotropic disorders are diagnosed with the help of:

- **CSF analysis**: raised protein, and pleocytosis
- **MRI brain scan**: cerebral atrophy
- **Nerve conduction studies**: distal symmetric sensory neuropathy

AIDS dementia is the most frequent neurological condition of HIV infection, and is directly caused by the virus. Impairment of concentration and memory leads to progressive decline in widespread cognitive function. Occasionally psychiatric symptoms may be prominent. The EEG shows generalised slowing with no specific features, and imaging demonstrates cortical atrophy.

Sensorimotor neuropathy associated with HIV/AIDS usually has mild sensory symptoms and signs. Less commonly, a mononeuritis multiplex or a chronic painful myelopathy may develop.

8.5.2 Neurological infections

Opportunistic infections of the CNS are common.

Causes of focal neurological disease

- ***Toxoplasma gondii***
  - Cerebral abscess
- ***Mycobacterium tuberculosis***
  - Meningitis
  - Tuberculosis abscess

Causes of generalised neurological disease

- *Cryptococcus neoformans*
  - Meningitis
- **Virus family (papovavirus)**
  - Progressive multifocal leucoencephalopathy
- **Cytomegalovirus**
  - Encephalitis/retinitis
  - Peripheral neuropathy

Specific CNS infections

Cerebral toxoplasmosis is the most common CNS infection (90% of focal lesions) and occurs in 10% of AIDS patients. The organism is the crescentic trophozoite form of *Toxoplasma gondii*.

- **Investigations**: CT brain scan shows solitary or multiple ring-enhancing lesions. *Toxoplasma* IgG serology is positive in >90% of cases
- First-line anti-*Toxoplasma* therapy is pyrimethamine plus sulfadiazine (with folinic acid to prevent bone marrow suppression)
- **Prognosis**: 10% mortality with first episode; 25% of patients have residual neurological deficit
- It is important to differentiate from primary CNS lymphoma causing a space-occupying lesion

Cryptococcal meningitis is due to a 'budding' yeast; it occurs in 5%–10% of AIDS patients. It presents with a subacute meningitic illness.

- Cryptococcal antigen is present in blood and CSF in most cases
- **India ink stain**: positive in 70% of CSF samples

Neurosyphilis: the co-existence of HIV and syphilis can result in aggressive and atypical neurosyphilis. Previous syphilis infection may reactivate. The following features are recognised:

- Myelopathy
- Retinitis
- Meningitis
- Meningovascular

Diagnosis: from syphilis serology (rising VDRL and TPHA) and CSF, although serology may be modified by immune dysfunction.

Treatment: The first-line therapy is intramuscular procaine penicillin and oral probenecid for 17 days.

8.5.3 Ophthalmic disorders

AIDS may affect the lids or any layer of the eye.

Ophthalmic features of AIDS

- **Molluscum contagiosum of lids**
- **Episcleritis and keratitis**
- **Uveitis**
- **Choroidal granulomata**
- **CMV retinitis**
- **Neuro-ophthalmic manifestations** (eg cranial nerve palsies, optic neuritis, sequelae to CNS infection or space-occupying lesion)
- **Kaposi's sarcoma of the eyelids or conjunctiva**
- **Retinal changes**: haemorrhages, cotton-wool spots, oedema and vascular sheathing
- **Toxoplasmosis**: may develop acquired disease or reactivation of pre-existing disease
- *Candida* **endophthalmitis**

Retinitis is common and may be caused by HIV itself (non-specific microangiopathy which is present in 75% of HIV patients) or by CMV.

CMV retinitis usually occurs when the CD4 count is <50/mm^3. This is the most common AIDS-related opportunistic infection in the eye (occurring in 25% of patients).

- **Symptoms**: blurred or loss of vision; floaters
- **Signs**: soft exudates, and retinal haemorrhages
- **Prognosis**: initially unilateral eye involvement; ultimately both eyes are affected

8.6 MALIGNANT DISEASE IN PATIENTS WITH HIV/AIDS

Despite the introduction of HAART, the incidence of malignant disease in patients with HIV/AIDS has increased in recent years. The most frequently occurring malignancies are:

- Kaposi's sarcoma (83%)
- Non-Hodgkin's lymphoma (13%)
- Primary CNS lymphoma (4%)

8.6.1 Kaposi's sarcoma (KS)

This occurs in 10%–15% of HIV patients as the first AIDS-defining presentation. The tumour is derived from vascular or lymphatic endothelial cells and is due to infection with human herpesvirus type 8 (HHV8). This virus is closely related to EBV and is transmitted sexually, vertically and via organ transplantation.

- **Clinical presentation**: Kaposi's sarcoma (KS) can have cutaneous and visceral involvement. Lesions appear as purple plaques or nodules. The most common systems involved are the gastrointestinal tract (30% of patients with KS of the skin also have gastrointestinal involvement), lymph nodes and the respiratory system. Patients with pulmonary KS have cough, dyspnoea and infiltrates, lymphadenopathy or effusion on chest X-ray. KS is now quite uncommon owing to the effect of the new antiretroviral combination therapies
- **Diagnosis**: clinical appearance (or biopsy in difficult cases)
- **Prognosis**: depends on stage of sarcoma: tumour (T), extent of systemic involvement (ie gastrointestinal, pulmonary) and level of immune status, immunosuppression (I), as indicated by level of CD4 lymphocyte count. The best prognosis occurs when disease is confined to skin or lymph nodes, when there is minimal oral disease, and when the CD4 lymphocyte count is >150/mm^3

8.7 HIV/AIDS-RELATED SKIN DISEASE

Dermatological diseases are extremely common in HIV patients (affecting 75%), especially in those who have AIDS. During the acute HIV illness, patients may develop an asymptomatic maculopapular eruption affecting the face and trunk. During seroconversion, they may also develop marked seborrhoeic dermatitis. As the disease progresses to AIDS, the development of tumours and atypical infections is seen.

Dermatological associations of HIV disease

- **General inflammatory dermatoses**
  - Psoriasis
  - Eczema
  - Seborrhoeic dermatitis
  - Folliculitis
- **Fungal/yeast infections**
  - *Pityrosporum ovale**
  - Candidiasis*
  - *Cryptococcus neoformans*
  - *Histoplasma capsulatum*
- **Malignancy**
  - Kaposi's sarcoma
  - Lymphomas
  - Cervical intraepithelial neoplasia*
- **Viral infections**
  - Herpes zoster/herpes simplex
  - Human papilloma virus*
  - Cytomegalovirus
  - Molluscum contagiosum*
- **Bacterial infections**
  - Tuberculosis
  - Syphilis
  - Bacillary angiomatosis
  - *Staphylococcus aureus*

*Features common in HIV patients

Other skin diseases that are recognised include:

- **Generalised maculopapular rash** (due to drugs): co-trimoxazole (25%), nevirapine (14%), efavirenz (4%), abacavir (5%), dapsone (5%)
- **Nail pigmentation**: zidovudine, indinavir
- **Stevens–Johnson syndrome** (due to drugs): nevirapine, co-trimoxazole

8.8 DRUG THERAPIES IN HIV/AIDS PATIENTS

8.8.1 Specific therapy of common opportunistic infections

Opportunistic infections in HIV/AIDS and their treatment are outlined in Table 8.1.

8.8.2 Antiretroviral therapy

Antiretroviral therapy is usually given as combination therapy with the following aims:

- Suppression of viral replication
- Reducing the risk of viral resistance emerging with three or more drugs
- Improving patient immunity with reduction of morbidity and mortality

Highly active antiretroviral treatment (HAART)

This involves combinations of at least three drugs; for example, two different nucleoside/nucleotide reverse transcriptase inhibitors (NRTI) in addition to a protease inhibitor (PI), or a non-nucleoside reverse transcriptase inhibitor (NNRTI).

Table 8.1. Opportunistic infections, their treatment and side-effects in HIV/AIDS

Infection	First-line drugs	Side-effects
Pneumocystis pneumonia	Co-trimoxazole (oral, or IV for moderate to severe infection) Pentamidine (IV)	Rash, bone marrow toxicity, nausea and fever Hyper/hypoglycaemia, pancreatitis, hypotension
Cerebral toxoplasmosis	Pyrimethamine and sulfadiazine (in combination)	Bone marrow suppression, fever, gastrointestinal reactions, rash
Cryptococcal meningitis	Amphotericin and flucytosine (in combination)	Chills, fever, gastrointestinal reactions, renal impairment (amphotericin), bone marrow toxicity, liver toxicity
CMV retinitis	Ganciclovir or valganciclovir Foscarnet Cidofovir	Bone marrow suppression Renal impairment Nephrotoxicity

There are three main classes of antiretroviral drugs currently licensed in the UK. Their modes of action are by inhibition of the viral reverse transcriptase enzyme or by inhibition of protease enzymes.

- Between 20% and 25% of ward admissions in patients with known HIV are due to drug toxicity
- Patients who fail combination therapy switch to salvage regimens, which might include drugs from all classes (sometimes combinations of four to six drugs are used)

Reverse transcriptase inhibitors

- **Nucleoside/nucleotide analogues (NRTI)**: zidovudine, lamivudine, didanosine, abacavir, tenofovir
- **Non-nucleoside analogues (NNRTI)**: efavirenz, nevirapine,
- **Protease inhibitors (PI)**: These act by inhibiting a protease that is needed to make the virus viable outside the cell. Particular PIs include saquinavir, ritonavir, fosamprenavir, lopinavir, atazanavir

Other drugs used as antiretrovirals

- **Interleukin-2**: this is used to boost CD4 counts in those patients who have had good HIV suppression with therapy, but who have failed to recover CD4 counts. The agent has little effect on HIV viral load
- **Enfuvirtide (T-20)**: amino acid peptide (GP41) competes with the HIV viral envelope protein for fusion to the cell membrane (therefore, a fusion receptor inhibitor). This is used in conjunction with HAART salvage therapy

Newer antiretroviral drug classes currently licensed for use

- Integrase inhibitors (inhibit cellular integration of viral DNA), eg raltegravir
- CCR5 inhibitors (classed as entry uptake inhibitors), eg maraviroc

Side-effects of antiretroviral drugs

- **Nucleoside/nucleotide analogues**
  - Zidovudine: myopathy, anaemia, fatigue, bone marrow toxicity, nail changes
  - Stavudine: peripheral neuropathy, lactic acidosis, lipoatrophy
  - Lamivudine: peripheral neuropathy, fatigue
  - Abacavir: hypersensitivity reaction (can be fatal on re-challenge)
  - Didanosine: pancreatitis, peripheral neuropathy
- **Non-nucleoside analogues**
  - All agents: potential for drug interactions via the CYP 450 cytochrome family; they can act as inhibitors or inducers
  - Nevirapine: rash, hepatitis
  - Efavirenz: rash, vivid dreams, hallucinations and depression
- **Protease inhibitors**
  - All agents: diabetes, hypertriglyceridaemia and hypercholesterolaemia (except atazanavir), central adiposity, buffalo hump, peripheral fat loss (lipodystrophy syndrome); there is also great potential for drug interaction via the CYP 450 cytochrome family (ritonavir is the most potent inhibitor known)
  - Indinavir: nephrolithiasis, asymptomatic hyperbilirubinaemia
  - Atazanavir: no effect on lipids but hyperbilirubinaemia occurs in 5%

Monitoring of HIV patients on treatment

- **Clinical assessment**: examination of mouth (for ulcers and candidiasis), skin, lymph nodes, chest, fundoscopy and weight
- Renal and hepatic function
- CD4 lymphocyte count
- HIV viral RNA load
- Viral resistance assay

- HLA B5701 – a genotypic allele which is carried in up to 4%–6% of the population (lower in African origin ~1%) which can predict severe abacavir hypersensitivity
- Cholesterol, blood sugar, triglycerides
- Lactate if symptoms of lactic acidosis (muscle pains, malaise, gastrointestinal symptoms, breathlessness) are present
- **Adherence to treatment**: >90%–95% of therapy must be taken to maintain adequate viral suppression and this will also reduce the chance of resistance developing to therapy. If there is evidence of virological failure (increased viral load on >2 tests) then HIV **resistance testing** is indicated. The latter involves viral genotype assay of point mutations associated with antiretroviral resistance to specific drugs

8.8.3 Prognosis of patients with HIV/AIDS

HIV was previously the leading cause of death in the USA in people aged 25–40 years (40 deaths/100 000). The prognosis of HIV/AIDS patients has now been revolutionised by HAART (introduced 1997) and the death rate has reduced.

- Life expectancy may surpass 25 years after diagnosis
- All opportunistic illnesses have been reduced dramatically; however, the incidence of **lymphoma** has increased steadily
- The new antiretroviral agents also significantly reduce mother-to-baby transmission of the virus from 20% to <1% (if breast-feeding is avoided)
- Individual prognosis depends on viral resistance (10% of new infections in Europe involve a resistant virus), side-effects and adherence to treatment; prognosis is worse if treatment is started when the CD4 count is below 200 cells/mm^3
- Evidence from the SMART Study suggests that the optimum time to commence HAART is when the CD4 count falls to around 350/mm^3. Prognosis is worse in patients who present late with AIDS (mainly heterosexuals who may have no obvious risks); death is due to delay in diagnosis
- Coronary heart disease, end-stage liver failure (due to co-infection with hepatitis B and C) and malignancy (lymphoma) are now common causes of death in patients with HIV/AIDS

HIV has now become a treatable chronic illness rather than a fatal disease.

CONTENTS

Haematology

9.1 ANAEMIAS

9.1.1 Definition and clinical features

Anaemia is defined as a reduction in the concentration of circulating haemoglobin. The normal haemoglobin level varies with age and sex; neonates having a relative polycythaemia, infants having a lower haemoglobin level than adults, and women lower levels than men.

Common features of anaemias
• Pallor • Decreased oxygen-carrying capacity (shortness of breath on exertion, tiredness) • Increased cardiac output (palpitations, 'haemic' ejection murmurs, cardiac failure in the elderly)

Anaemia may be classified by its cause, for example iron-deficiency anaemia, but often the cause is not known at the start of investigations so the usual method of classification uses the red cell size (MCV):

- **Microcytic**: anaemia with small red cells
- **Normocytic**: anaemia with normal red cell size
- **Macrocytic**: anaemia with large red cells

9.1.2 Causes of macrocytosis

Macrocytosis with a megaloblastic bone marrow

Examination of a bone marrow aspirate allows microscopic examination of the maturing erythroid cells. Normal maturation is termed **normoblastic erythropoiesis**. In conditions where there is interference with DNA synthesis, for example due to lack of vitamin B_{12} or folate, morphological abnormalities are seen. These include chromatin deficiency, premature haemoglobinisation, giant metamyelocytes and other morphological features which, put together, are termed **megaloblastic erythropoiesis**.

- **B_{12} deficiency**: pernicious anaemia most common
- **Folate deficiency**
- **Drugs**: methotrexate, hydroxycarbamide, cytosine, azathioprine. Many other chronically administered cytotoxics also affect nucleic acid synthesis

Macrocytosis with a normoblastic bone marrow

- **Reticulocytosis**: young cells are big cells
- **Liver disease**
- **Alcohol**
- **Myxoedema** (but check not due to the associated autoimmune disease pernicious anaemia!)
- **Pregnancy**: usually mild

Liver disease is associated with anaemia because of interference with manufacture of the lipid envelope of red cells, associated with abnormal liver function tests and target cells on blood film. Alcohol has a direct toxic effect on the marrow and may cause liver disease or be associated with dietary folate deficiency.

Macrocytosis associated with haematological diseases with their own special features

- **Myelodysplasia**: associated with cytopenias, monocytosis and dysplastic morphology (with blasts when transforming to acute myeloid leukaemia (AML))
- **Myeloma**: look for paraprotein, high erythrocyte sedimentation rate (ESR), leucoerythroblastic blood picture

*Central haemoglobin
concentration*

- **Myeloproliferative disorders**: polycythaemia rubra vera, essential thrombocythaemia, myelofibrosis, chronic myeloid leukaemia (CML)
- **Aplastic anaemia**: look for pancytopenia with hypoplastic bone marrow

9.1.3 Causes of microcytosis

- **Iron-deficiency anaemia**: look for pencil cells, check iron/total iron binding capacity (TIBC) or ferritin
- **Thalassaemia trait**: look for Mediterranean/Asian origin, check HbA2 level (elevated)
- **Anaemia of chronic disease**: often normocytic, usually obvious disease
- **Sideroblastic anaemia**: the MCV in this disorder may be low, normal or high
- **Aluminium toxicity**: affecting some haemodialysis patients (now uncommon)

9.1.4 Red cell morphology

Sometimes morphological abnormalities of the red cells are sufficiently characteristic to suggest a diagnosis. These may be commented on in blood film reports. Abnormalities of red cell shape are termed **poikilocytosis** (Table 9.1).

Other red cell morphological changes

- **Spherocytes**: found in any cause of haemolysis but particularly hereditary spherocytosis and autoimmune haemolytic anaemia

*Dense
No central pallor*

- **Target cells**: found in liver disease, post-splenectomy, iron deficiency, thalassaemia and haemoglobinopathies
- **Polychromasia**: young red cells, implies a high reticulocyte count if this is measured
- **Dimorphic blood picture**: two populations of red cells. Easily spotted using modern blood counters, which can provide a graph of cell size and/or haemoglobin content. It is caused by treatment of a haematinic deficiency (the new normal red cells contrast with the persisting cells characteristic of the anaemia); it may also be seen after transfusion of normal red cells into a patient with macro- or microcytosis and occasionally in combined deficiency when separated in time (eg patient with folate deficiency then becomes iron deficient). In primary sideroblastic anaemia the clone of abnormal erythroblasts produces abnormal red cells which contrast with those being produced by residual normal erythropoiesis

9.1.5 Sickle cell disease

The sickle cell diseases consist of homozygous sickle cell anaemia (HbSS), haemoglobin SC disease (HbSC) and haemoglobin S beta thalassaemia trait (HbS Thal). The clinical manifestations of sickle cell disease are mainly due to occlusion of small blood vessels by logjams of sickled red cells. Precipitating causes may be hypoxaemia, infection and dehydration, but often no cause is identified for a vaso-occlusive crisis.

Table 9.1. Poikilocytosis

Type of poikilocytosis	Found in
Teardrops	Myelofibrosis
Helmet cells and fragmented cells	Microangiopathic haemolysis
Pencil cells	Iron deficiency (with hypochromic microcytes)
Elliptocytes	Hereditary elliptocytosis
Sickle cells	Sickle cell diseases (with target cells)

Clinical syndromes recognised in sickle cell disease

- **Simple pain crisis**: due to infarction of red bone marrow, a common problem in sickle cell disease. Deep-seated bone pain often requires opiate analgesia. Vigorous hydration may shorten the duration of the crisis. Hypoxaemia should be corrected and infection treated with antibiotics
- **Sickle dactylitis**: infarction of the small bones of the hands or feet may be the earliest manifestation of sickle cell disease. Local pain and swelling result, with possible long-term deformity
- **Splenic sequestration crisis**: in adults the spleen has usually atrophied by repeated infarction but children may have enlarged spleens and sometimes the spleen may rapidly enlarge (over hours) and be painful. This is associated with massive retention of sickled red cells in the spleen resulting in severe anaemia with requirement for urgent transfusion
- **Localised areas of splenic infarction**: results in pleuritic pain in the left hypochondrium radiating to the left shoulder, sometimes associated with audible rubs
- **Thrombotic stroke**: fortunately this is relatively rare but it may be catastrophic and is an indication for urgent exchange transfusion
- **Pulmonary infarction–chest syndrome**: may be associated with infection. It is another serious complication of sickle cell disease, often requiring exchange transfusion
- **Priapism**: painful sustained penile erection due to sickling of red cells in the corpora cavernosa. It may require surgical intervention and lead to impotence
- **Other areas of sickle infarction**: the retina may be affected, particularly in haemoglobin SC disease, leading to retinal detachment and blindness. Infarction of the placenta may lead to fetal loss and small-for-weight babies. Intractable leg ulcers are common in countries where the ankles are not protected by shoes and socks. Avascular necrosis of the head of femur may be seen in adults

- **Aplastic crisis**: this is a syndrome of severe anaemia with a lower reticulocyte count and bilirubin level than usual for the patient. It is usually due to parvovirus B19 infection. In normal people this infection results in a mild febrile illness with infection of red cell precursors in the bone marrow causing shutdown of marrow red cell production for a few days. In patients with increased red cell turnover, such as sickle cell disease, a precipitous drop in haemoglobin level may result from a short shutdown in red cell production. Aplastic crisis may be found in other congenital haemolytic anaemias associated with a high red cell turnover

Transfusion in sickle cell disease

Because the oxygen dissociation curve of sickle haemoglobin is shifted to the right, oxygen is more easily released from haemoglobin to the tissues. Anaemia is therefore well tolerated and blood transfusion for the correction of anaemia is rarely required except in aplastic or sequestration crises. For severe sickle problems exchange transfusion with non-sickling HbA-containing red cells is required. To be effective the percentage of haemoglobin A needs to be raised to 80%–90% and care needs to be taken not to increase the haematocrit, which may lead to stagnation and increased sickling. Use of ABO-compatible red cell units matched for rhesus and Kell antigens will inhibit the development of atypical red cell antibodies. Commonly accepted indications for exchange transfusion are:

- Recurrent, severe, simple pain crisis
- Central nervous system sickling
- Priapism
- Preoperatively for large operations where the patient has a severe sickle history
- Chest syndrome not responding to conservative management
- Pregnancy with a history of sickling in previous pregnancy

Haemoglobin F in sickle cell disease

Elevated levels of haemoglobin F protect against sickling, hence clinical manifestations of sickle cell disease are not seen before 1 year of age, after which the physiological switch from fetal to haemoglobin S becomes complete. Hydroxycarbamide, an oral cytotoxic mainly used for the treatment of myeloproliferative diseases, has the side-effect of increasing haemoglobin F levels and is sometimes used for the amelioration of sickle cell disease; however, this use has to be balanced against its other side-effects of teratogenicity, marrow suppression and reduction of fertility. New drugs without these detrimental side-effects are in development.

Treatment of simple sickle pain crisis

- Vigorous hydration – the most effective intervention for shortening a pain crisis
- Analgesia – usually with opiates, preferably diamorphine, with roles for patient-controlled analgesia and non-steroidal anti-inflammatory drugs (NSAIDs)
- Oxygen if hypoxaemia is demonstrated by pulse oximetry
- Antibiotics – if evidence of infection

9.1.6   Thalassaemia

In contrast to the true haemoglobinopathies such as sickle cell disease (which are associated with abnormal substitutions of amino acids in the globin chains), in thalassaemia the globin chains are normal in structure but **not enough of the globin chains can be manufactured**. The disorder may affect α chains (**alpha thalassaemia**) or β chains (**beta thalassaemia**). Both types of thalassaemia may be severe (homozygous, major) or mild (heterozygous, minor).

- In the first year of life adult haemoglobin (HbA) gradually replaces fetal haemoglobin (HbF) as the major circulating haemoglobin
- About 3% of haemoglobin is the second adult haemoglobin (HbA2)
- These normal haemoglobins differ from each other in the nature of the polypeptide chains that make up the globin part of the molecule (Table 9.2)

Table 9.2. The globin chain contents of haemoglobin

Haemoglobin type	Globin chain content
HbF	$2\,\alpha + 2\,\gamma$
HbA	$2\,\alpha + 2\,\beta$
HbA2	$2\,\alpha + 2\,\delta$

Thalassaemia major

It may be seen that α chains are required in all the normal haemoglobins. It follows that in **alpha thalassaemia major**, where there is major failure of α chain manufacture, none of the haemoglobins are made and death in utero results. In **beta thalassaemia major** the blood is normal at birth, since β chains are not required for the production of fetal haemoglobin. During the first year of life there is failure to switch over from fetal to adult haemoglobin and the syndrome of anaemia, stunting of growth and hepatosplenomegaly arises.

Treatment of beta thalassaemia major

- Effective treatment depends on regular transfusions, which leads to iron overload
- Iron overload results in cardiomyopathy, endocrine failure and cirrhosis, but can be prevented by iron chelation therapy
- **Desferrioxamine** (Desferal®): is given by overnight subcutaneous infusion (using a syringe driver or balloon infuser) on two to five nights of the week, depending on the degree of iron overload. The aim of therapy is to maintain the ferritin level at about 1000 µg/l
- **Deferasirox** (Exjade®): orally active iron chelator that removes iron mostly in the bile and faeces. Because of its cost, it is only available in the UK for desferrioxamine treatment failures

In women with beta-thalassaemia trait, intrauterine diagnosis is possible, allowing the option of therapeutic abortion of a fetus with thalassaemia major.

Thalassaemia trait

Beta thalassaemia trait is associated with ~~minor suppression of β-chain manufacture~~ and a mild microcytic hypochromic anaemia difficult to distinguish from iron deficiency, although the MCV is often surprisingly low for the level of haemoglobin (which is usually over 9 g/dl). Besides assessing iron status (Section 9.2.1) an elevated HbA2 is also a useful marker of this trait.

In alpha-thalassaemia trait the clinical picture is more complex as four genes control α-chain production compared to the two genes that control β-chain production.

- The mildest varieties of alpha-thalassaemia trait are manifested by a microcytosis without anaemia
- More severe cases have a microcytic anaemia with splenomegaly and **HbH** in the red cells

In **haemoglobin H** a tetramer of β chains (that are unable to pair with α chains) replaces the α2β2 chains of HbA. Haemoglobin H may be detected by haemoglobin electrophoresis or by the presence of characteristic inclusion bodies in red cells (HbH inclusions) seen on an incubated reticulocyte stain.

9.1.7 Aplastic anaemia

This is a pancytopenia secondary to marrow hypoplasia. The reticulocyte count measured by high-precision (automated) techniques is lower than normal.

Aplastic anaemia

Causes:

- **Idiopathic**: most cases are in fact autoimmune
- **Drugs**: an idiosyncratic reaction to drugs such as gold, phenylbutazone and chloramphenicol
- **Post-hepatitis**: viruses that are toxic to hepatocytes may also kill bone marrow stem cells
- As a predictable reaction to chemotherapy or radiation

Treatment:

- **Remove the cause** if known (eg causative drugs)
- **Supportive**: red cell transfusion for correction of anaemia, antibiotics for infections, platelet transfusion for thrombocytopenic bleeding. Granulocyte colony-stimulating factor (G-CSF) does not improve stem cell numbers but may boost the numbers and function of later myeloid cells
- **Immunosuppression**: high-dose steroids, anti-lymphocyte globulin, ciclosporin
- **Stimulation of residual marrow activity**: anabolic steroids
- **Bone marrow transplantation**: only in severe cases; most successful in children with an HLA-matched sibling. A reduced-intensity conditioning regimen may be used, without total body irradiation, because the bone marrow is already empty and there are no malignant cells to eradicate

9.2 IRON METABOLISM

A representation of the body's iron economy is shown in Figure 9.1.

Iron absorption may be greatly increased in iron deficiency, but iron excretion cannot be increased in the case of iron overload. Most iron in the body is contained within red cells, so chronic bleeding is a potent cause of iron deficiency.

The marrow normally contains stainable iron but it is possible to have no stainable iron in the bone marrow but a normal haemoglobin level. The converse is not true – in iron-deficiency anaemia the marrow will not contain stainable iron. In megaloblastic anaemias, haemoglobinopathies and myelodysplasia, red cells may die and enter the reticuloendothelial system without leaving the bone marrow – this is termed 'ineffective erythropoiesis'.

9.2.1 Assessment of iron status

- **Transferrin saturation**: may be calculated by dividing the serum iron by TIBC and multiplying

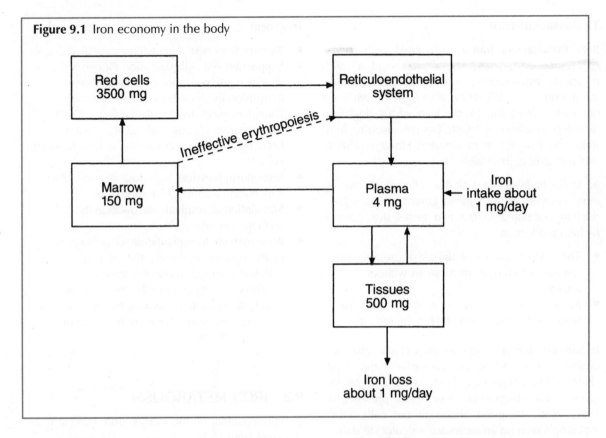

Figure 9.1 Iron economy in the body

by 100%. Neither the serum iron nor the TIBC is particularly helpful on its own, so transferrin saturation should always be requested. This is low in iron deficiency and high in iron overload

- **Serum ferritin**: a major transport and storage form of iron that is high in iron overload states and low in iron depletion. It is one of the acute phase proteins, and so, like C-reactive protein (CRP), fibrinogen and immunoglobulins, it is increased in inflammatory illness. If the ESR is increased then the serum ferritin may not be an accurate reflection of iron stores. It is also released from damaged liver cells, so if the patient has a transaminitis then it will be falsely elevated
- **Iron stain**: on particles from bone marrow aspirate. This is the gold standard, but it is invasive and expensive so rarely performed in the diagnosis of iron deficiency

- **Serum soluble transferrin receptor**: the latest index for measuring iron status, being high in iron deficiency and low in iron overload. It is still a research tool but shows promise
- **Trial of oral iron**. In some patients it is difficult to establish iron status with certainty and a trial of oral iron for about a month is justified, and will do no harm if the patient is not iron overloaded

9.2.2 Sideroblastic anaemia

In this disorder there is a failure to incorporate iron into the haemoglobin molecule, due to a biochemical block, and it accumulates in the mitochondria. These become poisoned and are visible as iron granules lying in a ring around the erythroblast nucleus. Hence the diagnostic feature is **ring sideroblasts** in the bone marrow.

Causes of sideroblastic anaemia:

- **Congenital**: rare, pyridoxine responsive
- **Acquired – primary**: one of the myelodysplastic disorders
- **Acquired – secondary**: alcohol, malignancy in the body, drugs (eg antituberculous), connective tissue disorders, heavy metal poisoning

9.3 HAEMOLYSIS

Destruction of red cells may occur in the:

- Circulation (*intravascular*)
- Reticuloendothelial system (*extravascular*)

If haemolysis is intravascular then the haemoglobin liberated from red cells will be conserved in the body by binding to plasma proteins. Initially this will be haptoglobin, so haptoglobin levels will be reduced. Then albumin will bind free haemoglobin, forming methaemalbumin, which may be detected by a positive Schumm test. Without a protein to bind to, the haemoglobin will pass through the glomerulus to appear in the urine – **haemoglobinuria**. This will give a positive stick test for haemoglobin but red cells will not be seen on microscopy of urine. In extravascular haemolysis the red cells are engulfed by macrophages in spleen and liver. In cases of severe haemolysis both mechanisms may occur together.

9.3.1 General features and causes of haemolysis

The anaemia is commonly macrocytic and associated with:

- **Elevated reticulocyte count**: >2%
- **Jaundice**: pre-hepatic, unconjugated, water-insoluble bilirubin; therefore NOT found in urine. However, **urobilinogen** may be found in urine – due to increased breakdown products of porphyrins secreted into the bile and reabsorbed from the bowel. Detected by simple stick test
- **Abnormal red cell morphology**: particularly spherocytes (see above)

Causes of haemolysis

- **Mainly intravascular**
  - Some delayed haemolytic transfusion reactions
  - Immediate haemolytic transfusion reaction
  - Paroxysmal cold haemoglobinuria
  - Microangiopathic haemolytic anaemia
  - Glucose-6-phosphate dehydrogenase deficiency
  - Infections – malaria
  - Phosphokinase deficiency
  - Paroxysmal nocturnal haemoglobinuria
- **Mainly extravascular**
  - Warm autoimmune haemolytic anaemia
  - Cold haemagglutinin disease
  - Haemolytic disease of the newborn
  - Hereditary spherocytosis
  - Some delayed haemolytic transfusion reactions
  - Haemoglobinopathies (eg sickle cell disease)

9.3.2 The antiglobulin (Coombs') test

The direct antiglobulin test detects antibody on the patient's red cells. The antibody coating on the red cells may be:

- **Opsonising**: making the red cells attractive to the phagocytes of the reticuloendothelial system
- **Complement fixing**: causing a local enzymatic explosion, blowing a hole in the red cell envelope
- **Agglutinating**: in which case the red cell clumping may be visible in the test tube or blood film without resorting to a Coombs' test to discover the antibody

The indirect antiglobulin test detects antibody in the patient's serum. This involves incubation of serum with test red cells bearing various surface antigens. This test is most frequently used as part of the 'cross-match' or compatibility test. The donor's red cells are mixed with the recipient's serum and if there is incompatibility a positive, indirect antiglobulin test will result.

9.3.3 Microangiopathic haemolytic anaemia (MAHA)

Fibrin strands are laid down in small blood vessels and these chop up red cells (like a wire cheese cutter). The red cells reseal themselves if not too badly damaged and circulate as helmet cells or, if multiply chopped, as fragmented cells. All the features of haemolysis will be present, as well as reticulocytosis due to increased marrow activity.

Haematological features of microangiopathic haemolytic anaemia:

- Anaemia
- Helmet cells
- Fragmented cells
- Polychromasia
- Reticulocytosis
- Spherocytes

Sometimes thrombocytopenia and consumption coagulopathy may be associated, depending on diagnosis.

Causes:

- Disseminated intravascular coagulation (DIC) (*see* Section 9.7.4)
- Haemolytic uraemic syndrome (HUS)
- Thrombotic thrombocytopenic purpura (TTP)
- Malignant (accelerated-phase) hypertension
- Severe pre-eclampsia

Thrombotic thrombocytopenic purpura (TTP) and haemolytic uraemic syndrome (HUS)

The general features of microangiopathic haemolytic anaemia, as described above, are present in these overlapping syndromes. However, in addition there is often fever, renal impairment and cerebral dysfunction (*see also* Chapter 15, Nephrology).

- In TTP neurological symptoms dominate the clinical picture and adults are frequently affected

- In HUS renal failure and fever are the predominant clinical problems and children are usually affected. Infection with verotoxin-producing strains of *Escherichia coli* due to faecal contamination of food (in particular, meat) is a well-recognised cause (diarrhoea-associated HUS), but many cases are idiopathic or familial

Pathogenesis of TTP and HUS

The essential problem is an excess of sticky high-molecular-weight von Willebrand factor (vWF) in the plasma, which causes the platelets to adhere to vascular endothelium. This results in thrombocytopenia and the blockage of small capillaries in the brain and kidney by platelet thrombi. Activation of the coagulation system causes fibrin strands to be laid down and these shred passing red cells, causing the classic features of microangiopathic haemolysis.

- In normal plasma high-molecular-weight vWF is cleaved to less sticky vWF by a plasma protease
- Low levels of this protease have been found in many cases of TTP and, in some cases, antibody directed against the protease has been found
- In contrast to DIC, the screening tests of coagulation (but not the platelet count) are normal
- In sporadic HUS (not associated with diarrhoea), 20% of patients are shown to have a genetic defect for the complement regulatory protein factor H

Treatment of TTP and HUS

The mainstay of treatment is large-volume infusion of fresh frozen plasma (FFP) which contains the vWF-cleaving protease, coupled with **plasma exchange**. The latter has the advantage of removing any antibodies and toxins involved in the pathogenesis of disease. Cryo-poor FFP (from which cryoprecipitate and hence vWF has been removed) may be used for the plasma exchange, and solvent/detergent-inactivated FFP may confer less risk of transfusion-transmitted infection.

- High-dose steroids may be of benefit in cases with an autoimmune aetiology and are often given (except in the epidemic form of HUS).
- Once the platelet count has exceeded $50 \times 10^9/l$, aspirin may be used to inhibit further adhesion of platelets to vascular endothelium
- In cases with autoimmune aetiology the anti-CD20 antibody rituximab is effective
- Other specific therapies may be indicated for particular disease sequelae (eg haemodialysis for acute renal failure)

9.3.4 Paroxysmal nocturnal haemoglobinuria (PNH)

This is a rare, acquired disorder that may affect all haematological cells. There is increased sensitivity of the cell membranes to the action of the patient's own complement, which damages red cells, white cells, platelets and stem cells. This results in intravascular haemolysis with haemoglobinuria, leucopenia, thrombocytopenia and (sometimes) pancytopenia with an 'empty bone marrow' – aplastic anaemia. Other clinical features:

- In addition to episodes of haemoglobinuria, the release of tissue thromboplastin from damaged cells leads to an **acquired thrombophilia** when thrombosis may present in unusual sites such as the hepatic or portal veins
- There is an increased incidence of **acute myeloid leukaemia**

Pathogenesis and diagnosis of PNH

A transmembrane glycoprotein is missing from the blood cell surface in PNH, and this 'fence post' would carry molecules that inactivate complement approaching the cell membrane.

- This glycoprotein would normally carry various CD antigens (eg CD55 and CD59) and so these are missing from the cell surface in PNH. This allows diagnosis by **immunophenotyping** of red cells, white cells or platelets
- The classic diagnostic test is the **Ham acid serum haemolysis test**, in which the patient's red cells are placed in hydrochloric acid with

fresh complement. The red cells will haemolyse, but normal control red cells do not
- The Ham acid lysis test will be negative if the patient has recently been transfused, but immunophenotyping of white cells or platelets may still allow detection of a PNH clone
- Unlike many other causes of haemolysis, iron deficiency is common as haemoglobin is lost in the urine
- A minor clone of PNH cells can be demonstrated by immunophenotyping of blood in haematological diseases associated with a 'stressed' marrow, such as aplastic anaemia

Treatment of PNH

This consists of:

- **Red cell transfusion**: the correction of anaemia often requires the use of washed red cells as the transfusion of complement in the donor plasma may exacerbate haemolysis
- **Anticoagulation**: thrombosis is the commonest cause of death so anticoagulation with warfarin is usual if the platelet count permits
- The **monoclonal antibody eculizumab**, directed against the complement component C5, reduces haemolysis, rendering most patients transfusion-independent, and decreases thrombosis. It is currently too expensive for general use outside clinical trials in the UK
- **Other therapies**: erythropoietin, steroids and danazol are of unproved value, although folate (and sometimes iron) supplements should be given. Bone marrow transplantation is curative but risky, so usually reserved for patients developing acute myeloid leukaemia

9.4 MEASUREMENT OF INFLAMMATION

Many medical disorders are associated with inflammation and measurement of inflammatory markers is useful in screening for disease and in following the clinical progress of inflammatory diseases. The three most popular measurements are ESR, CRP and plasma viscosity.

9.4.1 Erythrocyte sedimentation rate (ESR)

An increased concentration of inflammatory proteins affects the dielectric of the suspending plasma so that erythrocytes can more closely approach each other. Normally their surface negative electrical charge causes them to repel each other and remain in suspension. When they touch they adhere face to face, forming stacks of red cells like piles of coins – rouleaux. These rouleaux may be seen on the blood film, where they suggest the presence of an inflammatory process or paraprotein. Alterations in the volume to surface area ratio mean that rouleaux sediment more rapidly than individual red cells. When spherocytes are present rouleaux cannot form, so the ESR may be falsely depressed.

- Despite the complex underlying mechanism, the ESR is a simple test to do and can be performed in the clinic using long, thin, citrated blood-taking tubes placed vertically in a rack. The ESR is measured as the depth (in mm) that the red cell meniscus has dropped after 1 hour
- Normal ESR is 2–20 mm/hour. The normal range is age related, rising with advancing years. An ESR > 100 mm/hour is usually due to a paraprotein, collagen disease or tuberculosis
- There will be a delay of a few weeks after cure of an inflammatory condition before return of the ESR to normal levels
- The ESR is not stable overnight in citrate tubes, but EDTA tubes can be used for up to 24 hours providing citrate anticoagulant is added in the laboratory
- The ESR is frequently used as a screening test to distinguish diseased from non-diseased patients – a normal ESR does not exclude disease but an elevated one suggests an inflammatory process

9.4.2 C-reactive protein (CRP)

The name refers to the original finding of a protein that reacted with the C-polysaccharide of pneumococci but CRP is released by hepatocytes and fat cells in response to high levels of the cytokine interleukin-6 (IL-6) and appears to attach to dead and dying cells and bacteria, assisting in their removal by macrophages that bear receptors for CRP. The assay is relatively complex and performed in the laboratory. CRP levels rise after a few hours in response to inflammation and reach their peak in 2 days. CRP levels drop more rapidly than ESR as inflammation improves.

A modest elevation of CRP level is also a marker for increased cardiovascular risk.

9.4.3 Plasma viscosity

Providing a viscometer is available this is a reliable and inexpensive way of assessing acute phase proteins, which include relatively large molecules such as immunoglobulins and fibrinogen. The sample is stable for several days.

9.5 DISORDERS OF LEUCOCYTES

9.5.1 Leucocytosis

An elevated white cell count may be due to an increase in any of the individual types of white cell in the blood and should prompt a differential count to determine if there is a neutrophilia, lymphocytosis or, more rarely, an increase in other types of white cell underpinning the leucocytosis.

Neutrophilia ($>7.5 \times 10^9$/l)

This is by far the commonest cause of a leucocytosis. If acute it may be associated with young neutrophils (band cells) in the blood or 'left shift'.

Causes of neutrophilia

- **Bacterial infections**
  Localised or generalised
- **Trauma**
- **Metabolic disorders**
  (eg uraemia, acidosis, gout, eclampsia, poisoning)
- **Malignant neoplasms**
  Particularly when associated with tissue necrosis
- **Inflammation or necrosis**
  (eg myocardial infarction, trauma, vasculitis)
- **Corticosteroid therapy**
- **Myeloproliferative disorders**
  (eg chronic granulocytic leukaemia, myelofibrosis, essential thrombocythaemia, polycythaemia rubra vera)

Lymphocytosis ($>3.5 \times 10^9$/l)

The morphology of the lymphocytes may give valuable clues. For example, in acute viral infections the lymphocytes may show morphological abnormalities termed 'reactive changes' and in chronic lymphocytic leukaemia the mature-looking small lymphocytes characteristic of the disease are fragile and become crushed during the spreading of the blood film – 'smear cells'.

Causes of lymphocytosis

- **Acute viral infections** (eg influenza, glandular fever, rubella, mumps, acute HIV)
- **Chronic lymphocytic leukaemia**
- **Thyrotoxicosis**
- **Chronic infections** (eg TB, *Brucella*, hepatitis, syphilis)
- **Other chronic leukaemias and lymphomas**
- **A lymphocytosis is normal in infancy**

Eosinophilia ($>0.5 \times 10^9$/l)

In the developed world allergic disorders are the main cause of eosinophilia.

Causes of eosinophilia

- **Allergies**
  (eg asthma, hay fever, drugs)
- **Skin diseases**
  (eg eczema, psoriasis, dermatitis herpetiformis)
- **Tropical eosinophilia**
  (usually multiple parasitic infections)
- **Hypereosinophilic syndrome**
  (see below)
- **Eosinophilic leukaemia**
  (very rare)
- **Parasites**
  (eg ankylostomiasis, ascariasis, filariasis, trichinosis, toxocariasis)
- **Neoplasms**
  (eg Hodgkin's disease)
- **Miscellaneous conditions**
  (eg sarcoidosis, polyarteritis nodosa, eosinophilic granuloma)

Hypereosinophilic syndrome

This condition is associated with a high eosinophil count, up to 100×10^9/l. The aetiology is obscure. Some cases are myeloproliferative disorders equivalent to eosinophilic variants of chronic myeloid leukaemia, some are T-cell lymphomas which produce large amounts of cytokines such as interleukin-5 (IL-5), which stimulate eosinophil proliferation. Treatment is with steroids and hydroxyurea. Cases which are associated with a FIP1L1/PDGRF translocation in haemopoietic cells may respond to imatinib.

Hypereosinophilic syndrome

- **Clinical features**
  - Weight loss
  - Rashes
  - Fever
  - Peripheral neuropathy
  - Oedema
  - Cardiac disturbances
- **Pathological features**
  - Acute arteritis
  - Pericarditis
  - Cardiac mural thrombus
  - Chronic endocardial fibrosis
  - Pulmonary abnormalities
  - Splenomegaly

Monocytosis ($>0.8 \times 10^9$/l)

Monocytes are tissue phagocytes ('dustbin lorries') en route to the tissues to phagocytose and digest dead cells and other debris.

Causes of monocytosis

- **Recovery**
  (from chemotherapy, radiotherapy, trauma, operation)
- **Chronic inflammatory disease**
  (eg sarcoidosis, Crohn's, ulcerative colitis, rheumatoid arthritis, systemic lupus erythematosus (SLE))
- **Myelodysplastic syndromes**
  (and chronic myelomonocytic leukaemia)
- **Infections**
  (eg TB, *Brucella*, kala-azar, typhus, bacterial endocarditis, malaria, trypanosomiasis)
- **Hodgkin's disease**
  (and other neoplasms)
- **Acute myelomonocytic leukaemias**
  (when it will be associated with increased blast cells)

9.5.2 Leucoerythroblastic change

This is defined as the presence of nucleated red cells and primitive white cells of any type in the peripheral blood. There are two major causes: either the normal cells inhabiting the bone marrow are being evicted by a marrow infiltration, or the patient has acute severe illness.

Causes of a leucoerythroblastic blood picture

- **Invasion of marrow space**
  - Tumour (metastatic carcinoma), leukaemia, myeloma, lymphoma, myelofibrosis, osteopetrosis, storage disease (eg Gaucher's disease)
- **Severe illness**
  - For example, severe haemolysis, massive trauma, septicaemia

9.5.3 Neutropenia

This is defined as a neutrophil count of less than 2×10^9/l. Below 1×10^9/l, some risk of infection exists; below 0.5×10^9/l this may be severe and such patients, if in hospital, will usually be isolated and subject to a regimen of care including prophylactic antiseptic mouthwashes and antifungal agents and avoidance of foods with a high bacterial load. In the event of significant fever a broad-spectrum antibiotic regimen reserved for 'febrile neutropenia' is instituted.

Causes of neutropenia

- **Associated with intercurrent viral infections** (usually a mild neutropenia)
- **Idiosyncratic drug reactions**
  (eg carbimazole)
- **Collagen diseases**
  (eg SLE, rheumatoid)
- **Myelodysplasia**
- **After chemotherapy or radiotherapy**
- **Benign ethnic neutropenia** (eg in blacks or Arabs)

- **Hypersplenism**
  (Often low platelet count and haemoglobin as well)
- **Marrow infiltration**
  (May be associated with leucoerythroblastic change)

9.6 HAEMATOLOGICAL MALIGNANCIES

These may be broadly divided into:

- Leukaemias
- Lymphomas
- Myelodysplasias
- Myeloproliferative disorders

Acute leukaemias are characterised by primitive blast cells in the bone marrow and blood; chronic leukaemias show an excess of mature cells in the marrow and blood. In leukaemias the malignant cells lie mainly in marrow and blood, whereas in the lymphomas they lie mostly in lymph nodes. There is an overlap, however, so many cases of lymphoblastic lymphoma have marrow involvement by cells of the disease in addition to enlargement of thymus and lymph nodes.

9.6.1 Leukaemias

Acute

- Myeloblastic (AML)
- Lymphoblastic (ALL)

Chronic

- Myeloid (CML (CGL))
- Lymphoid (CLL)

Acute lymphoblastic leukaemia:

- Predominantly affects children
- Remission may be induced with non-myelosuppressive chemotherapy
- CNS involvement common
- >80% cure rate with chemotherapy
- Further classified by immunological surface markers.

Acute myeloid leukaemia:

- Predominantly affects adults
- Marrow hypoplasia required to induce remission
- CNS involvement rare
- >30% cure rate with chemotherapy
- Further classified by morphological appearance (see below)

How to identify the leukaemic blast cell

- **Morphology**: often this is not helpful as myeloblasts look similar to lymphoblasts. One give-away is the presence of Auer rods which are diagnostic of AML
- **Cytochemistry**: the leukaemic cells are tested for their biochemical activities. Important cytochemistry tests in acute leukaemia: Sudan black (stains lipid material in AML); periodic acid–Schiff (PAS) (stains carbohydrate material in ALL); esterase (stains monocytic variants of AML)
- **Immunological surface markers**: these are particularly useful in ALL when they allow classification into T-cell, B-cell and other immunological types

Treatment strategies in acute leukaemia

Bone marrow transplantation is a powerful treatment for acute leukaemia, as it also harnesses the power of graft-versus-leukaemia effect. It is a risky treatment, however, and this risk increases with age. The total body irradiation also results in sterility. Chemotherapy also carries major risks and so patients with acute leukaemia are stratified by **risk of relapse**. This allows the selective application of stronger, and hence riskier, chemotherapeutic regimes for those patients who require them, and less stringent chemotherapy in patients with a better prognosis (see below).

Prognostic factors in acute leukaemia

Acute lymphoblastic leukaemia

- Age: <1 year or over 10 years worsens prognosis; adults do particularly badly (highest presenting white cell count, age and sex may be combined in the Medical Research Council's algorithm)
- Height of highest pre-treatment white cell (blast) count (a higher count = a higher tumour load and worse prognosis, particularly in children)
- Cytogenetics (see below)
- Sex (in children, boys do worse)
- Immunophenotype (T-cell ALL usually has a high presenting white cell count – see below)
- Response to treatment is measured by blast cell count in the marrow, or by assessment of minimal residual disease (MRD). Morphological remission is defined as less than 5% blast cells in the bone marrow. MRD assessment uses the polymerase chain reaction (PCR) to amplify clonal rearrangements of immunoglobulin genes or T-cell receptor genes characteristic of that patient's disease. In children the persistence of more than one malignant cell per 10^4 marrow cells after 1 month into chemotherapy mandates the use of a more intensive chemotherapy protocol

Acute myeloid leukaemia

- Cytogenetics (see below)
- Age (over-60s do worse)
- Response to first course of chemotherapy

9.6.2 Specific chromosome abnormalities in leukaemia/lymphoma

Cytogenetic techniques

Morphological examination of the chromosomes of malignant haematological cells is possible by culturing them in tissue culture medium and then 'freez-ing' the cell in division with the chromosomes spread out (metaphase arrest) by adding colchicine or vincristine, which poison the spindle apparatus. The cells are then swollen in hypotonic salt solution and the cell suspension is dripped onto glass microscope slides so that the cells split open, releasing a cloud of contained chromosomes. This is examined under the microscope and usually analysed with the aid of a computerised image analysis system. The chromosomes are arranged in order of their length to form a karyotype (see Chapter 7, Genetics). Cytogenetic abnormalities are found in two-thirds of cases of AML and in three-quarters of cases of ALL.

Chromosome abnormalities in leukaemia and lymphoma are important for the following reasons:

- They act as a marker of the disease, indicating remission or relapse
- Some have a prognostic significance. If the prognosis is especially bad (eg Philadelphia chromosome in childhood ALL) then a high-risk treatment such as bone marrow transplantation may be employed early in treatment. If the prognosis is especially good (eg t(8;21) in adult AML) then conventional chemotherapy may be employed without a transplant unless the patient relapses
- Some of the abnormal DNA sequences that result from chromosomal translocation can be amplified by PCR to allow the detection of incredibly small amounts of residual leukaemia. Within individual clinical trials detection of MRD may mandate for increased intensity or duration of chemotherapy. This varies with the molecular abnormality being detected

Many of the chromosomal abnormalities in leukaemia and lymphoma are translocations, involving the exchange of material between chromosomes (Table 9.3). For example, t(9;22) involves a reciprocal translocation between chromosomes 9 and 22. Chromosome 22 comes off worst in this exchange, gaining only a small amount of extra material. The abnormally shortened long arms of this chromosome are visible morphologically as the Philadelphia chromosome (see Section 9.6.4).

Table 9.3. Cytogenetic abnormalities associated with malignant haematological disease

Cytogenetic abnormality	Found in
t(9;22)	Philadelphia chromosome (Ph) in CML
t(15;17)	Acute promyelocytic leukaemia (M3) – *see* Section 9.6.3
t(8;21)	AML with differentiation (M2) – better prognosis
inv(16)	Inversion of the long arm of chromosome 16 – better prognosis
	Acute myelomonocytic leukaemia (AML M4) with marrow eosinophilia (M4Eo)
Hyperdiploidy	(More than 47 chromosomes) Childhood ALL – better prognosis
t(1;19)	Childhood pre-B ALL
t(8;14)	ALL L3 Burkitt type
5q–	Myelodysplastic syndrome (refractory anaemia) with abnormal megakaryocytes particularly in women (loss of part of the long arm of chromosome 5)
t(14;18)	Follicular NHL – found in three-quarters of cases

9.6.3 The French–American–British (FAB) classification of acute leukaemia

This morphological classification (Table 9.4) is widely used for AML but in ALL has been largely supplanted by the immunophenotype. It depends on the degree of differentiation of the leukaemic cells and whether a recognisable tendency to differentiate along one of the myeloid pathways (eg monocytic) is present. As with any morphological classification it is rather subjective and there will be some cases which would be best classified between grades, eg M2$\frac{1}{2}$!

Acute promyelocytic leukaemia (AML M3)

- Majority of leukaemic cells are abnormal hypergranular promyelocytes
- Auer rods and collections of Auer rods (faggots) common
- Strongly Sudan black/peroxidase positive
- Characteristic chromosome abnormality t(15;17), involving retinoic acid receptor gene alpha (RARA)
- Variant M3 (M3v) is **hypo**granular but otherwise the same

The disease and its treatment are associated with acute fibrinolysis/DIC – heavy platelet and FFP

Table 9.4. The FAB classification of acute leukaemia

FAB type	Description
M0	Acute myeloid leukaemia undifferentiated – no morphological feature to distinguish it from ALL
M1	Acute myeloid leukaemia with recognisable myeloid features such as Auer rods
M2	Acute myeloid leukaemia with a few cells differentiating to the promyelocyte stage
M3	Acute promyelocytic leukaemia
M4	Myelomonocytic leukaemia
M5	Pure monocytic leukaemia
M6	Acute erythroleukaemia
M7	Acute megakaryoblastic leukaemia

support are needed. Remission can be induced with all-*trans* retinoic acid (ATRA) – a differentiating agent that also helps with the coagulopathy. Prognosis is good providing death from DIC does not occur during induction.

9.6.4 Chronic myeloid leukaemia (CML)

CML is a disease of middle age, the majority of patients presenting with tiredness, weight loss and sweating. Splenomegaly is found in 90% of cases. If the white cell count is very high (over $500 \times 10^9/l$) then problems associated with hyperleucocytosis may be found: visual disturbance, priapism, deafness, confusion. Gout may be a presenting symptom. Eventually almost all patients not treated with therapy directed at the Ph-positive cells transform to blast crisis in 1–10 years. This may be myeloid, lymphoid or mixed transformation. At this stage it is very difficult to treat.

Blood and marrow features of CML

- High white cell counts ($100–500 \times 10^9/l$)
- Absolute basophilia and eosinophilia
- Platelet count high, normal or low
- Low neutrophil alkaline phosphatase (NAP) score
- Increased blood colony-forming cells (stem cells)
- High serum B_{12} due to production of a B_{12} binding protein by white cells
- Massive neutrophilia with left shift
- Anaemia in relation to height of WBC
- Philadelphia chromosome (see following text)
- Marrow hyperplasia sometimes with increased reticulin (fibrosis)

Philadelphia chromosome (Ph)

This is an abnormally truncated chromosome 22 that has lost part of its long arms, which have become attached to chromosome 9, with a smaller portion of chromosome 9 becoming attached to 22. There is thus a translocation between chromosomes 9 and 22, termed t(9;22). More than 95% of cases of CML have Ph chromosome; the breakpoints are at the *BCR* gene on 22 and *ABL* gene on 9. The majority of Ph-negative CML cases have a translocation at the *molecular* level although abnormal chromosome morphology is not present.

Ph is also found in:

- 5% childhood ALL
- 25% adult ALL
- 1% adult AML

It carries a bad prognosis if found in these acute leukaemias. The protein product of the hybrid gene has protein tyrosine kinase activity.

Treatment of CML

The aims of treatment of CML are reduction of hypercatabolic symptoms and splenomegaly (clinical remission), normalisation of the blood count (haematological remission), disappearance of the Philadelphia chromosome from bone marrow cells (cytogenetic remission) and non-detectability of the *BCR/ABL* abnormal gene as measured by PCR (molecular remission).

Imatinib, an inhibitor of the abnormal tyrosine kinase enzyme produced by *BCR/ABL*, is the treatment of first choice and produces haematological remission in 90% of cases, cytogenetic remission in 60% and molecular remission in 20%.

Imatinib and interferon can inhibit the proliferation of Philadelphia-positive marrow precursors, allowing return of normal haematopoiesis. **Interferon** is associated with a high incidence of systemic side-effects including malaise, myalgia and arthralgia, and it has to be given by injection.

Drugs such as **hydroxycarbamide** and **busulfan** do not modify the underlying cytogenetic abnormality or prevent transformation into acute blast crisis, but may be used to normalise the blood count whilst confirmation of Philadelphia status is being obtained.

Quarterly PCR measurements of blood *BCR/ABL* are usually performed, with excellent cytogenetic response being defined as a three-log reduction in

BCR/ABL percentage, ie less than 0.1% (assuming 100% at presentation). Patients who are resistant to imatinib should be assessed for mutations of *BCR/ABL* associated with imatinib resistance and can be treated by newer tyrosine kinase inhibitors such as dasatinib or nilotinib.

The tyrosine kinase inhibitors are being trialled in the treatment of many other malignancies.

Bone marrow transplantation remains a curative option for young and fit patients who are not fully responsive to imatinib, but who have a suitable donor.

9.6.5 Chronic lymphocytic leukaemia (CLL)

This is the most indolent of the chronic leukaemias. Many cases are discovered as an incidental finding when blood counts are done for some other reason, such as health screening.

- Commonest cause of a lymphocytosis in the elderly
- 95% of cases are of B-cell lineage
- Diagnosis is confirmed by immunophenotyping – CD19- and CD23-positive B cells which express the T-cell antigen CD5
- Mature-looking lymphocytes and smear cells on the blood film
- Progression through lymphocytosis to lymphadenopathy, hepatosplenomegaly and marrow failure, though patients may skip stages in this progression
- Increased incidence of certain antibody-mediated autoimmune disorders such as warm autoimmune haemolytic anaemia and immune thrombocytopenia (in B-cell CLL)

Treatment of CLL

Many patients with CLL require no treatment, living at peace with their lymphocytosis to die of an unrelated complaint. Early antibiotic treatment of intercurrent infection is indicated because of the associated immunoglobulin deficiency, and some patients with recurrent infections may benefit from immunoglobulin administration, particularly during the winter months. Annual influenza immunisation should be given.

Chemotherapy is indicated for:

- Patients with bulky disease or B symptoms (see below)
- Cytopenias due to marrow infiltration
- A short lymphocyte doubling time

The most commonly used chemotherapy is single-agent oral **chlorambucil** or **fludarabine**. The latter is highly immunosuppressive, and *Pneumocystis* prophylaxis with co-trimoxazole should accompany its use. The MRC CLL 4 trial demonstrated that the most effective disease-shifting chemotherapy is a combination of cyclophosphamide and fludarabine.

- High-dose methylprednisolone is effective at shrinking enlarged lymph nodes and can be combined with rituximab (MabThera®) anti-CD20 antibody
- Another monoclonal antibody, alemtuzumab (Campath®) directed against the CD56 antigen is useful in cases with resistance to conventional chemotherapy or cytogenetic abnormalities associated with such resistance, particularly deletion of 17p. It is effective in clearing marrow-based disease but less so for lymph node disease. As the CD56 antigen is present on both T cells and B cells this treatment is very immunosuppressive and monitoring for cytomegalovirus (CMV) infection by blood PCR is appropriate
- Isolated enlarged lymph nodes can be treated with local radiotherapy
- Young patients who require treatment and who have a suitable donor may benefit from bone marrow transplantation with reduced intensity conditioning

The antibody-mediated autoimmune disorders are treated along conventional lines when they occur.

9.6.6 Hodgkin's disease (HD)

Prognosis of Hodgkin's disease is related to clinical stage (Table 9.5), bulk of tumour and histopathological type.

The clinical stage may be given the letter suffix A or B, to reflect presence or absence of symptoms:

- **A**: no 'B' symptoms
- **B**: B symptoms consist of significant fever (>38°C), night sweats (drenching) or weight loss of more than 10% in the last 6 months

Pruritus and alcohol-induced pain are not B symptoms, although they are useful indicators of relapse.

Table 9.5. Ann Arbor clinical staging of Hodgkin's disease

Stage I	One involved lymph node group
Stage II	Two nodal areas on one side of the diaphragm
Stage III	Lymph nodes on both sides of the diaphragm
Stage IV	Involvement of extranodal* tissues, such as liver or bone marrow

*The spleen is an 'honorary' lymph node, ie if involved this is not necessarily stage IV

Investigation

- Many patients have neutrophilia, thrombocytosis and anaemia of chronic disease; some patients have eosinophilia
- The ESR and other inflammatory markers are elevated
- Lactate dehydrogenase (LDH) is elevated and provides a useful guide to bulk of disease in high-grade lymphomas; 'bulky disease' is a node mass more than 10 cm in diameter
- Clinical examination and CT scanning are used to establish clinical stage; there is almost no role for staging laparotomy if suitable imaging facilities are available
- Residual masses are common after treatment and it is often difficult to decide whether or not they represent active disease. Positron emission tomography (PET) scanning using radioactive glucose helps distinguish tissue that is metabolically active. False-positive results may

be found if the PET scan is performed within 6 weeks of completion of chemotherapy due to healing activity within nodes

Histological types of Hodgkin's disease

The Reed–Sternberg (RS) cell is the most useful diagnostic feature. This is a giant cell, often with twin mirror-image nuclei and prominent 'owls eye' nucleoli. Histological typing depends on the other cells within the involved tissue:

- **Lymphocyte predominant**: there is an infiltration with reactive T lymphocytes
- **Nodular sclerosing (NS)**: bands of fibrous tissue separate nodules of the Hodgkin's tissue
- **Mixed picture**
- **Lymphocyte depleted**: no infiltrating lymphocytes

The prognosis worsens through the histological types from lymphocyte predominant (best) to lymphocyte depleted (worst). With the benefit of modern immunophenotyping methodology (which uses monoclonal antibodies) many cases of Hodgkin's disease that were historically classified as lymphocyte-predominant Hodgkin's disease are now recognised to be non-Hodgkin's lymphomas. More than two-thirds of cases of Hodgkin's disease are of the NS type; this category can be subdivided into grade I and grade II NS Hodgkin's disease, depending on the number of RS cells and other histological features.

Treatment

Clinical stage I Hodgkin's disease can be treated with radiotherapy, and later stages with combination chemotherapy. The dividing line depends on national and institutional preferences. The currently most used chemotherapy is ABVD which contains **a**driamycin, **b**leomycin, **v**inblastine and **d**acarbazine.

- Many relapsed patients can be salvaged with second-line chemotherapy and stem cell autografts, particularly if the relapse occurs more than 1 year after completion of initial treatment. The most popular second-line chemotherapy regimen is ESHAP (etoposide, cytosine, methylprednisolone and cisplatin)

9.6.7 Non-Hodgkin's lymphoma (NHL)

Despite several international reclassifications of the histology, the categorisation of non-Hodgkin's lymphoma (NHL) remains in a state of flux. For clinical purposes the NHLs are divided into three groups: indolent, high grade and lymphoblastic.

Indolent NHL

- The cells are relatively mature and the disease pursues an indolent course without treatment. In many cases it is acceptable to watch and wait for symptoms or critical organ failure
- Local radiotherapy to involved nodal regions is effective and is usually given in stage I disease (infrequent) as some patients can be cured by this treatment
- Rituximab (MabThera®) anti-CD20 monoclonal antibody therapy is effective as most cases are of B-cell lineage. It is commonly given with other chemotherapy regimens for both aggressive and indolent B-cell lymphomas, and its addition usually improves response by about 10%
- Single-agent chemotherapy (eg chlorambucil) is usually used for diffuse disease
- Interferon may prolong remission duration

High-grade NHL

- The cells are immature and the disease is rapidly progressive without treatment
- Combination chemotherapy is usual from the outset (eg CHOP regime: **c**yclophosphamide, adriamycin (**h**ydroxydaunorubicin), vincristine, (**O**ncovin®) **p**rednisolone)
- It is usual to give four to eight (3-weekly) courses, although bone marrow suppression may cause delay
- Maintenance therapy with rituximab (see above) may be used
- Multi-agent, alternating and hybrid regimes may be advantageous

Lymphoblastic NHL

- The cells of the disease are very immature and have a propensity to involve the CNS
- Treat as for ALL with CNS prophylaxis

High-dose therapy with haemopoietic stem cell rescue may salvage some younger patients with aggressive chemotherapy-responsive lymphomas.

Prognosis

Low-grade (indolent) lymphomas are readily controllable initially but relapse usually occurs even after many years of remission. Approximately 40% of high-grade lymphomas are cured.

9.6.8 Myeloma

In myeloma there is a clonal proliferation of plasma cells and the clinical manifestations of disease are related to substances secreted by the plasma cells as much as to the effects of marrow infiltration. **Clonality** (all diseased cells originating from one parent plasma cell) may be confirmed by either of the following:

- The presence of a paraprotein (monoclonal) band on serum electrophoresis
- Immunophenotyping the increased numbers of plasma cells in the bone marrow, and finding that they all express either κ or λ light chains rather than a mixture of the two

The incidence of the different types of myeloma is related to the relative number of molecules of the different immunoglobulins in the blood, ie because IgG is present in the highest concentration it is the most common type of myeloma, with IgA next and IgM myeloma the rarest.

Plasma hyperviscosity syndrome may be found when plasma viscosity exceeds 4 CpA. This consists of confusion, capillary bleeding, oedema and renal impairment. The incidence of hyperviscosity syndrome relates to the size of the immunoglobulin molecule as well as its concentration. As IgM is the largest molecule (750 000 daltons) this syndrome is seen relatively frequently in IgM myeloma, less frequently in IgA myeloma and rarely in IgG myeloma. However, see comment above regarding the relative incidence of the different types of myeloma. Transfusion should be avoided if possible in patients with plasma hyperviscosity syndrome, as it will cause a big increase in whole blood viscosity.

- **Cryoglobulin**: rarely, the paraprotein may be a cryoglobulin, so that the protein precipitates from plasma in the cold. This may be a cause of vasculitis. Do not confuse cryoglobulin with **cold agglutinin** – the latter has antibody activity against red cells causing them to agglutinate in the cold
- Some myeloma paraproteins precipitate within tissue to form amyloid

Bence Jones protein
Sometimes, the malignant plasma cells are so defective that they cannot make a complete immunoglobulin molecule and are only able to make light chains. The latter are small enough to be filtered within the glomerulus and to appear in the urine as Bence Jones proteinuria. They may obstruct the renal tubules and contribute to the renal failure which is often found in myeloma (*see* Chapter 15, Nephrology).

Role of cytokines in myeloma
Osteoclast-activating factors stimulate the normal osteoclasts to dissolve bone and lead to bone pain, hypercalcaemia and pathological fractures in myeloma. In other myeloma cases, IL-6 may be produced in excess by bone marrow stromal cells infected with human herpesvirus (HHV8).

Treatment of myeloma

In younger patients, most centres use continuous infusional low-dose combination chemotherapy such as VAD (**v**incristine, **a**driamycin and **d**examethasone) or ZDex (oral idarubicin and dexamethasone). Malignant cells are most sensitive to the action of chemotherapy when they are dividing; as plasma cells divide relatively infrequently, it is helpful to administer the chemotherapy over several days in order to maximise the chances of treating dividing cells.

Patients who respond are commonly consolidated with stem cell autografting, in which stem cells are mobilised into the peripheral blood during blood count recovery following cyclophosphamide chemotherapy, with the assistance of granulocyte macrophage colony stimulating factor (GM-CSF). Stem cells are harvested from the blood on a cell separator and frozen. They are transfused back to the patient after treatment with high-dose melphalan.

Older patients (over 70 years) are usually treated with oral single-agent therapy, such as the alkylating agents melphalan or cyclophosphamide. Locally painful areas, eg vertebral involvement, can be treated with radiotherapy. Many alkylating agents, such as melphalan, are toxic to stem cells and their use can preclude later stem cell mobilisation.

- **Thalidomide** has a proved role in myeloma treatment although its mechanism of action remains uncertain. It is likely to inhibit cytokine release, but an anti-angiogenesis activity is also possible. Because its use as a sedative anti-emetic in pregnancy resulted in the birth of many children with severe limb defects there is a strict programme of prescription control to prevent use in patients who might become pregnant. Side-effects of somnolence, constipation, peripheral neuropathy and skin rash can be troublesome, and a derivative of thalidomide, **lenalidomide**, has been developed with fewer of these side-effects, but its expense limits general use
- **Bortezomib** (Velcade®) is the newest chemotherapy agent used in relapsed myeloma. It targets the proteasome enzyme complex within the cell, encouraging apoptosis and inhibiting plasma cell adhesion
- **Bisphosphonates**, such as monthly intravenous pamidronate, have an important role in the prevention of pathological fractures and in the treatment of myeloma-associated hypercalcaemia

Prognosis

Almost all patients with myeloma will die of their disease, except for the small minority of young, fit patients who can access allogeneic stem cell transplantation after successful disease-bulk reduction. The median 5-year survival is about 35%. Prognostic factors include β2-microglobulin, serum albumin, percentage plasma cell infiltration in bone marrow, paraprotein level, creatinine, haemoglobin and platelet count. An international prognostic scoring system is available.

Monoclonal gammopathy of undetermined significance (MGUS)

A common clinical problem is the differentiation between myeloma and MGUS (benign monoclonal gammopathy) in patients found to have a paraprotein. Ten per cent of patients with MGUS develop myeloma at 5 years, and 50% at 15 years. It is probable that most patients would eventually develop myeloma but many die of other causes before this occurs. MGUS does not require treatment but needs monitoring as some cases turn into myeloma.

Differentiation of myeloma from MGUS

- **MGUS**
  - Low level of paraprotein (< 20 g/l for an IgG paraprotein)
  - Paraprotein level remains stable over a period of observation (months or years)
  - Other immunoglobulin levels are normal
  - No clinical evidence of myeloma (bone disease, renal disease)
- **Myeloma**
  - High level of paraprotein level rises
  - Other immunoglobulin levels are depressed
  - Clinical evidence of myeloma

9.6.9 Monoclonal antibodies in the treatment of haematological diseases

Monoclonal antibodies that are directed against various antigens on haemopoietic cells are now established in the treatment of a variety of haematological diseases (Table 9.6). In many cases these are being used on a trial basis. Such antibodies may be administered in their native state or after conjugation to cell poisons or radioactive isotopes.

9.6.10 Polycythaemia

Polycythaemia refers to an increase in red cell count, haematocrit and (usually) haemoglobin. There are two main types of polycythaemia, the classification depending on the results of measurement of red cell mass and plasma volume:

- **Relative (pseudo) polycythaemia**: due to a decrease in plasma volume
- **True polycythaemia**: the red cell mass is increased

True polycythaemia may be either primary or secondary.

Primary true polycythaemia

In the myeloproliferative disorder polycythaemia rubra vera (PRV), there is uncontrolled production of red cells by the bone marrow, even though erythropoietin is switched off.

- **Clinical features**: hypertension, splenomegaly, arterial and venous thrombosis, pruritus, plethoric features, peptic ulceration, gout
- **Laboratory features**: there is high red cell count, haemoglobin, haematocrit, whole blood viscosity and uric acid. The white cell count, platelet count and neutrophil alkaline phosphatase are also increased, and these last three parameters help to distinguish PRV from secondary polycythaemia. The majority of patients with primary polycythaemia have an acquired gene mutation, *JAK-2*, detectable by PCR on blood cells

Table 9.6. Monoclonal antibodies in haematology treatment

Antibody	Disease treated	Antibody specificity	Comments
Rituximab	B-cell non-Hodgkin's lymphoma	CD20	In routine use
Campath®	Immunosuppression in bone marrow transplantation	CD56	In routine use
	Lymphoproliferative disorders		CD56 is present on both T and B cells
Gemtuzumab	Acute myeloid leukaemia	CD33	Coupled to an anthracycline cell poison
Anti-D	Prevention of rhesus sensitisation in pregnancy	Anti-D	In trial – no risk of infectious disease transfer

Secondary true polycythaemia

This condition is associated with increased levels of erythropoietin, which is produced either by the kidney or by an ectopic tumour. Causes of secondary polycythaemia are given in Table 9.7.

Relative polycythaemia

A reduction in circulating plasma volume can be due to pyrexia, diarrhoea, vomiting and diuretic therapy.

Gaisböck's polycythaemia refers to a form of 'stress polycythaemia'; this has been noticed in middle-aged men who have stressful occupations, a chronically reduced plasma volume of uncertain cause.

Treatment of polycythaemia

Treatment is indicated for polycythaemia as high blood viscosity leads to an increased incidence of thrombosis, hypertension, stroke and atheromatous vascular disease.

The main treatment options are:

- **Venesection to a target haematocrit**: the packed cell volume is more closely related to the blood viscosity than is the haemoglobin (as repeated venesection may result in iron-deficient red cells with a low haemoglobin content). Venesection may be traditional or **isovolaemic** (with saline replacement). The latter is used in patients with cardiovascular risk factors (eg angina or hypertension), in those who are taking drugs that may impair physiological response to venesection (angiotensin-converting enzyme (ACE) inhibitors, β-blockers), or in patients with relative polycythaemia
- **Cytotoxic agents** (particularly hydroxycarbamide): this suppresses erythropoiesis and causes a macrocytosis that is not related to vitamin B_{12} or folate deficiency. Unlike other cytotoxic agents (eg busulfan) it does not appear to precipitate leukaemic change
- **Aspirin and anticoagulants**: if the patient presents with thrombosis

9.6.11 Thrombocytosis (platelets >500 × 10⁹/l)

Primary (essential) thrombocythaemia

In practice it is often difficult to distinguish between essential thrombocythaemia and reactive causes of thrombocytosis unless other markers of either a

Table 9.7. Causes of secondary polycythaemia

Increased renal erythropoietin production due to hypoxia		Inappropriate erythropoietin production	
Physiological:	Adaptation to altitude	**From the kidney:**	(eg pyonephrosis, renal cysts, renal artery stenosis after renal transplantation***)
Congenital cyanotic heart disease:	In neonates (eg tetralogy of Fallot, Eisenmenger complex)	**From a tumour (ectopic erythropoietin secreted in an uncontrolled fashion):**	(eg carcinoma of the kidney, giant uterine fibroids, hepatoma, cerebellar haemangioma)
Respiratory-related:	Smoking* COPD		
High-affinity haemoglobins:	(eg haemoglobin M**)		

* Inhaled carbon monoxide combines irreversibly with haemoglobin, forming carboxyhaemoglobin, which is unavailable for oxygen transport
** An abnormal structure of the globin chains decreases the ability of the haemoglobin to release oxygen to hypoxic tissues (including the kidney), so more erythropoietin is released
*** All these pathologies result in decreased oxygen delivery to the juxtaglomerular apparatus, either by increasing the pressure within the renal capsule or by reducing blood supply to the whole kidney

myeloproliferative disorder (polycythaemia, spleno-megaly, basophilia, increased bone marrow reticulin, cytogenetic abnormality) or hyposplenism (due to multiple splenic infarcts) are present.

It is often necessary to treat any potential cause of secondary thrombocytosis that may be present and see what happens to the platelet count over months.

Causes of secondary (reactive) thrombocytosis

- Bleeding
- Infection
- Trauma
- Thrombosis
- Infarction
- Iron deficiency (even if not due to bleeding)

9.6.12 Myelodysplasias (myelodysplastic syndromes – MDS)

This group of haematological malignancies is being seen with increasing frequency as the mean age of the population rises and general practitioners perform screening blood counts more frequently on their patients. As a group, they hang together less well than other haematological malignancies, but they do have the following features in common:

- More common in the elderly, but no age is exempt
- Cytopenias – anaemia most common, also leucopenia and thrombocytopenia or combinations of these
- Dysplastic changes seen in blood and bone marrow. These include hypogranular

neutrophils, abnormal neutrophil nuclear lobulation, changes in red cell precursors mimicking megaloblastic change ('megaloblastoid') with vacuolated erythroblasts and mononuclear megakaryocytes
- A monocytosis in the blood. This may be found in all the myelodysplastic disorders but is most marked ($>1 \times 10^9$/l) in chronic myelomonocytic leukaemia (CMML)
- Propensity to transform into acute myeloid leukaemia. This may be an acute transformation but usually takes a number of years
- Cytogenetic abnormalities as seen in AML may be seen in MDS. A rare variant of MDS with a relatively good prognosis is 5q minus syndrome found mainly in women with a normal or even high platelet count and deletion of part of the long arm of chromosome 5
- Mainstay of treatment is support – transfusion for anaemia, antibiotics for infection, platelet transfusion for bleeding

Classification of myelodysplastic syndromes

A classification of myelodysplastic syndromes is given in Table 9.8.

9.6.13 Bone marrow transplantation

Bone marrow or stem cell transplantation works by using a strong (myeloablative) treatment such as high-dose cyclophosphamide with total body irradiation to wipe out residual malignant disease. In addition, the donor's transplanted immune system may recognise malignant cells and destroy them – graft-versus-leukaemia (GVL) effect. The downside of GVL is that the donor immune system may attack the recipient's tissues, particularly liver, intestine and skin, causing graft-versus-host disease (GVHD).

Peripheral blood stem cells

In the rebound after marrow recovery from chemotherapy, stem cells appear in the peripheral blood. They can be made to appear in larger numbers by using growth factors such as granulocyte colony-stimulating factor (GM-CSF). They can then be harvested using a cell separator and frozen. Peripheral blood stem cells are further down the differentiation pathway to mature cells than marrow stem cells, so their use is associated with quicker haematological recovery than seen when bone marrow is used. The types of donor and stem cells used are shown in Table 9.9.

Table 9.8. Classification of myelodysplastic syndromes

MDS	Special features
Refractory anaemia	Dysplastic morphological features seen (see text) but difficult to diagnose in early stages
Refractory anaemia with excess of blasts (RAEB)	As above plus increased number of blast cells in marrow (5%–20%)
Refractory anaemia with excess of blasts in transformation to AML (RAEB-t)	As above but 20%–30% blasts in marrow
Chronic myelomonocytic leukaemia (CMML)	Monocytosis in marrow and blood leukaemia
Primary acquired sideroblastic anaemia	Ring sideroblasts in marrow

Table 9.9. Types of donor and stem cells used

Type	Advantages	Disadvantages
Autologous	Donor available!	Poor GVL, possibility of residual marrow disease being harvested and returned to patient
Syngeneic (identical twin)	Full-house HLA match – no GVHD	Reduced GVL effect
HLA-matched sibling	Controllable GVHD but some GVL	GVHD unpredictable
Matched volunteer unrelated donor	Available if no family match	GVHD unpredictable

GVHD = Graft-versus-host disease; GVL = graft-versus-leukaemia effect

The following are conditions in which a bone marrow allograft is a useful treatment if a matched sibling is available and the recipient is fit enough for the procedure:

- **Acute myeloid leukaemia**: in first or subsequent remission. However, if good prognosis, cytogenetics are present (see Section 9.6.2) and the patient is in remission after the first course of chemotherapy, then bone marrow transplant (BMT) may not be necessary
- **Acute lymphoblastic leukaemia**: in second or later remission unless adverse prognostic features (such as age beyond childhood or adverse cytogenetic abnormality) are present, in which case BMT should be performed in first remission
- **Chronic myeloid leukaemia**: in first chronic phase if imatinib does not induce complete cytogenetic response and a donor is available with a recipient fit enough for the procedure. BMT is also indicated when a patient who has suffered transformation reaches remission
- **Other indications**: BMT for thalassaemia major and sickle cell disease remains controversial
- **Others**, eg storage diseases

9.7 COAGULATION

9.7.1 The coagulation mechanism and detection of factor deficiencies

A representation of the coagulation cascades is shown in Figure 9.2. It consists of an **extrinsic pathway** (in which tissue thromboplastin plays an important part) and an **intrinsic pathway** (intrinsic to the blood itself – what happens when blood clots away from the body in a tube). These two pathways share a final **common pathway** resulting in the production of a fibrin clot.

The system can be divided into boxes, each box representing one of the following three basic screening tests of coagulation:

- **Prothrombin time** (PT) measures the extrinsic system and final common pathway
- **Activated partial thromboplastin time** (APTT) measures the intrinsic system and final common pathway. It is also known as the kaolin cephalin clotting time (KCCT) and the partial thromboplastin time (PTT), which are technical variations of the same test

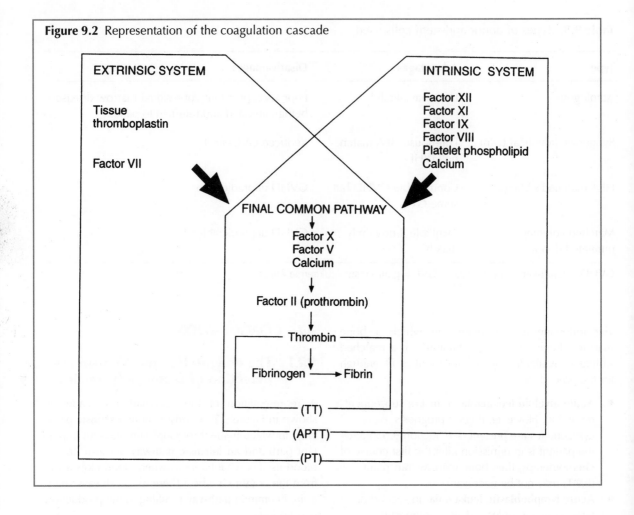

Figure 9.2 Representation of the coagulation cascade

- **Thrombin time** (TT) measures the final part of the final common pathway. It is prolonged by lack of fibrinogen to convert to fibrin, and by inhibitors of this conversion, including heparin and high levels of fibrin degradation products

If one of these screening tests of coagulation is significantly prolonged then it should be repeated using a mixture of 50% patient plasma and 50% normal plasma. If the cause of the prolonged time is factor deficiency then the abnormal time should correct more than halfway back to the control value. If it does not, this suggests the presence of an inhibitor such as the lupus anticoagulant. Figure 9.2 shows which factors should be assayed after finding a prolonged, correctable coagulation time. For example, an isolated prolonged APTT should prompt assay of the coagulation factors XII, XI, IX and VIII in the intrinsic system.

9.7.2 Haemophilia

This disease is characterised by deep muscular haematomas and haemarthroses with prolonged bleeding after trauma or operation. It is caused by a deficiency of clotting factor VIII (classical haemophilia A) or factor IX (Christmas disease) and is classed as severe if the factor VIII level is less than 1% of normal (<1 unit/dl).

There is a sex-linked inheritance but a third of cases have no family history, and are due to spontaneous mutation. Carriers may be detected as they have half the amount of clotting factor measured by a coagulation assay than they have measured by an immunological assay. Also, restriction fragment length polymorphisms (RFLP) can track the affected chromosome. Diagnosis is by prolonged APTT, with low factor VIII or IX. The range of treatments is shown in Table 9.10.

Complications of treatment include hepatitis, HIV, factor VIII antibodies and opiate addiction.

9.7.3 von Willebrand's disease

This is the commonest inherited coagulopathy in the UK. It is coded for on chromosome 12 – hence it shows an autosomal dominant inheritance pattern. It is caused by a quantitative or qualitative abnormality of von Willebrand factor (vWF) production. vWF is made in endothelial cells and forms variable-size polymers in plasma.

vWF acts as a protective carrier for factor VIII in the circulation and is responsible for gluing the platelets to exposed vascular subendothelium. Hence, the factor VIII coagulation factor level in vWD is often reduced but (in contrast to the haemophilias) the disease manifests as a platelet-type bleeding disorder, with bruising, superficial purpura, menorrhagia, nosebleeds and bleeding from cuts and mucous membranes.

Diagnosis

- Low factor VIIIc (c for 'clotting' activity, measured by a coagulation test)
- Low vWF Ag (von Willebrand factor antigen, measured in an immunological assay)
- Prolonged template bleeding time
- Deficient ristocetin-induced platelet aggregation

Ristocetin is an antibiotic that clumps platelets in normal plasma but fails to clump them in vWF-deficient plasma. The disease may be divided into types according to the size of vWF multimers present.

Treatment is with DDAVP® if mild, and with vWF concentrate. Many intermediate-purity factor VIII concentrates contain enough vWF for treatment; otherwise cryoprecipitate is used.

Table 9.10. Treatment of haemophilia

Treatment	Rationale
Viral inactivated coagulation factor concentrate	Should be given early in the course of a bleed, ideally home treatment
DDAVP® (a synthetic ADH analogue)	Releases factor VIII from storage sites in endothelial cells, so can temporarily boost blood level in mild haemophilia A
Fibrinolytic inhibitors (eg tranexamic acid)	Useful for bleeding wounds and tooth sockets but avoid in haemarthrosis, muscle haematomas and urinary bleeding as may lead to resolution by local fibrosis
Ancillary treatments (part of 'total haemophilia care')	Physiotherapy, hydrotherapy, immunisation against hepatitis B, dental and orthopaedic advice

9.7.4 Disseminated intravascular coagulation (DIC)

This disorder is caused by the release into the circulation of a pro-coagulant – something that makes the blood clot. There is massive activation of coagulation factors and platelets, with laying down of fibrin. This fibrin clot is immediately removed as the fibrinolytic system is also put into overdrive, worsening the haemorrhagic tendency.

The treatment is to remove the cause if possible, and transfuse with blood, platelets, fresh frozen plasma or cryoprecipitate.

Features and causes of disseminated intravascular coagulation (DIC)

- **Laboratory features of DIC**
  - Prolongation of all coagulation times (prothrombin, APTT and thrombin)
  - Activation of the fibrinolytic system leading to high fibrin degradation products
  - Thrombocytopenia
  - Microangiopathic blood film with fragmented red cells and helmet cells
- **Obstetric causes**
  - Retroplacental haemorrhage
  - Retained dead fetus
  - Amniotic fluid embolus
  - Severe pre-eclampsia
- **Other causes**
  - Crush injury
  - Septicaemia
  - Haemolytic transfusion reaction
  - Malignancy

9.7.5 Vitamin K-dependent coagulation factors (II, VII, IX, X)

Vitamin K is a fat-soluble vitamin essential for the carboxylation of inactive coagulation factors into their active functional form. These coagulation factors are manufactured in the liver, so levels are low in liver disease, obstructive jaundice and when there is fat malabsorption (loss of vitamin K). Levels are also low in the neonate due to liver immaturity – this can lead to haemorrhagic disease of the newborn, particularly when breast-fed. These coagulation factors are also reduced by warfarin anticoagulation. Deficiency causes prolonged prothrombin time and APTT.

9.7.6 Thrombocytopenia

There is overcapacity in haemostasis, including the platelet count (Table 9.11).

Young platelets tend to be relatively large and efficient compared with old platelets. Hence bleeding at a given platelet count is more severe in **underproduction** thrombocytopenia than in **peripheral destruction** thrombocytopenia. In the latter, the bone marrow produces more platelets and if the platelet count is $<50 \times 10^9/l$ an elevated reticulated platelet count is a useful marker of peripheral destruction, removing the need to examine the number of megakaryocytes in the marrow.

When thrombocytopenia is associated with other blood count abnormalities there is a wide differential diagnosis, including most of the haematological malignancies described in Section 9.6.

When it is associated with abnormalities of coagulation the differential diagnosis includes DIC (Section 9.7.4, above).

Table 9.11. Clinical risks of different platelet counts

Platelet count $\times 10^9/l$	Clinical effect
140	Start of normal range
100	Normal haemostasis, including surgery
50	Normal haemostasis unless challenged
20	Minor risk of bleeding
<10	Significant risk of bleeding

Isolated thrombocytopenia is usually the result of increased peripheral platelet destruction.

Causes of isolated thrombocytopenia

Artefactual: clot in the sample or platelet clumping. This can be confirmed by examination of the sample and the blood film. When platelets are clumped, sometimes a more accurate count can be obtained by using citrate or heparin-anticoagulated tubes, or by performing an 'instant' blood count with equipment located near to the patient.

Idiopathic or immune thrombocytopenia: very common (see below).

Drugs: heparin, abciximab, quinine, valproate, sulphonamides, DOPA, interferons. Suspected causative drugs should be stopped or changed if possible.

Hypersplenism: the spleen contains about a third of the circulating platelets and if the spleen is enlarged this can be associated with thrombocytopenia (*see* Section 9.9.1 for the causes of splenomegaly).

Gestational thrombocytopenia: platelet count is usually $>70 \times 10^9$/l and the patient is clinically well with no symptoms of pre-eclampsia or liver function abnormality. HELLP syndrome (**h**aemolysis with **e**levated **l**iver enzymes and **l**ow **p**latelet count, manifest as haemolytic anaemia with liver function abnormality and thrombocytopenia) is associated with pre-eclampsia and should be included in the differential diagnosis.

Immune thrombocytopenia (ITP)

This is the commonest cause of an isolated thrombocytopenia and it is an autoimmune disease. However, obtaining sufficient platelets to prove this is difficult, so a diagnosis of ITP is usually made in the absence of other causes. When the platelet count is $>100 \times 10^9$/l, without evidence of other disease, it is reasonable not to perform marrow examination but to observe the platelet count at follow-up (with decreasing frequency if it is stable). The following medical disorders are associated with ITP and they need to be excluded:

- Systemic lupus erythematosus
- Autoimmune haemolytic anaemia (Evans syndrome)
- Viral infection: HIV, EBV, hepatitis
- Antiphospholipid syndrome

Where the platelet count is $<20 \times 10^9$/l, or the thrombocytopenia is associated with significant bleeding, treatment is indicated and it is usual to examine the marrow to confirm normal or increased numbers of megakaryocytes. Sometimes the immune reaction is directed against the megakaryocyte, so marrow examination is most important for excluding other haematological disease as the cause of the thrombocytopenia.

Initial treatment is usually with prednisolone $(1 \text{ mg} \cdot \text{kg}^{-1} \cdot \text{day}^{-1})$ and may need to be continued for 1–3 months for maximum effect. The steroid dose is reduced as the platelet count rises. The aim of treatment is to obtain a haemostatic, not necessarily normal, platelet count. Azathioprine may have a useful steroid-sparing action.

For refractory cases other treatments are as follows:

Splenectomy: about two-thirds of patients benefit from splenectomy, either because this enables discontinuation of steroids, or because lower doses are then required to achieve a haemostatic platelet count. *See* Section 9.9 for post-splenectomy precautions.

High-dose intravenous immunoglobulin: will improve the platelet count in a few days but its effects are often short-lived; it is indicated prior to surgery and for emergency treatment.

Intravenous anti-D: Only applicable to the 80% of patients who are rhesus positive. The anti-D coats their red cells, which are preferentially destroyed by the spleen and reticuloendothelial system, sparing the platelets. A drop of 1–2 g in haemoglobin level is to be anticipated, but note that anti-D does not seem to be effective in splenectomised patients.

Rituximab: This anti-CD20 monoclonal antibody has an emerging role in the treatment of refractory cases.

9.8 THROMBOSIS

There are many well-recognised risk factors associated with venous thromboembolism, and in these situations it may be appropriate to take prophylactic measures.

Therapeutic ranges for warfarin anticoagulation

The necessary degree of anticoagulation will vary depending on the indication (Table 9.12) and whether the causes (eg bedrest, fracture) can be removed.

General clinical risk factors for venous thrombosis
• Increasing age
• Immobility
• Obesity
• Major abdominal and hip operations
• Oestrogen/contraceptive pill therapy
• Post-myocardial infarction or CVA
• Nephrotic syndrome
• Cigarette smoking
• Varicose veins
• Previous family history of thrombosis
• Cancer
• Trauma to the lower limbs
• Pregnancy and puerperium
• Diabetic hyperosmolar state
• Paroxysmal nocturnal haemoglobinuria
• Thrombophilia: see below

9.8.1 Thrombosis and the pill

Administration of oestrogen-containing pills:

• Increases fibrinogen and vitamin K-dependent coagulation factors
• Decreases antithrombin levels
• Gives a four times greater risk of thromboembolism

The risk of thromboembolism is increased by eight times if factor V Leiden is present – it is important to screen all women with a history of thrombosis if starting on the combined oral contraceptive pill.

Hormone replacement therapy is also associated with a small risk of thrombosis and patients with a previous history of thromboembolism should be screened for thrombophilia.

9.8.2 Thrombophilia

This may be defined as recurrent venous thromboembolism without any of the usual predisposing causes outlined above. Inherited or acquired prothrombotic abnormalities of the blood should be considered:

• Factor V Leiden mutation
• Protein S, C or antithrombin deficiencies
• Polycythaemia or other myeloproliferative disease
• Prothrombin gene mutations
• Lupus anticoagulant
• Hyperhomocystinaemia

Table 9.12. Indications for warfarin and the desired INR

Indication	INR
Treatment of deep vein thrombosis (DVT), pulmonary embolism (PE), systemic embolism, post-myocardial infarction (MI), mitral stenosis with embolism, transient ischaemic attacks, atrial fibrillation	2.0–3.0
Recurrent DVT and PE, arterial disease, including MI, mechanical prosthetic valves	3.0–4.5

Congenital causes of thrombophilia

The blood contains clotting factors that promote the formation of thrombus when activated. The blood also contains natural *anticoagulant* factors that inhibit the formation of clot. These factors are:

- Antithrombin
- Protein C
- Protein S

A congenital deficiency of these factors results in a tendency to thrombosis, so they should be tested for when screening for congenital thrombophilia.

Normally, activated clotting factor V is inhibited by the anticoagulant protein C. Approximately 3%–5% of Europeans have an abnormal structure to their clotting factor V caused by a single point mutation in the factor V gene. This means that protein C cannot bind to it and inactivate it. This abnormal factor V is called V Leiden, after its place of discovery, and it is found in 30% of patients with recurrent venous thrombosis. Screening for V Leiden may be done by PCR (looking for the abnormal gene) but this is expensive, so it is usual to screen using the activated protein C resistance test. In this test, protein C is added to the patient's plasma and an APTT is performed. In normal subjects the added protein C has an anticoagulant action, resulting in prolongation of the APPT. In a patient with factor V Leiden the added protein C cannot bind to activated factor V so the APTT coagulation time will not be prolonged by protein C.

Other causes of inherited thrombophilia include:

- Abnormal prothrombin molecule
- Dysfibrinogenaemia
- Fibrinolytic defects

Acquired causes of thrombophilia

- Polycythaemia and essential thrombocythaemia
- Lupus anticoagulant/antiphospholipid antibodies

Antiphospholipid antibodies and lupus anticoagulant, which are not always the same molecules, have a strong association with each other and with immune thrombocytopenia. Paradoxically, lupus anticoagulant, causing venous thrombosis, is detected by a prolonged coagulation test such as the APTT (or the more sensitive DRVT – **d**ilute **R**ussell **v**iper venom **t**ime). The coagulation times are prolonged because antiphospholipid antibodies neutralise phospholipids that are essential for the coagulation reaction. Although it may be found in patients with systemic lupus erythematosus (SLE), most patients with lupus anticoagulant do not have SLE. The disorder may present with recurrent venous thromboembolism or recurrent miscarriages. (*See also* Chapter 12, Maternal medicine.)

9.8.3 Therapeutic fibrinolysis

Therapeutic fibrinolysis

- **Action**
  - Conversion of plasminogen to plasmin, which dissolves fibrin to fibrin degradation products
- **Indications**
  - Early stage of myocardial infarction, young patient with proximal deep venous thrombosis (DVT, eg ilio-femoral), survivors of massive pulmonary embolism, peripheral arterial thrombosis
- **Drugs**
  - Streptokinase, urokinase, tissue plasminogen activator (tPA), anisoylated plasminogen streptokinase activator complex (APSAC)
- **Unwanted effects**
  - Bleeding
- **Reversal**
  - Administration of tranexamic acid, cryoprecipitate

9.8.4 Low-molecular-weight heparins (LMWH)

Conventional heparin is a mixture of different-sized polymers. Low-molecular-weight fractions can be separated by various chemical and physical methods. Low-molecular-weight heparin (LMWH) has a molecular weight of 5000 daltons, compared with 15 000 daltons for unfractionated heparin. LMWH has a strong anti-Xa and relatively weak antithrombin action compared with conventional heparin. It is claimed that this gives it more antithrombotic effect with less risk of bleeding. It certainly means that no significant prolongation of APTT is found, so this test is not used for monitoring therapy. Measurement of its anti-Xa effect is possible, though this is only necessary if prolonged treatment is required.

Advantages

- Long half-life – once or at most twice a day administration
- Laboratory assays are not required for short-term administration
- Less heparin-induced thrombocytopenia and osteopenia than conventional heparin

Disadvantages

- Expensive
- Different doses for different brands
- When given for more than a few weeks requires (relatively) complicated anti-Xa assay for monitoring

9.9 THE SPLEEN

9.9.1 Causes of splenomegaly

- **Myeloproliferative disorders**
  - Myelofibrosis
  - Chronic myeloid leukaemia
  - Polycythaemia rubra vera
  - Essential thrombocythaemia (splenic atrophy also common)
- **Portal hypertension**
  - Cirrhosis
  - Congestive cardiac failure
- **Infection**
- **Bacterial** (eg typhoid, *Brucella*, TB)
- **Collagen diseases**
- **Chronic haemolytic anaemias**
  - Autoimmune haemolytic anaemia
  - Cold haemagglutinin disease
  - Hereditary spherocytosis
  - Haemoglobinopathies
- **Lymphoproliferative disorders**
  - Most lymphomas
  - Chronic lymphocytic leukaemia
  - Hairy cell leukaemia
- **Viral** (eg glandular fever, hepatitis)
- **Tropical** (eg malaria, kala-azar)
- **Storage diseases**

9.9.2 Splenectomy

Often performed because of traumatic injury or haematological disease, this operation results in a characteristic blood film appearance and a well-recognised predisposition to sudden overwhelming bacterial infection with capsulated organisms such as *Pneumococcus* or *Haemophilus*.

Clinical indications for splenectomy

- **Traumatic rupture**: but surgeons may preserve splenic function by surgical repair of capsular tears, omental patches, and sometimes implantation of some splenic tissue in the retroperitoneum
- **Autoimmune destruction of blood cells**: immune thrombocytopenic purpura and warm autoimmune haemolytic anaemia after failure of steroid treatment
- **Haematological malignancies**: low-grade lymphoproliferative disorders associated with painful splenomegaly, hypersplenism and not much disease outside the spleen. Also sometimes performed in the myeloproliferative disorders, particularly in myelofibrosis when the enlarged or painful spleen is destroying more blood cells than it is producing
- **Congenital haemolytic anaemias**: such as hereditary spherocytosis and elliptocytosis and some cases of hypersplenic thalassaemia major
- **Staging of Hodgkin's disease and NHL**: this is no longer performed where adequate imaging is available (CT or MRI)

Haematological and immune changes after splenectomy

- **Howell–Jolly bodies**
  - Nuclear remnants in the red cells – the spleen is responsible for removing particulate material from red cell cytoplasm – pitting function
- **Enhanced neutrophilia** in response to infection
- **Target cells**, increased platelet count and occasionally spherocytes with increased aniso- and poikilocytosis
- **Decreased IgM level**

9.9.3 Causes of hyposplenism

- Splenectomy (see above)
- Sickle cell disease
- Coeliac disease
- Myeloproliferative diseases, particularly essential thrombocythaemia
- Congenital asplenism (rare)

Infection prophylaxis necessary in hyposplenism (recent UK working party report)

Pneumococcal vaccine, one dose of *Haemophilus influenzae* vaccine (Hib), and one dose of meningitis C vaccine are required at least 2 weeks before planned splenectomy; if the operation is unplanned then these should be given as soon as possible afterwards.

Postoperatively, prophylactic lifelong penicillin V 250 mg bd is necessary (or erythromycin if the patient is penicillin-allergic). Meticulous malaria prophylaxis is vital, including insect repellent and mosquito nets. A warning card and explanatory pamphlet is now available from the Department of Health.

The above applies to hyposplenic patients (eg adult sickle cell disease) as well as previously splenectomised patients (recognised by the film comment 'Howell–Jolly bodies' on routine blood count) who have not been taking prophylaxis. If penicillin prophylaxis is refused then they should keep a supply of amoxicillin at home.

9.10 BLOOD TRANSFUSION

9.10.1 Better blood transfusion

The recent UK government 'Better Blood Transfusion' initiatives have promoted the importance of reduced blood component use in several ways:

- Routine pre-admission assessment including blood count and correction of haematinic deficiencies before elective operations
- Establishment of maximum blood order schedules with agreed quantities of cross-matched blood being provided for specified operations. In general, if the chance of blood being needed for an elective operation is <30% then only a 'group and screen' should be performed
- Increased use of 'group and screen' with accelerated compatibility testing rather than the issuing of cross-matched blood for operations
- Adoption of lower haemoglobin thresholds for postoperative transfusion. There is usually no indication for red cell transfusion if the haemoglobin is over 10 g/dl. Transfusion is usually given if the haemoglobin is below 7 g/dl in otherwise fit patients or below 9 g/dl in patients with cardiovascular disease or aged over 70 years
- Intraoperative and postoperative red cell salvage and autologous transfusion

- Use of erythropoietin to stimulate erythropoiesis in diseases associated with anaemia, such as myelodysplasia, myeloma, myelofibrosis and advanced chronic kidney disease

9.10.2 Transfusion-transmitted infection

Periodically, transfusion-transmitted infections hit the headlines, resulting in patient's reluctance to accept blood products. The infection which is of most concern currently is **variant Creutzfeldt–Jakob disease** (vCJD or 'mad cow disease'), the prion protein of which is not destroyed by conventional heat-detergent viral inactivation processes. A screening test for carriers of this disease is being developed, although it is feared that introducing such a test may shrink the donor pool, as potential donors would not wish to have a test for a disease for which no treatment is currently available.

All cellular blood products issued by the UK blood service have been leucodepleted at source for some years so as to reduce the possibility of transmitting vCJD.

Leucocyte depletion at source has:

- Reduced the incidence of non-haemolytic febrile blood transfusion reactions due to HLA antigen sensitisation in recipients
- Decreased transmission of CMV to CMV-negative blood transfusion recipients
- Reduced the risk of third-party graft-versus-host disease caused by the transfusion of immunocompetent lymphocytes to immunodeficient recipients

Testing donations for transfusion-transmitted infection in the UK

- HIV antibodies – there remains a small risk of viral transmission from infected donors, when they donate in the 8-week period after HIV infection and before antibody production
- Hepatitis B surface antigen
- Hepatitis C nucleic acid (antigen)
- Syphilis screen
- Human T-lymphotropic virus (HTLV) antibody

- CMV antibody – (some donations only) to ensure enough CMV-negative products for transfusion to premature neonates and immunosuppressed patients who would be at risk of transfusion-transmitted CMV

9.10.3 Platelet transfusion in marrow failure

Platelet transfusion is usually administered when the platelet count is $<10 \times 10^9/l$ in cases of thrombocytopenia due to marrow failure after chemotherapy or radiotherapy. The platelet transfusion threshold may be reduced as a result of clinical criteria such as bleeding, fever, splenomegaly or planned operative procedures.

- Platelet transfusion should not be used in conditions with peripheral platelet destruction (eg idiopathic (immune) thrombocytopenic purpura (**ITP**)), where efforts should be directed to reducing platelet destruction with immunosuppression (except in cases of haemorrhagic emergency)
- Platelet transfusion is contraindicated in TTP and HUS as it will contribute to the microvascular occlusion in the brain and kidneys which is associated with these conditions
- Platelet preparations are obtained by the thrombocytopheresis of donors who have a high platelet count on the cell separator. One adult unit of platelets contains more than 2×10^{11} platelets
- Less commonly, the unit of platelets is prepared by pooling the platelets extracted from four to six units of fresh blood

Platelet refractoriness is defined as an increment of platelet count less than $20 \times 10^9/l$ 1 hour after transfusion of an adult dose (see above). This may be due to the following:

- Non-immune consumption (eg bleeding, DIC, hypersplenism)
- Immune consumption due to HLA antibodies directed against class I HLA antigens present on platelets (90%): give HLA-matched cell separator platelets and consider platelet-pheresis of relatives
- Immune platelet-specific antibodies (10%): use double doses of random platelets

9.10.4 Indications for the transfusion of fresh frozen plasma

Indications for transfusion of FFP

- Correction of multiple coagulation factor deficits as in DIC or after massive transfusion
- Correction of single coagulation factor deficiency where a heat-detergent virus-inactivated concentrate is not available
- Emergency correction of warfarin over-anticoagulation associated with bleeding, when II, VII, IX, X concentrate is not available and intravenous vitamin K would be too slow (a few hours)
- Treatment of TTP or HUS with or without large-volume plasma exchange

The 'formula replacement' of coagulation factors by FFP after large-volume blood transfusion (eg approximately 20% of the transfused volume being FFP) is no longer recommended – it is better to perform a coagulation screen and blood count, and to give FFP as required.

Chapter 10
Immunology

CONTENTS

Immunology

10.1 COMPLEMENT AND ITS ACTIVATION

This is a plasma protein sequence cascade triggered by one of three distinct pathways: classical, alternative or lectin-binding. Each pathway produces protein complexes capable of cleaving the C3 component into its active metabolites, C3a and C3b, which activate the terminal complement components to produce a membrane attack complex (MAC) capable of cell lysis.

The complement cascade slowly ticks over and is never completely inactive. This produces small quantities of active complement components. Positive feedback loops would be triggered and cause tissue damage if it were not for important regulatory components.

The biologically active complement products have three main effects:

- Opsonisation – mediated by C3b
- Chemotaxis and inflammation – mediated by C3a, C5a
- Cell lysis (MAC) – C5, C6, C7, C8, C9

10.1.1 Complement activation

All complement pathways are activated during infection (bacterial, viral, fungal) and it is unlikely that any particular pathway is predominant (Figure 10.1). The classical pathway is thought to be the most recently evolved, and is the only pathway to require antibodies for activation. The alternative and lectin-binding pathways can activate complement in the absence of antibody.

Classical pathway

- Initiated by antigen–antibody complexes containing IgM, IgG1, IgG2 or IgG3
- Components involved: C1q, C1r, C1s, C4, C2, C3
- The C4b2b complex cleaves and activates C3

Alternative pathway

- Initiated by the binding of C3b and factor B to polysaccharide components of cell walls (Gram-negative bacteria, pneumococci and yeasts)
- IgA is also a weak activator of this pathway
- Components involved: properdin, factor D, factor B, C3
- The C3bBb complex cleaves and activates C3

Lectin-binding pathway

- Initiated by bacterial cell wall mannose, which binds to mannose-binding lectin (MBL)
- Binding activates proteases (MASP1 and MASP2), which cleave C2 and C4
- C4b2b complex cleaves and activates C3

Figure 10.1 Complement activation pathways

10.1.2 Terminal membrane attack sequence

Components of C5, C6, C7, C8 and C9 join to form a rosette-like MAC. This structure forms on cell surfaces and will cause cell lysis unless specific inhibitors are present.

10.1.3 Regulating proteins

Classical pathway

- C1 inhibitor blocks C1s and C1r irreversibly
- C4-binding protein inhibits cleavage of C3

Alternative pathway

- Factor H, decay accelerating factor (DAF) and complement receptor 1 inhibit cleavage of C3

Others

- Factor I and membrane co-factor protein degrade C3b
- Anaphylotoxin inactivator degrades C3a and C5a
- The terminal sequence is regulated by homologous restriction factor (HRF), membrane inhibitor of reactive lysis (MIRL) and S-protein

10.2 COMPLEMENT DEFICIENCY

Inherited or acquired deficiencies of complement components or regulatory proteins can produce disease states. Although complement deficiency is common, most cases do not cause disease.

10.2.1 Deficiency of complement components

- Deficiencies of classical pathway components can produce disorders that resemble systemic lupus erythematosus (SLE). This may reflect impaired clearance of immune complexes
- C3 deficiency allows life-threatening infections by encapsulated organisms (eg pneumococci)
- Patients with deficiencies of the terminal complement proteins, C5, C6, C7, C8 or C9, are usually healthy but are unable to prevent *Neisseria* infections from becoming disseminated

10.2.2 Deficiency of regulatory proteins

- C1 inhibitor deficiency causes **hereditary angi-oedema**, in which there are recurrent acute episodes of non-inflammatory oedema mediated by vasoactive C2 fragments. Uncontrolled complement activation and consumption lead to low levels of C2 and C4. Danazol, a synthetic anabolic steroid, can raise levels of the inhibitor sufficiently to prevent attacks. Fifteen per cent of affected patients have normal levels of C1 inhibitor – but functional assays show it to be inactive in these cases
- **Paroxysmal nocturnal haemoglobinuria** occurs in patients who are unable to bind the regulatory proteins DAF, HRF or MIRL on their red cell surfaces. Spontaneous complement-mediated lysis of erythrocytes occurs

10.2.3 Acquired deficiency

Complement consumption in inflammatory disorders such as lupus nephritis can lead to low levels of C3 and C4. This is associated with an increased susceptibility to infection with encapsulated organisms such as *Pneumococcus*.

10.3 IMMUNOGLOBULINS

The actions of immunoglobulins include complement activation, stimulation of phagocytic cells and precipitation of antigen. Immunoglobulins are produced by B lymphocytes and secreted by plasma cells. They are made up of two identical light chains and two identical heavy chains joined covalently by disulphide bonds (Figure 10.2). Papain splits the Ig molecule into two **a**ntigen **b**inding **f**ragments (Fab) and one Fc fragment containing the complement fixation site.

IgG

The most abundant immunoglobulin in internal body fluids. Important in the secondary immune response. It is the only isotype to cross the placenta and the neonatal intestinal wall; levels fall at age 3 months as maternal IgG is catabolised.

- Fc portion activates complement by the classical pathway
- Four subclasses – differing in Fc portions of the heavy chains
- Molecular weight 150 000 daltons

IgA

The major immunoglobulin of seromucous secretions, produced predominantly in mucosa-associated lymphoid tissue (MALT). It is present in monomeric form in plasma but as a dimer in secretions. Levels are undetectable at birth but reach adult levels by puberty. Deficiency produces auto-immune disorders, chronic diarrhoea and respiratory infections.

- Activates the **A**lternative complement pathway
- Two subclasses – IgA1 and IgA2
- Molecular weight 160 000 daltons

IgM

A pentameric molecule, the main immunoglobulin of the primary immune response. It is very effective against bacteria which it agglutinates and then lyses by complement activation. It is undetectable at birth; adult levels are reached at 1 year of age.

- Secretion does not require T_H2 lymphocytes
- Includes blood group antibodies
- Molecular weight 750 000 daltons

Figure 10.2 IgG molecule showing heavy (H) and light (L) chains, constant (C) and variable (V) regions and the antigen-binding site. The fragments produced by the action of papain and pepsin are shown

IgD

- Monomer present on the B-cell surface and involved in B-cell activation
- Molecular weight 175 000 daltons

IgE

- Immediate (type I) hypersensitivity reactions
- Present on mast cells and basophils, but produced by plasma cells
- Molecular weight 190 000 daltons

10.3.1 Cryoglobulins

These are immunoglobulins (IgM, IgG or IgA) that precipitate when cooled to 4°C, and dissolve when reheated to body temperature. They may be monoclonal or polyclonal. Precipitation in small cool blood vessels within the peripheries and skin produces complement activation and inflammation. In high concentrations they may cause Raynaud's phenomenon, or vasculitis. Treatment of cryoglobulinaemia is of the underlying disorder, but may require corticosteroids, cytotoxic agents, plasmapheresis or monoclonal antibodies directed against B lymphocytes (rituximab).

Causes

- Essential (ie unexplained) – 33%
- Lymphoma

- Hepatitis C
- Paraproteinaemia
- Connective tissue disorders, particularly SLE

10.3.2   Cold agglutinins

These are IgM immunoglobulins which agglutinate red blood cells when cooled to between 0°C and 4°C. They may be monoclonal or polyclonal. The clinical manifestations are Raynaud's phenomenon, acrocyanosis and mild haemolytic anaemia.

Causes

- Idiopathic (mainly in the elderly)
- Bacterial infection (*Mycoplasma*)
- Viral infection (coxsackie)
- Lymphoma
- Paraproteinaemia

10.4   CELLS AND THE IMMUNE SYSTEM

10.4.1   Polymorphonuclear cells

Neutrophils, eosinophils and basophils. Their principal actions are phagocytosis and release of inflammatory mediators.

Neutrophils

- Stored in the bone marrow
- Rapidly released into the bloodstream in response to infection
- Surface receptors for IgG, IgA and complement components
- Their principal action is phagocytosis and destruction of bacteria

Basophils and mast cells

- Basophils circulate and mast cells are tissue-bound
- Surface receptors for C3, C5 and IgE
- Produce histamine, prostaglandins, leukotrienes and proteases

- Involved in the immune response to parasites
- Interaction of antigen with bound IgE produces immediate hypersensitivity

Eosinophils

- Commonly increased in patients with allergic disease
- Surface receptors for IgG, C3 and C5
- Also bind IgE but less avidly than mast cells or basophils
- Phagocytose antigen–antibody complexes

10.4.2   Lymphocytes

T lymphocytes

Characteristics of T lymphocytes

- 70%–80% of the total lymphocyte population
- Active in intracellular infections, tumour surveillance and graft rejection
- Precursors form in the bone marrow and undergo maturation in the thymus
- CD3 (part of the T cell receptor) is present on all T-cells
- CD4 is a glycoprotein that recognises major histocompatibility complex (MHC) class II antigens on antigen-presenting cells. It is present on the cell surface of T-helper cells and monocytes
- CD8 is a glycoprotein on cytotoxic T cells which recognises class I antigens on target cells

CD4 (helper) T cells only recognise antigen presented with class II MHC antigens (Figure 10.3). They make up 60% of the circulating T-cell population. Important in providing help for B-cell differentiation and type IV hypersensitivity. The following are subsets of CD4 cells:

- T_H1 **(helper) cells** support cell-mediated immunity. They recognise antigen presented by macrophages or other phagocytic cells and

when activated secrete interleukin-2 (IL-2) and interferon. They are suppressed by IL-10
- **T$_H$2 (helper) cells** support humoral immunity. They recognise antigen presented by B lymphocytes and when activated secrete IL-4, IL-5, IL-6 and IL-10, causing B-lymphocyte proliferation and secretion of IgG, IgA or IgE. They are suppressed by interferon

CD8 (cytotoxic) T cells make up 35% of the circulating T-cell population. They interact with cells expressing class I MHC antigens (eg virus-infected cells) and are crucial to the elimination of those cells (Figure 10.3).

B lymphocytes

- Initially formed in the bone marrow
- Further maturation in the spleen and lymph nodes
- Express immunoglobulin on the cell surface, but immature cells cannot secrete antibody
- Activation requires both antigen and T-helper cells. Some antigens, eg bacterial lipopolysaccharide, can activate B lymphocytes alone, but without T-helper involvement low-affinity antibodies are produced and immunological memory is poor

---

Figure 10.3 Antigen recognition by CD4 and CD8 T cells

CD4 T cells recognise antigen taken up by antigen-presenting cells

CD8 T cells recognise and kill virally infected cells

Natural killer cells

- Large granular lymphocytes
- Recognise and destroy cells bearing viral or tumour surface markers

10.5 TRANSPLANT IMMUNOLOGY

10.5.1 The major histocompatibility complex

The major histocompatibility complex (MHC) is an area on chromosome 6 (see Figure 10.4) containing the genes for HLA antigens and some complement components. The HLA antigens are important in the recognition of self, control of immune reactivity and graft rejection. There are three MHC classes:

- **Class I** (HLA A, B, C) are expressed as transmembrane peptides associated with β2-microglobulin. They are present on virtually all cells and, with antigen, signal to CD8 cytotoxic T cells that their carrier cell is a suitable target for destruction
- **Class II** molecules (HLA DR, DP, etc) are heterodimers of two α and two β chains. They are present on B cells, macrophages and some

endothelial cells. They signal to CD4 helper T cells, and protect their carrier cells from destruction by cytotoxic T cells
- **Class III** includes the complement proteins C4 and factor B

10.5.2 The immunology of transplantation

Graft rejection requires MHC antigens and can be mediated by several mechanisms (Table 10.1).

Privileged sites exist where rejection is rarely a problem even when there is no MHC matching:

- **Cornea**: avascular and does not sensitise the patient
- **Bone and artery**: even if the grafts die, they provide a structure for host cells to colonise

In the kidney, HLA DR and HLA B matching are the most important. After these, matching for HLA A, and to a lesser extent HLA C, produces only small improvements in graft survival. Heart and liver grafts survive well with immunosuppression with only limited matching (eg at one HLA site).

Figure 10.4 Major histocompatibility complex on chromosome 6

Table 10.1. Mechanisms of graft rejection

Rejection type	Timing	Mechanism
Hyperacute	Within minutes	Preformed antibody
Acute	Up to 10 days	CD8 lymphocytes
Acute late	After 10 days	Igs and complement
Late	Weeks, months, years	Immune complex deposition

10.6 HYPERSENSITIVITY

Hypersensitivity reactions are immune responses with excessive or undesirable consequences, such as tissue or organ damage. There are five types.

- **Type I: Anaphylactic or immediate**
  - *Antigen + cell surface IgE* (on mast cells and basophils) leads to release of vasoactive substances, histamine, leukotrienes, interleukins and chemotactic factors. Reactions usually occur within 30 minutes of exposure to antigen
  - *Examples:* asthma, atopy, some acute drug reactions
- **Type II: Antibody-dependent cytotoxicity**
  - *Cell-bound antigen + circulating IgG or IgM* antibody produce complement activation, phagocytosis, killer cell activation and cell lysis
  - *Examples:* transfusion reactions, rhesus incompatibility, Goodpasture syndrome, immune thrombocytopenia
- **Type III: Immune complex-mediated or Arthus reaction**
  - *Free antigen + free antibody* produce complement activation, platelet aggregation, chemotaxis and inflammation
  - In *antibody excess* the antigen–antibody complexes precipitate close to the site of entry into the body, activate complement and cause localised disease, as in farmer's lung, pigeon fancier's lung and allergic bronchopulmonary aspergillosis
  - In *antigen excess* the complexes remain soluble. They are cleared by binding to red blood cells via CR1 complement receptors.

If the classical complement pathway is deficient or becomes overwhelmed, immune complexes continue to circulate and are deposited in the small blood vessels of the kidneys, skin and joints. Complement is activated, producing both local tissue damage (eg glomerulonephritis) and systemic illness. The systemic features produced are those seen in serum sickness: pyrexia, lymphadenopathy, urticarial rash, swollen joints and hypocomplementaemia about a week after injection of foreign serum

- **Type IV: Cell-mediated or delayed-type hypersensitivity**
  - *Antigen (with class II MHC) + sensitised (memory) T cells* produce lymphokine release and T-cell activation. Reactions take 24 hours to develop
  - *Examples:* tuberculin reaction, Kveim test, contact dermatitis, graft-versus-host disease, graft rejection
- **Type V: Stimulatory**
  - *Antibody + cell surface receptor:* stimulates the receptor
  - *Example:* Graves' disease

10.7 CYTOKINES

Cytokines are low-molecular-weight peptides (10–45 kDa) with non-enzymatic biological activity. Produced by lymphocytes (mainly T cells), macrophages and fibroblasts, they include interleukins, interferons and colony-stimulating factors. The interleukin family is broadly divided into those with local (paracrine or autocrine) effects and those with systemic activity (IL-1, IL-6, tumour necrosis factor (TNF)), which produce fever, increased C-reactive protein (CRP) production and thrombocythaemia. They also mediate cytotoxic T-cell, natural killer (NK) cell and osteoclast activity.

10.7.1 Patterns of cytokine production

Cytokines produced by T-helper cells (Figure 10.5) and their patterns of production are shown in Table 10.2.

10.7.2 Therapeutic uses of cytokines

- **Interferon α**
  - Hepatitis B
  - Hepatitis C
  - Kaposi's sarcoma in acquired immunodeficiency syndrome (AIDS)
  - Hairy cell leukaemia
  - Cutaneous T-cell lymphoma
  - Recurrent or metastatic renal cell carcinoma
  - Condylomata acuminata

Figure 10.5 Cytokine production by T-helper cells

Table 10.2. Patterns of cytokine production

Immune response	Important cytokines	Derived from
Acute phase response	IL-1, IL-6, TNF	Macrophages
Cell-mediated immunity	IL-2, interferon	T_H1 helper cells
Antibody-mediated	IL-4, IL-5, IL-6, IL-10	T_H2 helper cells

- **Interferon β**
  - Relapsing/remitting multiple sclerosis or secondary progressive multiple sclerosis
- **Interferon γ**
  - Serious infections in chronic granulomatous disease
- **Granulocyte macrophage colony stimulating factor (GM-CSF)**
  - Correction of cytopenias, eg during chemotherapy
- **Interleukin 2**
  - Metastatic renal cell carcinoma

10.8 EICOSANOIDS

Eicosanoids are biologically active lipids synthesised in cells by the oxygenation of arachidonic acid. This is released from cellular lipid stores by the action of the enzyme phospholipase A_2. Omega-3 fatty acids, from fish oils, may act as an alternative substrate. There are two main enzymatic pathways:

- 5-lipoxygenase – producing leukotrienes
- Cyclo-oxygenase – producing prostaglandins and thromboxane (Figure 10.6)

10.8.1 Prostaglandins

- **PGD_2** is the major cyclo-oxygenase product of mast cells and produces some of the features of anaphylaxis: vasodilatation, bronchoconstriction and inhibition of platelet aggregation
- **PGI_2** (prostacyclin) is a potent vasodilator and inhibitor of platelet aggregation synthesised in vascular epithelium. Used therapeutically in primary pulmonary hypertension, haemolytic uraemic syndrome and severe Raynaud's disease
- **PGE_2** has predominantly immunomodulatory effects, inhibiting lymphocyte proliferation, cytokine production and neutrophil function

Non-steroidal anti-inflammatory drugs (NSAIDs) and aspirin inhibit cyclo-oxygenase (COX) and therefore reduce prostaglandin production. There are three isoenzymes of cyclo-oxygenase:

- COX-1 is a constitutive enzyme present in many tissues (constitutive genes are those that are continuously expressed without any regulation)
- COX-2 is predominantly induced at sites of inflammation
- COX-3 is present in brain and heart

Figure 10.6 The pathway of arachidonic acid metabolism

The NSAIDs that are more specific for COX-2 would be expected to have anti-inflammatory effects with fewer adverse gastrointestinal effects.

10.8.2 Leukotrienes

- **LTB$_4$** causes neutrophil chemotaxis, increases mucus secretion and modulates cell growth
- **LTC$_4$, LTD$_4$, LTE$_4$** increase vascular permeability, contract intestinal and bronchial wall smooth muscle, increase mucus production and modulate cell growth. These were previously known as slow-reacting substances of anaphylaxis

Leukotriene receptor antagonists are useful for the treatment of asthma (eg montelukast).

10.9 IMMUNODEFICIENCY

Primary immunodeficiency can be classified according to the parts of the immune system that are compromised:

- Complement deficiency
- Neutrophil disorders
- B-cell disorders
- T-cell disorders
- Combined B- and T-cell disorders

10.9.1 Complement deficiency

Disease may occur due to lack of complement components or their regulatory proteins:

- Hereditary angioedema due to C1 inhibitor deficiency
- SLE-like syndromes due to deficiencies of classical pathway components
- Paroxysmal nocturnal haemoglobinuria due to regulator protein defects
- Impaired response to encapsulated organisms (eg pneumococci) with C3 deficiency
- Impaired response to *Neisseria* infection with deficiency of terminal complement components

10.9.2 Neutrophil disorders

Allow recurrent infections with pyogenic bacteria, especially *Staphylococcus aureus*, but also some Gram-negative bacilli and fungi, such as *Aspergillus* and *Candida*. Treatment is with antibiotics.

Examples:

- **Chronic granulomatous disease**: normal phagocytosis but failure to kill the micro-organism intracellularly due to an X-linked defect of nicotinamide adenine dinucleotide phosphate (NADPH) oxidase
- **Chediak–Higashi disease**: normal phagocytosis but failure to kill the intracellular microorganism because lysosomes lack elastase and cathepsin G
- **Hyper IgE syndrome** (Job syndrome): impaired neutrophil chemotaxis
- **Myeloperoxidase deficiency**: associated with a susceptibility to systemic candidiasis
- **Lazy leucocyte syndrome**: defective responses to chemotactic stimuli
- **Leucocyte adhesion deficiency**: CD18 deficiency

10.9.3 B-cell disorders

These disorders lead to failure of antibody synthesis (hypogammaglobulinaemia or agammaglobulinaemia) and recurrent infections with pyogenic bacteria and fungi such as *Candida*. Where necessary, regular immunoglobulin infusions are used to maintain levels of circulating immunoglobulin.

Examples:

- **Common variable immunodeficiency** is likely to represent more than one disorder. The marrow contains normal numbers of immature B cells but there is a failure in maturation. Immunoglobulin levels vary from patient to patient. It is not familial
- **IgA deficiency** is the commonest isolated Ig deficiency in the UK (1 in 700), and is often asymptomatic. There is an increased susceptibility to giardiasis

- **Bruton's X-linked agammaglobulinaemia**. No circulating B cells are found. Usually presents between 3 months and 2 years of age

10.9.4   T-cell disorders

These disorders produce impaired cell-mediated immunity. There is an increased susceptibility to viruses, mycobacteria and fungi. Though common bacterial infections can be dealt with, infections with measles, vaccinia or even BCG immunisation can prove fatal. Malignancy is increased. Treatment may require bone marrow transplants or thymus grafts.

Examples:

- **DiGeorge syndrome**: primary, non-familial, T-cell deficiency due to a defect in the development of the thymus and third and fourth branchial arches. The parathyroids are absent, causing severe hypocalcaemia, and the usual presentation is with neonatal convulsions. Cardiovascular anomalies may also be present
- **Nezelof syndrome**: absent thymus, though there is often some B-cell involvement
- **Purine nucleoside phosphorylase deficiency**: prevents the development of T cells

10.9.5   Combined B- and T-cell disorders

- **Severe combined immunodeficiency** (SCID) is due in some cases to lack of the enzyme adenosine deaminase. It is autosomal recessive
- **Reticular dysgenesis**: lymphopenia, neutropenia and absence of monocytes
- **Ataxia telangiectasia**: an autosomal recessive disorder presenting in childhood with cerebellar ataxia and telangiectasia. There is defective cell-mediated immunity and low levels of IgE and IgA. Malignancy is increased due to defective DNA repair mechanisms
- **Wiskott–Aldrich syndrome**, due to lack of sialophorin, produces low IgM levels and impaired cell-mediated immunity. Malignancy is increased and there is thrombocytopenia,

lymphopenia and eczema. The disorder is X-linked

10.9.6   Acquired immunodeficiency

Humoral (immunoglobulin) deficiency

- **Drugs (unusual, idiosyncratic reactions)**
  - Gold (aurothiomalate)
  - Phenytoin
  - Penicillamine
- **Haematological malignancy**
  - Chronic lymphocytic leukaemia (CLL)
- **Protein loss**
  - Nephrotic syndrome
  - Protein-losing enteropathy

Cell-mediated immune dysfunction

- **Drugs (common and dose-related)**
  - Ciclosporin
  - Cytotoxic agents
  - Corticosteroids
- **Haematological malignancy**
  - Lymphoma
- **HIV/AIDS**
- **Malnutrition and old age**

HIV infects T-helper cells leading to a progressive fall in the number of CD4 T cells. The crucial immunological feature is impaired cell-mediated immunity with increased vulnerability to normally non-pathogenic organisms such as *Pneumocystis* but also viruses (cytomegalovirus (CMV), herpes simplex and Epstein–Barr virus (EBV)), fungi (*Candida*, *Aspergillus* and *Cryptococcus*) and protozoa (*Toxoplasma*). There is often an associated polyclonal activation of B cells and hypergammaglobulinaemia.

10.10   IMMUNISATION

There are several ways of enhancing the immune system to produce added protection against infection. Most are used prophylactically to prevent or reduce the severity of infection, but some can prevent the development of disease even after contact with the organism (eg rabies vaccine).

The benefits of immunisation depend on several factors:

- Likelihood of contracting disease: prevalence of disease, level of immunity in other individuals (herd immunity), presence of immunodeficiency
- Severity of disease
- Adverse effects: more common with preformed antibodies and live attenuated vaccines

10.10.1 Preformed antibodies

These are obtained from a previously infected individual, and they provide passive immunity. Used particularly in immunocompromised patients early after contact with infection and to inhibit the actions of bacterial toxins in tetanus, diphtheria and botulism. The transfer of maternal IgG to the fetus is an example of physiologically occurring protection by preformed antibodies. The antibody is catabolised, however, so protection against infection is temporary. When the source of antibody is a different species there is a risk of serum sickness with repeated doses (see box below for examples).

- Tetanus
- Rabies
- Hepatitis B
- Varicella
- Botulism
- Diphtheria

10.10.2 Killed organism vaccines

Immunisation with killed organism is effective against a variety of bacteria and viruses (see box below). Influenza vaccine is usually offered to those who would fare badly with infection, such as patients with chronic obstructive pulmonary disease (COPD), heart disease, chronic renal disease, the elderly and the immunocompromised.

- Cholera
- Polio (Salk)
- Pertussis
- Influenza
- Typhoid
- Rabies

10.10.3 Live attenuated vaccines

Live vaccines (see box below) are superior to killed vaccines. They deliver a larger sustained dose of antigen and produce a better immune response. Cytotoxic T-cell memory needs viral replication and is better acquired with live vaccine. The main concern is that attenuation may fail and actual infection occur, especially in the immunocompromised.

- BCG
- Mumps
- Vaccinia
- Rubella
- Measles
- Polio (Sabin)

10.10.4 Subunit vaccines

These are purified components of the infective organism (see box below). Only the antigens that produce a protective response are used so the vaccinated host is not challenged with other antigens that may have deleterious effects such as hypersensitivity. Immunisation against hepatitis B is reserved for high-risk groups such as health workers. Pneumococcal vaccination is important in asplenic patients and those with hypocomplementaemia.

- *Haemophilus influenzae* (HIB)
- *Streptococcus pneumoniae*
- *Neisseria meningitidis*
- Hepatitis B

Chapter 11
Infectious Diseases and Tropical Medicine

CONTENTS

Infectious Diseases and Tropical Medicine

11.1 CLASSIFICATION OF BACTERIA AND VIRUSES

11.1.1 Bacteria

Classification is largely based on microscopic appearance, staining characteristics and biochemical tests. For example, Gram staining differentiates bacteria based on differences in cell wall thickness and therefore retention of the stain. Some relevant bacteria are classified here; more clinical detail is given in other sections as infections affecting the systems are discussed.

Classification according to Gram staining and aerobic/anaerobic metabolism is shown in Table 11.1.

Table 11.1. Gram staining and aerobic/anaerobic metabolism

	Gram positive	**Gram negative**
Aerobic cocci	Staphylococci* (in clusters) Streptococci** (in chains) Enterococci	*Moraxella* *Neisseria* (eg *N. meningitidis*, *N. gonorrhoeae*, both Gram-negative diplococci)
Aerobic bacilli	*Listeria monocytogenes* *Nocardia* spp. *Corynebacterium diphtheriae* *Bacillus cereus*	*Enterobacter* *Escherichia coli* *Klebsiella* *Proteus* Salmonellae (including *S. typhi*) *Shigella* *Yersinia*
Anaerobic bacilli	Clostridia (including *C. difficile*, *C. perfringens*)	*Bacteroides*

*Staphylococci are further classified by the coagulase test, into *S. aureus* (coagulase-positive) and 'coagulase-negative staphs', often skin contaminants when grown in blood cultures, most commonly *S. epidermidis,* but can cause pathology. Staphs are mostly resistant to penicillins due to production of β-lactamases and are treated with β-lactamase-resistant penicillins such as methicillin and flucloxacillin, or with antibiotics including a β-lactamase inhibitor, such as co-amoxiclav. Methicillin-resistant *S. aureus* (MRSA) requires treatment with other antibiotics, including the glycopeptides **vancomycin** and **teicoplanin**, which are also active against other Gram-positive infections

**Streptococci are further classified by the type of haemolysis seen on blood agar: α, β, or γ haemolysis. Viridans-type streptococci are mostly α-haemolytic and commonly cause endocarditis. β-haemolytic streptococci (and others) are classified using Lancefield groups

The most important β-haemolytic streptococci are given in Table 11.2.

Table 11.2. Lancefield classification of β-haemolytic streptococci

Lancefield group	Name	Clinical relevance
A	*S. pyogenes*	Cellulitis Necrotising fasciitis Pharyngitis and tonsillitis Rheumatic fever (immunological reaction to pharyngeal infection) Glomerulonephritis (post-streptococcal infection, >1 week after infection) Scarlet fever (toxin-mediated)
B	*S. agalactiae*	Puerperal and neonatal sepsis (therefore treated if found on high vaginal swab in pregnancy)
D	Previously 'enterococci'	Includes *S. bovis*, which causes infective endocarditis associated with colonic cancer

Bacteria that are not identified by Gram stain are often diagnosed by serology or other stains (Table 11.3).

Table 11.3. Classification by serology or stains other than Gram stain

Obligate intracellular bacteria	*Chlamydia* *Coxiella* *Rickettsia* *Legionella*
No cell wall	*Mycoplasma*
Spirochaetes (coiled bacteria)	*Borrelia burgdorferi* *Leptospira* Treponemes (eg *T. pallidum*; syphilis)

11.1.2 Viruses

Knowledge of the herpesvirus family is required for MRCP. This includes herpes simplex virus 1 and 2 (HSV1 and HSV2), varicella zoster virus (VZV), cytomegalovirus (CMV), Epstein–Barr virus (EBV) and human herpesvirus 8 (HHV8). Diagnosis is by polymerase chain reaction (PCR) or serology. Their clinical associations are described in Table 11.4.

11.2 TREATMENT AND PREVENTION OF INFECTIONS

11.2.1 Antibacterial agents

Antimicrobial groups, their mechanisms of action, indication, side-effects and mode of excretion are given in Table 11.5 (*see also* Chapter 2, Clinical Pharmacology, Toxicology and Poisoning).

Table 11.4. Clinical associations of herpesviruses

HSV1	Initial infection may be asymptomatic or present with gingivostomatitis; leads to lifelong latency and recurrence as herpes labialis (cold sores)
HSV2	Genital herpes with lifelong latency and recurrences
	HSV 1 and 2 (1>2) cause aseptic meningitis or encephalitis, localised to the temporal lobes. Treatment is with aciclovir. In utero infection can cause severe malformations and neonatal infection has a high mortality
VZV	Primary infection is chickenpox (varicella) with an incubation period of around 14 days. The virus is then latent in the sensory ganglia Reactivation causes shingles (more common in immune compromise) Complications of chickenpox are more common in adults and include pneumonitis, especially in smokers. Permanent calcification can be seen on the chest X-ray. Cerebellar ataxia and meningo-encephalitis may be due to VZV
CMV	Primary infection is often asymptomatic (or causes a glandular fever-type syndrome, which may be complicated by Guillain–Barré or Bell's palsy) and seroprevalence is >80% by age 60. CMV is problematic if the individual becomes immune-suppressed, eg after transplant, chemotherapy or due to HIV infection. In HIV-infected individuals with low CD4 counts, CMV can cause sight-threatening retinitis, oesophagitis, colitis, hypoadrenalism, neuritis, CNS disease and cholangitis. Treatment is with antivirals, eg ganciclovir
EBV	Primary infection causes glandular fever (infectious mononucleosis; IM) and the virus is then latent in B cells, sometimes causing transformation to lymphoma. Adult seroprevalence is >90% and around 50% of acute infections cause symptomatic IM. It is associated with Burkitt's lymphoma and lymphoma in HIV, nasopharyngeal carcinoma and oral hairy leukoplakia (white lesions of the lateral tongue borders in HIV)
HHV8	Also known as 'Kaposi's sarcoma-associated virus,' this sexually transmitted virus is found in Kaposi's lesions in HIV and in endemic Kaposi's sarcoma. It is also associated with primary effusion lymphoma in immunosuppressed individuals

Table 11.5. Characteristics and use of the main groups of antibacterial agents

Antimicrobial group	Mechanism of action	Indications	Side-effects	Excretion
Penicillins (eg benzylpenicillin)	Block cell wall synthesis	Streptococci, respiratory infections, syphilis	Anaphylaxis, interstitial nephritis (rare), encephalopathy (rare)	Renal (adjust dose in renal failure)
Cephalosporins (eg ceftriaxone)	Block cell wall synthesis	Streptococci and Gram-negative infections Meningitis	Anaphylaxis	Renal (adjust dose in renal failure)
Quinolones (eg ciprofloxacin)	Inhibit bacterial DNA synthesis	Gram-negative infections, TB in combination, gastrointestinal infections	Hallucinations, psychosis, convulsions, tendon damage and inflammation	Renal and hepatic
Sulphonamides (eg sulfamethoxazole in co-trimoxazole)	Inhibit enzymes converting para-aminobenzoic acid (PABA) into folic acid (anti-folate)	Co-trimoxazole in *Pneumocystis pneumonia* prophylaxis and treatment. Sulfadiazine in combination for toxoplasmosis	Agranulocytosis, bone marrow suppression, Stevens–Johnson syndrome	Hepatic
Tetracyclines (eg doxycycline)	Inhibit bacterial protein synthesis	Respiratory infections, *Rickettsia*, Q fever, malaria prophylaxis	Photosensitivity, renal impairment, deposition in growing teeth and bones, dental hypoplasia	Renal
Macrolides (eg erythromycin)	Inhibition of bacterial protein synthesis	Gram-positive infections, atypical pneumonias, *Mycobacterium avium* (clarithromycin, in combination)	Thrombophlebitis, cholestatic hepatitis	Hepatic (some renal; reduce in severe renal failure)

(continued)

Table 11.5. *(continued)*

Antimicrobial group	Mechanism of action	Indications	Side-effects	Excretion
Aminoglycosides (eg gentamicin)	Inhibit bacterial protein synthesis	Gram-negative infections, synergistic action in streptococcal endocarditis	Ototoxicity, renal tubular damage (monitor levels to avoid toxicity)	Renal
Glycopeptides (eg vancomycin)	Inhibit cell wall synthesis	Gram-positive infections, MRSA, *C. difficile* (vancomycin)	Nephrotoxicity, ototoxicity, 'red man' syndrome (vancomycin)	Renal

11.2.2 Other agents used to counteract infection

Immunoglobulins

Normal human immunoglobulin has many applications, particularly in passively immunising patients with humoral immunodeficiency. Kawasaki disease (possibly due to an infectious agent) is one application. There are also specific immunoglobulins for specific situations (eg tetanus, rabies, diphtheria, hepatitis B and varicella zoster immunoglobulin).

Vaccines

The UK vaccination schedule aims to provide protection for children against the following infections:

- Diphtheria
- Tetanus
- Pertussis
- *Haemophilus influenzae* type b
- Polio
- *N. meningitidis* serogroup C
- Measles
- Mumps
- Rubella
- *S. pneumoniae*

Immunisation of individuals with chronic medical conditions

HIV infection: Inactivated vaccines are given according to schedule although response may be sub-optimal. Some live vaccines (BCG, oral polio) are contraindicated in HIV infection. Others (yellow fever, MMR, varicella) are given only if the individual is asymptomatic and the current CD4 count is >200 cells/mm^3.

Chronic respiratory, heart, renal, liver disease and diabetes: Annual influenza vaccine; single pneumococcal vaccine.

(*See also* Chapter 10, Immunology.)

11.3 INFECTIONS IN SPECIFIC SITUATIONS

11.3.1 Pregnancy and congenital infections

Infections exacerbated by pregnancy

- Urinary tract infection
- *Salmonella* spp.
- *Listeria*
- Varicella (pneumonitis is life-threatening, especially in third trimester)
- Hepatitis E (25% mortality)
- Falciparum malaria

Other infections important in pregnancy

Transplacental transmission may lead to fetal damage.

- *Rubella:* Adults may be symptomatic of infection, with headache, fever, upper respiratory symptoms and a rash. First trimester infection leads to congenital rubella syndrome, with deafness, cataracts and patent ductus arteriosus. Some have less severe features initially but may have developmental delay
- *Toxoplasmosis: Toxoplasma gondii* is transmitted from ingestion of oocysts from cat faeces, with seroprevalence up to 35% in the UK. Infection in early pregnancy can cause miscarriage and in later pregnancy chorioretinitis, intracerebral calcification, mental and psychomotor retardation, jaundice and fever
- *CMV:* Asymptomatic in pregnant women, CMV infection infects 30%–40% of fetuses, causing disease in few. It may cause intracerebral calcification, hepatosplenomegaly, retinitis and pulmonary infiltration
- *Varicella (chickenpox):* Infection in early pregnancy causes congenital varicella syndrome, with limb hypoplasia and scarring of dermatomes. Pregnant women with varicella have a higher risk of pneumonitis. If a pregnant woman is exposed to varicella and is unsure of her history, serum should be tested for varicella IgG and, if negative, varicella zoster immunoglobulin (VZIG) can be given to prevent infection
- *Parvovirus B19:* First trimester infection causes fetal anaemia, hydrops fetalis and fetal death

11.3.2 Intravenous drug use

- **Endocarditis**: Repeated injection into veins carries a risk of right-sided endocarditis. Infections in intravenous drug users can be polymicrobial; often *Staphylococcus aureus*, less commonly streptococci and enterococci. Tricuspid valve endocarditis can lead to septic embolisation into the pulmonary circulation, causing pneumonia with patches of consolidation in both lungs (which may

cavitate). *See* Section 11.5.4, Cardiac infections and Chapter 1, Cardiology
- **Blood-borne viruses**: Sharing of needles or any other equipment leads to transmission of HIV, hepatitis B and hepatitis C. Almost half of intravenous drug users in the UK have been infected with hepatitis C. A positive hepatitis C PCR test is required to diagnose current infection (a positive antibody test only indicates exposure). (*Also see* Chapter 6, Gastroenterology)
- **Soft tissue infections**: Infections at injection sites, such as groin abscesses, are common, as is limb cellulitis and there is a risk of gas gangrene (*see* Section 11.5.5, Soft tissue infections)
- **Clostridial infections**: Although more commonly seen in other groups, disease due to Gram-positive bacilli, *Clostridium botulinum* and *C. tetani*, has recently increased in incidence among intravenous drug users
- **Botulism**: *C. botulinum* produces a toxin, which causes the clinical syndrome of botulism. It is usually transmitted through food contaminated with the toxin. However, wound botulism can occur in intravenous drug users when the toxin is produced at the wound site. It causes an acute, descending (unlike Guillain–Barré), symmetric, flaccid paralysis affecting primarily cranial and autonomic nerves. The incubation period (IP) is usually 12–72 hours and presenting symptoms may be blurred vision, diplopia, weakness, vomiting or urinary retention, progressing to respiratory failure requiring ventilation. There may be ophthalmoplegia and specific muscle weakness. Diagnosis is by detection of toxin and treatment with antitoxin and antibiotics (penicillin and metronidazole)
- **Tetanus**: Tetanospasmin is the toxin produced by *C. tetani*, which travels via motor neurones to the central nervous system (CNS) where it blocks neurotransmitter release. *C. tetani* is a soil commensal and tetanus is often seen in the elderly or other individuals who have not been immunised. The IP is 3–21 days. Trismus (lockjaw) may be followed by restlessness, irritability, dysphagia, opisthotonus (extreme

hyperextension of the neck, back and lower limbs caused by spasm of skeletal muscles) and seizures. Diagnosis is clinical, plus culture of the organism. Treatment is with anti-tetanus immunoglobulin, wound debridement if required and intravenous benzylpenicillin for 10 days. Vaccination is by three doses of tetanus toxoid as a primary course, and then repeat doses every 10 years until five doses in total have been given

11.3.3 Splenectomy

The spleen accounts for approximately 25% of all lymphatic tissue; absence of its function causes particular vulnerability to systemic infection with capsulate organisms such as:

- *S. pneumoniae*
- *H. influenzae*
- *N. meningitidis*
- *Capnocytophaga canimorsus*, a Gram-negative bacillus characteristically acquired from dog bites

Splenectomised patients are also vulnerable to malaria and to **babesiosis** *(Babesia* spp.), a protozoal infection transmitted by ixodid ticks (as is Lyme disease, *see* Section 11.8.2) from an animal reservoir comprising small rodents. It is found in Europe and the US. Babesiosis causes a mild malaria-like disease in the immunocompetent, but is potentially life-threatening in splenectomised individuals. Diagnosis is by blood film.

Vaccinations and prophylaxis in splenectomised individuals

- Vaccination against *H. influenzae* type b, *N. meningitidis* group C and *S. pneumoniae* is recommended, as is an annual influenza vaccine
- Antibiotic prophylaxis with penicillin (or erythromycin if allergic) is required until at least age 16 or for at least 2 years following splenectomy. Appropriate malaria prophylaxis is vital if travelling to an endemic area

11.3.4 Sickle cell disease

Sicklers (ie SS homozygotes) often have functional hyposplenism and also a reduction in complement-mediated serum opsonising activity. This gives rise to vulnerability to:

- Pneumococcal infection (and other encapsulated organisms such as meningococci)
- Other forms of bacterial sepsis – pneumonia and meningitis in particular
- Osteomyelitis (due to *Salmonella* spp.)
- Morbidity and mortality from falciparum malaria, which precipitates haemolytic and infarctive crises (in contrast to AS heterozygotes, who are relatively resistant to malaria)
- Parvovirus B19 can cause life-threatening aplastic anaemia in sickle cell homozygotes

11.4 SYSTEMIC INFECTIONS AND SEPSIS

11.4.1 Sepsis

- Sepsis is defined as the association of systemic inflammatory responses with evidence of (or suspicion of) a microbial origin. In the absence of infection, eg in pancreatitis, this syndrome may be referred to as systemic inflammatory response syndrome (SIRS). 'Severe sepsis' is the above plus hypoperfusion or dysfunction of at least one organ system and 'septic shock' is all of the above plus hypotension refractory to fluid resuscitation
- Shock is the result of a cascade of inflammatory mediators such as tumour necrosis factor (TNF) and interleukin-1 (IL-1) and the origin is usually bacterial, although often not confirmed by culture
- There are some host factors conferring susceptibility to sepsis of particular cause: deficiency of mannose-binding lectin is associated particularly with pneumococcal sepsis; terminal complement deficiencies are associated with meningococcal sepsis; agammaglobulinaemia predisposes to

pneumococcal and *H. influenzae* type B sepsis; immunological defects associated with sepsis include Chediak–Higashi syndrome (autosomal recessive), leucocyte adhesion molecule deficiency and Job syndrome (hyperimmunoglobulin E syndrome)

- Early antibiotic treatment and supportive care are the mainstays of management. International guidelines recommend goal-directed therapy in the first 6 hours, sending samples for culture and providing broad-spectrum antibiotic cover within 1 hour, low-dose hydrocortisone in septic shock, consideration of activated protein C for patients with severe sepsis and high risk of death, a target haemoglobin of 7–9 g/dl and good glycaemic control

11.4.2 Toxic shock syndrome

- Toxic shock has been associated with tampon use in menstruating women, but can be due to other staphylococcal foci, eg surgical wound infection. Toxin-producing *Staphylococcus aureus* (producing eg toxic shock syndrome toxin-1 (TSST-1) or enterotoxin B) is usually implicated but a similar syndrome can follow infection with exotoxin-producing streptococci
- **Clinical features**: Fever, diffuse macular rash (followed by desquamation after 1–2 weeks), hypotension, plus evidence of multiorgan involvement such as vomiting or diarrhoea, renal failure, thrombocytopenia or altered mental state
- **Diagnosis**: Organisms may not be identified on culture and so treatment is on suspicion and exclusion of other causes of shock, eg meningococcaemia
- **Treatment**: Flucloxacillin, plus clindamycin, which may inhibit toxin production, with supportive care

11.5 INFECTIONS OF MAJOR SYSTEMS

11.5.1 Respiratory infections

Most respiratory conditions are covered in Chapter 19 on respiratory medicine. Some specific infections are covered here. For mycobacterial infections, *see* Section 11.6.

Infectious mononucleosis

(*Also see* Section 11.1.2, viruses.)

Infectious mononucleosis (IM) (also known as glandular fever) is caused by EBV, which is transmitted by saliva. Asymptomatic viral shedding is common and the IP is 30–45 days. Symptoms are sore throat, fever and malaise, with signs of exudative tonsillitis, lymphadenopathy and sometimes splenomegaly or a widespread maculopapular rash. An associated EBV hepatitis can cause jaundice. Treatment with ampicillin (for presumed streptococcal infection) causes a maculopapular rash. Possible complications include thrombocytopenia, haemolytic anaemia, traumatic rupture of an enlarged spleen and, rarely (<1%), Guillain–Barré syndrome, cerebellar ataxia, aseptic meningitis, encephalitis, pneumonitis, pericarditis or lymphoma.

Diagnosis

IM causes a lymphocytosis, with atypical lymphocytes seen on the blood film, positive monospot (Paul–Bunnell) test for heterophile antibodies, and increased transaminase and bilirubin levels if there is associated hepatitis. Specific tests for EBV are also positive, including antiviral capsid IgM in recent infection.

Treatment

There is no specific treatment. Steroids are given if tonsillitis threatens airway obstruction.

Differential diagnosis of glandular fever

Includes acute CMV, toxoplasmosis, primary HIV infection, plus other causes of pharyngitis such as group A streptococcal infection or diphtheria

Diphtheria

Corynebacterium diphtheriae is a spore-forming Gram-positive bacillus that can produce an exotoxin. It is transmitted by respiratory droplets. It is very rare in the UK due to the vaccination schedule which includes diphtheria vaccination along with tetanus, polio, *Haemophilus influenzae* type b and pertussis at 2, 3 and 4 months of age with booster doses later in childhood. It occurs more frequently in countries with lower vaccination coverage.

The IP is 2–5 days and infection presents with fever, lymphadenopathy, soft tissue oedema, giving a 'bull neck' appearance and a membranous pharyngitis; the 'pseudomembrane' may cause airway obstruction. In vaccinated individuals, milder infection may resemble streptococcal pharyngitis. The toxin can rarely cause paralysis and heart block or cardiac failure.

Diagnosis

Culture from throat swab or PCR for the gene encoding the exotoxin.

Treatment

Antitoxin, plus IV penicillin or erythromycin (if penicillin-allergic). Vaccinate if this has not previously been done. Notify public health authority.

'Atypical' pneumonia

This term is usually applied to pneumonias not conforming to a lobar pattern and 'typical' clinical features (symptoms and signs of acute lower respiratory tract infection, fever, focal chest signs and, if diagnosed in hospital, radiological features) and includes pneumonia caused by the following organisms:

- *Mycoplasma pneumoniae*
- *Legionella pneumophila*

- *Chlamydia pneumoniae*
- *Chlamydia psittaci* (psittacosis)
- *Coxiella burnetii* (Q fever)

Investigations for these infections differ from those for 'typical' pneumonia in that the organisms are not cultured from blood or sputum. Serological tests are required, ideally acutely and during convalescence, demonstrating an increasing antibody titre due to the infection.

Urinary antigen detection is useful for *L. pneumophila*, particularly as it can give a rapid diagnosis.

For Q fever, *see* Section 11.8, Important zoonoses.

Clinical features of pneumonia are described in Chapter 19, Section 19.3.1.

11.5.2 Neurological infections

Infections of the **brain and spinal cord** can cause focal, space-occupying lesions, meningitis or encephalitis. The **peripheral nerves** are less susceptible to direct bacterial infection (with the exception of leprosy). Most bacterial infections that affect peripheral nerves do so by the action of specific toxins (eg botulinum, diphtheria). Some viruses (particularly enteroviruses, eg poliovirus) can damage peripheral nerves.

Meningitis

Acute meningitis presents with headache, fever and meningism. The level of consciousness is normal unless there is encephalitis. Urgent treatment (ceftriaxone or cefotaxime) is required for bacterial meningitis and UK guidelines now recommend glucocorticoid treatment (dexamethasone) with antibiotics; evidence is strongest for benefit in pneumococcal meningitis. Meningococcal disease may be in the form of meningitis or septicaemia or both. In meningococcal septicaemia the diagnosis is made by blood culture and/or blood PCR for *Neisseria meningitidis*. Coagulopathy due to disseminated intravascular coagulation (DIC) may preclude lumbar puncture.

Common causes of acute bacterial meningitis in adults are *N. meningitidis* (meningococcus), *Streptococcus pneumoniae* (pneumococcus) and *Haemo-*

philus influenzae. Listeria monocytogenes is an important, though less common, cause in the elderly or very young and ampicillin should be added to cover this for adults over 55 years old. (*See* Section 11.1.1 for Gram-staining characteristics.) Spread from local ear, nose or throat infections is often implicated in pneumococcal meningitis.

Cerebrospinal fluid (CSF) characteristics in meningitis are given in Table 11.6.

Other causes of meningitis

- **Viral meningitis** due to:
  - Enteroviruses (coxsackie A and B, echoviruses)
  - Herpesviruses (HSV1 and 2, EBV, VZV)
- More rarely:
  - Characteristically **with lymphocytic cerebrospinal fluid (CSF)**
    - Leptospirosis (*Leptospira* spp.)
    - Syphilis (*Treponema pallidum*)
    - Lyme disease (*Borrelia burgdorferi*)
    - Fungal meningitis (eg *Cryptococcus neoformans, Histoplasma capsulatum*)

- Characteristically **with polymorphs in CSF**
  - *Mycobacterium tuberculosis* (less common than chronic lymphocytic type; acute onset with CSF polymorphs)
  - *Staphylococcus aureus*
- Acute viral
  - Mumps, enteroviruses (eg polio)
  - Measles

Note on prophylaxis of contacts

Antibiotic prophylaxis with rifampicin (licensed) or ciprofloxacin (unlicensed) is offered to close (household) contacts of an individual with meningococcal disease or to those who have had contact with respiratory droplets/secretions at the time of admission to hospital, eg staff involved in airway management

Encephalitis

Encephalitis is inflammation of the brain parenchyma, often due to infection. The level of consciousness is therefore altered. In the UK, the commonest cause is HSV (1>2), which is treatable with aciclovir.

Table 11.6. CSF characteristics in meningitis

	Appearance	Cells	Glucose	Protein	Organisms
Acute bacterial	Cloudy, turbid	Neutrophils	↓	↑	On Gram stain/culture
Viral	Clear	Lymphocytes ↑	↔	↑ or ↔	Not seen
Tuberculous	Cloudy/turbid	Lymphocytes ↑	↓	↑↑	On Ziehl–Neelsen stain/culture
Cryptococcal*	Clear	Lymphocytes ↑	↑ or ↔	↑ or ↔	India ink

* Often high opening pressure

Clinical features

There may be fever and headache with focal (often temporal lobe) signs, or seizures or coma.

Diagnosis

By PCR of CSF. The EEG may show abnormalities in the temporal lobes and magnetic resonance imaging (MRI) may show enhancement of the temporal lobes.

Treatment

Prompt treatment with aciclovir reduces mortality from up to 70% to around 25%. It also reduces long-term neurological disability. In studies of aciclovir treatment 38% of patients recovered to normality or minor neurological impairment, 9% had moderate impairment and 53% severe impairment or death.

Causes of encephalitis

- **Viral**
  - Herpes simplex (high mortality/morbidity, mainly type 1)
  - Enteroviruses, flaviviruses (eg Japanese encephalitis, West Nile)
  - VZV
  - HIV
  - Rabies
- **Others**
  - Toxoplasmosis
  - African trypanosomiasis

Space-occupying lesions

Brain abscesses

Often with an identifiable route of infection, such as recent surgery, parameningeal infection (otitis media, sinusitis, dental abscess) or metastatic spread from, for example, endocarditis, suppurative lung disease or congenital heart disease with right-to-left shunt.

Organisms

Often mixed, including one or more of: *Staphylococcus aureus*, *Streptococcus milleri* group, coliforms, *Streptococcus pneumoniae*, *Haemophilus influenzae*, *Pseudomonas aeruginosa*, anaerobes.

Treatment

Broad-spectrum initially, eg cephalosporin plus metronidazole, then antibiotic therapy guided by results of aspiration.

Parasitic lesions

Neurocysticercosis (*see* Section 11.7.7), neuroschistosomiasis (*see* Section 11.7.4), hydatid (*see* Section 11.5.3, Liver).

Other focal lesions

Toxoplasmosis or cryptococcoma in the immunecompromised; tuberculomas.

(*See also* Chapter 16; Neurology.)

11.5.3   Gastrointestinal infections

Bowel

The majority of gut infections cause diarrhoea (Table 11.7); as a general rule, small-bowel infection usually manifests as toxin-mediated watery diarrhoea with no blood whilst large-bowel infections (with exceptions) are invasive of colonic mucosa and may cause bloody diarrhoea with mucus and sometimes pus – 'dysentery'. (*See also* Chapter 6, Gastroenterology.)

- Food poisoning should be notified to public health on suspicion. Other notifiable diseases include malaria, meningococcal disease, measles, enteric fever, TB, viral hepatitis, tetanus and diphtheria

E. coli O157

Verotoxin-producing; may lead to epidemics of haemolytic uraemic syndrome.

Amoebiasis

See Section 11.7.3.

Giardiasis

The protozoon *Giardia lamblia* causes a minority of travellers' diarrhoea. It is transmitted by ingestion of cysts from faecally contaminated water or person to person. The IP is 3–20 days and symptoms may persist for several weeks. Initially causing diarrhoea,

Table 11.7. Organisms causing vomiting and/or diarrhoea

Symptom	Organisms	IP	Source
Vomiting	*Bacillus cereus*	1–6 hours	Toxin from rice or meat
	Staphylococcus aureus	2–7 hours	Toxin from dairy or meat products
Diarrhoea	*Escherichia coli* (enterotoxigenic)	12–72 hours	From milk, salads, water (major cause of travellers' diarrhoea)
	Campylobacter jejuni	1–10 days	From meat, especially poultry, dairy products
	Salmonella spp.	8–48 hours	From eggs, poultry
	Shigella spp.	12–96 hours	Faecal contamination
	Yersinia enterocolitica	3–7 days	From pork, dairy products

symptoms may progress to nausea, cramps, abdominal pain, bloating and burping. Some individuals develop chronic diarrhoea with significant weight loss.

Diagnosis: Cysts seen on stool microscopy or trophozoites seen on biopsy of small-bowel mucosa.

Treatment: Tinidazole (2 g single dose) or metronidazole (eg 2 g daily for 3 days; different regimens vary from 3 to 10 days) plus supportive treatments.

Tropical sprue

Also known as post-infective malabsorption. *E. coli*, *Klebsiella* and *Enterobacter* spp. are implicated in causing this chronic (>2 months) malabsorption of nutrients, which may lead to haematinic and protein deficiency states. It is mostly found in South and South-East Asia.

Cryptosporidiosis

A protozoal infection (*Cryptosporidium parvum*), which causes watery diarrhoea. The IP is 2–14 days. It occurs in water-borne epidemics worldwide but may cause severe, prolonged, watery diarrhoea in the immune-suppressed, particularly HIV-infected individuals. There is no reliable antimicrobial therapy and, in HIV, treatment is aimed at restoring T-cell levels with antiretroviral therapy. Nitazoxanide has some effect in the immune-competent and may be considered in the immune-suppressed, although evidence is weak.

Diagnosis: Red cysts on Ziehl–Neelson staining of stool.

Antibiotic-related diarrhoea and *C. difficile*

Older age, antibiotic use (particularly clindamycin, co-amoxiclav, cephalosporins) and use of proton-pump inhibitors predispose to antibiotic-associated diarrhoea. It is mostly due to toxin-producing *C. difficile*, growth of which is increased by the reduction in normal bowel flora. *C. difficile* is a spore-forming, anaerobic bacterium. Spores are found in hospital environments and are secreted by affected patients or asymptomatic individuals. Severe disease can cause pseudomembranous colitis, toxic mega-colon and perforation. A high leucocyte count and low albumin are typical.

Diagnosis: Toxin is detected in stool

Treatment: Metronidazole (oral or IV) or vancomycin (oral). Infection control measures are vital.

Liver

Amoebic liver abscess

- *See* Section 11.7.3.

Hydatid disease

Echinococcus granulosus is a dog tapeworm. Ingested eggs from contact with dogs or contamination of food hatch into larvae and penetrate the bowel wall into the portal bloodstream. They mature into liver cysts and can also disseminate to other sites, eg lung, brain. Liver cysts present insidiously as a liver mass. Rupture can cause life-threatening anaphylaxis and cysts must not be aspirated due to the risk of spreading the protoscolices around the body. People working with dogs or sheep farming may be at risk.

Diagnosis: Liver ultrasound, serology.

Treatment: Surgical removal of the cysts (with care not to spill contents into the abdominal cavity, as this can cause recurrence) and anthelmintic drugs; albendazole/mebendazole, praziquantel pre- and postoperatively. Asymptomatic cysts may not need treatment.

Leptospirosis

This zoonotic spirochaete infection is transmitted by contact with the urine of infected mammals (dogs, rats) through broken skin, usually in contaminated water. There is often a history of occupational (sewage or agriculture workers) or recreational (fishing, water sports) exposure. *Leptospira interrogans* is one species, of which serovar *icterohaemorrhagiae* is one responsible for disease from rats. The IP is 7–12 days.

Clinical features: Usually headache, fever, myalgia, rigors and neck stiffness for 4–5 days due to leptospiraemia. Some recover after this phase, but for others as the organism localises and causes vasculitis and capillary injury, further fever, suffused conjunctivae, aseptic meningitis (*Canicola fever*) and jaundice with renal impairment and proteinuria (*Weil's disease*) follow. Some have cardiac involvement with arrhythmias or cardiac failure. There is typically a neutrophilia, raised creatine kinase (CK) and lymphocytic CSF.

Diagnosis: Culture of blood/CSF/urine, serology, PCR.

Treatment: Penicillin, tetracycline with supportive measures.

(*See* Section 11.8 for other zoonoses.)

Viral hepatitis

See Chapter 6, Gastroenterology.

11.5.4 Cardiac infections

Infective endocarditis

Infective endocarditis is most commonly caused by bacterial infection affecting damaged or prosthetic heart valves, particularly streptococci which colonise the mouth and upper respiratory tract. For example, viridans-type streptococci, a group including *S. sanguis* and *S. oralis*, are the commonest cause of native valve endocarditis. Organisms may originate from dental disease or intravenous lines. Streptococcal endocarditis presents more indolently than staphylococcal endocarditis. Right-sided, staphylococcal endocarditis occurs in intravenous drug users, as above. The HACEK group of organisms (**H**aemophilus *aphrophilus* and *paraphrophilus*, **A**ctinobacillus *hominis*, **C**ardiobacterium *hominis*, **E**ikenella *corrodens*, **K**ingella *kingae* and *denitrificans*) are fastidious Gram-negative organisms that less commonly cause endocarditis. Diagnosis of infective endocarditis can be made using the Duke criteria (see box; the importance of positive blood cultures in diagnosis and treatment means that samples must be taken before antibiotics are given).

Cases are 'definite' if they fulfil two major criteria, one major and three minor, or five minor; 'possible' if they fulfil one major and one minor or three minor criteria:

Major criteria
• **Microbiological** • Typical infective endocarditis organism from two separate blood cultures (viridians-type streptococci, *Streptococcus bovis*, HACEK group, *Staphylococcus aureus*, community-acquired enterococcal bacteraemia without obvious source) OR • Organism consistent with infective endocarditis from persistently positive blood cultures OR • Single positive blood culture for *Coxiella burnetii* or serology positive for *C. burnetii* *Continues...*

Continued...
- **Cardiological**
  - New valvular regurgitation
  OR
  - Positive echocardiogram

Minor criteria

- Predisposition to infective endocarditis (intravenous drug use, cardiac abnormality)
- Fever
- Vascular phenomena
- Immunological phenomena
- Positive blood cultures not meeting major criteria

Treatment

Until an organism is known, and unless staphylococcal infection is suspected, IV benzylpenicillin with synergistic doses of gentamicin can be given. Duration of treatment depends on the organism; for some cases (eg uncomplicated streptococcal disease) 2 weeks of intravenous antibiotic may be sufficient.

Possible causes of 'culture-negative' endocarditis

If blood cultures are negative and there is a strong suspicion of infective endocarditis, consider causes of culture-negative infective endocarditis such as *Coxiella burnetii, Chlamydia psittaci, Brucella* spp., fungi, *Bartonella* spp., *Legionella* spp.

Antibiotic prophylaxis

Prophylaxis is indicated for individuals with rheumatic heart disease, congenital heart disease, history of valve repair, prosthetic valves or other cardiac surgery who are having procedures such as dental extraction, upper respiratory tract surgery or genito-urinary tract procedures. Amoxicillin is sufficient for most cases.

Pericarditis and myocarditis

Pericarditis and myocarditis present with chest pain and typical widespread, concave ST elevation on the ECG. They are caused by viruses, including enteroviruses (eg coxsackie A and B and echoviruses). Pericarditis may be caused by bacteria in individuals with severe septic illness or by *Mycobacterium tuberculosis*, often in combination with pulmonary tuberculosis.

Rheumatic fever

Rheumatic fever is very rare in the UK, but occurs in developing countries. It is an immunological response to group A streptococcal infection. Although not a cardiac infection in itself, it is included here because of its association with later risk of endocarditis and initial carditis which may include valvular disease.

Diagnosis can be made according to the Jones criteria, by the presence of evidence of streptococcal infection plus either two major criteria or one major and two minor criteria as shown in the following box.

A Evidence of recent group A streptococcal infection

- Positive throat swab culture or streptococcal antigen test
- Elevated or rising streptococcal antibody titre

B Major manifestations

- Carditis
- Polyarthritis
- Chorea
- Erythema marginatum
- Subcutaneous nodules

C Minor manifestations

- Arthralgia
- Fever
- Elevated acute phase response (C-reactive protein (CRP) or erythrocyte sedimentation rate (ESR))
- Prolonged PR interval in ECG

Q fever

For Q fever, *see* Section 11.8, Important zoonoses.

11.5.5   Soft tissue infections

Staphylococcus aureus and *Streptococcus pyogenes* (Lancefield group A β-haemolytic streptococci, as in Table 11.2) are mainly responsible for community-acquired soft tissue infection in otherwise healthy patients.

Necrotising fasciitis

This is an acute necrotising infection of the skin, subcutaneous tissues and superficial fascia. It may involve muscle. Clinically there is soft tissue erythema or dusky appearance with severe pain. Risk factors are diabetes, advanced age, obesity and intercurrent illness. It is often a mixed infection, with *Streptococcus pyogenes,* anaerobes and coliforms. It requires **aggressive surgical debridement** as well as antibiotics (covering anaerobes, Gram-negatives and streptococci; clindamycin may have benefit in inhibiting production of streptococcal toxins). Fournier's gangrene is a type of necrotising fasciitis involving the male genitalia.

Clostridial gas gangrene

Muscles are involved in this infection with *Clostridium perfringens* or other clostridia. There is systemic illness and gas in the tissues. It often follows trauma or surgery with wound contamination. The organisms are anaerobic and so impaired perfusion increases risk of disease. Urgent debridement is required.

11.6   MYCOBACTERIAL INFECTIONS

11.6.1   Tuberculosis (TB)

Mycobacterium tuberculosis disease, although most commonly pulmonary, can affect any organ. *M. tuberculosis* can also produce latent infection, said to affect a third of the world population, with the potential to reactivate and cause disease years later.

Transmission is by respiratory droplets from an individual with smear-positive ('open') TB. Globally, TB control has been hampered by the HIV pandemic, which increases the risk of TB disease by impairing cell-mediated immunity. Other risk factors include contact with a known case of pulmonary TB, history of living in an institution (eg prison) and originating from a country with high incidence of TB disease.

Note on drug-resistant tuberculosis

Multidrug-resistant (MDR) TB is defined by resistance to at least isoniazid and rifampicin. It occurs if treatment has been wrongly prescribed, intermittent or incomplete. The highest proportions of drug resistance among tuberculosis cases are found in Eastern Europe, Russia and Asia

Diagnosis

The mainstay of diagnosis is identification of acid and alcohol-fast bacilli (AAFBs) in sputum, fluid (eg pleural fluid, pus) or tissue by Ziehl–Neelsen or auramine staining and by culture to confirm *M. tuberculosis* (rather than a non-tuberculous or opportunistic mycobacterium) and to establish drug-susceptibility. Culture is on Löwenstein–Jensen solid medium or in liquid culture media, in which mycobacteria grow more quickly, allowing faster confirmation of diagnosis. PCR is increasingly being used on some samples (sputum, CSF). Rapid PCR-based tests for genes conferring drug resistance can give a prompt indication of susceptibility. A test for genes conferring rifampicin resistance is a useful indicator of possible MDR TB, as rifampicin monoresistance is rare.

Interferon γ tests

These blood tests measure the release of IFN-γ in the laboratory in response to antigens found only in *M. tuberculosis* (and not BCG or mycobacteria other than tuberculosis (MOTT)). They are used to differentiate latent TB from a positive Mantoux test due to previous exposure or vaccination. IFN-γ testing is recommended for those who would be considered for treatment of latent TB infection, eg those planning to receive anti-TNF α for rheumatological conditions, in whom TB reactivation is a risk.

Treatment

Drug-susceptible TB is treated with rifampicin and isoniazid for 6 months, adding pyrazinamide and ethambutol for the first 2-month intensive phase ('*RIPE*'). The exception is CNS TB disease in which case the total treatment is 12 months, with a 2-month intensive phase and a 10-month continuation phase (*see* Section 11.5.2 for CSF values in TB meningitis). Pyridoxine (vitamin B_6) can be added to prevent peripheral neuropathy due to isoniazid. Antituberculous drugs are given in Table 11.8.

Steroids in TB treatment

The addition of glucocorticoids is currently recommended for meningeal and pericardial TB.

BCG vaccination

BCG vaccination contains live attenuated *Mycobacterium bovis*. UK BCG policy no longer recommends vaccination at age 10–14; since 2005, the policy is targeted vaccination of high-risk individuals. Those for whom BCG is recommended include:

- Neonates born in, or with parents or grandparents from, an area with TB notification rates >40/100 000 per year
- Neonates with a recent family history of TB
- Mantoux-negative (tuberculin skin test) close contacts of those with active TB
- Mantoux-negative new entrants to the UK, aged <16, from an area with notification rates >40/100 000
- Unvaccinated, Mantoux-negative individuals at occupational risk (eg health care workers)

BCG is contraindicated in:

- Immunocompromised individuals, eg receiving oral steroid treatment, HIV infection, haematological malignancies

Table 11.8. Antituberculous drugs

	Pharmacokinetics	Side-effects	Use
Rifampicin	Potent liver enzyme inducer – interactions with HIV drugs, methadone, steroids, anticoagulants	Drug-induced hepatitis, orange secretions, influenza-like syndrome	TB, meningococcal prophylaxis, staphylococcal infections, *Legionella*
Isoniazid	Potentiates phenytoin, carbamazepine	Peripheral neuropathy, hepatitis	TB (treatment and prophylaxis)
Pyrazinamide	Good meningeal penetration (for TB meningitis)	Liver toxicity, arthralgia, gout	TB
Ethambutol	Renal excretion – reduce dose in renal failure	Reduced visual acuity, colour blindness (*monitor vision on treatment*)	TB and other mycobacteria
Streptomycin	Avoid in renal failure	Nephrotoxic, ototoxic	Drug-resistant TB (as part of combination)

11.6.2 Opportunistic mycobacteria

Also called non-tuberculous, atypical or 'mycobacteria other than tuberculosis' (MOTT), this group includes mycobacteria other than *M. tuberculosis* complex (which includes *M. tuberculosis, M. africanum* and *M. bovis*). Some clinical associations of commoner opportunistic mycobacteria are given in Table 11.9.

Diagnosis

UK guidelines for management of these infections give guidance on assessing the significance of a laboratory isolate, depending on the sample from which it is cultured, the number of isolates, degree of growth and the patient's clinical condition. Those with established, chronic lung disease, such as emphysema, bronchitis or cavitation from previous TB are at increased risk of opportunistic mycobacterial disease, as are the immunocompromised, for example those with HIV infection. Pulmonary disease is diagnosed when two specimens, at least 7 days apart, are isolated from a patient whose chest X-ray is consistent with mycobacterial disease, with or without symptoms or signs.

Treatment

Treatment is with combinations of antimycobacterial drugs, depending on the site of disease, HIV status of the patient and the organism isolated. Treatment regimens are longer than for TB and may be up to 2 years or longer if a patient remains immunosuppressed or continues to have positive cultures.

Mycobacterium avium complex

This subgroup of opportunistic mycobacteria includes *M. avium, M. intracellulare* and a few other minor species, but is usually referred to as 'MAC' or MAI (*Mycobacterium avium intracellulare*). These are ubiquitous environmental organisms and are not acquired by person-to-person spread.

In immunocompetent people MAC can cause pulmonary infection in one of two patterns:

- Disease resembling tuberculosis in elderly smokers with chronic lung disease
- Nodular infiltrates and a bronchiectasis-like pattern in those without chronic lung disease ('Lady Windermere syndrome') with a productive cough but no systemic symptoms

Paediatric infection can cause lymphadenopathy.

Table 11.9. Clinical associations of commoner opportunistic mycobacteria

Pulmonary disease resembling tuberculosis	*M. kansasii*
	M. malmoense
	M. avium complex
	M. xenopi
	M. fortuitum
Lymphadenitis	*M. avium* complex
	M. malmoense
	M. scrofulaceum
Cutaneous disease	*M. marinum* (fish-tank granuloma)
	M. ulcerans (Buruli ulcer)
	M. fortuitum
Disseminated disease	*M. avium* complex (particularly in advanced HIV infection)
	M. kansasii

Since the start of the HIV pandemic, MAC is commonly seen in HIV-infected individuals with low CD4 counts. It causes systemic symptoms, fever and sweats. A full blood count may show pancytopenia. It can be cultured from blood or bone marrow in addition to sputum and stool. Primary prophylaxis with azithromycin is recommended for those with a CD4 count below 50 cells/mm^3 until the CD4 count is improved by antiretroviral therapy. MAC is treated using combinations of antimycobacterial drugs as above.

Mycobacterium leprae

For *Mycobacterium leprae, see* section 11.7.5, Leprosy.

11.7 SPECIFIC TROPICAL INFECTIONS

11.7.1 Malaria

Four *Plasmodium* species commonly affect humans: *Plasmodium falciparum, P. vivax, P. ovale* and *P. malariae (P. knowlesi* is increasingly recognised as a human infection in South-East Asia). *P. falciparum* is the only one of these four to cause severe disease, and therefore the majority of deaths. All are transmitted by female *Anopheles* mosquitoes, which require blood for the development of their eggs and all can be transmitted by blood transfusion. Worldwide, the majority of malaria mortality is in sub-Saharan Africa, but it occurs throughout the tropics. IPs vary between species: for *P. falciparum* the IP is usually 7–14 days, but may be longer. IPs are longer for other species.

Diagnosis

Thick-film examination (higher sensitivity), then thin-film examination (to determine species and, if *P. falciparum*, parasitaemia). Trophozoites are the form seen on blood films, inside red cells. Schizonts seen on a film are a marker of severity. Antigen tests are used and can differentiate between species. Repeat films are required if negative and there is a high clinical suspicion.

Falciparum malaria

Falciparum malaria is defined as severe if the *parasitaemia* (percentage of red cells on a thin film which contain a malaria parasite) is above 2% or if there are complications (evidence of multisystem involvement, as below).

Clinical features

Clinical features are: fever, headache, rigors, myalgia, thrombocytopenia (common in non-severe malaria). May present with gastrointestinal symptoms and commonly presents with jaundice, which is mostly pre-hepatic, due to haemolysis (the jaundice often leads to initial misdiagnosis as viral hepatitis, a potential trap in clinical practice and MRCP questions). May be complicated by:

- *Cerebral malaria:* reduced level of consciousness (strictly defined as 'coma'), seizures, focal neurological disorders, but not meningism
- *Renal failure:* which may be severe and require haemodialysis, with *blackwater fever* or haemoglobinuria due to haemolysis
- *Pulmonary oedema:* and acute respiratory distress syndrome (ARDS). It is vital not to overload with fluid
- *Severe anaemia:* due to haemolysis and bone marrow suppression, particularly in children
- *Hypoglycaemia:* regular glucose monitoring is important, particularly as quinine can also cause hypoglycaemia
- *Algid malaria:* is malaria complicated by sepsis due to infection with Gram-negative organisms
- *Coagulopathy:* in addition to thrombocytopenia
- *Hyper-reactive malarial splenomegaly* ('tropical splenomegaly syndrome') is massive splenomegaly secondary to malaria, which may resolve with continuing antimalarial therapy

Treatment

Quinine, intravenously for severe and oral for non-severe falciparum, for 5 days or until blood films are negative. This must be followed by a second agent: doxycycline 200 mg daily for 7 days, is preferable to Fansidar® (pyrimethamine and sulfadoxine) single dose. Artemether is very effective in severe malaria and oral artemether combinations are useful in non-severe falciparum. Chloroquine is no longer recommended due to widespread resistance.

Benign malaria

P. vivax, P. ovale and P. malariae present with symptoms similar to falciparum malaria, but lack the complications or high degree of parasitaemia. Most West Africans are protected against *P. vivax* by the lack of Duffy antigen, the receptor via which the merozite stage of the parasite gains entry to red blood cells. The survival advantage conferred by the lack of this antigen accounts for its widespread absence of *P. vivax* in this region. Treatment is with oral chloroquine, followed with primaquine for 14 days to eliminate liver hypnozoites in *P. vivax* and *P. ovale* (but not *P. malariae*). Before giving primaquine, glucose-6-phosphatase dehydrogenase (G6PD) deficiency and pregnancy should be excluded. Primaquine can cause severe haemolysis in those G6PD deficiency; if it is required then dose and interval adjustments can be made to avoid haemolysis.

Prophylaxis against malaria

Drugs used for **prophylaxis** of malaria when travelling to endemic areas include: doxycycline, mefloquine, Malarone® (atovaquone and proguanil), and chloroquine and proguanil. The last combination is not recommended for travel to sub-Saharan Africa or parts of South and South-East Asia, due to resistance.

11.7.2   Enteric fever ('typhoid')

Enteric fever is caused by *Salmonella typhi* and *Salmonella paratyphi* (types A, B or C).

Incubation period

The IP is 1–3 weeks, depending on inoculating dose.

Transmission

Transmission is by ingestion of contaminated food or water. Enteric fever is endemic in areas with poor sanitation. Risk is increased with gastric acid suppression.

Clinical features

Enteric fever is a syndrome of fever, myalgia, cough, constipation, abdominal pain and headache. Features worsen with time and peak in the third week. Deafness and diarrhoea can occur and there is a classically described 'relative bradycardia'. Hepatosplenomegaly and 'rose spots' (pale pink, blanching spots on the trunk) may be found. Complications include psychosis or altered mental state, hepatitis, cholecystitis, pneumonia, pericarditis and meningitis. Leucopenia is typical. Untreated, mortality is from septicaemia or GI perforation. Steroids may reduce mortality in severe cases.

Diagnosis

Diagnosis is made by culture of the organism, a Gram-negative rod, from blood, bone marrow, stool or urine. Serology/Widal test is not useful.

Treatment

Prompt antibiotic therapy reduces mortality. Chloramphenicol, amoxicillin and co-trimoxazole have been used but there is some resistance, so fluoroquinolones (eg ciprofloxacin) may be preferred. In those returning from South Asia, ceftriaxone or azithromycin are alternatives due to fluoroquinolone resistance. Treatment is for 14 days. Relapse is relatively common and the organism can persist in the gallbladder.

Vaccination

Polysaccharide vaccine is given intramuscularly; it lasts 3 years (alternatives are oral live attenuated or killed whole-cell injectable vaccines), and is recommended for travellers to endemic areas.

11.7.3   Amoebiasis

The protozoon *Entamoeba histolytica* is transmitted by ingestion of food or water contaminated by amoebic cysts secreted in the faeces of asymptomatic individuals. It is found wherever sanitation is poor. Amoebae multiply in the gut and can cause invasive colitis and amoebic dysentery or amoebic liver abscess (containing 'anchovy sauce' pus), which if untreated can discharge into a cavity such as the peritoneum, pleural cavity or pericardium. The incubation period can be as long as several months.

Clinical features

Amoebic dysentery with blood and mucus in stools. Amoebic liver abscess can cause right upper quadrant pain and tenderness, right shoulder tip pain, with fever and leucocytosis. There may be hepatomegaly or signs of rupture of the abscess into a cavity, such as peritonitis or pericardial effusion.

Diagnosis

Amoebic trophozoites seen on stool microscopy, serology for invasive disease.

Treatment

Metronidazole, with diloxanide furoate to eradicate intestinal cyst carriage. Aspiration of abscess if large or causing severe pain or swelling.

11.7.4 Schistosomiasis ('Bilharzia')

These trematode, or blood fluke, infections cause much mortality and morbidity worldwide. Schistosomiasis is commonest in Africa, particularly in freshwater lakes, and in the Middle East. *Schistosoma mansoni* is also found in South America and *S. japonicum* in East Asia.

Transmission to humans occurs by exposure to fresh water infested with larvae (cercariae) from infected snails. The cercariae penetrate the skin and migrate as developing worms towards the venous plexuses of the bladder or mesenteries, depending on the species, where they remain as adult pairs and lay eggs, which are in turn passed in the urine or faeces. There are three main species affecting humans:

- *S. haematobium* (urinary tract)
- *S. mansoni* and *S. japonicum* (bowel and liver)

Clinical features

- **Acute**: cercarial dermatitis ('swimmers' itch') is an acute reaction to cercarial penetration, causing a self-limiting, pruritic, papular rash, within 24 hours of freshwater exposure. Katayama fever, or acute schistosomiasis, is less common but more severe and develops between 4 and 8 weeks after exposure, when the first eggs are produced. An immune complex-mediated syndrome, features may include fever, urticaria, eosinophilia, diarrhoea, hepatosplenomegaly, cough and wheeze
- **Chronic**: the large numbers of eggs produced by adult worms are the cause of pathology in chronic schistosomiasis. The eggs cause granulomatous reactions and fibrosis in affected organs, leading to pathology as follows:
  - *Urinary tract:* haematuria ('terminal haematuria') as eggs pass through the bladder epithelium, fibrosis and calcification of the bladder (visible on plain X-ray), obstructive uropathy and, usually after at least 20 years of infection, squamous cell carcinoma of the bladder
  - *Bowel and liver:* haemorrhagic polyps and colitis, hepatomegaly, periportal fibrosis causing portal hypertension (with splenomegaly, varices and ascites)
  - Other sites: eggs can transit via the pulmonary and systemic circulation to cause pathology in other organs, such as **pulmonary hypertension** (eg *S. haematobium*), **paraparesis** (eg *S. mansoni*), or **seizures** (eg *S. japonicum*)

Diagnosis

Microscopic identification of eggs in the urine (terminal urine sample) or faeces or in a tissue biopsy. Serological diagnosis is useful and would usually be positive in Katayama fever.

Treatment

Praziquantel with steroids ± anticonvulsants for CNS disease.

11.7.5   Leprosy

Leprosy (Hansen's disease) is caused by the slow-growing, intracellular, acid-fast bacillus *Mycobacterium leprae*, which is transmitted person to person by respiratory droplets from the nasal mucosa. It is associated with overcrowding and poverty and the majority of cases are found in South Asia (more than in Africa and South America). Unlike TB, the risk of developing leprosy is not increased by HIV infection. BCG offers some protection.

Incubation period

The IP is 2–12 years (shorter for tuberculoid leprosy, longer for lepromatous leprosy). Of those who are infected, 95% develop an effective immune response and clear the organism; others develop disease.

Clinical features

The organism grows well at lower temperatures and thus affects the skin, upper respiratory mucosa, superficial nerves, anterior chamber of the eye, lymph nodes and testes. Features are depigmented, anaesthetic skin patches or other, sometimes nodular, skin lesions; thickened superficial nerves (eg ulnar nerve); or signs of involvement of other organs, such as blindness.

There is a **spectrum** of disease from tuberculoid (paucibacillary) to lepromatous (multibacillary) types, depending on the degree of the T cell-mediated immune response to the organism, as shown in Table 11.10.

Diagnosis

Diagnosis is based on the clinical features in a patient from an area where leprosy is endemic, plus a skin smear from a lesion, stained for mycobateria. *M. leprae* cannot be grown in vitro.

Treatment

The World Health Organisation recommends combination drug treatment of rifampicin, dapsone and clofazimine for 12 months for multibacillary leprosy and rifampicin and dapsone for 6 months for paucibacillary leprosy. Clofazimine can cause ichthyosis.

Other aspects of care, such as protection of anaesthetic feet and hands, are also important.

Reactions

These are due to a shift in the individual's immune response, usually during treatment, either up or down the spectrum.

Reversal reaction (type 1)

Erythematous skin lesions and nerve damage with pain and loss of function occur in patients with delayed-type hypersensitivity and an increasing cell-mediated immune response to *M. leprae*. Prednisolone treatment can reduce nerve damage.

Erythema nodosum leprosum (ENL) (type 2)

This occurs in patients at the lepromatous end of the spectrum. Reactions comprise fever, erythema nodosum leprosum and occasionally life-threatening glomerulonephritis and renal failure due to

Table 11.10. Spectrum of disease in leprosy

Tuberculoid	Brisk T-cell responses	Well-defined lesions or one/few nerves affected
Borderline		Many lesions, widespread nerve involvement, with sensory and motor function loss
Lepromatous	Poor T-cell responses; humoral immune response	Numerous, nodular lesions, not anaesthetic, thickened skin

immune complex deposition. Chronic or severe ENL can lead to amyloidosis. Treatment is with prednisolone or, in chronic reactions, higher dose clofazimine or thalidomide.

11.7.6 Filariasis

Filarial worm larvae, most commonly *Wuchereria bancrofti* or *Brugia malayi,* are transmitted throughout the tropics by mosquitoes and cause debilitating deformities of the limbs caused by lymphatic damage. This can lead to 'elephantiasis' of the limbs. Microfilariae produced by adult worms can cause tropical pulmonary eosinophilia.

Diagnosis

Diagnosis is made by clinical appearance, microfilariae on blood film, serology and the presence of an eosinophilia.

Treatment

Diethylcarbamazine (DEC), and supportive treatment for lymphoedema.

11.7.7 Cysticercosis

The pork tapeworm *Taenia solium* differs from the beef tapeworm, *T. saginata*, in that it can cause invasive disease in the human host. Intestinal infection with adult tapeworms is caused by ingestion of larval cysts in undercooked pork. In addition, ingestion of eggs from faecal–oral contamination can cause migration of the parasite to the tissues, most notably the muscles and CNS. *Neurocysticercosis* is a common cause of epilepsy worldwide.

Clinical features

Calcified subcutaneous or muscle cysts, visible on X-ray; epilepsy or spinal symptoms from CNS lesions.

Diagnosis

Diagnosis is made by imaging and serology for cysticercosis (eggs on stool microscopy for intestinal tapeworm infection).

Treatment

Albendazole or other anthelmintic drugs for intestinal tapeworm infection. Neurocysticercosis may require anticonvulsants and steroids before using anthelmintic drugs.

11.7.8 Trypanosomiasis

African trypanosomiasis

Trypanosoma brucei spp. are transmitted by tsetse flies and cause *sleeping sickness*, which occurs in sub-Saharan Africa. Trypanosomes invade the CNS from the blood and cause a meningo-encephalitis, ultimately causing death in weeks or up to years, depending on the subtype. It is rarely seen in the UK.

Diagnosis

Trypanosomes seen on blood or CSF microscopy; serology.

Treatment

Melarsoprol (high rate of fatal complications) or eflornithine.

South American trypanosomiasis

Trypanosoma cruzi is transmitted by reduviid bugs and causes *Chagas disease*, which occurs in central and south America. It can also be transmitted by blood transfusion.

Clinical features

Acute infection gives non-specific symptoms. Chronic complications include megaoesophagus, megacolon and cardiomyopathy with arrhythmias.

Diagnosis

Serology, or trypanosomes seen on blood films.

Treatment

Benznidazole or nifurtimox. Surgery for GI complications or symptomatic treatment for cardiac disease.

Note on eosinophilia

In parasitic infections, eosinophilia is related to the tissue migration phase of the life cycle of a multicellular parasite. It therefore occurs in schistosomiasis, strongyloidiasis and filariasis, but not in malaria, amoebiasis or giardiasis. Also note the non-infective causes of eosinophilia, including some malignancies and connective tissue diseases.

11.7.9 Hookworm

Ancylostoma duodenale and *Necator americanus* are helminths, transmitted by penetration of larvae in the soil through the skin. Infection is common where sanitation is poor and hookworm is a common cause of anaemia worldwide. The worms mature in the intestines then attach to the mucosal surface, causing bleeding and iron-deficiency anaemia.

Diagnosis

Characteristic eggs are seen on stool microscopy.

Treatment

Anthelmintic drugs, such as mebendazole.

11.7.10 Viral haemorrhagic fevers

This group of infections includes the arenavirus, Lassa fever, and the filoviruses, Marburg and Ebola. They are transmitted person to person, cause outbreaks in West and Central Africa and should be considered in returning travellers with fever developing *within 3 weeks* of visiting these regions, particularly if they have visited rural areas. Special isolation procedures are required for suspected cases. Malaria is an important and much more common differential diagnosis.

Diagnosis

Serology or PCR.

Treatment

Ribavirin in Lassa fever.

11.8 IMPORTANT ZOONOSES

11.8.1 Brucellosis

Brucella spp. (*B. abortus* from cattle, *B. melitensis* from goats or sheep, *B. suis* from pigs) are Gram-negative coccobacilli which can cause disease if humans come into contact by handling animal carcasses or ingesting unpasteurised milk. Farm and veterinary workers are therefore at risk. The organisms spread through blood and lymphatics and localise in the reticuloendothelial system, causing granulomata. It is commonest in Mediterranean and Middle Eastern countries and South America and rare in the UK.

Clinical features

The IP may be 5–60 days and presenting features include fever, malaise, sweats and weight loss. Hepatosplenomegaly and lymphadenopathy may be present. Less commonly there is arthritis, osteomyelitis, orchitis, meningo-encephalitis, endocarditis or granulomatous hepatitis. The acute phase may be followed by a relapsing/remitting course ('undulant fever').

Diagnosis

The organism may be grown in prolonged culture of blood or bone marrow. Serology is an alternative.

Treatment

Doxycycline and rifampicin or, if more severe, then intravenous aminoglycosides. Treatment is for 3–6 weeks.

11.8.2 Lyme disease

Lyme disease is caused by the spirochaete *Borrelia burgdorferi*, transmitted by hard ticks (ixodid ticks) from an animal reservoir. It is found in large parts of

Europe, including the UK (forest areas) and in the USA (north-east), China, Japan and Australia.

Clinical features

Early features include a characteristic rash at the site of the tick bite, called *erythema chronicum migrans*, which is an expanding erythematous plaque with central clearing. There may be local lymphadenopathy. Later features (weeks–months later) may include focal neurological symptoms (eg Bell's palsy), encephalitis, meningitis, cardiac involvement with AV block, or arthritis.

Diagnosis

Serology (most positive after 4 weeks), or PCR of serum or CSF. CSF is lymphocytic in Lyme meningitis.

Treatment

Doxycycline or erythromycin for erythema chronicum migrans. Intravenous penicillin or cephalosporins for neurological or cardiac manifestations.

11.8.3   Q fever

Q fever refers to syndromes caused by infection with the rickettsial organism, *Coxiella burnetii*. It is usually transmitted by exposure to cattle or sheep, by aerosol or direct contact, or from contaminated milk. It occurs worldwide.

Clinical features

Fever, pneumonia, or hepatitis. A few individuals suffer a chronic infection with 'culture-negative' endocarditis and possibly myocarditis. Other features or less common presentations include rash, arthralgia, meningo-encephalitis and glomerulonephritis.

Diagnosis

Acute and convalescent serology.

Treatment

Tetracyclines for 2–3 weeks. Longer, combination therapy is required for cardiac involvement.

Chapter 12
Maternal Medicine

CONTENTS

Maternal Medicine

12.1 PHYSIOLOGY OF NORMAL PREGNANCY

Pregnancy impacts upon every system in the body, and each system adapts in order to accommodate the demands of the feto-placental unit. Consequently, pregnancy can adversely affect many pre-existing medical conditions and, likewise, many pregnancy complications arise because physiological adaptation does not occur.

12.1.1 Cardiovascular system

- There is an increase in plasma volume from 2600 ml to approximately 3800 ml, reaching a plateau by 32 weeks' gestation
- Cardiac output rises by about 40%, from about 4.5 l/min to 6 l/min, reaching a plateau by 24–30 weeks' gestation. This occurs because of an increase in heart rate (from approximately 80 beats per minute to 90 beats per minute) and an increase in stroke volume
- Left ventricular **hypertrophy** and **dilatation** facilitate this change in cardiac output but **contractility** remains unchanged. The structural changes revert to normal early post-partum and definitely by 6 weeks
- Together with the **upward displacement of the diaphragm**, the apex is moved anterior and to the left
- These changes may result in ECG findings of left axis deviation, **depressed ST segments** and inversion or flattening of the T wave in lead III
- Echocardiogram may show a small pericardial effusion ± mild valvular regurgitation. The valvular regurgitation is a reflection of dilatation
- There is a decrease in total peripheral resistance that outstrips the increase in cardiac output, and this results in a fall in blood pressure (between 8 and 36 weeks' gestation). This generalised vasodilatation accommodates the increased

blood flow to the uterus and other organs. A nadir in diastolic BP is typically seen at about 20 weeks' gestation, coincident with second wave spiral artery dilatation
- Symptoms of pregnancy may mimic cardiac disease, such that dyspnoea, peripheral oedema and palpitations are all common complaints in normal pregnancy
- A benign ejection systolic murmur occurs in 96% of pregnant women – due to increased blood volume and flow together with anaemia

12.1.2 Respiratory system

Vital capacity does not change during pregnancy but the tidal volume expands into the expiratory and inspiratory reserve volume.

Consequently, ventilation increases by 40% in pregnancy. This increase in ventilation exceeds the increase in oxygen consumption and there is a proportional fall in pCO_2.

The bicarbonate level falls to maintain a normal pH and there is a concomitant fall in sodium.

12.1.3 Haematological system

- There is an increase in red cell mass, from a non-pregnant level of 1400 ml to 1650–1800 ml
- Plasma volume increases proportionately more than red cell mass, resulting in a fall in the haematocrit and haemoglobin concentration in normal pregnancy, such that a haemoglobin level of 10.5 g/dl may be within 'normal' limits – *physiological anaemia*
- There is an increased demand for iron, mainly to meet the demands of the increased red cell mass and to a lesser extent the requirements of the developing fetus and placenta. This demand

is not quite matched by an increase in dietary absorption
- There are increases in the levels of factors VII, VIII and X, and in the level of plasma fibrinogen, such that in late pregnancy the fibrinogen concentration is at least double that in the non-pregnant state
- White blood cell count increases and may peak at over 20×10^9/l in stressful conditions such as labour. This can make the diagnosis of infection difficult in pregnancy
- A decrease in platelet concentration to around $100-150 \times 10^9$/l can also be seen

12.1.4 Renal system

- Kidneys increase in length by about 1 cm in pregnancy
- Ureters become dilated, secondary to increased progesterone and to the obstructive effect of the gravid uterus
- Renal blood flow increases from about 1.2 l/min in the non-pregnant state to at least 1.5 l/min in pregnancy. This results in an increase in glomerular filtration rate (GFR)
- Increased GFR leads to a fall in blood urea (from 4.3 to 3.1 mmol/l) and creatinine (from 73 to 47 µmol/l)
- Increased GFR also increases the filtered load of glucose and benign glycosuria is common in pregnancy

12.2 PHARMACOKINETICS IN PREGNANCY

The physiological changes of normal pregnancy profoundly affect pharmacokinetics.

Physiological changes in pregnancy which affect drug pharmacokinetics

- Renal blood flow increases and leads to increased renal clearance
- Increased plasma volume and fluid retention lead to an increased volume of distribution and decreased plasma concentration
- Induction of liver enzyme pathways increases the hepatic metabolism of certain drugs and results in a decreased plasma concentration

---

The concept of placental transfer is unique to pregnancy. Essentially, every drug (with the exception of heparin) crosses the placenta and has the potential to cause unwanted side-effects, including teratogenic effects in the unborn fetus. Under most circumstances, drugs cross the placenta and will equilibrate between the fetal and maternal compartments. In view of this, drug therapy is best avoided unless absolutely necessary during the period of organogenesis in the first trimester (ie between conception and 12 weeks). If unavoidable, older drugs with established safety data should be the agents of first choice. Specific drugs are discussed in more detail later in this chapter.

12.3 PRE-EXISTING MEDICAL DISORDERS AND PREGNANCY

12.3.1 Diabetes and pregnancy

Before the advent of insulin, women with type 1 diabetes who survived to the age of reproduction and were then able to become pregnant had a less than 50% chance of having a successful pregnancy.

Today maternal mortality is rare, but both fetal and neonatal morbidity and mortality remain higher compared with the general pregnant population. In 1989 the St Vincent Task Force, together with the WHO, endeavoured to 'achieve pregnancy outcomes in women with diabetes that approximate to those in women without diabetes'. This necessitates achieving normogylcaemia.

Terminology and definitions

Pregnancy induces profound metabolic alterations. To maintain stable concentrations of plasma glucose, insulin secretion must double from the end of the first to the third trimester. In pregnancy, glucose concentrations:

- Increase post-prandially
- Decrease with fasting
- Decrease with gestation

Pregnancy is associated with insulin resistance. This is a post-receptor defect, mediated by an increase in pregnancy-associated hormones and cortisol. Changes in insulin also cause accelerated starvation, with an increase in triglyceride breakdown resulting in raised free fatty acids and ketone bodies.

The diagnosis of diabetes in pregnancy is based on a 75-g oral glucose tolerance test (GTT) (Table 12.1).

Women with gestational diabetes are those who are found, during pregnancy, to have a GTT that meets the threshold for diagnosing diabetes (see Table 12.1). A small proportion of these women will inevitably have true, previously undiagnosed, diabetes.

Effects of diabetes on the fetus

Congenital malformations

- Overall there is a 4- to 10-fold increase in the incidence of congenital abnormalities in infants of diabetic mothers compared with the normal pregnant population
- Cardiac and neural tube defects are among the commonest abnormalities
- Caudal regression: an embryological defect that occurs during the third week of intrauterine development and is strongly *associated* with maternal diabetes, although it is rare compared with cardiac and neural tube defects. Although the syndrome is highly variable in severity, it can result in fusion of the lower limbs and urogenital and anorectal abnormalities
- The exact mechanism underlying the increase in congenital abnormalities is unknown but may reflect an abnormal metabolic environment around the time of organogenesis
- Tight glucose control can significantly reduce the risk of congenital abnormalities

Spontaneous miscarriage

- Poorly controlled diabetes is associated with an increased risk of miscarriage, but women with moderately well-controlled diabetes have only a minimally increased risk

Perinatal mortality

- In a multidisciplinary setting, excluding deaths from congenital malformations, perinatal mortality rates are similar between infants of diabetic mothers and those of normal pregnant women

Table 12.1. Interpreting the oral glucose tolerance test in pregnancy

Diagnosis	Fasting blood glucose (mmol/l)	Two-hour blood glucose (mmol/l)
Diabetes	$\geqslant 7$	$\geqslant 11$
Impaired glucose tolerance	6–6.9	9–10.9

Unexplained fetal death in utero

Despite improvements in care, death in utero of a normally formed fetus still occurs. The aetiology of these deaths is complex but includes alterations in:

- Placental oxygen transfer (reduced red cell oxygen release mediated through 2,3-diphosphoglycerate (2,3-DPG))
- Fetal acid–base balance (tendency towards metabolic acidosis, worsened by increasing maternal glucose concentrations)
- Organomegaly (results in increased metabolic demand)
- Fetal thrombosis (more likely because of fetal polycythaemia)

Effects of diabetes on the neonate

Birth weight

- There is an increased incidence of both small- and large-for-gestational-age fetuses born to diabetic mothers
- Approximately 25%–40% of infants of mothers with diabetes have birth weights above the 90th centile and as many as 35% have birth weights greater than the 95th centile. This leads to an increase in intrapartum complications, including an increase in both the caesarean section rate and the incidence of shoulder dystocia
- Increased growth rates may be seen as early as 20–24 weeks' gestation
- Subcutaneous fat deposits correlate with maternal plasma glucose concentrations and glycosylated haemoglobin levels, amniotic fluid C-peptide levels and fetal serum insulin/glucose ratios
- Fetal growth restriction is more frequently seen in diabetic women with long-standing disease and evidence of microvascular complications

Respiratory dysfunction

- Reduced phosphatidylglycerol production results in surfactant deficiency; this in turn predisposes the infant to hyaline membrane disease

Hypoglycaemia

This arises because of:

- Endogenous hyperinsulinaemia developed in utero
- Reduced hepatic phosphorylase activity
- Reduced glucagons and catecholamines resulting in reduced glucose release from the liver

Polycythaemia and jaundice

Polycythaemia occurs in 29% of infants of diabetic mothers, compared with 6% of infants of normal pregnant women; there is a direct correlation with diabetic control. Polycythaemia results in an increased viscosity, which may cause the following:

- Increased cardiac work
- Microvascular abnormality, leading to respiratory distress, renal vein thrombosis and necrotising enterocolitis
- Jaundice occurs in about 19% of infants due to an increase in red cell destruction as well as liver immaturity and poor handling of bilirubin

Hypocalcaemia and hypomagnesaemia

Calcium and magnesium levels are lower in infants born to diabetic mothers, predisposing to neonatal seizures; the exact mechanism is unknown.

Hypertrophic cardiomyopathy

As many as 30% of infants may have an enlarged heart, and 10% of these may have associated cardiac dysfunction. This correlates with maternal diabetic control. The heart shows features similar to that of hypertrophic obstructive cardiomyopathy, but the dysfunction tends to resolve in the neonatal period.

Management of pregnancy in the diabetic patient

All patients should be counselled regarding the risks of pregnancy and the need for vigilant clinical management.

Pre-pregnancy

- Switch to insulin if the patient is on oral hypoglycaemics
- Encourage tight glucose control (eg preprandial levels 4–6 mmol/l)
- HbA1c should be maintained <6%
- Treat any retinopathy
- Screen for nephropathy

Antenatal care

It is very important to involve the multidisciplinary team in the care of the patient. Patients should be booked in the antenatal clinic at a very early stage with organisation of an ultrasound scan to accurately date the pregnancy (crown–rump length (CRL) at 8–12 weeks gives expected date of delivery (EDD) ± 5 days). Patients should be given dietary advice and baseline renal function should be assessed. Other important aspects of management include:

- Maintain tight glucose control (preprandial levels 4–7 mmol/l); the patient should be warned about the possibility of hypoglycaemic episodes
- Serum screening should be interpreted with care as α-fetoprotein (AFP) levels are lower in diabetic pregnancies. Nuchal translucency (NT) screening (performed between 11 weeks 6 days and 13 weeks 6 days of gestation) is a more reliable alternative
- A detailed anomaly scan, including fetal echocardiography, should be performed
- Regular review with blood pressure measurement and urinalysis
- Serial fetal growth and liquor volume assessment
- Cardiotocograph (CTG) may be useful after 36 weeks to assess fetal well-being, in the light of possible risk of fetal death in utero
- In view of the increased risk of pre-term delivery (induced or spontaneous) patients may require high-dose intramuscular fluorinated steroids (eg betamethasone 12 mg, 2 doses 12–24 h apart) to accelerate fetal lung maturation (by stimulating surfactant secretion). A sliding scale of insulin would be necessary during this

treatment. Tocolytics are used to stop uterine activity (ie in the treatment of pre-term labour). Ritodrine and salbutamol have been used in the recent past for this indication and can interfere with glycaemic control. These agents have largely been superseded by nifedipine and atosiban (an oxytocin receptor antagonist)

The timing and mode of delivery will be individualised according to the patient and health of the fetus.

Labour

Good diabetic control should be maintained in labour. This will often necessitate the use of a sliding scale for insulin administration. The following are also important:

- Continuous CTG
- Watch for obstructed labour
- Beware possible shoulder dystocia
- High caesarean section rate (as high as 60%–65%)

Post-partum

- Reduce insulin back to pre-pregnancy levels following delivery of placenta
- Encourage breast-feeding
- Discuss contraception (see below)

Gestational diabetes/impaired glucose tolerance in pregnancy

Initially, glycaemic control may be achieved through diet (total calories between 1800 and 2000/day). Fibre intake should be increased and >50% of energy should be derived from carbohydrates.

- If preprandial blood glucose levels are > 6 mmol/l then insulin is introduced, usually twice daily
- The fetus is at risk of macrosomia and hence birth trauma
- Insulin requirements cease following delivery of the placenta
- It is vital that a glucose tolerance test (GTT) is performed at 6 weeks after delivery

The patient should be counselled with regard to their weight, diet and exercise. Without attention to this, more than 50% of women with gestational diabetes will develop true diabetes over the next 20 years.

Contraception for patients with diabetes

The following are important considerations:

- Combined pill (COP): associated with an increased risk of thrombosis, both venous and arterial. Nevertheless this would be suitable for the young, well-controlled diabetic with no evidence of vascular disease
- Progesterone-only pill: lower efficacy compared with the COP; greater likelihood of menstrual irregularities
- Intrauterine contraceptive device (IUCD): an effective method of contraception in diabetics. No evidence of reduced efficacy. A Mirena® IUS could also be considered
- Sterilisation: this is suitable for diabetic women who have completed their family, or wish to avoid pregnancy because of associated microvascular complications (severe retinopathy or nephropathy)

12.3.2 Cardiac disease and pregnancy

The overall incidence of heart disease in pregnancy is approximately 1% and is increasing, reflecting recent advances in cardiac management that have allowed greater numbers of women with congenital heart disease to reach child-bearing age. The haemodynamic changes that occur in pregnancy can be dangerous for women with cardiac disease. However, although the prognosis for pregnancy is generally good, in women with cardiac disease the exact level of risk posed by the pregnancy depends upon the underlying pathology:

- In general, regurgitant valvular lesions and mild/ moderate left-to-right shunts are well tolerated due to the decrease in total peripheral vascular resistance which occurs in pregnancy

- Conversely, stenotic valvular lesions, pulmonary hypertension and right-to-left shunts are poorly tolerated

It is therefore helpful to categorise heart disease in terms of mortality risk, as this will optimise accurate counselling, evaluation and management (Table 12.2).

Symptoms and signs in normal pregnancy

Symptoms of pregnancy may mimic cardiac disease, and dyspnoea, peripheral oedema and palpitations are all common complaints in normal pregnancy. A benign ejection systolic murmur occurs in 96% of pregnant women.

ECG and echocardiographic changes in normal pregnancy

- **ECG changes**
  - Sinus tachycardia
  - Leftward or rightward shift of the QRS axis
  - Premature atrial or ventricular beats
- **Echocardiographic changes**
  - An increase in heart size and left ventricular mass
  - A small pericardial effusion
  - Mild valvular regurgitation

Management of the pregnant woman with cardiac disease

Pre-conception

Management should take place in a multidisciplinary setting, preferably in a tertiary centre, and this should involve the obstetrician, cardiologist, anaesthetist and if necessary the cardiothoracic surgeon.

Pre-conception evaluation will allow for appropriate counselling regarding maternal and fetal risks, optimisation of drug therapy and/or pre-pregnancy surgery if indicated.

- Most cardiac drugs are safe, but angiotensin-converting enzyme (ACE) inhibitors should be avoided as they are associated with fetal and neonatal renal failure and death

Table 12.2. Categorisation of heart disease in terms of mortality risk

Risk	Condition
High (mortality 25%–50%)	Eisenmenger complex
	Cyanotic heart disease (tetralogy of Fallot, Ebstein's anomaly, transposition of the great vessels)
	Pulmonary hypertension
	Acute myocardial infarction
	Hypertrophic obstructive cardiomyopathy
	Heart failure (including peripartum cardiomyopathy)
Moderate to high (mortality 5%–15%)	Valvular stenosis
	Coarctation of the aorta
	History of myocardial infarction
	Marfan syndrome
	Mechanical prosthetic valve
Low (mortality <1%)	Acyanotic heart disease
	Mild to moderate valvular regurgitation
	Mitral valve prolapse
	Small ventricular septal defect (VSD)
	Small atrial septal defect (ASD)

- **Anticoagulation**: due to the hypercoagulable state of pregnancy, there is an increased risk of valve thrombosis and embolism in women with prosthetic valves. Warfarin is teratogenic, particularly in the first trimester, and is also associated with fetal haemorrhage throughout pregnancy. Heparin does not cross the placenta, but is associated with maternal bone demineralisation and thrombocytopenia. In addition, heparin has also been associated with a higher risk of thromboembolic complications. Anticoagulation in these patients should be determined on an individual risk basis

Antenatal management

Consideration should be given to the genetic implications of maternal cardiac disease. Congenital heart disease has a multifactorial inheritance. There is a small increase in the risk of congenital heart disease occurring in the fetus but this risk increases sharply if more than one member of the family is affected. Consequently, high-resolution ultrasound with fetal echocardiography is advised in the second trimester.

- Once pregnant, the majority of women will have no haemodynamic problems. Cardiac decompensation, however, is an indication for termination of pregnancy
- Fetal growth should be assessed regularly, particularly in women with severe heart disease and cyanotic congenital heart conditions
- Indications for cardiac surgery are the same as for the non-pregnant woman
- If surgery is required, it should be performed with the patient in the left decubitus position with provision for caesarean section if the gestation is greater than 24 weeks
- Standard cardiopulmonary bypass may compromise the placenta and fetus due to hypothermia, reduced arterial perfusion and

alterations in coagulation and acid–base balance. To avoid these complications, cardiopulmonary support should be high-flow, normothermic and initiated without hyperkalaemic arrest

Intrapartum management
In general, spontaneous vaginal delivery is preferred but selected patients with severe heart disease may benefit from elective caesarean section. In labour, care must be taken to avoid supine hypotension due to aortocaval compression by the gravid uterus.

- In the majority of patients with adequate cardiac reserve, epidural anaesthesia is effective and well tolerated. It should, however, be used with extreme caution in women with restricted cardiac outputs such as in primary pulmonary hypertension or right-to-left shunts. Under these circumstances, general anaesthesia and abdominal delivery may be preferred
- Fluid balance requires special attention and high-risk cases may warrant pulmonary wedge pressure monitoring with a pulmonary catheter
- Under certain circumstances, ergometrine should be avoided during the third stage of labour. The tonic contraction of the uterus caused by this drug will force approximately 500 ml of blood into the circulation, causing a rise in left atrial pressure. This would be particularly detrimental in patients with significant mitral stenosis
- Delivery is associated with a transient asymptomatic bacteraemia. Therefore, women with structural heart disease *may* benefit from antibiotic prophylaxis (see guidelines from the National Institute for Health and Clinical Excellence). This is mandatory in women with prosthetic valves

12.3.3 Renal disease and hypertension in pregnancy

Pregnancy outcome in women with renal disease has improved markedly in recent years. The main risks of pregnancy in a patient with renal disease are of **adverse pregnancy outcome** and **deteriora-**

tion of renal function accompanying the pregnancy. The risks depend upon the:

- Degree of renal impairment at conception
- Presence of hypertension at conception or in early pregnancy
- Degree of proteinuria

Risk is best determined by accurate assessment of renal function.

Mildly impaired renal function

In the presence of mildly impaired renal function (serum creatinine <125 μmol/l or GFR 50–70 ml/min), the live birth rate approaches 95%. There is a slightly increased risk of pre-term delivery, pre-eclampsia and intrauterine growth retardation (IUGR), but pregnancy does not seem to adversely influence renal function. Therefore, women in this category should not be discouraged from becoming pregnant.

Moderately impaired renal function

In the presence of moderately impaired renal function (serum creatinine 125–250 μmol/l or GFR 25–50 ml/min), there is a significantly increased risk (up to 50%) of pre-term delivery, pre-eclampsia and IUGR. The success of the pregnancy depends upon adequate control of blood pressure.

- Uncontrolled hypertension is associated with significantly increased rates of fetal and neonatal loss
- There is a 25%–50% chance of decline in renal function, which may be permanent
- Nevertheless, in a multidisciplinary setting and with rigorous control of blood pressure, the live birth rate approaches 84%

Severely impaired renal function

In the presence of severely impaired renal function (serum creatinine >250 μmol/l or GFR <25 ml/min), fertility is reduced. Spontaneous conception may occasionally occur. Again, the key to successful outcome is largely dependent upon adequate control of maternal blood pressure. However, the risks to both the fetus and mother are such that termination of pregnancy may be offered.

- In women who continue with the pregnancy, there is a 90% chance of antenatal complications
- Uncontrolled hypertension is associated with a 10-fold increase in perinatal mortality
- The live birth rate is 50%–80% (depending on underlying diagnosis and management)

End-stage renal disease

Patients who are receiving dialysis have very low fertility, and even if conception is successful, there is a high rate of miscarriage. There have only been a handful of reported cases of successful pregnancies in women receiving dialysis.

- In patients with functioning renal transplants, the outcomes are again determined by the level of graft (ie renal) function, as described above.

Ideally, pregnancy should be avoided until 12 months post-transplant, by which stage graft function has stabilised and immunosuppressants are at maintenance levels only

- Most of the commonly used immunosuppressant agents (eg ciclosporin A, tacrolimus, prednisolone and azathioprine) are considered to be safe for administration during pregnancy. Again, optimal blood pressure control is the key to a successful pregnancy. **Mycophenolate mofetil (MMF)** should be avoided (both during pregnancy and for 3 months pre-conception), as teratogenic effects, including microtia (of one or both ears ± hearing loss), cleft lip and palate, have been reported with its use

Specific renal diseases and pregnancy

Specific renal diseases and their effects and outcome in pregnancy are given in Table 12.3.

Table 12.3. Specific renal diseases and pregnancy

Renal disease	Effects and outcome	Risk of pre-eclampsia
Chronic glomerulonephritis	Usually no adverse effect in the absence of hypertension Urinary tract infection (UTI) more frequent The renal lesion may be affected by the coagulation changes of pregnancy	Mild
IgA nephropathy	Risk of hypertension and worsening of renal function	Moderate–severe
Pyelonephritis	Bacteriuria in pregnancy may lead to exacerbation Multiple organ dysfunction can occur	Mild
Reflux nephropathy	Risks of hypertension/worsening of renal function	Mild–moderate

(continued)

Table 12.3. *(continued)*

Renal disease	Effects and outcome	Risk of pre-eclampsia
Urolithiasis	UTI more frequent Avoid lithotripsy Natural history not affected	Mild
Diabetic nephropathy	Increased UTI, oedema Natural history not affected	Moderate–severe
Polyarteritis nodosa	Poor fetal prognosis Risk of maternal death	Severe
Polycystic disease	Minimal risk of functional impairment and hypertension	Mild at most
Systemic lupus erythematosus	More favourable prognosis if in remission >6 months prior to conception Controversy regarding steroid dosing	Severe
Scleroderma	If onset during pregnancy, rapid deterioration may occur Reactivation of quiescent scleroderma may occur post-partum	Severe
Previous urinary tract surgery	Possible associations with other urinary tract malformations Renal function may worsen	Mild
After nephrectomy, solitary kidney and pelvic kidney	Possible associations with other malformations of urogenital tract Pregnancy well tolerated	Mild
Wegener's granulomatosis	Proteinuria (± hypertension) is common from early pregnancy Avoid cytotoxics but immunosuppressives safe	Moderate–severe
Renal artery stenosis	May present as chronic hypertension or recurrent isolated pre-eclampsia Transluminal angioplasty in pregnancy if appropriate	Mild–moderate

The table above has been reproduced from *Hypertension in Pregnancy*, Belfont M et al 2003, by kind permission of Marcel Dekker

Management of pregnancy in patients with pre-existing renal disease

The patients with pre-existing renal disease should be managed in a multidisciplinary setting. Where possible, the patients should be referred for pre-conception evaluation and counselling prior to embarking upon a pregnancy. At this stage, there needs to be a consideration of possible genetic causes of renal impairment (eg polycystic kidney disease or Alport syndrome) which may affect the fetus. Once pregnant, the patient with renal disease should undergo the following management:

- Early referral for antenatal clinic booking with accurate dating ultrasound scan
- Baseline biochemistry and urinalysis (including urea, creatinine, electrolytes, urate, lactate dehydrogenase and 24-hour urine protein excretion). These investigations should be repeated at least every 4 weeks
- Preferred antihypertensive drugs include labetalol, methyldopa and long-acting nifedipine
- ACE inhibitors should be discontinued pre-conceptually or at the earliest opportunity (see earlier)
- The patient should be assessed frequently (fortnightly until 28 weeks, then weekly until delivery)
- Regular fetal surveillance with growth scans, commencing at 24 weeks (particularly if on antihypertensive medication)
- Indications for pre-term delivery are deteriorating renal function, the development of superimposed pre-eclampsia and/or severe IUGR. Hence, appropriate specialised paediatric services will be required

12.3.4 Antiphospholipid syndrome and pregnancy

The antiphospholipid syndrome is defined as a clinical disorder with recurrent arterial and venous thrombotic events, pregnancy wastage and/or thrombocytopenia in the presence of the lupus anti-coagulant and/or a moderate to high positive anti-cardiolipin test.

- **The lupus anticoagulant** is an inhibitor of the coagulation pathway. Its presence is a good predictor of poor fetal outcome
- **Anticardiolipin antibodies** are antibodies active against certain phospholipid components of cell walls. They may be IgG or IgM
- Both a **primary form** (patients without clinical or serological evidence of autoimmune disorders), and a **secondary form** (usually in patients with SLE) of the antiphospholipid syndrome are recognised

Diagnosis of antiphospholipid syndrome requires two positive tests, at least 12 weeks apart, **plus** at least one of the following clinical scenarios:

- Recurrent miscarriage
- Fetal loss after 10 weeks' gestation (no fetal heart demonstrated on scan)
- Early-onset (<34 weeks' gestation) pre-eclampsia and/or IUGR (secondary to placental dysfunction)
- Placental abruption
- Fetal death in utero or stillbirth

The mechanism of pregnancy loss/adverse pregnancy outcome is not clearly elucidated. Current theories include damage to placental vascular endothelium, platelet deposition, imbalance in the thromboxane/prostacyclin (PGI_2) ratio and inhibition of protein C and tissue plasminogen. Inflammatory cytokines may also be implicated.

Treatment

The treatment options include oral therapy with low-dose aspirin and/or subcutaneous low-molecular-weight heparin (LMWH). Even with treatment the pregnancies can be complicated by hypertension and fetal growth restriction, and hence they require careful monitoring.

- Clinical trials indicate a 'take-home baby rate' of 70% with combined therapy versus 40% with aspirin alone. With no treatment success is in the region of only 10%
- *See also* Chapter 9, Haematology

12.3.5 Thyroid disease and pregnancy

Thyroid disease is relatively common in women of child-bearing age. Physiological changes during normal pregnancy include:

- Increased thyroxine-binding globulin (TBG)
- Increase in triiodothyronine (T_3) and thyroxine (T_4)
- Relative iodine deficiency, increased renal excretion
- Free T_4/T_3 falls in the third trimester
- Thyroid-stimulating hormone (TSH) falls in first/second trimester, increases in third trimester

Serum screening is less accurate in hypothyroidism. Raised fetal TSH concentrations may falsely elevate both fetal and maternal serum α-fetoprotein (AFP). This results in false-positive screening for neural tube defects and false negatives for trisomy 21 screening.

Hyperthyroidism

Untreated hyperthyroidism is associated with subfertility and reduced libido. It occurs with an incidence of approximately 2/1000 pregnancies and is most frequently due to autoimmune thyrotoxicosis (Graves' disease).

Effect of pregnancy on hyperthyroidism

- Flares are seen in both the first trimester and the puerperium
- Typically remits in the second and third trimester, which results in a reduction in medication for many, and cessation of therapy in about 30%
- The change in disease activity reflects the maternal immune state and titres of thyrotropin receptor-stimulating antibodies

Effect of hyperthyroidism on pregnancy

- If hyperthyroidism is well controlled before and throughout pregnancy, outcomes are good for mother and baby
- Poor control is associated with congestive cardiac failure, pre-eclampsia, pre-term labour, IUGR and stillbirth

Treatment

The treatment of choice is propylthiouracil or carbimazole. The dose is titrated against biochemical results (free T_4 at the upper limit of normal) and the maternal condition:

- About 30% of women require dose reduction or discontinuation in the second/third trimester, with possible increase/recommencement in the puerperium
- A blocking/replacement regime should be avoided in pregnancy

Fetal and neonatal risks in thyrotoxicosis

In pregnancy the aim of therapy is to reduce the dose of any drugs to the minimum required to control maternal disease. However, both propylthiouracil and carbimazole cross the placenta. High dosage may be associated with fetal goitre, which usually resolves postnatally.

- 10%–20% of babies have transient biochemical hypothyroidism which is rarely symptomatic and resolves on day 4–5
- The fetal and neonatal risk of Graves' disease is proportional to the titre of maternal TSH-receptor-stimulating antibodies. These should be measured in the first and third trimester in women with active disease, or in those with a history of disease treated with surgery and/or radioactive iodine

Fetal hyperthyroidism develops between 20 and 24 weeks' gestation.

Complications of fetal hyperthyroidism

- Fetal tachycardia (>160 beats/min)
- Increased fetal movements
- IUGR
- Fetal goitre
- Craniosynostosis
- Hydrops
- Polyhydramnios
- Pre-term labour

Treatment is dependent upon gestation and is either delivery or anti-thyroid agents, titrated against fetal heart rate, movements and growth rate.

Neonatal hyperthyroidism occurs in 1% of cases of maternal thyrotoxicosis. The clinical presentation may be delayed, but treatment with anti-thyroid drugs or β-blockers is rarely needed for more than a few months.

Clinical features of neonatal hyperthyroidism

- Jitteriness
- Failure to gain weight
- Poor feeding
- Poor sleeping
- Bossing of frontal bones
- Liver dysfunction
- Jaundice

Hypothyroidism

Hypothyroidism is the commonest pre-existing endocrine disorder in pregnancy. The incidence is 9 in 1000 pregnancies. The commonest cause is Hashimoto's thyroiditis.

Treatment

Thyroxine is the mainstay treatment, as it is safe in pregnancy and in breast-feeding.

- Thyroid function tests should be measured at 8–12 weeks if stable, and every 4–6 weeks if the dosage is being adjusted
- Thyroxine should be altered according to the free T_4 levels; TSH may remain raised after the correct dosage has been achieved (especially in the third trimester)
- If the patient is stable pre-pregnancy, they are likely to remain stable without requiring any dose adjustment during the pregnancy
- Suboptimal maternal treatment (ie a low free T_4 in the first trimester) may be associated with adverse neurodevelopment in the child
- Neonatal hypothyroidism is rare and transient and is caused by TSH receptor-blocking antibodies

Post-partum thyroiditis

This has an autoimmune aetiology and hence it is associated with other autoimmune diseases. Thyroid antiperoxidase antibodies are seen in 90% of sufferers. The histology of the thyroid gland is typical of autoimmune thyroiditis with focal/diffuse thyroiditis, lymphocytic infiltration, follicular destruction and hyperplasia.

There are three phases of post-partum thyroiditis:

- **Thyrotoxicosis**: 1–3 months post-partum. This is associated with low uptake of radioactive iodine (unlike Graves' disease). Treatment is rarely required, but if needed involves only β-blockers
- **Hypothyroidism**: 3–8 months post-partum. This may be associated with symptoms which include lethargy, poor memory and cold intolerance, and treatment with thyroxine may be indicated
- **Normal thyroid function**: by 1 year post-partum

The mother may experience one, two or all of these phases. The recurrence risk in another pregnancy is about 70%. Patients will need long-term surveillance as the risk of permanent hypothyroidism is about 3%–5% per year.

12.3.6 Epilepsy and pregnancy

Epilepsy occurs in 1 in 200 women of child-bearing age, and is the commonest neurological disorder in pregnancy. In general, the longer a woman has been free of fits prior to pregnancy the less likely it is that her epilepsy will deteriorate during pregnancy.

Factors influencing fit frequency in pregnancy

- Disease pattern pre-pregnancy
- Sleep deprivation, especially in the third trimester
- Vomiting in pregnancy
- Altered protein binding, and increased volume of distribution of anticonvulsants
- Altered drug compliance
- Altered metabolism and excretion of anticonvulsant drugs

Effect of maternal epilepsy upon the fetus

The fetus is very tolerant of isolated, short-lived fits. Repeated fits can result in fetal hypoxia and lactic acidosis, which may be associated with fetal brady-cardia. In rare instances, fetal intraventricular hae-morrhages and death have been attributed to maternal convulsions. The effect may be remote and only detected in developmental delay years later. Status epilepticus doubles the risk of maternal death and is associated with a 50% miscarriage rate.

- **Birth defects**: epilepsy is associated with an increased incidence of certain congenital malformations (3.5%–4.4%); the risk is multifactorial and increases with the number of anticonvulsants used
- **Risk of epilepsy in the newborn**: about 4% if one parent is affected, rising to 10% if both are affected
- **Neonatal coagulopathy**: associated with maternal use of phenytoin, phenobarbital and primidone; maternal coagulation studies are usually normal

Management of the epileptic in pregnancy

Pre-pregnancy counselling should be given to the patient regarding the risks of pregnancy. Where possible, anticonvulsant monotherapy should be used.

- High-dose folic acid (5 mg daily) should be advised pre-conceptionally and for the first 3 months of pregnancy (particularly for those women on hepatic enzyme-inducing anti-epileptics such as phenytoin)
- A detailed fetal anomaly scan should be performed
- If fits occur during pregnancy, the anticonvulsant levels should be monitored
- If the patient is receiving phenytoin, then vitamin K should be administered to the mother from 36 weeks' gestation in order to counteract possible neonatal coagulopathy

12.4 MEDICAL COMPLICATIONS OF PREGNANCY

12.4.1 Hypertensive disorders of pregnancy

Definitions

Hypertension in pregnancy is defined as:

- Diastolic BP $\geqslant$110 mmHg on any one occasion
  or
- Diastolic BP $\geqslant$90 mmHg on two or more consecutive occasions $\geqslant$4 hours apart

Blood pressure should be measured in the sitting position with a sphygmomanometer cuff size appropriate for the size of the patient's arm.

Phases I and V of the Korotkoff sounds identify the systolic and diastolic limits, respectively, correlating more accurately with outcome than phase IV.

Proteinuria in pregnancy is defined as:

- Total protein excretion $\geqslant$300 mg per 24 hours
  or
- Two 'clean-catch – midstream' or catheter specimens of urine collected $\geqslant$4 hours apart with $\geqslant$2+ on reagent strip

Hypertension is associated with between 6% and 8% of pregnancies and can have serious repercussions for both fetal and maternal well-being. Hypertension can pre-date the pregnancy (**essential** or **chronic hypertension**) or arise in pregnancy (**pregnancy-induced hypertension** or PIH).

• The majority of women with PIH have non-proteinuric PIH, a condition associated with minimal maternal or perinatal mortality/ morbidity
• Approximately 2% of pregnancies are complicated by proteinuric PIH (**pre-eclampsia**)

Pre-eclampsia is a serious pregnancy complication that causes significant maternal and perinatal morbidity and it remains one of the leading causes of maternal and fetal/neonatal deaths. It is therefore imperative that every effort is made to accurately classify the nature of hypertension occurring in pregnancy as the aetiology and management of the three conditions, chronic hypertension, non-proteinuric PIH and pre-eclampsia, are very different (Table 12.4).

Pre-eclampsia

Although the primary events leading to pre-eclampsia are still unclear, it is now thought that the pathophysiology involves a cascade of events which leads to the clinical syndrome.

Pathophysiology of pre-eclampsia

• Genetic predisposition
• Faulty interplay between invading trophoblast and decidua
• Decreased blood supply to feto-placental unit
• Release of circulating factor(s)
• Endothelial cell alteration

Pre-eclampsia is associated with hypertension, proteinuria and IUGR.

Maternal mortality rate is about 2% in the UK and, worldwide, 100 000 women die of pre-eclampsia each year. Perinatal mortality is also increased, and this is associated with IUGR and iatrogenic pre-term delivery. In the most recent Confidential Enquiry

Table 12.4. The ISSHP classification (modified and abbreviated)

1. **Gestational hypertension and/or proteinuria developing during pregnancy, labour or the puerperium in a previously normotensive non-proteinuric woman:**	Gestational hypertension (without proteinuria) Gestational proteinuria (without hypertension) Gestational proteinuric hypertension (pre-eclampsia)
2. **Chronic hypertension (before the 20th week of pregnancy) and chronic renal disease (proteinuria before the 20th week of pregnancy):**	Chronic hypertension (without proteinuria) Chronic renal disease (proteinuria with or without hypertension) Chronic hypertension with superimposed pre-eclampsia (new-onset proteinuria)
3. **Unclassified hypertension and/or proteinuria**	
4. **Eclampsia**	

into Maternal and Child Health (CEMACH) hypertensive disorders of pregnancy remain the second leading cause of maternal death.

Screening for pre-eclampsia

It is important to take a full history, as several factors can be associated with an increased risk of pre-eclampsia.

Risk factors associated with pre-eclampsia

- **Increased risk**
  - Family history, 4–8 times higher in first-degree relatives
  - Primigravidas 15 times higher than multiparous
  - Longer pregnancy interval
  - Change in partner
  - Teenage pregnancy
  - Donor insemination
  - Medical disorders such as chronic hypertension, renal disease
- **Decreased risk**
  - Previous termination of pregnancy
  - Previous miscarriage
  - Non-barrier contraception
  - Increased duration of sexual cohabitation

Biophysical tests

All currently available tests are of limited clinical value. The uterine artery may appear 'notched'. Doppler waveforms may be of significance but they are only of sufficient sensitivity and specificity when used in a preselected high-risk population.

Prophylaxis of pre-eclampsia

Several agents have been investigated:

- **Aspirin** (and other antiplatelet agents): a cyclo-oxygenase inhibitor. A Cochrane review of 42 randomised trials demonstrated a 15% relative reduction in the risk of pre-eclampsia with the use of aspirin or other antiplatelet agents

- **Calcium**: 10 randomised trials have investigated the role of calcium in prophylaxis of pre-eclampsia. A moderate reduction in incidence could be demonstrated with calcium supplementation but only in women with an inadequate calcium intake prior to the study
- **Fish oils**: fish oils containing omega-3 fatty acids are thought to inhibit platelet thromboxane A_2. However, trials to date have not shown any reduction in pre-eclampsia
- **Vitamins C and E**: in patients at high risk of developing pre-eclampsia, a 50% reduction could be demonstrated with the use of these agents. Multicentre trials in high- and low-risk populations are now ongoing to determine whether the potential benefit extends to all pregnant women, particularly primigravida

Maternal assessment in pre-eclampsia

Several different organ systems can be affected in the pregnant woman:

- **Platelets**: consumed due to the endothelial activation. Although a platelet count of $>50 \times 10^9/l$ will support normal haemostasis, a falling platelet count, particularly to $<100 \times 10^9/l$ may indicate a need to deliver
- **Hypovolaemia**: results in an increased haematocrit, with an apparent rise in the haemoglobin
- **Clotting disorders**: pre-eclampsia can cause disseminated intravascular coagulation, and clotting disorders must be assessed, particularly in the face of falling platelet numbers
- **Renal tubular function**: uric acid is a measure of 'fine' renal tubular function. It is used to assess the disease severity, although severe disease can still occur with a normal uric acid level. Spuriously high levels of uric acid are associated with acute fatty liver of pregnancy (see below)
- **Renal impairment**: raised urea and creatinine are associated with late renal involvement and hence are not useful as an early indicator of disease severity. However, serial measurements will identify renal disease progression.

Proteinuria is a hallmark of pre-eclampsia; protein excretion may increase progressively as the pre-eclamptic process evolves

- **Liver involvement**: pre-eclampsia can cause subcapsular haematoma, liver rupture and hepatic infarction. Aspartate aminotransferase (AST) and other transaminases indicate hepatocellular damage. Elevated levels may again indicate a need to deliver. It should be remembered that the normal range for transaminases is approximately 20% lower than the non-pregnant range

The circulating albumin may fall, especially if urinary protein excretion is high (eg >3 g/24 hours); hypoalbuminaemia increases the risk of pulmonary oedema. Note that a raised AST can be associated with either **haemolysis** or liver involvement; lactate dehydrogenase (LDH) levels are also elevated in the presence of haemolysis (see HELLP syndrome, below).

Fetal assessment in pre-eclampsia

Fetal well-being must be carefully assessed in all cases of pre-eclampsia. This involves:

- **Clinical assessment**: the symphyseal–fundal height should be carefully measured and an enquiry as to fetal movements undertaken
- **Investigations**: regular ultrasound assessment of fetal growth and amniotic fluid volume should be performed. Umbilical artery Doppler waveforms may be of use (see above)

Suspected fetal compromise is a frequent indication for delivery in pre-eclampsia.

Management of pre-eclampsia

Pre-eclamptic hypertension can cause direct arterial injury which can, in turn, predispose to possibly fatal cerebral haemorrhage. In order to prevent this injury severe hypertension should be avoided. Blood pressures greater than 170/110 mmHg (mean arterial pressure (MAP) of $\geq$140 mmHg) require urgent therapy. The rationale for treating moderate hypertension (BP >140/90 mmHg but <170/110

mmHg) is less clear. Nevertheless in the most recent CEMACH report attention was particularly drawn to the importance of treating systolic hypertension (ie SBP $\geq$160 mmHg), irrespective of the MAP, because of the risk of maternal cerebral haemorrhage.

- **Choice of antihypertensive agents**: methyldopa, labetalol and nifedipine are the mainstay in therapy. In practice, the choice of agent probably matters less than the clinician's familiarity with it

Timing of delivery: in women with established pre-eclampsia, delivery should be considered once fetal lung maturity has been achieved. However, in asymptomatic women with pre-eclampsia presenting between 26 and 32 weeks, management can often be conservative in an attempt to achieve improved perinatal survival, without substantial risk to the mother. This does, however, require close in-patient supervision in a unit with adequate numbers of appropriately skilled staff. Trials have confirmed the advantages of this cautiously expectant approach. As stated previously, fetal compromise will indicate the need for delivery.

Indications for delivery in pre-eclampsia

- Inability to control hypertension
- Deteriorating liver or renal function
- Progressive fall in platelets
- Neurological complications
- Abnormal CTG
- Deteriorating fetal condition

HELLP syndrome

HELLP (**h**aemolysis, **e**levated **l**iver enzymes and **l**ow **p**latelets) syndrome is a severe form of pre-eclampsia, associated with:

- Haemolysis
- Elevated liver enzymes (ALT/LDH)
- Low platelets

It complicates about 10%–15% of cases of pre-eclampsia. Mortality rates vary from 0% to 25%, and mortality is associated with cerebral haemorrhage and disseminated intravascular coagulation (DIC), correlating with the extent of thrombocytopenia. HELLP syndrome and acute fatty liver of pregnancy are two conditions which are very similar and there is a recognised degree of overlap in both aetiology and pathophysiology, such that a definitive diagnosis can be difficult to make.

Acute fatty liver of pregnancy

Acute fatty liver of pregnancy typically occurs in obese women or in the third trimester of pregnancy. It is associated with pre-eclampsia (30%–100% of cases), twin pregnancy and is more common in women with male fetuses.

Symptoms develop acutely and include abdominal pain, nausea/vomiting, headache and jaundice. Other clinical features which may occur include pruritus, fever, enterocolitis, ascites or pancreatitis.

Investigations in acute fatter liver of pregnancy

- **Laboratory findings**
  - Neutrophil leucocytosis
  - Increased fibrin degradation products
  - Low platelets
  - Microangiopathic haemolytic anaemia
  - Increased bilirubin
  - Raised AST (3–10 times above normal)
  - Hypoglycaemia
  - Increased uric acid
- **Liver pathology**
  - The liver is small and yellow
  - Histology reveals microvesicular steatosis with intrahepatic cholestasis and canalicular plugs of bile; distribution is panlobar with sparing of periportal areas
  - Extramedullary haematopoiesis

- **Imaging**
  - Increased reflectivity of liver on ultrasound scanning and lower attenuation on MRI are both indicative of 'fat' within the liver
  - Infarction appears as multiple non-enhancing lesions of low attenuation, with mottled appearance

Management of acute fatty liver of pregnancy

Early diagnosis is important, followed by transfer of the patient to tertiary care. The patients may need to be transferred to intensive care for correction of hypertension, hypoglycaemia and bleeding diathesis. The baby needs to be delivered as a matter of urgency.

The neonate is at risk of fatty infiltration of the liver and this is associated with impaired liver function, hypoglycaemia, thrombocytopenia and neutropenia.

Eclampsia

Eclampsia is defined as convulsions occurring in a woman with pre-eclampsia in the absence of any other neurological cause. The maternal mortality rate associated with eclampsia in the UK is approximately 1 in 50. It complicates 1 in 2000 pregnancies in the UK. In about 40% of cases it is totally or partially unheralded by prodromal signs or symptoms. In 10% of cases the only warning sign is proteinuria, and in another 20% there is hypertension only. Most cases occur during labour or after delivery. Such cases are usually at term and in hospital. Pre-term eclampsia is more likely to be antepartum.

Management of eclampsia

The aim of management is to protect the maternal airway, control the convulsions and extreme hypertension, as well as to expedite delivery.

- **Choice of anticonvulsant**: most fits stop quickly and spontaneously. In the Collaborative Eclampsia Trial (1995) magnesium sulphate was shown to be the anticonvulsant of first choice. A bolus of 4 mg is given intravenously over 10 minutes. About 10% of all fits will not be controlled by magnesium sulphate. A brain scan should be performed if presentation is atypical, if any focal signs develop, or in the case of repeated or prolonged seizures

Magnesium sulphate treatment in eclampsia

- **Toxic side-effects**: muscular weakness; respiratory paralysis; heart failure and death
- **Monitor**: check deep tendon reflexes
- **Therapeutic levels**: 2–3.5 mmol/l
- **Antidote**: calcium gluconate 1 g over 10 minutes, intravenously

Chronic hypertension

Chronic hypertension (CHT) is detected either by an antecedent medical history or by a raised blood pressure in the first half of pregnancy. The physiological decline in the blood pressure in early pregnancy is exaggerated in women with CHT so that they may be normotensive. Conversely, in later pregnancy the normal rise in blood pressure is exaggerated in patients with CHT. Hence a woman with CHT may be normotensive initially, with hypertension only appearing in the third trimester.

- CHT in pregnancy is a major predisposing factor for pre-eclampsia. This risk is about five times greater than in normotensive women
- Women with CHT who do not develop pre-eclampsia can usually expect a normal, uncomplicated perinatal outcome, although there is some evidence for a modest increase in the incidence of IUGR in these women. Perinatal morbidity and mortality is related to treatment and so cautious discontinuation of

pharmacological agents may be appropriate (see later)
- **Antihypertensive treatment**: ACE inhibitors should be avoided, as this class of drug is associated with fetal and neonatal renal failure and death. Women with mild to moderate hypertension should discontinue treatment prior to conception because of the risk of IUGR. There is no evidence that treating CHT reduces the risk of superimposed pre-eclampsia, nor is there any evidence to support a particular fetal benefit. Long-term use of antihypertensive drugs has been associated with IUGR; it is uncertain whether this is a specific drug effect (eg β-blockers) or a consequence of a reduction in placental perfusion following a lowering of arterial pressure

12.4.2 Thrombotic complications in pregnancy

Thromboembolic disease

Pulmonary embolism is the commonest cause of maternal mortality in the UK. Pregnancy increases the risk of thromboembolism about sixfold. The absolute incidence varies widely between 0.1% and 1.2% of all pregnancies. Deep vein thrombosis (DVT) is about twice as common as pulmonary embolism. The risk of thrombosis is as common in the first trimester as in the third.

Aetiology

Pregnancy is a hypercoagulable state due to an increase in Factors VII, VIII and X as well as fibrinogen and prothrombin. This is exacerbated by venous stasis as the gravid uterus obstructs the inferior vena cava, causing a decrease in venous tone in the lower limbs, which is greater on the left than the right (hence 80% of DVTs occur on the left). Immobility during labour and in the post-partum period, particularly after operative delivery, further exacerbates the situation. Other factors are listed in Table 12.5.

Table 12.5. Other factors increasing the risk of thromboembolism in pregnancy

---

Increased with age (>35 years)
Increased with rising parity
Increased body mass index (3 times increased risk if BMI >29)
Smoking, as it causes inhibition of fibrinolysis
Sickle cell disease
Anaemia
Dehydration
Blood group other than O
Thrombophilic conditions (see below)

Thrombophilia

Thrombophilic tendencies may be more significant in women of reproductive age as pregnancy may uncover a hitherto unrecognised condition. The main conditions to consider are:

• Antithrombin deficiency
• Antiphospholipid deficiency/lupus anticoagulant syndrome
• Protein C deficiency
• Protein S deficiency
• Prothrombin gene variant (see below)
• Factor V Leiden (see below)
• Homocystinuria (see below)

Hereditary thrombophilic states may be associated with an adverse pregnancy outcome including early pregnancy loss odds ratio (OR 1.40–6.25); late pregnancy loss (OR 1.31–20.09); pre-eclampsia (OR 1.37–3.49); placental abruption (OR 1.42–7.71) and IUGR (OR 1.24–2.92). Low-dose aspirin plus heparin was the most effective in preventing pregnancy loss in thrombophilic women (OR: 1.62). However, despite the increase in relative risk, the absolute risk of venous thromboembolism (VTE) and adverse outcomes remains low. There is also a lack

of controlled trials of antithrombotic intervention to prevent pregnancy complications.*

The association with recurrent miscarriage is also probably limited to those women with acquired rather than hereditary thrombophilias or those with compound thrombophilias.**

Similarly there is now evidence to suggest that a single gene variant (eg heterogygosity for factor V Leiden) alone is in itself a relatively weak risk factor for VTE (and/or adverse pregnancy outcome) and is therefore not an indication for low-molecular-weight heparin (LMWH). Rather it should be considered in the light of other risk factors for VTE.

Antithrombin deficiency
Two types of antithrombin deficiency exist:

• Type I – a deficiency of a normal molecule
• Type II – associated with an abnormal molecule

The risk of thromboembolism is as high as 40%–70% and necessitates lifelong warfarin. The risk is greater in type I than in type II antithrombin deficiency.

In pregnancy, patients with types I and II antithrombin deficiency (plus additional risk factors; see Table 12.5 for other factors increasing the risk of thromboembolism) should receive therapeutic levels of LMWH. Antithrombin concentrate may be required to cover labour and if thrombosis occurs earlier in pregnancy. Cord blood should be taken to assess neonatal status at birth; tests should be repeated at 6 months.

Antiphospholipid syndrome
Antiphospholipid deficiency/lupus anticoagulant have been considered earlier (see Section 12.3.4).

Protein C deficiency
Protein C deficiency may be inherited in autosomal dominant and recessive forms. Patients will often have a history of thrombosis. These patients require thromboprophylaxis with anti-embolic stockings

---

*Robertson L et al. Thrombophilia in pregnancy: a systematic review. *Br J Haematol* 2006;**132**:171–96
Coulam CB. Multiple thrombophilic gene mutations rather than specific gene mutations are risk factors for recurrent miscarriage. *Am J Reprod Immunol* 2006;55**:360–8

and LMWH throughout the antenatal period and for 6 weeks post-partum. In those women without a personal history of thrombosis additional risk factors need to be considered (eg BMI >30, age >35 years, parity >3, immobility >4 days) in deciding whether to use LMWH – ALL women require anti-embolic stockings. Warfarin is avoided because it is associated with skin necrosis (purpura fulminans in those women with the homozygous form) and both teratogenicity (greatest risk between 6 and 12 weeks' gestation) and fetal intracerebral bleeding (throughout the second and third trimesters). Prenatal diagnosis is achieved by cordocentesis in the second trimester.

Protein S deficiency

Protein S is a co-factor for protein C and levels normally fall in pregnancy, making diagnosis difficult. Deficiency of protein S is associated with a 0%–6% risk of thrombosis antenatally and 7%–22% postnatally. The usual approach is to treat with prophylactic doses of LMWH in the post-partum period only, unless additional risk factors exist.

Factor V Leiden

Factor V Leiden is caused by a single point mutation. It is resistant to activated protein C, causing thrombosis. Two forms of Factor V Leiden exist:

- **Heterozygous**: more common; risk of thrombosis 0.25% (see Table 12.6)

- **Homozygous**: rare; risk of thrombosis 50–80 times greater than in non-carriers

The risk of thrombosis is low in heterozygotes, particularly in the absence of a personal history of thrombosis and/or additional risk factors. Prophylaxis, in the form of compression stockings, may be all that is required. LMWH is usually reserved for those women who are homozygous for the gene or who have additional risk factors. Recent evidence refutes its association with recurrent miscarriage and/or poor pregnancy outcome (see earlier).

Prothrombin gene variant

Similar to factor V Lieden above. Heterozygous and homozygous forms.

Homocystinuria

Homocystinuria is an inborn error of metabolism that is associated with increased risk of both arterial and venous thrombosis. It should be considered alongside other risk factors.

Table 12.7 gives the prevalence and risk of VTE during pregnancy in relation to inherited thrombophilias.

Diagnosis of thromboembolic disorders in pregnancy

Table 12.8 outlines the diagnosis of thromboembolic disorders in pregnancy.

Table 12.6. Thrombophilic or hereditary hypercoagulable disorders in the general population and in people with venous thrombosis

Condition	Prevalence in general population (%)	Prevalence in people with venous thrombosis (%)	Increased risk for thrombosis
Factor V Leiden	5–15	20	3.8
Prothrombin 20210A	1–6	2	3.0
Protein C	0.2	3	25–50
Protein S	Unknown	1–2	10–15
Antithrombin III	0.02	1	10

Table 12.7. Prevalence and risk of venous thromboembolism (VTE) associated with pregnancy in relation to inherited thombophilias

Thrombophilia	Prevalence among women with VTE associated with pregnancy (%)	Relative risk of VTE
Factor V Leiden (heterozygous)	8–44	5–10
Factor V Leiden (homozygous)	9–17	10–80
Prothrombin gene mutation (heterozygous)	3–17	2–5
Prothrombin gene mutation (homozygous)	–	–
Compound heterozygote (factor V Leiden and prothrombin gene mutation)	4–9	9–107
Antithrombin deficiency (<80% activity)	12–60 AN; 11–33 PP*	10 to unknown
Protein C deficiency (<75% activity)	3–10 AN; 7–19 PP*	Unknown**
Protein S deficiency (<65% activity)	0–6 AN; 7–22 PP*	Unknown**

AN = antenatal; PP = post-partum
*For women with protein C or protein S deficiency the risk of VTE is greater post-partum. Conversely, with antithrombin deficiency the risk of VTE is greatest during pregnancy
Overall **annual incidence of VTE in patients with protein S deficiency or protein C deficiency is 3.5% and 2.5% respectively (Pabinger, IPA et al. The risk of thromboembolism in asymptomatic patients with protein C and protein S deficiency: a prospective cohort study. *Thromb Haemost* 1994;**71**:441–5)

Treatment of thromboembolic disorders

Warfarin is generally avoided in pregnancy. In the first trimester it is associated with an increased risk of miscarriage and teratogenic side-effects which include chondrodysplasia punctata, asplenia and diaphragmatic hernia. In the second and third trimester it is associated with retroplacental and intracerebral fetal haemorrhage, as well as fetal microcephaly, optic atrophy and developmental delay.

LMWH is the mainstay of treatment (but also note use of aspirin in antiphospholipid syndrome). LMWH is preferred to unfractionated heparin as it is less frequently associated with bleeding, thrombocytopenia and osteopenia.

Table 12.8. Diagnosis of thromboembolic disorders in pregnancy

Disorder	Diagnostic tool	Description
Deep vein thrombosis	Clinical and laboratory	The clinical diagnosis of DVT in pregnant women is as difficult as it is in non-pregnant women (50% of pregnant women with a tender, swollen painful leg do not have a DVT) D-dimers are raised in normal pregnancy and therefore of minimal use in aiding the diagnosis of thromboembolism. They do however provide a useful negative
	Plethysmography	Used in left lateral position to detect blood flow in the limb. Normal blood flow is reduced in pregnancy; a negative test excludes DVT, but a positive test requires further evaluation
	Doppler ultrasound	Most widely used technique; effective in diagnosis of symptomatic, proximal DVT. If clot is present the vein is incompressible and does not dilate during Valsalva manoeuvre; sensitivity/specificity about 97%. Insensitive for thrombosis within the calf, or above the inguinal ligament
	Venography	Can be performed with adequate shielding of uterus with minimal risk to the fetus. Useful for confirming femoral and more distal vein thrombosis
Pulmonary embolism	Chest X-ray	Confers minimal risk to fetus. Often normal but may demonstrate an effusion, decreased vascularity
	ECG	Note that changes can occur within normal pregnancy. In PE the ECG may be normal, or it may demonstrate a sinus tachycardia, right heart strain or the classic features of a deep S wave in I, Q wave and inverted T wave in III
	Blood gas analysis	May be normal but in the presence of a PE will typically demonstrate hypoxia with reduced PaO_2, and normal or reduced PaCO_2
	$\dot{V}/\dot{Q}$ scan	The isotopes used have short half-lives and so exposure of the fetus is minimal. The $\dot{V}/\dot{Q}$ scan can be safely performed in breast-feeding mothers. False negatives are rare and hence a normal scan excludes PE. The typical features are perfusion defect with normal ventilation. Moderate probability scans should be discussed with a respiratory physician. Consider leg Doppler $\pm$ CTPA CTPA should also be considered first line in those patients with additional lung pathology $\pm$ abnormal CXR, or following a low probability scan when the clinical picture fails to improve or worsens despite thromboprophylaxis when the underlying diagnosis is not established

Chapter 13
Metabolic Diseases

CONTENTS

Metabolic Diseases

13.1 DISORDERS OF AMINO ACID METABOLISM

Most of the inherited metabolic diseases are mendelian, single-gene defects, transmitted in an autosomal recessive manner. Disease expression requires the affected individual to be homozygous – inheriting a mutant gene from each of their parents, who are both heterozygous for the defect. Although heterozygotes may synthesise equal amounts of normal and defective enzymes they are usually asymptomatic.

- Even the major inborn errors of amino acid metabolism are rare – phenylketonuria, one of the most common, has an incidence of 1/20 000
- Complete penetrance is common and the onset is frequently early in life
- The consequences of these enzyme deficiencies are varied and frequently multisystem but expression tends to be uniform

The more common of these conditions are listed in the box below and the major inborn errors of amino acid metabolism are then discussed.

Inborn errors of amino acid metabolism

- Albinism
- Alkaptonuria
- Cystinosis
- Cystinuria
- Homocystinuria
- Histidinaemia
- Maple syrup urine disease
- Oxalosis
- Phenylketonuria

13.1.1 Alkaptonuria (ochronosis)

This is a rare autosomal recessive disease with an incidence of 1/100 000. Homogentisic acid accumulates as a result of a deficiency in the enzyme homogentisic acid oxidase.

- The homogentisic acid polymerises to produce the black–brown product alkapton, which becomes deposited in cartilage and other tissues (ochronosis)
- Classic features include pigmentation (dark blue, grey or black) of the sclerae, ears, arthritis, intervertebral disc calcification and dark sweat-stained clothing
- Life expectancy is normal but there is significant morbidity from joint complications. Onset of back pain is around 30 years
- Rarer manifestations include renal stone disease as well as aortic valve and ocular involvement
- The urine darkens on standing because homogentisic acid conversion to alkapton is accelerated in alkaline conditions
- There is a high prevalence of alkaptonuria in Slovakia (1/19 000) due to novel mutations, which have resulted in geographical clustering
- The molecular basis of the disorder is known but there is no specific treatment. Arthritis may require joint replacement

13.1.2 Cystinosis

Cystinosis is an autosomal recessive lysosomal storage disease which occurs with an approximate frequency of 1/100 000 to 1/200 000 live births. In cystinosis, cystine accumulates in the reticulo-endothelial system, kidneys and other tissues. There is a defect of cystine transport across the lysosomal membrane resulting in widespread intralysosomal accumulation of cystine. The causative gene (*CTNS*), which encodes for an integral membrane protein called cystinosin, has been identified on chromosome 17p13. Unlike cystinuria, stones do not occur in this condition.

Clinical features of cystinosis
• Fanconi syndrome (often with severe hypophosphataemia and consequent vitamin D-resistant rickets) • Lymphadenopathy • Severe growth retardation • Insulin deficiency • Corneal opacities and photophobia • Abnormalities of cardiac conduction • Hypothyroidism • Bone marrow failure • Central nervous system involvement

Onset is usually in the first year of life and chronic kidney disease (CKD) is progressive, often resulting in end-stage renal disease by the age of 10 years. Corneal or conjunctival crystals usually suggest the diagnosis, which can be confirmed by measuring the cystine content of neutrophils or cultured fibroblasts. Specific therapy with cysteamine bitartrate is effective at reducing cystine accumulation and delaying CKD. Cysteamine eye drops can be used to help with corneal disease. Supportive care, including dialysis and transplantation, is usually needed. Cystinosis does not recur in the transplant but extrarenal disease is progressive. Antenatal testing for cystinosis can be performed by measuring cystine levels in chorionic villi or cultured amniotic fluid cells.

• **Ocular non-nephropathic cystinosis**: this is a variant of the classic disease and is due to different mutations of the cystinosis gene *CTNS*. It is an autosomal recessive lysosomal storage disorder characterised by photophobia due to corneal cystine crystals

13.1.3 Cystinuria

Cystinuria is an autosomal recessive disorder with a prevalence of about 1/7000. The transport of cystine and the other dibasic amino acids lysine, ornithine and arginine is abnormal in the proximal renal tubule and the jejunum.

• No malnutrition occurs as sufficient dietary amino acids are absorbed as oligopeptides
• Presentation is usually in the second or third decade of life with renal stones
• Cystine accumulates in the urine. It is highly insoluble at acid pH and this results in the formation of radio-opaque calculi. (Cystine stones account for 1%–2% of all urinary tract stones)

A urinary cystine concentration >1 mmol/l (at pH 7.0) is supersaturated and leads to calculi formation.

Diagnosis requires measurement of urinary cystine and/or chromatographic analysis of the stone. Pathognomic hexagonal crystals can be found on urine microscopy.

Management

Management involves large fluid intake, alkalinisation of urine and D-penicillamine (which chelates cystine and increases its solubility). Tiopronin is a newer cystine chelator that is better tolerated than D-penicillamine. Captopril is a thiol angiotensin-converting enzyme (ACE) inhibitor and consequently can bind to cystine and increases its solubility.

13.1.4 Homocystinuria

This rare autosomal recessive abnormality results from reduced activity of cystathionine β-synthase. The resulting homocystine and methionine accumulation interferes with collagen cross-linking. Nearly a quarter of patients die as a result of vascular thrombosis before the age of 30.

Clinical features of homocystinuria

- Downward lens dislocation
- Venous and arterial thromboses
- Spontaneous retinal detachment
- Developmental and mental retardation
- Osteoporosis
- Seizures and psychiatric syndromes
- Skeletal abnormalities (eg marfanoid stature, arachnodactyly, chest deformities)

The main differential diagnosis is Marfan syndrome, as patients can have similar skeletal manifestations and ectopia lentis (although this is classically upward lens dislocation in Marfan syndrome). Osteoporosis, mental retardation and vascular thrombosis do not occur in patients with Marfan syndrome.

Investigations

Tests show elevated plasma free methionine and homocystine. Diagnosis is established by the cyanide-nitroprusside test that detects elevated urinary homocystine and reduced cystathionine β-synthase enzyme activity in tissue (liver or skin biopsy). Heterozygous carriers have elevated serum homocystine but no homocystinuria. Premature cardiovascular risk is also increased in heterozygotes.

Management

- Early detection (of younger siblings)
- Methionine restriction and cystine-supplemented diets
- Pyridoxine supplements (effective in 50%)
- Some variants are responsive to folate or vitamin B_{12} supplements
- Antenatal screening for enzyme deficiency is available

Other causes of elevated plasma homocystine

Plasma homocystine levels can be elevated in the elderly, in postmenopausal women and in patients with advanced CKD and hypothyroidism. Drug treatments such as methotrexate can also increase levels. Elevated homocystine levels have been associated with an increased risk of cardiovascular disease (eg in dialysis populations) and deep vein thrombosis.

13.1.5 Primary hyperoxaluria (oxalosis)

There are two inborn errors of metabolism that cause overproduction of oxalate. Both are autosomal recessive and can lead to hyperoxaluria with stones and tissue deposition of calcium oxalate.

- Type I is due to a deficiency of hepatic peroxisomal alanine:glyoxylate aminotransferase
- Type II is due to a deficiency of D-glyceric acid dehydrogenase

Clinical features of oxalosis

- Oxalate renal stones
- Severe arterial disease (due to deposition of oxalate crystals in the vessel wall)
- Nephrocalcinosis
- Cardiac disease (conduction delay)
- Bone disease (and bone marrow invasion leading to pancytopenia and fractures)

Diagnosis

Oxalosis should be suspected if there is increased urinary oxalate excretion, but the latter can also occur with pyridoxine deficiency (as this is a necessary co-enzyme in oxalate metabolism), ileal disease, ethyl glycol poisoning and excess oxalate ingestion.

Confirmation of diagnosis requires:

- Plasma oxalate
- Liver biopsy to demonstrate enzyme deficiency in type I
- Demonstration of enzyme deficiency in peripheral blood leucocytes in type II
- Genetic testing by mutation and linkage analysis is useful for identifying other affected family members, as well as in prenatal diagnosis and carrier testing

Treatment of oxalosis

This initially involves high fluid intake, urinary calcium crystallisation inhibitors (eg citrate) and the use of pyridoxine. Only 10%–30% of patients respond to pyridoxine. In primary hyperoxaluria type I early diagnosis and pre-emptive isolated liver transplantation can be curative. In patients who already have advanced CKD (CKD stages 4 and 5), intensive dialysis therapy is appropriate. Concomitant liver and renal transplantation is often performed, but in this situation the renal transplants can be lost due to rapid oxalate crystal deposition (prior liver transplantation is preferable as it would allow clearance of the oxalate load before consideration of renal transplantation).

13.1.6 Phenylketonuria (PKU)

There are several variants of PKU due to different allelic mutations. For example, mutations of the gene that encodes phenylalanine hydroxylase (and associated enzymes) are found on chromosome 12. Only severe deficiency of the enzyme results in classic PKU with neurological damage. PKU affects between 1/10 000 and 1/14 000 live births.

The biochemical abnormality is an inability to convert phenylalanine into tyrosine due to lack of phenylalanine hydroxylase. This results in hyperphenylalaninaemia and increased excretion of its metabolite, phenylpyruvic acid ('phenylketone') in the urine.

Clinical features of PKU

- Affects children, usually manifesting by 6 months of life
- Irritability
- Decreased pigmentation* (pale skin, fair-haired and blue-eyed phenotype)
- Eczema
- Mental retardation

* This is due to reduced melanin formation

Diagnosis

The Guthrie screening test is a bacterial inhibition assay named after its inventor. Blood applied from a heel prick is applied to filter paper that is subsequently incubated with *Bacillus subtilis* in the presence of β2-thienylalanine (an analogue that inhibits utilisation of phenylalanine). The amount of bacterial growth is proportional to the phenylalanine concentration in the neonatal blood.

Phenylalanine levels can also be measured by spectrofluorometric methods or using a form of mass spectrometry that has the ability to analyse many amino acids, fatty acids and short-chain organic acid metabolites simultaneously.

Management

A diet low in phenylalanine, with tyrosine supplementation in infancy and childhood is now also recommended for adults. Commencing the diet as soon as possible after birth can prevent the deleterious consequences, which are irreversible. PKU females should be advised to reinstitute strict dietary control prior to conception and throughout pregnancy and breast-feeding. Fish oil supplementation can also improve symptoms.

13.2 DISORDERS OF PURINE METABOLISM

Uric acid is the end product of purine metabolism. Purines can be synthesised de novo or salvaged from the breakdown of nucleic acids of endogenous or exogenous origin. Increased de novo synthesis of purines is thought to be responsible, at least partly, for primary gout. Deficiency of hypoxanthine guanine phosphoribosyl transferase (HGPRT), which is involved in the salvage pathway, results in the Lesch–Nyhan syndrome.

Disorders of purine metabolism

- Primary gout
- Lesch–Nyhan syndrome
- Secondary hyperuricaemia

(*See also* Chapter 20, Rheumatology.)

13.2.1 Gout

More than 10% of the population of the western world has hyperuricaemia, which can be due to a variety of genetic and environmental factors. Gout develops in less than 0.5% of the population. (*See also* Chapter 20, Rheumatology.)

- Primary hyperuricaemia is more common in males and postmenopausal females than in pre-menopausal females
- It is rare in childhood
- It is probably polygenic, involving both increased purine synthesis and reduced renal tubular secretion of urate
- Gout can be precipitated by thiazide diuretics, alcohol and high purine (meat) intake
- Treatment is with non-steroidal anti-inflammatory drugs (NSAIDs) and colchicine for acute episodes. NSAIDS or colchicine may be contraindicated or poorly tolerated by some groups of patients (eg CKD); short courses of oral steroids, or a long-acting IM steroid injection, can be prescribed as an alternative. Longer-term lowering of uric acid is achieved with allopurinol. The selective non-purine xanthine oxidase inhibitor febuxostat has also been shown to effectively lower serum uric acid levels
- Hyperuricaemia is associated with increased cardiovascular risk
- Hyperuricaemia is also a sensitive marker for pre-eclampsia. Elevated levels correlate with maternal and fetal mortality and morbidity

13.2.2 Lesch–Nyhan syndrome

Lesch–Nyhan syndrome is an uncommon X-linked recessive disease (therefore seen only in males) due

to complete lack of hypoxanthine guanine phosphoribosyl transferase (HPRT). This results in accumulation of both hypoxanthine and guanine, both of which are metabolised to xanthine and subsequently to uric acid.

Clinical features of Lesch–Nyhan syndrome

- Mental retardation
- Self-mutilation
- Athetosis
- Renal calculi
- Gout
- CKD due to crystal nephropathy
- Spasticity

- Neurological manifestations are usually present in early infancy and consequently patients present with delayed motor development; death from end-stage renal disease in adolescence is common
- Kelley–Seegmiller syndrome is a variant, with mild neurological symptoms, due to a partial deficiency of HPRT
- Treatment of the uric acid overproduction is with allopurinol. Treatments for the neurological and behavioural symptoms are limited
- Carrier and prenatal diagnosis is possible by mutation detection and linkage analysis for probands and their families. Biochemical measurement of HPRT enzyme activity is also possible for at-risk pregnancies

13.3 DISORDERS OF METALS AND METALLOPROTEINS

Iron and copper play central roles in the function of a number of metalloproteins, including cytochrome oxidase, which is essential in cellular aerobic respiration; haem, based on iron, is the key molecule in oxygen transport. Excessive accumulation can, however, promote free radical injury (eg Wilson's disease and haemochromatosis) and disorders of haem synthesis result in porphyria.

Disorders of metals and metalloproteins

- Wilson's disease
- Secondary iron overload
- Haemochromatosis
- The porphyrias

13.3.1 Wilson's disease

This autosomal recessive disorder has a gene frequency of 1/400 and a disease prevalence of approximately 1/200 000. The responsible defective gene (*ATP 7B*) is on chromosome 13, and this codes for a copper-transporting P-type adenosine triphosphate.

In normal subjects 50% of ingested copper is absorbed and transported to the liver loosely bound to albumin. Here copper is incorporated into an $\alpha2$-globulin to form caeruloplasmin, which is the principal transport protein for copper, and necessary for biliary excretion. In Wilson's disease copper absorption is normal but intrahepatic formation of caeruloplasmin is defective. Total body and tissue copper levels rise due to failure of biliary excretion and urinary excretion of copper is increased.

Clinical features of Wilson's disease

- **Onset in childhood or adolescence**
- **Hepatic dysfunction**
  - Acute hepatitis
  - Cirrhosis (most common)
  - Chronic hepatitis
  - Massive hepatic necrosis
- **Hypoparathyroidism**
- **Haemolysis**
- **CNS involvement** (often presents later than hepatic dysfunction)
  - Behavioural problems/psychosis
  - Mental retardation
  - Tremor/chorea
  - Seizures
- **Kayser–Fleischer corneal rings**
  - Due to copper deposition in Descemet's membrane

- **Fanconi syndrome**
- **Musculoskeletal**
  - Degenerative arthropathy resembling premature osteoarthritis
  - Osteopenia (50%)
  - Osteoporosis
  - Chondrocalcinosis

Diagnosis

Wilson's disease should be considered in any patient with unexplained hepatic dysfunction and neurological/neuropsychiatric symptoms. Diagnosis is based on a decrease in serum caeruloplasmin and increases in hepatic copper content and urinary excretion of copper. However, biochemical diagnosis is increasingly recognised to have low sensitivity. Molecular diagnosis is now available to identify presymptomatic individuals. Serum copper levels are of no diagnostic value.

Management

Early detection permits lifelong use of medications that can prevent the deleterious effects of copper accumulation. Copper chelators (eg penicillamine and trientine) are used to remove copper in symptomatic patients. In patients who have no symptoms, zinc is used to prevent the build up of copper. Zinc works by preventing copper absorption in the gut. It is also used in patients who have responded to treatment with chelators as maintenance therapy. Fulminant hepatic failure and end-stage liver disease necessitate liver transplantation, which is curative (but CNS sequelae may persist). First-degree relatives should be screened for Wilson's disease. (*See also* Chapter 6, Gastroenterology.)

13.3.2 Haemochromatosis

In the normal adult the iron content of the body is closely regulated. Haemochromatosis is the excessive accumulation of iron. Primary (or idiopathic) haemochromatosis is a common autosomal recessive disorder in which iron accumulates in parenchymal cells, leading to damage and fibrosis. Haemosiderin is an insoluble iron–protein complex found in macrophages (it is relatively harmless to them) in the bone marrow, liver and spleen. Secondary iron overload, which has many causes, is often referred to as 'haemosiderosis'.

- The gene for haemochromatosis (*HFE*) is located on chromosome 6 close to the HLA locus. *HFE* codes for a transmembrane glycoprotein that modulates iron uptake. Ninety per cent of Caucasian patients are homozygous for the *HFE* C282Y mutation
- The gene frequency is 6% and disease frequency 1/220 people, but the severity of the disease seems to vary
- Males are affected earlier and more severely than females (as menstrual loss/pregnancy protects females)
- Heterozygotes are at greater risk of secondary haemosiderosis than non-carriers if they have a predisposing condition
- Thirty per cent of patients with cirrhosis develop hepatocellular carcinoma. (*See also* Chapter 6, Gastroenterology)

Clinical features of haemochromatosis

- Presentation above the age of 40 years
- Hepatomegaly preceding micronodular cirrhosis
- Chondrocalcinosis and pseudogout
- Cardiomyopathy and arrhythmias
- Bronze skin pigmentation
- Diabetes mellitus and (rarely) exocrine pancreas failure
- Hypopituitarism, hypogonadism and testicular atrophy

Diagnosis

Serum iron is elevated with greater than 60% transferrin saturation. Serum ferritin is >500 µg/l but it is important to note that the most common causes of elevated ferritin (an acute phase reactant) are inflammation, alcohol and many other conditions. Molecular genetic diagnosis for *HFE* mutation is now widely used. Liver iron concentration >180 µmol/g is also indicative of haemochromatosis.

Liver biopsy is now used as a prognostic indicator rather than a diagnostic one. Factors associated with increased progression of hepatic fibrosis include increased serum ferritin and alcohol abuse.

Management

- Venesection
- Chelation therapy with desferrioxamine
- Screening of first-degree relatives (serum ferritin)
- Screening cirrhotic patients for hepatocellular carcinoma is recommended (6-monthly ultrasound and serum α-fetoprotein)
- Liver transplantation (for end-stage liver disease)

13.3.3 Secondary iron overload

Secondary haemochromatosis is due to iron overload, which can occur in a variety of conditions. The pattern of tissue injury is similar to that in primary haemochromatosis. In the inherited haemolytic anaemias iron overload can present in adolescence; the features are often modified by the underlying disease. Treatment is with desferrioxamine.

Secondary causes of iron overload

- **Anaemia due to ineffective erythropoiesis**
  - Beta-thalassaemia
  - Sideroblastic anaemia
  - Aplastic anaemia
  - Pyruvate kinase deficiency
- **Parenteral iron overload**
  - Transfusions
  - Iron–dextran
- **Liver disease**
  - Alcoholic cirrhosis
  - Chronic viral hepatitis
  - Porphyria cutanea tarda
- **Increased oral iron intake** (Bantu siderosis)
- **Congenital transferrinaemia**

13.3.4 The porphyrias

The porphyrias are a rare heterogeneous group of conditions caused by abnormalities of enzymes involved in the biosynthesis of haem, resulting in overproduction of the intermediate compounds called porphyrins. Most porphyrias are hereditary, although some can be acquired. Excess production of porphyrins can occur in the liver or bone marrow and is classified as acute or non-acute.

The haem metabolic pathway and the type of porphyria resulting from different enzyme deficiencies are shown in Figure 13.1. The two most important porphyrias are porphyria cutanea tarda and acute intermittent porphyria – these are described in more detail.

Porphyria cutanea tarda

This is the most common hepatic porphyria. There is a genetic predisposition but the pattern of inheritance is not established. It is more common in men and usually presents after the age of 40. Many sporadic cases are due to chronic liver disease, usually alcohol-related.

- There is reduced uroporphyrinogen decarboxylase activity

- Uroporphyrinogen accumulates in blood and urine
- Manifests as photosensitivity rash with bullae. Porphyrins produce free radicals when exposed to ultraviolet light which results in damage to sun-exposed skin

Diagnosis
Based on elevated urinary uroporphyrinogen (urine is normal in colour).

Treatment

- The underlying liver disease
- Chloroquine
- Venesection

Acute intermittent porphyria

This causes attacks of classic acute porphyria, often presenting with abdominal pain and/or neuropsychiatric disorders. It is an autosomal dominant disorder.

- There is reduced hepatic porphobilinogen deaminase activity

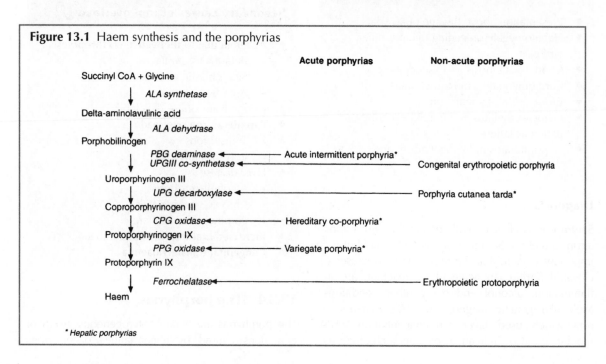

Figure 13.1 Haem synthesis and the porphyrias

- The gene (and disease) frequency is between 1/10 000 and 1/50 000
- Episodes of porphyria are more common in females (?due to the effects of oestrogens)
- There is no photosensitivity or skin rash
- There is increased urinary porphobilinogen and aminolaevulinic acid, especially during attacks
- Urine turns deep red on standing

Clinical features of acute intermittent porphyria

- Onset in adolescence
- Females more affected
- Polyneuropathy (motor)
- Hypertension and tachycardia
- Episodic attacks
- Tubulointerstitial nephritis
- Abdominal pain occurs in 95% of acute episodes, vomiting, constipation
- Neuropsychiatric disorders

Precipitating drugs:

- Alcohol
- Benzodiazepines
- Rifampicin
- Oral contraceptives
- Phenytoin
- Sulphonamides

Other precipitating factors:

- Stress
- Pregnancy
- Changes in the menstrual cycle (especially premenstrual)
- Infection
- Fasting

Management

- Supportive: maintain high carbohydrate intake; avoid precipitating factors
- Gonadotrophin-releasing hormone analogues to prevent cyclical attacks

- Sertraline and other psychotropic drugs have been used without precipitating acute porphyria, but care is advisable with use of all drugs
- Early detection of the signs and symptoms of an acute episode
- Acute episodes are treated with daily haem arginate infusions for 3–4 days as well as treatment/withdrawal of any precipitating agents
- 10% of patients die as a result of hepatocellular carcinoma

13.4 DISORDERS OF LIPID METABOLISM

Hyperlipidaemia, especially hypercholesterolaemia, is associated with cardiovascular disease (Table 13.1).

Table 13.1. Cholesterol level and relative risk of myocardial infarct

Total cholesterol (mmol/l)	Relative risk of myocardial infarct
5.2	1
6.5	2
7.8	4

Although lipid metabolism is complex, and many inherited or acquired disorders can disrupt it, the end result is usually elevated cholesterol and/or triglyceride concentrations. These can be managed by dietary and pharmacological means.

13.4.1 Lipid metabolism

Cholesterol and triglycerides are insoluble in plasma and circulate bound to lipoproteins. The lipoproteins consist of lipids, phospholipids and proteins. The protein components of lipoproteins are called apolipoproteins (or apoproteins) and they act as cofactors for enzymes and ligands for receptors. Figure 13.2 is a schema of lipoprotein structure and lipid metabolism is shown in Figure 13.3.

Figure 13.2 Schema of lipoprotein structure

There are four major lipoproteins:

- **Chylomicrons**: large particles that carry dietary lipid (mainly triglycerides) from the gastrointestinal tract to the liver. In the portal circulation lipoprotein lipase acts on chylomicrons to release free fatty acids for energy metabolism
- **Very low-density lipoprotein (VLDL)**: carries endogenous triglyceride (60%), and to a lesser extent cholesterol (20%), from the liver to the tissues. The triglyceride core of the VLDL is also hydrolysed by lipoprotein lipase to release free

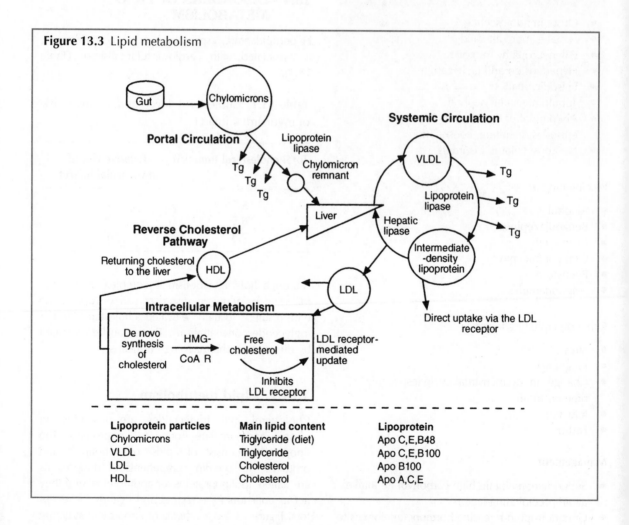

Figure 13.3 Lipid metabolism

Lipoprotein particles	Main lipid content	Lipoprotein
Chylomicrons	Triglyceride (diet)	Apo C,E,B48
VLDL	Triglyceride	Apo C,E,B100
LDL	Cholesterol	Apo B100
HDL	Cholesterol	Apo A,C,E

fatty acids. The VLDL remnants are called intermediate-density lipoprotein

- **Low-density lipoprotein (LDL)**: formed from the intermediate-density lipoproteins by hepatic lipase. LDL contains a cholesterol core (50%) and lesser amounts of triglyceride (10%). LDL metabolism is regulated by cellular cholesterol requirements via negative feedback control of the LDL receptor
- **High-density lipoprotein (HDL)**: carries cholesterol from the tissues back to the liver. HDL is formed in the liver and gut and acquires free cholesterol from the intracellular pools. Within the HDL, cholesterol is esterified by lecithin cholesterol acyltransferase (LCAT). HDL is inversely associated with ischaemic heart disease

The LDL receptor

Circulating LDL is taken up by the LDL receptor. Cells replete in cholesterol reduce LDL receptor expression. In contrast, inhibition of 3-hydroxy-3-methylglutaryl co-enzyme A (HMG CoA) reductase, the enzyme that controls the rate of de novo cholesterol synthesis, leads to a fall in cellular cholesterol and an increase in LDL receptor expression.

Lipoprotein (a)

Lp(a) is a specialised form of LDL. Lp(a) inhibits fibrinolysis and promotes atherosclerotic plaque formation. It is an independent risk factor for ischaemic heart disease.

13.4.2   The hyperlipidaemias

Population studies have consistently demonstrated a strong relationship between both total and LDL cholesterol and coronary heart disease. HDL is protective. A total cholesterol:HDL ratio of >4.5 is associated with an increased risk. Intervention trials (for example, the Cholesterol Treatment Trialists' (CTT) Collaborators) have shown that a reduction of LDL cholesterol of 1 mmol reduces cardiovascular events by 21% and reduces mortality by 12%.

Triglycerides are also associated with cardiovascular risk; very high triglycerides are also associated with pancreatitis, lipaemic serum and eruptive xanthomata. Triglycerides must be measured fasting.

A genetic classification of lipid disorders has now replaced the Fredrickson (WHO) classification, which was based on lipoprotein patterns. The primary hyperlipidaemias can be grouped according to the simple lipid profile. Secondary causes of hyperlipidaemia need to be excluded and are discussed below.

Primary hypercholesterolaemia (without hypertriglyceridaemia)

Familial hypercholesterolaemia (FH) is a monogenic disorder resulting from LDL receptor dysfunction.

- There are many different mutations in different families, all resulting in LDL receptor deficiency/dysfunction and producing isolated hypercholesterolaemia
- Heterozygote prevalence is 1/500; these individuals have cholesterol levels of 9–15 mmol/l and sustain myocardial infarctions at about age 40 years (M = F)
- Homozygous FH is rare. Cholesterol levels are in excess of 15 mmol/l and patients suffer myocardial infarction in the second or third decades
- Other typical clinical features are Achilles tendon xanthomata (can also occur in other extensor tendons) and xanthelasma
- All patients with FH should have lipid-lowering therapy titrated upwards until there has been at least a 50% reduction in LDL cholesterol

LDL-lowering apheresis (plasma exchange)

LDL apheresis can lower plasma LDL by up to 65% after each treatment. This procedure involves the extracorporeal removal of LDL in a process similar to dialysis. The treatment is lifelong and is performed weekly to fortnightly. It can be used to lower LDL cholesterol in homozygous FH patients who have not responded to drug treatment or have evidence of coronary heart disease. It can also be used in exceptional cases for patients with heterozygous FH, ie progressive coronary heart disease despite maximal medical and surgical intervention. ACE inhibitors should not be used in patients undergoing LDL apheresis due to the increased risk of anaphylaxis.

Liver transplantation

- Patients who have had maximal medical treatment and LDL apheresis can be considered for liver transplantation. The new liver provides functionally normal LDL receptors, thereby reducing plasma cholesterol levels

In **polygenic hypercholesterolaemia** the precise nature of the metabolic defect(s) is unknown.

These individuals represent the right-hand tail of the normal cholesterol distribution. They are at risk of premature atherosclerosis. Depressed HDL levels are a risk factor for vascular disease.

Factors modifying HDL levels

- **Decreasing**
  - Familial deficiency of HDL
  - Hyperandrogenic state
  - Post-pubertal males
  - Obesity
  - Hypertriglyceridaemia
  - Diabetes mellitus
  - Sedentary states
  - Cigarette smoking
- **Increasing**
  - Familial hyper-α-lipoproteinaemia
  - Low triglyceride levels
  - Thin habitus
  - Exercise
  - Oestrogens
  - Alcohol

Primary hypertriglyceridaemia (without hypercholesterolaemia)

- **Polygenic hypertriglyceridaemia** is analogous to polygenic hypercholesterolaemia. Some cases are familial but the precise defect is not known. There is elevated VLDL

- **Lipoprotein lipase deficiency** and **apoprotein CII deficiency** are both rare. They result in elevated triglycerides due to a failure to metabolise chylomicrons
- These patients present in childhood with eruptive xanthomata, lipaemia retinalis, retinal vein thrombosis, pancreatitis and hepatosplenomegaly
- Chylomicrons can be detected in fasting plasma

Primary mixed (or combined) hyperlipidaemia

- **Familial polygenic combined hyperlipidaemia** results in elevated cholesterol and triglycerides
- The prevalence is 1/200
- There is premature atherosclerosis
- **Remnant hyperlipidaemia** is a rare cause of mixed hyperlipidaemia (palmar xanthomata and tuberous xanthomata over the knees and elbows are characteristic). It is associated with apoprotein E_2. There is a high cardiovascular risk

Secondary hyperlipidaemias are usually mixed but either elevated cholesterol or triglycerides may predominate.

Causes of secondary hyperlipidaemias

- **Predominantly increased triglycerides**
  - Alcoholism
  - Obesity
  - CKD
  - Diabetes mellitus
  - Liver disease
  - High-dose oestrogens
- **Predominantly increased cholesterol**
  - Hypothyroidism
  - Renal transplant
  - Cigarette smoking*
  - Nephrotic syndrome
  - Cholestasis

*Cigarette smoking reduces HDL

13.4.3 Lipid-lowering drugs

Cholesterol and triglyceride levels should be considered in combination with other risk factors (*also see* Chapter 1, Cardiology). Potential secondary causes of hyperlipidaemia should be corrected.

Dietary intervention can be expected to reduce serum cholesterol by a maximum of 30%. Dietary measures should be continued with pharmacological therapy. Table 13.2 shows the impact that can be expected with the various agents.

The side-effect profile of the older agents (see Table 13.3) made them unpopular and reduced compliance. In the majority of cases, hypercholesterolaemia will respond to dietary intervention and statin therapy; and mixed or isolated hypertriglyceridaemia, to diet and a fibrate. Treatment of hyperlipidaemia can reduce the risk of coronary heart disease by 30%. The side-effects and interactions of lipid-lowering drugs are given in Table 13.3.

HMG-CoA reductase inhibitors (statins)

Statins are widely used to lower cholesterol and have been shown to reduce cardiovascular events. Simvastatin is now available in a generic formulation; consequently many patients are having their current statin treatment 'switched' to simvastatin on the assumption that all statins are the same, which

they are not. Whilst switching patients to generic simvastatin is more often than not complication-free, care should be taken to avoid potential drug interactions, eg protease inhibitors used in antiretroviral regimens inhibit the metabolism of simvastatin and are contraindicated. However, protease inhibitors do not interact with atorvastatin or pravastatin.

Ezetimibe

Ezetimibe is a new class of drug that selectively inhibits intestinal absorption of cholesterol. It is indicated for patients with primary hypercholesterolaemia who are intolerant of statins or when there is a contraindication to statin use. It is also used in combination with a statin to enable patients to lower LDL cholesterol to the target level.

Sterols and stanols, eg Flora Pro-activ™ Benecol™

These substances inhibit cholesterol absorption in the gut and thereby lower LDL cholesterol. They are found naturally in a number of foods including extra virgin olive oil. They have no effect on HDL cholesterol or triglycerides. Sterols and stanols are being increasingly used commercially as an additive to margarines. Although studies have shown a reduction in LDL cholesterol, further research is required to show whether this translates into a reduction in cardiovascular events.

Table 13.2. Impact of lipid-lowering drugs

Drug class	↓LDL (%)	↑HDL (%)	↓TGs (%)
HMG-CoA reductase inhibitors	20–40	5–10	10–20
Fibrates	10–15	15–25	35–50
Ezetimibe	15–20	No change	No change
Sterols and stanols	10–20	No change	No change
Anion-exchange resins	15–30	No change	No change
Nicotinic acid	10–25	15–35	25–30
Probucol	10–15	↓20–25	No change
Neomycin	20–25	No change	No change
Fish oil	5–10	No change	30–50

Table 13.3. Side-effects and drug interactions of lipid-lowering drugs

Drug class	Side-effects/interactions
HMG-CoA reductase inhibbdors	Headache, nausea, insomnia, abnormal LFTs. Myositis and rhabdomyolysis (when in combination with gemfibrozil or ciclosporin A) Simvastatin (but not pravastatin) potentiates warfarin and digoxin
Fibrates Gemfibrozil Bezafibrate	Potentiates warfarin. Gemfibrozil absorption is impaired by anion-exchange resins
Ezetimibe	Headache, abdominal discomfort. Rarely, hypersensitivity, thrombocytopenia, myositis, pancreatitis and abnormal LFTs
Sterols and stanols	Well tolerated as naturally occurring substances but may cause lower GI symptoms: diarrhoea, constipation
Anion-exchange resins (aka bile acid sequestrants) Colestyramine Cholestipol	GI side-effects: nausea, cramping, abnormal LFTs Impaired absorption of digoxin, warfarin, thyroxine and fat-soluble vitamins
Nicotinic acid	Flushing, headaches, upper GI symptoms, acanthosis nigricans and myositis
Probucol	Diarrhoea, eosinophilia, long QT syndrome, angioneurotic oedema
Neomycin	Ototoxicity, nephrotoxicity
Fish oil	Halitosis, bloating, nausea Impaired glycaemic control in non-insulin-dependent diabetes mellitus

Primary prevention

- Statins can be prescribed for primary prevention in patients who are at high risk (>20%) of developing cardiovascular disease,* eg diabetes. If patients are unable to tolerate a statin then ezetimibe, fibrates or anion-exchange resins should be offered

- There is no target LDL or cholesterol and consequently high-dose statins are not recommended
- All patients with familial hyperlipidaemia should be offered lipid-lowering therapy

* Current UK guidelines recommend that cardiovascular risk should be estimated using the Framingham 1991 10-year risk equations. However the Framingham risk equation was developed from North American patients and consequently they have been shown to overestimate cardiovascular risk in northern European populations by up to 50% and underestimate cardiovascular risk in patients who are socially deprived. Alternative risk equations are available, eg QRISK (UK), ASSIGN (Scotland). The QRISK equations have been developed using data from the UK population. Published data suggest QRISK equations may be better predictors of cardiovascular events than the Framingham equation in the UK. The QRISK equations take family history and social deprivation into consideration. These equations are currently in evolution and it is likely that future guidelines will use QRISK or similar equations to calculate cardiovascular risk in England and Wales.

Secondary prevention

- It is recommended that all patients with established cardiovascular disease should be treated with a statin as first-line agent
- If total cholesterol is above 4 mmol/l or LDL remains above 2 mmol/l statin treatment should be titrated upwards

13.4.4 Rare lipid disorders

A multitude of rare inborn errors of lipid metabolism can lead to multisystem diseases. The most common (all very rare) are shown in Table 13.4.

Table 13.4. Rare inborn errors of lipid metabolism

13.5 DISORDERS OF BONE, MINERAL METABOLISM AND INORGANIC IONS

Bone is a unique type of connective tissue that mineralises. Biochemically it is composed of matrix (35%) and inorganic calcium hydroxyapatite (65%). Bone and mineral homeostasis are tightly regulated by numerous factors, so as to maintain skeletal integrity and control plasma levels.

Disorder	Serum lipid abnormality	Clinical features	Pathogenesis	Treatment
Abetalipoproteinaemia	Low cholesterol Low triglycerides	Onset in childhood Fat malabsorption Acanthocytosis (of RBCs) Retinitis pigmentosa Ataxia and peripheral neuropathy	Defective ApoB synthesis	Vitamin E
Tangier disease	Low cholesterol	Onset in childhood Large orange tonsils Polyneuropathy No increased IHD risk	Increased ApoA catabolism	None
LCAT deficiency	↑ Triglycerides Variable cholesterol	Affects young adults CKD	Reduced LCAT activity	Low-fat diet
Cerebro-tendinous xanthomatosis	None	Affects young adults Cerebellar ataxia Dementia, cataracts Tendon xanthomata	Not known	None
β-Sitosterolaemia	None	Affects adults	Increased β-sitosterol absorption	Low plant-fat diet

(continued)

Table 13.4. *(continued)*

Disorder	Serum lipid abnormality	Clinical features	Pathogenesis	Treatment
Fabry's disease	None	Affects young male adults (mild disease in females)	Deficiency of α-galactosidase A	Human recombinant α-galactosidase A therapy
		Angiokeratomas	X-linked recessive	Renal replacement therapy if end-stage renal failure develops
		Periodic crises Thrombotic events CKD		
Adrenoleukodystrophy (ALD)	None	Children <2 years	X-linked	Lorenzo's oil (a combination of oleic acid and euric acid) can reduce or delay symptoms
		Addison's disease and progressive brain damage	Accumulation of very long-chain fatty acids (VLCFA) in the brain and adrenal cortex	
Adrenomyeloneuropathy	A milder form of ALD that can be seen in men in their 20s and 30s. Presentation is similar to multiple sclerosis			Restrict dietary VLCFA intake Hormone replacement for adrenal insufficiency

13.5.1 Calcium homeostasis

Calcium homeostasis is linked to phosphate homeo-stasis to maintain a balanced calcium phosphate product.

- Hypocalcaemia activates parathyroid hormone (PTH) release to restore serum ionised calcium;

other stimuli to PTH release include hyperphosphataemia and decreased vitamin D levels
- Hypercalcaemia switches off PTH release
- Vitamin D promotes calcium and phosphate absorption from the GI tract
- Bone stores of calcium buffer the serum changes

The metabolism and effects of vitamin D, and the actions of PTH are shown schematically in Figures 13.4 and 13.5.

13.5.2 Hypercalcaemia

In over 90% of cases hypercalcaemia is due to either hyperparathyroidism or malignancy. Hypercalcaemia normally suppresses PTH and so PTH is therefore the best first test to identity the cause of hypercalcaemia – if it is detectable (in or above the normal range) the patient must have hyperparathyroidism.

- Primary hyperparathyroidism is common, especially in women aged 40–60 years. It is usually due to an adenoma of one of the four parathyroid glands
- PTH-related protein (PTH-rP) is responsible for up to 80% of hypercalcaemia in malignancy
- PTH-rP acts on the same receptors as PTH and shares the first (N-terminal) 13 amino acids with PTH; however, they are coded from two separate genes
- Common malignancies secreting PTH-rP are squamous cell tumours, breast and kidney

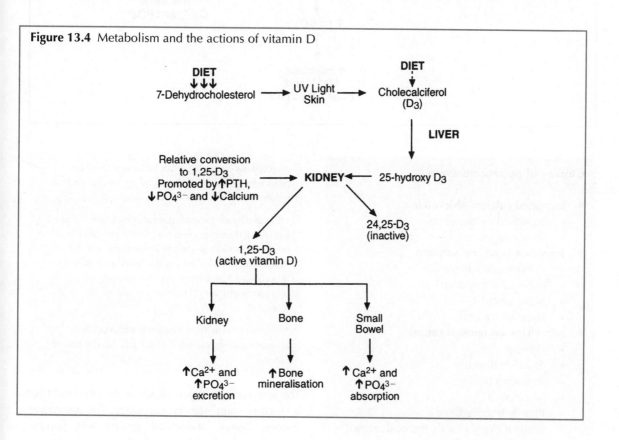

Figure 13.4 Metabolism and the actions of vitamin D

Figure 13.5 Control and actions of parathyroid hormone (PTH)

Causes of hypercalcaemia

- **Increased calcium absorption**
  - Increased calcium intake
  - Increased vitamin D
- **Increased bone reabsorption**
  - Primary and tertiary hyperparathyroidism
  - Malignancy
  - Hyperthyroidism
- **Miscellaneous unusual causes**
  - Lithium
  - Thiazide diuretics
  - Addison's disease
  - Sarcoidosis*
  - Phaeochromocytoma
  - Familial hypocalciuric hypocalcaemia**
  - Theophylline toxicity
  - Milk-alkali syndrome***
  - Vitamin A toxicity (rarely)

*Sarcoidosis causes hypercalcaemia due to excess production of 1,25-D₃ by macrophages in the sarcoid lesions

**Familial hypocalciuric hypercalcaemia (FHH) is an autosomal dominant condition. Most cases of FHH are a result of mutations in the calcium-sensing receptor. Patients are often incorrectly diagnosed with primary hyperparathyroidism. In contrast to primary hyperparathyroidism FHH does not require any treatment

***Hypercalcaemia can be seen in patients who consume excess quantities of 'Rennies' bought over the counter

The symptoms of hypercalcaemia are often mild but a range of manifestations can occur. The mnemonic 'stones, bones, abdominal groans and psychic moans' can be used to describe these symptoms.

Clinical manifestations of hypercalcaemia

- Malaise/depression
- Lethargy
- Muscle weakness
- Confusion
- Peptic ulceration*
- Pancreatitis
- Constipation
- Nephrolithiasis
- Nephrogenic diabetes insipidus
- Distal renal tubular acidosis (RTA)
- CKD**
- Short QT syndrome
- Band keratopathy
- Diabetes insipidus

*Peptic ulceration is due to excess gastrin secretion

**CKD is due to chronic tubulointerstitial calcification and fibrosis

The **management** of acute hypercalcaemia (serum calcium >3 mmol/l) involves:

- Adequate rehydration – 3–4 litres saline/day
- Intravenous bisphosphonates (eg pamidronate disodium)
- Identification of the cause, and its subsequent specific treatment (eg corticosteroids for sarcoid) if indicated

13.5.3 Hyperparathyroid bone disease

Hyperparathyroidism has a prevalence of about 1/1000. It results in bone reabsorption due to excess PTH action.

Primary hyperparathyroidism is caused by a single (80%+) or multiple (5%) parathyroid adenomas or by hyperplasia (10%). Parathyroid carcinoma is rare (<2%). It results from abnormal regulation of PTH by calcium because of an increase in the calcium set point. Familial cases (as seen in MEN type 1) have a higher incidence of hyperplasia and, like parathyroid carcinoma, can be associated with ab-

normalities of chromosome 11 (usually deletions in the little q13 region).

Biochemically there is increased PTH, serum and urinary calcium, reduced serum phosphate and increased alkaline phosphatase. Histologically there is an increase of both osteoblasts and osteoclasts resulting in 'woven' osteoid, increased resorption cavities ('osteitis fibrosa cystica') and marrow fibrosis. The definitive treatment of primary hyperparathyroidism is by surgical parathyroidectomy.

Secondary hyperparathyroidism is physiological compensatory hypertrophy of all four glands due to hypocalcaemia (eg CKD, malabsorption). PTH levels are raised, calcium is low or normal. The secondary hyperparathyroidism in CKD is controlled by phosphate restriction, phosphate binders and with use of 1-α-hydroxylated vitamin D preparations (*see also* Chapter 15, Nephrology). Cinacalcet is a calcimimetic which acts on calcium sensing receptors to increase receptor sensitivity to calcium, which in turn results in a decrease in PTH. Cinacalcet is licensed for the treatment of advanced secondary hyperparathyroidism.*

Tertiary hyperparathyroidism is the development of autonomous parathyroid hyperplasia in the setting of long-standing secondary hyperparathyroidism – usually in CKD. Calcium levels are raised. Treatment is in the form of parathyroidectomy or cinacalcet.*

13.5.4 Hypocalcaemia

Hypocalcaemia is usually secondary to CKD (increased serum phosphate), hypoparathyroidism or vitamin D deficiency.

---

* UK NICE guidelines do not recommend cinacalcet for the routine treatment of secondary hyperparathyroidism as it has not been shown to be cost-effective. It can be used in patients who have failed to respond to other treatments or in patients with tertiary hyperparathyroidism in whom parathyroidectomy is not possible.

Causes of hypocalcaemia

- **Decreased calcium absorption**
  - Hypoparathyroidism
  - Hypovitaminosis D
  - Malabsorption
  - Sepsis
  - Fluoride poisoning
  - Hypomagnesaemia*
- **Acute respiratory alkalosis**
- **Hyperphosphataemia (by reduction in ionised calcium)**
  - CKD
  - Phosphate administration
  - Rhabdomyolysis
  - Tumour lysis syndrome
- **Deposition of calcium**
  - Pancreatitis
  - Hungry bone syndrome
  - EDTA infusion
  - Rapidly growing osteoblastic metastases

*Cause of functional hypoparathyroidism

Hypoparathyroidism can be spontaneous (auto-immune), post-surgical or due to a receptor defect (pseudo-hypoparathyroidism). Autoimmune hypoparathyroidism may be part of **autoimmune polyglandular failure type I** (mucocutaneous candidiasis, with adrenal, gonadal and thyroid failure). Treatment is with calcium and vitamin D supplements.

Recombinant human 1-34-PTH (teriparatide) is available but is not used in clinical practice for hypoparathyroidism because of its cost, need for parenteral administration and short half-life. It has been used for post surgical hypoparathyroidism over a short-term period but it is more routinely used in the management of osteoporosis.

In **pseudohypoparathyroidism** there is a characteristic phenotype with short stature, short metacarpals and intellectual impairment. The disorder is due to a G-protein abnormality (*see* Chapter 14, Molecular Medicine).

Vitamin D deficiency can occur in several settings, including:

- Dietary deficiency/lack of sunlight
- Malabsorption
- CKD (failure of 1-α-hydroxylation)
- 1-α-hyroxylase deficiency (vitamin-D-dependent rickets type I)
- Vitamin D-receptor defect (vitamin D-dependent rickets type II)

Rickets without vitamin D deficiency and with normal calcium may be due to hypophosphataemia, as in X-linked dominant hypophosphataemic vitamin D-resistant rickets.

The symptoms of hypocalcaemia are mainly those of neuromuscular irritability and neuropsychiatric manifestations. Signs include Chvostek's (tapping the facial nerve causes twitching) and Trousseau's (precipitation of tetanic (carpopedal) spasm in the hand by sphygmomanometer-induced ischaemia). Trousseau's sign is a more specific test for hypocalcaemia. The development of symptoms depends on how quickly the level of calcium falls as well as the serum concentration.

Clinical manifestations of hypocalcaemia

- **Neuromuscular**
  - Tetany
  - Seizures
  - Confusion
  - Extrapyramidal signs
  - Papilloedema
  - Psychiatric
  - Myopathy
  - Prolonged QT syndrome
- **Ectodermal**
  - Alopecia
  - Brittle nails
  - Dry skin
- **Cataracts**
- **Dental hypoplasia**

Table 13.5 lists the causes of hypocalcaemia and the related biochemical findings

The **management** of hypocalcaemia involves:

- Intravenous calcium gluconate if severe (tetany/seizures)

Table 13.5. Causes of hypocalcaemia – biochemical findings

Cause	Serum PTH	Vitamin D levels	Phosphate	Alkaline phosphatase
Hypoparathyroidism	Low	Normal	High	Normal
Vitamin D deficiency	High	Low	Low	High
Pseudohypoparathyroidism	High	Normal	High	Normal
CKD	High	Low	High	High

- Oral calcium supplements
- Vitamin D (for hypoparathyroidism, vitamin D deficiency and CKD)
- Normalise serum magnesium levels. Hypocalcaemia is difficult to correct if serum magnesium levels are low
- Thiazide diuretic and low-sodium diet

13.5.5 Hypercalciuria

Hypercalciuria is the commonest cause of kidney stones and contributes to the development of osteoporosis. Hypercalciuria occurs as a result of excessive duodenal calcium absorption (normally the duodenum only absorbs 20% of ingested calcium), renal calcium leak or excessive bone absorption (eg hyperparathyroidism) resulting in excess serum calcium and subsequent hypercalciuria. Excessive calcium absorption is the commonest cause of hypercalciuria, although the causes often overlap.

Causes of hypercalciuria

- Absorptive
  - Excess calcium ingestion
  - Milk-alkali syndrome
  - Vitamin D excess
  - Sarcoidosis*
- Renal hypercalciuria (renal leak)
  - Medullary sponge kidney (30%–50%)
  - Bartter syndrome**
  - Dent's disease***
  - Autosomal-dominant hypercalciuric hypocalcaemia****

- Resorptive
  - Hyperparathyroidism
  - MEN-1 (with hyperparathyroidism)
- Miscellaneous
  - Hyperthyroidism
  - Renal tubular acidosis
  - Prolonged immobilisation
  - Paget's disease
  - Pregnancy

*Excess 1,25-vitamin D_3 production results in hypercalcaemia and hypercalciuria

**Rare autosomal recessive condition caused by mutations in the genes involved in the active absorption of chloride in the loop of Henle. This results in excess sodium and potassium loss in the urine. Secondary hyperaldosteronism occurs with hypokalaemic alkalosis. Blood pressure is usually normal

***aka X-linked recessive hypophosphataemic rickets

****Mutation in the calcium-sensing receptor

Investigations

- 24-hour urinary calcium
- Serum calcium, phosphate, creatinine and PTH
- Calcium loading test in patients who have not responded to dietary calcium restriction. Patients are fasted and then administered a calcium load. Urine calcium is checked at intermittent periods to distinguish the cause of hypercalciuria, eg patients with renal leak hypercalciuria will not change the amount of calcium excreted, whereas patients with absorptive hypercalciuria will increase calcium excretion in response to the calcium load

Treatments

- Most hypercalciuria can be managed with dietary calcium restrictions
- Reduce sodium intake (elevated sodium intake increases calcium excretion, raises urinary pH and reduces urinary citrate excretion, thereby increasing stone formation)
- Thiazide diuretics are used in patients with renal leak or who have not responded to dietary restriction alone. Thiazide diuretics reabsorb calcium in the renal tubule
- Bisphosphonate can be used in patients who have hypercalciuria as a result of excessive bone resorption (especially patients with osteoporosis)
- Orthophosphates reduce hypercalciuria by reducing vitamin D_3 levels and increasing tubular reabsorption of calcium. Side-effects include GI disturbance

13.5.6 Osteomalacia

Osteomalacia (adults) or rickets (children) result from inadequate mineralisation of osteoid. The biochemical features are: elevated alkaline phosphatase (95%), hypocalcaemia (50%) and hypophosphataemia (25%). It is usually caused by a defect of vitamin D availability or metabolism. Approximately 1 billion people have osteomalacia worldwide. In the UK the prevalence increases with age, with a prevalence of 30% in the over-65s.

Causes of osteomalacia

- Vitamin D deficiency
  - Dietary*
  - Sun exposure**
  - Malabsorption
  - Gastrectomy
  - Small-bowel disease
  - Pancreatic insufficiency
- Defective 25-hydroxylation
  - Liver disease
  - Anticonvulsant treatment***
- Loss of vitamin D-binding protein
  - Nephrotic syndrome

- Defective 1-α-hydroxylation
  - Hypoparathyroidism
  - CKD****
- Defective target organ response
  - Vitamin D-dependent rickets (type II)
- Mineralisation defects
  - Abnormal matrix
  - Osteogenesis imperfecta
  - CKD****
  - Enzyme deficiencies
  - Hypophosphatasia
- Inhibitors of mineralisation
  - Fluoride
  - Aluminium
  - Bisphosphonates
- Phosphate deficiency
  - Decreased GI intake
    - Antacids (reduce absorption)
  - Impaired renal reabsorption
    - Fanconi syndrome
    - X-linked hypophosphataemic rickets (vitamin D-resistant rickets)

*Vegans in particular may not benefit from dietary vitamin D

**Asian immigrants in Western countries are at increased risk because melanin in skin decreases D_3 formation and certain foods (eg chapattis) bind calcium, unmasking vitamin D deficiency

***Especially phenytoin

****Patients with CKD can have mixed bone disease where there is hyperparathyroid bone disease in combination with osteomalacia

The **management** of osteomalacia involves:

- Diagnosis and treatment of the underlying disorder
- Vitamin D therapy to correct hypocalcaemia and hypophosphataemia
- Beware iatrogenic hypercalcaemia when alkaline phosphatase begins to fall at the time of bone healing

Oncogenic osteomalacia

This is a paraneoplastic syndrome usually caused by benign tumours of mesenchymal origin. Patients have osteomalacia, bone pain, phosphaturia and hypophosphataemia.

13.5.7 Paget's disease

Paget's disease is a focal (or multifocal) bone disorder characterised by accelerated and disorganised bone turnover resulting from increased numbers and activity of both osteoblasts and osteoclasts. A viral aetiology has not been confirmed.

- Rare in patients aged under 40 years
- Prevalence of 1%–2% in Caucasians over the age of 55 years. The UK has the highest prevalence (4.6%) in Europe
- Familial clustering and HLA linkages (15% have a positive family history)
- Biochemically characterised by raised alkaline phosphatase, osteocalcin and urinary hydroxyproline excretion. X-rays and radionuclide bone scans aid diagnosis

Paget's disease is usually diagnosed because of asymptomatic sclerotic changes (which can mimic sclerotic bone metastases) but a number of complications can arise.

Clinical manifestations of Paget's disease

- Bone pain
- Fractures (and pseudofractures)
- Secondary arthritis
- Neurological compression syndromes*
- Osteosarcoma (rare)
- High-output congestive cardiac failure
- Hypercalcaemia (only with immobilisation)
- Skeletal deformity

*Including deafness, other cranial nerve palsies and spinal stenosis

---

Treatment is indicated for bone pain, nerve compression, disease impinging on joints and immobilisation hypercalcaemia. Options include:

- Bisphosphonates
- Calcitonin
- Surgery

Causes of a raised bone alkaline phosphatase

- **With high calcium**
  - Hyperparathyroidism
- **With high or normal calcium**
  - Malignancy
  - Paget's disease
- **With normal calcium**
  - Puberty
  - Fracture
  - Osteogenic sarcoma
- **With low calcium**
  - Osteomalacia

13.5.8 Osteoporosis

A very common disorder characterised by reduced bone density and increased risk of fracture. The most common form is postmenopausal osteoporosis, which affects 50% of women aged 70. Common sites of fracture are the vertebrae, neck of femur (trabecular bone) and the distal radius and humerus (cortical bone); these fractures can occur with minimal trauma.

Diagnosis is by bone mineral densitometry, measured by dual-energy X-ray absorptiometry (DEXA), single-photon absorptometry (SPA) or quantitative computed tomography (QCT) (Table 13.6).

The measured bone density is compared with the mean population peak bone density (ie that of young adults of the same sex) and expressed as the number of standard deviations from that mean, the T score. The bone mineralisation and serum biochemistry are normal.

- T scores down to -1 are regarded as normal
- T scores between -1 and -2.5 represent osteopenia
- T scores below -2.5 are osteoporotic

Table 13.6. Comparison of DEXA,* SPA and QCT

Method	Measurements	Pros and cons	Cost
DEXA	Spine, hip, radius	Most widely available	££
QCT	Spine, hip, radius	Most accurate	£££
		Better for patients with extensive osteoarthritis	
		Increased radiation	
		Expensive	
SPA	Radius, calcaneum	Not as accurate as DEXA and QCT	£

Fracture risk

The risk of future fractures is dependent on both bone quality (strength and resilience) and the risk of falling. Fractures increase twofold with each standard deviation of the T score and independently with age by 1.5-fold per decade.

Aetiology

From the age of 30, bone loss occurs at about 1% per year. This is accelerated to about 5% per year in the 5 years after the menopause. Persistent elevations of parathyroid hormone will accelerate bone loss further. This occurs both in primary hyperparathyroidism but also in secondary hyperparathyroidism arising in vitamin D deficiency, or in negative calcium balance (eg hypocalcaemia, hypercalciuria).

Aetiology of osteoporosis

- **Primary**
  - Type 1: postmenopausal
  - Type 2: age-related or involutional
  - Osteoporosis of pregnancy
- **Secondary**
  - *Endocrine:* premature menopause, Cushing syndrome, hypopituitarism, hyperparathyroidism, prolactinomas, hypogonadism, hyperthyroidism
  - *Drugs:* steroids, heparin, ciclosporin A, anticonvulsants
  - *Malignancy:* multiple myeloma, leukaemia
  - *Inflammatory:* rheumatoid arthritis, ulcerative colitis
  - *GI:* gastrectomy, malabsorption, primary biliary cirrhosis
  - *CKD*
  - *Immobilisation,* eg space flight
  - *Other:* osteogenesis imperfecta, homocystinuria, Turner syndrome (oestrogen deficiency), rheumatoid arthritis*, scurvy
- **Additional risk factors for osteoporosis**
  - Race: white/Asian
  - Short stature and low body mass index
  - Positive family history
  - Multiparity
  - Amenorrhoea >6 months (other than pregnancy)
  - Poor calcium and vitamin D intake
  - Excess alcohol and smoking

*In rheumatoid arthritis osteoporosis is multifactorial but corticosteroids and immobility are major contributors

In the absence of a recent fracture or secondary cause of osteoporosis, bone biochemistry should be normal.

Treatment of osteoporosis

- **General measures**
  - Correct any secondary cause
  - Weight-bearing exercise
  - Adequate dietary calcium and vitamin D intake
- **Specific drug treatments**
  (These may reduce fractures by approximately 50%)
  - Oestrogens (HRT)
  - Vitamin D
  - Testosterone (in males)
  - Bisphosphonates*
  - Selective oestrogen receptor modulators (SERMs), eg raloxifene
  - Teriparatide (1-34-PTH)
  - Strontium
  - Denosumab (novel human monoclonal antibody) **
- **Other**
  - Fluoride (increases bone density, but reduces bone microstructure quality). Fluoride accumulates in peripheral bone and increases the risk of microfractures (stress fractures) and fracture in peripheral weight-bearing bones
  - Calcitonin

*Prophylaxis with bisphosphonates is now recommended for patients receiving high-dose (eg relapsing nephrotic syndrome) or long-term (eg asthma) steroids

**Denosumab is a human monoclonal antibody against RANKL (receptor activator of nuclear factor κB ligand). RANKL is involved in bone resorption. The drug is currently undergoing phase III drug trials

13.5.9 Disorders of magnesium

Magnesium is principally found in bone (50%–60%) as an intracellular cation and plasma levels are maintained within the range 0.7–1.1 mmol/l. It plays an important role in many metabolic pathways. Disorders of magnesium balance usually occur in association with other fluid and electrolyte disturbances, in particular calcium and potassium.

Hypomagnesaemia

Hypomagnesaemia is frequently accompanied by hypocalcaemia, hypophosphataemia and hypokalaemia. Patients are often asymptomatic but may complain of weakness or anorexia, and features of neuromuscular irritability have been described. Hypomagnesaemia is an important risk factor for ventricular arrhythmias.

Causes of hypomagnesaemia

- **Gastrointestinal losses**
  - Diarrhoea
  - Malabsorption
  - Small-bowel disease
  - Acute pancreatitis*
- **Loop of Henle dysfunction**
  - Acute tubular necrosis**
  - Renal transplantation
  - Post-obstructive diuresis
  - Bartter syndrome
  - Gitelman syndrome
- **Renal losses**
  - Loop and thiazide diuretics
  - Volume expansion
  - Alcohol***
  - Diabetic ketoacidosis
  - Hypercalcaemia****
- **Nephrotoxins**
  - Aminoglycosides
  - Amphotericin B
  - Cisplatin
  - Pentamidine
  - Ciclosporin A
- **Primary renal magnesium wasting*****

*Due to the formation of magnesium soaps in the areas of fat necrosis

**Diuretic phase

***Alcohol acutely increases urinary magnesium excretion; in chronic alcoholism this is compounded by ketoacidosis and phosphate depletion

****Hypercalciuria increases magnesium excretion; if saline and diuretics are given to treat hypercalcaemia then the three stimuli together predispose to hypomagnesaemia

*****Primary magnesium wasting is a rare familial disorder

Hypermagnesaemia

Hypermagnesaemia is rare. It is usually due to magnesium ingestion or infusion in the setting of CKD (ie when the kidney cannot excrete a magnesium load).

- At concentrations above 4 mmol/l symptoms develop, including lethargy, drowsiness, areflexia, paralysis, hypotension, heart block and finally cardiac arrest
- Toxic effects can be temporarily reversed by intravenous calcium (antagonises the neuromuscular and cardiac effects of hypomagnesaemia). In patients with normal renal function, intravenous normal saline with forced diuresis using loop diuretics can increase renal magnesium loss. Dialysis can also be used in patients with CKD or in severe hypermagnesaemia

Causes of hypermagnesaemia

- CKD
- Adrenal insufficiency
- Magnesium infusion
- Milk-alkali syndrome
- Oral ingestion
- Lithium
- Magnesium enemas
- Theophylline intoxication
- Familial hypocalciuric hypercalcaemia
- Tumour lysis syndrome (release of intracellular magnesium)
- Rhabdomyolysis

13.5.10 Disorders of phosphate

Serum phosphate is maintained between 0.8 and 1.4 mmol/l largely by renal regulation of excretion. Bone accommodates 85% of body stores; the rest is found extracellularly as inorganic phosphate and intracellularly as phosphate esters, eg phospholipids, nucleic acids and high-energy compounds such as adenosine triphosphate (ATP).

Hypophosphataemia

Hypophosphataemia can occur in a variety of settings, due to redistribution, renal losses or decreased intake.

- Symptoms rarely develop unless phosphate is below 0.6 mmol/l; below 0.3 mmol/l rhabdomyolysis is likely
- Hypophosphataemia leads to reduced oxygen delivery (via reduced levels of 2,3-diphosphoglycerate (2,3-DPG)) and also impairs intracellular metabolism (by depleting ATP)
- Symptoms include weakness (especially respiratory muscles – a particular problem when weaning certain ICU patients from respiratory support), confusion, coma, heart failure and rhabdomyolysis

Causes of hypophosphataemia

- **Internal redistribution**
  - Acute respiratory alkalosis
  - Hyperinsulinaemia
  - Post renal transplantation
- **Decreased intestinal absorption**
  - Inadequate intake (especially alcoholism, persistent vomiting)
  - Antacids containing aluminium or magnesium
  - Steatorrhoea and chronic diarrhoea
- **Increased urinary excretion (phosphate wasting)**
  - Primary and non-renal secondary hyperparathyroidism
  - Vitamin D deficiency/resistance
  - Fanconi syndrome
  - X-linked hypophosphataemic rickets
  - Miscellaneous – osmotic diuretics, thiazide diuretics
  - Acute volume expansion
  - Heavy metal poisoning
  - Oncogenic osteomalacia
- Treatment is dependent on the underlying condition and phosphate supplementation is commonly used. Vitamin D levels should be corrected

Hyperphosphataemia

Hyperphosphataemia is common in acute and advanced CKD. It can also occur in massive tissue breakdown (eg rhabdomyolysis) and if there is increased tubular reabsorption of phosphate.

- It is usually asymptomatic. If symptoms do occur, they are secondary to a reduction in ionised calcium
- In acute hyperphosphataemia (with normal renal function), saline infusion to volume replete with forced diuresis using a loop diuretic can be used to increase phosphate excretion
- In CKD a low-phosphate diet, phosphate binders and dialysis may be required. The high serum phosphate in CKD is a major vascular risk factor in this population

Causes of hyperphosphataemia

- **Massive acute phosphate load**
  - Tumour lysis syndrome*
  - Rhabdomyolysis
  - Lactic and ketoacidosis
  - Exogenous phosphate
  - Vitamin D intoxication
- **CKD**
- **Increased tubular reabsorption of phosphate**
  - Hypoparathyroidism
  - Pseudohypoparathyroidism
  - Severe hypomagnesaemia (results in PTH resistance)
  - Acromegaly
  - Thyrotoxicosis
  - Bisphosphonates

*The tumour lysis syndrome results in release of phosphate, potassium, purines (metabolised to uric acid) and proteins (metabolised to urea). It can result in acute kidney injury due to uric acid crystal deposition

13.6 NUTRITIONAL AND VITAMIN DISORDERS

In the developed countries the most common nutritional problem is obesity (*see also* Chapter 4,

Endocrinology). In contrast, in the developing countries, protein-energy malnutrition is common.

- In developed countries the long-term sequelae of fetal and childhood undernutrition are increased cardiovascular disease in adult life

13.6.1 The obesity and diabetes epidemic

- Body mass index (BMI) = weight (kg)/(height in metres)^2
- Obesity is defined as a BMI of >30 kg/m^2 in males and >28.6 kg/m^2 in females

Obesity is associated with increased risks of cardiovascular disease, diabetes mellitus, osteoarthritis and gallstones. A BMI of 25 kg/m^2 has been estimated to reduce life expectancy by 2 years in English men.

Previously obesity was more often than not a problem of high-income countries; however, the prevalence of obesity is now increasing in other countries such as Brazil, India and China. WHO projects that by 2015 the number of overweight adults will be 2.3 billion and over 700 million people will be obese. As the rate of obesity has increased, so too has the prevalence of diabetes. In 2000 it was estimated that 171 million adults had diabetes. This is projected to rise to 366 million by 2030 (4.4% of the world population). WHO has also projected that the number of deaths attributable to diabetes will increase by 50% between 2005 and 2015.

Certain countries will also face a 'double burden' of disease. Middle-income countries (eg India) are seeing an increase in obesity in urban settings whilst still having to manage problems associated with undernutrition.

13.6.2 Protein-energy malnutrition (PEM)

Starvation is common in the developing world. In the developed countries PEM frequently complicates severe sepsis, cachexia, liver cirrhosis, advanced CKD and malabsorption. In these circumstances undernutrition is a risk factor for death. The elderly and in particular the institutionalised individual are at a markedly increased risk of malnutrition. Protein-energy malnutrition in both adults and children can be divided into undernutrition, kwashiorkor and marasmus (Table 13.7).

Table 13.7. Wellcome Trust classification of protein-energy malnutrition

Weight (% of standard for age)	Oedema present	Oedema absent
60–80	Kwashiorkor*	Undernutrition
<60	Marasmic kwashiorkor	Marasmus

*Kwashiorkor literally means 'disease of the displaced child'

- **Marasmus** results from severe deficiency of both protein and calories
- **Kwashiorkor** results primarily from protein deficiency (ie diet entirely of carbohydrate)
- Oedema is the cardinal sign separating marasmus from kwashiorkor; fatty liver also develops in kwashiorkor
- Growth failure is more severe in marasmus

13.6.3 Vitamin deficiencies

Multiple vitamin deficiencies frequently accompany PEM. Isolated or grouped vitamin deficiencies (for example, of fat-soluble (Table 13.8) or water-soluble (Table 13.9) vitamins) can also occur in specific circumstances.

13.7 METABOLIC ACID–BASE DISTURBANCES (NON-RENAL)

The kidneys and the lungs are intimately involved in the regulation of hydrogen ion concentration. Metabolic acid–base disturbances arise from abnormalities in the regulation of bicarbonate and other buffers in the blood. Acidosis results from an increase in hydrogen ion concentration and alkalo-

sis from a fall in H^+. pH is the negative logarithm of H^+ – a small change in pH represents a large change in H^+ concentration – this is often poorly appreciated in clinical practice.

13.7.1 Metabolic acidosis

The metabolic acidoses are conveniently divided on the basis of the anion gap.

$$\text{Anion gap} = Na^+ + K^+ - (Cl^- + HCO_3^-)$$

The normal anion gap is 10–18 mmol/l and represents the excess of negative charge (unmeasured anions) present on albumin, phosphate, sulphate and other organic acids, eg lactic acid.

Relationship of metabolic acid to anion gap

- **Normal anion gap**
  - Diarrhoea (or other GI loss)
  - Renal tubular acidosis
  - Hypoaldosteronism
  - Treatment of ketoacidosis
- **Increased anion gap**
  - Lactic acidosis
  - Ketoacidosis
  - Acute kidney injury and advanced CKD
  - Hepatic failure
  - Toluene ingestion
  - Intoxications, eg methanol, aspirin, ethylene glycol

Specific metabolic acidoses

Metabolic acidosis with diarrhoea

The gastrointestinal secretions (below the stomach) are relatively alkaline and have a high potassium concentration. There is usually hypokalaemia, low urinary potassium loss (<25 mmol/l) and low urine pH (<5.5). Causes include:

- Villous adenoma
- Enteric fistula
- Obstruction
- Laxative abuse

Table 13.8. Deficiencies of fat-soluble vitamins

Vitamin	Causes of deficiency syndromes	Roles of vitamin	Deficiency
Vitamin A	Severe PEM*	Component of visual pigment Maintenance of specialised epithelia Bitot's spots**	Night blindness Xerophthalmia*** Follicular hyperkeratosis Keratomalacia****
Vitamin D	Vegans[†] Elderly with poor diet CKD	Absorption of calcium and phosphate Bone mineralisation	Rickets Osteomalacia
Vitamin E	Severe (near-total) fat malabsorption[††] Abetalipoproteinaemia	Antioxidant Scavenger of free radicals	Spinocerebellar degeneration
Vitamin K	Oral antibiotics[‡] Biliary obstruction	Cofactor in carboxylation of coagulation cascade factors	Bleeding tendency

* Although vitamin A is fat-soluble and deficiency can occur in any chronic malabsorptive state, this is rare unless there is severe protein-energy malnutrition
** Conjunctival foamy patches are an early sign of vitamin A deficiency
*** Xerophthalmia – dryness of the cornea
**** Keratomalacia – corneal ulceration and dissolution
[†] Vitamin D_3 is produced in the skin by photoactivation of 7-dehydrocholesterol. If sun exposure is sufficient, dietary vitamin D is not essential
[††] Vitamin E deficiency is rare. It can complicate biliary atresia. In abetalipoproteinaemia (see earlier section) chylomicrons cannot be formed
[‡] Antibacterial drugs interfere with the bacterial synthesis of vitamin K

Table 13.9. Deficiencies of water-soluble vitamins

Vitamin	Causes of deficiency	Roles of vitamin	Deficiency syndromes
Vitamin B_1* (thiamine)	Alcoholism	Nerve conduction	Dry beri-beri – symmetrical
	Dietary Bariatric surgery	Co-enzyme in decarboxylation	Polyneuropathy Wernicke–Korsakoff syndrome Wet beri-beri** – peripheral vasodilatation, heart failure
Vitamin B_2 (riboflavin)	Severe PEM***	Enzyme cofactor	Angular stomatitis Glossitis Corneal vascularisation
Niacin (nicotinic acid)	Carcinoid syndrome[+] Alcoholism Low-protein diets Isoniazid[++]	Incorporated into NAD and NADP	Pellagra – dementia, dermatitis and diarrhoea (the three Ds)
Vitamin B_6[‡] (pyridoxine)	Isoniazid Hydralazine	Enzyme cofactor	Peripheral neuropathy Dermatitis Glossitis
Vitamin B_{12} (cyanocobalamin)	Pernicious anaemia Post-gastrectomy Vegan diet Terminal ileal disease Blind loops	Co-enzyme for DNA synthesis; co-enzyme in myelin metabolism	Pernicious anaemia Subacute combined degeneration of the spinal cord
Vitamin C[‡‡]	Dietary	Redox reactions Collagen formation	Scurvy – bleeding, joint swelling, hyperkeratotic hair follicles, gingivitis

* Thiamine deficiency is confirmed by reduced red cell transketolase activity
** In alcoholics, wet beri-beri must be distinguished from alcoholic cardiomyopathy
*** Riboflavin deficiency usually occurs with multiple deficiencies
[+] In the carcinoid syndrome (and to a lesser extent in phaeochromocytoma) tryptophan metabolism is diverted from nicotinamide to form amines
[++] Isoniazid can lead to deficiency of pyridoxine, which is needed for the synthesis of nicotinamide from tryptophan
[‡] Dietary deficiency of pyridoxine is extremely rare
[‡‡] Deficiency of vitamin C is confirmed by low white cell (buffy coat) ascorbic acid levels

Renal tubular acidosis

Renal tubular acidosis (RTA) describes diseases/conditions in which there is a net urinary reduction in acid excretion, resulting in metabolic acidosis. This can be due to reduced acid excretion (reduced H^+ secretion in type 1), increased bicarbonate excretion (as a result of loss of bicarbonate reabsorption in type 2 RTA) or reduced ammonia production (type 4 RTA). In type 4 RTA the kidney is either resistant to aldosterone or plasma aldosterone levels are low. This results in hyperkalaemia, reduced ammonia production and acidosis. It is the most common RTA and occurs in patients with tubulo-interstitial disease such as diabetes. The RTAs are covered in more detail in Chapter 15, Nephrology.

Metabolic acidosis with ureteric diversion and ileal loop diversion

This results in hyperchloraemic acidosis in 80% of ureterosigmoid diversions. The mechanism is due to urinary chloride exchange for plasma bicarbonate, which is then lost in the urine. Urinary ammonia is also absorbed across the sigmoid epithelium. Ileal loop diversions also result in significant hyperchloraemic acidosis but less so than ureterosigmoid diversions.

Metabolic acidosis accompanying poisoning

Metabolic acidosis often accompanies poisoning (eg toluene, ethylene glycol, salicylates, paracetamol). *See also* Chapter 2, Clinical Pharmacology, Toxicology and Poisoning.

13.7.2 Metabolic alkalosis

Metabolic alkalosis is less common than metabolic acidosis because metabolic processes produce acids as by-products, and also because renal excretion of excess bicarbonate is very efficient. Many causes of metabolic alkalosis are associated with hypokalaemia.

Metabolic alkaloses

- **Gastrointestinal hydrogen ion loss**
  - Vomiting/pyloric stenosis
  - Nasogastric suction
  - Antacids (in CKD)
- **Intracellular shift of hydrogen ion**
  - Hypokalaemia
- **Alkali administration**
- **Renal hydrogen ion loss**
  - Mineralocorticoid excess, eg Cushing syndrome
  - Loop or thiazide diuretics
  - Post-hypercapnic alkalosis
  - Hypercalcaemia and the milk-alkali syndrome
- **Contractional alkalosis**
  - Volume depletion

Specific metabolic alkaloses

Gastric loss of hydrogen ions

In protracted vomiting (eg pyloric stenosis) or nasogastric suction there can be complete loss of up to 3 litres of gastric secretions per day. The gastric secretions contain:

- Hydrogen ions: 100 mmol/l
- Potassium: 15 mmol/l
- Chloride: 140 mmol/l

Alkalosis will result but, paradoxically, acid urine is produced due to renal tubular sodium bicarbonate reabsorption to maintain plasma volume. Patients respond to volume expansion with normal saline and correction of hypokalaemia.

Milk-alkali syndrome

This is defined as the triad of hypercalcaemia, metabolic alkalosis and ingestion of large amounts of calcium with absorbable alkali (traditionally for peptic ulcer pain). The hypercalcaemia increases renal bicarbonate reabsorption, exacerbating the alkalosis. Clinical presentation is with symptoms of hypercalcaemia or metastatic calcification.

Post-hypercapnic alkalosis

Chronic respiratory acidosis leads to a compensatory increase in urinary hydrogen ion secretion, resulting in a rise in plasma bicarbonate concentration. Rapid lowering of a raised pCO_2 (usually by mechanical ventilation) is not immediately accompanied by a fall in plasma bicarbonate. There is often an accompanying chloride loss that must be replaced before bicarbonate can fall to normal.

13.8 HYPOTHERMIA

Hypothermia is defined as a fall in core temperature to below 35°C. It is frequently fatal if the core temperature falls below 32°C.

Causes of hypothermia

- Exposure to low external temperatures
  - Elderly with inadequate heating
  - Immersion in cold water
  - Mountaineers
- Medical conditions
  - Hypothyroidism
  - Hypoglycaemia
  - CNS disorders, eg stroke, hypopituitarism
  - Post cardiac arrest and unconscious patients
- Drugs
  - General anaesthetics
  - Alcohol

Mild hypothermia (32–35°C) causes shivering and intense feeling of cold, altered judgement and ataxia.

Moderate hypothermia (28–32°C): patients are often unconscious and lose the ability to shiver. The risk of arrhythmias increases.

Severe hypothermia (<28°C) increases the risk of asystole, coma, apnoea, fixed pupils, pulmonary oedema and death.

- **Clinical features of hypothermia** include bradycardia, hypoventilation, muscle stiffness, cold diuresis, hypotension and loss of reflexes. The pupils can be fixed and dilated in recoverable hypothermia
- **Metabolic acidosis** due to lactate accumulation is common; pancreatitis can complicate hypothermia
- **Electrocardiograph changes**: include J waves, prolonged PR interval, prolonged QT and QRS complexes. Death results from ventricular arrhythmias or asystole

In certain medical situations therapeutic hypothermia (cooling to 32–34°C) can be induced (eg after cardiac arrest, complex cardiac surgery). This reduces tissue oxygen requirements and can improve patient outcomes.

13.8.1 Treatment of hypothermia

Hypothermia >30°C: Surface rewarming is usually adequate with removal of wet clothes, and provision of warm blankets and heaters.

Hypothermia <30°C: Active internal warming until core temperature is at least 32°C using warm IV fluids and warm humidified oxygen. If necessary, peritoneal lavage, pleural lavage and haemodialysis can also be helpful. Cardiac bypass can be used in patients who are in ventricular fibrillation or who have profound hypothermia and are deteriorating.

Cardiac arrest in the hypothermic patient

Severe hypothermia can mimic death. Consequently cardiopulmonary resuscitation should be continued in hypothermic patients until the patient has been rewarmed or until all attempts have failed to improve core temperature. The hypothermic heart has reduced responsiveness to cardiac drugs, pacemakers and defibrillation. Cardioactive drugs can also accumulate as drug metabolism is decreased. Therefore, IV drugs are often withheld until core temperature is above 30°C. Hypothermia protects the brain during cardiac arrest, so patients can have a full neurological recovery despite prolonged cardiac arrest.

Chapter 14
Molecular Medicine

CONTENTS

Molecular Medicine

14.1 MOLECULAR DIAGNOSTICS

The diagnostic process in medicine is entering a new and important historical phase. Increasingly, diagnostic entities are being reclassified according to the molecules that are central to the disease process and also according to changes in the expression of genes which code for these molecules. With the advent of the complete human gene sequence we now have the tools for a complete understanding of how cells develop and how they function in health and disease.

14.1.1 Genomes, transcriptomes, proteomes and metabolomes

The genome of an organism is its complete complement of coding genes. Comparing the organisms in Table 14.1 reveals that the level of complexity of an organism is not explained by the number of genes predicted to code for protein. Fruit flies (*Drosophila melanogaster*, a favourite organism for geneticists) have more complex behaviours than nematode worms (*Caenorhabditis elegans*) but fewer genes. One reason for this is that flies process genes in a more complex way. Humans and mice have the same number of predicted genes and 98% of these

are **orthologues** (have a common ancestral gene and code for equivalent proteins). Biological complexity is explained by:

- The **transcriptome**: this is the name given to the total complement of expressed mRNA sequences in an organism. In lower organisms this will be the same as the number of genes. In mammals genes are transcribed in a more complex way, with transcription being initiated from different exons in different tissues and alternative splicing (post-transcriptional processing). The temporal (*when* in development) and spatial (in *which* cells) expression of genes allows significant diversity which is not evident just from looking at gene number. It is likely therefore that the transcriptomes of mice and humans contain significant differences
- Processed mRNA is translated into protein. Similarly, differences in mRNA transport, localisation and stability mean that the **proteome** cannot be inferred directly from the transcriptome
- **Post-translational processing**: proteins can be modified by glycosylation, sialydation, etc. Protein stability and turnover may be very

Table 14.1. The genomes of various organisms

Organism	Number of proteins	Approx. genome size	Introns	Splicing
Human	30 000	3×10^9 (3 Gb)	Yes	Highly complex
Mouse	30 000	3 Gb	Yes	Complex
Fruit fly	13 500	40×10^6 (40 Mb)	Yes	Yes
Nematode	19 000	96 Mb	Very few	Very little
Fission yeast	6 000	12 Mb	Rare	Absent
Bacterium	2 000–6 000	2–6 Mb	Absent	Absent

different in different cell types and between similar cells in different organisms

- Finally, the progressive diversity of the proteome with evolution leads to an exponential amplification of combinatorial possibilities between proteins. Therefore, while the human genome may have 30 000 information units (genes) the final number of information units needed to explain human biological complex is theoretically several orders of magnitude greater

The Human Genome Project

The Human Genome Project (HGP) was possibly the greatest scientific undertaking in recent history. The project began in 1990 and sequencing was completed in 2003. Analysis of the vast amounts of data generated by the project is still ongoing, but medical science has already profited from the results. As a direct consequence of the HGP, genetic tests are now available that show predisposition to a range of diseases, including breast cancer, cystic fibrosis and liver diseases.

The main goals of the HGP were to:

- *Identify* all the approximately 20 000–25 000 genes in human DNA
- *Determine* the sequences of the 3 billion chemical base pairs that make up human DNA
- *Store* this information in databases
- *Improve* tools for data analysis
- *Transfer* related technologies to the private sector
- *Address* the ethical, legal, and social issues (ELSI) that may arise from the project

The HGP created the field of **genomics**, that of understanding genetic material on a large scale. The field of medicine is profiting from the HGP as we learn more about the genetic contribution to disease.

Fluorescent in-situ hybridisation

Fluorescent in-situ hybridisation (FISH) is a technique that, using fluorescently labelled DNA probes (often derived from fragments of DNA that were isolated during the HGP), can detect and confirm gene and chromosome abnormalities beyond the resolution of routine cytogenetics.

Sample DNA is first denatured, converting double-stranded to single-stranded DNA. The fluorescently labelled probe (complementary to the DNA sequence of interest) is then added to the single-stranded DNA. If the DNA sequence of interest is present in the sample the probe hybridises with the complementary bases as the DNA re-forms back into a double helix. The probe signal can then be detected through a fluorescence microscope and the sample DNA scored for the presence or absence of the signal.

FISH can be performed using two sample types: metaphase chromosomes and interphase nuclei.

Metaphase FISH

FISH can be performed on metaphase chromosomes to detect specific microdeletions undetectable by routine cytogenetics, or to identify chromosome translocations or extra material of unknown origin.

Microdeletion syndromes currently detectable using FISH

- **Cri-du-chat syndrome**
  - A syndrome that results from the deletion of part of the short arm of chromosome 5. The main clinical feature is the presence of a high-pitched 'cat-like' cry present in the newborn that may disappear with age. Other features include a round, full face, widely spread eyes (hypertelorism), an extra fold of skin at the inner corners of the eyes (epicanthal folds), a flattened and widened nasal bridge and ears that are positioned low on the head, severe cognitive, speech and motor delays and feeding problems from birth which may lead to poor growth
- **Miller–Dieker syndrome**
  - A congenital malformation syndrome that results from the deletion of several adjacent genes in the short arm of chromosome 17 (17p). Clinical features include lissencephaly and a characteristic facial appearance (prominent forehead with bitemporal hollowing, short nose with upturned nares, thickened upper lip with a thin vermilion upper border, widely spaced eyes, low ears, and small jaw). The syndrome may result in mental retardation, epilepsy, pre- and postnatal growth retardation, and reduced lifespan. There may also be multiple abnormalities of the brain, kidneys, heart, and gastrointestinal tract
- **Smith–Magenis syndrome**
  - Results from a microdeletion in the short arm of chromosome 17 [del(17)(p11.2 p11.2)]. As well as characteristic facial abnormalities (short flat head, prominent forehead, broad square face, upslanting eyeslits, deep-set eyes, underdeveloped midface, broad nasal bridge, short nose and tented upper lip) the syndrome may also cause mild to moderate mental retardation
- **Steroid sulphatase deficiency**
  - Also known as X-linked ichthyosis, it is a genetic disorder of the skin that occurs only in males. The condition develops in infancy and manifests as tan or grey scales on the skin that are a result of a deficiency in the enzyme steroid sulphatase due to genetic mutations of the gene
- **DiGeorge syndrome** (also known as velo-cardio-facial/CATCH-22/Shprintzen syndrome) (*see* Chapter 7, Section 7.1.3 and Chapter 10, Section 10.9.4)
- **Kallman syndrome** (*see* Chapter 4, Section 4.8.3)
- **Williams syndrome** (*see* Chapter 1, Section 1.3.5 and Chapter 7, Section 7.1.3)
- **Wolf–Hirschhorn syndrome**
  - Results from a partial deletion of the short arm of chromosome 4. Many parts of the body are affected by this syndrome as the deletion affects fetal growth and development. Common features include profound mental retardation, microcephaly, seizures, low muscle tone and poor muscle development, heart defects and cleft lip and/or palate
- **Prader–Willi/Angelman syndrome** (*see* Chapter 7, Section 7.6)

Interphase FISH

FISH can be used in interphase cells to determine the chromosome number of one or more chromosomes as well as to detect some specific chromosome rearrangements characteristic of certain cancers. The advantage of interphase FISH is that it can be performed very rapidly as cell growth is not required.

An example of interphase FISH is the **aneuploid screen test** performed on amniotic fluid cells to determine the presence of the common trisomies. Sample nuclei are denatured and incubated with probes for chromosomes 13, 18, 21, X and Y.

Transcriptomics

The gene expression profile (**transcriptome**) of a particular tissue is the key to understanding the cell phenotype in health and disease. An average cell expresses about 16 000 genes throughout its lifetime but clearly the range of genes expressed in the lifetime of an individual cell will vary during development, maintenance and ultimately cell death. Inevitably the genes expressed by a neurone in the cerebellum will be very different from those expressed by a lymphocyte, though **housekeeping genes** are common to many cells and encode constitutive cellular processes.

The **transcriptome** of a cell can be captured using a technique known as **microarray analysis**. This depends on the same hybridisation reaction as other nucleic acid techniques but represents dramatic scaling up of the procedure such that many thousands of hybridisation reactions occur on a single medium and changes in transcription in many genes can be assessed simultaneously. RNA is prepared from the tissue of interest (for example, a tumour biopsy specimen) and from a control sample (eg normal tissue from the same organ from which the biopsy was obtained). The RNA is hybridised to a 'DNA chip'. This consists of a silicon slide 1–2 cm in size onto which have been spotted oligonucleotides, 20–30 base pairs long. Each oligonucleotide represents a particular gene. The RNAs from the abnormal and control tissues are labelled with different colour fluorescent dyes (eg red and green) and the level of expression of many thousands of genes can then be analysed by computer software which compares the differences in intensity generated by the hybridisation reaction.

- The power of this technology is such that it is not necessary to know anything about the function of the particular gene spotted onto the chip
- As the sequence of every gene is now known, DNA chips with a representative coverage of the whole human genome can be produced commercially
- It is also possible to produce tissue-specific chips (eg human CNS) or chips with a limited

number of genes of interest for use in diagnostics, when a specific question is being asked
- DNA microarrays can in principle identify a whole array of downstream genetic consequences of a particular gene mutation and provide a **molecular profile** of a disease state that can act as a marker of therapeutic effect

Practical applications

- Rapid sequencing for many genetic mutations can be performed simultaneously in a high-throughput approach. For example, specific oligonucleotides that recognise all of the mutations responsible for a particular disease can be spotted onto a chip and DNA from an affected individual analysed
- Tumours or other abnormal tissue can undergo molecular profiling in order to identify patterns of gene expression. For example, it is now possible in clinical practice to use microarrays to analyse the expression of panels of key genes that determine the clinical response to chemotherapeutic agents in lymphoma. Also, tissue or fluid from infections can be analysed for the expression of genes conferring antibiotic resistance before organisms have even been cultured
- Though still a research tool it is likely that microarrays will be routinely used in the near future in **genotyping** large numbers of genes simultaneously to look at specific disease risk (eg cardiovascular) associated with single nucleotide polymorphisms (SNPs) or other genetic variants
- Individual responses to common drug treatments (eg antihypertensive agents) are likely to have a basis in genetic variation. The application of knowledge acquired through genetic profiling such as with microarrays is known as **pharmacogenomics**

Proteomics

As discussed above, the total protein content of a cell or tissue may be a more meaningful target for analysis in certain situations than either the genome or transcriptome. Protein from whole tissue or from subcellular fractions (eg membrane, nuclear, mitochondrial) can be separated by physical methods, such as on a **2-D gel**, in which proteins are resolved by charge and mass to produce individual spots on a polyacrylamide gel which can then be silver-stained. Individual spots of interest can be removed and eluted from the gel. The protein within can then be identified using **tandem mass spectrometry** which can sequence short peptides. A known protein can then be identified by reference to protein sequence databases.

Where the oligopeptide does not produce a match, a search can be made of the **human genome sequence databases** – computer programmes have been used to predict genes and therefore protein sequences from the primary data (an example of what is known as **bioinformatics**). Currently, proteomics is largely a research tool, but with time and improved technology it will inevitably be used in clinical practice.

Potential applications include

- The identification of all of the proteins expressed in a particular cell, groups of cells or whole tissues throughout the whole development of an organism from conception to death. Ultimately a complete description of the ontogeny of the cell will be possible allowing virtual modelling and computer-based drug design
- Comparisons can be made between healthy and diseased tissue in the same way as for mRNA with microarrays. However, the advantage with proteomics is that it may be possible to detect differences at the protein level which are not reflected at the transcriptional level due to changes in turnover or post-translational processing. As with RNA techniques, protein from different sources can be differentially labelled with fluorescent dyes to aid the detection of differences
- **Protein chips** contain antibodies spotted onto silicon-based media similar to microarrays. Several hundred targeted proteins can be analysed in this way

Metabolomics

Metabolomics is the study of the specific and unique metabolite profile left behind by cellular processes. In different disease states it is thought that this profile of small metabolites changes. If characteristic profiles for specific diseases can be determined, it may be used as a diagnostic tool.

The metabolome is the complete set of small-molecule metabolites found in an organism. Like the transcriptome and proteome, the metabolome is constantly changing. At present the Human Metabolome Project (http://metabolomics.ca) has identified and quantified over 300 metabolites in cerebrospinal fluid, over 1000 metabolites in serum, over 400 metabolites in urine and approximately 300 metabolites in other tissues and biofluids, but the major limiting factor in the application of this technology is the incomplete characterisation of the human metabolome. With many of the molecules being small and difficult to extract, further work is required so we can use the 'whole' metabolome in disease diagnosis. The metabolome of an organism is related to both its genotype and physiology and can also be affected by its environment (what it eats and breathes). This complex interaction therefore allows us to look at genotype–phenotype as well as phenotype–environment relationships.

Metabolomics technology is increasingly used in a variety of health applications, including pharmacology, preclinical drug trials, toxicology, transplant monitoring, newborn screening and clinical chemistry.

There are four key steps:

1. Efficient and unbiased extraction of the metabolites from biological samples
2. Separation of the analytes (typically by chromatography, either gas or high-performance liquid chromatography)
3. Detection of the metabolites following separation (usually by either mass spectrometry (MS) or nuclear magnetic resonance (NMR))
4. Identification and quantification of detected metabolites

Physicians are now coming to understand that metabolic profiling can be used in the diagnosis, prediction, prevention and monitoring of many genetic, infectious and environmental diseases. In practice, complex computer software looks for patterns and changes in the metabolic profile from samples taken from patients with a particular disease compared with healthy controls. Having been 'taught' that a particular pattern is characteristic of a disease, samples from patients with unknown disease status can then be screened comparatively.

14.1.2 The polymerase chain reaction (PCR)

PCR is an amplification reaction in which a small amount of target DNA (the **template**) is amplified to produce enough to perform analysis. This might be the detection of a particular DNA sequence, such as that belonging to a pathogenic microorganism or an oncogene, or the detection of differences in genes, such as mutations causing inherited disease. Therefore, the template DNA might consist of total human genomic DNA derived from peripheral blood lymphocytes, amniocentesis or chorionic villus sampling; alternatively, it might consist of a tumour biopsy or a biological fluid from a patient with an infection.

- Two unique oligonucleotide sequences, known as **primers**, are mixed with a DNA template and a thermostable DNA polymerase (**Taq** **polymerase**, derived from an organism that inhabits thermal springs). Sometimes more than two primers can be used if more than one gene is to be amplified (multiplex PCR) or the region of DNA to be amplified needs special definition ('nested' PCR) – for example, if it is similar to other sequences in the genome which may give spurious reaction products
- In the initial stage of the reaction the DNA template is heated (typically for about 30 seconds) to make it single-stranded and then as the reaction cools the primers will anneal to the template if the appropriate sequence is present
- Then the reaction is heated to 72°C (for about a minute) and the DNA polymerase synthesises

new DNA between the two primer sequences. During 30 or so cycles (each typically lasting a few minutes) the target sequence will have been amplified exponentially

The crucial feature of PCR is that to detect a given sequence of DNA it only needs to be present in one copy (ie one molecule of DNA); this makes it extremely powerful.

Clinical applications of PCR

- Mutation detection
- Detection of viral and bacterial sequences in tissue (herpes simplex virus in CSF, hepatitis C, HIV in peripheral blood, meningococcal strains)
- Single-cell PCR of in vitro fertilised embryo to diagnose genetic disease before implantation

In the example in Figure 14.1, some CSF from a patient suspected of having herpes simplex encephalitis is used in a PCR reaction in an effort to detect the presence of the virus directly.

Small amounts of target DNA are amplified with a thermostable DNA polymerase.

14.1.3 Reverse transcription PCR (rt PCR)

Conventional PCR looks at genomic DNA. Every cell in our body contains our total genome in two copies. However, the phenotype of a cell (what makes a hepatocyte different from a Purkinje cell) depends on which genes are being expressed at any one time. To look at the expression of genes we must therefore analyse only those genes that are being transcribed into mRNA.

- RNA is too unstable to be used in PCR so it must first be converted to complementary DNA (cDNA) using **reverse transcriptase**, a retroviral enzyme that makes a precise copy of the mRNA
- PCR is then performed in the normal way but, because the template reflects the mRNA of the

> **Figure 14.1** The polymerase chain reaction (PCR)
>
> Cerebrospinal fluid from a patient with encephalitis is heated up and any viral DNA is liberated and separated into single-stranded DNA
>
> The primers specific for herpes simplex virus DNA bind to the virus-specific sequences if present
>
> *Taq* DNA polymerase synthesises a new daughter strand on the DNA template, resulting in double the number of copies of the starting DNA
>
> After 30 cycles, the PCR product is analysed by agarose electrophoresis. In this example, lane 1 contains a DNA size marker, lane 2 a PCR reaction product using pure viral DNA as a control. Lane 3 was generated using CSF from a patient with HSV encephalitis and lane 4 is a control with no CSF in the reaction to assess contamination
>
>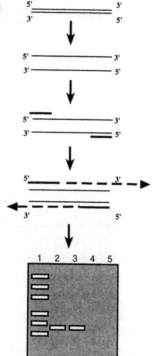

starting material, this technique can look at **gene expression** in individual tissues

---

Clinical applications of rt PCR

- Detection of the expression of particular genes in tumour tissue carries important prognostic information
- Basic scientific research into normal function of disease genes by understanding their spatial and temporal expression

---

14.1.4 Monoclonal antibodies

The detection of specific proteins in molecular diagnosis relies on the fact that the antibody used has a high specificity for the target protein. An immune response to an antigen consists of a polyclonal proliferation of cells giving rise to antibodies with a spectrum of specificity for the target. Therefore, useful diagnostic and therapeutic antibodies must be selected from this complex immune response before they can be used.

Myeloma is a malignantly transformed B-cell lineage that secretes a specific antibody. This fact is used to produce unlimited amounts of specific antibodies directed towards an antigen of choice.

- A laboratory animal is injected with the antigen of choice (Figure 14.2); it mounts an immune response and its spleen, which contains B-cell precursors with a range of specificity for the antigen, is harvested

Figure 14.2 Monoclonal antibody production

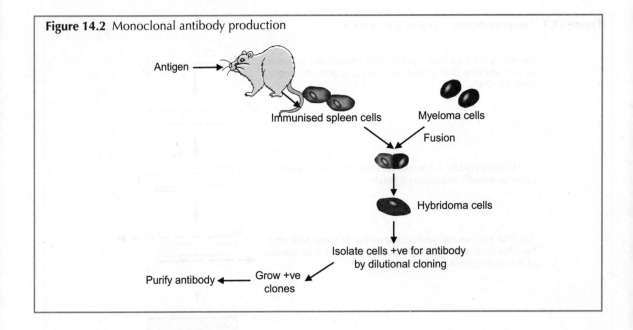

- The spleen cells are fused en masse to a specialised myeloma cell line that no longer produces its own antibody
- The resulting fused cells, or **hybridomas**, grow in individual colonies, are immortal and produce antibodies specified by the lymphocytes of the immunised animal. These cells can be screened to select for the antibody of interest which can then be produced in limitless amounts

Clinical applications of monoclonal antibodies

- Diagnosis of cancer and infections
- Imaging of tumours, radiotherapy
- As a 'magic bullet' to direct drugs to target
- Transplantation and other immune modulations (eg OKT3)

14.1.5   Antibody-based assays

An assay is defined as a procedure where a property or concentration of an analyte is measured. In medicine the specific binding of labelled antibodies is used to assay for a huge range of analytes that may aid in the diagnosis of disease. Assays are available for numerous serum proteins (growth factors, cytokines, clotting factors, etc) as well as for proteins found on infectious organisms (bacterial and viral). Previous radioactive methodology (radio-immunoassay (RIA) and immunoradiometric assay (IRMA)) is being replaced by enzyme immuno-assays, the most common of which is the enzyme-linked immunosorbent assay (**ELISA**).

1. A plate is coated with capture antibody specific to the analyte of interest (Figure 14.3)
2. Sample is added and incubated for sufficient time to allow any analyte present to bind to the capture antibody; non-specific, unbound proteins are washed off
3. Secondary antibody is added that also recognises the antigen, but which has been raised against a different part of the protein – so both antibodies can bind at the same time. Excess secondary antibody is washed off
4. Enzyme-linked tertiary antibody is added that recognises the secondary antibody; excess tertiary antibody is washed off

Figure 14.3 The ELISA assay process

5. Substrate is added and is converted by the linked enzyme to a detectable form (fluorescent or colorimetric). The intensity of signal is directly proportional to the amount of analyte present. Concentration is calculated by constructing a standard curve with known amounts of analyte

14.2 CELL SIGNALLING

Central to all cellular processes is the conversion of external signals (first messengers) via intermediates (second messengers) into changes that alter the state of that cell. This often involves adjustment in the expression of genes in the cell nucleus and new protein synthesis. In the following example (see Figure 14.4) a photon of light is the external stimulus that produces, via second messengers, a change in the resting state of the rod cell, leading it to transmit a signal to the visual cortex.

14.2.1 Types of receptor

The chief function of the cell membrane is to provide a barrier to ion flux and therefore to maintain the internal milieu of the cell. There are, as described below, certain lipophilic modules which travel freely into the cell. However, most external

signals can only effect changes inside the cell by interaction with membrane-bound receptor modules. This biologically ubiquitous system of signal transduction by receptors underlies the action of many hormones, growth factors and drugs.

Figure 14.4 A typical signalling pathway (the rod receptor). This involves a G-protein-coupled membrane receptor which activates a second messenger pathway

Ligand-gated ion channel

For example, **acetylcholine receptor** (nicotinic):

- Five non-covalently assembled subunits ($\alpha_2\beta\gamma\delta$) are located at the post-synaptic neuromuscular junction
- Each subunit is coded for by a different gene which enables mixing and matching of subunits between different tissues and in embryological development to generate a repertoire of responses
- On binding of acetylcholine to the α subunits the whole complex undergoes a conformational change leading to the passage of sodium ions into the cell and cellular depolarisation

Other examples include some **glutamate** receptors (excitatory), γ-aminobutyric acid (GABA) and **glycine** (inhibitory: the passage of chloride ions into the cell renders it more resistant to depolarisation).

Receptors that contain cytoplasmic domains with protein-tyrosine-kinase activity

- **Insulin** binds to its receptor which then undergoes dimerisation and autophosphorylation at a tyrosine residue
- The tyrosine kinase activity intrinsic to the receptor is then activated and the result is the phosphorylation of cytoplasmic proteins and initiation of an intracellular cascade
- This ultimately leads to the action of insulin on glucose uptake, etc

Other examples include platelet-derived growth factor, insulin-like growth factor 1 (IGF-1), macrophage colony-stimulating factor, nerve growth factor.

G-protein-coupled receptors

Guanine nucleotide-binding proteins are a ubiquitous cellular mechanism for coupling an extracellular signal to a second messenger, such as cyclic AMP (Figure 14.5).

- G-proteins have three non-covalently associated subunits: α, β, γ. In the inactive state GDP is bound to the α subunit of the G-protein
- When the receptor is activated by ligand binding, the G-protein is activated by the hydrolysis of GTP to GDP
- In this active state the α subunit dissociates from the β and γ subunits. Either of these two complexes (the GTP-α or the β-γ) can then interact with second messengers
- The α subunit is rapidly inactivated by hydrolysis of GDP to GTP (this is an intrinsic property of the α subunit, which is therefore known as α-GTPase) and then re-associates with the β and γ subunits, resetting the whole system to the inactive state

G-proteins can be inhibitory (Gi) or stimulatory (Gs) and the overall activity of a second messenger such as adenylate cyclase is likely to be regulated by the differential activation of these different forms. The **muscarinic acetylcholine receptor**, the α and β **adrenergic receptor** and the retinal photoreceptor **rhodopsin** are all G-protein-coupled receptors.

Figure 14.5 G-proteins are activated by ligand binding to a transmembrane receptor

These can be linked to a variety of second messenger systems or sometimes directly to ion channels.

14.2.2 Protein kinases and phosphatases

Protein kinases catalyse the transfer of a phosphate group from ATP to a serine, threonine or tyrosine residue on a target protein (the substrate). Phosphorylation of this amino acid residue results in an alteration in the conformation of the target protein and thus leads to its activation or inactivation. Many **growth factor receptors** are protein tyrosine kinases (see above). Many of the 'downstream' intracellular pathways that are initiated by the activation of a second messenger system involve protein kinases (usually serine kinases in the cytoplasm). In this way an external signal can, through the activation of one receptor, influence a vast array of cellular processes due to a cascade of protein interactions.

14.2.3 Nuclear hormones

Not all extracellular signals use second-messenger systems to effect changes to the cell. Important exceptions are **steroid hormones** that bind to an intracellular receptor, allowing the receptor to be freed from its cytosolic membrane-bound anchor (Figure 14.6). The receptor–hormone complex then travels to the nucleus where it binds to specific regions of DNA called **hormone-responsive elements (HRE)**, thereby effecting alterations in the transcription of DNA.

Examples of nuclear hormones

- Corticosteroids
- Vitamin D
- Retinoic acid
- Sex steroids

14.2.4 Transcription factors and the regulation of gene expression

The human genome is present in two copies in every cell in the body, and is estimated to consist of around 30 000 genes. The spatial and temporal expression of a proportion of these genes (typically 10 000–15 000 genes are expressed in any one cell at any time) determines the differentiation, morphology and functional characteristics of each cell type (the **cellular phenotype**). Clearly, for cells to maintain a specific identity, this process must be very tightly regulated.

Eukaryotic genes consist of **exons**, which are transcribed into the mRNA template, which is translated into protein (Figure 14.7). Exons are separated by **introns**, which do not code for protein but have a role in mRNA stability and are spliced out of the pre-mRNA prior to translation. Sometimes exons are also spliced out to produce variant forms of the protein with tissue-specific functional elements (splice variants).

Clearly some genes have a fundamental biological role and will be expressed in all cells at all times ('housekeeping genes'). However, the transcription of most genes only proceeds when a macromolecular complex (the initiation complex) binds to a region of the 5' end of genes called the **promoter**. The assembly of this complex is directed by the presence of transcription factors and facilitates the binding of RNA polymerase, which leads to transcription. Muscle, for example, will contain specific transcription factors that lead to the expression of

Figure 14.6 The nuclear hormone superfamily of receptors act by controlling gene transcription in the nucleus

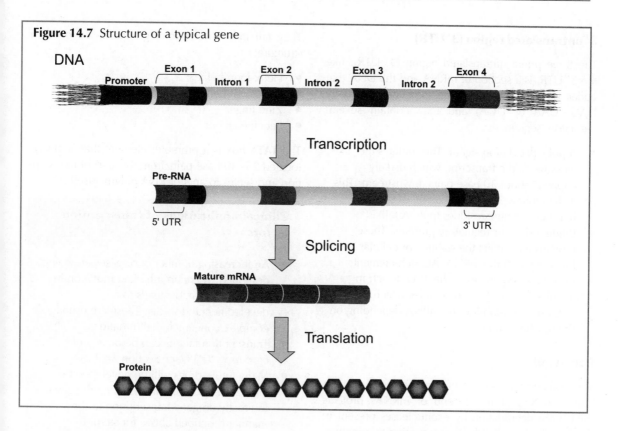

Figure 14.7 Structure of a typical gene

muscle-specific genes which determine the muscle phenotype.

The promoter

- A modular arrangement of different elements that act as a binding site for RNA polymerase II and the initiation of transcription
- The initiation of transcription involves a large complex of multimeric proteins (RNA polymerase II plus the general transcription factors (GTFs): TFII A–H)
- The GTFs can activate transcription of any gene that has a TATA box (see below)

Enhancers

- Elements that can be at the 5′ or the 3′ end of genes and can vary in distance from the coding sequence itself

- Enhancers are not obligatory for the initiation of transcription but alter its efficiency in such a way as to lead to an increase in gene expression

5′ untranslated region (5′ UTR)

The five prime untranslated region (5′ UTR) is a section of mRNA and the DNA that codes for it. It starts at the transcription start site and ends just before the transcription start codon (usually AUG). The region can contain several regulatory sequences:

- A ribosome-binding site
- Binding sites for proteins that may affect the stability or translation rate of the mRNA
- Sequences that promote the initiation of translation

3′ untranslated region (3′ UTR)

The three prime untranslated region (3′ UTR), like the 5′ UTR, is a section of mRNA and the DNA that codes for it. It starts after the stop codon (usually UAG, UAA or UGA) and may contain several regulatory sequences:

- A polyadenylation signal. This initiates the cleavage of the transcript, which usually happens about 30 base pairs downstream. This is then followed by the addition of several hundred adenine residues (poly-A tail)
- Binding sites for regulatory proteins. These proteins may affect the stability or cellular localisation of the mRNA. AU-rich elements (AREs) are sequences in the 3′ UTR rich in adenine and uridine nucleotides which can stabilise or destabilise the mRNA depending on the protein bound

Poly-A tail

The addition of a stretch of adenine residues (typically 50–200) at the 3′ end of mRNAs protects them from degradation by exonucleases present in the cytoplasm, and aids in transcription termination, export from the nucleus and translation. The length of the adenine repeat may also have an effect on stability; when the tail is shortened the mRNA is enzymatically degraded.

Transcription factors

Transcription factors are proteins that bind to sequence-specific regions of DNA at the 5′ end of genes called **response elements** to regulate gene expression. These elements can form part of promoters or enhancers. They can be divided into:

- Basal transcription factors – involved in the constitutive activation of so-called 'housekeeping genes'
- Inducible transcription factors – involved in the temporal and spatial expression of genes that underlie tissue phenotype and developmental regulation

They fall into a number of groups based on their structure:

- Helix-loop-helix
- Helix-turn-helix
- Zinc finger
- Leucine zipper

The **TATA box** is a promoter element that is always located 25–30 base pairs from the start of transcription and serves to anchor RNA polymerase II.

Clinical applications of transcription factors

- An increasing number of diseases are being described where an inherited mutation in transcription factors leads to a developmental disorder. These are usually complex congenital malformations
- Transcription factors can be oncogenes, eg *c-myc*, *TP53* (*see* Section 14.3.2)
- Many future drugs will be developed to alter gene transcription by acting directly or indirectly on gene transcription in the manner described above for steroids

---

14.3 THE MOLECULAR PATHOGENESIS OF CANCER

14.3.1 Somatic evolution of cancer

Cancer cells are a clonal population. The accumulation of mutations in multiple genes results in escape from the strictly regulated mechanisms that control the growth and differentiation of somatic cells. It will be evident that some of these genetic 'errors' will be inherited and form the basis of a familial tendency to cancer. For cancer to develop, in most cases, an environmentally driven genetic mutation is necessary. Genotoxic damage from ionising radiation and some of the constituents of tobacco smoke fall into this category. In addition, all somatic cell division requires the copying of

DNA and this can result in the spontaneous mutations of genes. It is a combination of these three types of genetic mutation (inherited, spontaneous and environmentally determined) which leads to cancer. Therefore, cancer evolution is a complex, multifactorial process.

Most tumours show visible abnormalities of chromosome banding on light microscopy, suggesting that as tumours develop they become more bizarre and more prone to genetic error. Although there are some cancer genes that lead to Mendelian (ie monogenic) inheritance of specific tumours, most cancers result from a complex mixture of polygenetic and environmental influences.

14.3.2 Oncogenes

Originally identified as genes carried by cancer-causing viruses that are integrated into the host genome and, when expressed, lead to loss of growth control (viral oncogenes are denoted v-onc). They have cellular homologues, **proto-oncogenes** (denoted c-onc), found in the normal human genome and expressed in normal tissue, that are usually highly conserved in evolution and have central roles in the signal-transduction pathways that control cell growth and differentiation. They can be thought of as exerting a dominant effect in that they cause cancer in the presence of the normal gene product because, in mutating, they have gained a new function.

- **Ras** is a small, monomeric G-protein and is likely to be involved in the transduction of growth-promoting signals. The relative abundance of the active and inactive forms of **Ras** is controlled by positive and negative regulators of GTP–GDP exchange (GAP and GNRF) (Figure 14.8). Mutations affecting the GTP-binding site prevent GTP hydrolysis and prolong **Ras** activation. At least a third of sporadic tumours contain acquired somatic mutations in the *ras* gene

- Further downstream, after a number of protein kinase steps have been activated, the transduction of growth signals culminates in the activation of the transcription factors **Fos** and **Jun** which in turn induce the transcription of the proto-oncogene *myc*, which commits the cell to a round of DNA replication and cell division

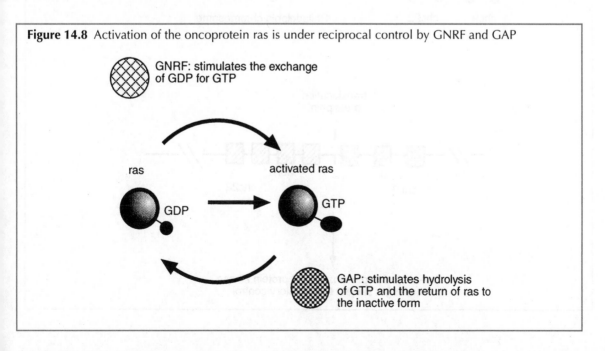

Figure 14.8 Activation of the oncoprotein ras is under reciprocal control by GNRF and GAP

Mutant forms of these proteins can induce tumour growth
- The 9:22 balanced translocation (Philadelphia chromosome) found in chronic myeloid leukaemia (**CML**) generates a composite gene comprising exons from the **bcr** locus on chromosome 22 and the **c-abl** locus on chromosome 9, generating a **fusion protein** with distinct biochemical properties which presumably promote tumour growth
- In **Burkitt's lymphoma** the **c-myc** gene is transposed from its normal position into the immunoglobulin heavy-chain locus on chromosome 14, resulting in a gross increase in its expression and a potent molecular signal for cells to undergo mitosis (see Figure 14.9)

14.3.3   Tumour suppressor genes

- In contrast to oncogenes these exert a recessive effect, in that both copies must be mutated before tumorigenesis occurs
- Mutation results in loss of function
- These genes normally function to inhibit the cell cycle and therefore, when inactivated, lead to loss of growth control

p53 is a protein that occupies a pivotal role in the cell cycle and its gene is the most commonly mutated gene in tumours (breast, colon, etc). It encodes a transcription factor, the normal function of which is to downregulate the cell cycle. Inactivation of **p53** is the primary defect in the Li–Fraumeni syndrome (a dominantly inherited monogenic can-

Figure 14.9 In CML the Philadelphia chromosome leads to the production of an oncoprotein

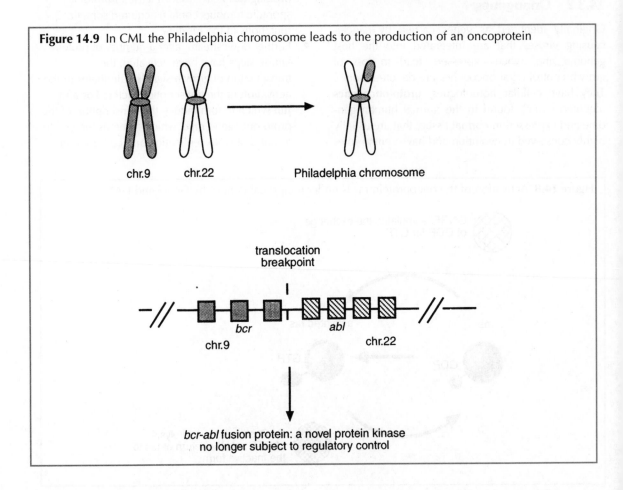

cer syndrome characterised by breast carcinoma, sarcomas, brain and other tumours), and is a central regulator of **apoptosis** (see below).

14.4 APOPTOSIS AND DISEASE

It has only recently been fully appreciated that widespread cell death occurs in human development and in the normal regulation of cell number in the adult organism. In embryonic development cells are lost, for example, as finger webbing disappears or as neurones are 'selected' for survival by making the appropriate synaptic contact. In postnatal life, the expansion of lymphocyte numbers in response to antigen stimulation must be regulated by the subsequent death of these cells or clonal proliferation would continue unabated. It turns out that this process of naturally occurring cell death is regulated by the activation of a specific set of genes in response to external signals in a process referred to as **programmed cell death**. The morphological change that accompanies this process is called **apoptosis** (Figure 14.10).

- Cells undergo shrinkage, compaction of chromatin, nuclear and cytoplasmic budding to form membrane-bound apoptotic bodies and finally phagocytosis by surrounding macrophages
- The activation of intracellular nucleases can be detected by the 'laddering' of DNA on

electrophoresis gels, which serves as a marker for apoptosis

In contrast to necrosis, apoptosis does not induce the release of destructive proteolytic enzymes and free radicals and is thus a non-inflammatory process. Therefore, collateral damage to neighbouring cells is not seen. Most cells seem to rely on a constant supply of survival signals without which they will undergo apoptosis. These are provided by neighbouring cells and the extracellular matrix. The absence or withdrawal of these molecular signals is a trigger to apoptosis.

The 'cell death programme' is genetically regulated and there are specific proteins that promote or inhibit apoptosis.

- A family of proteases called **caspases** (ICE, or interleukin-1β-converting enzyme, is the best-studied example) is central to apoptosis in mammals and is responsible for driving all the structural changes in the nucleus that accompany apoptosis. Caspases have been shown to be present in all cells and thus to prevent apoptosis there must be specific inhibitors of these proteases
- The **Bcl-2** family of molecules inhibit apoptosis by a variety of mechanisms and are thus cytoprotective survival signals. Over-expression of **Bcl-2** specifically prevents cells from entering apoptosis and its high expression has been correlated with poor survival from cancer

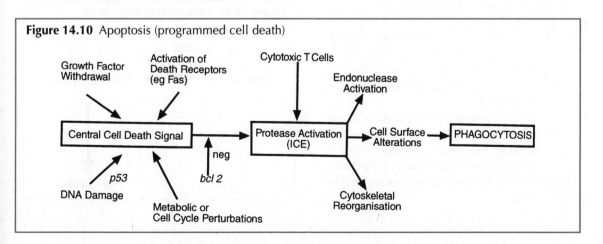

Figure 14.10 Apoptosis (programmed cell death)

- **Fas**, or CD95, is a transmembrane receptor that belongs to the tumour necrosis factor (TNF) receptor family. The binding of TNF-like ligands to Fas is coupled to the activation of intracellular caspases. Some tumours express the Fas ligand on their surface, thus activating Fas on cytotoxic T lymphocytes, leading to their death (a way of evading immune surveillance)
- **p53** is required for the apoptosis of cells in which DNA has been damaged. The failure of tumour cells to die in the face of genotoxic damage may be due to the accumulation of p53 gene mutations

Programmed cell death can be stimulated by a variety of triggers and leads to the activation of proteases such as ICE that initiate a cascade of morphological changes (collectively known as apoptosis) which result in inevitable phagocytosis.

- Certain disorders (cancer, autoimmunity and some viral illnesses) are associated with increased cell survival (and therefore a failure of programmed cell death). Metastatic tumour cells have circumvented the normal environmental cues for survival and can survive in foreign environments
- Physiological cell death is necessary for the removal of potentially autoreactive T cells during development and for the removal of excess cells after the completion of the immune response. Animal models of SLE (CD95/Fas knockout mice) have implicated apoptosis genes in the pathogenesis of autoimmunity
- Death by apoptosis can be seen as an evolutionary adaptation to prevent the survival of virally infected cells. Therefore, viruses have developed strategies for circumventing this. Pox viruses appear to inhibit apoptosis by producing an inhibitor of ICE
- Excessive cell death due to an excess of signals promoting apoptosis has been hypothesised to occur in many degenerative disorders where cells have been observed to die by apoptosis. Direct evidence that this actually occurs has yet to be found

14.5 MOLECULAR REGULATION OF VASCULAR TONE

Both the regulation of systemic arterial blood pressure and the local control of the microcirculation in organs such as the kidney and the brain are vital for the maintenance of homeostasis. Recently there has been an explosion of knowledge concerning the molecular mediators of blood flow and this is already having an impact in the therapy of some common disorders.

Two important principles should be kept in mind:

- The regulation of vascular tone is predominantly a **paracrine** process, where molecules are released to act in adjacent cells
- Vascular control is often a balance between competing vasodilators and vasoconstrictors

14.5.1 Nitric oxide (NO)

Previously called endothelium-derived relaxant factor (EDRF), NO is an important transcellular messenger molecule that is involved in a diverse range of processes.

NO is synthesised from the oxidation of nitrogen atoms in the amino acid L-arginine by the action of NO synthase (NOS) (Figure 14.11).

Figure 14.11 Formation of nitric oxide

Cell types which synthesise nitric oxide

Vascular endothelium

- Platelets
- Macrophages
- Vascular smooth muscle
- Neutrophils
- Hepatocytes
- Central and peripheral nerve cells

NO acts on target cells close to its site of synthesis where it activates guanylate cyclase leading to a rise in intracellular cGMP, which acts as a second messenger to modulate a variety of cellular processes. It has a very short half-life.

There are at least three distinct **isoforms** of NO synthase:

- Neuronal (constitutive)
- Endothelial (constitutive)
- Macrophage (inducible)

Constitutive NO production is involved in regulation of vascular tone and neurotransmission and is calcium/calmodulin-dependent. **Inducible NO production** is mainly involved in cell-mediated immunity and is activated by cytokines.

Synthetic nitrates, such as GTN and sodium nitroprusside, act after their conversion into NO.

Functions of nitric oxide

- Vasodilator tone modulation in the regulation of systemic blood pressure
- CNS neurotransmission, including the formation of new memories
- Inhibition of platelet aggregation
- Cytotoxic action utilised in the generation of the host immune response in activated macrophages
- Organ-specific microregulatory control (eg kidney)

- Peripheral nervous system 'non-adrenergic, non-cholinergic neurotransmission' (NANC), mediating neurogenic vasodilatation

Diseases related to abnormalities in the generation or regulation of NO

- **Septic shock:** NO is released in massive amounts and correlates with low blood pressure
- **Atherosclerosis:** NO synthesis may be impaired more than endothelin synthesis, leading to tonic vasoconstriction and vasospasm
- **Primary and secondary pulmonary hypertension:** inhaled NO reverses pulmonary hypertension
- **Hepatorenal syndrome** and the **hypertension of chronic renal failure:** failure of breakdown and secretion of endogenous antagonists of NO leads to a microcirculatory imbalance between NO and endothelin (see below)
- **Excitotoxic cell death in the CNS:** glutamate is the principal excitatory neurotransmitter in the CNS. NO is the transduction mechanism when glutamate binds to NMDA (*N*-methyl-D-aspartate) receptors on neurones. The final event in the presence of excess glutamate is a rise in intracellular calcium and the cell becomes vulnerable to dying. This process, in which NO is now implicated, is thought to be important in neuronal loss in many neurodegenerative conditions such as Alzheimer's disease and also in acute brain injury such as stroke
- **Tissue damage in acute and chronic inflammation** (probably by interacting with oxygen-derived free radicals)
- **Adult respiratory distress syndrome** (ARDS)

14.5.2 Endothelin-1

This is the most potent vasoconstrictor substance yet described. It is manufactured following vascular endothelial 'stress' (shear, hypoxia, growth factors, expansion of plasma volume). It is produced from pre-pro ET by the action of endothelin-converting enzyme (ETCE). Very little endothelin reaches the circulation and serum levels do not generally carry any diagnostic significance.

There are endothelin receptors:

- On the vascular endothelium and on some smooth muscle cells (gut and heart), including coronary arteries where they cause constriction
- On capillary endothelium where they cause vasodilatation

When ET-1 is infused intravenously it causes a transient vasodilatation followed by a long period of intense vasoconstriction lasting up to 2 hours. The normal function of endothelin is in the regulation of vascular tone. The endothelin-receptor blockers sitaxsentan and bosentan have been developed to counter pulmonary hypertension. Bosentan is a non-selective endothelin-receptor blocker whilst sitaxsentan is selective for the endothelin-A receptor. As endothelin receptor-B activation is thought to be beneficial, it is thought that sitaxsentan could be a more effective treatment. More diverse functions of endothelin are indicated by the recent finding of mutations in the endothelin-B receptor in some patients with Hirschsprung's disease.

Disorders whose pathogenesis may be related to endothelin

- Essential hypertension
- Primary pulmonary hypertension
- Renovascular hypertension
- Hepatorenal syndrome
- Acute renal failure
- Chronic heart failure
- Raynaud's phenomenon
- Vasospasm after subarachnoid haemorrhage

14.6 MOLECULAR MEDIATORS OF INFLAMMATION, DAMAGE AND REPAIR

The process of tissue injury, inflammation and subsequent repair is highly conserved in evolution and represents part of the 'primitive' repertoire of protective mechanisms against invasion by foreign organisms and other insults. This is in contrast to the more sophisticated mechanisms of defence mediated by the immune system. Some of the same molecules are involved in both processes but they are considered here to emphasise the enormous importance of inflammation as a pathological process central to many diseases. These molecular interactions are to a certain extent therefore independent of the immune system.

The principal molecules involved are termed **cytokines**, because they function in the immune system as products secreted by one cell to act on another cell to direct its movement ('kinesis'). In the context of inflammation it is the **pro-inflammatory cytokines** that are relevant. (*See also* Chapter 10, Immunology.)

14.6.1 Interleukin 1 (IL-1)

This molecule has a broad spectrum of both beneficial and harmful biological actions and, as a central regulator of the inflammatory response, has been implicated in many diseases.

There are three structurally related polypeptides in the interleukin 1 family:

- IL-1α
- IL-1β
- IL-1-receptor antagonist

IL-1α and IL-1β are synthesised by mononuclear phagocytes that have been activated by microbial products or inflammation:

- IL-1α stays in the cell to act in an autocrine or paracrine fashion

- IL-1β is secreted into the circulation and cleaved by interleukin-1β-converting enzyme (ICE)

IL-1β levels in the circulation are undetectable except:

- After strenuous exercise
- With sepsis
- With acute exacerbation of rheumatoid arthritis
- In ovulating women
- With acute organ rejection

IL-1 in disease

- **Rheumatoid arthritis**: IL-1 is present in the synovial lining and fluid of patients with rheumatoid arthritis and it is thought to activate gene expression for collagenases, phospholipases and cyclo-oxygenases. It is thus acting as a molecular facilitator of inflammatory damage in the joint but is not an initiator
- **Atherosclerosis**: the uptake of oxidised LDL by vascular endothelial cells results in IL-1 expression, which stimulates the production of platelet-derived growth factor. IL-1 is thus likely to play a role in the formation of the atherosclerotic plaque
- **Infection**: IL-1 has some host defence properties, inducing T and B lymphocytes, and reduces mortality from bacterial and fungal infection in animal models
- **Septic shock**: IL-1 acts by increasing the concentration of small mediator molecules such as platelet-activating factor (PAF), prostaglandins and nitric oxide, which are potent vasodilators

14.6.2 Tumour necrosis factor (TNF)

This is a pro-inflammatory cytokine that has a wide spectrum of actions. Either through neutralising anti-bodies (anti-TNFα) or inhibitor drugs it is the target of therapy in disorders such as rheumatoid arthritis and multiple sclerosis.

Two non-allelic forms of TNF, α and β, are expressed in different cells.

- TNFα is produced by macrophages, eosinophils and NK cells
- TNFβ is made by activated T lymphocytes

Its name is derived from the early observation that it can have a cytotoxic effect on tumour cells in vitro. Trials with TNFα as a therapeutic agent were soon stopped due to the severe toxicity of the substance. In fact in certain situations it can promote tumour growth.

Its action in diseases such as **rheumatoid arthritis** depends on a synergistic effect with IL-1. Both are found in the synovial membrane of patients with the disease. TNFα strongly induces monocytes to produce IL-1 at a level comparable to that stimulated by bacterial lipopolysaccharide (LPS).

Actions of TNF

- TNFα is a potent stimulator of prostaglandin production
- TNF is a key cytokine in the pathogenesis of multiorgan failure
- It induces granulocyte-macrophage colony stimulating factor (GM-CSF) and thus is an activator of monocytes and macrophages in diseased tissue

14.6.3 Transforming growth factor β (TGFβ)

A key cytokine that initiates and terminates tissue repair and whose sustained production underlies the development of tissue fibrosis.

TGFβ is released by platelets at the site of tissue injury and is strongly chemotactic for monocytes, neutrophils, T cells and fibroblasts. It induces monocytes to begin secreting fibroblast growth factor (FGF), TNF and IL-1, but inhibits the functioning of T and B cells and their production of TNF and IL-1. It also induces its own secretion. This **autoinduction** may be important in the pathogenesis of fibrosis.

TGFβ in disease

- TGFβ-deficient (knockout) mice die of an autoimmune disease in which levels of TNF and IL-1 are very high
- It has a potent effect on cells to induce the production of extracellular matrix (a dynamic superstructure of self-aggregating macromolecules including fibronectin, collagen and proteoglycans to which cells attach by means of surface receptors called **integrins**). Extracellular matrix is continually being degraded by proteases which are inhibited by TGFβ
- In **mesangioproliferative glomerulonephritis**, glomerular immunostaining for TGFβ correlates well with the amount of mesangial deposition
- In **diabetic nephropathy**, increased TGFβ is found in the glomeruli, and TGFβ may be central to the pathogenesis of progression of many chronic renal diseases
- Elevated plasma levels of TGFβ are highly predictive of **hepatic fibrosis** in bone marrow transplant recipients. mRNA for TGFβ is found in areas of active disease in liver biopsy samples of patients with chronic liver disease
- In patients with **idiopathic pulmonary fibrosis**, TGFβ is increased in the alveolar walls. It is also implicated in **bleomycin lung**

14.6.4 Heat shock proteins (HSPs)

The **heat shock response** is a highly conserved and phylogenetically ancient response to tissue stress that is mediated by activation of specific genes, leading to the production of specific heat shock proteins that alter the phenotype of the cell, and enhance its resistance to stresses.

Some HSPs are extremely similar to constitutively activated proteins that have essential roles in unstressed cells. Their diverse functions include:

- Export of proteins in and out of specific cell organelles (acting as **molecular chaperones**)
- Catalysis of protein folding and unfolding
- Degradation of proteins (often by the pathway of ubiquitination)

As well as heat, HSP expression can be triggered by cytotoxic chemicals, free radicals and other stimuli. The unifying feature that leads to the activation of HSPs in these situations is thought to be the accumulation of damaged intracellular protein.

Clinical relevance

- Tumours have an abnormal thermotolerance which is the basis for the observation of the enhanced cytotoxic effect of chemotherapeutic agents in hyperthermic subjects
- Stress proteins are prominent amongst the bacterial antigens recognised by the immune response of humans to bacterial and parasitic infections and are thought to be involved in some autoimmune diseases
- Mutations in small heat shock proteins (sHSPs) have been associated with diseases as diverse as cataract (α-crystallin) and forms of motor neurone degeneration (sHSPs 22 and 27)

14.6.5 Free radicals and human disease

Free radicals have been implicated in a large number of human diseases and are currently the subject of much interest. Therapeutic trials have been undertaken with putative free-radical scavengers such as vitamin E. A free radical is literally any atom or molecule that contains one or more unpaired electrons, making it more reactive than the native species.

Free radical species produced in the human body

- – $HOO^{\cdot}$ (peroxide radical)
- – $\dot{O}_2$ (superoxide radical)
- – $HO^{\cdot}$ (hydroxyl radical)
- – $N\dot{O}$ (nitric oxide)

The hydroxyl radical is by far the most reactive species but the others can generate more reactive species as breakdown products.

When a free radical reacts with a non-radical a chain reaction ensues, which results in the formation of further free radicals and direct tissue damage by lipid peroxidation of membranes. This is particularly implicated in **atherosclerosis**, and **ischaemia-reperfusion injury** (eg acute tubular necrosis within the kidney) within tissues. Hydroxyl radicals can cause mutations by attacking purines and pyrimidines. Also:

- Activated phagocytes generate large amounts of superoxide within lysosomes as part of the mechanism whereby foreign organisms are killed. During chronic inflammation this protective mechanism may become harmful
- **Superoxide dismutases** (SOD) convert superoxide to hydrogen peroxide and are thus part of an inherent protective antioxidant strategy. **Catalases** remove hydrogen peroxide. **Glutathione peroxidases** are major enzymes that remove hydrogen peroxide generated by SOD in cytosol and mitochondria
- **Free-radical scavengers** bind reactive oxygen species. Alpha-tocopherol, urate, ascorbate and glutathione remove free radicals by reacting directly and non-catalytically. Severe deficiency of α-tocopherol (vitamin E deficiency) causes neurodegeneration

Clinical relevance

There is growing evidence that cardiovascular disease and cancer can be prevented by a diet rich in substances that diminish oxidative damage.

Principal dietary antioxidants
- Vitamin E - Vitamin C - Beta-carotene - Flavonoids

Epidemiological studies have demonstrated an association between increased intake of vitamins C and E and morbidity and mortality from coronary artery disease. This supports models where atherogenesis is initiated by lipid peroxidation of LDL.

Patients with dominant familial forms of amyotrophic lateral sclerosis (motor neurone disease) have mutations in the gene for Cu-Zn SOD-1, suggesting a link between failure of oxidative damage and neurodegeneration.

14.7 TRANSMISSIBLE SPONGIFORM ENCEPHALOPATHIES (TSEs)

The transmissible spongiform encephalopathies (TSEs) are a group of diseases that are characterised by progressive spongiform degeneration in the brain and neuronal loss. While these conditions are rare, they are the subject of intense interest because of an epidemic of human infection which is linked to the cattle disease bovine spongiform encephalopathy (BSE). The biologically unique features of these diseases are, firstly, that they can be simultaneously inherited and also infectious, and, secondly, that the agent of transmission is thought to be a protein only rather than an 'organism' containing DNA or RNA. This protein has been called a **prion**; it is encoded by the host genome and cannot replicate.

Diseases caused by TSEs

- **Sporadic Creutzfeldt–Jakob disease (CJD)**: rare ($1/10^6$), causes rapid dementia with myoclonus and characteristic EEG
- **Variant CJD (vCJD)**: 167 cases had occurred in the UK up to 1 September 2008 with 164 deaths and 3 additional probable cases reported. This affects young people and has a slower course than sporadic CJD; it has characteristic pathological features
- **Autosomal dominant CJD**: familial form of classic CJD
- **Gerstmann–Straussler–Scheinker syndrome (GSS)**: familial spongiform encephalopathy with prominent ataxia
- **Fatal familial insomnia**

- **Kuru**: previously endemic in New Guinea highlanders who performed ritual cannibalism. This condition is now disappearing

Molecular features of TSEs

The accidental or deliberate inoculation of affected brain tissue from a case of inherited or sporadic TSE results in the passage of the disease to the recipient. Procedures that destroy nucleic acid do not prevent this passage, which has led to the proposition that the prion protein itself causes the disease by interacting with the host-encoded protein, leading to its conversion to the mutant form of the protein. Other important considerations for the TSEs are:

- **Prion protein**: This is encoded by a gene on chromosome 20, exact function unknown. Curiously, mice lacking this gene only have subtle neurological defects. Prion proteins are not destroyed by boiling, UV irradiation or formaldehyde, nor do they elicit an immune response of any recognisable kind
- **Species barrier**: This means that the diseases are, to some extent, species-specific. For example, scrapie in sheep has never been passed on to humans as far as is known. Similarly, the transmission of a spongiform encephalopathy from one species to another is very difficult. If CJD brain tissue is injected into the brain of a monkey then there is very little cell death, but if brain tissue from that same monkey is injected into another monkey (second passage) then there is severe neuronal loss. This suggests that the pathological process leading to spongiform change depends on the host protein
- **Susceptibility polymorphism**: At codon 129 of the prion protein the amino acid can either be a valine or a glycine residue. Given that there is one copy of the gene on each chromosome we can either be heterozygous (valine/glycine) or homozygous (valine/valine or glycine/glycine). It turns out that homozygosity at this residue is vastly over-represented in affected individuals in sporadic CJD and in variant CJD. It would appear that the one amino acid can confer susceptibility to the disease

- **Strain type**: When the protein from affected brains is electrophoretically separated and blotted onto a membrane (Western blotting) and then incubated with anti-prion protein antibody, different patterns can be seen. This is what is referred to as the 'strain' of the infective agent but is really a surrogate marker. It is the fact that the observed pattern with variant CJD is identical to that observed with BSE, and different from sporadic CJD, that provides the strongest evidence of a link between the two

14.8 ADHESION MOLECULES

The way in which cells communicate with each other is fundamental to the maintenance of homeostasis in the developing and adult organism. In particular, the molecular basis of neural connectivity, the immune response and the prevention of cancer are all dependent on **adhesion molecules**. Adhesion involves the interaction of one molecule, for example a cell surface molecule, with a specific ligand which may be on another cell or a part of the extracellular matrix. These can be divided into four groups on the basis of structure and function:

- The immunoglobulin superfamily
- The cadherin superfamily
- Integrins
- Selectins

The **immunoglobulin superfamily** is so-called because at the genetic level it has a sequence similarity that suggests that it arose from the same set of ancestral genes by duplication. These molecules are involved as cofactors in antigen presentation and are present as cell surface receptors on leucocytes (eg CD2, CD3, T-cell receptor) and some function as **integrin ligands** (eg ICAM, NCA: intercellular and neural-cell adhesion molecule, respectively).

Cadherins are involved in the interaction between muscle and nerve in the developing embryo.

Integrins are heterodimeric (two subunits, different from each other) transmembrane glycoproteins which are widely distributed in different tissues and serve to interact with molecules of the extracellular matrix (laminin, fibronectin, collagen).

Selectins are expressed on leucocytes and are thought to be involved in leucocyte adherence to endothelium during acute inflammation and coagulation.

Expression of adhesion molecules is dynamic and can be upregulated by pro-inflammatory cytokines (IL-1, TNF), viral infection, T-cell activation and many other stimuli.

Clinical relevance of adhesion molecules

Adhesion molecule expression is upregulated in many forms of solid organ inflammation (eg autoimmune and viral hepatitis, and also in organ rejection after transplantation). The adhesion molecule intercellular adhesion molecule-1 (ICAM-1) is a receptor for the integrin lymphocyte function-associated molecule-1 (LFA-1) and may be involved in the recruitment and maintenance of activated lymphocytes in tissue inflammation.

- It is theoretically possible to block these molecules to treat inflammation (eg in acute renal failure and in transplant rejection)
- The integrin $\alpha_{IIb}\beta$ is the platelet receptor for fibrinogen
- Mutations in its gene lead to the congenital bleeding disorder **Glanzmann's thrombasthenia**
- In another genetic disease, **leucocyte adhesion deficiency** (LAD), lack of β2-integrins leads to failure of leucocyte migration to sites of infection and hence to recurrent bacterial sepsis
- Conversely, antibodies against $\alpha_{IIb}\beta$ are routinely used in clinical practice (ie abciximab) as antithrombotic agents in coronary artery disease

14.9   STEM CELLS

A number of tissues in the body contain progenitor cells which are capable of producing progeny, or daughter cells, to replenish cell populations. The most obvious example is the bone marrow where red and white cells are constantly being replaced to match turnover in the peripheral blood. It is now known that a number of other tissues contain stem cells:

- **Embryonic stem cells** are totipotential and hence can give rise to any tissue type. There are ethical difficulties in the acquisition and use of these cells which may limit their therapeutic use. Embryonic stem cells from mice are a powerful investigative tool in basic science
- **Bone marrow stem cells** can be easily accessed and purified by antigen sorting with CD34 antibodies. If these cells undergo **transdifferentiation** they can then function as a replacement for degenerating cells of non-haematological origin (eg neurones)

14.10   THE MOLECULAR BASIS OF SOME IMPORTANT DISEASES

The following conditions have been highlighted either because their molecular basis is well understood (eg **myasthenia gravis, α1-antitrypsin deficiency**) or because they are caused by novel mechanisms (eg **trinucleotide repeat disorders**). Others are included because the identification of their molecular basis is historically important (as for dystrophin in **Duchenne muscular dystrophy**, which was the first disease to be worked out by identifying the gene through positional cloning). Overall, the following diseases serve to illustrate the importance of the molecular mechanisms of disease outlined in the above sections.

14.10.1   Amyloidosis

A pathological process characterised by the accumulation of extracellular fibrils of insoluble protein. The aggregated protein is specific to the different amyloid diseases listed overleaf, but in all cases the fibrillar component is associated with a non-fibrillar constituent called **amyloid-P component** which is derived from the acute phase protein **serum amyloid P** (SAP). Figure 14.12 outlines the classification of amyloidosis. (*See also* Section 15.12.1, Chapter 15, Nephrology.)

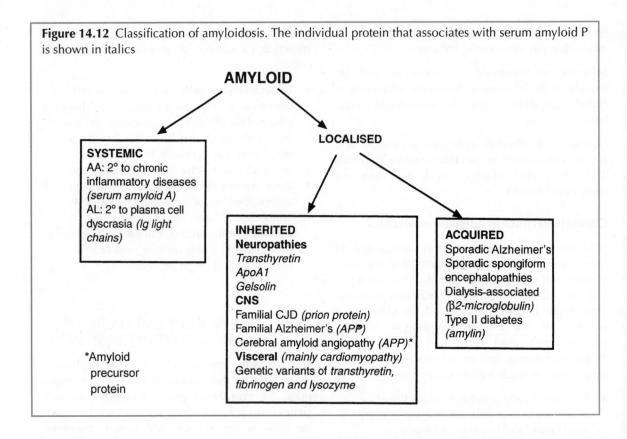

Figure 14.12 Classification of amyloidosis. The individual protein that associates with serum amyloid P is shown in italics

AMYLOID

SYSTEMIC
AA: 2° to chronic inflammatory diseases *(serum amyloid A)*
AL: 2° to plasma cell dyscrasia *(Ig light chains)*

LOCALISED

INHERITED
Neuropathies
Transthyretin
ApoA1
Gelsolin
CNS
Familial CJD *(prion protein)*
Familial Alzheimer's *(APP)*
Cerebral amyloid angiopathy *(APP)**
Visceral *(mainly cardiomyopathy)*
Genetic variants of *transthyretin, fibrinogen and lysozyme*

ACQUIRED
Sporadic Alzheimer's
Sporadic spongiform encephalopathies
Dialysis-associated *(β2-microglobulin)*
Type II diabetes *(amylin)*

*Amyloid
  precursor
  protein

Pathogenesis

Whilst the inherited forms of amyloid are rare, the accumulation of amyloid fibrils is a central part of the pathological process of a number of common diseases such as Alzheimer's and type 2 diabetes, where amyloid is found in the islets of Langerhans. Many individuals on long-term haemodialysis eventually develop amyloid arthropathy. The key event in amyloid fibril formation is a change in conformation of the respective precursor protein which leads to its aggregation into an insoluble fibrillar form. The exact mechanism of this conformational change is unclear but it is thought to involve partial proteolytic cleavage of the precursor, and/or its overproduction. Using ^{131}I-labelled SAP, amyloid deposits can be localised using scintigraphy. Amyloid may cause organ dysfunction by progressive replacement of functional parenchyma or it may possibly be inherently cytotoxic.

14.10.2 Alpha-1 antitrypsin deficiency

Deficiency of α1-antitrypsin is one of the most common hereditary diseases affecting Caucasians. The prime function of the enzyme is to inhibit neutrophil elastase and it is one of the serpin superfamily of protease inhibitors. Patients with deficiency present with emphysema (*see* Chapter 19, Respiratory Medicine) because low protein levels fail to protect the lung from proteolytic attack. A proportion of individuals also develop liver cirrhosis, but this does not appear to be directly due to enzyme deficiency.

• The most common mutation that changes a glutamate residue to a lysine at position 342 of the protein (the Z mutation) results in the accumulation of protein in the endoplasmic reticulum of the liver

- The formation of these hepatic inclusions results from a protein–protein interaction between the reactive centre loop of one molecule and the β-pleated sheet of a second
- This leads to polymerisation and aggregation. Similar mechanisms have been found to be responsible for deficiency of C-1 esterase inhibitor (hereditary angioneurotic angiooedema) and antithrombin III
- Since not all patients who are homozygously deficient develop liver damage, other factors, such as the way the mutant protein is broken down in the liver, must be relevant to the manifestation of the liver component

14.10.3 Alzheimer's disease

A neurodegenerative disease of inexorable cognitive decline characterised histologically by intraneuronal **neurofibrillary tangles** and extracellular **amyloid plaques**. Most cases are sporadic.

- About 5% of cases are inherited as an autosomal dominant with at least three genes responsible
- Mutations in the amyloid precursor protein (APP) gene on chromosome 21 are a rare cause of familial Alzheimer's disease (AD). The βA4 protein is a proteolytic product of APP and the principal constituent of senile plaques
- Mutations in two closely related genes, the presenilins *PS1* and *PS2*, are responsible for other cases of AD
- Inheritance of the ε-4 allele of apolipoprotein E is an important determinant of age of onset in familial AD and a risk factor for sporadic AD. (*See also* Chapter 16, Neurology)

Molecular markers

Neurofibrillary tangles consist of highly ordered intraneuronal structures called paired helical filaments (PHF) which are assembled from the microtubule associated protein **tau**.

This suggests that neurones die because tau is handled in some abnormal way which leads to dysfunction of the microtubular network. Tau pro-

tein from PHFs is abnormally phosphorylated but it is not yet known whether this is part of the primary pathological process leading to AD. APP is cleaved into a β and a γ fragment. It is thought that plaque formation occurs when the Aβ fragment becomes insoluble and aggregates. Aggregated Aβ has been shown to induce free radical-mediated damage to neurones.

14.10.4 Trinucleotide repeat disorders

A new class of genetic disease has been recognised in recent years, in which the responsible genetic mutation is a repetitive sequence of three nucleotides which can undergo expansion (and occasionally contraction). It has therefore become known as a **dynamic mutation**.

Examples of trinucleotide repeat disorders

- Huntington's disease
- Fragile X syndrome*
- X-linked bulbospinal neuronopathy (Kennedy syndrome)
- Myotonic dystrophy
- Friedreich's ataxia
- Spinocerebellar ataxias (there are a number of variants)

*See Chapter 7, Genetics

As a consequence of dynamic mutation, mutant alleles arise from a population of pre-mutant alleles that have a repeat number at the upper limit of the normal range (usually <35) which then become unstable and undergo sudden expansion into the mutant range (>50). Two key genetic characteristics are illustrated by trinucleotide repeat disorders.

Anticipation

The phenomenon whereby the severity of a disease becomes worse, and the age of onset earlier, in successive generations.

Somatic instability

The length of the expansion continues to increase as cells divide throughout life. This may partly explain why a disease such as myotonic dystrophy gets worse as the patient gets older.

For a particular disease the length of the expansion corresponds with the age of onset of the disease.

There are two main types of trinucleotide repeats (Figure 14.13): trinucleotide repeats can occur in the non-coding region or within exons, giving different effects.

It will be evident from Figure 14.13 that the consequence of a type I expansion is loss of gene expression because the gene cannot be transcribed due to stereochemical interference from the expanded region. Type II disorders are thought to be so-called **gain of function** dominant mutations. That is, the trinucleotide expansion leads to the accumulation of an abnormal protein which is toxic to cells. In several of these disorders it has now been demonstrated that toxic protein accumulates in intraneuronal inclusions which stain positive for ubiquitin. (*See also* Chapter 7, Genetics.)

14.10.5 Mitochondrial disorders

The mitochondrial genome is circular and approximately 16.5 kb in length. It encodes genes for the mitochondrial respiratory chain and for some species of transfer RNA. Nucleic acids cannot move in and out of mitochondria, so all of the mRNA synthesised from the mitochondrial genome must be translated in the organelle itself. However, many nuclear encoded proteins are transported into mitochondria and are absolutely necessary for mitochondrial function. (*See also* Chapter 7, Genetics.)

- Mitochondrial DNA (mtDNA) mutates 10 times more frequently than nuclear DNA; as there are no introns, a mutation will invariably strike a coding sequence
- **Maternal inheritance**: no mitochondria are transferred from spermatozoa at fertilisation and so each individual only inherits mtDNA from the mother
- Because there are 10^3–10^4 copies of mitochondrial DNA in each cell (each mitochondrion has 2–10 copies of mtDNA) normal and mutant mtDNA may co-exist within one cell (known as heteroplasmy). This may be one explanation why mitochondrial diseases show a **poor genotype–phenotype correlation**
- There is evidence that mtDNA mutations are accumulated throughout life, as mitochondrial DNA has no protective DNA repair enzymes, and that this may contribute to the changes of ageing

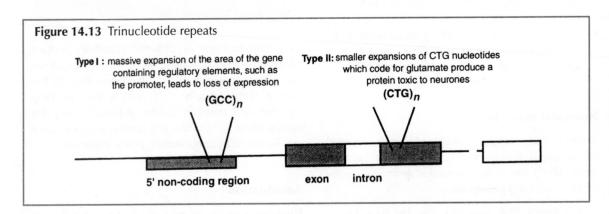

Figure 14.13 Trinucleotide repeats

Type I : massive expansion of the area of the gene containing regulatory elements, such as the promoter, leads to loss of expression

$(GCC)_n$

Type II: smaller expansions of CTG nucleotides which code for glutamate produce a protein toxic to neurones

$(CTG)_n$

5' non-coding region   exon   intron

Phenotypes due to mitochondrial DNA mutations

- Sensorineural deafness
- Optic atrophy
- Stroke in young people
- Myopathy
- Cardiomyopathy and cardiac conduction defects
- Diabetes mellitus
- Chronic progressive external ophthalmoplegia
- Lactic acidosis
- Pigmentary retinopathy

Virtually all tissues in the body depend on oxidative metabolism to a greater or lesser extent and so these phenotypes can often occur together (for example, diabetes and deafness). As mentioned above the relationship between the mutations and the clinical features is poorly understood.

14.10.6 Myasthenia gravis

This relatively rare disease (incidence 1 case per 8000–20 000) has a molecular pathogenesis that is well understood, and it serves as a model for other autoimmune diseases. Specific antibodies are directed against the nicotinic acetylcholine (ACh) receptor which is present on the post-synaptic membrane of the neuromuscular junction (Figure 14.14). This results in:

- Complement-mediated destruction of acetylcholine receptors and a loss of the normal convolution of the muscle membrane (an important morphological hallmark of the disease); this leads to the loss of surface area for ACh to interact with its receptors
- Accelerated endocytosis and degradation of receptors
- Functional blockade of receptors

These abnormalities lead to fatiguable weakness (*see also* Chapter 16, Neurology). Ptosis and diplopia

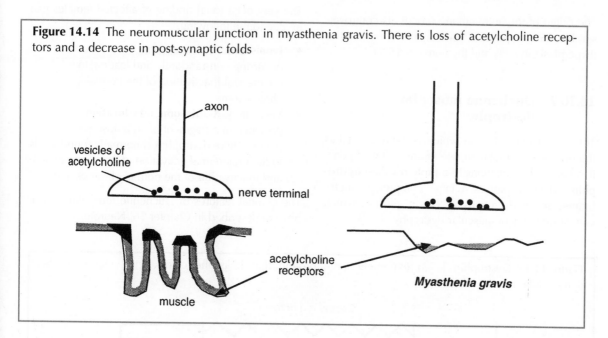

Figure 14.14 The neuromuscular junction in myasthenia gravis. There is loss of acetylcholine receptors and a decrease in post-synaptic folds

are the commonest symptoms. In 10%–15% of sufferers, symptoms are confined to the eyes (ocular myasthenia). Fatiguability occurs because of a combination of the normal rundown of ACh release which occurs physiologically, and a decreased number of ACh receptors.

Over 80%–90% of patients have detectable antibodies to the ACh receptor and the others are presumed to have antibodies not detectable by current assays. Antibody negativity is more common in the ocular form.

- Passive transfer of antibodies from patients to mice reproduces the disease features
- Reduction of antibody levels by plasmapheresis or treatment with immune globulin ameliorates the disease
- The antibody titre in patients does not always correlate with disease severity, suggesting that anti-ACh receptor antibodies have different functional consequences depending on the exact epitope to which they are directed

The origin of the autoimmune process is controversial but 75% of patients have thymic abnormalities (hyperplasia in 85% and thymoma in 15%).

14.10.7 Duchenne muscular dystrophy

This is a genetic disease which is X-linked; it has the highest new mutation rate of any X-linked gene. It is caused by mutations in a protein called **dystrophin**, which is part of a large complex of membrane-associated proteins, defects in most of which can cause forms of muscular dystrophy.

Dystrophin is a very large protein indeed (>400 kDa) which is attached at its C-terminus to laminin on the inner aspect of the muscle membrane and at its N-terminus to actin, thus providing a connection between the extracellular matrix and the muscle cytoskeleton (Figure 14.15). Therefore, its role is probably structural.

The most common mutations are large deletions which can be either of the following:

- **In frame** in which the C-terminus and N-terminus of the molecule are preserved and a truncated form of dystrophin missing some of the rod domain is produced leading to Becker's dystrophy, a milder form of the disease compatible with a normal lifespan and prolonged ambulation
- **Out of frame** which results in total abolition of dystrophin production because one or both of the binding sites for actin or laminin is disrupted. This is the abnormality which leads to typical Duchenne muscular dystrophy

The very occasional finding of affected females can be due to the following:

- **Lyonisation**: X-chromosome inactivation occurring non-randomly and leading to preferential inactivation of the normal chromosome
- Very rarely, **X-autosome translocation**. The presence of a fragment of an autosome in the region where dystrophin is normally found leads to the preferential activation of this chromosome and inactivation of the normal chromosome

The clinical features of Duchenne muscular dystrophy are described in Chapter 16, Neurology.

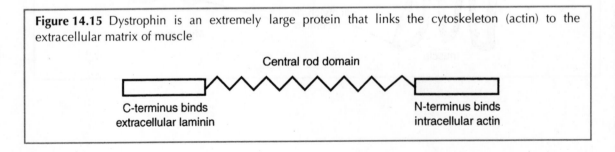

Figure 14.15 Dystrophin is an extremely large protein that links the cytoskeleton (actin) to the extracellular matrix of muscle

Central rod domain

C-terminus binds extracellular laminin

N-terminus binds intracellular actin

14.10.8   Sickle cell disease

It has been known for five decades that haemoglobin from patients with this disease undergoes abnormal electrophoretic mobility. The basis for this is the presence, in all patients with the disease, of a single amino acid substitution of valine for glutamic acid in the haemoglobin (HbS) β-globin subunit. Haemoglobin has to be highly soluble to pack into red cells at high concentrations and the sickle mutation leads to polymerisation of HbS and consequent loss of solubility. The reason that polymerisation takes place is that, in its deoxygenated form, the HbS β-globin subunit can bind to a partner β subunit on another strand, leading to the formation of large polymers (see Figure 14.16), which deform the red cell by damaging the membrane and interfering with ion flux. The polymerisation process is a dynamic event under the influence of the oxygenation state of the cell and the intracellular concentration of haemoglobin which accounts in part for the variable clinical manifestations of the disease.

- The unpredictable nature of the vaso-occlusive events observed in patients has been explained because the SS red cells have a greater propensity for attachment to vascular endothelium. The degree of stickiness to endothelium is determined primarily by the rapidity of polymer formation which in turn is dependent on the rapidity of deoxygenation
- The binding of sickle red cells to endothelium appears to be mediated by the interaction between integrins on the cell membrane and adhesion molecules expressed on the vascular endothelial surface
- The presence of pro-inflammatory cytokines such as TNF stimulates this process, which explains why infection of any kind can provoke a sickle crisis
- One factor that has been shown to modify the rate of polymer formation is the presence of fetal haemoglobin (HbF), which slows the rate of polymer formation
- Certain ethnic subpopulations have higher amounts of fetal haemoglobin persisting in the circulation and milder SS disease
- This suggests that pharmacological upregulation of HbF could ameliorate the disease. Hydroxyurea has been shown to increase the amount of HbF and is now widely used in the prevention of sickle crises. The risk of tumours from this cytotoxic drug appears to be small and any myelosuppression is reversible

The clinical features of sickle cell disease are discussed in Chapter 9, Haematology.

Figure 14.16 Sickle cell disease. In sickle cell disease HbS undergoes abnormal polymerisation when deoxygenated

14.11 GLOSSARY OF TERMS IN MOLECULAR MEDICINE

Allele	One of several different forms of a gene occupying a given genetic locus
Annealing	The pairing of complementary strands of DNA to form a double helix
Apoptosis	The morphological changes accompanying the process of programmed cell death
Autocrine	Secretion of substances by cells which then act on the cells themselves rather than on a distant target
cDNA	A single-stranded DNA complementary to an RNA, synthesised from it by the enzyme reverse transcriptase in vitro
Cell cycle	The period from one cell division to the next
Cytokines	Act locally and their effect can be positive or negative depending on the environment, other cytokines, the physiological state of the cell and the extra-cellular matrix. This variable response of cytokines underlies the ability of the organism to maintain a wide repertoire of responses to tissue injury
DNA polymerase	An enzyme that synthesises a daughter strand of DNA on a DNA template
ELISA	Enzyme-linked immunosorbent assay, a method of quantifying circulating proteins
Exon	Any segment of an interrupted gene which is represented in the mature RNA product
FISH	Fluorescent in-situ hybridisation, a method of characterising gross chromosomal abnormalities
Gene family	Consists of a set of genes the exons of which are related; the members were derived from a common ancestral gene by duplication and subsequent variation
Gene targeting	The creation of animals (usually mice) which are null mutants for a particular gene. That is, the gene has been 'knocked out' and the 'knockout' mouse contains no copy of the gene at all
G-protein	Heterotrimeric membrane protein that is activated by the exchange of GDP for GTP and dissociates on activation into an α and $\beta\gamma$ subunits. It has intrinsic GTPase activity which mediates its inactivation
Growth factor	A hormone that induces cell division and differentiation
Heterozygote	An individual with different alleles on each chromosome at a given locus
Housekeeping genes	Constitutively expressed genes in all cells because they provide basic functions needed for survival of all cell types

Hybridoma	A cell line produced by fusing a myeloma with a lymphocyte; it can indefinitely express the immunoglobulin of both cells, unless the myeloma has been selected to be deficient in Ig expression
Introns	Sequences of DNA that are transcribed but removed from nascent mRNA by splicing
Isoform	One of a number of different forms of a protein that may be derived from one gene by splicing or from separate closely related members of a gene family
Oligonucleotide	A short sequence of (synthetic) DNA, typically 18–22 base pairs in length, which acts as a primer for PCR reactions or a molecular probe when detecting gene sequences
Oncogene	A gene whose protein product (the oncoprotein) has the ability to transform eukaryotic cells so that they grow in a manner analogous to tumour cells
Paracrine	Secretion by one cell of substances that act on adjacent cells
Programmed cell death	The process whereby unwanted cells die under the control of a genetic programme
Promoter	A region of DNA involved in the binding of RNA polymerase to initiate transcription
Protein kinase	An enzyme that phosphorylates (adds a phosphate group) to a substrate (an amino acid in another protein)
Protein phosphatase	An enzyme that removes phosphate groups from substrates
Proto-oncogene	The normal counterpart in eukaryotic genomes of retroviral genes which can transform cells
Response elements	Specific nucleotide recognition sequences in the 5′ regulatory regions of genes which recognise transcription factors that have been activated by upstream signals such as steroid hormones
Somatic cells	All the cells of an organism except the germ cells
Transcription factor	A protein that binds to the promoter region of a gene to influence its transcription
Tumour suppressor gene	A gene that, when activated, will produce a protein that inhibits cell division. Mutations of these genes therefore lead to loss of control of cell division and contribute to tumorigenesis
UTR	Untranslated region

Chapter 15
Nephrology

CONTENTS

Nephrology

15.1 RENAL PHYSIOLOGY

The chief functions of the kidneys are:

- Excretion of water-soluble waste
- Maintenance of electrolyte balance
- Maintenance of water balance
- Acid–base homeostasis
- Endocrine: renin–angiotensin–aldosterone system, erythropoietin, vitamin D activation

15.1.1 Glomerular filtration rate (GFR)

Glomerular filtration is a passive process which depends upon the net hydrostatic pressure acting across the glomerular capillaries, countered by the oncotic pressure, and is also influenced by the intrinsic permeability of the glomerulus (K_f); the latter may vary due to mesangial cell contraction, as in the response to angiotensin II. The mean values for GFR in normal young adults are 130 ml·min^{-1}·1.73 m^{-2} (men) and 120 ml·min^{-1}· 1.73 m^{-2} (women), the 1.73 m^2 being mean body surface area of young adults. However, variation between individuals is large and accepted ranges of GFR at this age are 70–140 ml·min^{-1}·1.73 m^{-2}. In health, the GFR remains stable until around 40 years of age but thereafter declines at a rate of approximately 0.5–1 ml·min^{-1}·year^{-1}; by the age of 80 years the mean GFR is approximately 50% of that of a young adult.

- GFR increases by 50% during pregnancy due to plasma volume expansion (*see* Chapter 12, Maternal Medicine)
- GFR has a diurnal rhythm, values being 10% greater in the afternoon than at midnight. This may be partly related to protein intake (which increases GFR)
- GFR falls transiently during exercise

- In patients with reduced renal reserve, GFR will be lower in the fasting than in the fully hydrated state (relevant in the context of blood sampling)

There are several means of estimating GFR:

- **Plasma creatinine**: creatinine is produced from muscle cells at a constant rate, and so its plasma concentration at steady state depends upon its excretion, which reflects GFR. Plasma creatinine is therefore useful to crudely assess GFR. However, when renal function is well preserved, small changes in creatinine are associated with large changes in GFR, and so plasma creatinine is an insensitive marker of early renal disease
  - When considering plasma creatinine values, the patient's age, sex and weight should be taken into account – elderly and malnourished patients may have low GFR but plasma creatinine close to the normal range
- All UK laboratories now provide estimated GFR (eGFR) routinely; it is calculated from the four-variable MDRD (Modification of Diet in Renal Disease (Study)) equation (which includes age and sex)
- **Creatinine clearance**: calculated from a 24-hour urine collection with a consecutive blood sample – this is now used infrequently. This tends to overestimate GFR as creatinine is not just filtered, but also secreted into the tubule from the post-glomerular circulation; the error increases with declining renal function. Note that certain drugs (eg trimethoprim and cimetidine) compete for this secretion mechanism, and so will increase plasma creatinine
- **Cockcroft and Gault formula**: this also assesses eGFR (based upon creatinine clearance) and requires knowledge of the patient's age, weight

and plasma creatinine:

$$GFR \ (ml/min) = \frac{(140 - age \ in \ years) \times weight \ (kg)}{plasma \ creatinine \ (\mu mol/l)}$$

$$\times 1.23 \ (men) \ or \ 1.04 \ (women)$$

- This formula overestimates creatinine clearance in obese patients and in those patients adhering to a strict low-protein diet (in both of these groups the endogenous creatinine production will be less than that predicted by overall body weight). A correction should be undertaken for body surface area

The most accurate laboratory techniques for assessing GFR are:

- **Inulin clearance**: inulin is a small molecule, freely filtered by the glomerulus, and with no tubular secretion
- **Chromium-labelled EDTA**: the most frequently used isotopic technique

15.1.2 Tubular physiology

The renal tubule has many reabsorptive and secretory functions (see Figure 15.1); these are energy-consuming and hence tubular cells are those most vulnerable to ischaemic damage (the acute tubular necrosis (ATN) of ischaemic acute renal failure).

Proximal tubule

Fifty per cent of filtered sodium is reabsorbed within the proximal tubule (via Na-K-ATPase); the Na-H antiporter secretes H^+ into the lumen and is responsible for 90% of bicarbonate and some chloride reabsorption. All of the filtered glucose and amino acids are reabsorbed here. Other important characteristics are as follows:

- Phosphate reabsorption occurs under the influence of parathyroid hormone (PTH)
- Some important drugs are secreted into the tubular filtrate here: trimethoprim, cimetidine, most β-lactams and most diuretics (note that

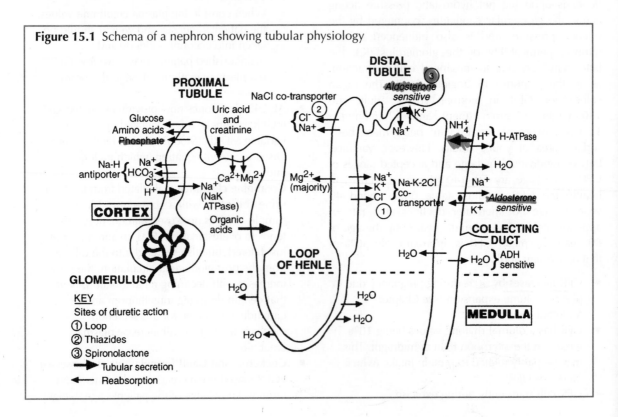

Figure 15.1 Schema of a nephron showing tubular physiology

diuretics such as thiazides, amiloride and loop diuretics are highly protein-bound and are not filtered at the glomerulus)
- Creatinine and urate are secreted into the lumen

Loop of Henle

The medullary thick ascending limb (mTAL) is impermeable to water, and the medullary concentration gradient is generated here (allowing concentration of the urine). Forty per cent of sodium is reabsorbed (via the Na-K-2Cl co-transporter). Loop diuretics compete for chloride-binding sites on this transporter.

Distal tubule

In this segment of the nephron 5% of sodium is reabsorbed (NaCl co-transporter); thiazide diuretics compete for these chloride-binding sites. As loop diuretics increase sodium delivery to the distal tubule, their combination with a thiazide (eg metolazone) can provoke a massive diuresis in resistant oedema. There are aldosterone receptors in both the distal and collecting tubules (see below).

Collecting duct

Aldosterone-sensitive sodium channels are responsible for 2% of all sodium reabsorption; spironolactone binds to the cytoplasmic aldosterone receptor. Atrial natriuretic peptide (ANP) is also anti-aldosterone in action (and hence is increased in renal failure and in patients with congestive cardiac failure (CCF), where it is thought to be counteractive against secondary hyperaldosteronism). Other important collecting duct functions are as follows:

- H^+ is secreted into the lumen, so acidifying the urine by forming ammonia/NH_4^+
- Antidiuretic hormone (ADH, or vasopressin) increases water reabsorption by opening 'water channels'. Receptors on the basolateral membrane (non-luminal) of the collecting duct cell are stimulated by ADH, leading to insertion of **aquaporins** into the luminal membrane. The aquaporins then allow water uptake by the cell

- Lithium enters the collecting duct cells via the sodium channels and inhibits the response to ADH (so nephrogenic diabetes insipidus (NDI) results)

15.1.3 Renin–angiotensin– aldosterone (RAA) system

This is covered in Chapter 4, Endocrinology. The RAA system is very important in normal health, helping to control blood pressure, sodium balance and circulating volume. However, it has a central role in the pathogenesis of secondary renal hypertension, and also in propagating progressive chronic kidney disease (CKD) (see below). Remember that intrarenal perfusion will become critically dependent upon the RAA system when hypovolaemia and hypotension supervene; this explains why patients can be vulnerable to acute renal failure induced by agents blocking the RAA system (ie angiotensin-converting enzyme (ACE) inhibitors, angiotensin-receptor blockers (ARBs) and renin inhibitors) even in the absence of renovascular disease.

- The RAA system is of key importance in the pathogenesis of progressive renal disease, irrespective of the primary disease aetiology
- Agents which block the RAA system are therefore now considered to be essential therapy in patients with a variety of chronic nephropathies

15.2 RENAL INVESTIGATION

15.2.1 Urinalysis

Urinary dipstick

Standard dipsticks assess the presence of protein, blood and glucose. 'Multi-stix' will also assess pH (range 4.5–8 but normally 5–6; pH>8 suggests renal tubular acidosis, for example) and leucocytes (most commonly raised because of vaginal contamination of urine or urinary tract infection).

- The sticks register positive for 'blood' in the presence of erythrocytes, as well as free myoglobin (eg in rhabdomyolysis) and haemoglobin. Many cases of 'dipstick +ve, microscopy –ve (absence of red cells on MSU) haematuria' are seen, and these are presumably due to haemoglobinuria (eg exercise, low-grade haemolysis)
- Standard dipsticks do not detect Bence Jones proteins, and so if free urinary light chains are to be identified immunoelectrophoresis of urine is necessary
- Microalbuminuria will usually not be detected with standard dipsticks

Proteinuria

Normal urinary protein excretion is <150 mg/day, which should consist of <20 mg albumin, tubular secreted proteins (40–60 mg), such as the Tamm–Horsfall or tubular glycoprotein and immuno-globulin, and various filtered low-molecular-weight proteins.

- **Microalbuminuria**, which is the hallmark of early diabetic nephropathy but which is also prognostically important for cardiovascular disease and mortality risk when present in hypertensive patients, is defined as albumin excretion of 30–250 mg/day
- Proteinuria should be quantified by either **urinary albumin creatinine ratio (uACR)** or **protein creatinine ratio (uPCR)**. As a rough guide, average individuals pass around 10 mmol urinary creatinine each day. Hence:
  - uPCR or ACR 25 = 250 mg protein or albumin/day
  - uPCR or ACR 100 = 1000 mg protein or albumin/day
  - uACR 5 = 50 mg albumin/day = micro-albuminuria (note that in this instance uPCR would be 'normal' and urine dipstick testing –ve)

Significant non-nephrotic proteinuria (eg dipstick + to +++, 0.2–3.5 g/24 h) is usually indicative of renal parenchymal disease (unless due to urinary tract infection). **Nephrotic-range proteinuria** (>3.5

g/24 h, dipstick ++++) is always due to glomerular disease.

Non-renal causes of proteinuria:

- Fever
- Severe exercise
- Skin disease (eg severe exfoliation, psoriasis)
- Lower urinary tract infection (eg cystitis)

Orthostatic proteinuria

This describes proteinuria detectable after the patient has spent several hours in the upright posture; it disappears after recumbency, and so the first morning urine should test negative. Proteinuria is usually <1 g/24 h, there is no haematuria and renal function and blood pressure are normal. Renal biopsy samples are usually normal and nephrologi-cal consensus suggests this is a benign condition.

Urine microscopy

Microscopic examination of a fresh specimen of urine may yield many helpful pointers to intrinsic renal pathology:

- **Red cells**: >2–3/high-power field is pathological (microscopic haematuria); cells are usually dysmorphic in glomerular bleeding, but appear normal when derived from the lower urinary tract
- **Leucocytes**: infection, and some cases of glomerular and interstitial nephritis
- **Crystals**: eg oxalate, struvite (*see* Section 15.10.1 on renal calculi), cystine and, with polarised light, uric acid
- **Casts**: there are several types of cast:
  - *Tubular cells* – acute tubular necrosis (ATN) or interstitial nephritis
  - *Hyaline* – Tamm–Horsfall glycoprotein (ie in healthy people)
  - *Granular* – non-specific
  - *Red cell* – glomerulonephritis or tubular bleeding
  - *Leucocytes* – pyelonephritis or ATN

Causes of urinary discoloration

- Haematuria
- Myoglobinuria (brown)
- Beetroot consumption
- Alkaptonuria (urine brown on exposure to the air)
- Obstructive jaundice (yellow)
- Haemoglobinuria
- Drugs (eg rifampicin, para-aminosalicylic acid)
- Porphyria (urine dark brown or red on standing)

15.2.2   Renal radiology

The essential first-line radiological investigation for acute kidney injury (AKI), chronic kidney disease (CKD) and most other nephrological conditions is **renal ultrasound**. This will demonstrate:

- **Bipolar renal length**: in most cases of **CKD**, the kidneys are small (<8 cm) – the exceptions are polycystic kidney disease (very large with multiple cysts), and sometimes in diabetic renal disease and amyloid (normal size). In **AKI** the kidneys are usually normal size (8.5–13.5 cm), but slight enlargement is common due to swelling. Asymmetry (>1.5 cm disparity) is seen in unilateral renal artery stenosis (RAS), but also in chronic pyelonephritis and other causes of renal atrophy
- **Obstruction**
- **Cortical scarring**: for example in reflux nephropathy or following segmental ischaemic damage
- **Calculi**: within the substance of the kidney and collecting systems
- **Mass lesions and cysts** (eg renal tumour, polycystic disease or simple renal cysts)

Doppler ultrasound is useful to assess renal blood flow and to measure the resistive index within the kidney; specific patterns are observed in, for example, RAS, acute tubular necrosis and acute transplant rejection.

Intravenous urography (IVU) is reserved for investigation of urinary tract bleeding (eg to detect urothelial tumours of the renal pelvis, ureters and bladder), UTI and for some cases of obstructive uropathy. IVU can exacerbate AKI (*see* Section 15.4.3, Radio-contrast nephropathy), and has very limited value in advanced CKD (eg eGFR <25 ml/min) because of poor concentration of the dye.

Isotope renography

Two major types of renograms are commonly utilised:

- **Static scans (eg DMSA)**: the isotope is concentrated and retained within the renal parenchyma, and elimination is slow. DMSA will therefore demonstrate aspects of structure (eg scars in reflux nephropathy) and split function of the two kidneys
- **Dynamic scans (eg MAG$_3$, DTPA, hippuran)**: these isotopes are rapidly taken up and eliminated by the kidneys; such scans are used to assess renal blood flow, split function and also to investigate obstruction (eg to show whether urinary tract dilatation is due to obstruction)

Renal angiography

The most frequently used techniques are:

- **Magnetic resonance angiography (MRA)**: non-invasive and used in screening for RAS. Gadolinium (Gd) is used as the 'contrast' agent. Since 2006 there has been recognition that Gd-MR scanning can occasionally lead to a serious condition, **nephrogenic systemic fibrosis (NSF)**, which has some similarities to scleroderma and can be fatal. The patients at greatest risk are those with stage 5 CKD (*see* Section 15.5.1) receiving dialysis, or patients who have AKI; the nature of the Gd preparation (linear structure, eg Magnevist® and Omniscan®) and use of multiple doses are additional risk factors. Current guidance recommends that Gd-MR should only be used with caution in patients with eGFR <30 ml/min

- **CT angiography (CTA)**: non-invasive and readily available, but risk of contrast nephropathy in renal impairment, diabetics, etc
- **Digital subtraction angiography (DSA)**: provides excellent detail of intrarenal vasculature; invasive and risk of contrast nephropathy

Renal tract CT and MR

These imaging modalities are commonly used in nephro-urology in the investigation of many conditions, including:

- Delineation of cause of obstruction
- Assessment of renal tract tumours, including staging
- Assessment of renal cyst structure

15.3 ACID–BASE, WATER AND ELECTROLYTE DISORDERS

15.3.1 Acidosis and alkalosis

Respiratory acidosis (eg carbon dioxide retention due to chronic or acute-on-chronic lung disease) and **alkalosis** (eg due to hyperventilation) are common, and well understood by all.

Metabolic alkalosis and **metabolic acidosis** are covered in detail in Chapter 13, Metabolic Diseases. The width of the anion gap can help differentiate the likely causes of a metabolic acidosis; the bicarbonate will be low, and the anion gap can be either wide (normal chloride and exogenous acid) or normal (increased chloride and, hence, hyperchloraemic acidosis). Renal failure is associated with a wide-gap acidosis (due to excess ammonia and organic acids), whereas **renal tubular acidosis** is worth consideration as a cause of a normal-gap acidosis.

15.3.2 Renal tubular acidosis (RTA)

Distal or **type 1 RTA** is fairly common, and can complicate many renal parenchymal disorders, particularly those which predominantly affect the me-

dullary regions. Note that the latter may also be associated with nephrogenic diabetes insipidus, and sometimes with salt-wasting states. **Proximal** or **type 2 RTA** is uncommon. GFR is often normal in both conditions.

- **Nephrocalcinosis and renal calculi formation**: urinary calcium excretion is increased in severe acidosis, and calcium salts are more insoluble in alkaline urine, and hence calculi develop frequently in distal but not in proximal RTA (which is usually associated with a lower urinary pH and less severe acidosis)

The two types of RTA can be differentiated by several parameters (Table 15.1), but the hallmark associations are severe acidosis, hypokalaemia and renal calculi/nephrocalcinosis in **distal RTA**, and proximal tubular dysfunction, osteomalacia/rickets and less severe acidosis in **proximal RTA**.

Treatment of RTA: this is usually straightforward (compared with an understanding of the condition!), and consists of oral potassium and bicarbonate replacement therapy. Close monitoring is needed to prevent major imbalances in electrolyte concentrations, especially during intercurrent illness.

Causes of distal RTA

- **Primary**
  - Genetic (dominant) or idiopathic
- **Secondary to autoimmune diseases**
  - Systemic lupus erythematosus (SLE), Sjögren syndrome, chronic active hepatitis
- **Tubulointerstitial disease**
  - Chronic pyelonephritis, transplant rejection, obstructive uropathy, chronic interstitial nephritis
- **Nephrocalcinosis**
  - Medullary sponge kidney, hypercalcaemia
- **Drugs and toxins**
  - Lithium, amphotericin, toluene

Table 15.1. Differentiation between type 1 and type 2 renal tubular acidosis

	Type 1 (Distal)	Type 2 (Proximal)
Defect	Impaired urinary (H^+) acidification	Failure of HCO_3 reabsorption
Urine pH	>5.3 (ie urine never 'acidifies')	Variable
Plasma HCO$_3$	<10 mmol/l	14–20 mmol/l
Plasma K	Usually ↓	Normal or ↓
Complications	Nephrocalcinosis Calculi	Osteomalacia (phosphate wasting) Rickets
Other features	Growth failure Urine infection	Fanconi syndrome (ie phosphaturia, glycosuria, aminoaciduria)

Causes of proximal RTA

- **Occurring alone**
  - Idiopathic
- **With Fanconi syndrome**
  - Wilson's disease, cystinosis, fructose intolerance, Sjögren syndrome
- **Tubulointerstitial disease**
  - Interstitial nephritis, myeloma, amyloidosis
- **Drugs and toxins**
  - Outdated tetracyclines, streptozotocin, lead and mercury (and other heavy metals), acetazolamide, sulphonamides

Type 4 RTA: this describes a metabolic acidosis that is associated with hyperkalaemia and mild renal impairment (eGFR usually >30 ml/min). It is commonly due to **mineralocorticoid deficiency**:

- Low renin, low aldosterone (hyporeninaemic hypoaldosteronism): diabetes mellitus, and drugs (non-steroidal anti-inflammatory drugs (NSAIDs) and ciclosporin)
- High renin, low aldosterone: adrenal destruction, congenital enzyme defects and drugs (ACE inhibitors and ARBs)

Abnormal collecting duct function (eg due to absent/defective mineralocorticoid receptor, chronic tubulointerstitial disease or drugs such as spironolactone or amiloride) is responsible for other cases.

15.3.3 Polyuria

Polyuria (urine output >3 l/day) may result from:

- Diuretic usage
- Large fluid intake
- Alcohol: inhibits ADH release and alcohol is an osmotic diuretic
- Cranial diabetes insipidus: osmolality high
- Nephrogenic diabetes insipidus: osmolality high; note that polyuria (often manifest as nocturia) is often the first symptom of CKD
- Psychogenic polydipsia: osmolality usually low

- Atrial natriuretic peptide release: post-arrhythmia, cardiac failure

The causes of **cranial** and **nephrogenic diabetes insipidus** are listed in Chapter 4, Endocrinology; hyponatraemia as well as other disorders of water balance, including syndrome of inappropriate ADH (**SIADH**), are also discussed in that chapter.

15.3.4 Hypokalaemia

Acute hypokalaemia can lead to muscle weakness and direct renal tubular cell injury. Chronic hypokalaemia is a cause of interstitial nephritis. The causes can be classified according to the **presence** or **absence** of **hypertension** with reference also to the **plasma renin activity** and **urinary potassium excretion**.

Causes of hypokalaemia

- **With hypertension** (potassium excretion usually >30 mmol/day)
  - *High plasma renin activity*
    - Renovascular disease
    - Accelerated-phase hypertension
    - Cushing syndrome
    - Renin-secreting tumour
  - *Low plasma renin activity*
    - Primary hyperaldosteronism (including Conn syndrome)
    - Carbenoxolone*
    - Liquorice excess*
    - 11-β-hydroxy steroid dehydrogenase deficiency* ('apparent mineralocorticoid excess')
    - Liddle syndrome (see text)
    - Glucocorticoid-suppressible hyperaldosteronism (GSH)**

- **Without hypertension** (usually high plasma renin activity)
  - *High plasma renin activity*
    - Diuretic usage (urinary potassium excretion may be high or low)
    - Gastrointestinal tract losses (potassium excretion <30 mmol/day)
    - Salt-wasting CKD (high sodium and potassium excretion)
    - Bartter syndrome (high potassium excretion – see text)
    - Gitelman syndrome (see text)
    - Secondary hyperaldosteronism (eg cardiac or hepatic failure – increased potassium excretion)

*11-β-hydroxy steroid dehydrogenase metabolises cortisol and prevents it from binding to the mineralocorticoid receptor. Acquired or congenital conditions in which this enzyme is inhibited have a Conn's phenotype (including patients taking liquorice in excess, and carbenoxolone). Patients may have acidosis rather than alkalosis

**GSH is rare and is due to a gene fusion which makes the hyperaldosteronism completely ACTH-sensitive. The clue to diagnosis is a strong family history (autosomal dominant). Treatment is with glucocorticoids, which lower the blood pressure

Bartter syndrome

Severe hypokalaemia is consequent upon a salt-wasting state (increased sodium delivery to the distal tubule) that is due to defective chloride reabsorption (at the Na-K-2Cl co-transporter) in the loop of Henle; inheritance is usually autosomal recessive. Patients have normal or low blood pressure and severe hyper-reninaemia (with hypertrophy of the juxtaglomerular apparatus) with consequent hyper-aldosteronism; GFR is usually normal. Treatment is with large-dose potassium replacement; NSAIDs may also be beneficial.

Liddle syndrome

This is an autosomal dominant syndrome of hypertension and variable degrees of hypokalaemic metabolic alkalosis. The patient appears to have primary hyperaldosteronism, but renin and aldosterone are suppressed and there is no response to spironolactone. The pathogenesis is associated with enhanced reabsorption of sodium in the distal nephron (amiloride-sensitive sodium channel). Treatment consists of salt restriction, potassium supplements and use of either amiloride or triamterene.

Gitelman syndrome

This condition can be either autosomal recessive or dominant, and is characterised by hypokalaemic metabolic alkalosis and also with hypocalciuria and hypomagnesaemia. Patients present at a later age than those with classic Bartter syndrome and, like the latter, the blood pressure is low or normal and patients have hyper-reninaemic hyperaldosteronism. The metabolic abnormalities may lead to muscular weakness and tetany. Treatment is with magnesium and potassium supplements.

15.4. ACUTE KIDNEY INJURY (AKI)

15.4.1 Pathogenesis and management of acute kidney injury

AKI is the term now used interchangeably to describe acute renal failure (ARF). Acute deterioration of renal function is seen in up to 5% of all hospital admissions. The incidence of severe AKI (eg creatinine >500 μmol/l) increases with age; the overall annual incidence is approximately 150 per million in the UK, but this figure is six times greater in the >80-year-old group. Oliguria is usual, and is defined as a daily urine output of <400–500 ml; this is the minimum volume to enable excretion of the daily waste products of metabolism.

Non-oliguric AKI accounts for about 10% of cases; this may be associated with drug toxicity (eg gentamicin or amphotericin), radio-contrast nephropathy and acute interstitial nephritis.

The majority (60%) of cases of AKI result from renal hypoperfusion and ischaemic damage; the resulting renal histopathological lesion is **acute tubular necrosis** (ATN). Many other patients can have similar ischaemic insults to the kidneys, with an initial period of oliguria, but renal perfusion can then be restored by vigorous haemodynamic management before severe tubular injury ensues; this is termed **pre-renal uraemia**. In the latter, physiological mechanisms (ie stimulation of the RAA system) are preserved within the kidney, and so the urinary manifestations of sodium and water reabsorption allow differentiation from established ATN (Table 15.2). In practice, the two conditions may sometimes only be differentiated by the clinical response to fluid resuscitation – patients with ATN will remain oliguric, whereas those with pre-renal uraemia will usually start diuresing. A large number of

Table 15.2. Urinary findings in acute tubular necrosis and pre-renal uraemia

Urinary findings	ATN	Pre-renal uraemia
Urine sodium	>40 mmol/l	<20 mmol/l
Urine:plasma osmolality	<1.1:1	>1.5:1
Fractional sodium excretion (FeNa)*	>1%	<<1%
Urine: plasma urea	<7:1	>10:1
Urine volume	Oligo-anuric or polyuria (recovery phase)	<1.5 litres

*FeNa is the percentage of sodium that is filtered at the glomerulus (normally 1000 mmol/h) which actually appears in the urine (normal <6 mmol/h, ie <0.6%)

patients with ATN can be managed without the need for dialysis.

Many patients with pre-existing CKD present with acute deterioration of renal function ('**acute-on-chronic kidney disease**') and require similarly intensive support and clinical management.

The causes of ARF, with approximate relative frequency, are summarised below (excluding acute-on-chronic cases).

Classification of ARF

- **Pre-renal factors leading to renal hypoperfusion and ATN (60%)**
  - Reduced circulating volume: blood loss; excess GI losses; burns
  - Low cardiac output states: toxic or ischaemic myocardial depression
  - Systemic sepsis
  - Drugs inducing renal perfusion shutdown: (eg ACE inhibitors; NSAIDs)
- **Toxic ATN (5%)**
  - Rhabdomyolysis with urinary myoglobin
  - Drugs: (eg gentamicin; amphotericin)
  - Radio-contrast nephropathy
- **Structural abnormalities of renal vasculature (5%)**
  - Large-vessel occlusion (renovascular disease)
  - Small-vessel occlusion: accelerated-phase hypertension; disseminated intravascular coagulation (DIC); haemolytic uraemic syndrome (HUS); thrombotic thrombocytopenic purpura (TTP); pre-eclampsia; systemic sclerosis
  - Acute cortical necrosis
- **Acute glomerulonephritis and vasculitis (15%)**
  - Idiopathic crescentic glomerulonephritis
  - ANCA-positive vasculitis
  - Goodpasture syndrome
  - Other proliferative glomerulonephritis (eg SLE; endocarditis; Henoch–Schönlein nephritis)
- **Interstitial nephritis (<5%)**
  - Idiopathic, immunologically mediated
  - Drug-induced hypersensitivity
  - Infection (eg pyelonephritis; leptospirosis; Hanta virus)
- **Myeloma/tubular cast nephropathy (<5%)**
- **Urinary tract obstruction (10%)**

Pathophysiology of ATN

After an ischaemic insult there is intense afferent arteriolar vasoconstriction, mediated by the release of vasoconstrictors (particularly endothelin) and by loss of intrinsic vasodilators (nitric oxide and prostaglandin I_2 (PGI_2)); this contributes to the loss of GFR and the redistribution of blood flow within the kidney. Hypoxic injury to the energy-consuming cells of the proximal tubule and thick ascending limb of Henle occurs; calcium- and oxygen-free-radical-mediated cell necrosis results in cell shedding from the tubular basement membrane, with the formation of casts that block urine flow.

Investigation of AKI

The history may point to the cause of AKI (eg drugs, skin rash); assessment of the haemodynamic status is imperative, and appropriate fluid resuscitation should be given.

- **Urinary examination**: ATN and pre-renal uraemia can sometimes be differentiated by urinary biochemistry (see Table 15.2); microscopic haematuria and red cell casts will point to acute glomerulonephritis as the cause
- A **renal ultrasound** scan will usually show normal-sized kidneys, and will identify obstruction (the latter should be urgently treated to reduce irreversible renal injury)
- **Autoantibody profile**: ANF, ANCA, anti-GBM, complement and plasma and urinary electrophoresis should all be routinely performed (unless the cause of AKI is obvious, eg post-myocardial infarction or renal obstruction)
- **Percutaneous renal biopsy** is essential if an intrinsic lesion (eg vasculitis, glomerulonephritis,

interstitial nephritis) is suspected, or if no ischaemic cause is apparent, especially if there is no sign of improvement in renal function and/or if the oliguric phase is delayed

Management of AKI

The mainstay of treatment involves **optimisation of fluid balance** and avoidance of either hypovolaemia or fluid overload. Patients with single-organ AKI are best managed in an HDU setting. Blood pressure should be controlled, haemoglobin maintained above 9 g/dl and sepsis should be promptly and vigorously treated. 'Renal dose' dopamine and loop diuretics are often given in ATN, although there is no evidence that they alter the outcome of AKI in humans. Some cases of ATN can be managed without dialysis, with the adoption of careful fluid balance and dietary control; however, many patients with ATN also have multi-organ failure (MOF) and they can only be managed on an ICU.

Key to AKI management is attention to **intensive nutritional support** of the sicker patients, and the use of **continuous renal replacement therapies** (eg CVVH: continuous veno-venous haemofiltration) which are less likely to provoke haemodynamic instability.

Other more specific treatments in AKI depend upon the causative condition and include the following:

- Specific **immunosuppressive therapy**, and sometimes plasma exchange, may be appropriate for some conditions (eg Goodpasture syndrome, ANCA +ve vasculitis)
- **Obstruction**: bladder catheterisation for bladder outflow obstruction; nephrostomy drainage for renal obstruction
- **Other**: eg steroids in acute interstitial nephritis (AIN), plasma exchange in HUS and TTP, chemotherapy in myeloma

Indications for urgent dialysis in AKI

- **Severe uraemia**
  - eg vomiting, encephalopathy, urea > 60 mmol/l
- **Hyperkalaemia**
  - K^+ >6.5 mmol/l (or less, if ECG changes apparent)
- **Severe acidosis**
  - pH <7.1
- **Uraemic pericarditis**
- **Pulmonary oedema**

Prognosis of AKI

The overall survival for patients with AKI remains relatively poor; 55%–60% of patients who require dialytic therapy survive, but this figure partly reflects the very poor outcome of patients who have ATN as a component of MOF who are managed on the ICU. For example, only 10%–20% of those with three- or four-organ failure will survive, yet 90% of patients who have AKI in isolation survive.

The prognosis for **recovery of renal function** varies according to the causative condition; renal recovery occurs in <50% of cases with autoimmune vasculitis. In survivors of ATN, renal function will return to the normal range in 60%, whereas 30% will be left with CKD and 10% will be dialysis-dependent.

15.4.2 Rhabdomyolysis

Muscle damage with release of myoglobin can cause severe, hypercatabolic AKI. Serum potassium and phosphate (released from muscle) rapidly rise, calcium is typically low and the creatine kinase massively elevated; serum creatinine may be disproportionately higher than urea. Primary management involves intravascular fluid expansion with the encouragement of diuresis; alkalinisation of the urine (with IV bicarbonate) may help to solubilise the myoglobin pigment within the renal tubules. Sometimes the source of the rhabdomyolytic process requires specific therapy (eg fasciotomy for compartment syndrome, debridement of dead tissue and amputation of non-viable limbs).

Causes of rhabdomyolysis

- **Crush injury**
  - Trauma; unconsciousness with compression
- **Metabolic myopathies**
  - eg McArdle syndrome
- **Infections**
  - Viral necrotising myositis, infectious mononucleosis (eg coxsackie influenza)
- **Uncontrolled fitting**
- **Drugs**
  - eg statins
- **Overdose**
  - Barbiturates, alcohol, heroin
- **Severe exercise, heat stroke, burns**
- **Inflammatory myopathies**
  - Polymyositis
- **Malignant hyperpyrexia**

Prognosis of rhabdomyolysis

Patient survival in rhabdomyolysis depends upon the nature and extent of the underlying causative pathology. However, in survivors the prognosis for full renal functional recovery is usually good.

15.4.3 Radio-contrast nephropathy

Mild renal dysfunction may complicate up to 10% of angiographic procedures and IVUs. Radio-contrast nephropathy is manifest by non-oliguric AKI, typically occurring 1–5 days after the procedure. Intrarenal vasoconstriction, mediated largely by endothelin, and tubular cell toxicity (with ATN) are important in the pathogenesis. The AKI is usually fully reversible. Recent attention has been direc-

ted to prevention of radio-contrast nephropathy:

- Pre-hydrate patients at greatest risk (eg with N-saline infusion before and during the procedure)
- There is some limited evidence that *N*-acetyl cysteine (given orally for 2–3 days, from before to 24 hours post-procedure) may be of benefit in high-risk patients

---

Risk factors for radio-contrast nephropathy

- High contrast load
- High iodine content of contrast
- Hypovolaemia
- Diabetes mellitus*
- Myeloma
- Hypercalcaemia
- Age
- Pre-existing CKD
- Hyperuricaemia

*Especially if the patient is taking metformin – this should be withdrawn before injection of radio-contrast

---

15.5 CHRONIC KIDNEY DISEASE (CKD) AND RENAL REPLACEMENT THERAPY

15.5.1 Chronic kidney disease (CKD)

CKD is defined as evidence of kidney damage (eg urinary abnormality such as haematuria or proteinuria; scars or polycystic change on a renal scan) or eGFR <60 ml/min (see below). It is very common, and latest data suggest that it affects about 8% of the UK adult population. The incidence of end-stage renal disease (ESRD) patients joining renal replacement therapy (RRT) programmes in the UK is about 125/million each year; the figure is almost 300/million in parts of the USA (because of racial factors and increased population prevalence of diabetes mellitus and hypertension). The prevalence of patients on UK RRT programmes is around 600/million, but as ageing constitutes one of the major risk factors for CKD and ESRD, the prevalence is greatest in people aged >65 years (eg 1000/million, or 0.1%, receiving RRT).

There are several recognised stages of **CKD** (Table 15.3):

- **Stage 1** – although renal function is entirely normal (eGFR >90 ml/min) this group should be identified, as a proportion of patients will be at risk of progression of CKD in the future (eg type 1 diabetics with microalbuminuria)
- **Stage 2** – the same argument applies for identification and then follow-up of patients with eGFR 60–90 ml/min and urinary/renal structural abnormalities. Note that patients with CKD stages 1 and 2:
  - Will not have renal-related anaemia – if anaemia is present, another cause should be sought
  - Will not have renal bone disease
  - May have hypertension
- **Stage 3** – accounts for the largest proportion of CKD patients (eg 5% of the UK adult population). Over 95% of this group will not be at risk of future progressive CKD, being classed as having CKD simply because they are elderly (age being a denominator in the MDRD eGFR equation). In recognition of this, stage 3 has been divided into 3A (eGFR 45–59 ml/min) and 3B (eGFR 30–44 ml/min), with 3A patients being considered at low risk (unless they have associated proteinuria). However, a high proportion of stage 3 patients will be hypertensive, as this too is associated with ageing

- Renal-related anaemia and secondary hyperparathyroidism may begin during stage 3B CKD, as it is at this level of renal function that perturbations in erythropoietin production and vitamin D metabolism start to occur (see below)
- **Stage 4** – most patients will be hypertensive, and many are anaemic. Hyperphosphataemia may develop during this stage. A far higher proportion of stage 4 patients will be at risk of progression compared to those with stage 3 CKD. Hence, the majority of patients will be referred to the nephrology service, and those with progressive CKD will be given patient education with discussion of treatment options (ie RRT or conservative care)
- **Stage 5** – this is ESRD. The majority of patients will have progressive renal dysfunction such that consideration of treatment options becomes essential. The patient will normally be managed in secondary care, and attention will be given to the following:
  - In patients opting for haemodialysis therapy, a goal of management is to have a mature arteriovenous fistula in situ before dialysis needs to commence
  - Suitable patients will be activated on the renal transplant waiting list (by eGFR 15 ml/min), or, where relevant, transplantation from a live kidney donor arranged
  - In those who have opted for treatment, and where a renal transplant is not imminent, most need to commence dialysis when eGFR falls below 10 ml/min

Table 15.3. Classification of CKD

Stage	Description	eGFR (ml·min^{-1}·1.73 m^{-2})
1	Kidney damage with normal or ↑ GFR	≥90
2	Kidney damage with mild ↓ GFR	60–89
3A	Moderate ↓ GFR	45–59
3B		30–44
5	Severe ↓ GFR	15–29
5	Kidney failure	≤15

Although many cases of CKD progress insidiously, such that very abnormal biochemistry is relatively well tolerated by the patient, about 25% of dialysis patients initially present as uraemic emergencies (which carries a twofold worse prognosis). The key **parameters that differentiate CKD from AKI** are:

- Small kidneys at imaging
- Anaemia
- Renal bone disease
- Clinical tolerance of very severe uraemia

Causes of progressive CKD (approximate relative frequencies)

- **Most common causes of ESRD in UK***
  - Diabetic nephropathy (25%)
  - Chronic glomerulonephritis (15%)
  - Hypertension (15%)
  - Chronic pyelonephritis (12%) – most often due to reflux nephropathy, but also renal calculi (nephrolithiasis) with infection
  - Polycystic kidney disease (8%)
  - Obstructive uropathy (5%)
  - Chronic interstitial nephritis (4%) – eg sarcoidosis, lithium toxicity, myeloma
  - Post-acute kidney injury (3%)
  - Amyloidosis (1%)
- **Rarer causes of CKD**
  - Analgesic nephropathy
  - Other hereditary disorders – eg Alport syndrome
  - Toxic nephropathy
  - Following nephrectomy for renal tumours

*In at least 10% of cases of ESRD, the aetiology remains unknown. These are patients presenting with small kidneys on ultrasound, and in whom renal biopsy will be diagnostically unhelpful. Most likely diagnoses are hypertension, chronic glomerulonephritis or pyelonephritis, or dysplastic kidneys

---

Pathogenesis and management of progressive renal dysfunction in CKD

Although the majority of cases of CKD are slowly progressive towards ESRD, patients with particular pathologies (eg post-obstructive atrophy, and hypertension – when controlled) may manifest stable CKD for many years. When progression occurs its pathogenesis is multifactorial. It is thought that the RAA system plays a major role: the vasoactive mediator angiotensin and aldosterone exacerbate the intraglomerular hypertension seen in remaining nephrons, and they probably stimulate fibrosis within the tubulointerstitium and increase proteinuria, which itself may also directly damage tubular cells (see Figure 15.2). Hence the **management** of patients with CKD requires attention to:

- **Control of blood pressure**: it is imperative to optimise blood pressure control. Target blood pressures for patients with CKD are <130/80 mmHg (without significant proteinuria) and <125/75 mmHg if significant proteinuria (eg uACR >50) is present. Hypertension control can slow the progression towards ESRD, and **ACE inhibitors and ARBs** are logical agents to choose because of their effects upon the RAA system. The importance of optimal blood pressure control has been shown in observational studies; for example, diabetic patients with optimal control may lose GFR at a rate of only 1–2 ml/min per year whereas those with poor blood pressure and glycaemic control deteriorate rapidly towards ESRD, losing GFR at 8–16 ml/min per year
- **Reduction of proteinuria**: heavy urinary protein losses are associated with an increased rate of progression in many cases of CKD. Amelioration of proteinuria by blockade of the RAA system may also slow progression
- **Dietary modification**: patients with advanced CKD should maintain a normal protein and high calorie intake to avoid malnutrition (and a consequent increased likelihood of morbidity) in

Figure 15.2 Role of angiotensin II (AII) in the pathogenesis of progressive CKD

↑ANGIOTENSIN II

Efferent
arteriole

GLOMERULI

- ↑AII release from damaged renal tissue
- Leads to intraglomerular hypertension in remaining nephrons
- Leads to ↑proteinuria (toxic to tubules) and further glomerular injury
- Problem exacerbated by systemic and intrarenal hypertension

COLLAGEN

FIBROBLAST

AII

TUBULE

↑Aldosterone release

TUBULOINTERSTITIUM

- AII increases release of aldosterone from zona glomerulosa of adrenal gland
- Both have deleterious effects in the renal tubulointerstitium mediated in part by pro-scarring cytokines (eg TGFβ)

the phase leading up to RRT. Restricted protein intakes are now only used as a conservative means of limiting uraemia in a minority of patients. However, phosphate restriction and dietary modification of salt and potassium intake should be instituted at an early stage of CKD

- **Endocrine complications**: anaemia and renal osteodystrophy may begin during CKD stages 3 and 4, and hence early attention should be directed to these endocrine complications (see below)

- **Cardiovascular disease prevention**: CKD creates a pro-atherosclerotic environment due to factors such as hypertension, mixed hyperlipidaemia, hyperhomocystinaemia, anaemia, hyperparathyroidism and, when present, diabetes mellitus. The resulting accelerated atherogenesis will result in coronary artery

disease, stroke and peripheral vascular disease but other cardiovascular complications include congestive cardiomyopathy, left ventricular hypertrophy (LVH), and vascular calcification (which results in arterial stiffness). Patients with CKD therefore have a marked increase in CVS mortality compared to the general population; the importance of early treatment with statins is now the subject of a multicentre trial

15.5.2 Anaemia of CKD

The anaemia of CKD usually first appears when GFR is <50 ml/min; if untreated, it is a major contributor to morbidity in patients with advanced CKD. The major cause is the lack of endogenous erythropoietin secretion by the damaged kidneys, but other factors which predispose to the anaemia are listed in the box overleaf.

- Reduced dietary iron intake due to anorexia
- Impaired intestinal absorption of iron
- Uraemia has a toxic effect upon precursor cells in bone marrow
- Blood loss due to capillary fragility and platelet dysfunction (probably of minor importance)
- Reduced RBC survival (particularly in haemodialysis patients)

In general, haemodialysis patients have more severe anaemia, and a poorer response to erythropoiesis-stimulating agents (ESA) than their counterparts receiving continuous ambulatory peritoneal dialysis (CAPD). This may be because haemodialysis represents an 'inflammatory state' with cytokine release being stimulated by interaction of blood cells with the artificial dialysis membranes.

Recombinant erythropoiesis-stimulating agents (ESA)

Endogenous erythropoietin is normally synthesised by renal peritubular cells; it stimulates proliferation and maturation of erythroid lines within the marrow. Recombinant ESA preparations are now widely available and are used to correct anaemia in patients with CKD. It is imperative that these patient groups avoid repeated blood transfusion, so that future renal transplantation will not be precluded by allo-sensitisation.

Before initiation of an ESA the patient should be iron-replete. The serum ferritin and the transferrin saturation need monitoring as most patients require supplemental IV iron. Targets for treatment include:

- Haemoglobin: 10.5–12.5 g/dl
- Ferritin: >200 µg/l in haemodialysis patients, or >100 µg/l in CAPD and pre-dialysis patients
- Transferrin saturation: >20% (a figure of less than this may indicate functional iron deficiency)

One of the key aims of therapy is to limit or reverse the LVH which is prevalent in RRT patients. Haemoglobin correction will also have a positive effect

upon sexual function and other quality of life measures.

Causes of resistance to ESA therapy

- Iron deficiency
- Hyperparathyroidism
- Sepsis or chronic inflammation
- Aluminium toxicity (rare)
- Occult GI tract blood loss
- Pure red cell aplasia (PRCA; see below)

Main side-effects of ESA therapy: accelerated hypertension with encephalopathy (aim for a monthly Hb increase of <1.5 g/dl), bone aches, flu-like syndrome, fistula thrombosis (rare) and, most recently, PRCA (see below).

Pure red cell aplasia (PRCA)

A few cases of unresponsive and progressive severe anaemia have been identified in patients treated with ESA, who have antibodies directed at endogenous and exogenous erythropoietin; they become transfusion-dependent. Other marrow functions remain intact.

15.5.3 Hyperparathyroidism and CKD mineral and bone disorder (CKD-MBD)

The regulation of vitamin D and parathyroid hormone (PTH) metabolism are discussed in Chapter 13, Metabolic Diseases. Renal bone disease (CKD-MBD) is common in patients with CKD and those receiving dialysis. The pathogenesis is fairly intricate (see Figure 15.3) but the most important components are:

- **High serum phosphate**: phosphate clearance is reduced in renal failure
- **Low plasma ionised calcium**: due to several factors. There is lack of 1,25-dihydroxy-vitamin D (the 1-α-hydroxylation, which markedly increases activity of vitamin D, normally occurs in the kidney). Malnutrition may contribute, but hyperphosphataemia

Figure 15.3 Pathogenesis of CKD-bone mineral disorder (CKD-BMD). In CKD there is phosphate retention and reduced 1-α-hydroxylation of 25-hydroxy vitamin D. These abnormalities both lead to reduced plasma [Ca^{2+}] and all three factors independently stimulate PTH release from the parathyroid glands. The net effect is demineralisation of bone with release of calcium and more phosphate into the circulation; bony abnormalities include osteomalacia and high-turnover bone disease. (Figure courtesy of Dr Helen Eddington, Salford Royal Hospital)

(imbalancing the ionic product of $Ca^{2+} \times PO_4{}^{3-}$) is also very important

- **Stimulation of PTH release: secondary hyperparathyroidism** is very common and is the direct response of the glands to hypocalcaemia, hyperphosphataemia and low 1,25-dihydroxy-vitamin D levels. The latter three factors feed back independently on the parathyroid glands to stimulate PTH release, and hence correction of all of them (phosphate perhaps the most important) is necessary before the hyperparathyroidism can be optimally controlled. PTH has end-organ effects on bones (leading to osteoclastic resorption cavities) and also the heart, contributing to LVH, and it is also

a major cause of ESA resistance. **Tertiary hyperparathyroidism** is defined by the presence of elevated PTH and non-iatrogenic hypercalcaemia; it is due to autonomous PTH secretion from generally hyperplastic parathyroid glands (90%) or an adenoma (10%). Note that **primary hyperparathyroidism** is only rarely associated with renal failure (due to the nephrotoxic effects of hypercalcaemia or to renal calculus disease)

- **Low vitamin D levels**: this not only results in reduced absorption of calcium by the gut, but also in osteomalacia
- **Acidosis**: increases the severity of bone disease

Histological findings at bone biopsy in osteodystrophy

Several different histological lesions often co-exist in the same patient:

- **Osteomalacia**: due to vitamin D deficiency
- **Hyperparathyroid bone disease**: osteoporosis and cystic resorption; also termed 'osteitis fibrosa cystica' (von Recklinghausen's disease of bone). Subperiosteal erosions on the radial border of phalanges are characteristic
- **Osteoporosis**: due to relative malnourishment; steroid use
- **Osteosclerosis**: a component of the 'rugger jersey' spine appearance at X-ray (bone denser at the vertebral end-plates and thin in the middle of the vertebrae)
- **Adynamic bone disease**: bone with low turnover; PTH levels (and serum alkaline phosphatase) are usually subnormal. Over-treatment of secondary hyperparathyroidism with excess vitamin D (totally suppressing PTH release) may be contributory. Although the exact clinical significance is uncertain there is perhaps a greater likelihood of fracturing
- **Aluminium bone disease**: now much less common with the use of specially treated water supplies for dialysis (reverse osmosis) and non-aluminium-containing phosphate binders

Prevention and treatment of CKD-MBD

The basic principles are to improve the diet, reduce hyperphosphataemia and acidosis, and to reduce the PTH level (see below). This is brought about by use of phosphate binders, oral bicarbonate, dialysis where necessary, and by giving vitamin D at doses that do not provoke hypercalcaemia.

- **Phosphate binders**: aluminium-containing binders are now infrequently used and the mainstay of treatment has been calcium-based binders (calcium carbonate or calcium acetate). However, practice is changing, and with the awareness that CKD patients are at risk of vascular calcification and aortic valve calcification, non-calcimimetic agents (eg sevelamer, a polymer, and lanthanum carbonate) are increasingly used
- **Treatment targets**: serum phosphate <1.7 mmol/l, calcium low–normal range (2.2–2.45 mmol/l) and PTH <3 times above the normal range (eg <200 pg/ml when range is 25–65 pg/ml)

Most cases (>97%) of secondary hyperparathyroidism can be controlled with this standard medical treatment. For resistant cases (usually those with a large parathyroid gland mass (eg >1 cm^3), who have had chronic and poorly treated secondary hyperparathyroidism) and in patients with tertiary disease, the treatment options are now:

- Cinacalcet (a calcium-sensing receptor agonist)
- Selective vitamin D receptor agonist (eg paricalcitol)
- Parathyroidectomy

15.5.4 Maintenance dialysis

In the UK, the dialysis population is approximately 25 000, or 450/million. In the UK approximately 70% of patients receive **haemodialysis**, and the remainder peritoneal dialysis (**CAPD, or automated PD, APD**). Ideally, a patient should be given the opportunity to choose dialysis modality according to lifestyle factors (employment, home environment), their capability and local resources.

Factors which would favour haemodialysis in preference to peritoneal dialysis

- Recent abdominal surgery, or irremediable hernia
- Recurrent or persistent peritonitis (eg *Pseudomonas* or fungal)
- Peritoneal membrane failure: inability to ultra-filtrate the necessary fluid volume to maintain fluid balance in the patient
- Age and general frailty (ie physically or mentally incapable of PD)
- Severe malnutrition: protein losses in the dialysis effluent may be 3–10 g/day on CAPD (>15 g/day during peritonitis)
- Intercurrent severe illness with hypercatabolism
- Chronic severe chest disease: respiratory function may be compromised by PD
- Loss of residual renal function: it is now recognised that many patients only obtain adequate dialysis with CAPD during the early stages after development of ESRD. As residual function is lost, underdialysis becomes a reality, especially in larger body weight patients

Peritoneal dialysis

A standard **CAPD** regime would involve four 2-litre exchanges/day. The concentration of dextrose within the dialysate can be altered so that differing ultrafiltration requirements can be addressed. Although a few patients manage CAPD for many years, in most there is a finite length of time (eg 3–6 years) for its efficacy as a form of RRT. This is determined by gradual loss of **residual renal function** (ie a patient will commence CAPD with a GFR of 10–15 ml/min, which is a major contributor to waste-product clearance; over time, the GFR falls to zero, with corresponding inadequacy of the CAPD technique) and deterioration of peritoneal membrane function. **Automated peritoneal dialysis (APD)** is performed overnight, and can maintain

fluid homeostasis in patients with ultrafiltration failure (see below). APD may also be chosen for its convenience by some patients with normal peritoneal membrane characteristics.

The main **complications of PD** treatment are:

- **Bacterial peritonitis**: most cases are treatable. The most common infecting organisms are coagulase-negative staphylococci, Gram-negative bacteria and *Staphylococcus aureus*. The rate of PD-peritonitis should be no greater than 1 episode/30 patient-months. Patients who have repeated episodes of peritonitis, and hence several courses of intraperitoneal antibiotics, are prone to develop resistant organisms (eg *Pseudomonas* or fungal peritonitis) and catheter loss, necessitating a switch to haemodialysis. If the dialysis fluid culture yields more than one organism (especially Gram-negatives and anaerobes) during a peritonitis episode, then intra-abdominal pathology (eg bowel perforation, diverticular abscess) should be suspected and expediently diagnosed and treated
- **Ultrafiltration failure**: some patients are identified as 'high transporters' of glucose; the osmolar benefit of their PD dialysate is rapidly lost and hence these patients have difficulty with fluid removal (ultrafiltration). The latter may also develop after several years of PD treatment. APD may help maintain fluid balance in such patients, but polymer-based dialysis solutions can also be beneficial
- **Encapsulating peritoneal sclerosis (EPS)**: an increasingly recognised and serious complication of long-term PD. Risk factors include repeated episodes of peritonitis and duration of PD (eg 5% incidence in patients treated with PD for >3 years). The peritoneal membrane thickens and encases the bowel. Clinical features include CAPD ultrafiltration failure, but, in more severe cases, life-threatening bowel obstruction and malnutrition. Surgery can be of benefit in some cases
- **Malnutrition**: renal failure is an anorexic condition; patients often need nutritional supplements

Haemodialysis

This therapy has been available for several decades; it is an intrinsically more efficient means of RRT than PD and so many patients have lived for >20 years whilst being supported by haemodialysis. As this is an intermittent therapy (typically, 4 hours of dialysis three times each week) water restriction and dietary modification are even more important than for patients receiving PD (who with CAPD would be receiving continuous dialysis). Successful haemo-dialysis relies upon adequate **vascular access**:

- This is ideally provided by arterio-venous fistulae. An appropriate blood flow rate would be 250–400 ml/min into the dialyser circuit. Fistulae take 4–6 weeks to mature and so vascular access surgery should be planned in timely fashion, when at all possible
- Patients who present late with severe uraemia and patients with fistula complications inevitably require use of temporary or semi-permanent (tunnelled) vascular access catheters. The most frequent complication is line-related sepsis (in particular, *S. aureus* and coagulase-negative staphylococci), and the incidence of bacterial endocarditis is increased in haemodialysis patients. Repeated use of antibiotic courses increases the risk of MRSA and *Clostridium difficile* infection in dialysis patients
- The other main complication of haemodialysis catheters is venous stenosis or occlusion, most commonly seen after subclavian insertion. Consequently, most temporary catheters are now inserted into the femoral (for the very ill) or internal jugular veins, and the jugular veins are the preferred sites for tunnelled catheter insertion
- Complications relating to insertion can be minimised by using ultrasound scanning to locate the vein for all insertions, and the use of fluoroscopy with left internal jugular vein insertion (as anatomical variants are common)

Long-term complications in dialysis patients

Although dialytic therapies will keep patients alive and, with the additional use of ESA, relatively well,

many of the metabolic abnormalities of the uraemic condition persist and these patients are at increased risk of:

- **Vascular disease**: dialysis patients have a high risk of cardiovascular events and death compared to the general population, the relative risk of mortality being >100 in dialysis patients aged <30 years, and it remains three times that of the general population even in patients aged >80 years. The risk is increased further in diabetic dialysis patients (eg mean survival of 2 years). Pathogenetic factors have been discussed earlier in this section. The majority of deaths are due to cardiac disease but this is more often due to arrhythmia or congestive cardiomyopathy (which is exacerbated by fluid overload) than to overt myocardial infarction. **Vascular calcification** is a major component of the vascular disease affecting patients with renal failure; it is associated with arterial stiffness and LVH, which in turn correlate with increased mortality
- **Cardiac valve calcification**: this affects the aortic valve in particular, and is frequently seen in haemodialysis patients. As with vascular calcification, it is thought to be associated with perturbations in serum phosphate and calcium product
- **Dialysis-related amyloid**: β2-microglobulin is a small-molecular-weight (about 11 000 Da) protein normally metabolised and excreted by the kidney. Plasma levels increase greatly in patients on long-term (eg >10 years) haemodialysis, and the protein is deposited as amyloid within carpal tunnels, joints and bones. Dialysis with more biocompatible membranes can alleviate the β2-microglobulin burden
- **Arthritis**: pyrophosphate arthropathy (pseudogout) and gout (*see* Section 15.5.5 on transplantation below) are common in patients with renal failure

15.5.5 Renal transplantation

About 2000 UK patients benefit from renal trans-plantation each year, and over half of transplants derive from **cadaveric donors**. However, a shortage of organs available for transplantation persists and the rate of **living-donor transplants** (related or unrelated) is ever-increasing. All potential living renal donors have to be screened carefully to ensure that they are clinically fit; absolute contraindications include pre-existing renal disease, a disease of unknown aetiology (eg multiple sclerosis or sarcoidosis), recent malignancy and overt ischaemic heart disease. Hypertensive patients may be considered provided that they have no evidence of end-organ damage, and the blood pressure is well controlled. All donors require careful counselling before the donor operation.

Screening and preparation of potential recipients

All dialysis patients and those with advanced CKD are considered for transplantation. However, less than half will be suitably fit for listing.

- Exclusion criteria include current or recent malignancy (eg <2 years) and severe co-morbidity (debilitating chronic obstructive pulmonary disease (COPD) or stroke, dementia, etc). Advanced age is not a contraindication but few patients aged >75 years are eventually listed
- As the transplant is inserted in the iliac fossa, anastomosed to the iliac vessels, vascular calcification of the latter should be sought with pelvic X-ray. This is especially important in patients with a history of peripheral vascular disease
- Patients with major risk factors (long-standing diabetes, previous IHD, heavy smoking) should undergo **CVS screening** prior to referral. This would include echocardiography (LV ejection fraction must be >30%) and non-invasive imaging for reversible coronary ischaemia (eg myocardial perfusion imaging or stress echocardiography). Selected patients then undergo coronary angiography and, if necessary, angioplasty or coronary artery bypass grafting (CABG) prior to transplantation
- Patients with obstructed and persistently or recurrently infected urinary tracts (eg severe

reflux, patients with spina bifida) need bilateral native nephrectomy prior to transplantation

Matching and incompatible transplants

The majority of cadaveric organs are transplanted to blood group-compatible patients with the best available tissue match, but the national allocation scheme will give preference to 'long-waiters' who are often highly sensitised to the majority of HLA allotypes.

- HLA antigens are coded from chromosome 6 (*see also* Chapter 10, Immunology)
- Class I antigens are A, B and C; class II are the D group antigens
- Relative importance of HLA matching: DR>B>A>C; most centres accept 1 DR or 1 B mismatch
- Transplants to **'incompatible'** recipients (eg blood group incompatibility or those pre-sensitised to donor antigens) are possible with use of 'desensitisation therapy' (eg plasma exchange and B-lymphocyte suppressive therapy) for the recipient a week or so before a planned living donor transplant

Combined kidney–pancreas transplantation

This is now increasingly performed for patients with type 1 diabetes mellitus; recipient fitness is of paramount importance. The pancreas is usually transplanted onto the opposite iliac vessels to the kidney, with its duct draining into the bladder.

- Acute rejection of the pancreas is manifest by worsening of glycaemic control and by a rise in urinary amylase, but responds to pulsed steroid therapy
- Long-term results are encouraging – normalisation of glycaemic status is expected, and most diabetic microvascular complications (particularly retinopathy and neuropathy) can be stabilised, although not reversed

- Pyonephrosis or any suppuration within the urinary tract (see above). If this is due to bladder dysfunction (eg spina bifida) a resting ileal conduit will need to be created prior to transplantation
- Massive polycystic kidneys
- Uncontrollable hypertension (rare with modern drug therapies)
- Renal/urothelial malignancy: patients must remain free of recurrence for >2 years before transplantation

Post-transplantation renal function

It is common to see **acute renal transplantation dysfunction**, especially in the first 2 weeks after engraftment. Nevertheless, overall graft survival is 90% at 1 year, 70% at 7 years and 50% at 14 years. **Chronic graft dysfunction** is common and is re-sponsible for the majority of graft losses beyond 1 year after transplantation. The causes of acute and chronic graft dysfunction are shown in Table 15.4.

Acute transplant rejection

This is very common, and should be anticipated in the early weeks after transplantation. The risk of acute rejection episodes may be less with use of tacrolimus rather than ciclosporin. Most cases respond rapidly to pulsed IV methylprednisolone therapy. Steroid-resistant rejection occurs in about 5% and usually requires therapy with monoclonal antibody therapy (eg ATG or OKT3).

Chronic allograft nephropathy (CAN)

This accounts for the majority of graft losses occurring beyond the first year after transplantation. It is usually manifest by the development of proteinuria and slowly progressive graft dysfunction, and is thought to be due to both low-grade immunological and non-immunological (hypertension, hyper-

Table 15.4. Causes of graft dysfunction after transplantation

Acute graft dysfunction (1 day to 4 months after transplantation)
- **Delayed graft function** (ATN of the graft): increased with prolonged cold ischaemia time (seen in about 25% of all transplants – usually resolves by 2–3 weeks)
- Ureteric leakage (breakdown of anastomosis)
- Vascular thrombosis (arterial or venous thrombosis of the transplant vessels – usually irremediable); this may be associated with **primary non-function** (ie the transplant never functions)
- Urinary tract infection
- Acute ciclosporin or tacrolimus toxicity – resolves rapidly with alteration in dosage
- CMV infection (diagnosed with PCR for the virus)
- **Acute rejection**: occurs in about 30% of all transplants

Chronic graft dysfunction (4 months after transplantation onwards)
- **Chronic allograft nephropathy**: by far the most common cause of chronic dysfunction of the transplant
- Recurrent primary disease within the graft
- Calcineurin inhibitor (CNI; ciclosporin or tacrolimus) nephrotoxicity: changes on transplant biopsy are rarely pathognomonic. Withdrawal of the calcineurin inhibitor in such patients will often stabilise graft function
- Polyomavirus infections (eg BK or JC virus)

cholesterolaemia, vascular disease within the graft, CNI toxicity) factors. Management involves:

- Optimising hypertension control
- Limiting proteinuria (use of ACE inhibitors and ARBs)
- **Modification of immunosuppressive therapy**: despite their excellent track record in transplantation, CNIs are associated with CAN, partly because of their tendency to provoke vasoconstriction and vasculopathy (and consequent ischaemia) within the graft. There is increasing evidence that reduction in CNI dose or complete withdrawal, with introduction of antiproliferative therapy (eg mycophenolate mofetil (MMF) or sirolimus; see below), can ameliorate, or even stabilise, progressive graft dysfunction in patients with CAN

Polyomavirus infection

Subacute graft dysfunction is increasingly recognised in association with polyomavirus infection within the graft. BK and JC virus are named after the initials of the patients in whom they were first identified. The mainstay of treatment is a reduction in immunosuppressive therapy, particularly the antiproliferative drugs (eg **MMF**); specific antiviral therapy with **cidofovir** may be beneficial in selected cases, but this agent can be nephrotoxic and doses must be reduced according to eGFR. Successful treatment allows stabilisation of graft function at the level noted at the time of polyomavirus diagnosis; return to baseline graft function is rare.

Post-transplantation: non-renal complications

Although the quality of life of most patients is significantly improved after transplantation, patients are still at risk of:

- **Malignancy**: **non-Hodgkin's lymphoma** (usually EB virus-associated) is 20–50 times and **skin cancer** 5–20 times commoner in transplant recipients than in age-matched general populations, and the increased incidence is thought to be due to the effects of immunosuppression (especially azathioprine

with skin and CNIs with lymphoma). All other malignancies are slightly more prevalent (1.5-fold increase)

- **Cardiovascular**: ischaemic heart disease is 10–20 times more prevalent (due to effects of immunosuppression and hyperlipidaemia, as well as persistence of the CVS risk accompanying the patient's previous 'uraemic state') than in an age/sex-matched equivalent population. Mortality is 2% in the first year after transplantation, half of which is due to CVS disease, and half to infection (see below)
- **Infections**: all infections are commoner but patients are also at risk from opportunistic infections such as *Pneumocystis carinii* pneumonia (PCP), and especially cytomegalovirus (CMV)
  - **CMV** occurs in about 30% and is anticipated in CMV antibody-negative recipients of a CMV-positive graft at 6–12 weeks after transplantation. Patients at risk of CMV receive prophylaxis with oral ganciclovir, and oral valganciclovir is used to treat mild infections (leucopenia and mild pyrexia are typical). Severe infections occur in 10%, and can be associated with myocarditis, encephalitis, retinitis and renal dysfunction; these patients require treatment with systemic ganciclovir
  - **PCP** is uncommon, but patients receive co-trimoxazole prophylaxis for the first 6 months post-transplantation
  - Patients of Asian origin, or those with a previous TB history, are given anti-tuberculous prophylaxis with isoniazid for the first year after transplantation
- **Osteoporosis**: the risk is increased because of immunosuppressant (particularly steroid) usage. Many patients receive bisphosphonate prophylaxis
- **Gout**: all patients with reduced renal function are at increased risk of hyperuricaemia and acute gout. However, prophylaxis with allopurinol is not widely implemented, largely because this agent has many unwanted effects. Treatment of acute gout in patients with CKD is problematic: there are no non-nephrotoxic

NSAIDs available, and patients with transplants (or with CKD) are at risk of serious renal dysfunction with their usage. Colchicine can be used, but it also has frequent GI side-effects; temporary treatment with moderate-dose steroids (eg a single IM injection of 125 mg methylprednisolone, or 30 mg prednisolone orally for 1 month) will provide an excellent anti-inflammatory effect and provides cover for the introduction of allopurinol

- **New-onset diabetes after transplantation (NODAT)**: the incidence is increased in transplanted patients (3%–5% may develop it per year); immunosuppressants (particularly tacrolimus) are thought to be responsible

Recurrent renal disease after transplantation

Patients with Alport syndrome are at risk of developing anti-glomerular basement membrane antibody syndrome after transplantation, as they have no prior tolerance to the Goodpasture antigen. Vasculitis may recur, and monitoring of serum ANCA is recommended in these patients. All types of primary glomerulonephritis may recur in the graft, but particularly:

- Focal segmental glomerulosclerosis (FSGS) – 15% recurrence rate, with graft loss in 50% of these
- IgA nephropathy – 30%–60% have evidence of histological recurrence; graft loss in 15% of these
- Membranous glomerulonephritis – <10% recurrence rate, but 50% graft loss if affected
- Mesangiocapillary glomerulonephritis: 30%–80% risk of recurrence

Commonly used immunosuppressants for renal transplantation

Immunosuppressive regimes vary from centre to centre. Most now involve induction with monoclonal antibody (eg basiliximab, directed against CD25, given at induction and day 4), followed by a CNI-based regime (eg tacrolimus with MMF). Patients who have at least two steroid-responsive acute rejections will usually receive oral cortico-

steroids for up to 12 months after transplantation. Particular considerations with immunosuppressants are:

- **Ciclosporin A**: this agent inhibits a T-cell phosphatase, calcineurin, which is needed for T-cell activation, and hence the term 'CNI'. Its introduction around 1980 completely revolutionised the outcome of transplantation. Common side-effects include hirsutism, liver dysfunction and gum hypertrophy, hypertension and CAN
- **Tacrolimus**: this is also a CNI. Compared with ciclosporin, it reduces the incidence of acute rejection episodes in the initial post-transplant period. Also, the number of steroid-resistant rejection episodes is seen to be reduced, and hypertension may be less frequent or severe. However, the risk of CAN with long-term use appears to be similar to that of ciclosporin. Approximately 5% of patients receiving this agent develop diabetes mellitus (NODAT) per year
- **Azathioprine**: this traditional antiproliferative agent is commonly associated with mild bone marrow suppression. It should only be used with caution in patients receiving allopurinol because of the risk of life-threatening bone marrow suppression
- **Mycophenolate mofetil (MMF)**: the main side-effects of this antiproliferative agent are gastrointestinal, in particular diarrhoea, and bone marrow suppression (but less frequently than azathioprine). It is usually used in combination with a CNI; it has a major role in the management of CAN, being used to facilitate reduction or withdrawal of the CNI
- **Sirolimus (rapamycin)**: this is related to erythromycin, and it inhibits T-cell division. It is not associated with nephropathy, but it can provoke hyperlipidaemia
- **Corticosteroids**: these agents have been the mainstay of immunosuppressive regimes for several decades, but now there is concern about long-term dosing. This is particularly relevant to cardiovascular complications after transplantation, as well as to post-transplant

bone metabolism (osteoporosis). Some centres now use regimes that withdraw steroid at 6–12 months post-transplantation

Optimal immunosuppressive regime

Some centres now try to tailor immunosuppressive regimes in order to maximise the chances of good long-term graft function, but with limitation of recipient vascular risk; this involves reducing or complete withdrawal of CNI dose, and sparing steroid use. Although there is no current consensus view, the following would be a logical strategy:

- Induction with monoclonal antibody and large CNI dose
- Maintenance therapy with CNI coupled with either MMF or sirolimus
- If more than one steroid-sensitive acute rejection episode, prednisolone for 6–12 months
- At 1–2 years post-transplant, reduce CNI dose
- If CAN develops, then reduce/withdraw CNI, and introduce MMF or sirolimus (if not receiving one or other)

15.6 GLOMERULONEPHRITIS AND ASSOCIATED SYNDROMES

15.6.1 Clinical presentation of glomerulonephritis

The term glomerulonephritis implies inflammatory disease primarily affecting the glomeruli (but note that no inflammation is seen in minimal-change disease) – but other **glomerular** diseases exist which do not involve glomerulonephritis (eg diabetic nephropathy). Most glomerulonephritis develops as a result of **immune dysregulation**, either due to an inappropriate immune response to a 'self-antigen' (autoimmunity, eg anti glomerular basement membrane (anti-GBM) disease, ANCA +ve vasculitis), or to an inappropriate or exaggerated response to a foreign antigen (eg membranous glomerulonephritis secondary to hepatitis B infection).

- This 'immune dysregulation' pathogenesis explains why there is a genetic predisposition to some forms of glomerulonephritis (eg IgA nephropathy)
- Immune complexes are often deposited in the glomeruli (eg SLE nephritis, mesangiocapillary glomerulonephritis), but in some glomerulonephritides immune complexes form in situ within the glomerulus (eg anti-GBM disease)
- Inflammation leads to proliferation of cellular structures (mesangial, endothelial or epithelial cells) and/or scarring
- Glomerulonephritis may be **idiopathic** (**primary**), or **secondary** to systemic disease (eg malignancy, infections), drugs, etc
- The long-term clinical outcome often depends more upon the severity of tubulointerstitial damage rather than on the extent of glomerular injury
- The type of glomerulonephritis is defined by light microscopic, immunofluorescent and electron microscopic (ultrastructural) characteristics (see below)

Screening for glomerulonephritis

- Dipstick for proteinuria; urinary ACR (or PCR)
- Dipstick for haematuria; urine microscopy for red cells and casts
- Hypertension

Attenuation of progression of glomerulonephritis

- Control blood pressure: for all types of glomerulonephritis. The target blood pressure for patients with chronic renal disease and significant proteinuria is <125/75 mmHg
- ACE inhibitors and ARBs: decrease proteinuria and blood pressure, and may ameliorate progressive scarring (*see* Section 15.5 on CKD)
- Progression depends on degree of co-existent scarring in the tubulointerstitium

Classification of glomerulonephritis

Diabetes mellitus is the most common cause of glomerular pathology but it causes glomerulosclerosis and is therefore not a 'glomerulonephritis'. The commoner forms of glomerulonephritis (GN) are:

- Minimal-change disease
- Membranous glomerulonephritis
- Focal segmental glomerulosclerosis (FSGS)
- IgA nephropathy (mesangioproliferative glomerulonephritis)
- Crescentic glomerulonephritis (eg associated with Goodpasture syndrome or vasculitis)
- Focal segmental proliferative glomerulonephritis (eg associated with vasculitis or endocarditis)
- Mesangiocapillary glomerulonephritis
- Diffuse proliferative glomerulonephritis (eg post-streptococcal)

Renal syndromes and their relationship to glomerulonephritis

There is often confusion regarding the relationship of the various glomerulonephritides to the different renal syndromes. A particular type of glomerulonephritis may manifest several different clinical syndromes (see Table 15.5). For example, membranous glomerulonephritis may be responsible for CKD, persistent proteinuria, nephrotic syndrome and hypertension; any combination of these may be present during the course of the disease. However:

- Certain glomerulonephritides are characteristically associated with typical clinical presentations (eg minimal-change disease and nephrotic syndrome, IgA nephropathy and recurrent macroscopic haematuria)
- It should also be borne in mind that a particular syndrome can be due to some conditions other than glomerulonephritis (eg the nephrotic syndrome can be due to accelerated-phase hypertension, pre-eclamptic toxaemia or amyloid)

Definitions of the common renal syndromes

- **Asymptomatic proteinuria**
  - <3 g/day
- **Nephritic syndrome**
  - Characterised by hypertension, oliguria, haematuria and oedema
- **Hypertension**
- **Nephrotic syndrome**
  - >3 g proteinuria/day with serum albumin <25 g/l; oedema; hypercholesterolaemia
- **Haematuria**
  - Microscopic or macroscopic
- **Acute or chronic kidney disease**
  - (Discussed in previous sections)

Table 15.5. Clinical presentation of glomerulonephritis

	Proteinuria	Nephrotic	Nephritic	Haematuria	AKI	CKD
Minimal-change disease	+	+++	−	−	−	−
Membranous GN	+++	++	−	±	−	++
Focal segmental glomerulosclerosis	++	++	±	−	±	++
Mesangioproliferative (IgA)	++	+	+	+++	±	++
Mesangiocapillary GN	++	++	+	+	+	++
Diffuse proliferative GN	+	±	+++	++	+++	+
Diabetic glomerulosclerosis	+++	++	−	−	−	+++
Crescentic nephritis	+	±	+++	++	+++	+
Focal segmental proliferative GN	+	++	++	++	++	+

+++ = Very common presentation; − = Never seen/extremely rare

Causes of the nephrotic syndrome

- **Common**
  - Primary glomerulonephritis
  - Diabetes mellitus
  - Basement membrane nephropathy (eg Alport syndrome)
  - Infections (eg leprosy, malaria, hepatitis B – associated with secondary GN)
  - Pre-eclampsia
  - Accelerated hypertension
  - Myeloma
  - Amyloidosis
  - Drugs (eg gold, penicillamine, captopril, NSAIDs, mercury – associated with secondary GN)
  - Connective tissue disease (eg SLE – anther secondary GN)
- **Rare**
  - Vesico-ureteric reflux
  - Constrictive pericarditis
  - Sickle cell disease
  - Allergies (eg bee sting, penicillin)
  - Hereditary glomerulonephritis (eg 'Finnish type' nephrotic syndrome)

Causes of macroscopic haematuria*

- Urinary infections
- Renal papillary necrosis
- Acute glomerulonephritis
- Loin-pain haematuria syndrome
- IgA nephropathy
- Prostatic hypertrophy (dilated prostatic veins)
- Renal calculi
- Urinary tract malignancy

*It is usually imperative to exclude urinary tract malignancy (urine cytology, cystoscopy, IVU and ultrasound) in patients aged > 40 years presenting with macroscopic haematuria

15.6.2 Notes on particular glomerulonephritides

Minimal-change disease

The clinical presentation is almost always nephrotic. Although most common in children (causing >80% of nephrotic syndrome due to glomerulonephritis in under-15-year-olds), it also accounts for 28% of nephrotic syndrome in adults. Highly selective proteinuria (ie loss of mainly smaller protein molecules as evidenced by IgG/transferrin <0.1; see below) is typical, and the majority of cases are steroid-responsive. Other features include:

- Normal renal function and renal histology (by light microscopy – but epithelial cell foot-process fusion on electron microscopy)
- May be due to NSAIDs or gold; rare associations are with Hodgkin's lymphoma and thymoma
- May frequently relapse (10%), but renal prognosis is excellent

Monitoring: patients with frequently relapsing disease are taught to dipstick their urine on a regular basis; three consecutive days of +++ proteinuria is the trigger to commence steroids, which are continued at high dose until urinalysis has remained negative for 3 consecutive days.

Treatment: the mainstay is with short courses of high-dose prednisolone. Most relapses are steroid-sensitive; cyclophosphamide (usually orally in children, pulsed IV in adults) is used for frequent relapsers or steroid-resistant disease. A distinct subgroup of frequently relapsing (eg 2–4 relapses/year) teenagers enter adult nephrological care and prove quite difficult to manage. Avoidance of long-term steroid side-effects (particularly osteoporosis) is important and so the relapse rate can be reduced by treatment with ciclosporin (taken for several years), in the knowledge that, in the majority of these patients, the presumed underlying immune perturbation resolves by their late 20s. However, a small group of these patients are eventually found to have FSGS (see below).

Urinary protein selectivity

The index of urinary protein selectivity is used mainly in paediatric nephrological practice; highly selective proteinuria is likely to result from minimal-change disease, and so its detection may obviate the need to perform renal biopsy of the child. In adults the range of possible renal diagnoses in patients with significant proteinuria usually makes biopsy essential. The index is calculated from the respective concentrations of different molecular weight proteins within the urine:

$$\frac{\text{IgG (mol. wt. 150 kDa)}}{\text{Transferrin (mol. wt. 40 kDa)}}$$

Highly selective (ie minimal-change) proteinuria is defined as an index of <0.1; unselective proteinuria >0.3.

Membranous glomerulonephritis

This is one of the commonest types of glomerulonephritis in the adult; there are two peaks of disease (patients in their mid-20s and those aged 60–70 years). The clinical presentation may be nephrotic syndrome, asymptomatic proteinuria or CKD.

- Renal histology is characterised by granular IgG and complement deposition on the glomerular basement membrane; immune complexes are subepithelial (outer aspect of basement membrane) and appear as 'spikes' with silver stain
- Immunosuppressive therapies have been trialled in patients with nephrotic syndrome and/or evidence of progressive CKD. About a third will progress through CKD to ESRD, a third respond to immunosuppressive therapy (eg cytotoxic regimes such as the Ponticelli regime: chlorambucil alternating with corticosteroids), and the disease remits spontaneously in a similar proportion of patients

- In all proteinuric patients a cornerstone of treatment is optimal blood pressure control and limitation of proteinuria with ACE inhibitors and/or ARBs
- Renal vein thrombosis may occur in up to 5% of patients. Patients at greatest risk are those with serum albumin <20 g/l, and these should receive prophylactic-dose heparin. Unfractionated heparin is generally safe, but note that there have been reports of serious haemorrhagic complications in patients with renal failure who have been treated with 'normal' doses of low-molecular-weight heparin (reduced doses can safely be used)
- Membranous glomerulonephritis may be idiopathic, or secondary to other conditions (see below)
- As stated before, the condition can recur in renal transplants

Secondary causes of membranous glomerulonephritis

- **Malignancy**
  - Bronchus, stomach, colon, lymphoma, chronic lymphoid leukaemia (CLL) (high suspicion of these in elderly patients)
- **Connective tissue disease**
  - SLE, rheumatoid arthritis, Sjögren syndrome, mixed connective tissue disease
- **Chronic infections**
  - (eg hepatitis B or C, malaria, syphilis)
- **Drugs**
  - Gold, penicillamine, captopril, NSAIDs
- **Others**
  - Sarcoidosis, Guillain–Barré syndrome, primary biliary cirrhosis (all rare)

Causes of renal vein thrombosis

- **Acute thrombosis**
  - Infantile gastroenteritis
  - Acute pyelonephritis (high mortality)
  - Renal cell carcinoma (with renal vein invasion)
- **Chronic thrombosis**
  - Amyloidosis
  - Nephrotic syndrome due to glomerulonephritis (particularly membranous glomerulonephritis)

Focal segmental glomerulosclerosis (FSGS)

The **primary form of FSGS** accounts for <10% of nephrotic syndrome in children and the elderly, but up to 20% in young adults. It can also frequently present with proteinuria and/or CKD. In childhood the clinical pattern is often identical to minimal-change disease, and it may be misdiagnosed as such. There are also familial forms of FSGS. Focal glomerular deposits of IgM are seen at biopsy.

Secondary FSGS: this can be seen in patients with heroin abuse, those with HIV infections and AIDS, and it is recognised in patients with obesity or when the functioning renal mass is reduced (eg after nephrectomy). In the latter cases, the glomerulosclerosis probably occurs as a result of haemodynamic stress and/or ischaemic changes within the glomeruli, which also explains why it has been associated with renovascular disease.

Treatment of primary FSGS: it is important to distinguish this clinically from secondary FSGS, as patients with the latter should not be treated with immunosuppression, but with optimal blood pressure control with RAA blockade. In nephrotic patients with primary disease >40% will respond to moderate-dose steroids given for 3–6 months. Frequent relapsers are treated in a similar way to those with minimal-change nephropathy.

Outcome of FSGS: a rapidly deteriorating clinical course is seen in 2%, and 25% of all patients will eventually progress to ESRD. There is a high rate of recurrence in transplants.

Mesangioproliferative glomerulonephritis (IgA nephropathy or Berger's disease)

This is a very frequent condition, the commonest primary glomerulonephritis in adults. It typically affects young adults, presenting with microscopic or recurrent macroscopic haematuria. The haematuric episodes are usually 'synpharyngitic' (ie occurring 0–3 days after upper respiratory tract infection (URTI)). There are likely to be many undiagnosed cases as most nephrologists would not undertake renal biopsy in patients with isolated microscopic haematuria. The serum IgA is increased in 50% of patients; the condition is considered to be auto-immune, perhaps due to dysregulation of IgA metabolism. Other features of IgA nephropathy are:

- An increased incidence in the Far East (associated with HLA DQW7)
- IgA nephropathy can be associated with cirrhosis, dermatitis herpetiformis, coeliac disease and mycosis fungoides. It occurs in the Wiskott–Aldrich syndrome
- Renal biopsy features show proliferation of mesangial areas of the glomerulus; immunological staining is strongly positive for IgA in these areas. A similar histological picture may be seen in **Henoch–Schönlein nephritis**, and the pathogenesis is thought to be similar in the two conditions. Crescents may be present during haematuric episodes

Treatment of IgA nephropathy: nephrotic presentations should be treated as for minimal-change nephropathy. Patients with progressive CKD may show stabilisation of renal function with a 6-month regime of alternate-day steroids. The possible beneficial effects of fish oil (ω-3 fatty acids) remain uncertain. Otherwise the mainstay of treatment is optimal blood pressure control with RAA blockade, as for other chronic nephropathies.

Outcome of IgA nephropathy: 25% of patients will progress to ESRD by 20 years after disease onset; however, the overall prognosis for IgA nephropathy is certain to be better than this as the mildest cases are likely to remain undiagnosed. Clinical criteria help identify patients with better prognosis – those with proteinuria <1 g/24 h at presentation have

98% renal survival at 15 years, compared to 65% of patients with proteinuria >1 g/24 h. The disease frequently recurs in transplants.

Mesangiocapillary glomerulonephritis (MCGN)

There are three forms of mesangiocapillary (also termed membranoproliferative) glomerulonephritis:

- **Type I**: immune deposits in the subendothelial space and mesangium. This can occur in association with or without mixed **cryoglobulinaemias**, and **hepatitis C** may underlie the problem in 70%–90%; other causes are hepatitis B, subacute bacterial endocarditis (SBE), shunt nephritis, malaria, SLE, Sjögren syndrome, sickle cell disease, α-antitrypsin deficiency, hereditary complement deficiencies and malignancy (CLL, non-Hodgkin's lymphoma)
- **Type II**: dense deposits in the mesangium ('dense deposit' disease) leading to characteristic double-contouring of the basement membrane on renal biopsy. This is usually familial, and associated with partial lipodystrophy or factor H deficiency. Patients have reduced serum complement and the presence of circulating C3 nephritic factor. The latter binds to the alternative pathway C3 convertase, preventing its inactivation by factor H; continued complement activation results
- **Type III**: immune deposits diffusely present in subendothelial space and mesangium. Often associated with hepatitis C or B infections (and the secondary causes as for type I MCGN)

Patients present with microscopic haematuria and dipstick proteinuria (most common), nephrotic syndrome (35%), CKD, or with rapidly deteriorating renal function (10%). The overall prognosis is fairly poor, with 50% progressing to ESRD; steroids are only occasionally effective, but are used in childhood nephrotic presentations. There is a high rate of recurrence of MCGN in transplants.

Diffuse proliferative glomerulonephritis

This is the histological pattern of the classic post-streptococcal glomerulonephritis which usually presents with the nephritic syndrome or AKI; children and young adults are most often affected. The disorder is typically preceded (by 10–21 days) by a sore throat, or (most often in third world countries) skin disease (impetigo).

- Serum C3 is low and there is diffuse proliferation within glomeruli at biopsy
- Post-infective cases usually recover spontaneously with restoration of full renal function
- The same histological picture may be seen in patients with SLE nephritis (but immune complex deposition is characteristic in the latter)

Rapidly progressive glomerulonephritis (RPGN) – including Goodpasture syndrome

The term 'rapidly progressive' glomerulonephritis is a clinical description of rapidly deteriorating renal function due to an underlying glomerulonephritis. The histological counterpart is a **crescentic glomerulonephritis**, and so the two terms are (sometimes incorrectly) used interchangeably. They refer to the renal lesions which excite great interest from the nephrologist, not least because patients are often very sick with hypercatabolic AKI and possibly associated systemic disease (eg pulmonary haemorrhage), but also because the underlying disease processes are potentially treatable provided that investigation and therapy are expedient. All age groups may be affected and the presentation is usually with AKI or nephritic syndrome.

- Causes of RPGN include Goodpasture syndrome, ANCA +ve vasculitis and lupus nephritis
- Crescentic nephritis may be 'idiopathic' but is more often associated with Goodpasture syndrome, ANCA +ve vasculitis or SLE

ANCA +ve vasculitis and lupus nephritis are both considered in detail in Section 15.12, 'Systemic disorders and the kidney', and hence the remainder of this section will concentrate on Goodpasture syndrome and its treatment, which is similar to that for the former conditions.

Goodpasture syndrome

This is characterised by the presence of circulating anti-GBM antibodies (the GBM antigen is a component of type IV collagen), which localise to the glomerular and pulmonary capillary basement membranes. The condition is rare (<1 case/million per year), tends to affect the elderly or patients in their 20–30s, is commoner in smokers and in some cases may be triggered by inhaled hydrocarbons.

- **Pulmonary haemorrhage** occurs in 50% of patients with Goodpasture's; the most vulnerable are young male smokers. It is also seen in ANCA +ve disease (Wegener's and microscopic polyangiitis), which is considered later. The occurrence of pulmonary haemorrhage confers a greater mortality and is a definitive indication for plasma exchange
- Specific biopsy changes are seen in Goodpasture syndrome, with IgG deposited on the glomerular basement membrane in a linear pattern. The glomerulonephritis is of the diffuse proliferative type, and typically there is extensive crescent formation (epithelial cell proliferation arising from Bowman's capsule)
- **Prognosis**: renal functional recovery is rarely seen if the patient presents with advanced AKI (eg creatinine >600 μmol/l) and/or anuria. Overall mortality is 20%. Elderly patients are at particular risk from infective complications after immunosuppression; patients who have pulmonary haemorrhage are at greatest risk of mortality. Transplantation is possible once the patient is rendered autoantibody negative

Treatment of RPGN and crescentic nephritis

The following is applicable to most diseases causing RPGN and/or crescentic glomerulonephritis. Treatment is with early and high-dose immunosuppressive therapy with or without **plasma exchange**. The latter is essential for patients with pulmonary haemorrhage who have a circulating autoantibody (ie anti-GBM or ANCA) in high titre, and it is used in most cases of Goodpasture syndrome and those with ANCA +ve disease who have AKI. The aim of plasma exchange is to rapidly remove these auto-antibodies, allowing time for the immunosuppressive drugs to act to reduce their formation (eg cyclophosphamide) or to diminish tissue inflammation (with steroids). A typical regime for Goodpasture syndrome would be:

- **Induction therapy**: high-dose steroids (IV methylprednisolone 1 g on three consecutive days, followed by prednisolone 1 mg/kg) with 7 × 4-litre plasma exchanges within the first 10–14 days. Pulsed IV cyclophosphamide (0.7–1 g each month) is given for the first 6 months, by which stage the steroid dose will have been tapered to around 10–20 mg/day
- **Maintenance therapy**: low-dose steroid and azathioprine are continued for a further 12–18 months (or even longer in some cases of cANCA +ve vasculitis (see later), or Goodpasture's with persistence of anti-GBM antibody)

Plasma exchange in renal disease

- **Agreed benefit**
  - Goodpasture syndrome
  - ANCA +ve diseases: especially with pulmonary–renal presentation (mandatory with pulmonary haemorrhage); also for severe AKI
  - Idiopathic crescentic glomerulonephritis
  - Cryoglobulinaemias
  - Myeloma: cases with hyperviscosity
  - Thrombotic thrombocytopenic purpura (TTP)
- **Possible benefit**
  - SLE nephritis: severe lupus with AKI
  - Henoch–Schönlein nephritis: with crescentic forms and AKI
  - Myeloma: with AKI due to cast nephropathy (see later)
  - Haemolyticuraemic syndrome (HUS)

Hypocomplementaemia and glomerulonephritis

The following disorders are often associated with glomerulonephritis coupled with *low serum complement* (C3).

- **SLE**
- **Shunt nephritis (rare)**
  - Focal segmental proliferative glomerulonephritis (or MCGN); classically associated with coagulase-negative staphylococcal infection of ventriculo-atrial shunts
- **Primary complement deficiency (eg C1q, C2 or C4 deficiency)**
  - Associated with lupus-like syndromes, glomerulonephritis (usually mesangiocapillary type) and increased risk of bacterial infection
- **Endocarditis**
  - Focal segmental proliferative glomerulonephritis
- **Post-streptococcal glomerulonephritis**
- **Mesangiocapillary glomerulonephritis**
  - (See earlier section)
- **Cryoglobulinaemia**
  - Especially type II (see below)

Cryoglobulinaemia

Immunoglobulins which precipitate on cooling may be monoclonal or polyclonal (*see* Chapter 10, Immunology). They can induce a small-vessel vasculitis, particularly affecting skin and kidneys. Type II (mixed monoclonal) and type III (polyclonal) cryoglobulinaemias are associated with glomerulonephritis (mesangiocapillary or membranoproliferative).

15.7 INHERITED RENAL DISEASE

The commonest inherited renal diseases are polycystic kidney disease and Alport syndrome. Rarer disorders include other renal cystic disease, disorders of amino acids and familial glomerulonephritis; the latter conditions are encountered much more often in paediatric nephrology.

15.7.1 Autosomal dominant polycystic kidney disease (ADPKD)

Autosomal dominant polycystic kidney disease (ADPKD) is the most common inherited renal condition, and the genes have now been identified:

- **PKD1**: chromosome 16 in 86% of PKD patients (mean age of ESRD: 57 years)
- **PKD2**: chromosome 4 in 10% (ESRD mean age: 69 years)

The diagnosis is usually made by ultrasound; cysts usually develop during the teenage years so that first-degree relatives aged >20 years, with a normal scan, can be >90% confident of being disease-free; the confidence level rises to 98% at 30 years of age. Cysts develop from all segments of the nephron. The prevalence of ADPKD is 1 in 1000; the condition accounts for about 10% of RRT patients in the UK.

Diagnostic criteria for ADPKD

In a patient known to be at 50% risk because of family history, diagnosis would be suggested by the following ultrasound findings:

- Two cysts, either unilateral or bilateral, if aged <30 years
- Two cysts in each kidney in patients aged 30–59 years
- Four cysts in each kidney in patients >60 years

Sporadic cases (no family history) are also commonly seen.

Clinical features

Patients may present with abdominal pain or mass, hypertension, urinary tract infection (UTI), renal calculi (10%), macroscopic haematuria or CKD.

- The age of onset of CKD varies widely (eg 25–60 years); not all patients develop ESRD
- In patients known to have ADPKD, intermittent presentation with severe abdominal pain is

common, but, apart from UTI and calculi, the exact cause may be difficult to identify (cyst expansion, cyst rupture, intracystic haemorrhage)

- **Treatment** of the progressive CKD in ADPKD is as for other chronic nephropathies (ie hypertension control, RAA blockade, prevention of CVS complications). New therapeutic agents that limit cyst development and expansion, and possibly progressive CKD, are currently under investigation

Associations of ADPKD*

- Liver cysts: 70%
- Hepatic fibrosis (rare)
- Berry aneurysms: 8% (see below)
- Diverticular disease
- Pancreatic cysts: 10%
- Mitral valve prolapse or aortic incompetence

*There is no increased incidence of renal malignancy in ADPKD (see von Hippel–Lindau syndrome below)

Intracranial aneurysms in ADPKD

These occur in 5% of ADPKD patients, but familial clustering is seen (ie if family history of aneurysms, then >20% of patients with ADPKD will have them). The majority are asymptomatic; the risk of rupture increases with aneurysm size (eg 4% per year if >10 mm). Rupture is associated with a 30%–50% chance of severe morbidity/mortality. Most patients have normal renal function at the time of rupture. There is currently some debate as to the value of screening (with MR angiography) for intra-cranial aneurysms in ADPKD.

15.7.2 Other renal cystic disorders

- **Autosomal recessive PKD**: rare (1/10 000 births). The gene is localised to chromosome 6. ESRD develops early in childhood; 100% have hepatic fibrosis. The prognosis is poor
- **von Hippel–Lindau (VHL) syndrome**: autosomal dominant, the gene is localised on chromo-

some 3. Renal cysts are premalignant (>50%) and prophylactic bilateral nephrectomy is often necessary. It is likely that patients previously thought to have renal malignancy in association with ADPKD actually had VHL. Patients are also at risk of multiple spinocerebellar haemangioblastomas (which can be severely debilitating and are the main determinant of outcome in patients who are successfully transplanted), retinal angiomas, pancreatic cysts, islet cell tumours and phaeochromocytoma

- **Tuberous sclerosis**: dominantly inherited (either chromosome 9 or 16), and affects 1 in 10 000 individuals; patients develop epilepsy (80%), mental retardation (50%), hamartomas, renal cysts and angiomyolipomas (usually do not require surgery). Skin lesions include shagreen patches, ash-leaf spots and adenoma sebaceum
- **Juvenile nephronophthisis-medullary cystic disease complex**: two different terms are used for two similar diseases which differ only in their age of onset and mode of transmission. Cysts occur in the renal medulla, and patients have chronic tubulointerstitial nephritis, salt-wasting and progressive CKD. **Juvenile nephronophthisis (NPH)** occurs in children, is autosomal recessive, and accounts for up to 15% of childhood ESRD; 10%–15% of children have retinal abnormalities (a form of retinitis pigmentosa). In adults a histopathologically identical disease, **autosomal dominant medullary cystic disease**, leads to ESRD in the third and fourth decades; it is uncommon and is not associated with extrarenal abnormalities
- **Medullary sponge kidney (MSK)**: sporadic; the cysts develop from ectatic collecting ducts. These may calcify, leading to the classic nephrocalcinosis associated with MSK. The disease runs a benign course except that renal calculi and upper urinary tract infections are commonly associated
- **Acquired cystic disease**: cystic change is common in the rudimentary kidneys of dialysis patients, and especially in scarred kidneys; most cysts develop from proximal tubules. They are present in >5% of patients at the onset of RRT, and in >80% after 10 years of dialysis.

Malignant change is thought to occur with an annual incidence of about 1%

- **Simple cysts**: fluid-filled, solitary or multiple, these are usually harmless, incidental findings at ultrasound or IVU. The cysts may grow to a considerable size (eg >10 cm). They occasionally require percutaneous drainage because of persistent loin pain. Simple cysts are very common, affecting 2% of patients aged <50 years, 11% aged 50–70 years and >20% of the elderly. The **Bosniak system** is used to classify the malignant risk of renal cysts (categorisation depends upon the presence of cyst wall thickening, calcification, septations and solid components). A Bosniak I cyst is simple; category IV, malignant. Category II and III cysts are 'indeterminate' and may require more investigation and follow-up

15.7.3 Alport syndrome

The prevalence of Alport syndrome is 1/5000 individuals. Genetic associations vary; 85% have X-linked dominant inheritance, but other families may show dominant or recessive inheritance. The primary defect is an abnormal GBM (seen at electron microscopy) with variable thickness and splitting ('basket weave' appearance); the Goodpasture antigen is absent in the GBM (hence the predisposition of patients to anti-GBM glomerulonephritis after transplantation).

- Clinical presentation is with deafness (see below), persistent microscopic haematuria, proteinuria and CKD; 30% develop nephrotic syndrome
- Renal failure develops in all affected males; the rate of progression is heterogeneous between families (ie ESRD before 30 years in some, yet only by 60 years in others)

- Carrier females may have urinary abnormalities (haematuria, proteinuria), and usually do not develop renal failure
- **Bilateral sensorineural deafness** is characteristic, but the hearing loss may only be mild; familial progressive nephritis may occasionally occur without deafness
- **Other extrarenal manifestations**: ocular abnormalities occur in 40% (**lenticonus** – conical or spherical protrusion of the surface of the lens into the anterior chamber, retinal flecks or cataracts); macrothrombocytopenia; leiomyomata (rare)
- The molecular defect involves the gene encoding for the α5 chain of type IV collagen; alteration of this chain is thought to prevent integration of the α3 chain into the GBM

15.7.4 Benign familial haematuria (BFH) and thin-membrane nephropathy

Up to 25% of patients referred to a nephrologist for investigation of microscopic haematuria have this condition. It is common in families, when it is termed '**benign familial haematuria**'; the inheritance pattern is dominant although the gene has not been identified. Sporadic cases are designated as '**thin-membrane nephropathy**'. The normal thickness of the GBM is around 450 nm; patients with BFH/thin-membrane nephropathy have an average GBM thickness of <250 nm. Patients usually have normal blood pressure and renal function; long-term follow-up is recommended as there appears to be a very small risk of renal failure (perhaps because some patients represent variants of Alport syndrome, or IgA nephropathy may co-exist).

15.7.5 Other inherited disorders associated with renal disease

The list is far from comprehensive as many rare disorders have been described.

- **Conditions associated with renal structural disorders**
  - Cystic renal diseases (see above)
  - Brachio-oto-renal syndrome (AD)
  - Dandy–Walker syndrome (polycystic kidneys (AR))
- **Inherited conditions with glomerular disease**
  - Alport syndrome and variants (see above)
  - Congenital nephrotic syndrome (eg Finnish-type (AR))
  - Nail–patella syndrome (AD)
  - Familial glomerulonephritis (eg some forms of FSGS or IgA nephropathy; Wiskott–Aldrich syndrome (XL))
  - Inherited complement deficiency
  - Charcot–Marie–Tooth disease (?AD)
- **Metabolic disorders with renal involvement**
  - Fabry disease (XL)
  - Primary amyloidosis (AD)
  - Familial Mediterranean fever (AR)
  - Cystinosis (AR)
  - Primary oxalosis (AR)
- **Inherited tubular disorders**
  - Cystinuria (AR)
  - Shwachman syndrome (AR)
  - Marble brain disease (AR)
  - Hypophosphatasia (AR)
- **Renal diseases which have genetic influence**
  - Benign familial haematuria (AD)
  - Reflux nephropathy

AD = autosomal dominant; AR = autosomal recessive; XL = X-linked

15.8 RENAL INTERSTITIAL DISORDERS

15.8.1 Interstitial nephritis

Inflammation of the renal tubulointerstitium may be acute or chronic; a recognised precipitating cause can be found in the majority of patients.

Acute interstitial nephritis (AIN)

AIN accounts for about 2% of all AKI cases, but for 25% of all drug-induced AKI. Most cases are due to an immunologically induced hypersensitivity reaction to an antigen – classically a drug (see below) or an infectious agent. The presentation is usually with mild renal impairment and hypertension or, in more severe cases, AKI which is often non-oliguric. Systemic manifestations of hypersensitivity may occur and include fever, arthralgia, rash, eosinophilia and raised IgE.

- **Diagnosis**: urinalysis may be unremarkable (eg minor proteinuria), although urinary eosinophils may be present. If >1% of urinary white cells are eosinophils, then this suggests the diagnosis. Renal biopsy shows oedema of the interstitium with infiltration of plasma cells, lymphocytes and eosinophils; there is often ATN with variable tubular dilatation. Occasionally there is a granulomatous reaction (sarcoidosis can cause AIN). Note that AIN may need to be distinguished from acute pyelonephritis, in which condition most of the inflammatory infiltrate will be composed of neutrophils
- **Treatment**: cessation of precipitating cause (eg drugs). Most cases will improve without further treatment, but studies show that moderate-dose oral steroids (eg 1 mg/kg, tapered over 1 month) can hasten recovery of renal function. Most patients make a near-complete renal functional recovery

Causes of acute interstitial nephritis

- **Idiopathic** (rare – can be associated with anterior uveitis)
- **Infections**
  - Viral (eg Hanta virus), bacterial (eg leptospirosis), mycobacterial
- **Drugs**
  - eg rifampicin, allopurinol, methicillin, **penicillin**, **cephalosporins**, sulphonamides, furosemide, thiazides, cimetidine, amphotericin, aspirin, **NSAIDs**
- **Others**, eg sarcoidosis, Sjögren syndrome

Causes of chronic interstitial nephritis

- **Immunological diseases**
  - eg SLE, Sjögren syndrome, rheumatoid arthritis, systemic sclerosis
- **Haematological disorders**
  - Myeloma, light-chain nephropathy, sickle cell disease
- **Heavy metals (and other toxins)**
  - eg lead, cadmium, Chinese herb nephropathy (*see* Section 15.13.3 Toxic nephropathy)
- **Metabolic disorders**
  - eg hypercalcaemia, hypokalaemia, hyperuricaemia
- **Other**
  - Irradiation, chronic transplant rejection
- **Granulomatous disease**
  - Wegener's, TB, sarcoidosis
- **Drugs**
  - Ciclosporin A, cisplatin, lithium, iron, analgesics (*see* Section 15.8.2)
- **Chronic infections**
  - Chronic pyelonephritis (TB)
- **Hereditary disorders**
  - eg nephronophthisis, Alport's
- **Endemic disease**
  - Balkan nephropathy (see below)

Chronic tubulointerstitial nephritis (TIN)

Many diverse systemic and local renal conditions can result in chronic inflammation within the tubulointerstitium. Patients present with CKD or ESRD; some patients may also manifest RTA (usually type 1), nephrogenic diabetes insipidus (DI) or salt-wasting states. Renal biopsy findings involve a chronic inflammatory infiltrate within the interstitium (granulomatous in sarcoid and TB), often with extensive scarring and tubular loss; the latter indicates that renal function can never be fully recovered.

Certain common causes of CKD are associated with TIN and macroscopically abnormal kidneys – eg reflux nephropathy, analgesic nephropathy, obstructive and cystic renal disease. However, **TIN with macroscopically normal kidneys** accounts for about 3% of all ESRD, and is seen with Sjögren syndrome, lithium toxicity, urate nephropathy, heavy metal nephropathy and Balkan nephropathy (see following box).

Treatment of TIN

This is of the underlying condition (or drug/toxin withdrawal); steroids may be beneficial in some autoimmune or inflammatory disorders. The progressive CKD is treated as for other chronic nephropathies.

Balkan nephropathy

A chronic interstitial renal disease endemic in villages along the tributaries of the River Danube (eg in Romania, Bulgaria, Bosnia, Croatia). There is extensive scarring, and patients progress to ESRD.

- Urothelial malignancy is increased 200-fold
- Patients have coppery yellow pigmentation of palms and soles
- **Aetiology**: initially thought to be a chronic toxic nephropathy (eg trace metals in water) or viral infection. Although recent evidence has suggested that chronic exposure to a fungal toxin (eg ochratoxins, products of the fungus *Penicillium*, which may grow in stored maize) may be important, genetic studies suggest an underlying dominant inheritance pattern, with a marker on chromosome 3. It is suspected that the environmental factors modify the expression of the genetic predisposition

15.8.2 Analgesic nephropathy and papillary necrosis

Analgesic nephropathy

In the 1950s to 1970s analgesic nephropathy was the most common cause of both AKI and CKD in parts of Europe and Australia (eg 25% of ESRD in Australia). The condition is now uncommon, especially since the withdrawal of phenacetin from the pharmaceutical market; aspirin and NSAIDs are now the most common causative agents. The hallmarks of the condition are the history of chronic analgesic usage (eg for backache, pelvic inflammatory disease, headache) and of addictive or dependent personality traits, renal pain (due to papillary necrosis) and CKD. There is a classic radiological appearance on IVU – 'cup and spill' calyces due to papillary necrosis, with renal scarring.

- Renal biopsy is of no diagnostic value
- Women are affected more often than men (4:1)
- As with other TIN, nephrogenic DI, salt-wasting and distal RTA can be associated
- Increased risk of urothelial malignancy (there may be multiple synchronous lesions)

- Patients are at a threefold increased risk of CVS disease (contributed to by hypertension, hyperlipidaemia, smoking and formation of atherogenic oxidised LDL)

Causes of renal papillary necrosis

- **Toxic**
  - Classic analgesic nephropathy
  - TB
- **Ischaemic**
  - Sickle cell disease
  - Acute pyelonephritis
  - Accelerated hypertension
  - Profound shock
  - Diabetes mellitus
  - Urinary tract obstruction
  - Hyperviscosity syndromes
  - NSAID-induced

15.9 REFLUX NEPHROPATHY AND URINARY TRACT INFECTIONS

15.9.1 Vesico-ureteric reflux and reflux nephropathy

Reflux nephropathy is the term applied when small and irregularly scarred kidneys (**chronic pyelonephritis, CPN**) are associated with **vesico-ureteric reflux (VUR)**. It is the commonest cause of CPN, but other disorders such as obstructive injury and analgesic nephropathy can also result in CPN. Renal scarring is necessary for the diagnosis of reflux nephropathy and this almost only occurs during the first 5 years of life. The end result of reflux nephropathy is hypertension, proteinuria, CKD and, sometimes, ESRD; reflux nephropathy still accounts for at least 10% of adult patients entering RRT programmes, and is the commonest cause of ESRD in children.

- **Epidemiology**: VUR is very common in utero, and 0.5% of all neonates are affected. Around 1% of children will have VUR, but this disappears in 40% by the age of 2 years. In young children VUR usually presents with a complicating UTI. About 30% of children with UTI will have some degree of VUR and 10% will have evidence of reflux nephropathy; 5% of women with symptomatic UTI will have reflux nephropathy. However, documented UTI occurs in <50% of adults with reflux nephropathy

- **Grading**: reflux can be graded: from grade I (involving reflux into the ureter only) to grade V (gross dilatation and tortuosity of ureter, renal pelvis and calyces with severe scarring) – see Figure 15.4
- **Diagnosis** is by micturating cystography (radionuclides can be used in children); scarring can be demonstrated by ultrasound and DMSA
- **Pathogenesis of renal scarring**: scars will only form if there is intrarenal reflux accompanied by urinary infection. The scars form at the sites of the intrarenal reflux; severity of scarring is proportional to the degree of VUR. Note that there is no evidence that UTI occurring without VUR will lead to scarring

- **Genetic predisposition**: first-degree relatives of patients with reflux have a greatly increased (eg > 25%) chance of VUR; it is recommended that offspring or siblings (if a child) of affected patients undergo screening. The gene is thought to be dominant but its effect is modified by environmental factors; the gene frequency has been estimated to be 1 in 600

Management of VUR and reflux nephropathy

All children with UTI should be investigated for VUR. The aim of treatment for patients with VUR is to prevent renal scars. As these occur early in life there is no place for anti-reflux surgery to prevent renal scars in adults who have VUR. Few surgeons operate on children with grades I–III reflux as these tend to resolve spontaneously; those with grade II or worse reflux should receive prophylactic antibiotic therapy (eg low-dose nitrofurantoin, trimethoprim or co-trimoxazole, or cefalexin in those with CKD) until puberty in order to limit UTIs.

Figure 15.4 Classification of vesico-ureteric reflux

Grade I: Ureter only
Grade II: Up to pelvis and calyces, but with no dilatation
Grade III: Mild-moderate dilatation, but with only minimal blunting of fornices
Grade IV: Moderate dilatation, with obliteration of sharp angles of fornices
Grade V: Gross dilatation and tortuosity of ureter and pelvi-calyceal system. Calyces severely clubbed

There is now debate as to the best management of patients with grades IV and V VUR. Surgery (eg endoscopic injection of collagen behind the intravesical ureter, lengthening of the submucosal ureteric tunnel and ureteric re-implantation) has its protagonists. However, other clinicians would advocate long-term antibiotics (as above). Whichever the approach, UTI should be treated promptly and, as with all forms of chronic, potentially progressive renal disorders, hypertension must be controlled properly (with RAA blockade favoured). Patients with reflux nephropathy have an increased incidence of renal calculi.

15.9.2 Urinary tract infection (UTI)

Apart from the outer one-third of the female urethra, the urinary tract is normally sterile. UTIs are the commonest bacterial infections managed in general practice; they predominantly affect women (except in infants, patients aged >60 years, and those with co-morbid diseases). Coliforms are by far the most common pathogens. Several important definitions are applied:

- **Acute uncomplicated UTI**: **acute cystitis** and **acute pyelonephritis**. The incidence of cystitis is 0.5% per year in sexually active women. It may recur in 40% of healthy women, even when their urinary tracts are normal. Three-day antibiotic treatment regimes are recommended for acute cystitis because of cost, compliance and efficacy. In those with recurrent cystitis, attention to hygiene, post-coital micturition and fluid intake are recommended; in post-menopausal women, intravaginal oestrogen pessaries may be beneficial, probably because of alteration of vaginal flora
- **Complicated UTI**: these occur in patients with abnormal urinary tracts (eg stones, obstruction, ileal conduits, VUR, neuropathic bladder) and very commonly in patients with urinary catheters (see below). The definition also incorporates UTI in patients with advanced CKD and renal transplants
- **Asymptomatic bacteriuria**: two separate urinary specimens showing bacterial colony counts of >10^5/ml of the same organism in an asymptomatic patient. The prevalence may be 3%–5% in adult women (and 0.5% in men); it increases greatly in the elderly (eg 50% of women) and in institutionalised patients. The vast majority of cases require no treatment, but it should always be treated if detected in pregnant women, as 15%–20% will otherwise develop acute pyelonephritis (*see* Chapter 12, Maternal Medicine)
- **Urethral syndrome**: patients have 'abacterial' cystitis. Causes include true recurrent UTI (but with low bacterial counts), and genital (eg *Chlamydia*), vaginal (eg *Trichomonas* or *Candida*) or fastidious organism (eg *Ureaplasma*, *Lactobacillus*) infections. Postmenopausal women may develop the syndrome because of atrophic vaginitis due to oestrogen deficiency

Long-term antibiotic treatment regimes: these may be appropriate for patients prone to recurrent UTI, and especially in those with an underlying predisposition (except those with urinary catheters). The regimes may involve rotating monthly antibiotic courses (eg amoxicillin, a quinolone and a cephalosporin) or low-dose, once-daily, long-term nitrofurantoin or trimethoprim.

Predispositions to urinary tract infection

- **Abnormal urinary tract**
  - eg calculi, VUR, reflux nephropathy, analgesic nephropathy, obstruction, atonic bladder, ileal conduit, indwelling catheter
- **Pregnancy** (where the urinary tract abnormality – eg ureteral dilatation – is temporary)
- **Impaired host defences**
  - Immunosuppressive therapy (including transplanted patients), diabetes mellitus, atrophic vaginitis
- **Virulent organisms**
  - (eg urease-producing *Proteus*)

Other specific forms of UTI

- **Urinary catheter-associated infection**: up to 5% of all hospital admissions may be due to nosocomial UTI, and the majority of these occur in patients with long-term indwelling catheters. The incidence of bacteriuria is 3%–10% per day of catheterisation, and so the duration of catheterisation is the greatest risk factor. Most infections are asymptomatic, but catheter-associated infections are the commonest source of Gram –ve septicaemia in hospitalised patients. Most cases of 'infection' do not require treatment; if lower urinary tract symptoms occur, a single antibiotic dose may be as effective as a full course of therapy (which predisposes to bacterial resistance), and the catheter should be changed. For prevention of UTI in patients with long-term catheters, regular (eg 3-monthly) catheter change is recommended as organisms are harboured within the biofilm lining of the catheter
- **Prostatitis**: prostatitic symptoms are experienced by 50% of men, but are caused by bacteria in only a minority. **Acute bacterial prostatitis** is rare; patients present with symptoms of cystitis and the prostate is swollen and tender. There will be pyuria and a positive urine culture. The commonest pathogens are the Gram –ve bacilli, *Escherichia coli*, *Proteus* and *Klebsiella*. Antibiotic treatment is needed for 1 month. **Chronic prostatitis** is manifest by recurrent UTI with the same organism. It is characterised by a qualitative difference in the first voided urine (no pyuria), compared with that passed after prostatic massage (>10 white blood cells per high-power field, bacterial colony count 10-fold greater). Treatment is with quinolone antibiotics for 1–3 months
- **Renal abscess**: usually due to *Staphylococcus aureus* after haematogenous spread to the kidney. May present as a renal mass but renal abscesses are often insidious and non-specific. CT is needed for diagnosis. Treatment is with antibiotics, percutaneous drainage for larger abscesses and sometimes nephrectomy

- **Emphysematous pyelonephritis**: this is a necrotising, life-threatening form of acute pyelonephritis caused by gas-forming organisms (including *E. coli*, *Pseudomonas*, *Klebsiella* and *Proteus*); 90% of cases occur in diabetics. Plain X-ray will demonstrate the gas, but CT will localise this better. Emergency nephrectomy and broad-spectrum antibiotics are required, but even then mortality is 20%
- **Xanthogranulomatous pyelonephritis**: this is a rare chronic renal infection that is associated with obstruction. Renal tissue is replaced with lipid-laden infiltrating macrophages (foam cells); the xanthomatous tissue may extend beyond the renal capsule into neighbouring structures. Patients are usually middle-aged women with flank pain, fever, a palpable renal mass and positive MSU. Nephrectomy provides the only chance of cure

15.9.3 Tuberculosis of the urinary tract

TB reaches the urinary tract via haematogenous spread. Most patients are 20–40 years of age, with men affected twice as commonly as women. Twenty-five per cent of patients are asymptomatic; a further 25% have asymptomatic pyuria or microscopic haematuria, and painless macrohaematuria is common. Hypertension is unusual, but genital involvement (epididymitis and prostatitis in men, salpingitis and pelvic pain in women) is commonly associated.

- The renal medullary regions are most commonly affected. In the early stages, ulcerating lesions and granulomas are seen in the renal pyramids and collecting systems; renal histology shows chronic interstitial nephritis with granulomas
- As the disease progresses scarring occurs with ureteric strictures, hydronephrosis, subcapsular collections, perinephric abscesses or renal atrophy. The bladder may be fibrotic and small. The caseating material may eventually calcify
- **Treatment**: standard anti-tuberculous therapy is recommended. Surgery may be indicated for obstruction and strictures. Nephrectomy for

non-functioning kidneys is no longer routine as prolonged anti-TB therapy can render the calcified, caseous masses ('cement kidney') sterile

15.10 RENAL CALCULI AND NEPHROCALCINOSIS

15.10.1 Renal calculi (nephrolithiasis)

Renal stones are common, with an annual incidence of approximately 2 per 1000 and a prevalence of 3% in the UK. Calcium-containing stones account for >70%.

Stone composition

- Calcium oxalate: 25%
- Mixed calcium oxalate/phosphate: 40%
- Calcium phosphate: 5%
- Urate: 10% (radiolucent)
- Cystine: 2%
- Xanthine: 1% (radiolucent)
- Staghorn ('struvite' containing magnesium ammonium phosphate and sometimes calcium): 20%; associated with infection with urease-producing bacteria (eg *Proteus* spp.)

Basic investigations

This should include stone analysis, MSU, assessment of renal function, serum calcium and phosphate, and a qualitative test for urinary cystine. The 24-hour urinary excretion of oxalate, calcium, creatinine and uric acid may also be helpful, and RTA should be excluded (urine pH).

Conditions predisposing to urolithiasis

- **Metabolic abnormalities**
  - Idiopathic hypercalciuria (most common)
  - Primary hyperparathyroidism (and other causes of hypercalcaemia)
  - Renal tubular acidosis
  - Cystinuria
  - Hyperoxaluria (primary or secondary)
  - High dietary oxalate intake (eg glutinous rice or leafy vegetables in Thailand)
  - Uric aciduria
  - Hypocitraturia (eg chronic diarrhoea, excess laxative and diuretic use)
- **Renal structural abnormalities**
  - Polycystic kidney disease
  - Medullary sponge kidney
  - Reflux nephropathy
  - Nephrocalcinosis (*see* Section 15.10.2)
- **Other causes**
  - Chronic dehydration - common (eg chronic diarrhoea, warm climates)
  - Triamterene
  - Industrial exposure to cadmium or beryllium

Treatment

General measures: increased fluid intake and low protein diet; reduced dietary oxalate intake. Associated urinary infection should be eradicated where possible (very difficult with staghorn calculi). Treat other underlying causes (eg allopurinol for urate stones, surgery for hyperparathyroidism).

Thiazide diuretics (eg chlortalidone): increase tubular absorption of calcium in patients with hypercalciuria, and will therefore reduce the likelihood of super-saturation of calcium products within the urine. Citrate may be beneficial for calcium oxalate stones.

The specific treatment of patients with **cystinuria** is described in Chapter 13, Metabolic Diseases.

Stone removal: ureteric calculi <0.5 cm may be passed spontaneously. Lithotripsy alone may be used for larger ureteric stones and for pelvicalyceal stones <4 cm (obstruction being prevented by double J-stent insertion); larger calculi can be 'de-bulked' by this technique before surgical extraction.

15.10.2 Nephrocalcinosis

This is defined as the deposition of calcium salts within the renal parenchyma; it may be associated with urinary calculi.

Causes of nephrocalcinosis

- **Cortical nephrocalcinosis**
  - Cortical necrosis – after very severe acute ischaemic injury to the kidneys (see 'tram-line' calcification)
  - Chronic glomerulonephritis
- **Medullary nephrocalcinosis**
  - Hypercalcaemia (eg primary hyperparathyroidism, sarcoidosis, hypervitaminosis D, milk–alkali syndrome)
  - Idiopathic hypercalciuria
  - Renal tubular acidosis
  - Primary hyperoxaluria
  - Berylliosis
  - Thyrotoxicosis
  - Sulphonamides
  - Medullary sponge kidney
  - Tuberculosis

15.11 URINARY TRACT OBSTRUCTION AND TUMOURS

15.11.1 Urinary tract obstruction

Chronic urinary tract obstruction (most often due to prostatic disease, calculi and bladder lesions) is a common cause of CKD; obstruction must also be excluded in every case of unexplained AKI. The causes of renal tract obstruction are shown in the box opposite. The term **obstructive nephropathy** refers to pathological renal damage resulting from obstruction.

Acute obstruction

This is often painful due to distension of the bladder, ureter(s) or pelvicalyceal systems. Complete obstruction will result in anuria and AKI; anuria may also occur even when obstruction is unilateral, due to an intense afferent arteriolar vasoconstriction (similar to that seen in ischaemic AKI).

- **Diagnosis**: obstruction is one of the few truly reversible causes of renal failure, but diagnosis and treatment need to be expedient in order to allow renal functional recovery. Ultrasound is the chief mode of diagnosis, but it may only show minimal pelvicalyceal dilatation in the early stages of acute obstruction
- **Treatment and prognosis**: temporary drainage can often be achieved by percutaneous nephrostomy or by endoscopic ureteric stenting, pending definitive surgical correction. Relief of obstruction may be followed by massive diuresis (temporary nephrogenic DI), but if the obstruction has been relieved within 2 weeks then full renal functional recovery is likely, unless there is complicating pyonephrosis

Chronic obstructive nephropathy

This is usually associated with CKD or ESRD and it is often complicated by chronic UTI. Obstruction accounts for 5% of all cases of ESRD. Salt-wasting nephropathy and chronic metabolic acidosis are common, the latter contributing to the advanced renal bone disease recognised in some patients.

- **Differential diagnosis**: there may be diagnostic uncertainty when the upper tracts are dilated (but non-obstructed). This is seen in VUR, post-obstructive atrophy, congenital mega-calyces and mega-ureters and in some cases of CPN. In such cases diuresis renography or retrograde pyelography will exclude obstruction. Occasionally, the Whitaker test, which involves puncture of the collecting system followed by pressure flow studies, is necessary to diagnose obstruction
- **Pathology and outcome**: there is permanent renal histopathological damage that results from a combination of parenchymal compression, renal ischaemia and sometimes infection. In severe cases severe tubular loss, interstitial fibrosis and cortical atrophy are observed. If the obstruction is relieved (eg in <12 weeks), renal functional decline can stabilise and dialysis may be prevented

Causes of urinary tract obstruction

- **Within the lumen**
  - Tumour (eg urothelial lesions of bladder, ureter or renal pelvis)
  - Renal calculi
  - Papillary necrosis (sloughed papilla)
  - Blood clot
- **External compression**
  - Malignancy: retroperitoneal neoplasia including para-aortic lymphadenopathy and pelvic cancer (eg cervical or prostatic carcinoma)
  - Other 'tumours': aortic aneurysm; pregnancy (hydronephrosis of pregnancy is very common, is usually asymptomatic, and resolves fully after delivery); haematomas
  - Aberrant arteries (PUJ obstruction)
  - Retroperitoneal fibrosis (eg malignant, idiopathic, peri-aortitis, drugs (see below))
  - Prostatic disease: benign hypertrophy or malignancy

  - Inflammatory disorders (eg diverticulitis, Crohn's disease, pancreatitis)
  - Iatrogenic, eg accidental surgical ligation of the ureter
- **Within the wall of urinary tract structures**
  - Neuromuscular dysfunction (eg pelvi-ureteric junction (PUJ) obstruction, neuropathic bladder (spina bifida, spinal trauma – see below))
  - Ureteric or vesico-ureteric stricture: TB, schistosomiasis, previous calculi, after surgery, congenital, irradiation (eg for seminoma of testis), malignancy, ureterocele
  - Urethral stricture (eg gonococcal) following instrumentation
  - Posterior urethral valves (see below)
  - Congenital bladder neck obstruction

Neuropathic bladder

In childhood, **spina bifida** with myelomeningocele is by far the commonest cause of a neuropathic bladder. Spina bifida has an incidence of around 1–2 per 1000 births; siblings of affected individuals have a 10- to 20-fold chance of having the condition. Urinary tract complications are present at birth in 15%, and will develop in 50%, often over many years. Most of these patients have incomplete bladder emptying due to urethral sphincter dyssynergia, but those with the mildest neurological lesions are paradoxically able to generate very high pressures within the bladder, with greatest risk of renal damage.

- The main urinary tract abnormalities are incontinence, infection and reflux with upper tract dilatation, the latter leading to CKD and ESRD
- Patients often have associated bowel dysfunction
- **Treatment** is with anticholinergic drugs, intermittent self-catheterisation and, in more severe cases, urinary tract diversion into an ileal conduit. Note that chronically infected urinary tracts will need to be removed prior to renal transplantation

Posterior urethral valves (PUV)

These occur in male infants and account for 10% of childhood hydronephrosis; the valves are mucosal diaphragms in the posterior urethra at the level of the prostate. PUV can now be detected antenatally with ultrasound. Fifty per cent of patients present before the first year of life with poor urinary stream, distended bladder and failure to thrive (due to renal failure). Most have VUR and dilated upper tracts.

- **Treatment**: urinary diversion should be avoided; self-catheterisation is usually necessary. Approximately 20% of affected individuals will progress to ESRD, largely because of late initial presentation

15.11.2   Retroperitoneal fibrosis (RPF)

An uncommon, progressive condition in which the ureters become embedded in dense fibrous tissue (the ureters are drawn medially) often at the junction of the middle and lower thirds of the ureter, leading to obstruction. The majority of cases are thought to result from an immunologically mediated peri-aortitis, and steroids are of benefit in these 'idiopathic' forms of RPF.

- **Other associations**: retroperitoneal malignancy (eg colonic, bladder or prostatic cancer, lymphoma), previous irradiation, inflammatory abdominal aortic aneurysm, other fibrosing conditions (eg mediastinal fibrosis, sclerosing cholangitis), drugs (eg methysergide and some β-blockers) and granulomatous disease (TB or sarcoidosis)
- **Investigation**: ESR is often very high, IVU shows medial deviation of the ureters and a peri-aortic mass may be seen at CT scan
- **Treatment**: ureterolysis (with tissue biopsy) with long-term steroid therapy (as relapse is common). Malignant RPF can be palliated with ureteric stenting, or with percutaneous nephrostomy

15.11.3   Urinary tract tumours

Benign renal tumours: include adenomata, which are very common (however, just as with thyroid adenoma and carcinoma, their histological differentiation from malignant lesions can be difficult), hamartomas and renin-secreting (juxtaglomerular cell) tumours.

Renal cell carcinoma (hypernephroma): arise from the tubular epithelium; they are more common in smokers, and at least 50% of patients with von Hippel–Lindau syndrome will develop them (usually multiple and bilateral). As mentioned previously, **acquired cystic kidney disease** in patients with renal failure is also a risk factor; the cumulative incidence of malignant change is about 1%, and accounts for 80% of renal cell carcinomas in dialysis patients.

- Renal cell carcinoma has a propensity to invade the renal veins, with passage of tumour emboli to the lung
- Other unusual clinical features include pyrexia of unknown origin (PUO), left varicocele (renal vein invasion leads to left testicular vein occlusion), and endocrine effects (secretion of erythropoietic factor resulting in polycythaemia (3%), PTH-like substance, renin and ACTH). Five-year survival is about 50%

Wilms' tumour (nephroblastoma): these are tumours of early childhood, and are derived from embryonic renal tissue (so containing combinations of poorly differentiated epithelium and connective tissues). They can become enormous and metastasise early. Treatment is with nephrectomy and actinomycin D, providing a 3-year survival rate of 65%.

Urothelial tumours: very common and usually derived from transitional epithelium, although squamous carcinoma (worse prognosis) is recognised. The usual presentation is with bleeding or urinary tract obstruction. Tumours are often multiple, and so investigation of the complete urinary tract is indicated.

- Several carcinogens (eg smoking, rubber and aniline dye exposure, analgesic nephropathy) have been aetiologically linked to this type of malignancy
- Other risk factors include renal calculi, cystic kidney disease, chronic cystitis and *Schistosoma haematobium* infection (note that *Schistosoma mansoni* is associated with glomerulonephritis)
- Nephro-ureterectomy is indicated for lesions of ureter or renal pelvis, and cystectomy with resection of urethral mucosa for advanced bladder cancer; surgery combined with radiotherapy provides a 5-year survival rate of 50%

Metastatic disease (involving the kidney): most commonly from breast, lung, stomach, lymphoma or melanoma.

15.12 SYSTEMIC DISORDERS AND THE KIDNEY

15.12.1 Amyloidosis

Amyloidosis occurs when certain proteins, most of which are normal constituents of plasma, develop a particular conformational pattern (β-pleated sheet) and are deposited in an organised formation within organs. Twenty-five different amyloid proteins are now recognised: some are abnormal, others genetically derived, and in the commoner forms of amyloid there is over-production of the protein. Kidney involvement leads to presentation with proteinuria, nephrotic syndrome or CKD; biopsy demonstrates characteristic Congo-red-staining extracellular fibrillar material within the mesangium, interstitium and vessel walls. Radionuclide scan (amyloid fibrils labelled with ^{123}I localise to amyloid deposits after injection) is used to demonstrate the full extent of disease in all organs. Amyloid is classified according to the amyloid proteins involved, as well as the underlying disease process.

Immunologoglubulinic amyloid (AL-amyloidosis)

The incidence of AL-amyloidosis is 9 per million/year. Free immunoglobulin light chains (hence the 'L') are secreted by a clone of B cells; 25% of patients have an underlying immunoproliferative disease (usually myeloma), but many more probably have a monoclonal gammopathy (MGUS). Median age of presentation is above 60 years.

- Nephrotic syndrome, postural hypotension and peripheral neuropathy are more likely in cases without myeloma
- AL-amyloid may infiltrate any organ other than the brain – eg heart (restrictive cardiomyopathy in 30%, sick sinus syndrome and arrhythmias), macroglossia, GI tract (motility disturbance, malabsorption, haemorrhage), neuropathy (peripheral and autonomic) and bleeding diathesis
- **Treatment**: cases associated with myeloma receive conventional therapy. In 'primary amyloid', regimes involving prednisolone with either melphalan or colchicine have been shown to extend survival duration by only 50% (see below). Autologous bone marrow transplantation (after high-dose chemotherapy) provides the only prospect of cure
- **Prognosis**: when patients present with renal complications prognosis is poor, with a median survival of 12 months, and only 25% alive at 3 years. Survival is shorter in those with myeloma, heart disease and autonomic neuropathy. Cardiac involvement accounts for half of deaths

AA-amyloidosis

Chronic infections (eg TB, empyema) now account for fewer cases than previously; 70% are due to autoimmune inflammatory conditions (eg rheumatoid arthritis). In these conditions the amyloid protein A is derived from acute phase reactants, and is made in the liver. In AA-amyloidosis the kidney is the main target organ – cardiac involvement and neuropathy are uncommon. Prognosis is consequently better than for AL-amyloidosis, with median survival of 25 months and 40% 3-year survival.

Treatment: the underlying inflammatory or infective disorder should be treated. Although previously there has been little apparent benefit from specific drug therapy, colchicine has been shown to prevent disease progression in **familial Mediterranean fever** (another form of AA-amyloidosis), which is encouraging. It has been trialled in patients with rheumatoid arthritis with some success. A few patients with AA-amyloidosis have received renal transplants; recurrent amyloid is seen in >10%.

Classification of amyloidosis

- **Primary amyloid**
- **AL type**, which is serum amyloid protein A coupled with immunoglobulin light chains
- **Hereditary amyloid** (eg familial Mediterranean fever)
  - Fibrils are formed from other proteins (lysosomes, apolipoproteins, fibrinogen); the amyloid is of **AA type**
- **Secondary amyloid** (this is usually **AA type** (fibrils derived from acute phase proteins)
- **Secondary to chronic suppurative disorders**
  - Tuberculosis, osteomyelitis, empyema, bronchiectasis, syphilis, leprosy
- **Secondary to chronic inflammatory disorders**
  - *Rheumatological conditions* – rheumatoid arthritis, psoriatic arthritis, ankylosing spondylitis, Still's disease, Reiter syndrome, Sjögren syndrome, Behçet's disease
  - *Gastrointestinal conditions* – Whipple's disease, inflammatory bowel disease
  - *Paraprotein-related conditions* – myeloma (AL type), benign monoclonal gammopathy (AL type)
- **Other secondary amyloid**
  - Heroin abuse, paraplegia, renal cell carcinoma
- **Dialysis-related amyloid**
  - This does not deposit in the kidneys, as it is a complication of long-term dialysis. It is due to failure of clearance of β2-microglobulin (*see* Section 15.5.4)

15.12.2 Renovascular disease

Atherosclerotic renovascular disease (ARVD)

ARVD accounts for >90% of all renovascular disease. It is increased with ageing and is associated with common atherogenic risk factors (hypertension, hypercholesterolaemia, smoking, diabetes, etc) as well as with the presence of generalised vascular disease – it can be demonstrated in >10% of patients undergoing coronary angiography, >40% with peripheral vascular disease, and it affects 30% of patients with CCF aged >70 years. As older patients are now readily admitted to RRT programmes, ARVD is commonly detected in ESRD patients (15%–20%), although it probably only accounts for the renal failure in the minority (see below).

Clinical presentation is with hypertension, CKD or ESRD, 'flash' pulmonary oedema (5%), and AKI due to acute arterial occlusion, ischaemic ATN or related to ACE-I. Prognosis is poor (5-year survival <20%) due to co-morbid vascular events. Many cases of ARVD are thought to be incidental, the arterial narrowing occurring in association with prior hypertension and CKD (pro-atherogenic state), rather than being the cause of them. Around 90% of RAS lesions are 'ostial' (occurring within the first 1 cm of the renal artery origin).

- **Flash pulmonary oedema**: sudden onset of acute heart failure in the absence of a myocardial ischaemic event. The mechanism probably involves reduced natriuretic ability, coupled with left ventricular hypertrophy and severe hypertension, in patients who usually have severe bilateral renal artery disease. The episodes of pulmonary oedema are more common at night, largely because of posture-related redistribution of fluid, but possibly also because of diurnal variations in vasoactive peptides
- **Pathogenesis of CKD**: the correlation between severity of proximal lesions (ie degree of renal artery stenosis (RAS) or occlusion) and renal function is poor; this explains why revascularisation procedures are only variably successful. Parenchymal disease, manifest by

intrarenal atheroma, ischaemic change and cholesterol embolisation ('ischaemic nephropathy'), is now being recognised as a major determinant of renal functional outcome

- **Radiological diagnosis**: MR angiography (MRA) was the optimum non-invasive screening test for ARVD diagnosis until the advent of cases of gadolinium-related **NSF** (*see* Section 15.2.2, Renal radiology). MRA can still be performed safely in most patients with CKD stages 3 and 4. **CT angiography** is commonly used, but can be complicated by radio-contrast nephropathy in patients with CKD. **Duplex ultrasound** combines measurement of proximal renal artery blood flow velocity with intrarenal resistive index and although time-consuming and highly operator-dependent, it is an accurate test for detection of ARVD and assessing RAS severity. **Conventional intra-arterial angiography** is now reserved for patients with complex anatomy, and when confirming RAS severity prior to revascularisation

- **Revascularisation**: around 16% of American ARVD patients undergo revascularisation therapy and endovascular techniques (renal angioplasty with stenting) account for >95% of these procedures (the remainder being surgical reconstructions – especially indicated with complicated lesions, eg related to aortic aneurysm). The ASTRAL trial, a randomised trial involving >800 patients, has shown that revascularisation added to standard medical therapy (statins, aspirin and antihypertensives) does not improve renal function, blood pressure control, CVS event rate or mortality when compared with medical therapy alone. This finding is applicable to the majority of patients with ARVD; significant RAS occurring in patients with AKI or flash pulmonary oedema is, however, a definitive indication for revascularisation

Fibromuscular dysplasia (FMD)

FMD accounts for about 10% of all renovascular disease; it occurs in the young (20–35 years), and the majority of patients are female. The RAS lesions may be long and can be distal in the renal artery; they appear as a 'string of beads' at angiography. Patients usually present with severe hypertension, but renal failure is unusual. As the kidney beyond a fibromuscular stenosis is usually healthy, revascularisation may cure the hypertension, and it often restores renal function completely in the subgroup of patients with renal impairment. FMD is associated with other arterial lesions (eg carotid stenosis in 10%).

15.12.3 Connective tissue disorders and the kidney

Most of the connective tissue disorders have the propensity to cause renal disease, and characteristic features are described below (*see also* Chapter 20, Rheumatology); lupus nephritis and systemic sclerosis merit more detailed coverage.

- **Mixed connective tissue disease**: membranous or diffuse proliferative glomerulonephritis (uncommon)
- **Sjögren syndrome**: renal involvement is most often manifest by renal tubular dysfunction (RTA 1 or 2) with interstitial nephritis; cryoglobulinaemia and membranous or focal proliferative glomerulonephritis are less common
- **Rheumatoid arthritis**: renal disease is common, and usually due to amyloid or less often the effects of drug therapy. Rheumatoid-related glomerulonephritis (typically mild mesangio-proliferative change) is fairly common and is manifest by microscopic haematuria and mild proteinuria. Membranous glomerulonephritis is also recognised (not just an association with gold or penicillamine therapy)
- **Seronegative spondylarthropathies**: ankylosing spondylitis and Reiter syndrome can be associated with IgA nephropathy
- **Relapsing polychondritis**: this rare disorder is associated with cartilage inflammation leading to destruction and deformity (eg saddle nose, floppy ears). Crescentic, mesangioproliferative or membranous glomerulonephritis may occur

SLE nephritis

Over 5% of patients with SLE have renal involvement at presentation, and around 60% of patients will develop overt renal disease at some stage. Lupus nephritis is commoner in black patients and in women (10-fold greater incidence than in men), and 90% will have ANF antibodies. Renal disease can be manifest by any syndromal picture (eg proteinuria, nephrotic syndrome, rapidly progressive glomerulo-nephritis with AKI, CKD) but proteinuria is present in almost all patients with nephritis. Similarly, many different patterns of glomerular disease are recognised (the histological picture may even change, over time, within the same individual). Note that drug-induced SLE only rarely affects the kidneys. Although lupus nephritis can present with marked patient morbidity, most patients respond well to prompt immunosuppressive treatment.

Renal histology – WHO classification: the histological pattern has some prognostic value, with focal proliferative disease having a favourable renal outcome; diffuse proliferative or crescentic glomerulo-nephritis predicts the worst renal prognosis. 'Wire loop' lesions (thickened capillary walls – EM shows electron-dense deposits) are characteristic; immuno-fluorescence is positive for most immunoglobulins (IgG, IgM, IgA) and complement components (C3, C4, C1q). A synopsis of the WHO classification is :

- Class I: mild changes
- Class II: mesangioproliferative changes
- Class III: focal proliferative glomerulonephritis (variable severity)
- Class IV: severe diffuse proliferative glomerulonephritis
- Class V: membranous glomerulonephritis

Treatment: Patients with mild disease (eg WHO classes I and II) usually require no treatment. However, irrespective of the WHO class, most patients with significant proteinuria are likely to receive at least prednisolone and ACE inhibitor therapy. Acute SLE with AKI (classes III and IV – usually diffuse, crescentic or severe focal proliferative glomerulo-nephritis) should be treated as for 'RPGN/crescentic nephritis' (*see* Section 15.6, Glomerulonephritis and associated syndromes), with an intense induction regime (high-dose steroid, and usually pulsed IV cyclophosphamide) followed by maintenance therapy. Patients with class V histology who present with the nephrotic syndrome are treated similarly, although there is less evidence of conclusive benefit. Although plasma exchange has been used in patients with crescentic disease, and in those with severe extrarenal manifestations of SLE, there is again little evidence of improved outcome.

- Trials have shown a benefit with treatment regimes involving MMF; this is favoured over cyclophosphamide in the treatment of women of child-bearing age
- In many patients the immunosuppression can be tapered, and withdrawn by 5 years, even in those presenting with severe AKI

Prognosis of renal lupus: <10% of patients with nephritis now progress to ESRD (historically, renal disease used to be the commonest cause of death in SLE). The SLE syndrome often becomes quiescent once the patients reach RRT. Lupus nephritis rarely recurs in renal transplants.

Systemic sclerosis

Renal disease is always accompanied by hypertension; the hallmark presentation is 'scleroderma renal crisis' with accelerated hypertension, microangiopathic haemolytic anaemia and AKI. Prominent pathological changes are seen in the interlobular arteries (severe intimal proliferation with deposition of mucopolysaccharides – so-called 'onion skin' appearance); fibrinoid necrosis of afferent arterioles and secondary glomerular ischaemia are common. The essential treatment is with RAA blockade for hypertension control; some patients develop ESRD, but renal function can recover, particularly in those patients who presented with renal crisis. The overall prognosis is poor because of other organ involvement (especially restrictive cardiomyopathy and pulmonary fibrosis).

15.12.4 Diabetic nephropathy

Diabetic nephropathy is now the most common cause of ESRD in the UK, accounting for 25% of patients. In recent years there have been advances in the understanding of the natural history, pathogenesis and treatment of diabetic nephropathy, but the mortality of this group remains high, largely because of associated CVS disease.

Epidemiology

Established or clinical nephropathy (see below) is associated with macroalbuminuria (>300 mg/24 h, which equates to >500 mg/24 h of total proteinuria), and occurs with a cumulative incidence of 30% after 40 years in type 1 diabetics. In type 2 diabetics, nephropathy is already prevalent in 10% at the time of diabetes diagnosis (reflecting previous 'subclinical' hyperglycaemia), and there is a 25% 20-year cumulative incidence of nephropathy. About one-fifth of these latter patients will develop CKD and be at risk of ESRD (ie 5% of all type 2 diabetics) – the remainder succumb to other complications (usually CVS or infections) of diabetes before they develop significant CKD. As type 2 diabetes is 10–15 times more common than type 1 in Western populations, it accounts for 75% of the diabetics seen in CKD clinics or on RRT programmes. In a UK diabetic clinic, the prevalence of nephropathy is about 5% at any time.

- Genetic influence: diabetics in certain racial groups have a far greater risk of developing nephropathy (eg Asians, Pima Indians). In the UK, the likelihood of ESRD is three times greater in Asian and Afro-Caribbean diabetics than in Caucasians
- Nephropathy is usually associated with retinopathy (common basement membrane pathology); renovascular disease and other arterial pathology are common

Natural history of nephropathy

In type 1 diabetes the stages of development of nephropathy have been well characterised:

- **Stage 1**: at the time of diabetes diagnosis the GFR is elevated by >20% compared to age-matched controls. Urinary albumin excretion rate (UAER) is also increased; both are reduced by commencement of insulin

- **Stage 2**: GFR remains elevated (due to hyperfiltration) and kidneys are hypertrophied but blood pressure and UAER are normal. The GFR appears to be linked to glycaemic control, with greatest hyperfiltration associated with worse control. There are early histological changes with thickening of glomerular basement membranes and mesangial expansion. This stage typically lasts for 5–15 years after diabetes diagnosis
- **Stage 3**: microalbuminuria (or 'incipient nephropathy') is present (UAER 30–300 mg/day, or uACR 3–30). The GFR remains elevated or returns to the normal range. Blood pressure starts to rise (in 60%). Microalbuminuria occurs in 30%–50% of patients at 5–10 years after diabetes onset, and 80% of these patients go on to develop overt nephropathy (stage 4) over 10–15 years. Histological changes progress from those seen in stage 2
- **Stage 4**: 'established', (also known as 'clinical' or 'overt') nephropathy is associated with increasing macro-proteinuria, which may become nephrotic in 30%, and declining GFR (eg average 5–10 ml/min per year) in all patients. Hypertension is present in 80% and is correlated with the rate of decline of GFR. Renal histology typically shows diffuse glomerular sclerosing lesions (all patients) and vascular changes; 10% have Kimmelstiel–Wilson nodules (focal glomerular sclerosis)
- **Stage 5**: development of ESRD occurs at an average of 7 years from onset of stage 4

It is thought that the development of nephropathy occurs in a similar fashion in type 2 diabetes.

Screening and prevention

Patients should be **screened** for microalbuminuria in the diabetic clinic; the ACR can be assessed in an early morning specimen or equally well in random spot urine samples. An ACR of >2.5 is generally taken as the cut-off for microalbuminuria (equivalent to a UAER of > 30 mg/24 h).

- Studies in type 1 diabetics have shown that tight glycaemic control can reduce the likelihood of patients developing microalbuminuria (by 40%), and there is emerging evidence that intensive insulin regimes may prevent some microalbuminuric patients progressing to overt nephropathy

- The latter has been clearly shown in trials using ACE inhibitors in type 1 diabetes, and with ARBs in type 2. These agents also slow the time of doubling of serum creatinine and the time to ESRD in patients with established nephropathy; comparisons with other antihypertensive agents suggest that their renoprotective effects are partly independent of hypertension control
- It is now accepted that blood pressure should be targeted to 125/75 mmHg in patients with stage 4 nephropathy – this will slow, but not prevent, the inexorable decline of GFR in patients with overt nephropathy

Outcome

The mortality of these patients is very high (eg patients with type 1 diabetes have a 20-fold greater mortality than the general population) and this relative risk may be magnified a further 25-fold in those with proteinuria (eg 2-year mortality of 30% in patients with ESRD), largely due to co-morbid cardiovascular disease. Most patients with stage 4 nephropathy in type 2 diabetes will die before they reach ESRD.

- Microalbuminuria confers an excess risk of mortality compared to patients with normalbuminuria – eg 4-year mortality 28% in type 2 diabetics with microalbuminuria, compared to 4% in those without. It is thought that microalbuminuria represents the renal manifestation of a generalised vascular endothelial dysfunction
- All patients who reach ESRD are considered for RRT. Most patients require screening for coronary artery disease before listing for transplantation; combined renal and pancreatic transplantation is now feasible in selected patients (*see* Section 15.5.5 Renal transplantation). Five-year survival of transplanted diabetics is 45%–75%, compared to around 20% for those who remain on dialysis

15.12.5 Thrombotic microangiopathies

Haemolytic uraemic syndrome and **thrombotic thrombocytopenic purpura** share similar renal histological features and pathophysiology (*see also* Chapter 9, Haematology). In both conditions there is a microangiopathic haemolytic anaemia (MAHA), with anaemia, RBC fragments and schistocytes. Platelet clumping occurs within the intravascular thrombi, and hence thrombocytopenia is a major feature. The typical renal histological lesions include intraglomerular thrombi with ischaemia and arteriolar lesions.

Haemolytic uraemic syndrome (HUS)

HUS is the commonest cause of AKI in children (because AKI is rare in children), but it is also seen in adults (5 cases per million/year). Children aged <4 years account for 90% of cases. Two main forms of HUS are recognised:

Typical or diarrhoea-associated (D⁺) HUS: the onset is explosive, with AKI, and epidemics of the disease occur. A third of UK cases are due to verotoxin-producing *E. coli* O157:H7 (VTEC); the toxin damages vascular endothelium, predisposing to the microangiopathy. *Shigella dysenteriae* can also be associated. The intravascular abnormalities are largely confined to the kidneys. Ninety per cent of patients with D⁺HUS make a good recovery, but 5% die during the acute illness; up to 40% of patients have decreased GFR at long-term follow-up.

Atypical HUS: tends to affect older children and adults; most patients have no diarrhoea (D⁻HUS). Many D⁻HUS cases are thought to be familial, and there is progressive renal dysfunction with neurological episodes that can resemble TTP. **Familial forms** of HUS/TTP can be associated with factor H deficiency (which may limit cleavage of unusually large von Willebrand factors, leading to continued platelet activation and hence the pathogenesis of HUS or TTP). These forms have a poorer prognosis, with ESRD or death occurring in >50% of patients.

- **Monitoring of disease**: in typical HUS red cell fragmentation and the platelet count are the best means of monitoring disease activity. LDH levels are high (due to haemolysis), but this may also represent tissue infarction
- **Treatment**: the mainstay of therapy is infusion of fresh frozen plasma (FFP) and plasma exchange. These are more effective in adult D$^+$HUS than in childhood forms. In atypical HUS, FFP and plasma exchange may lower the risk of ESRD and mortality

Thrombotic thrombocytopenic purpura (TTP)

In TTP, explosive AKI is less prominent, but neurological abnormalities are usual (due to formation and release of microthrombi within the brain vasculature). Again two main forms are recognised:

- **Acute TTP**: 90% of patients with TTP present with abrupt onset with neurological signs, fever and purpura. Plasma exchange and FFP infusion are indicated for this condition. Previously invariably fatal, survival now approaches 90%
- **Relapsing TTP**: adults are usually affected and chronic disease is more likely – the condition can appear similar to atypical HUS. Some of these cases are probably familial HUS/TTP

Secondary causes of HUS and TTP

These include:

- Pregnancy-associated thrombotic microangiopathy (*see* Chapter 12, Maternal Medicine)
  - TTP
  - HELLP syndrome
  - Post-partum HUS
- HIV-associated thrombotic microangiopathy
- Cancer-associated thrombotic microangiopathy
- Drugs (eg ciclosporin)

15.12.6 Hypertension and the kidney

A detailed description of hypertension is beyond the scope of this chapter; but *see* Chapter 1, Cardiology. The kidney is often damaged by essential hyper-

tension, or it can be central to the pathogenesis of many cases of secondary hypertension.

Primary (essential) hypertension and renal damage

End-organ renal damage is common and is usually manifest as asymptomatic proteinuria and/or CKD (**hypertensive nephrosclerosis**). Microalbuminuria develops in 20%–40% of patients with essential hypertension, and persistent proteinuria (occasionally nephrotic) in a smaller proportion. Typical histological lesions include vascular wall thickening and luminal obliteration, with widespread interstitial fibrosis and glomerulosclerosis.

- Elevated creatinine develops in 10%–20% of patients; the risk is greater in African Americans, the elderly and those with higher systolic blood pressure
- Progression to ESRD occurs in 2%–5% over 10–15 years. Isolated hypertension accounts for about 30% of all ESRD in the USA and 15% in the UK
- It is thought that many patients who present with ESRD of unknown aetiology, especially with small, smooth kidneys visible at ultrasound, actually have long-standing hypertensive renal disease

Treatment and targets: all patients should have their blood pressure controlled to <140/85 mmHg. In those with CKD, or with significant proteinuria, the targets should be <130/80 and 125/75 mmHg, respectively. RAA blockers are specifically indicated for the reasons described earlier in the chapter.

'Malignant' or accelerated hypertension: this refers to presentation with severe diastolic hypertension (eg DBP >120 mmHg) with grade 3 or 4 retinopathy (haemorrhages and/or exudates (grade 3) with/without papilloedema). Patients may have AKI, significant proteinuria and non-renal complications such as encephalopathy or cardiac failure. The condition constitutes a medical emergency. Typical histological lesions include arterial fibrinoid necrosis (which also accounts for the retinal abnormalities) coupled with severe tubular and glomerular ischaemia.

Secondary hypertension

Over 90% of hypertension is idiopathic, approximately 5% is due to renal disease, 2%–3% due to primary hyperaldosteronism, and <1% has either an alternative rare endocrine or other cause.

Hypertension due to renal disease

Renal disease accounts for the majority of cases of secondary hypertension. The pathogenesis involves stimulation of renin release with activation of the RAA system, reduced natriuretic capacity (in advanced CKD), and disorganisation of intrarenal vascular structures. The majority of patients with CKD are hypertensive, and it is evident in at least 90% of the dialysis population and over 60% of transplant patients. It is the chief contributor to the LVH and associated high cardiovascular mortality of these patients.

- Most forms of renal disease are complicated by hypertension, but exceptions are some patients with chronic pyelonephritis who have salt wasting (typically with normal blood pressure although some can develop postural hypotension)
- Although ARVD is invariably associated with hypertension it may only be pathogenetically significant in the minority
- **Coarctation of the aorta**: hypertension is seen in the upper limbs only. Rib-notching may be seen on X-ray
- **Endocrine**: Cushing syndrome, phaeochromocytoma, acromegaly and apparent mineralocorticoid excess (*see* Section 15.3.4 Hypokalaemia) are all rare causes. It is now believed that **primary hyperaldosteronism** (associated with bilateral or unilateral adrenal hyperplasia) may account for about 3% of all hypertension (*see* Chapter 1, Cardiology and Chapter 4, Endocrinology)
- **Other secondary hypertension**: alcohol, obesity

15.12.7 Myeloma and the kidney

Myeloma occurs with an incidence of 30–40 cases/million, and at a median age of 70–80 years. Renal involvement may present with AKI, CKD and/or proteinuria. Note that Bence Jones proteinuria is not detected by standard urinary dipsticks.

Renal failure due to myeloma

AKI: some degree of renal impairment is observed in 50% of patients with myeloma; this is reversible in the majority (in those where it is secondary to hypercalcaemia, hypovolaemia, infection or nephrotoxic drugs), but 10% of patients may need dialysis. The latter cases are usually due to **light-chain or 'cast' nephropathy**.

CKD: due to amyloidosis, and cast nephropathy associated with chronic interstitial nephritis.

Cast nephropathy

In this, free kappa (the most nephrotoxic) and lambda light chains excreted in the urine damage the tubules by direct nephrotoxicity and by cast formation. The intratubular casts are composed of hard, needle-shaped crystals and excite an interstitial infiltrate, often with multinucleate giant cells. ATN and tubular atrophy occur, and hence the potential for some recovery from an AKI episode.

- Patients with light-chain-only myeloma are more likely to have renal involvement
- Cast nephropathy may also be seen in patients with MGUS (see below)

Treatment is with rehydration and supportive therapy. Hypercalcaemia should be treated with IV bisphosphonates. AKI may improve with plasma exchange – a clinical trial is currently ongoing. The myeloma should be treated with conventional regimes (eg dexamethasone, melphalan and thalidomide if the prognosis is >6 months; in younger patients, and those with lower tumour bulk and complications, VAD regimes are used, and patients may be considered for autologous stem cell transplantation).

Prognosis: renal recovery is only seen in about 15%–20% of patients with cast nephropathy who require dialysis. The remainder need RRT – the prevalence of myeloma patients on dialysis programmes is about 2%. Renal transplantation is not appropriate. Patients with myeloma and ESRD have poor survival (<50% at 1 year). Those with the greatest tumour mass have the worst prognosis.

Benign monoclonal gammopathy (MGUS)

(*See also* Chapter 9, Haematology.) This may be associated with light-chain nephropathy, interstitial nephritis, amyloid and also mesangiocapillary glomerulonephritis. A proportion of patients with MGUS will develop myeloma during long-term follow-up.

15.12.8 Renal vasculitis

The kidney is often involved in systemic vasculitic illness. Several disorders are recognised (*see also* Chapter 20, Rheumatology).

Small-vessel pauci-immune vasculitis

These conditions affect small vessels (arterioles and veins) and are associated with glomerulonephritis, and pulmonary and skin vasculitis. They are usually associated with +ve serum ANCA. Incidence is 10–20 cases/million each year. The major conditions are defined as:

- **Wegener's granulomatosis**: respiratory tract disease is characteristic and this involves necrotising granulomata within the upper respiratory tract (leading to sinusitis and nasal discharge, as well as damage to the nasal septum) and lungs (with haemoptysis). About 70% of patients are cANCA +ve, and 25% pANCA +ve
- **Churg–Strauss syndrome**: vasculitis that is associated with asthma, eosinophilia and necrotising inflammation; 60% have +ve pANCA; 30% are ANCA –ve
- **Microscopic polyangiitis (MPA)**: vasculitis occurring in the absence of evidence for the above two conditions (ie no asthma, eosinophilia or necrotising granulomatous

inflammation); 50% are pANCA +ve, and 40% cANCA +ve

In all conditions, **AKI** is the usual renal presentation; renal histology shows necrotising glomerulitis typically associated with focal proliferative and/or crescentic glomerulonephritis (*see* 'Treatment of RPGN and crescentic nephritis' in Section 15.6.2). Pulmonary involvement is common, but blood pressure may be normal. Various forms of vasculitic skin rash (ranging from purpura to skin necrosis) are seen.

Treatment: all of the above three conditions normally merit high-dose immunosuppressive therapy; typical regimes are described in 'Treatment of RPGN and crescentic nephritis' in Section 15.6.2. Patients with cANCA +ve disease are more likely to relapse after the cessation of maintenance therapy. In such cases, immunosuppression is continued for several further years.

Prognosis: 1-year renal and patient survival is >80%. Poorer renal prognosis is seen in patients with highest creatinine and/or oligo-anuria at presentation. Mortality is increased in patients with pulmonary haemorrhage. The risk of vasculitic relapse in transplanted patients is 20%.

Polyarteritis nodosa (PAN)

PAN is a rare, medium-sized arterial vasculitis which results in microaneurysm formation; hypertension is usually severe, and renal infarcts rather than glomerulonephritis are characteristic. Patients are usually ANCA –ve (unless there is also small-vessel involvement, ie PAN–MPA overlap – these patients can develop glomerulonephritis). Pulmonary (infiltrates and haemorrhage), GI tract (infarcts), neurological (mononeuritis multiplex) and systemic features (myalgia, PUO) are recognised, but the condition is notoriously difficult to confirm. A few cases are associated with hepatitis B infection. **Treatment** is as for small-vessel vasculitis/crescentic nephritis.

Other vasculitides that can affect the kidney

- **Henoch–Schönlein nephritis**: in addition to the typical systemic features of this condition, some

patients develop renal disease as a result of small-vessel (typically post-capillary venulitis with IgA deposition) vasculitis. Glomerular lesions range from mild mesangial hypercellularity (similar to idiopathic IgA nephropathy) through to crescentic nephritis
- **Kawasaki disease**: acute febrile illness, usually in children, associated with a desquamating erythematous rash and necrotising arteritis in some patients. It is the commonest cause of myocardial infarction in childhood, but significant renal disease is uncommon
- **Takayasu arteritis**: this can be associated with RAS and renovascular hypertension
- **Giant-cell arteritis**: has been associated with rapidly progressive glomerulonephritis (RPGN), but such cases may represent Wegener's granulomatosis with temporal artery involvement

15.12.9   Sarcoidosis and the kidney

Sarcoidosis (*see* Section 15.8.1 Interstitial nephritis) can be associated with:

- **AKI**: due to AIN. Ninety per cent of patients have systemic manifestations of sarcoidosis (eg hepatosplenomegaly, hypercalcaemia)
- **CKD**: associated with CIN and hypercalcaemia. Glomerular disease (membranous or proliferative glomerulonephritis) may rarely occur, and is associated with microscopic haematuria and significant proteinuria

Treatment: most patients respond promptly to oral steroids, which can be tapered at 3–6 months. Relapses occur, but are usually steroid-responsive. Serum ACE may be useful for monitoring disease activity and predicting likelihood of relapses.

15.13   DRUGS AND THE KIDNEY AND TOXIC NEPHROPATHY

(*See also* Chapter 2, Clinical Pharmacology, Toxicology and Poisoning.)

15.13.1   Renal elimination of drugs

Drugs may be eliminated via the kidneys by two main mechanisms:

- **Glomerular filtration**: a passive process; such drugs will be water-soluble
- **Active tubular secretion**: drugs act as substrates for secretory processes that are designed to eliminate endogenous molecules; the tubular pathways are different for organic anions (basolateral tubular membrane) and cations (located on the luminal brush border)

Examples of drugs which are secreted by the tubule

- **Anionic drugs**
  - Acetazolamide
  - Cephalosporins
  - Penicillin
  - Loop diuretics
  - Thiazide diuretics
  - Probenecid
  - Salicylates
- **Cationic drugs**
  - Amiloride
  - Cimetidine
  - Ranitidine
  - Metformin
  - Morphine
  - Quinine

15.13.2   Drug nephrotoxicity

Drugs can lead to renal damage in a number of different ways, and examples are given below.

Alterations in renal blood flow

- **NSAIDs**: alteration in prostaglandin metabolism can lead to a critical reduction in glomerular perfusion (particularly when there is reduced renal reserve or CKD). Interstitial nephritis may also result from NSAIDs
- **ACE inhibitors (and ARBs)**: AKI or renal impairment occurring in patients who are

critically dependent upon the RAA system (those with reduced renal perfusion (eg CCF, loop diuretics, hypovolaemia and severe ARVD) is well recognised with these agents

- **Ciclosporin A**: toxicity can be acute (due to renal vasoconstriction) or chronic. The latter is a common cause of transplant dysfunction, and is associated with arterial damage (intimal proliferation and hyaline degeneration of the vascular media), tubular vacuolation and atrophy and interstitial fibrosis

Direct tubular toxicity

- **Aminoglycosides**: disturbance of renal function is seen in up to a third of patients receiving aminoglycosides. Five per cent of filtered gentamicin is actively reabsorbed by proximal tubular cells, within which the drug is concentrated; binding to phospholipid results in disturbed intracellular regulation with inhibition of microsomal protein synthesis and, eventually, ATN
- **Cisplatin**: selectively toxic to proximal tubular cells, by inhibiting nuclear DNA synthesis; ATN results. The platinum component may not be the major damaging influence as carboplatin is less nephrotoxic
- **Amphotericin**: this is toxic to distal tubular cells in a dose-dependent manner; ATN results, and is accompanied by non-oliguric AKI. Liposomal formulations minimise the nephrotoxic risk

Glomerulonephritis

- **Gold**: although now much less commonly used in rheumatoid treatment, gold can lead to proteinuria in about 5% of patients, and this is not dose-related; proteinuria usually occurs within 6 months of the start of therapy. On cessation of the gold, resolution of proteinuria is seen by 6 months. Gold is found in the mesangial cells at renal biopsy; it is believed to induce an immune-complex glomerulonephritis (usually membranous, but occasionally minimal-change nephropathy)
- **Penicillamine**: risk of membranous glomerulonephritis is greater than with gold; it is dose-related, and the onset of proteinuria may be delayed to 18 months after the start of treatment

Other nephrotoxic effects of drugs

Interstitial nephritis and retroperitoneal fibrosis are covered in earlier sections, and drug-induced SLE syndromes in Chapter 20, Rheumatology. **Lithium** is commonly associated with CKD due to an interstitial fibrosis; this usually stabilises with dose reduction or drug withdrawal. Nephrogenic DI can also occur.

15.13.3   Toxic nephropathy

This refers to renal damage resulting from drugs (as above) or radio-contrast media (*see* Section 15.4.3) or environmental toxins (eg heavy metals) and poisons (eg paraquat).

Causes of environmental and occupational toxic nephropathy

- **Heavy metals**
  - Mercury
    - AKI, proteinuria and nephrotic syndrome (minimal-change or membranous nephropathy)
  - Lead
    - Acute poisoning leads to AKI with ATN; chronic interstitial nephritis and Fanconi syndrome are seen with chronic exposure
  - Cadmium
    - Similar renal pathology and clinical presentation as for lead
  - Arsenic
    - Acute poisoning causes AKI with ATN and cortical necrosis; interstitial fibrosis leads to CKD with chronic exposure
  - Bismuth
    - Proteinuria, Fanconi syndrome and AKI have been described
- **Hydrocarbons and organic solvents**
  - Carbon tetrachloride
    - AKI
  - Ethylene glycol
    - This is rapidly metabolised to oxalic acid, which crystallises within the renal tubules; ATN results
  - Petroleum-based hydrocarbons
    - These can predispose to glomerulonephritis (eg Goodpasture syndrome or membranous glomerulonephritis)
  - Paraquat
    - AKI, usually lethal due to irremediable pulmonary disease
- **Plant and animal toxins**
  - Snake, spider and hornet venoms
    - Directly nephrotoxic, or induce ATN, cortical necrosis (often associated with DIC), or muscle necrosis and rhabdomyolysis
  - Bee sting
    - Rare cause of nephrotic syndrome
  - Mushroom poisoning
    - AKI
  - Poison ivy or oak
    - Rare causes of nephrotic syndrome

Chapter 16
Neurology

CONTENTS

16.10 Investigations used in neurological disease

Neurology

16.1 CEREBRAL CORTEX

16.1.1 Cortical localisation

The cortical surface is divided into frontal, parietal, temporal and occipital lobes (Figure 16.1). Primary motor and sensory cortices are located as follows.

- **Motor**
  - Precentral gyrus (frontal lobe)
- **Auditory**
  - Superior temporal lobe
  - (Heschl's gyrus)
- **Olfactory**
  - Frontal lobe (orbitofrontal cortex)
- **Somatosensory**
  - Postcentral gyrus
- **Visual**
  - Occipital cortex (calcarine sulcus)

In general, primary sensory cortices receive input from subcortical structures. Signals reach the somatosensory cortex via the posterior limb of the internal capsule (the anterior limb carries descending motor output in the form of the corticospinal tracts). Auditory signals reach the temporal cortex via the medial geniculate nucleus of the thalamus. Visual signals reach the calcarine sulcus (V1) from the lateral geniculate nucleus (the geniculostriate pathway) although some also reach the visual cortex via the superior colliculus (the retinotectal pathway).

After processing in primary sensory areas, corticocortical connections carry signals into secondary association cortices. The pattern of connections of the visual cortex is best understood in the following way. From primary visual cortex (V1), parallel pathways carry signals to different cortical areas that carry out different types of processing (eg for colour or for motion). These areas are broadly organised

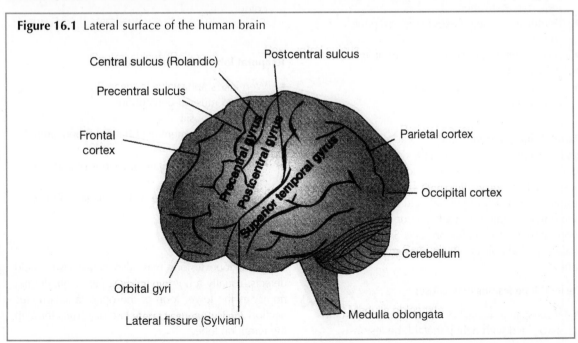

Figure 16.1 Lateral surface of the human brain

Central sulcus (Rolandic)

Postcentral sulcus

Precentral sulcus

Frontal cortex

Precentral gyrus

Postcentral gyrus

Superior temporal gyrus

Parietal cortex

Occipital cortex

Cerebellum

Orbital gyri

Lateral fissure (Sylvian)

Medulla oblongata

into two streams: a dorsal 'where' stream, passing into the parietal cortex and concerned with the location of objects in the environment, and a ventral 'what' stream passing into the temporal cortex and concerned with object identity. Damage to the dorsal stream can cause disorders of object localisation such as visual neglect; damage to the ventral stream leads to difficulties with identifying objects, such as agnosia.

A distributed network of cortical areas in the dominant hemisphere (usually the left in right-handed individuals; equally likely to be left or right hemisphere in left-handers) subserves **language function**. Two areas are especially important:

- **Broca's area**: in the dominant frontal lobe, which is concerned with speech output
- **Wernicke's area**: in the dominant posterior superior temporal gyrus, which is concerned with word comprehension

Frontal lobe lesions may cause:

- Anosmia
- Abnormal affective reactions
- Difficulties with planning tasks or those requiring motivation
- Primitive release reflexes (eg grasp, pout, rooting)
- Broca's aphasia ('telegraphic' output aphasia)
- Perseveration
- Personality change (apathetic versus disinhibited)

Parietal lobe lesions tend to cause disorders of spatial representation or apraxias (disorders of learned movement unrelated to muscular weakness), such as those described below. Parietal lobe lesions may also cause visual field defects, usually a homonymous inferior quadrantanopia, as the upper loop of the optic radiation (*see* Section 16.3 on neuro-ophthalmology) runs through the parietal lobe.

Parietal lobe lesions may cause:

- Visuospatial neglect or extinction (both usually associated with right parietal lobe lesions)

- Astereognosis (failure to recognise common objects by feeling them)
- Gerstmann syndrome (dominant parietal) consisting of alexia (inability to read), agraphia (inability to write), right/left confusion and finger agnosia (inability to identify fingers by name)
- Apraxia (dominant)
- Acalculia (inability to perform mental arithmetic; dominant)
- Agraphia (dominant)
- Dressing apraxia (dominant)
- Constructional apraxia (non-dominant)
- Anosognosia (denial of illness; non-dominant)

Occipital lesions may cause:

- Cortical blindness
- Homonymous hemianopia
- Quadrantanopia
- Visual agnosia (inability to comprehend the meaning of objects despite intact primary visual perception)
- Specific visual processing defects, eg akinetopsia (impaired perception of visual motion), achromatopsia (impaired perception of colour)

Temporal lobe lesions may cause:

- Wernicke's aphasia
- Impaired musical perception
- Auditory agnosia
- Memory impairment (eg bilateral hippocampal pathology)
- Cortical deafness (bilateral lesions of auditory cortex)
- Emotional disturbance with damage to limbic cortex

Temporal lobe lesions may also cause visual field defects, usually a homonymous superior quadrantanopia, as the lower loop of the optic radiation (*see* Section 16.3 on neuro-ophthalmology) runs through the temporal lobe.

16.1.2 Dementia

Dementia is an acquired, progressive loss of cognitive function associated with an abnormal brain condition. It is not a feature of normal ageing.

Other disorders may masquerade as dementia, including depression, post-ictal states, acute confusional states (including drug-induced) and psychotic illnesses of old age.

By far the commonest cause of dementia in adults is **Alzheimer's disease**. Other important dementias include:

- Dementia with Lewy bodies
- Vascular dementia
- Frontotemporal dementia (Pick's disease)

Rarer causes of dementia include:

- Creutzfeldt–Jacob disease
- Progressive supranuclear palsy
- AIDS-associated dementia
- Huntington's disease

Treatable causes of cognitive impairment (which can masquerade as dementia)

- Intracranial tumour
- Normal-pressure hydrocephalus
- Thiamine (vitamin B_1) deficiency
- Vitamin B_{12} deficiency
- Hypothyroidism
- Acute confusional state
- Depression
- Chronic drug intoxication

Dementia normally presents in primary care, and NICE guidelines suggest that a dementia screen should be carried out at initial presentation. This would include:

- Biochemistry tests (including electrolytes, calcium, glucose, and renal and liver function)
- Thyroid function tests
- Serum vitamin B_{12} and folate levels

In making the diagnosis, structural imaging (using magnetic resonance imaging (MRI)) and clinical cognitive assessment (including formal neuropsychological testing in cases of mild or questionable dementia) is required.

Alzheimer's disease

The earliest symptom of Alzheimer's disease (AD) is typically forgetfulness for newly acquired information. The disease progresses to disorientation, progressive cognitive decline with multiple cognitive impairments and disintegration of personality.

The neuropathology consists of:

- **Macroscopic**: the brain is atrophied with enlarged ventricles. Hippocampal atrophy is particularly prominent and can be one of the first signs of AD
- **Microscopic**: there is neuronal loss throughout the cortex and two distinctive pathological features: **plaques** (which contain a core of β-amyloid) and **neurofibrillary tangles** (which contain hyperphosphorylated tau protein). Tangles and plaques occur throughout the cortex in overlapping but separate distributions. The density of tangles **can** correlate with dementia severity
- **Neurotransmitter changes**: there is a loss of cholinergic neurones and a loss of choline acetyltransferase activity throughout the cortex, although other neurotransmitter systems are also affected

Genetic abnormalities associated with Alzheimer's disease

Fewer than 5% of AD cases are familial (typically autosomal dominant) and three main mutations are described. A point mutation to the presenilin-1 gene (chromosome 14) accounts for up to 50% of familial AD. Less common are mutations to the β-amyloid precursor protein (APP) gene (chromosome 21) or the presenilin-2 gene (chromosome 1).

- **Down** syndrome (trisomy 21) is associated with mental retardation and the formation of senile plaques and neurofibrillary tangles in the same brain regions commonly affected by AD.

Clinically, people with Down syndrome develop progressive cognitive impairment from their fifth or sixth decade. The gene coding for amyloid precursor protein is located on chromosome 21 and it is thought that there is overproduction of β-amyloid in these individuals

- **Apolipoprotein E** (ApoE) is a protein synthesised in the liver that serves as a cholesterol transporter. There are three major forms of ApoE that are specified by different alleles of the ApoE gene on chromosome 19 (η2, η3, η4). The η4 allele has a greatly increased frequency (around 50%) in patients with AD. The effect of this allele is to decrease the age of onset of AD. After the effect of age, ApoE4 is the most significant risk factor for AD

Pharmacological treatment of Alzheimer's disease

In recent years pharmacological agents have become available for the treatment of AD. In the UK, NICE guidelines (http://www.nice.org.uk/Guidance/CG42) recommend the use of three acetylcholinesterase inhibitors (donepezil, galantamine and rivastigmine) in mild to moderate AD (Mini Mental State Examination (MMSE) score of between 10 and 20).

- Treatment must be initiated by a dementia specialist
- Review should occur every 6 months, and this should include an MMSE score
- Treatment should be discontinued if MMSE drops below 10. (It is recognised in NICE guidelines that the MMSE score should not be relied upon in all circumstances (for example, where significant functional impairment is present despite moderately preserved MMSE) and so some professional discretion is allowed)

Frontotemporal dementia (Pick's disease)

Frontotemporal lobar degeneration (also known as Pick's disease) is a progressive dementia that is associated with focal atrophy of the frontal and temporal lobes. The disorder has histopathology that is distinct from that of AD, but quite heterogeneous. In a minority of patients with frontotemporal lobar degeneration, Pick bodies are seen within the cellular cytoplasm on light microscopy. Clinically, patients present with progressive language disturbance, often affecting output rather than comprehension, and behavioural changes. Frontal lobe features are prominent. Clinical variants include frontotemporal dementia, semantic dementia and progressive non-fluent aphasia.

Recently, advances in molecular genetics and immunohistochemistry have suggested that the microtubular protein **tau** plays a central role in the pathophysiology of frontotemporal lobar degeneration. This suggests the possibility of common pathologies (or tauopathies) with other neurodegenerative diseases, including corticobasal degeneration and progressive supranuclear palsy.

Creutzfeldt–Jakob disease

Creutzfeldt–Jakob disease (CJD) is clinically characterised by:

- Rapidly progressive dementia
- Myoclonus
- Young age of onset

Cerebrospinal fluid (CSF) examination is usually normal, though CSF protein may be mildly elevated. There is a **characteristic EEG** with biphasic high-amplitude sharp waves.

The most common cause is sporadic, but there are familial forms. A **new-variant CJD** (nvCJD) is recognised with a neurobehavioural presentation (often depression) in people aged under 40; this form is associated with interspecies transmission of the bovine spongiform encephalopathy (BSE) agent.

Invasive brain biopsy is currently the only definitive way of diagnosing CJD antemortem, though serological tests show some promise. The disease is rapidly progressive and most patients die within a year of diagnosis.

CJD is a **prion disease**.

Prion protein

- Prion protein is a normal product of a gene found in many organisms
- It is membrane-bound
- An abnormal isoform accumulates in the spongiform encephalopathies, and this abnormal isoform is thought to be the infectious agent
- The infectious agent is resistant to heat, irradiation and autoclaving

See also Chapter 9, Haematology (transfusion-transmitted infection) and Chapter 14, Molecular Medicine, which contain further discussion of prion diseases.

Normal-pressure hydrocephalus

This should be considered in the differential diagnosis of dementia and consists of the triad of dementia, gait abnormality and urinary incontinence. Urinary symptoms are initially of urgency and frequency, and progress to frontal lobe incontinence (patients indifferent to their incontinence). Gait and posture may mimic Parkinson's disease.

The syndrome appears to be due to a defect in absorption of CSF due to thickening of the basal meninges, or in the cortical channels over the convexity and near to the arachnoid villi. The aetiology may be secondary to meningitis, head injury or subarachnoid haemorrhage. The ventricles are dilated and radiologically hydrocephalus is found, but the pressure is only intermittently high.

Headaches are not usually a complaint and papilloedema is **not** found. Treatment with a ventriculoperitoneal shunt may improve symptomatology.

16.1.3 Multiple sclerosis (MS)

Clinical presentation of MS

Multiple sclerosis (MS) is thought to be a cell-mediated autoimmune disease associated with immune activity directed against central nervous system (CNS) antigens, principally myelin. Clinical

consensus identifies four different subtypes of MS, which may reflect different immunological subtypes:

- **Relapsing-remitting disease** is the most common form of MS (80%–85% of patients). Short-lasting acute attacks (4–8 weeks) are followed by remission and a steady baseline state between relapses. The average number of relapses is around 0.8/year
- **Secondary progressive disease**: about 30%–50% of patients with relapsing/remitting disease will subsequently show progressive deterioration with relapses becoming less prominent within about 10 years of MS disease onset
- **Primary progressive disease**: 10%–15% of patients show progressive deterioration from onset without any superimposed relapses. Age of onset is typically later than for relapsing/remitting disease
- **Progressive-relapsing disease**: a small number of patients with primary progressive disease also experience superimposed relapses associated with gradual disease progression

Good prognostic factors are:

- Relapsing-remitting course
- Female sex
- Early age at onset
- Presence of sensory symptoms

The aetiology of MS is still unclear but there is undoubtedly a genetic component, with an increased relative risk (20%–40%) in siblings compared to the general population. However, as the concordance rate in monozygotic twins is only 25%, there appears to be a substantial environmental component as well.

Optic neuritis is a common presentation of MS:

- Isolated optic neuritis: 40%–60% chance of subsequent MS
- A cause of painful visual loss
- Treat with methylprednisolone
- Colour vision is affected early and residual abnormality may persist after recovery

Diagnosis of MS

This typically requires the demonstration of brain or spinal cord lesions that are disseminated in time and anatomical location. A definitive diagnosis, therefore, is hard to make at the time of the first neurological episode, although if MRI reveals typical lesions this is highly suggestive. Supportive investigations may include:

- T_2-weighted MRI showing demyelinating plaques. The presence of gadolinium enhancing lesions is the most predictive MRI parameter, although these are not always present
- Delayed visual-evoked response potentials (VEPs)
- Oligoclonal bands in the CSF (but not the serum – see below)

Diagnosis of primary progressive disease is often hardest, as clear evidence for lesions disseminated in time and (anatomical) space is often obscured by the progressive course of the disease. Brain MRI may be normal in this form of MS, although multiple lesions may be visible in the spinal cord.

Oligoclonal bands in the CSF

Oligoclonal bands in the CSF indicate intrathecal immunoglobulin synthesis. These are not specific to MS and other causes include neurosarcoidosis, CNS lymphoma, systemic lupus erythematosus (SLE), neurosyphilis, subarachnoid haemorrhage (rare), subacute sclerosing panencephalitis (SSPE) – a rare, late complication of measles – and Guillain–Barré syndrome.

Treatments available for MS

Significant advances have been made in the treatment of MS in recent years, principally in the use of interferon preparations for relapsing-remitting MS. In the UK, treatment consensus guidelines have been prepared by NICE (http://www.nice.org.uk/Guidance/CG8) and by the Association of British Neurologists (http://www.theabn.org/downloads/ABN-MS-Guidelines-2007.pdf).

Steroids

NICE guidelines suggest that individuals suffering an acute relapse should be treated with methylprednisolone, either orally (500 mg to 2 g daily) or intravenously (500 mg to 1 g daily) for 3–5 days. Steroids have no effect on the incidence of relapses, and are not useful other than for treatment of acute attacks.

β-Interferon and glatiramer acetate

Clinical trial results guide recommendations for therapy, which should be offered to patients (aged 18 years or older), who are **ambulant** and have no contraindications to therapy, in the following clinical situations:

1. Patients with a **clinically isolated syndrome** (one episode) and an abnormal MRI typical of MS should be offered β-interferon (reduces relapses by about one-third over 2 years) if they are within 1 year of presentation
2. Patients with **relapsing-remitting MS** and active disease (two or more relapses in the last 2 years, or one disabling relapse, or MRI with new lesions in the last year) should be offered β-interferon or glatiramer acetate (reduces the relapse rate by one-third in relapsing-remitting MS)

In patients with relapsing **secondary progressive MS**, treatment (glatiramer acetate, and β-interferon reduce relapses) should only be considered when relapses are the dominant cause of the increasing disability. Treatment for **primary progressive MS** is not recommended.

Decisions on discontinuation of treatment are generally made clinically, on the basis of:

- Increasing severity of relapses
- Lack of relapse reduction on treatment compared to pre-treatment
- The development of non-relapsing secondary progressive MS with loss of ability to walk

Neutralising antibodies can develop to both interferon IFNβ-1b (40% of patients) and IFNβ-1a (20% of patients). These antibodies are associated with a reduction in the drug effects on relapse rate and also MRI lesions; in some patients the antibodies disappear subsequently, but in others they persist. It is unclear whether neutralising antibodies influence the progression of disability in any way.

These treatments modify disease and may reduce the development of disability through preventing relapses, although any effect has, to date, been modest. They do not affect progression of disability that is unrelated to relapse.

Other immunomodulatory agents for MS treatment

- **Copolymer 1** (glatiramer acetate) and **IV immunoglobulin** therapy both significantly reduce the frequency of attacks of relapsing-remitting MS
- **Oral low-dose methotrexate** therapy also slows down the progression of disability in secondary progressive MS (and possibly in primary progressive MS)
- A number of other treatments, eg mitoxantrone and natalizumab, are under study

16.1.4 Epilepsy

An epileptic seizure is a paroxysmal discharge of neurones sufficient to cause clinically detectable events apparent either to the subject or an observer. Epilepsy is a disorder where more than one such seizure (not including febrile seizures) has occurred. The prevalence of epilepsy is relatively constant at different ages and is around 0.7%, whereas the incidence follows a U-shaped curve with the highest incidence in the young and elderly.

A simplified classification of epilepsy

- **Generalised seizures**
  - Tonic-clonic
  - Absences (3-Hz spike-and-wave activity in ictal EEG)
  - Partial seizures secondarily generalised
- **Partial seizures**
  - Simple partial seizures
  - Complex partial seizures
- **Others**
  - eg myoclonic or atonic

- A typical **tonic-clonic** seizure begins without warning. After loss of consciousness and a short tonic phase, the patient falls to the ground with generalised clonic movements. There may be incontinence and there is post-ictal confusion
- **Simple partial seizures** may affect any area of the brain, but consciousness is not impaired and the ictal EEG shows a local discharge starting over the corresponding cortical area. Any simple seizure may progress (for example, motor seizures may show a Jacksonian march) and become secondarily generalised with a supervening tonic-clonic seizure
- Consciousness is impaired by **complex partial seizures** that typically have a medial temporal (often hippocampal) focus. An aura (sense of déjà vu, strong smell or rising sensation in the abdomen) may precede the seizure, followed by loss of consciousness. There may be automatisms (repetitive stereotyped semi-purposeful movements)

Imaging is usually carried out in most if not all patients with seizures; focal seizures usually imply a focal pathology and imaging is mandatory in such circumstances.

Anticonvulsant agents are discussed in Chapter 2, Clinical Pharmacology, Toxicology and Poisoning.

Treatment of epilepsy

Patients presenting with a first seizure have an overall risk of recurrence of about 35% at 2 years. Most neurologists do not therefore advocate routine treatment for a first seizure. However, some groups have a higher recurrence risk (eg 65% at 2 years for patients with a remote neurological insult and an EEG with epileptiform features) and in these subgroups treatment may be considered.

- After the second or subsequent seizures, drug treatment is routinely advised as the recurrence risk is much higher
- Carbamazepine and sodium valproate are widely accepted as drugs of first choice for partial and generalised seizures, respectively

- Note that 40% of patients with epilepsy will be women of child-bearing age. As valproate is associated with a higher incidence of neural tube defects than other agents, the choice of monotherapy may need to be reviewed (*see* Chapter 2, Clinical Pharmacology, Toxicology and Poisoning)

Any anti-epileptic should be introduced at a low dose and the clinician must be vigilant for idiosyncratic reactions. The dosage can then be escalated until either control is achieved or the maximum allowed dose is reached. If control is not achieved with monotherapy, then at least one additional trial of monotherapy is recommended before combination therapy is considered.

Epilepsy and driving

Current regulations are such that following a first seizure (whether diagnosed as epilepsy or not), driving is not permitted for 1 year with a medical review before restarting driving. Loss of consciousness in which investigations have not revealed a cause is treated in the same way as for a solitary fit.

Patients with epilepsy may be allowed to drive if they have been free from any epileptic attack for 1 year, or if they had an epileptic attack whilst asleep more than 3 years ago and attacks subsequently only when asleep.

To obtain a vocational (HGV, etc) driving licence patients should have been free of epileptic attacks AND off all anti-epileptic medication AND free from a continuing liability to epileptic seizures (eg structural intracranial lesion) for 10 years.

Epilepsy and pregnancy

Seizure rate in pregnancy is predicted by seizure rate prior to pregnancy. All epileptic drugs have teratogenic effects including:

- Cleft-lip/palate
- Congenital heart defects
- Urogenital defects
- Neural tube defects (especially valproate)

Teratogenic effects are more likely if more than one drug is used. Nevertheless, anti-epileptic drugs are not contraindicated in pregnancy, as the effects of uncontrolled epilepsy may be more risky.

There is no increase in infant mortality for epileptic mothers. Folic acid supplementation decreases the incidence of malformations.

16.2   MOVEMENT DISORDERS

16.2.1   Tremors, myoclonus, dystonia and chorea

Essential tremor is a postural tremor of the hands in the absence of any identifiable cause such as drugs.

- Autosomal dominant with incomplete penetrance (35% will have no family history)
- Propranolol is the most effective medication
- Stress will worsen the tremor
- Alcohol will improve the tremor

Resting tremor is seen when the limbs are completely supported and relaxed, and is typical of Parkinsonism ('pill-rolling').

An **action tremor** is typically caused by an ipsilateral cerebellar hemisphere lesion. **Myoclonus** is characterised by the occurrence of sudden involuntary jerks ('fragmentary epilepsy').

Causes of myoclonus
<ul><li>Physiological (normal) hypnic jerks whilst falling asleep</li><li>Drug-induced (eg amitriptyline)</li><li>Alzheimer's disease</li><li>Juvenile myoclonic epilepsy</li><li>Inherited as part of other myoclonic epilepsies (eg Lennox–Gastaut syndrome)</li><li>Metabolic (liver or renal failure)</li><li>Creutzfeldt–Jakob disease</li><li>Following anoxic cerebral injury (eg cardiac arrest)</li><li>As part of a progressive myoclonic encephalopathy (eg Gaucher's disease)</li></ul>

Dystonia is characterised by prolonged spasms of muscle contraction; focal dystonias include spasmodic torticollis, writer's cramp and blepharospasm. Myotonic dystrophy is discussed in Section 16.9.1.

Chorea is a continuous flow of small, jerky movements from limb to limb.

Causes of chorea

- Huntington's disease
- Rheumatic (Sydenham's) chorea
- SLE
- Polycythaemia rubra vera
- Neuroacanthocytosis
- Thyrotoxicosis
- Drug-induced (eg oral contraceptives, phenytoin, neuroleptics)
- Chorea gravidarum (during pregnancy)

Athetosis is a slow sinuous movement of the limbs, and is often seen after severe perinatal brain injury. In the past, athetosis was also used to describe movements that would now be called dystonic.

16.2.2 Parkinsonism

Parkinsonism refers to a triad of symptoms:

- Resting tremor
- Bradykinesia
- Rigidity

This pattern of symptoms comprises an akinetic-rigid syndrome.

Causes of an akinetic-rigid syndrome

- Idiopathic Parkinson's disease
- Drug-induced parkinsonism
- Normal-pressure hydrocephalus
- Progressive supranuclear palsy (PSP)
- Diffuse Lewy body disease
- Dementia pugilistica (secondary to boxing or chronic minor head injury)
- Post-encephalitic parkinsonism
- Depression with psychomotor retardation

- 'Parkinson's plus' syndromes
- Multiple system atrophy (eg Shy–Drager syndrome, olivopontocerebellar atrophy)
- Intoxications (eg carbon monoxide, MPTP, illegal narcotic, manganese)

The diagnosis of idiopathic Parkinson's disease is often inaccurate and there is no single diagnostic test.

Pointers include:

- An asymmetric onset
- Persistent asymmetry
- Good therapeutic response to levodopa initially (over 90% will improve symptomatically)

Pharmacological treatment of Parkinson's disease

In the UK, treatment follows NICE guidelines (http://www.nice.org.uk/Guidance/CG35).

Levodopa has been the mainstay of symptomatic treatment of Parkinson's disease since the 1970s. However, in recent years levodopa has been used less frequently as a first-line treatment, particularly for young patients, because of its involvement in the generation of long-term motor complications (eg end-of-dose wearing-off effect, unpredictable on/off switching). Such complications affect 10% of patients for every year of levodopa treatment.

- Modified-released levodopa has a similar rate of long-term motor complications
- **Selegiline** was commonly added to levodopa in later disease as initial studies suggest that it might have neuroprotective effects. However, this was not confirmed in subsequent trials and indeed one trial found increased mortality with selegiline (although this was not confirmed at follow-up)
- **Anticholinergics** (eg benzhexol) are frequently used for the control of tremor, but they are probably less efficacious than levodopa in respect of other motor symptoms (and they have a worse side-effect profile)

More recently, modern **dopamine agonists** (eg ropinirole, pramipexole, cabergoline and pergolide) have been introduced. Initial trial results suggest that monotherapy with these agents may be marginally less efficacious than with levodopa, but these agents generate fewer long-term motor complications. Many neurologists would now recommend that Parkinson's disease is initially treated with such dopamine agonist monotherapy, particularly for young patients, with small amounts of levodopa added as the disease progresses.

However, there is no single drug of choice for treating early-stage idiopathic Parkinson's disease and so the choice of drug prescribed must take into account clinical and lifestyle characteristics plus patient preference.

Similarly, in later idiopathic Parkinson's disease there is no single drug of choice. Most patients will develop motor complications over time and will require treatment with levodopa. A number of adjuvant drugs can be taken alongside modified-release levodopa preparations, including dopamine agonists, monoamine oxidase B (MAO-B) inhibitors, catechol-*O*-methyltransferase (COMT) inhibitors (eg entacapone, tolcapone), amantadine and apomorphine injections. The purpose of adjuvant therapy is to reduce motor complications and improve quality of life.

Surgical treatment of Parkinson's disease

Interventional surgery with deep brain stimulation, involving placing stereotactic electrodes surgically in the basal ganglia, has recently become available as a potential therapeutic option. Either subthalamic nucleus stimulation or globus pallidus interna stimulation may be considered as a therapeutic option in late-stage Parkinson's disease in patients with motor complications refractory to pharmacological treatment, who remain responsive to levodopa and who have no significant co-morbidities. At present it is not possible to decide which of these two surgical procedures is preferred, or if one form of surgery is more effective than the other.

Parkinson's plus syndromes

In the differential diagnosis of parkinsonism, two groups of Parkinson's plus syndromes are of particular importance: progressive supranuclear palsy and the multiple system atrophies.

Progressive supranuclear palsy (PSP)

Also known as Steele–Richardson syndrome, this presents in the seventh decade with parkinsonism, characteristic ophthalmoplegia and dementia.

The ophthalmoplegia is described in Section 16.3.3.

Other features of PSP may include pseudobulbar palsy, and dementia late in the course of the illness.

Multiple system atrophies

A number of disorders fall into this category, including Shy–Drager syndrome and olivopontocerebellar atrophy. They are clinically characterised by:

- Parkinsonism
- Autonomic failure
- Cerebellar and pyramidal features (olivopontocerebellar atrophy; OPCA)

16.2.3 Huntington's disease (Huntington's chorea)

Huntington's disease is inherited as an autosomal dominant disorder that normally begins in the third or fourth decade and which is clinically characterised by the triad of:

- Chorea (which patients can temporarily suppress)
- Cognitive decline
- Positive family history

Other motor symptoms include dysarthria, dysphagia, ataxia, myoclonus and dystonia. Childhood onset is atypical and may be associated with rigidity.

Genetics of Huntington's disease

- Autosomal dominant with complete penetrance
- There is expansion of the CAG trinucleotide repeat within this gene (see Chapter 14, Molecular Medicine)
- Gene is on chromosome 4 and codes for a protein, huntingtin
- Genetic testing in asymptomatic individuals is now available

Neuropathologically the disease causes neuronal loss in the cortex and striatum, especially the caudate. Treatment is unsatisfactory and relies on neuroleptics, which partially relieve chorea through interfering with dopaminergic transmission.

Other causes of chorea

- Levodopa-induced chorea in parkinsonism
- SLE
- Antiphospholipid syndrome
- Wilson's disease
- Sydenham's chorea (autoimmune, preceded by group A *Streptococcus* infection)
- Neuroacanthocytosis

16.2.4 Wilson's disease

This is an autosomal recessive condition. The responsible gene is *ATP7B*, located on chromosome 13. The gene sequence is similar to sections of the gene *ATP7A*, which is defective in Menke's disease (another disease caused by defects in copper transport). The similar sequences code for copper-binding regions, part of a P-type ATPase transmembrane protein. Clinically, the disease is characterised by abnormal copper deposition in the basal ganglia, as well as elsewhere in the brain, the eye and in the liver. This disorder should be considered in any young person presenting with an extrapyramidal syndrome. Psychiatric symptoms are particularly common in adults. (*See also* Chapter 13, Metabolic Diseases and Chapter 6, Gastroenterology).

16.3 NEURO-OPHTHALMOLOGY

This section should be read in conjunction with Chapter 17, Ophthalmology.

16.3.1 Visual fields

The optic pathways, and the visual defects resulting from various lesions at different sites are illustrated in Figure 16.2.

Optic nerve fibres leave the retina, and travel in the optic nerve to the optic chiasm. Lesions of the retina and optic nerve produce field defects in the ipsilateral eye alone. Lesions at the optic chiasm typically produce **bitemporal hemianopia**. Causes include:

- Pituitary tumour (compression from below)
- Craniopharyngioma
- Intracranial aneurysm
- Meningioma
- Dilated third ventricle

From the optic chiasm fibres run in the optic tract to the lateral geniculate nucleus (thalamus). **Retro-chiasmal** lesions produce **homonymous** field defects, the degree of congruity increasing with more posterior lesions. From the lateral geniculate nucleus fibres pass in the optic radiation to the primary visual cortex, located in the occipital cortex. The fibres from the lower and upper quadrants of the retina diverge, the upper fibres (lower half of the visual field) passing though the parietal lobes, the lower fibres (upper half of the visual field) through the temporal lobes. Hence:

- Temporal lobe lesions may cause superior quadrant homonymous hemianopia
- Parietal lobe lesions may cause inferior quadrant homonymous hemianopia

Note that the decussation of fibres at the optic chiasm means that the right visual field is represented in the left occipital cortex and vice versa.

- Within the **calcarine sulcus**, there is a topographic representation of the visual field with more peripheral regions represented anteriorly, and more central (foveal) regions located posteriorly

Figure 16.2 Optic pathway abnormalities and associated defects

Visual Fields

1. Central scotoma. Ipsilateral lesion due to optic nerve disease, eg optic neuritis

2. Complete loss of ipsilateral field, eg due to optic nerve transection

3. Bitemporal hemianopia – chiasmal lesion, pituitary craniopharyngioma

4. Homonymous superior quadrantanopia ('pie in the sky') - temporal lobe lesion

5. Homonymous inferior quadrantanopia - parietal lobe lesion

6. Homonymous hemianopia - less congruous, reflects more anterior lesion

7. Homonymous hemianopia - highly congruous - posterior lesion

optic nerve

optic chiasm

lateral geniculate nucleus

optic radiations

KEY

Vision spared — Area of vision loss

- At the very tip of the occipital lobe, the representation of the fovea (macula) is a vascular watershed, supplied by the posterior and middle cerebral arteries. Sparing of this area ('foveal sparing') may therefore occur with a posterior cerebral artery cerebrovascular accident

Cortical blindness

This is usually due to bilateral occipital infarcts and it results in severe or complete loss of vision. Other features are:

- Pupillary responses are preserved
- The patient may deny that they have visual loss (Anton syndrome)
- Macular sparing may occur and the patient may have a tiny island of preserved central field which will allow some useful reading vision. However, this central field may be so small as to be useless for distance vision

16.3.2 Pupils

Pupil size depends on both pupillodilator (sympathetic) and pupilloconstrictor (parasympathetic) fibres. Pupilloconstrictor fibres travel from the Edinger–Westphal nucleus in the midbrain to the orbit on the third nerve. The path of sympathetic fibres is described below.

The pupillary light reflex pathway has two parts:

- **Afferent**: retina, optic nerve, lateral geniculate body, midbrain
- **Efferent**: Edinger–Westphal nucleus (midbrain) to third nerve

Afferent pupillary defect

This is detected by the 'swinging flashlight' test. If the amount of light information carried by one eye is less than that from the contralateral side when the light is swung from the normal to the abnormal side, pupil dilatation is observed. This is also known as a Marcus Gunn pupil.

An afferent pupillary defect is a sign of **asymmetric disease anterior to the chiasm**.

Causes:

- Retinal disease (eg vascular occlusion, detachment)

- Optic nerve disease (eg optic neuritis, glaucoma) with asymmetric nerve damage

Causes of a small pupil (miosis)

Miosis can be caused by:

- Senile miosis
- **Pontine haemorrhage**
- **Horner syndrome**: see below
- **Argyll Robertson pupil**: bilateral (may be asymmetrical) small irregular pupils which do not react to light but accommodate normally. They dilate poorly in the dark and in response to mydriatics. Lesion is in the rostral midbrain near the Sylvian aqueduct, such that the light reaction fibres are interfered with, but the more ventral near fibres are spared
- **Drugs**: systemic (opiates); topical (pilocarpine)
- **Myotonic dystrophy**

Horner syndrome

Horner syndrome is caused by interruption of sympathetic pupillomotor fibres (see Table 16.1), and is one of the causes of a small pupil (miosis).

Table 16.1. Causes of Horner syndrome

Anatomical structures	Causes
Brainstem or spinal cord First-order neurone	Vascular, trauma, neoplastic demyelination, syringomyelia, ependymoma
Pre-ganglionic lesion Second-order neurone: anterior roots (C8–T3), sympathetic chain	**Chest lesion**: apical carcinoma, cervical rib, mediastinal mass **Cervical lesion**: lymphadenopathy, trauma, thyroid neoplasm **Surgical**: thyroidectomy, carotid angiography, endarterectomy
Post-ganglionic lesion Third-order neurone: stellate ganglion, carotid sympathetic plexus, fibres to eyelid in branch of III, fibres to pupil in ciliary nerve	Internal carotid artery dissection, cavernous sinus lesions, orbital apex disease

Clinical characteristics of Horner syndrome

- **Miosis**: hydroxyamphetamine differentiates between pre- and post-ganglionic (miosis more evident in dim light 'dilation lag')
- **Enophthalmos**: apparent, due to narrowing of the palpebral aperture by ptosis and elevation of the lower lid
- **Ptosis**: partial – levator palpebrae is 30% supplied by sympathetic
- **Anhidrosis**: whole face means lesion proximal to common carotid artery
- **Vasodilatation**

Congenital Horner syndrome is associated with difference in iris colour (heterochromia).

Causes of a large pupil (mydriasis)

Mydriasis can be due to:

- **Adie's (tonic) pupil**: idiopathic dilated pupil with poor reaction to light and slow constriction to prolonged near effort. Seventy per cent female, 80% initially unilateral, 4% per year becoming bilateral. Associated with decreased deep tendon reflexes (Holmes–Adie syndrome)
- **Third nerve palsy**: see later
- **Drugs**: systemic (eg antidepressants, amphetamines); mydriatrics (eg tropicamide, atropine)
- **Trauma**: sphincter pupillae rupture

16.3.3 The oculomotor system and its disorders

A mnemonic to remember oculomotor innervation is:

$$LR_6(SO_4)_3$$

The sixth nerve supplies the lateral rectus, the fourth supplies the superior oblique and the third nerve innervates the others.

Disorders of conjugate gaze

Symmetrical and synchronous movements of the two eyes together are known as **conjugate eye movements**.

Causes of oculomotor palsies

- Ischaemic infarction of a nerve
- Intracerebral aneurysm
- Head trauma
- Neurosarcoidosis
- Myasthenia gravis
- Tumours at the base of the brain (eg glioma, metastasis, carcinomatous meningitis)
- Ophthalmoplegic migraine
- Arteritides
- Meningitides (eg syphilitic or tuberculous)
- Orbital lymphoma
- Orbital cellulitis

Causes of bilateral ophthalmoplegia

- Dysthyroid disease
- Myasthenia gravis
- Myositis
- Midbrain tumour or infarction
- Guillain–Barré syndrome
- Basal meningitides (eg tuberculous)
- Wernicke's encephalopathy

The effects of paresis on diplopia are predicted by three rules:

- Paresis of horizontally acting muscles tends to cause horizontal diplopia, and vertical paresis leads to vertical diplopia
- The direction of gaze in which the separation of the images is maximum is the direction of action of the paretic muscles
- The image seen furthest from the centre of gaze (the **false** image) usually belongs to the paretic eye, so when covering the paretic eye, this image will disappear

Third nerve

The third nerve nucleus is a large nucleus located in the midbrain at the level of the superior colliculus. Fibres pass through the red nucleus and the pyramidal tract in the cerebral peduncle. The nerve then passes between the posterior cerebral and superior cerebellar arteries, through the cavernous sinus and into the orbit via the superior orbital fissure. The large nuclear size of the third nerve means that it is rarely entirely damaged by lesions and complete third nerve palsies tend to be caused by **peripheral lesions**. Complete third nerve palsy causes:

- Ptosis
- Eye deviated down (preserved superior oblique) and out (preserved lateral rectus)
- All other movements reduced or absent, dependent on whether partial or complete
- Pupil fixed and dilated

Lateral gaze is intact and attempted downward gaze causes intorsion (inwards rotation of the eye); normal downgaze requires not only superior oblique but also inferior rectus.

The pupil may be normal (pupil-sparing or 'medical' third) or dilated and fixed to light (so-called 'surgical' third). This is because parasympathetic pupilloconstrictor fibres run on the surface of the nerve; these are fed by the pial vessels and are therefore spared in palsies of vascular aetiology. However, they are affected early by a compressive lesion (when the pupil is involved in 95% of cases).

Causes of a third nerve palsy

- Posterior communicating artery aneurysm (usually but not always painful)
- Diabetes, usually pupil-sparing (75%)
- Arteriosclerotic
- Cavernous sinus pathology (eg thrombosis, aneurysm, fistula, pituitary mass). Frequently associated with lesions of cranial nerves IV, V and VI (*see* Section 16.3.5)

- Orbital apex disease, such as tumours, thyroid disease, orbital cellulitis, granulomatous disease; often associated with palsies of cranial nerves IV–VI and optic nerve dysfunction
- Trauma
- Uncal herniation; the third nerve travels anteriorly on the edge of the cerebellar tentorium and may be compressed by the uncal portion of the temporal lobe with increased intracranial pressure due to a supratentorial cause

Fourth nerve

The fourth nerve nucleus lies in the midbrain at the level of the inferior colliculus. The fourth nerve has the longest intracranial course; passing between the posterior cerebral and superior cerebellar arteries, lateral to the third nerve and into the orbit through the cavernous sinus and superior orbital fissure. It is the only nerve to exit the dorsal aspect of the brainstem. A fourth nerve lesion is the commonest cause of vertical diplopia. Looking down and in is most difficult and classically the patient notices diplopia descending stairs or reading.

Causes of a fourth nerve palsy

- Vascular (20%)
- Diabetes
- Vasculitis
- Cavernous sinus syndrome
- Congenital (decompensation causes symptoms) (30%)
- Trauma (susceptible to contrecoup injury, for example whiplash because of dorsal brainstem exit) (30%)
- Orbital apex syndrome

Sixth nerve

The sixth nerve nucleus lies in the mid-pons inferior to the fourth ventricle, and is motor to the lateral rectus. A sixth nerve palsy causes convergence of the eyes in primary position and diplopia maximal on lateral gaze towards the side of the lesion. The affected eye **deviates medially** due to the unopposed action of medial rectus.

Causes of a sixth nerve palsy

- Vascular
- Trauma
- Cavernous sinus syndrome
- Orbital apex syndrome
- Increased intracranial pressure (false localising sign due to stretching of the nerve)

Other disorders of conjugate gaze

Internuclear ophthalmoplegia is a disorder of horizontal eye movement due to a lesion in the medial longitudinal fasciculus which connects the IIIrd and VIth cranial nerve nuclei in the pons (see Figure 16.3).

Features of internuclear ophthalmoplegia

- Impaired adduction of the eye ipsilateral to the lesion (complete paralysis – minor slowing)
- Horizontal nystagmus in the abducting eye contralateral to the lesion
- Convergence normal (this differentiates it from a medial rectus lesion)
- Vertical gaze nystagmus occasionally present

Bilateral internuclear ophthalmoplegia results in defective adduction (bilaterally), with nystagmus in the abducting eye.

Figure 16.3 Pathology of internuclear ophthalmoplegia

* Lesion of left MLF

MR = medial rectus
LR = lateral rectus
PPRF = parapontine reticular formation
MLF = medial longitudinal fasciculus

* This causes deficient adduction during attempted conjugate gaze away from side of MLF lesion

Causes of internuclear ophthalmoplegia

- Multiple sclerosis (most common; may be bilateral in younger adults)
- Vascular
- Trauma
- Occlusion of the basilar artery
- SLE
- Miller–Fisher syndrome
- Drug overdose (barbiturates, phenytoin or amitriptyline)
- Wernicke's encephalopathy

Causes of **impaired vertical conjugate gaze** include progressive supranuclear palsy, Parinaud syndrome and thalamic or midbrain pathology.

Progressive supranuclear palsy (Steele–Richardson syndrome): the ophthalmoplegia is a paresis of vertical conjugate gaze which is supranuclear; downgaze cannot be elicited voluntarily but if the patient is allowed to fixate whilst the head is moved passively, the eyes have a full range of movements (doll's head movement). This pattern implies that while the oculomotor nuclei are intact, in that the eyes can be driven into eccentric positions within the orbit, the supranuclear descending control of voluntary eye movements is impaired.

Parinaud syndrome is also known as the dorsal midbrain syndrome, with damage to the midbrain and superior colliculus. It leads to:

- Impaired upgaze and accommodation
- Retraction of the eyelids
- Loss of light reflex with preserved convergence reflex
- Convergence retraction nystagmus
- Relative mydriasis

Possible causes include pineal tumour, stroke or haemorrhage, hydrocephalus or demyelinating disease.

Other causes of upgaze palsy

- Progressive supranuclear palsy
- Parinaud's syndrome
- Myasthenia gravis
- Miller–Fisher syndrome
- Thyroid eye disease – mimics upgaze weakness by causing fibrosis of inferior recti

16.3.4 Nystagmus

Nystagmus is a defect of control of ocular position that leads to a rhythmic involuntary to-and-fro oscillation of the eyes. There are three types:

- **Pendular**: no distinct fast and slow phases, both being of equal velocity
- **Jerk**: distinct fast and slow phases; the amplitude usually increases with gaze towards the direction of the fast phase
- **Rotatory**: combination of vertical and horizontal nystagmus

Causes of congenital nystagmus

- X-linked or autosomal dominant; usually horizontal
- Secondary to poor vision (eg albinism, untreated congenital cataract, congenital optic atrophy)

Causes of acquired nystagmus

- **Vestibular lesions**: the lesion may be in the VIIIth nerve, inner ear, brainstem or vestibular pathway; jerky nystagmus with fast phase away from the side of the lesion and made worse by gaze in that direction; typically improves with visual fixation
- **Cerebellar lesions**: fast phase towards the side of the lesion
- **Drug-induced** (eg alcohol, barbiturates, phenytoin)

Downbeat nystagmus (where the fast phase is down) is associated with foramen magnum lesions (eg Arnold–Chiari malformation, spinocerebellar degeneration, syringobulbia, platybasia), whereas upbeat nystagmus is typically due to intrinsic brain-stem disease, or, rarely, cerebellar vermis lesions or organophosphates.

16.3.5 Cavernous sinus syndrome

The major structures passing through the cavernous sinus are the IIIrd, IVth and VIth cranial nerves, the ophthalmic division of the Vth nerve, the sympathetic carotid plexus and the intracavernous carotid artery (see Figure 16.4). Lesions in this region may therefore produce a total internal and external ophthalmoplegia. The main causes of cavernous sinus syndrome are:

- **Trauma**
- **Vascular**: aneurysm of intracavernous carotid artery or the posterior communicating artery; cavernous sinus thrombosis; carotico-cavernous fistula

- **Neoplastic**: primary intracranial tumours, direct spread from nasopharyngeal tumours or metastatic
- **Inflammatory**: due to infection (eg sinusitis, tuberculosis, or inflammatory disease such as Wegener's granulomatosis).

Carotico-cavernous fistula

This may be either a high- or low-pressure shunt.

- **High pressure, high flow**: shunt due to a fistula between the cavernous sinus and the intracavernous carotid artery. Usually traumatic in origin, producing marked proptosis which may be pulsatile, palsies of the IIIrd, IVth and VIth nerves, an orbital bruit with an injected chemotic eye and elevated intraocular pressure secondary to raised episcleral venous pressure
- **Low pressure, low flow**: shunt occurs because of communication between the dural branches of the internal or external carotid arteries and the cavernous sinus. This type is more common in elderly patients, often occurring spontaneously in arteriosclerotic individuals, and results in a milder clinical picture

Figure 16.4 Main structures passing through the cavernous sinus

At the level of the pituitary fossa

At the level of the anterior clinoid process

Ophthalmic artery

ON

Anterior clinoid

Pituitary fossa

III

IV

IC

VI

V₁

Sphenoid sinus

Sphenoid sinus

III

IV

V₁

VI

V₂

IC - Internal carotid artery
ON - Optic nerve
Numbers indicate cranial nerves

16.4 OTHER BRAINSTEM AND CRANIAL NERVE DISORDERS

The brainstem and locations of the principal cranial nerve nuclei are illustrated in Figure 16.5.

16.4.1 Facial nerve

The facial nerve has the following functions:

- Motor to the muscles of facial expression
- Taste fibres from the anterior two-thirds of the tongue (in the chorda tympani)
- Taste from the palate (nerve of the pterygoid canal)
- Secretomotor parasympathetic fibres to parotid, submandibular and sublingual glands
- Nerve to stapedius

Taste fibres, the nerve to stapedius and to the facial muscles leave the nerve **below** the geniculate ganglion.

Causes of a facial nerve palsy

- Brainstem tumour
- Neurosarcoidosis
- Cerebellopontine angle lesions (eg acoustic neuroma)
- Cholesteatoma
- Lyme disease
- Stroke
- Multiple sclerosis
- Otitis media
- Ramsay Hunt syndrome
- Diabetes
- Guillain–Barré syndrome

If the palsy is bilateral, exclude myasthenia gravis, facial myopathy (look for ptosis) and neurosarcoidosis. Weakness of frontalis (forehead) indicates a nuclear or intranuclear (lower motor neurone, LMN) lesion.

Figure 16.5 Locations of the principal cranial nerve nuclei within the brainstem

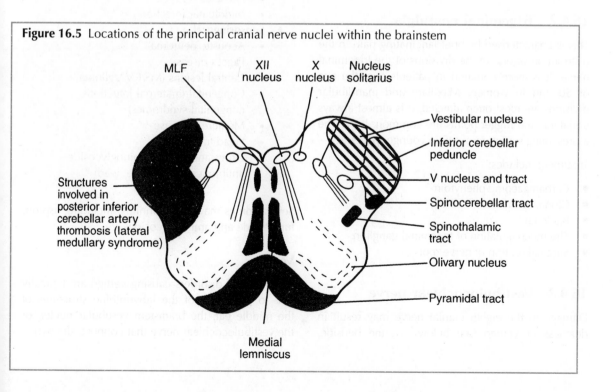

Bell's palsy

An isolated facial nerve palsy of acute onset, thought to be secondary to viral infection.

- Unilateral facial weakness
- Absent taste sensation on anterior two-thirds of tongue
- Pain behind the ear

Usually recovery begins by 2 weeks but the palsy may be prolonged and 10% have residual weakness. Electrophysiological tests can help predict the outcome and tapering dose of steroids (given from onset) improves the outcome. Tarsorrhaphy may be needed to prevent corneal damage.

Ramsay Hunt syndrome

Features include herpes zoster, affecting the geniculate ganglion, and facial palsy with herpetic vesicles in the auditory meatus. Deafness is a complication.

16.4.2 Trigeminal neuralgia

This is characterised by brief lancinating pain in the distribution of one of the divisions of the trigeminal nerve. It is more common in patients over the age of 50 and in women. Maxillary and mandibular divisions are most often affected, it is almost always unilateral and trigger points are common. It may be a presenting symptom of MS in younger patients.

Treatment includes:

- Carbamazepine/phenytoin
- Clonazepam
- Baclofen
- Thermocoagulation of trigeminal ganglion
- Surgical section of nerve root

16.4.3 Vestibulocochlear nerve

Damage to the eighth cranial nerve may result in deafness or vertigo (see below). At the bedside,

sensorineural and conductive deafness are distinguished by Rinne's and Weber's tests.

Rinne's test

- Air > bone conduction normally
- Hearing decreased and bone < air conduction in conduction deafness
- Hearing decreased and air > bone conduction in sensorineural deafness

Weber's test

- Central normally
- Lateralises to normal side in sensorineural deafness
- Lateralises to deaf side in conduction deafness

Causes of deafness

- **Conduction**
  - Ear wax
  - Otosclerosis
  - Middle ear infection
- **Sensorineural**
  - Acoustic neuroma
  - Paget's disease
  - Central lesions (MS/CVA/glioma)
  - Congenital (maternal infections, congenital syndromes)
  - Ménière's disease
  - Head trauma
  - Drugs and toxins (aminoglycoside antibiotics, furosemide, lead)

Several drugs may cause tinnitus, including aspirin, furosemide and aminoglycosides.

Vertigo

Neurological disorders causing vertigo are typically due to pathology of the labyrinthine structures of the middle ear, the brainstem vestibular nuclei, or the vestibulocochlear nerve that connects the two.

Common causes of vertigo

- **Labyrinthine (peripheral)**
  - Trauma (including barotrauma)
  - Ménière's disease
  - Acute viral infections
  - Chronic bacterial otitis media
  - Occlusion of the internal auditory artery
- **Brainstem (central)**
  - Acute vestibular neuronitis
  - Vascular disease
  - MS
  - Space-occupying lesions (eg brainstem glioma)
  - Toxic causes (eg alcohol, drugs)
  - Hypoglycaemia

Features of the lateral medullary syndrome

- Ipsilateral loss of pain and temperature sensation on the face (V)
- Ipsilateral paralysis of palate, pharynx and vocal cords (IX, X)
- Ipsilateral ataxia (inferior cerebellar peduncle)
- Contralateral loss of pain and temperature sensation on the body (spinothalamic tract)
- Ipsilateral Horner syndrome (descending sympathetic outflow)
- Vertigo, nausea and vomiting, nystagmus (vestibular nuclei)

Acoustic neuroma

Acoustic neuroma is a benign tumour arising on the eighth cranial nerve as it emerges from the brainstem in the cerebellopontine angle. It is a common cause of a **cerebellopontine angle syndrome**:

- Cranial nerve VIII is affected early, but the patient may not report hearing loss, tinnitus and vertigo
- Corneal reflex (cranial nerve V) is absent
- Facial sensation is abnormal (V nerve)
- The facial nerve is affected late

Investigation is by use of MRI or high-resolution CT scanning, and treatment is surgical removal.

16.4.4 Lateral medullary syndrome

The lateral medullary (Wallenberg) syndrome is usually due to vertebral artery or posterior inferior cerebellar artery occlusion, which damages the dorsolateral medulla and inferior cerebellar peduncle (see Figure 16.5).

16.4.5 Other causes of cranial nerve palsies

The cranial nerves may commonly be involved in the following neuropathies:

- **Diabetes mellitus**: CN III or other oculomotor
- **Guillain–Barré/Miller–Fisher**: CN VII, oculomotor
- **Diphtheria**: classically CN IX
- **Neurosarcoidosis**: CN VII and bilateral VII

16.5 SPINAL CORD DISORDERS

16.5.1 Neuroanatomy

The spinal cord ends at the lower border of L2. There is one principal descending pathway, the corticospinal tract, which crosses in the midbrain. The two principal ascending sensory pathways are the dorsal columns and spinothalamic tracts (see below).

Ascending sensory pathways

- **Dorsal (posterior) columns**
  - Joint position sense and vibration
  - Carry sensation from the same side of the body (ipsilateral – uncrossed)
  - Synapse in the brainstem at the cuneate and gracilis nuclei, then decussate
- **Spinothalamic tracts**
  - Pain and temperature
  - Incoming fibres cross immediately or within a few segments
  - Crossed tract results in **lamination**, with fibres from legs outside fibres from the arms

16.5.2 Brown–Séquard syndrome

This clinical syndrome is caused by lateral hemisection of the spinal cord, resulting in:

- Ipsilateral upper motor neurone weakness below the lesion (severed descending corticospinal tract fibres)
- Ipsilateral loss of joint position sense and vibration (severed ascending dorsal column fibres)
- Contralateral loss of pain and temperature sensation (severed crossed ascending spinothalamic tract fibres)

Light touch sensation is often clinically normal below the lesion, and the clinical syndrome is most commonly (but not exclusively) caused by multiple sclerosis.

16.5.3 Motor neurone disease

Motor neurone disease (MND) is a degenerative disorder affecting both lower motor neurones (LMN) and upper motor neurones (UMN) supplying limb and bulbar muscles. There is no involvement of sensory nerves, and the aetiology is unknown. There are three principal types.

- **Progressive muscular atrophy**: typically presents with LMN signs affecting a single limb that then progresses. Best prognosis (still poor)
- **Amyotrophic lateral sclerosis**: both LMN and UMN are involved; typical clinical picture would be LMN signs in the arms and bilateral UMN signs in the legs. Intermediate prognosis
- **Progressive bulbar palsy**: bulbar musculature affected with poor prognosis

Examination may initially show only fasciculation but progresses to widespread wasting and weakness, spastic dysarthria and exaggerated reflexes.

Diagnosis of MND

Diagnosis is largely clinical but confirmatory investigations include nerve conduction studies and EMG, which show evidence of chronic partial denervation and widespread fasciculation with normal sensory nerves and preserved motor nerve conduction velocity (these latter features distinguish the disorder from peripheral neuropathies). CSF protein concentration may be slightly increased. Prognosis is poor with death within 5 years typical.

Treatment of motor neurone disease

Riluzole is a drug which affects glutamate neurotransmission in a complex fashion. It is usually well tolerated, is associated with a modest improvement in survival (about 2–3 months at 18 months) and is NICE-approved for treatment of probable or definite MND. However, its effects upon quality of life remain unknown and it should be emphasised that the mainstay of treatment of MND remains symptomatic, with a multidisciplinary approach to problems such as nutrition and ventilation.

16.5.4 Absent knee jerks and extensor plantars

The causative lesion typically produces both LMN (diminished reflexes) and UMN (extensor plantars) signs.

Causes include:

- Friedreich's ataxia
- Subacute combined degeneration of the cord
- Motor neurone disease
- Taboparesis
- Conus medullaris compression (the conus represents the transition between spinal cord proper and the filum terminale at the lower end of the cord). Compression can cause UMN signs from cord compression and LMN signs from filum terminale (nerve root compression)

16.6 VASCULAR DISORDERS, CEREBRAL TUMOURS AND OTHER CNS PATHOLOGIES

This section considers vascular disorders of the CNS, the important causes of headache, cerebral tumours and a number of metabolic disorders affecting the CNS.

16.6.1 Transient ischaemic attacks

A transient ischaemic attack (TIA) is a focal CNS disturbance developing and fading over minutes or hours to give full recovery within 24 hours. Most TIAs are caused by embolism.

Differential diagnosis of TIA

- Migraine
- Malignant hypertension
- MS (unusual)
- Epilepsy
- Hypoglycaemia

Modifiable risk factors for TIA include hypertension, diabetes mellitus, cigarette smoking, drug use (drugs of abuse, oral contraceptive pill, alcohol), elevated haematocrit and carotid stenosis. Medical management with oral aspirin significantly decreases the chance of subsequent TIA or stroke.

Carotid arterial stenosis

If a severe (70%–99%) carotid stenosis is present then the existing evidence suggests that carotid endarterectomy (by an experienced surgeon) should be undertaken. Carotid endarterectomy carries a relatively high (about 8%) risk of perioperative stroke, so the patient trades a short-term increased risk of stroke for a significant long-term reduction in subsequent risk.

16.6.2 Stroke

A completed stroke is a focal CNS disturbance due to a vascular cause where the deficit persists. The aetiology may be embolic, thrombotic or haemorrhagic. The presenting symptoms depend on the vascular territory involved.

Lacunar strokes

Lacunar infarctions occur where small intracerebral arteries are occluded by atheroma or thrombosis. Typically, small low-density subcortical lesions are seen in the area of the internal capsule.

- Lacunar syndromes cause a pure motor, sensorimotor or pure sensory stroke, with no involvement of higher cortical functions
- Lacunar infarcts have a low mortality and relatively good prognosis for recovery; they are primarily associated with hypertension

Other types of stroke involve either the anterior or posterior cerebral circulation. **Intracerebral haemorrhage** is primarily associated with the rupture of microaneurysms situated in the basal ganglion or brainstem.

Risk factors for stroke

- Diabetes
- Hypertension
- Smoking
- Cocaine abuse
- Previous TIA or stroke
- Male sex
- Increased Hb, haemoglobinopathy
- Family history

Diagnosis of stroke is on clinical grounds supported by neuroimaging. (CT is commonly used initially in order to distinguish between haemorrhage and ischaemic causes, but note that up to 50% of early CT scans will be normal in acute ischaemic stroke.) Management of stroke is initially conservative, though patients with expanding cerebellar or cerebral haematoma may need surgical treatment. Aspirin is effective in secondary prevention. Mortality from stroke is between 20% and 30%, with poorer prognosis in old patients with depressed level of consciousness.

Factors associated with a poor prognosis in stroke

- Complete paralysis of a limb (MRC grade 0 or 1)
- Loss of consciousness at onset of stroke
- Higher cerebral dysfunction
- Coma or drowsiness at 24 hours
- Old age

Treatment of stroke

In the UK, NICE has recently published guidance on the diagnosis and management of TIA and acute stroke (http://www.nice.org.uk/Guidance/CG68). For **acute stroke** urgent treatment improves outcome. In general:

- All patients with acute stroke who have had a diagnosis of intracerebral haemorrhage ruled out by brain imaging should be given aspirin 300 mg as soon as possible and certainly within 24 hours

- Thrombolysis with alteplase can be given within appropriately equipped acute stroke services and is indicated if presentation is less than 3 hours from symptom onset and following brain imaging to rule out intracerebral haemorrhage
- In addition to specific pharmacological treatment of stroke, full supportive care (including treatments directed at the maintenance of cerebral blood flow, oxygenation and normoglycaemia) is recommended in the context of a multidisciplinary stroke unit

16.6.3 Subarachnoid haemorrhage

Around 5%–10% of all strokes are due to subarachnoid haemorrhage (SAH). Causes include:

- Ruptured arterial aneurysm
- Trauma
- Ruptured arteriovenous malformation
- Cocaine or amphetamine abuse
- Hypertension

Eighty per cent of intracranial aneurysms are located in the anterior circulation, most on the anterior communicating artery, and 15% are bilateral.

Investigation of subarachnoid haemorrhage

SAH is typically investigated with CT and lumbar puncture (LP):

- CT may be negative in up to 20% of suspected SAH, so a normal CT does not exclude the diagnosis
- LP shows xanthochromia (due to red cell breakdown products, only visible >4 hours after haemorrhage)
- Other recognised findings include transient glycosuria, low CSF glucose or lengthening of the QT interval (leading to tachyarrhythmias or torsades de pointes)

Treatment of SAH

The management of SAH depends upon making the diagnosis, locating the underlying aneurysm and occluding it. About a quarter of patients will die within a day of presentation, and a third of those who survive the first day will subsequently die of complications or rebleeding. At presentation, several factors have prognostic value for poor outcome, the most important of which are decreased level of consciousness, increasing age and amount of blood visible on CT scan.

- All patients are typically treated with oral nimodipine, which reduces intracranial vasospasm and so can prevent delayed cerebral ischaemia. It probably reduces the risk of poor outcome by about a third
- Early operative intervention to occlude the causative aneurysm is now usual practice for most patients in reasonable condition, but this is not supported by randomised controlled trial evidence

Complications of subarachnoid haemorrhage

- **Neurological**
  - Rebleeding
  - Hydrocephalus
  - Focal ischaemic injury from cerebral vasospasm
- **Systemic**
  - Fever
  - Tachyarrhythmias secondary to catecholamine release
  - Neurogenic pulmonary oedema (rarely)
  - Hyponatraemia secondary to syndrome of inappropriate antidiuretic hormone

Intracranial aneurysms are associated with:

- Polycystic kidney disease
- Ehlers–Danlos syndrome
- Fibromuscular dysplasia causing renal artery stenosis
- Medium-vessel arteritides (eg polyarteritis nodosa)
- Coarctation of the aorta

16.6.4 Headache

Headache is an extremely common symptom that has a multiplicity of causes. Leaving aside acute unexpected headaches caused by, for example, subarachnoid haemorrhage, important causes of chronic recurrent headache include:

- Tension headache
- Classic (accompanied by focal neurological symptoms) or common migraine
- Cluster headache
- Headaches in association with raised intracranial pressure

Migraine

Migraine is classically preceded by a visual aura followed by a unilateral throbbing headache with photophobia and nausea.

Features of migraine

- EEG and neurovascular abnormalities associated with the headache
- Rarely may result in stroke
- May have unilateral lacrimation
- Can be associated with (reversible) neurological signs (eg hemiplegic migraine)

The neurological symptoms suggest a vascular origin, and a popular hypothesis is that of 'spreading depression' of cortical blood flow. However, whilst changes in cerebral perfusion undoubtedly occur, it is presently not clear whether these are primary or whether brainstem neuroregulatory abnormalities of serotonergic or noradrenergic neurotransmitters are more important. Therapy is aimed at stopping an attack (abortive) or if the frequency of attacks is high enough, regular medication is given as a prophylactic agent.

Migraine therapy

- **Abortive**
  - Paracetamol
  - Codeine ± anti-emetic
  - Ergotamine*
  - Sumatriptan (5HT$_1$ agonist)
- **Prophylactic**
  - Propranolol
  - Pizotifen
  - Amitriptyline
  - Methysergide

*Ergotamine is contraindicated with cardiovascular/ peripheral vascular disease as it is a vasoconstrictor; also in pregnancy, Raynaud's or with renal impairment

Cluster headache

Cluster headache has a distinct pattern, with attacks occurring in clusters lasting days or weeks and remissions lasting months. Males are more often affected than females, and onset of attacks is typically between 25 and 50 years.

Typical features of cluster headache

- Unilateral severe headache lasting up to an hour
- Lacrimation
- Partial Horner's may occur
- Pain may be retro-orbital
- Redness of ipsilateral eye
- Nasal stuffiness

The aetiology is not known and treatment is difficult. Management of the acute attack includes inhaled oxygen (face mask), ergotamine and sumatriptan. Steroids may be helpful. Lithium treatment is used for prophylaxis.

16.6.5 Benign intracranial hypertension (BIH)

This term refers to a group of patients who present with headaches and profound papilloedema, yet have no focal neurological signs or intracranial

lesion on imaging. The most common presentation is in overweight young women and comprises:

- Headache
- Blurred vision
- Dizziness
- Transient visual obscurations
- Horizontal diplopia

Papilloedema is found on examination, with peripheral constriction of the visual fields and enlarged blind spot. The CSF pressure is elevated.

Iatrogenic (drug-induced) causes include:

- Oral contraceptive pill
- Steroids
- Tetracycline
- Vitamin A
- Nitrofurantoin
- Nalidixic acid

Treatment of BIH

This consists of weight loss, acetazolamide and repeated lumbar puncture to reduce the CSF pressure. In more resistant cases or those associated with regular recurrence, **ventriculoperitoneal shunt** may be necessary. **Optic nerve sheath fenestration** can be performed in patients whose sight is threatened.

16.6.6 Wernicke's encephalopathy

This is a neurological syndrome of acute onset characterised by:

- Ataxia
- Ophthalmoplegia
- Nystagmus
- Global confusional state
- Polyneuropathy (in some cases)

It may evolve into Korsakoff syndrome, with a dense amnesia and confabulation. The syndrome is commonly associated with alcoholism and may be precipitated by a sudden glucose load, but may also be caused by prolonged vomiting (eg hyperemesis gravidarum), dialysis or gastrointestinal cancer.

Red cell transketolase activity is reduced. Neuro-pathologically it is characterised by periaqueductal punctate haemorrhage. Treatment with thiamine should lead to rapid reversal of the neurological symptoms, though the memory disorder may endure. (*See* Chapter 18, Psychiatry, for further discussion.)

16.6.7 Cerebral tumours

Primary and secondary intracranial neoplasms have an approximately equal incidence. Both produce presenting symptoms through local neural damage giving rise to focal neurological symptoms, epilepsy or symptoms of raised intracranial pressure, such as headache. The most common presenting symptoms of a glioma are epilepsy and headache.

Gliomas

Gliomas are the most common primary intracranial neoplasm. Most commonly gliomas are derived from the astrocyte cell line, though less commonly oligodendrogliomas, ependymomas and ganglio-gliomas may occur.

- **Treatment**: confirmation of diagnosis necessary by brain biopsy. If possible, surgical removal should be undertaken followed by radiotherapy. Adjuvant chemotherapy for high-grade gliomas is under evaluation
- **Prognosis**: this is relatively poor. Even grades I and II astrocytomas have survival rates of 10%–30% at 5 years, whereas glioblastoma multiforme (grade IV astrocytoma) is usually rapidly fatal within a year

16.7 CNS INFECTIONS

CSF abnormalities in bacterial and viral meningitis are discussed in Section 16.10 and causative organisms are listed in Chapter 11, Infectious Diseases. For HIV-related neurological disease *see* Chapter 8, Genito-urinary Medicine and AIDS.

16.7.1 Encephalitis

Acute viral encephalitis involves not simply the meninges (a viral meningitis) but also the cerebral substance. Confusion and altered consciousness are thus prominent, and seizures and focal neurological signs may occur. Viral encephalitis is often secondary to herpes simplex, but may also be secondary to infection with mumps, zoster, EBV or coxsackie and echoviruses. *See also* Chapter 11, Infectious Diseases.

Herpes simplex encephalitis

Clinical features of herpes simplex encephalitis

- Fever
- Focal symptoms (eg musical hallucinations)
- Confusion
- Focal signs (eg right-sided weakness and aphasia)

Focal signs are related to anterior temporal lobe pathology, which may be visible on CT or MRI. Normal CSF findings are occasionally seen, but typically there is a lymphocytosis with red cells also present. In a minority (20%) of cases the CSF sugar may be low. Investigation with imaging or with EEG may confirm focal temporal lobe involvement, and definitive diagnosis can be made with polymerase chain reaction (PCR) to detect viral DNA in the CSF. Treatment with aciclovir should be started on suspicion of the diagnosis.

16.7.2 Lyme disease

Lyme disease, caused by the spirochaete *Borrelia burgdorferi*, is discussed in Chapter 11, Section 11.8.2. The illness can be subacute or chronic and evolves in poorly defined stages. A ring-like erythematous lesion (erythema migrans) at the site of the tick bite is accompanied by influenza-like symptoms, with neurological (or cardiac) symptoms appearing weeks to months later. Usually, neurological involvement appears as 'viral-like' meningitis with or without cranial mononeuropathies. Treatment is with oral doxycycline in the initial stages but the meningitis is usually treated with intravenous ceftriaxone.

Neurological abnormalities in Lyme disease

- Cranial neuropathies
- Bell's palsy
- Low-grade encephalitis
- Mononeuritis multiplex
- Meningitis
- Cerebellar ataxia

16.8   PERIPHERAL NERVE LESIONS

16.8.1   Mononeuropathies

A peripheral lesion of a single nerve is known as a mononeuropathy. Commonly mononeuropathies are associated with compressive lesions or have a vascular aetiology. Two of the most important mononeuropathies (other than oculomotor palsies) are carpal tunnel syndrome and common peroneal nerve palsy.

Carpal tunnel syndrome

The most common peripheral nerve entrapment syndrome. Symptoms are of numbness and dysaesthesia affecting the median nerve (lateral three-and-a-half fingers), and weakness of median nerve-innervated muscles (see below).

Conditions associated with carpal tunnel syndrome:

- Pregnancy
- Obesity
- Hypothyroidism
- Acromegaly
- Amyloidosis
- Rheumatoid arthritis

Treatment is with wrist splints, occasionally diuretics or surgical decompression.

Common peroneal nerve palsy

This nerve is motor to tibialis anterior and the peronei muscles. Patients usually present with foot drop and weakness of:

- Inversion of the foot (L4)
- Dorsiflexion (L5; tibialis anterior)
- Eversion (S1; peronei)

Sensory loss over the dorsum of the foot is usually present, but not prominent. Distinction from an L5 root lesion is made by demonstrating that foot eversion is intact (for a root lesion).

Causes of common peroneal palsy

- Compression at the fibula neck, where the nerve winds round the bone (eg below-knee plasters)
- Connective tissue disease/vasculitis
- Weight loss
- Diabetes mellitus
- Polyarteritis nodosa
- Leprosy

Other causes of (unilateral) foot drop include diabetes mellitus (other than due to common peroneal nerve palsy), stroke, multiple sclerosis and prolapsed intervertebral disc.

Other mononeuropathies affecting the hand and arm

The **median nerve** supplies some of the muscles of the thenar eminence (abductor pollicis, flexor pollicis brevis and opponens pollicis) and the lateral two lumbricals.

The **ulnar nerve** supplies the muscles of the hypothenar eminence (abductor digiti minimi), the medial two lumbricals and all the interossei (remember dorsal abduct, palmar adduct – 'dab and pad').

The **radial nerve** does not supply muscles in the hand. It supplies primarily the extensor compartment of the forearm.

Causes of wasting of the small muscles of the hand

- Arthritis
- Motor neurone disease
- Other cervical cord pathology
- Syringomyelia
- Polyneuropathies
- Brachial plexus injury (eg trauma, Pancoast's tumour)

Causes of fasciculation

- Motor neurone disease
- Thyrotoxicosis
- Cervical spondylosis
- Syringomyelia
- Acute poliomyelitis
- Metabolic – severe hyponatraemia, hypomagnesaemia
- Drugs (clofibrate, lithium, anticholinesterase, salbutamol)

16.8.2 Polyneuropathies

Polyneuropathies have a heterogeneous set of causes. Typically peripheral nerves are affected in a diffuse symmetrical fashion; symptoms and signs are most prominent in the extremities. Different aetiologies may be associated with involvement of mainly motor, mainly sensory or mainly autonomic fibres.

Causes of polyneuropathy

- **Mainly sensory neuropathies**
  - Diabetes mellitus
  - Leprosy
  - Amyloidosis
  - Vitamin B_{12} deficiency
  - Carcinomatous neuropathy
- **Mainly motor neuropathies**
  - Guillain–Barré syndrome (see below)
  - Porphyria
  - Lead poisoning
  - Diphtheria
  - Hereditary sensory and motor neuropathy (HSMN) types I and II
  - Uraemic neuropathy
  - Chronic inflammatory demyelinating polyneuropathy (CIDP)

Motor neuropathies cause partial denervation of muscle. An important sign of denervation is fasciculation, which is particularly prominent in disorders of the anterior horn cell in addition to the motor neuropathies described above.

Autonomic neuropathies

Autonomic neuropathy may present with:

- Postural hypotension
- Abnormal sweating
- Diarrhoea or constipation
- Urinary incontinence
- Absence of cardiovascular responses (eg to Valsalva manoeuvre)
- Impotence

Principal causes of autonomic neuropathy

- Diabetes mellitus
- Amyloidosis
- Chronic hepatic failure
- Guillain–Barré syndrome
- Renal failure
- Multiple system atrophies (ie Shy–Drager syndrome/OPCA)

Palpable peripheral nerves are recognised in the following polyneuropathies:

- Charcot–Marie–Tooth (HMSN II)
- Amyloidosis
- Lepromatous leprosy
- Acromegaly

Guillain–Barré syndrome

Guillain–Barré syndrome (GBS) is an uncommon acute post-infective polyneuropathy. A progressive ascending symmetric muscle weakness (ascending polyradiculopathy) leads to paralysis, maximal by 1 week in more than half of patients. Symptoms frequently begin after a respiratory or gastrointestinal infection; *Campylobacter jejuni* infection is associated with a worse prognosis.

Sensory symptoms may be present but are typically not associated with objective sensory signs. Papilloedema may occur. The condition may be associated with urinary retention or cardiac arrhythmia (autonomic involvement). Some patients will require intubation and artificial ventilation.

Investigation typically reveals:

- Elevated CSF protein (often very high)
- Normal CSF white cell count
- Slowing of nerve conduction velocity and denervation on EMG

Poor prognostic features include:

- Rapid onset of symptoms
- Age
- Axonal neuropathy on nerve conduction studies
- Prior infection with *Campylobacter jejuni*

Treatments include plasma exchange and intravenous immunoglobulin.

Miller–Fisher syndrome is a variant of Guillain–Barré syndrome and comprises ophthalmoplegia, ataxia and areflexia.

16.9 DISORDERS OF MUSCLE AND NEUROMUSCULAR JUNCTION

Disorders of muscle are known as myopathies. The most important feature is muscle weakness, variably accompanied by wasting, hypertrophy, pseudo-hypertrophy or other symptoms, such as myotonia. Signs are invariably symmetrical. Myopathies are usually painless (with the exception of inflammatory myopathies).

Note that fasciculations are signs of muscle denervation, and they indicate a disorder of motor nerves or of the neuromuscular junction. They are not a feature of myopathy.

16.9.1 Myopathies

There are a number of different types of myopathies.

Classification of myopathies

- **Inflammatory** (eg polymyositis; *see* Chapter 20, Rheumatology)
- **Metabolic** (eg mitochondrial)
- **Drug-induced**
- **Inherited – dominant** (eg dystrophia myotonica; see below); **recessive** (eg Duchenne; see below)
- **Secondary to endocrine disease** (principally thyrotoxicosis or hypothyroidism)

Muscular dystrophy

Duchenne muscular dystrophy is an X-linked disorder affecting about 1 in 3500 male births, though occasionally females may be affected (due to translocation of the short arm of the X chromosome, Xp21).

- The gene has now been isolated in this Xp21 region, and produces a protein named dystrophin that is normally present on the muscle sarcolemmal membrane. The pathogenesis is described in detail in Chapter 14, Molecular Medicine
- In Duchenne dystrophy, the dystrophin protein is absent
- Serum creatine kinase is elevated

In Duchenne muscular dystrophy, weakness occurs progressively from about 3–4 years of age. Thirty per cent of sufferers show intellectual impairment with the overall IQ curve being shifted to the left. There is no effective treatment at present and death usually occurs from cardiorespiratory failure in the second or third decade of life.

In the milder **Becker's dystrophy**, the dystrophic protein is seen but it is dysfunctional and present at a lower level than normal. Distinguishing features in muscular dystrophy are shown in Table 16.2.

Table 16.2. Distinguishing features in muscular dystrophy

	Duchenne	Becker's
Immunofluorescent dystrophin on muscle biopsy	Undetectable	Reduced/abnormal
Wheelchair dependence	95% at <12 years	5% at <12 years
Mental handicap	20%	Rare

Dystrophia myotonica

An inherited myopathy (autosomal dominant) with onset in the third decade.

Features of dystrophia myotonica

- Myotonic facies
- Myotonia (delayed muscular relaxation after contraction)
- Wasting and weakness of the arms and legs
- Frontal baldness
- Testicular/ovarian atrophy
- Diabetes mellitus
- Cataract
- Cardiomyopathy
- Mild cognitive impairment

Diagnosis depends on the characteristic myotonic discharge on EMG in association with the clinical features listed above. Usually severe disability results within 10–20 years, and there is no treatment available though phenytoin may be used for symptomatic relief of myotonia.

16.9.2 Neuromuscular junction

Neuromuscular transmission is dependent on cholinergic transmission between the terminals of motor nerves and the motor end plate.

Myasthenia gravis

This is an antibody-mediated autoimmune disease affecting the neuromuscular junction; antibodies are produced to the acetylcholine receptors. It is a relatively rare disorder with a prevalence of about 1 in 20 000. The pathogenesis is described in detail in Chapter 14, Molecular Medicine.

Most (but not all) patients have ptosis. Many have ophthalmoplegia, dysarthria and dysphagia, but any muscle may be affected. The pupil is never affected, but weakness of eye closure and ptosis is common. Quick lid retraction on refixation from downgaze is known as Cogan's sign.

Myasthenia gravis can mimic MND, mitochondrial myopathies, polymyositis, cranial nerve palsies or brainstem dysfunction.

Diagnosis of myasthenia gravis

- Tensilon® test
- ACh receptor antibodies (present in 85%–90%)
- Electrophysiology (repetitive stimulation gives rise to diminution in the amplitude of the evoked EMG response)
- Thyroid function tests (up to 10% have co-existent thyrotoxicosis)
- CT mediastinum

Treatment of myasthenia gravis

Primary treatment is with cholinesterase (ChE) inhibitors (eg pyridostigmine), and some patients will achieve control with these agents alone. The cause of the disease is usually modified with treatments directed at the **immune system**:

- **Immunosuppression**: steroids, azathioprine, cyclophosphamide, ciclosporin A
- Plasmapheresis
- Intravenous immune globulin infusion

In those with thymoma or hyperplasia of the thymus, up to 60% will improve or achieve remission after **thymectomy**. The benefits of surgery are greatest in patients aged less than 40 years.

Lambert–Eaton myasthenic syndrome (LEMS)

LEMS is commonly a paraneoplastic syndrome, most commonly associated with small-cell carcinoma of the lung (also breast and ovarian cancer). However, in a variable proportion (up to 50%) of patients no cancer is found.

Clinical features of LEMS

- Fatiguability
- Hyporeflexia
- Ocular and bulbar muscles rarely affected
- Autonomic symptoms (eg difficulty with micturition, dry mouth, impotence)

Unlike myasthenia gravis, ophthalmoplegia and ptosis are not features. Like myasthenia gravis, LEMS is an autoimmune disorder with antibodies produced to voltage-gated calcium channels in the muscle membrane. On examination, reflexes are absent but return **after** exercise (cf myasthenia gravis). EMG with repetitive stimulation shows an improvement in response.

16.10 INVESTIGATIONS USED IN NEUROLOGICAL DISEASE

16.10.1 Cerebrospinal fluid

Normal CSF findings

- **Pressure**
  - 60–150 mm of CSF (patient recumbent)
- **Protein**
  - 0.2–0.4 g/l
- **Cell count**
  - Red cells 0, white cells <5/mm^3 (few monocytes or lymphocytes)
- **Glucose**
  - More than 2/3rds of blood glucose

Abnormal CSF findings

- **Elevated protein**
  - Very high; >2 g/l
    - Guillain–Barré syndrome
    - Spinal block
    - TB meningitis
    - Fungal meningitis
  - High
    - Bacterial meningitis
    - Viral encephalitis
    - Cerebral abscess
    - Neurosyphilis
    - Subdural haematoma
    - Cerebral malignancy
- **Low CSF glucose**
  - Bacterial meningitis
  - TB meningitis
  - Fungal meningitis
  - Mumps meningitis (in 20% of cases)
  - Herpes simplex encephalitis (in 20%)
  - Subarachnoid haemorrhage (occasionally)
- **Polymorphs**
  - Bacterial meningitis
- **Lymphocytes**
  - Viral encephalitis/meningitis
  - Partially treated bacterial meningitis
  - Behçet syndrome
  - CNS vasculitides
  - HIV-associated
  - Lymphoma
  - Leukaemia
  - Lyme disease
  - Systemic lupus erythematosus

Oligoclonal bands in CSF

- Multiple sclerosis
- Neurosarcoidosis
- CNS lymphoma
- Systemic lupus erythematosus
- Subacute sclerosing panencephalitis: rare, late complication of measles
- Subarachnoid haemorrhage (unusual)
- Neurosyphilis
- Guillain–Barré syndrome

16.10.2 Neuroradiology

CT and MRI scanning of the brain and spinal cord are now widely used in the investigation of neurological diseases. A comprehensive account is beyond the remit of this section.

Causes of intracranial calcification (on CT scan or skull X-ray)

- Oligodendroglioma
- Craniopharyngioma
- Pineal gland (may be normal finding)
- Sturge–Weber syndrome
- Aneurysm
- Meningioma
- Tuberculoma
- Tuberous sclerosis
- Toxoplasmosis
- Hypoparathyroidism (basal ganglia)

16.10.3 Electrophysiological investigations

EEG

The EEG is characteristically abnormal in the following conditions:

- **Absence seizures**: 3-Hz spike-and-wave complexes
- **Creutzfeldt–Jakob**: periodic bursts of high-amplitude sharp waves

Nerve conduction tests

Nerve conduction tests are used to investigate peripheral neuropathies. The technique involves stimulating a peripheral nerve (sensory or motor) and recording the action potential latency and amplitude further along the same nerve. This allows calculation of the conduction velocity of the nerve. These measures can be used to distinguish (amongst other things) between axonal and demyelinating neuropathies.

- **Axonal**: reduced amplitude (loss of axons) but **preserved** conduction velocity
- **Demyelinating**: preserved amplitude but **reduced** conduction velocity (loss of myelin)

Electromyography (EMG)

EMG is useful in disorders of the neuromuscular junction or investigation of myopathic processes. The technique involves stimulating the motor nerves while recording the compound action potential from muscles.

Characteristic abnormalities:

- **Myasthenia gravis**: diminished response to repetitive stimulation
- **Lambert–Eaton syndrome**: enhanced response to repetitive stimulation
- **Polymyositis**: fibrillation due to denervation hypersensitivity, reduced amplitude and duration of motor units
- **Myotonic syndromes**: 'dive bomber' discharge (high-frequency action potentials)

Chapter 17
Ophthalmology

CONTENTS

Pupillary and eye movement disorders, nystagmus and visual field defects are all covered in the neuro-ophthalmology section of Chapter 16, Neurology

Ophthalmology

Pupillary and eye movement disorders, nystagmus and visual field defects are all covered in the neuro-ophthalmology section of Chapter 16, Neurology.

17.1 BASIC ANATOMY OF THE EYE

17.1.1 Orbit

The orbit houses the globe, extraocular muscles, lacrimal gland, orbital fat and attendant arteries, veins and nerves (Figure 17.1).

17.1.2 Extraocular muscles

The four rectus muscles and the superior oblique arise at the orbital apex and pass forward to insert into the globe. The inferior oblique arises from the anteromedial orbital floor and runs along the lower surface of the globe to insert into its posterolateral aspect.

The innervation and primary action of each muscle are shown in Table 17.1 – note all other movements are composite, ie due to the action of two muscles acting together.

Table 17.1. The innervation and primary action of the extraocular muscles

Muscle	Nerve supply	Primary action
Superior rectus	III	Elevation in abduction
Inferior rectus	III	Depression in abduction
Medial rectus	III	Adduction
Lateral rectus	VI	Abduction
Inferior oblique	III	Elevation in adduction
Superior oblique	IV	Depression in adduction

17.1.3 The globe

Key features of the constituent parts are:

- **Cornea**: clarity maintained by avascularity, the regular structural array of component fibrils and its relative dehydrated state (maintained by endothelium)
- **Conjunctiva**: thin mucous membrane covering anterior sclera and lining eyelids
- **Sclera**: tough fibroelastic coat
- **Uveal tract**: anterior uvea comprises iris and ciliary body. Posterior uvea is the choroid, a vascular layer lining the sclera which nourishes outer retinal layers
- **Retinal pigment epithelium**: cellular monolayer comprising the outermost layer of the retina
- **Retina**: light-sensitive innermost layer of the globe. Converts light energy into electrical energy. It comprises: (i) rods – more plentiful in the peripheral retina, sensitive to low light and movement detection; and (ii) cones – concentrated within the macular region, particularly at the fovea, important for acuity and colour vision. Vascular supply is from the central retinal artery. Capillaries have non-fenestrated endothelium and tight junctions forming a blood–retinal barrier (analogous to the blood–brain barrier), preventing the passage of large molecules
- **Lens**: positioned posterior to the iris and anterior to the vitreous, anchored by the zonules. It is enclosed by a capsule, the basement membrane of the lens epithelium. New lens fibres are continuously produced throughout life and the older fibres are compressed to form the lens nucleus. Reduced accommodation is found in later life because the lens becomes less deformable

Figure 17.1 Cross-section of the eye

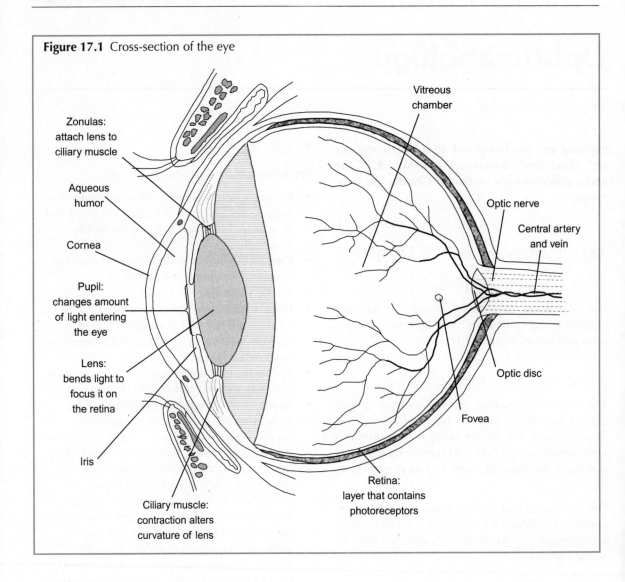

Zonulas: attach lens to ciliary muscle

Aqueous humor

Cornea

Pupil: changes amount of light entering the eye

Lens: bends light to focus it on the retina

Iris

Ciliary muscle: contraction alters curvature of lens

Vitreous chamber

Optic nerve

Central artery and vein

Optic disc

Fovea

Retina: layer that contains photoreceptors

17.2 RETINAL DISORDERS

17.2.1 Retinal venous occlusion

Retinal vein occlusion probably occurs due to a dynamic change in blood flow at arteriovenous crossings and may affect the central retinal vein (CRVO) or one of its branches (BRVO).

Risk factors

- Systemic hypertension (most common)
- Increased intraocular pressure (central occlusion only)
- Diabetes mellitus
- Hyperviscosity states
- Vasculitides

Clinical signs of retinal venous occlusion

- **Loss of vision**
  - Variable extent depending on macular involvement and degree of retinal ischaemia produced
- **Relative afferent pupillary defect**
  - With retinal ischaemia
- **Multiple retinal haemorrhages**
  - Mainly superficial, in nerve fibre layer ('blood and thunder' appearance)
- **Retinal venous dilatation**
- **Cotton-wool spots**
- **Vascular sheathing**
- **Neovascularisation**
  - May occur in 20% of CRVO and 1% of BRVO due to ischaemia, ie similar pathogenesis to diabetic retinopathy. This may affect the anterior segment producing neovascular glaucoma, or the retina causing vitreous haemorrhage or retinal traction. Treatment is by retinal laser to abolish the ischaemic stimulus

17.2.2 Retinal arterial occlusion

As the central retinal artery is an end artery, occlusion of the central artery or one of its branches produces retinal infarction and visual loss in the area supplied.

Aetiology of retinal artery occlusion

- **Embolic**
- **Sudden rapid increase in intraocular pressure**
  - To above central retinal arterial pressure
- **Arteritic**
  - Most commonly giant-cell arteritis (GCA). However, visual loss in GCA is only due to central retinal artery occlusion in 10% of cases; it usually affects vision by producing anterior ischaemic optic neuropathy, which damages the optic nerve head

Clinical signs of retinal arterial occlusion

- **Sudden, profound, painless loss of vision**
  - (Corresponding sector field loss if branch occlusion)
- **Pale oedematous retina with cherry-red spot at fovea (only lasts around 48 hours)**
  - This is due to the choroidal reflex showing through at the fovea as the retina is thinner here
- **Relative afferent pupillary defect**
- **Neovascular complications (occur later)**
  - Much rarer than with venous occlusions, probably because the retina is too severely damaged to produce angiogenic factor

Treatment is sometimes possible to dislodge the embolus if presentation occurs within a few hours of onset. Aims of treatment are to induce vascular dilatation secondary to hypercarbia by rebreathing, or more usually, inducing a rapid drop in intraocular pressure either pharmacologically or surgically.

17.2.3 Hypertensive retinopathy

Retinal abnormalities represent the severity of hypertension and are characterised by:

- Vascular constriction causing focal retinal ischaemia
- Leakage leading to retinal oedema, haemorrhage and lipid deposition

Arteriosclerotic changes reflect the duration of the hypertension. These include vessel wall thickening secondary to intimal hyalinisation, medial hypertrophy and endothelial hyperplasia.

Classification of hypertensive retinopathy

- **Grade 1**
  - Arteriolar attenuation
- **Grade 2**
  - Focal arteriolar attenuation (with 'arteriovenous nipping')
- **Grade 3**
  - Haemorrhages, cotton-wool spots (due to infarction of nerve fibre layer of retina)
- **Grade 4**
  - Disc swelling – 'malignant' or 'accelerated' phase

Grades 3 and 4 are associated with severe target organ damage and high mortality (accelerated-phase hypertension). Treatment is aimed purely towards the hypertension and any underlying cause.

17.2.4 Diabetic retinopathy

Diabetic retinopathy is related to the duration and control of the disease. It is the most common cause of blindness in patients aged 30–60 years. It is unusual in type 1 diabetes until 10 years after diagnosis, but eventually occurs in nearly all patients. It is present in 10% of type 2 patients at diagnosis, 50% after 10 years' disease and 80% after 20 years' disease.

Diabetic retinopathy is a **microvascular** disease. The following pathological changes are known to occur:

- **Loss of vascular pericytes**: thought to be responsible for the structural integrity of the vessel wall. A decrease therefore results in disruption of the blood–retinal barrier and leakage of plasma constituents into the retina
- **Capillary endothelial cell damage**
- **Basement membrane thickening** with carbohydrate and glycogen deposition

Changes in red cell oxygen-carrying capabilities and increased platelet aggregation are also thought to contribute. The production of an angiogenic factor by ischaemic retina is the likely cause of neovascularisation. At all stages, good control of diabetes and of any co-existing hypertension and stopping smoking have been shown to reduce serious sequelae.

Classification of diabetic retinopathy

- **Background retinopathy**
  - Does not affect visual acuity
  - Microaneurysms – first clinical change, saccular pouch, either leaks or resolves due to thrombosis
  - Haemorrhages – dot, blot and flame-shaped
  - Exudates – leakage of lipid and lipoprotein
  - No local treatment required; adequate control of diabetes only
- **Diabetic maculopathy**
  - Most common cause of visual loss
  - More common in type 2 diabetes
  - Retinopathy within the macular region
  - Oedematous retina that is in close proximity to the fovea may require laser treatment
- **Preproliferative retinopathy**
  - Cotton-wool spots – represent areas of axonal disruption secondary to ischaemia
  - Venous changes – dilatation and beading
  - Large deep haemorrhages
  - Treatment controversial: some advocate prophylactic laser treatment, others recommend improving disease control and more frequent monitoring
- **Proliferative retinopathy**
  - More common in type 1 diabetes
  - Retinal neovascularisation: new vessels occur in thin-walled friable clumps on the venous side of the retinal circulation; new vessels on the disc are more ominous than those on the vascular arcades; vitreous haemorrhage, fibrosis and tractional retinal detachment may occur
  - Iris neovascularisation: may be complicated by glaucoma
  - Treatment with laser photocoagulation to retina is designed to abolish the production of angiogenic factor from ischaemic retina and induce regression of new vessels

Diabetic retinopathy may progress rapidly in some situations:

- Pregnancy – 5% of patients with background changes develop proliferative retinopathy
- Sudden improvement in control in previously poorly managed disease

Diabetic papillopathy

Typically bilateral process in young type 1 diabetic patients. Associated with mild to moderate visual loss. Fundal examination reveals disc swelling, macular oedema with exudates and macular star. There is no specific management apart from control of the diabetes. Usually spontaneous recovery within 6 months.

Non-retinal eye disease in diabetics

The eye may be affected by diabetes in several other ways:

- **Visual changes**
  - Secondary to osmotic lens changes with fluctuating glucose levels
- **Mononeuropathies**
  - Leading to ophthalmoplegia
- **Snowflake cataract**
  - Poorly controlled juvenile diabetes
- **Early-onset senile cataract**
- **Increased external eye infections**
  - (eg conjunctivitis, styes)

17.2.5 Macular degeneration

Macular degeneration is the commonest cause of blindness in people aged >65 years. It can be broadly classified into 'wet' or 'dry' forms, according to the presence or absence of retinal oedema. **Wet degeneration** occurs due to subretinal choroidal neovascularisation. **Dry macular degeneration** can predispose to the wet form of disease.

Risk factors for macular degeneration include:

- Family history
- Myopia
- Smoking

Central visual loss, which may be severe, with preservation of the peripheral field occurs in both types. Dry degeneration tends to be slowly progressive, whereas the onset of wet degeneration may result in acute visual loss. There is no treatment for dry macular degeneration. Wet macular degeneration has previously been treated with laser therapy, either alone or more latterly in combination with photodynamic therapy. A new treatment involving the repeated intraocular injection of anti vascular endothelial growth factor (VEGF) substances, for example Lucentis® (ranibizumab), has recently been approved for use in selected individuals with recent-onset wet macular degeneration.

17.2.6 Retinitis pigmentosa

Retinitis pigmentosa (RP) is a term describing a group of progressive inherited diseases affecting the photoreceptors and the retinal pigment epithelium. These conditions are more correctly termed **photoreceptor dystrophies**. RP is characterised by the triad of:

- **Night blindness**: due to loss of rod function
- **Tunnel vision**: loss of peripheral field, also due to rod dysfunction; central visual acuity loss due to cone disease may also occur but tends to be a later feature
- **Pigmented 'bony spicule'** fundal appearance with associated disc pallor and blood vessel attenuation

There are three inheritance patterns: autosomal recessive, autosomal dominant and X-linked recessive.

Disease onset and progression vary between different groups and also between affected members within families. Autosomal recessive and X-linked recessive forms tend to be more severe.

Important systemic associations include:

- **Abetalipoproteinaemia (Bassen–Kornzweig syndrome)**: autosomal recessive disease

typically affecting Ashkenazi Jews. Treatment with high-dose vitamin E may help neurological and retinal disease. (*See* Chapter 13, Metabolic diseases)

- **Refsum's disease**: autosomal recessive disorder of phytanic acid metabolism leading to its accumulation in tissues, causing peripheral neuropathy, cerebellar ataxia, ichthyosis and deafness. Serum phytanic acid levels are elevated and examination of the cerebral spinal fluid (CSF) reveals elevated protein in the presence of a normal cell count. Refsum's disease is responsive to a phytanic-acid-free diet which excludes animal fats, dairy products and green leafy vegetables
- **Usher syndrome**: autosomal recessive condition with non-progressive sensorineural deafness
- **Bardet–Biedl (Laurence–Moon–Biedl) syndrome**: autosomal recessive disease with mental retardation, obesity, hypogonadism, polydactyly, deafness and renal cystic disease
- **Kearns–Sayre syndrome**: disorder of mitochondrial inheritance with progressive external ophthalmoplegia, ptosis and heart block

17.3 LENS ABNORMALITIES

17.3.1 Cataract

Cataract is an opacity of the lens. It is the most common cause of blindness worldwide. Many classifications exist according to type, aetiology and associations. Surgical intervention is indicated:

- When patient function is impaired because of decreased vision
- If the view of the fundus is impaired when monitoring or treating another condition (eg diabetic retinopathy)

Causes of cataracts

- **Congenital**
  - Autosomal dominant (25%)
  - Maternal infection – rubella, toxoplasmosis, cytomegalovirus (CMV), herpes simplex, varicella zoster
  - Maternal drug ingestion – corticosteroids, thalidomide
  - Metabolic – galactosaemia, hypocalcaemia, Lowe syndrome, hypoglycaemia
  - Chromosomal abnormalities (eg Down syndrome, Turner syndrome)
- **Toxic/drug-induced**
  - (eg steroids, chlorpromazine, busulfan, gold, amiodarone)
- **Senile**
- **Secondary to ocular disease**
  - (eg uveitis, high myopia)
- **Metabolic**
  - Diabetes, hypoglycaemia, mannosidosis, Fabry's disease, Lowe syndrome, Wilson's disease, hypocalcaemia, galactokinase deficiency
- **Traumatic**
  - Penetrating or blunt injury, infrared radiation, radiotherapy, electric shock
- **Miscellaneous**
  - Myotonic dystrophy, progeria, atopic dermatitis

17.3.2 Lens dislocation

Lens dislocation results from disruption of the zonules that anchor it in position. Depending on the lens shift this may produce myopia or hypermetropia, or elevated intraocular pressure.

Causes of lens dislocation

- Marfan syndrome: up and out
- Homocystinuria: down and in
- Ehlers–Danlos syndrome
- Autosomal recessive ectopia lentis
- Trauma
- Uveal tumours

17.4 OPTIC NERVE DISORDERS

17.4.1 Optic neuritis

Inflammation of the optic nerve may affect the:

- **Nerve head**: producing **papillitis** with optic disc swelling, hyperaemia and haemorrhages
- **Retrobulbar portion of the nerve**: producing retrobulbar neuritis in which the nerve appears normal ('the patient sees nothing, the doctor sees nothing')

It is the presenting feature of 25% of patients with multiple sclerosis (MS); the cumulative probability of developing MS by 15 years after an attack of optic nerve nueritis has been found to be 50% (strongly correlated to the presence of lesions on MRI of the brain). The clinical signs of optic neuritis are shown in Table 17.2.

Causes of optic neuritis/papillitis

- **Demyelination**
- **Post-viral syndromes**
- **Infections**: viral encephalitis (measles, mumps, chickenpox), infectious mononucleosis, herpes zoster
- **Inflammatory**: contiguous with orbital inflammation, sinusitis or meningitis secondary to granulomatous optic nerve inflammation (eg TB, sarcoid, syphilis)
- **Other systemic disease**, eg diabetes

Table 17.2. Clinical signs of optic neuritis (in order of frequency of occurrence)

Reduced visual acuity	In classic demyelination this is usually monocular (90%) and progresses rapidly over a few days; improves over 4–6 weeks, achieving virtually normal vision in 90%, although an RAPD usually persists
Pain	Present in demyelination, precedes visual loss by a few days, worsened by eye movements
Red colour desaturation	Red appears darker or brown to the patient
Relative afferent pupillary defect (RAPD)	Swinging flashlight test – *see* Section 16.3.2
Paracentral or central scotoma	Commonest defect, although any type of scotoma may occur
Visual-evoked potential prolonged	Reflecting delayed conduction in optic pathway
Optic atrophy	Develops within weeks, may be seen in contralateral eye as a sign of previous asymptomatic episode

17.4.2 Causes of optic atrophy

Causes of optic atrophy

- **Congenital**
  - Dominant or recessive
- **Secondary to optic nerve compression**
  - (eg pituitary mass, meningioma, orbital cellulitis)
- **Drugs**
  - Ethambutol, isoniazid, chloramphenicol, digitalis, chlorpropamide
- **Radiation neuropathy**
- **Carcinomatous**
  - Due to microscopic infiltrates of the nerve and its sheath
- **Post-papilloedema**
- **Post-optic neuritis**
  - See above
- **Post-trauma**
- **Toxic neuropathy**
  - (eg tobacco (cyanide), arsenic, lead, methanol)
- **Nutritional**
  - Vitamins B_1, B_2, B_6, B_{12}, folic acid and niacin deficiencies
  - Tobacco-alcohol amblyopia may be toxic or nutritional (mechanism not fully understood) with a good prognosis for recovery with withdrawal of tobacco and alcohol, and vitamin B and folate supplementation
- **Infiltrative neuropathy**
  - (eg sarcoid, lymphoma, leukaemia)

17.4.3 The swollen optic nerve head

Papilloedema

Papilloedema means optic nerve head swelling **secondary to increased intracranial pressure**. This may be due to:

- Space-occupying lesion
- Hydrocephalus
- CO_2 retention
- Idiopathic intracranial hypertension

Papilloedema is usually bilateral. Features include:

- Hyperaemia of the disc: due to capillary dilatation
- Splinter haemorrhages of retina
- Blurring of the disc margins: due to nerve fibre layer swelling
- Exudates and cotton-wool spots
- Loss of spontaneous venous pulsation: absent in 20% of normal people
- Loss of the cup is a late feature

On clinical examination papilloedema produces an enlarged blind spot. **Transient visual obscurations**, with blacking out of vision lasting a few seconds often due to positional change, also occur. Visual loss occurs late.

Foster–Kennedy syndrome is unilateral papilloedema with contralateral optic atrophy. It is due to a mass lesion compressing the optic nerve on one side causing ipsilateral atrophic changes and resulting in increased intracranial pressure and contralateral papilloedema.

Papillitis

This refers to inflammation of the optic nerve head (as distinct from retrobulbar neuritis) and is most frequently due to a demyelinative episode (*see* Section 17.4.1 above).

Anterior ischaemic optic neuropathy

Infarction of the anterior portion of the optic nerve results in acute severe visual loss which generally does not improve. This is the usual method by which giant-cell arteritis affects vision (90%), retinal artery occlusion occurring in the other 10% of cases. It is essential to exclude this condition as it rapidly becomes bilateral. Giant cells and loss of the internal elastic lamina are evident histologically on temporal artery biopsy.

Ischaemic optic neuropathy is not always due to inflammatory arteritis; it may be due to arteriosclerosis or to hypotensive events. If visual loss is incomplete an altitudinal (ie horizontal) field defect results.

Other causes of swelling of the optic nerve head

- Central retinal vein occlusion
- Orbital mass (eg optic nerve glioma, nerve sheath meningioma, thyroid eye disease and metastases)
- Accelerated-phase hypertension (see above)
- Infiltrative neuropathy (eg lymphoma)
- Toxic neuropathy

17.5 UVEITIS AND SCLERITIS

17.5.1 Uveitis

Uveitis is inflammation of the uveal tract, which may affect the anterior (iris and/or ciliary body) and/or posterior uvea (choroid).

Anterior uveitis typically presents with pain, photophobia, a red eye, lacrimation and decreased vision.

Posterior uveitis presents with floaters (due to inflammatory debris in the vitreous) or impaired vision (secondary to choroiditis if the inflammatory lesion is within the macula).

Uveitis of any cause may be complicated by cataract or glaucoma. Anterior uveitis is most commonly idiopathic but there are also many associations with systemic diseases.

Systemic diseases associated with uveitis (in order of frequency of occurrence)

- **HLA-B27-associated uveitis**
- **Ankylosing spondylitis**
- **Sarcoidosis**
- **Inflammatory bowel disease**
- **Juvenile idiopathic arthritis**
  - (Previously termed juvenile chronic arthritis)
- **Reiter syndrome**
- **Infections**
  - TB, syphilis, herpes simplex, herpes zoster, toxoplasmosis, toxocariasis, AIDS, leprosy
- **Behçet syndrome**
- **Malignancy**
  - Non-Hodgkin's lymphoma
  - Leukaemia
  - Retinoblastoma
  - Ocular melanoma

Characteristics of uveitis associated with particular systemic diseases are:

- **HLA B27 genotype**: present in 50%–60% of patients with anterior uveitis as compared to 6% of the population
- **Ankylosing spondylitis**: recurrent anterior uveitis occurs in approximately 30% of patients with ankylosing spondylitis, and about 30% of males with unilateral uveitis will have ankylosing spondylitis. The uveitis may precede or follow the joint involvement and does not correlate with disease severity; 88% of those with uveitis also have HLA B27
- **Sarcoidosis**: acute or granulomatous. Anterior or posterior. Frequently bilateral and complicated. (*See* Section 17.8.4)
- **Reiter syndrome**: anterior uveitis occurs in 30% of patients. Other ocular features include

conjunctivitis and keratitis; 85%–95% of patients with ocular involvement have HLA B27

- **Behçet syndrome**: ocular disease occurs in 70% of patients. Anterior uveitis is often severe and bilateral. Conjunctivitis and episcleritis are seen and the retina is frequently affected by retinal vasculitis with infarction, secondary venous occlusion, retinal oedema, exudates and neovascularisation
- **Juvenile idiopathic arthritis**: ocular involvement typically occurs in pauci-articular disease, particularly those patients who are ANA positive. Uveitic activity bears no relation to that of the arthropathy. The disease is usually bilateral and asymptomatic and therefore regular screening is required because of the high incidence of complications. These are cataract in 35% of patients, secondary glaucoma in 20% and band keratopathy in 40% (calcified band across cornea)

Common causes of **posterior uveitis** (chorio-retinitis) are:

- **Idiopathic**
- **Inflammatory**: sarcoid
- **Infections**: (*see* box above) TB, syphilis (congenital and tertiary), leprosy, toxoplasmosis, toxocariasis and AIDS
- **Malignancy**: leukaemia, lymphoma

Treatment of uveitis

Anterior uveitis is treated with topical steroids and often with cycloplegia. This dilation of the pupil helps reduce posterior synechiae formation which can be associated with elevated pressure; it also reduces pain produced by ciliary spasm.

Posterior uveitis is treated according to the extent of visual involvement, for example whether the macular area of the retina is threatened. Treatment varies according to the nature of the underlying cause but generally involves steroids and/or other immunosuppression.

17.5.2 Scleritis

Inflammation of the sclera may be caused by

- Herpes zoster
- Ankylosing spondylitis
- Sarcoidosis
- Inflammatory bowel disease
- Gout
- Vasculitis: PAN, SLE, Wegener's granulomatosis, relapsing polychondritis, dermatomyositis, Behçet syndrome

17.5.3 Causes of a painful red eye

- **Conjunctivitis** (bacterial is irritable, viral is painful)
- **Uveitis**
- **Scleritis** (causes listed above) severe boring pain which disturbs sleep
- **Corneal damage** (abrasion, keratitis, eg herpes simplex and herpes zoster)
- **Acute glaucoma** (due to angle closure or rubeosis)

17.6 SYSTEMIC DRUGS AND THE EYE

Blurred vision is very frequently reported as a side-effect of systemic medication. The following are common or sight-threatening complications. The list is not intended to be comprehensive of all ophthalmic side-effects.

- **Steroids**: the eye can be affected by systemic, local (eg to eyelids) or topical steroids. They cause cataract and can elevate intraocular pressure in some individuals, leading to glaucoma. For this reason steroid creams to the periocular skin are best avoided and the intraocular pressure should be monitored in all patients receiving steroid eye drops

- **Amiodarone**: causes vortex keratopathy in almost all patients. Epithelial deposits, which are reversible on cessation of the drug, occur. These swirl out from a point below the pupil but are inconsequential to vision
- **Chloroquine and hydroxychloroquine**: classically cause 'Bull's eye maculopathy'. There is central hyperpigmentation at the fovea surrounded by concentric rings of hypo- and hyperpigmentation. Fundal changes occur after subjective visual loss. Baseline visual function (corrected near and distance acuity, colour vision, visual fields) should be established and these parameters monitored throughout treatment. Toxicity is rare with a cumulative chloroquine dose of less than 300 g, and it is much less likely to occur with hydroxychloroquine. Once visual loss occurs it may be progressive despite cessation of the drug
- **Ethambutol**: causes optic neuropathy, more frequently when used in high doses or with renal impairment. The earliest feature is subjective reduction in visual acuity. Toxicity is usually reversible with early withdrawal of the drug. Visual acuity should be checked pre-treatment and during the course of drug usage
- **Tamoxifen**: causes maculopathy and refractile opacities, which are associated with a mild reduction in vision
- **Vigabatrin**: causes constriction of visual fields which may be severe. The onset is reported to occur from 2 months to 5 years after starting the drug. The field defect starts nasally and progresses to become concentric; the eyes are affected symmetrically. The aetiology is thought to be related to retinal toxicity, but this is not fully understood; the visual field defects usually persist on cessation of vigabatrin
- **Drugs with anticholinergic effects** (eg tricyclics and anaesthetic agents such as atropine, glycopyrrolate and hyoscine): these can precipitate angle-closure glaucoma in susceptible patients (usually those who are long-sighted)

17.7 INFECTIOUS AGENTS AND THE EYE

The following conditions may all be caused by infectious agents, as discussed in previous sections:

- Congenital cataracts (maternal infection)
- Optic neuritis/papillitis
- Uveitis
- Scleritis
- Conjunctivitis

17.7.1 Genito-urinary disease and the eye

All patients with genito-urinary disease affecting the eye warrant evaluation at a genito-urinary clinic for systemic investigation and treatment. Ophthalmic features of HIV/AIDS are covered in Chapter 8, Genito-urinary Medicine and AIDS.

Chlamydial conjunctivitis

This is sexually transmitted and most commonly found in young adults. It may be associated with non-specific urethritis or cervicitis. Typical features are:

- It causes bilateral acute conjunctivitis which can persist for several weeks
- This is often associated with pre-auricular lymphadenopathy
- It may lead to **ophthalmia neonatorum**. Affected newborns will require systemic treatment to prevent pneumonitis
- Diagnosis is by chlamydial culture or immunofluorescence

Gonococcal conjunctivitis

There is typically a hyperacute conjunctivitis with marked chemosis and lid swelling accompanied by copious discharge. This may be associated with corneal ulceration and the risk of perforation. A diagnostic swab may show Gram-negative diplococci, which may be grown on culture. Topical and systemic treatment are indicated.

Syphilis

The ophthalmic abnormalities are related to the particular stage of syphilis:

- **Congenital**: interstitial keratitis (leads to clouding of the corneas in the second decade of life), iritis, chorioretinitis and optic atrophy
- **Primary**: chancre may occur on the eyelid
- **Secondary**: iritis occurs in 4% of patients with secondary syphilis, usually bilateral; optic neuritis, chorioretinitis and scleritis are all associated
- **Tertiary**: associated with optic atrophy, chorioretinitis, iritis, interstitial keratitis and the **Argyll Robertson pupil** (small irregular pupils which react to accommodation but not light)

17.7.2 Herpetic disease and the eye

Herpes simplex (HSV)

Most HSV infections are subclinical as 90% of the adult population are seropositive.

- **Primary infection with HSV**: this usually occurs in children and causes conjunctivitis with lid swelling. Lesions heal without scarring
- **HSV reactivation**: this is associated with **epithelial keratitis**. The corneal ulceration may be 'dendritic', when lesions appear like the branch of tree, or 'geographic' when the lesions become much larger with an amoeboid shape. The corneal stroma may subsequently become involved. Treatment is with topical or long-term low-dose systemic antiviral agents, dependent on severity

Herpes zoster

The painful acute vesicular rash follows a dermatomal pattern, and so disease affecting the fifth cranial nerve can affect the eye. If the rash is present on the tip of the nose (Hutchinson's sign) this indicates involvement of the nasociliary nerve and implies a higher risk of ophthalmic involvement.

- The eye may be affected by conjunctivitis, corneal ulceration, uveitis, scleritis, retinitis and oculomotility abnormalities because of cranial nerve involvement

17.7.3 Tropical eye infections

Trachoma

Trachoma is the second commonest cause of blindness worldwide and the commonest infective cause. It is responsible for blindness in 6 million people but 146 million have active trachoma. *Chlamydia trachomatis* is spread through poor hygiene, close personal contact and flies. Geographically affected areas include Africa, Asia, the Middle East and parts of Aboriginal Australia. The resulting conjunctivitis clears after about a month but repeated infections occur with conjunctival and subconjunctival scarring. This causes:

- Reduced tear production
- Trichiasis – the eyelids scar such that the lashes abrade the cornea. This causes corneal epithelial damage, allowing secondary infection
- Blindness – due to corneal opacification, generally occurs in adulthood

Onchocerciasis (River blindness)

Caused by the filarial nematode *Onchocerca volvulus* and transmitted by flies in Africa and South America. The larval form of the worm is transmitted from host to host by the black fly. Over 1–3 months the larvae develop into adult worms, which can release up to 2000 microfilariae per day for up to 10 years. When the microfilariae die they produce an intense inflammatory reaction. Ocular involvement produces tearing, light hypersensitivity and foreign body sensation.

Signs include:

- Conjunctivitis
- Intraocular microfilariae – may be seen on slit lamp examination
- Keratitis – snowflake opacities
- Anterior uveitis and chorioretinitis
- Optic neuropathy or atrophy resulting in visual loss

17.8 MISCELLANEOUS DISORDERS

17.8.1 Thyroid eye disease

The ocular manifestations of Graves' disease may pre-date, coincide with or follow the systemic disease. In patients with no history of thyroid disease thyroid autoantibodies are frequently positive. The only treatment modality known to worsen or precipitate thyroid eye disease is radioactive iodine.

The classic triad of thyroid eye disease includes the association of ocular changes with thyroid acropachy (a form of pseudo-clubbing) and pretibial myxoedema (both of the latter are now rare). For ease of memory, eye disease may be divided according to Werner's classification ('NO SPECS'), although it is important to appreciate that there is not a step-like progression from one stage to the next, and that not all steps occur in all patients.

No signs or symptoms
Only signs (eg lid retraction/lag)
Soft tissue swelling
Proptosis – orbital fat proliferation and muscle changes; auto-decompresses orbital contents
Extraocular muscle changes – usually affect inferior and/or medial recti; lymphocytic infiltrate
Corneal exposure
Sight loss – secondary to corneal disease or optic nerve compression

Management of ocular manifestations may be divided into:

- **Surface abnormalities**: ocular lubricants, tarsorrhaphy
- **Muscle changes**: prisms or patches to control diplopia, surgery after defect stable for minimum of 6 months
- **Optic nerve compression**: presents with visual loss, red desaturation with/without a field defect. It requires urgent treatment to prevent permanent visual loss – management includes systemic steroids, radiotherapy or surgical decompression of the orbital apex
- **Cosmetic**: improve lid position, remove redundant tissue

17.8.2 Myotonic dystrophy

An autosomal dominant condition characterised by failure of relaxation of voluntary muscle fibres. Anticipation occurs over successive generations such that severity worsens, eg a family history of early-onset cataract may be relevant.

Ophthalmic features of myotonic dystrophy

- Ptosis, poor lid closure and orbicularis weakness
- Retinal pigmentary changes
- Presenile cataract
- Miotic pupils

17.8.3 Ocular features of the phacomatoses

This group of disorders affects the nervous system, skin, eye and other organs and they are characterised by the presence of hamartomatous lesions.

Sturge–Weber syndrome

Glaucoma occurs on the ipsilateral side to cutaneous angioma in 50%. Cavernous haemangioma may be seen in the choroid.

Neurofibromatosis

- The eyelid may be affected by cutaneous neuroma
- In the anterior segment, iris nodules are seen and glaucoma is more common
- Choroidal naevi may be seen on fundoscopy
- The optic nerve may be affected by glioma, and a pulsatile globe suggests a defect of the greater wing of the sphenoid

von Hippel–Lindau syndrome

Autosomal dominant condition with incomplete penetrance and variable expressivity, the abnormality being on the short arm of chromosome 3.

- Retinal haemangiomas develop bilaterally in 25% of patients and may leak (producing

exudates or a serous retinal detachment), or rupture (leading to vitreous haemorrhage). These are histologically identical to the cerebellar haemangioblastomas which also occur
- Indirectly, increased intracranial pressure due to posterior fossa haemangioblastoma may lead to papilloedema; hypertensive changes may be seen when phaeochromocytoma is present

Tuberous sclerosis

- Autosomal dominant condition linked to several chromosomal abnormalities; 50% are new mutations. Ocular features include retinal hamartomas and, rarely, papilloedema or sixth nerve palsy due to increased intracranial pressure secondary to CNS lesions

17.8.4 Sarcoidosis

This multisystem granulomatous disease affects the eye and ocular adnexae in about 30% of cases, and of these 25% will have posterior segment disease.

Ocular effects of sarcoidosis

- **Lids**
  - Lupus pernio, cutaneous granuloma
- **Lacrimal glands**
  - Granulomatous infiltrate, may cause sicca syndrome (Mikulicz syndrome when combined with parotid involvement)
- **Uveitis**
  - Acute or granulomatous, frequently bilateral, and complicated by glaucoma and cataract
- **Retinal involvement**
  - With periphlebitic 'candle wax exudates', haemorrhages, oedema and neovascularisation
- **Choroiditis and choroidal granulomata**
- **Optic nerve granuloma**
- **Disc oedema**
- **Nerve palsies: III, IV, VI**

17.8.5 Keratoconus

Keratoconus is an ectatic condition of the inferior paracentral cornea. which produces a 'cone-shaped' cornea (Figure 17.2). Onset is usually in the teens with progressive myopic astigmatism. Management is with spectacles and hard contact lenses when astigmatism progresses. A corneal graft may be required, but only in a minority of patients.

Systemic associations are:

- Atopy
- Down syndrome
- Turner syndrome
- Marfan syndrome
- Ehler–Danlos syndrome

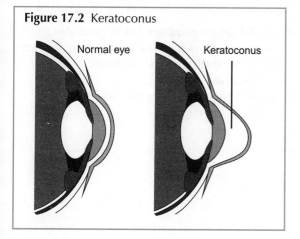

Figure 17.2 Keratoconus

Normal eye   Keratoconus

17.8.6 Glaucoma

Glaucoma describes the group of conditions in which intraocular pressure is sufficient to cause visual damage with a characteristic optic neuropathy. The normal intraocular pressure is <22 mmHg. Aqueous humour is formed by the ciliary body, and passes through the pupil and drains, via the trabecular meshwork, into the venous circulation through the episcleral venous system.

Acute glaucoma

- Rapid decrease in visual acuity associated with severe pain and vomiting

- More common in hypermetropes (those with long-sightedness)
- Due to closure of the drainage angle, resulting in a massive sudden elevation in intraocular pressure
- The cornea appears cloudy (due to oedema) and there is a mid-dilated non-reacting pupil
- Failure to treat pressure rapidly results in permanent visual loss

Chronic glaucoma

- Insidious asymptomatic disease
- Intraocular pressure elevated (usually not as markedly as in acute glaucoma), resulting in cupping of the optic nerve head and loss of visual field
- Classically an arcuate scotoma develops, which progresses to generalised field constriction
- Familial tendency but no strict inheritance
- More common in women and myopes (those with short-sightedness)

Secondary glaucoma

Glaucoma is a possible complication of almost any ocular disorder.

Secondary glaucomas may be generally classified as follows

- **Pre-trabecular**
  - (eg fibrovascular membrane in rubeosis as may occur in diabetes)
- **Trabecular**
  - Clogging of meshwork by, for example, inflammatory cells in uveitis or blood as in cases of trauma, or meshwork alteration due to inflammation in uveitis or scleritis
- **Post-trabecular**
  - Raised episcleral venous pressure preventing outflow (eg carotico-cavernous fistula, or cavernous sinus thrombosis)

17.8.7 Ocular tumours

Primary tumours

- **Choroidal melanoma:** this is the commonest primary intraocular tumour. It presents as a unilateral lesion with variable pigmentation (amelanotic to dark brown). It may be asymptomatic or can cause reduction in acuity or loss of visual field, depending on the site of the lesion
- **Choroidal haemangioma:** this appears as a red/orange lesion most frequently seen at the macula. A more diffuse lesion can be seen in Sturge–Weber syndrome, which gives a deep-red appearance to the fundus; this may only be appreciated by comparison with the other eye

Secondary tumours

The eye may be affected by metastases to the choroid or orbit and cerebral metastases may affect the visual pathway or cause oculomotility disorders.

- **Choroidal metastases** occur most frequently from breast, bronchial and renal primary tumours. They are frequently multiple and also bilateral. Lesions appear pale and are minimally elevated. They are associated with metastatic disease elsewhere. The effect upon vision depends on the site; macular lesions are most common and can cause marked visual loss. Palliative external beam radiation is usually successful in improving vision

17.8.8 Blind registration

Blind registration is completed by ophthalmologists and can facilitate rehabilitation and social services support. Monocular visual loss is not a criterion for registration. Two levels for blind registration exist:

- **Partial sight registration:** this is applicable when the visual acuity is ≤6/24 in both eyes, or when there is constriction of visual fields, including hemianopia
- **Blind registration:** when the visual acuity is ≤3/60 in both eyes

CONTENTS

Psychiatry

18.1 SCHIZOPHRENIA

Schizophrenia is characterised by disturbances of thought, perception, mood and personality. These lead to 'positive' symptoms, such as delusions, hallucinations and disorganisation of thoughts and speech, and 'negative' symptoms, including decreased motivation, poor self-care and social withdrawal. Patients do not have a 'split personality'. The lifetime risk is about 1% for men and women, although men consistently have an earlier age of onset. There is strong evidence of genetic predisposition, but not through a simple Mendelian model of inheritance (see Table 18.1).

Schizophrenia is a heterogeneous condition; signs and symptoms present to a highly variable degree between individuals. Despite this, generalisations can be made about certain 'core features'. Schneider's first-rank symptoms were an attempt to tighten diagnostic practice.

18.1.1 First-rank symptoms

Originally described by Schneider, these represent an attempt to identify symptoms that occur exclu-

Table 18.1. Lifetime risk of schizophrenia in relatives of patients with schizophrenia

Relationship	Per cent with schizophrenia
Monozygotic twin	50
Children (both parents schizophrenic)	46
Children	13
Dizygotic twin	10
Sibling	10
Uncles/aunts	3
Unrelated	0.9

sively in schizophrenia. In clinical practice they occur in approximately 70% of schizophrenic patients and in approximately 10% of manic patients. However, for the purpose of medical examinations, including the MRCP, they *should* be considered to be 'diagnostic of' or 'characteristic of' schizophrenia in the absence of obvious organic brain disease. A mnemonic for first-rank symptoms follows.

First-rank symptoms mnemonic: ATPD – Aim To Pass Definitely

Auditory hallucinations of a specific type:

- Third-person (ie two or more voices heard discussing the patient)
- Running commentary
- Thought echo

Thought disorder of a specific type (passivity of thought):

- Thought withdrawal
- Thought insertion
- Thought broadcasting

Passivity experiences (delusions of control):

- Actions/feelings/impulses under external control
- Bodily sensations being due to external influence

Delusional perception (two-stage process):

- Normal perception of commonplace object/ sight, leads to...
- Sudden, intense, self-referential delusion (eg finding coin on the ground leads to belief of messianic role)

There are many other important clinical features of schizophrenia, including impaired insight, suspiciousness, flat/blunted or incongruous affect, decreased spontaneous speech, general lack of motivation and poor self-care and abnormalities of motor activity such as dyskinesia and catatonia.

Auditory hallucinations which are not of the type covered by the first-rank symptoms may occur, as can other types of delusions, often bizarre and non-mood-congruent. These symptoms can be divided into two categories, as follows.

Positive symptoms

These include delusions, hallucinations and disorder of the form of thought. Temporal lobe epilepsy is one important differential diagnosis that should be considered in individuals who experience positive symptoms and hence an EEG may be useful in certain patients.

Negative symptoms

These include flat/blunted affect, decreased motor activity and speech, poor motivation and self-care. Patients with schizophrenia who manifest predominantly negative symptoms often have frontal cognitive deficits in attention and executive function (planning, goal-directed behaviour and monitoring of performance). CT and/or MRI studies of the brain in such patients have shown ventricular enlargement and cortical sulcal prominence.

18.1.2   Medical co-morbidities

There is increasing recognition that people with schizophrenia have high levels of medical co-morbidity and unhealthy lifestyle manifesting as higher rates of cardiovascular disease, HIV/AIDS, hepatitis and all malignancies. Obesity and diabetes are particularly prevalent, which may partly be explained by increasing prescription of atypical antipsychotics. Standardised all-cause mortality rates are 2–3 times those of the general population.

18.1.3   Principles of treatment

Treatment of schizophrenia involves a biopsychosocial model, but compliance with medication is the best predictor of relapse.

Biological treatments

- **Atypical antipsychotics** (eg clozapine, olanzapine, risperidone) are now considered to be first-line therapeutic agents. They have a preferential side-effect profile, particularly with regard to extrapyramidal side-effects. Use of **traditional antipsychotics** (chlorpromazine, haloperidol, trifluoperazine, etc) is limited by extrapyramidal (tardive dyskinesia occurs in >30% of patients on long-term treatment) and cardiac side-effects. Antipsychotics may be given orally, intramuscularly (IM) or depot IM; depot preparations aid compliance and are now available in atypical form (risperidone). 'Positive' symptoms respond better than 'negative' symptoms to antipsychotic therapy; the atypical antipsychotics are probably better for negative symptoms. **Electroconvulsive therapy (ECT)** may be needed for catatonic stupor
- **Psychological treatments**: three independent trials have recently shown that cognitive behavioural therapy (CBT) is a valuable adjunctive treatment for patients with persistent hallucinations and delusions. CBT can also aid compliance
- **Social interventions**: these should target accommodation, finances and daytime activities. Patients and relatives may both benefit from supportive psychotherapy, counselling and education. Early intervention by specialist teams for young people with psychotic illness is key

Predictors of long-term outcome

Lack of insight, long duration of untreated psychosis and poor response to early treatment predict poorer outcomes.

18.2   MOOD DISORDERS

Mood (affective) disorders are conditions in which a pathologically depressed or elated mood is the core feature. Depression is much more common than mania; those who suffer with mania almost invariably have one or more periods of depression at some stage in the course of their illness. Bipolar disorder has high heritability associated with multiple loci for genetic susceptibility.

18.2.1 Hypomania/mania (bipolar affective disorder)

Hypomania and mania are mood disorders characterised by pathologically elated or irritable mood. Lifetime prevalence is about 1% with a slight female predominance. Hypomania is a less severe form of mania – psychotic symptoms are absent. The majority of symptoms in both are 'mood congruent', ie understandable in the context of the pathological mood change. There is usually a previous episode of depression or there will be episodes of depression in the future, so hypomania/mania is part of a bipolar affective disorder. The main differential diagnoses are usually organic psychoses or schizophrenia. The clinical features of hypomania/mania are listed in the following box.

Clinical features of hypomania/mania

- **Mood**
  - Predominantly elevated/elated irritable
  - Expansive (but note transient depression common)
- **Speech and thoughts**
  - Pressured (fast)
  - Flight of ideas
  - Inflated self-esteem/grandiosity
  - Over-optimistic ideas
  - Poor attention, concentration
- **Behaviour**
  - Insomnia
  - Overactivity
  - Loss of normal social inhibitions: over-familiar, sexual promiscuity, risk-taking, overspending
  - Increased libido
  - Increased appetite, decreased weight
- **Psychotic symptoms (mania)**
  - Mood-congruent (eg delusions of special ability or status, grandiose delusions or auditory hallucinations)

Perhaps the most crucial decision to make in the management of bipolar disorder is the timing of the introduction of long-term prophylactic mood-stabilising medication (typically lithium or anticonvulsants). There are no hard and fast rules; this is a matter of clinical judgement.

Lithium is the most commonly prescribed mood stabiliser and it is particularly important to remember its therapeutic window. (*See* Chapter 2, Clinical Pharmacology, Toxicology and Poisoning.)

Biological/physical treatments of hypomania/mania

- **Short-term, acute episode**
  - Antipsychotics (olanzapine is licensed for the treatment of acute mania)
  - Benzodiazepines
  - Lithium (plasma level 1.0 mmol/l)
  - ECT
- **Long-term, prophylaxis**
  - Lithium (plasma level 0.5 mmol/l)
  - Carbamazepine (in patients unresponsive to lithium, particularly 'rapid cyclers': >4 episodes per year)
  - Valproic acid
  - Lamotrigine (effective where depressive episodes predominate)
  - Depot antipsychotics

18.2.2 Depression

Depression occurs with a wide range of severity and has a multifactorial aetiology. Lifetime incidence of depression varies from 1% to 20% according to severity. Evidence for a genetic contribution is most compelling in the most severe illness, whereas mild and moderate depression are usually best explained by psychosocial models. These latter disorders are rarely treated by psychiatrists unless they are complicated by co-morbidity with substance misuse or personality disorder. The variation in severity and symptomatology of depression has led to a number of classification systems:

- Endogenous versus reactive (more closely related to precipitating life events)
- Melancholic versus neurotic
- Unipolar (depression only) versus bipolar (depression with mania)

Clinical features of depression

'Biological' symptoms (shown in italics) are especially important because their presence predicts response to physical treatments. They are also known as 'somatic', 'endogenous' or 'melancholic' symptoms:

- **Mood**
  - Loss of reactivity
  - *Diurnal variation (worse in am)*
  - Pervasively lowered
  - Variable anxiety/irritability
- **Speech and thoughts**
  - Slowed speech, low volume
  - Reduced attention/concentration
  - Reduced self-esteem
  - Reduced confidence
  - Ideas of guilt, worthlessness, hopelessness
  - Bleak, pessimistic outlook
  - Ideas and acts of self-harm
- **Behaviour**
  - *Insomnia (early morning wakening)*
  - *Psychomotor agitation or retardation*
  - *Reduced libido*
  - *Loss of enjoyment (anhedonia)*
  - *Decreased appetite*
  - *Weight loss*
  - Decreased social interactions
  - Reduced energy/increased fatigue
  - Decreased activity
- **Psychotic symptoms**
  - Mood-congruent
  - Delusions of guilt, physical illness
  - Auditory hallucinations with derogatory content

18.2.3 Depression in the elderly

Depression in the elderly is often missed. This is in part due to the prejudice that depression is an inevitable consequence of increasing age, but also because older patients tend to present less with depressed mood and more with physical complaints. It is likely to be associated with social isolation, bereavement, financial problems, physical ill health and chronic pain. The most common presentations are physical symptoms (or hypochondriasis), insomnia (and psychomotor disturbances), and most commonly agitation, but stupor may occur. Neurocognitive deficits that are secondary to depression may mimic dementia (see below).

Treatment of depression on the elderly

Again, a biopsychosocial model is used:

- **Biological: selective serotonin re-uptake inhibitors** (SSRIs) are currently the most popular first-line agents. In the elderly, patients may be sensitive to the side-effects of tricyclic agents. **ECT** may be preferable in severe illness
- **Psychological**: CBT
- **Social**: decrease isolation

18.2.4 Differentiation of depression from dementia

The cognitive impairment seen in severe depression, sometimes called depressive pseudodementia, can lead to a misdiagnosis of primary dementia, particularly in elderly patients. Conversely, it is important to recognise that organic dementia often presents with depressive symptoms in the early stages.

Table 18.2 details differentiating clinical features.

Table 18.2. Clinical features of depression and dementia

Clinical features	Depression	Dementia
Family history	Affective disorder	Alzheimer's disease (in some)
Illness duration	Short	Long
Progression	Rapid	Slow
History of previous depression	Yes	No
Biological symptoms of depression	Present	Absent
c/o poor memory	Yes	No
History given	Detailed	Vague
Effort at testing	Poor	Good
Response at test results	Picks on faults	Pleased
Other behaviour	Contrary	Compatible
Examination of concentration/attention	Variable	Consistently poor
Orientation tests	'Don't know'	Poor
Memory loss	Global	Recent
Primitive reflexes	Absent	Present
Apraxias	Absent	Present
Word intrusions	Corrects	Unaware
Neuropsychological tests		
Test performance	Variable	Always poor
Pattern	Nil specific	Verbal IQ > performance IQ

18.2.5 Principles of treatment

Treatments in depression target the biological, psychological and social aetiologies. If biological symptoms are present then physical treatments are indicated, whatever the apparent psychosocial precipitants. *See also* Section 18.11, Treatments in psychiatry.

Treatment of depression

- **Biological treatments**
  - Antidepressants: for moderate to severe depression. SSRIs should be considered first-line (safer in overdose and better tolerated than other classes). Second-line choices include mirtazapine and reboxetine
  - Lithium (for augmentation of antidepressant effect, long-term prophylaxis or in treatment-resistant illness)
  - ECT (for severe or resistant depression)
  - Antipsychotics (if psychotic symptoms present)
  - Thyroid hormone (T_3; augmentation therapy in resistant depression)
- **Psychological treatments**
  - Cognitive therapy: for mild to moderate depression
  - Supportive psychotherapy/counselling
- **Social interventions**
  - Accommodation, finances, daytime activities

18.3 ANXIETY DISORDERS

18.3.1 Generalised anxiety disorder

The clinical features of generalised anxiety disorder are persistent and generalised, occurring across a range of daily circumstances. Patients never completely return to a baseline level of zero anxiety. Anxiety affects 1%–5% of the population (more common in females) and commonly co-exists with other psychiatric problems, particularly mood disorders. Organic causes of anxiety disorder include drugs (eg caffeine) and thyrotoxicosis.

Cognitive symptoms

- Apprehension
- Fear of death, losing control or going mad
- Hypervigilance

Somatic symptoms (associated with autonomic hyper-arousal)

- Palpitations
- Shortness of breath and hyperventilation
- Butterflies in the stomach, nausea, loose bowel motions
- Urinary frequency
- Muscle tension
- Headaches, dizziness, light-headedness, tingling in fingers and around mouth

Treatment of anxiety disorders

- **Biological**: specific SSRI antidepressants have been shown to be especially useful. Benzodiazepines (with care), β-blockers, buspirone ($5HT_{1A}$ partial agonist) and tricyclic antidepressants are also used in the short term
- **Psychological**: CBT (challenges dysfunctional thoughts and processes) and anxiety management (structured education, relaxation training)

18.3.2 Panic disorder

These patients suffer paroxysms of intense anxiety (panic) interspersed with periods of complete remission. Typical attacks last several minutes and occur without situational cues. Somatic symptoms are prominent. Patients may develop an anticipatory fear of the next attack.

Physical treatment includes short-term use of benzodiazepines with care, and SSRIs. CBT is an appropriate psychological treatment.

18.3.3 Phobic disorders

These patients suffer from intense anxiety which is reliably precipitated by a situational cue. The fear they experience is out of proportion to the situation and cannot be reasoned or explained away. This results in the avoidance of the feared situation and related situations and this, in turn, further reinforces the phobia.

Specific/simple phobias include fear of flying, heights, animals, etc. Agoraphobia is anxiety about being in places or situations from which escape may be difficult (for example, in crowds, on public transport, on a bridge). Social phobia is a persistent fear of humiliation or embarrassment in social situations.

Appropriate physical treatments include SSRIs, β-blockers and occasionally short-term use of benzodiazepines 'with care'. Patients may also benefit from psychological treatments, including:

- Behavioural psychotherapy: systematic desensitisation (controlled exposure to the feared situation), flooding, modelling
- Supportive psychotherapy
- Psychodynamic psychotherapy (*see* Section 18.11.5, The psychotherapies).

18.4 OBSESSIVE COMPULSIVE DISORDER

Obsessive compulsive disorder may also be called obsessional illness, or obsessional neurosis. Mild obsessional symptoms are very common and may actually be helpful for certain occupations (eg accountancy and medicine). Pathologically severe symptoms may be secondary to other psychiatric or neuropsychiatric disorders (see below). The lifetime prevalence of primary obsessive compulsive disorder is between 2% and 3%, with a slight excess of females affected. It is widely considered to be a neurobiological disorder associated with inadequate serotonin regulation.

Obsessions are ideas, thoughts (ruminations) or images that are:

- Recurrent
- Persistent and intrusive
- Occurring against the patient's will
- Regarded as absurd, but insight is maintained
- Recognised as a product of the patient's own mind (in contrast to psychosis, the patient recognises that their thoughts are abnormal)
- Resisted → anxiety

Compulsions are:

- Irresistible impulses to carry out a particular activity
- Usually triggered by an obsessional thought (with the belief that the compulsion will 'neutralise' the thought and thus lower anxiety levels)

OBSESSION → COMPULSION → RITUAL
hands dirty   must wash hands   washing

Compulsions and ritualised behaviours are sometimes referred to together as 'compulsions'. There is a large overlap with depressive disorder, and the two conditions often co-exist:

- 30% of patients with obsessive compulsive disorder have associated depression
- 25% of patients with depression develop obsessions

Other associations include:

- Schizophrenia (3%–5%)
- Anorexia nervosa
- Organic brain disease (frontal lobe syndromes, Sydenham's chorea, Tourette syndrome (obsessional symptoms in 11%–80%))

Treatment of obsessive compulsive disorders

- **Psychological**: in mild cases, CBT, which includes habituation training and thought

stopping (for obsessions), and exposure with response prevention (for compulsions), is first-line treatment
- **Biological**: in moderate disease SSRIs or clomipramine (to increase 5HT neurotransmission) combined with CBT. Antipsychotic augmentation can be used if the patient is resistant to SSRI alone. Very rarely psychosurgery may be effective for the extremely disabled patient

18.5   UNEXPLAINED PHYSICAL SYMPTOMS

Within a general hospital or general practice setting psychiatric referral may occur because no organic cause is found for physical symptoms. Somatic symptoms may be a manifestation of depression, anxiety or schizophrenia (rare) and these diagnoses should be excluded before a diagnosis of somatoform, conversion or factitious disorder is made.

18.5.1   Somatoform disorders

In this group of disorders there is repeated presentation of physical symptoms accompanied by persistent requests for medical investigations. If physical disorders are present, they do not explain the nature or extent of symptoms. Repeated negative findings and reassurance have little effect and patients usually refute the possibility of psychological causation. In somatisation disorder the emphasis is on particular symptoms (eg back pain); in hypochondriacal disorder, patients believe they have a specific disease process (eg cancer).

Somatisation disorder

- More than 2 years of **multiple physical *symptoms*** without adequate explanation
- Persistent refusal to accept advice or reassurance that there is no physical explanation
- Functional impairment due to the nature of symptoms and resulting behaviour
- Affects women much more often than men
- Is accompanied by a tendency to excessive drug use

Particularly common symptoms include gastrointestinal sensations (pain, belching, vomiting, nausea), abnormal skin sensations (itching, burning, tingling) and sexual and menstrual complaints.

Hypochondriacal disorder

- Persistent belief in the presence of at least one **serious physical *illness*** despite repeated negative investigations
- Typical illnesses include cancer, AIDS
- Persistent refusal to accept advice or reassurance
- Fear of drugs and side-effects

The principles of treatment for somatoform disorders are to exclude an organic basis for the complaint, acknowledge that the symptoms exist and then educate the patient about basic physiology and elicit and challenge the assumptions leading from the symptoms. Self-monitoring (by keeping a diary) can assist with the re-attribution of physical experiences.

18.5.2   Conversion disorder

This is a **rare** cause of unexplained physical symptoms. The theory is that intolerable psychic anxiety is **unconsciously** 'converted' to physical symptoms. The extent of 'motivation' or voluntary control is usually hard to assess, but there is a clear alteration or loss in physical function which is usually acute, but may be chronic.

Such 'psychogenic' symptoms usually follow an unresolved stressful event and their existence may lead to a reduction in psychological distress ('primary gain') and to a resolution of the stressful event. Although some patients experience the 'secondary gain' of attention from others, others may be indifferent to their loss of function ('la belle indifference'). Isolated conversion symptoms may be associated with schizophrenia or depression.

Convincing evidence of psychological causation may be difficult to find. It is vital to exercise caution in making a diagnosis of conversion disorder, especially in the presence of a known CNS or peripheral nervous system disorder.

Treatment of somatoform disorders

- CBT
- Psychotherapy: detection of the underlying conflict (may require hypnosis/abreaction)
- Antidepressants

18.5.3   Factitious disorder

Also known as Munchausen syndrome, this is the **intentional** production of physical or psychological symptoms. It is usually associated with severe personality disorder and treatment is extremely difficult.

18.6   EATING DISORDERS

Anorexia nervosa and bulimia nervosa share many clinical features (Figure 18.1, Table 18.3) and patients may satisfy criteria for anorexia or bulimia at different stages of their illness. Eating disorders are much more common in women, but 5%–10% of cases of anorexia are male. They are frequently undiagnosed and many such patients are not known to the healthcare system.

Figure 18.1 A schematic representation of the relationship between anorexia nervosa and bulimia nervosa. In clinical practice a diagnosis of bulimia is restricted to those with greater than average body weight. Those in the overlap are considered to have anorexia, bulimic subtype.

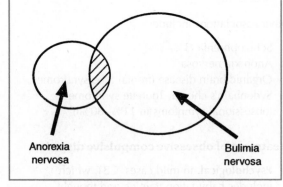

Anorexia nervosa

Bulimia nervosa

Table 18.3. Differentiation of eating disorders

	Anorexia nervosa (restricting subtype)	Anorexia nervosa (bulimic subtype)	Bulimia nervosa
'Nervosa' psychopathology	Yes	Yes	Yes
Behaviour to control weight	Yes	Yes	Yes
Bulimic episodes	No	Yes	Yes
Low weight (<15% average body weight)	Yes	Yes	No
Amenorrhoea	Yes	Yes	Possible

Anorexia nervosa is largely restricted to social groups in which thinness is coveted. Presentation is usually in adolescence and associated with childhood negative self-evaluation and perfectionism. The long-term outcome is poor, with only 20% making a full recovery and long-term mortality is around 15%–20%.

Bulimia nervosa has a prevalence in young women of 1%–2% and usually presents in the 20s. About one-third of patients have a previous history of anorexia. Outcome is highly variable but is worse if there is preceding anorexia or if the bulimia is part of a multi-impulsive personality disorder.

18.6.1 Anorexia nervosa and bulimia nervosa: diagnostic criteria

The diagnostic criteria of anorexia nervosa are shown in Table 18.4.

Table 18.4. Diagnostic criteria of anorexia nervosa

Loss of (>15%) normal body weight which is self-induced:	Extreme avoidance of foods considered 'fattening' Aggravated by self-induced vomiting, purging or exercise
A specific psychopathology ('nervosa'):	Overvalued idea that fatness is a dreadful state Extremely harsh definition of fatness Will not let weight rise above very low threshold
Specific endocrine associations: Female	Amenorrhoea Delayed puberty if very young (primary amenorrhoea)
Male	Loss of sexual interest and potency Delayed puberty if very young; arrest of secondary sexual characteristics

Bulimia nervosa: diagnostic criteria

Key features:

- Episodes of binge eating
- Persistent preoccupation with eating
- Irresistible craving for food

Specific psychopathology ('nervosa')

- Morbid fear of fatness
- Sharply defined weight threshold
- Earlier episode of anorexia nervosa

Attempts to counteract the 'fattening' effects of food

- Self-induced vomiting
- Periods of starvation
- Purgative and diuretic abuse
- Abuse of appetite suppressants
- Abuse of thyroid hormones
- Neglect to use insulin (diabetics)

18.6.2 Medical complications of anorexia nervosa

The medical complications of anorexia nervosa are mostly physiological adaptations to starvation and usually regress with refeeding (Table 18.5).

Table 18.5. Medical complications of anorexia nervosa

Cardiovascular	Bradycardia (87%)
	Hypotension (85%)
	Ventricular arrhythmias
	ECG abnormalities (including increased QT/RR slope)
	Congestive cardiac failure and cardiomyopathy
Gastroenterological	Eroded dental enamel/caries (secondary to vomiting)
	Enlarged salivary glands (secondary to vomiting)
	Oesophagitis, erosions, ulcers
	Oesophageal rupture
	Acute gastric dilatation with refeeding
	Decreased gastric emptying
	Constipation
	Duodenal dilatation
	Irritable bowel syndrome
	Melanosis coli (secondary to laxatives)
Renal	Decreased glomerular filtration rate
	Decreased concentration ability
	Hypokalaemic nephropathy
	Pre-renal uraemia

(continued)

Table 18.5. *(continued)*

Haematological	Pancytopenia
	Hypoplastic marrow
	Low plasma proteins
Musculoskeletal and skin	Early onset leads to shorter stature
	Osteoporosis and pathological fractures
	Muscle weakness and proximal myopathy
	Cramps
	Tetany
	Xerosis (dry scaly skin)
	Lanugo hair
	Hair loss
	Acne
	Carotenoderma (yellow-orange skin discoloration caused by increased serum carotenoids)
	Acrocyanosis
	Russell's sign – calluses on the dorsum of the hand, caused by using the fingers and hands to induce vomiting
Metabolic	Hypothermia and dehydration
	Electrolyte disturbance (especially hypokalaemia, hyponatraemia, hypomagnesaemia)
	Hypercholesterolaemia and carotinaemia
	Hypoglycaemia and raised liver enzymes
Neurological	Reversible brain atrophy (on CT scan)
	Abnormal EEG and seizures
Endocrine	Low follicle-stimulating hormone (FSH), luteinising hormone (LH), oestrogens, testosterone
	Low tri-iodothyronine (T_3)
	Raised cortisol and positive dexamethasone suppression test
	Raised growth hormone (GH)

18.6.3 Principles of treatment

The principles of treatment for anorexia nervosa are given in Table 18.6.

Table 18.6. Principles of treatment for anorexia nervosa

Biological/physical treatments	Psychological treatments
Anorexia nervosa • Restoration of weight as an inpatient, ideally in a specialist eating disorder unit • Drugs have a limited place in management • Enteral/parenteral nutrition is rarely indicated	**Anorexia nervosa** • Supportive psychotherapy • Family therapy • CBT
Bulimia nervosa • Selective serotonin re-uptake inhibitor (SSRI) may be useful • Reduce bingeing and self-induced vomiting • Effect not related to the presence of depressive symptoms	**Bulimia nervosa** • CBT • Cognitive analytic therapy • Self-help manuals

18.7 SELF-HARM AND SUICIDE

A good deal is known about the epidemiology of, and risk factors for, deliberate self-harm, both fatal and non-fatal. These are presented in Table 18.7. A decrease in the rate of suicide, particularly in patients with mental illness, has been the target of many government policies.

The incidence of completed suicide is reduced during wartime and in certain religious groups (eg Roman Catholics). The incidence is increased in springtime, amongst those working in certain high-risk occupations, such as farmers and doctors, and amongst those who are unemployed, and those who have a family history of suicide and have the means available to carry it out (ie weapons/drugs). Although the UK Suicide Policy focuses on reducing deaths by suicide in younger people (particularly young males) elderly males are still at highest risk of completed suicide.

- Non-fatal deliberate self-harm is a strong risk factor for eventual completed suicide
- Approximately 20% of non-fatal deliberate self-harm cases repeat within 1 year
- 1%–2% per year of non-fatal deliberate self-harm cases will lead to suicide within 1 year
- 10%–20% eventually commit suicide

Prevention of the above involves the identification and treatment of mental illness, increased awareness among GPs and in hospital staff, and the removal of the means to commit suicide (firearms restrictions, limit sales of paracetamol, catalytic converters).

Table 18.7. Features of suicide and non-fatal self-harm

	Suicide	Non-fatal self-harm
Annual incidence in UK	1/10 000 (5000 total)	20–30/10 000
Sex	M : F = 3 : 1	F > M
Age	Young and old males	Young, <35 years
Socioeconomic class	I, V	IV, V
Childhood	Parental death	Broken home
Physical health	Chronic or terminal illness, handicapped, pain	Nil specific
Mental illness	Depression ~ 60% Alcoholism ~ 20% Schizophrenia 10%	Depression ~ 10%
Pre-morbid personality	Usually well-adjusted	Antisocial, borderline personality disorder
Precipitants	Guilt, hopelessness	Situational
Setting	Premeditated, alone, warnings	Impulsive, others present
Method	Drug overdose. Males use more 'violent' methods, eg hanging	Drug overdose and cutting

18.8 ORGANIC PSYCHIATRY

Organic brain disorders can mimic any other functional mental disorder. Features that raise the possibility of an organic disorder include acute onset, visual perceptual abnormalities (illusions or hallucinations), cognitive deficit clearly preceding other symptoms, neurological signs and fluctuating symptoms.

18.8.1 Acute organic brain syndrome

This is also known as acute confusional state, or delirium. The young and the elderly are especially vulnerable. A breakdown of the blood–brain barrier is implicated. There are multiple possible aetiologies, both intra- and extracranial. Many of these converge in a final common pathway of profound cholinergic deficit.

Causes of acute organic brain syndrome

- **Extracranial**
  - Hypoxia (cardiac, respiratory)
  - Infection (respiratory, urinary, septicaemia)
  - Metabolic (electrolyte imbalance, uraemia, hepatic encephalopathy, porphyria, hypoglycaemia)
  - Hypovitaminosis (thiamine, B_{12})
  - Endocrine (hypo/hyperthyroid, hypo/ hyperparathyroid, diabetes, Addison's/ Cushing's, hypopituitarism)
  - Toxic (alcohol intoxication, alcohol withdrawal, all other illicit drugs, prescribed drugs (many), heavy metals)
- **Intracranial**
  - Trauma (head injury)
  - Infection (meningitis, encephalitis)
  - Vascular disease (transient ischaemic attack/stroke) hypersensitive encephalopathy, subarachnoid haemorrhage
  - Space-occupying lesion (tumour, abscess, subdural haemorrhage)
  - Epilepsy

Characteristic clinical features of acute organic brain syndrome

- Clouding of consciousness
- Disorientation
- Poor attention (digit span)
- Memory deficits
- Disturbed behaviour (especially at night)
- Mood abnormalities
- Disordered speech and thinking
- Abnormal perceptions (especially visual misperceptions and hallucinations)
- Abnormal beliefs
- Patients may be severely agitated or withdrawn and stuporose

EEG tests for this condition are sensitive but not specific; results may be abnormal (slowing of rhythm, low voltage trace) in the absence of clear cognitive abnormalities.

Principles of treatment are:

- Specific – to treat cause of confusional state
- General – to optimise immediate environment and reduce disorientation
- Symptomatic – careful use of sedatives if necessary

18.8.2 Dementia

Dementia is the global deterioration of higher mental functioning secondary to progressive neurodegenerative disease. Characteristic clinical features of dementia include episodic memory loss, apraxia, deterioration in self-care skills, temporal and topographical disorientation and personality changes in the presence of clear consciousness (cf acute confusional state). Delusions, hallucinations, agitation and aggression occur, particularly in the moderate stages before the dementia is very severe.

Aetiology

- Alzheimer's disease ~50%
- Lewy body dementia ~20%
- Vascular dementia (multi-infarct dementia) ~20%

For differentiation of dementia from depression, *see* Section 18.2.4.

Table 18.8 lists the features of Alzheimer's disease and multi-infarct dementia.

Table 18.8. Features of Alzheimer's disease and multi-infarct dementia

Clinical feature	Alzheimer's disease	Multi-infarct dementia
Age of onset	70–90 years	60–80 years
Sex	F > M	M > F
Family history	FAD* less than 1%	–
Aetiology	Genetic + environmental	Embolic
Onset	Insidious	Acute
Presenting symptoms	Cognitive	Emotional
Cognitive impairment	Diffuse	Patchy
Insight	Early loss	Preserved
Personality	Early loss	Preserved
Course of progression	Relentless	Stepwise
Focal neurological signs	Unusual	Common
Previous CVA** or TIA***	–	+++
Hypertension	–	+++
Associated ischaemic heart disease	–	+++
Seizures	+	+++
Most common cause of death	Infection	Ischaemic heart disease
Time to death from diagnosis	2–5 years	4–5 years

*FAD = familial Alzheimer's disease; **CVA = cerebrovascular accident; ***TIA = transient ischaemic attack

18.8.3 Physical illnesses particularly associated with mental disorders

Physical illnesses particularly associated with mental disorders

- **Neurological**
  - Parkinson's disease (depression, dementia)
  - Huntington's disease (personality change, depression, suicide, dementia)
  - Neurosyphilis (dementia, depression, grandiosity)
  - Epilepsy (depression, psychosis)
  - Multiple sclerosis (depression, elation, dementia)
  - Wilson's disease (affective disorder, aggression, cognitive impairment)
  - Prion diseases (depression, personality changes, dementia)
  - Brain tumour (location determines early symptoms)
  - Myasthenia gravis (depression)
  - Motor neurone disease (depression, dementia)
- **Endocrine**
  - **Cushing syndrome**: psychiatric disturbance in about 50% of hospital cases, depression, euphoria, confusion, paranoid psychoses, cognitive dysfunction in 66%
  - **Addison's disease**: psychiatric features in nearly 100%, depression, withdrawal, apathy, memory difficulties in up to 75%
  - **Hyperthyroidism**: psychological disturbance in 100%, restlessness, agitation, confusional state (rare), psychosis (very rare)
  - **Hypothyroidism**: mental symptoms universal at presentation, lethargy, cognitive slowing, apathy > depression, irritability, confusional state, dementia, affective or schizophreniform psychosis (very rare)
  - **Phaeochromocytoma**: paroxysmal anxiety
- **Other systemic causes**
  - Systemic lupus erythematosus (SLE) (acute confusional state, affective or schizophreniform psychosis); may be further complicated by the effect of steroids
  - Vitamin deficiency (B_1: Wernicke–Korsakoff syndrome; B_{12}: acute confusional state, depression)
  - Porphyria (especially AIP): acute confusional state, depression, paranoid psychosis
  - Paraneoplastic syndrome: depression, psychosis

18.8.4 Drug-induced mental disorders

Many drugs can lead to psychiatric conditions (Table 18.9).

Table 18.9. Mental disorders induced by drugs

Anxiety	Depression	Psychotic symptoms
Amphetamines	Reserpine	Amphetamines (including MDMA, 'ecstasy')
Cocaine	β-Blockers	LSD
Alcohol	Calcium antagonists	Cocaine
Phencyclidine (PCP)	Oral contraceptive pill	Marijuana
	Corticosteroids	Levodopa
	Alcohol	Anticholinergic drugs
	Furosemide	Anabolic steroids
		PCP

18.9 ALCOHOL ABUSE

The complications of alcohol are wide-ranging and cross social, psychological and neuropsychiatric domains. General medical problems are not covered here.

> **Alcohol dependence syndrome – seven key features**
>
> - Sense of compulsion to drink
> - Stereotyped pattern of drinking
> - Prominent drink-seeking behaviour
> - Increased tolerance to alcohol
> - Repeated withdrawal symptoms
> - Relief drinking to avoid withdrawal symptoms
> - Reinstatement after abstinence

18.9.1 Social consequences of alcohol abuse

- Family/marital problems
- Incest
- Absenteeism from work
- Accidents (major factor in ⩾10% of road traffic accidents)
- Crime (associated with acute abuse)
- Vagrancy

18.9.2 Acute withdrawal

Acute withdrawal causes a wide spectrum of symptoms. The fully developed syndrome is known as delirium tremens.

Delirium tremens

- **Definition of full syndrome**
  - Vivid hallucinations (often visual)
  - Delusions
  - Profound confusional state
  - Tremor
  - Agitation
  - Sleeplessness
  - Autonomic overactivity (including pyrexia)
- **Other clinical features**
  - Associated trauma or infection in 50%
  - Prodromal features may occur
  - Onset usually after 72 hours of abstinence
  - Visual illusions/hallucinations prominent
  - Duration ≤3 days in majority
  - Hypokalaemia common ± hypomagnesaemia
  - Mortality up to 5%

Treatment of alcohol withdrawal

- Inpatient
- Rehydration, antibiotics, parenteral high-potency B-complex vitamins, sedation
- Sedative drugs which facilitate GABA-ergic neurotransmission are cross-tolerant with alcohol and have anticonvulsant properties (eg a reducing dose of chlordiazepoxide, chlormethiazole oral/IV (only when patient in hospital)). Phenothiazine should be avoided because of the risk of seizure. If an antipsychotic drug is required, then haloperidol should be used

Relapse prevention and maintaining abstinence (outpatient)

- Pharmacological: disulfiram, acamprosate
- Psychosocial: essential to maintain abstinence, group therapy and support, ie Alcoholics Anonymous, '12-Step Programme' (specific principles guiding action for recovery from addiction)

18.9.3 Psychological consequences of alcohol abuse

These include dysphoric mood, pathological jealousy (Othello syndrome) and sexual problems (impotence, decreased libido). Other symptoms are alcoholic hallucinosis and alcohol dependence syndrome. Alcohol abuse commonly occurs secondary to other psychiatric illnesses, particularly bipolar disorder, depression, anxiety and post-traumatic stress disorder (PTSD).

Suicide is more common amongst this group (16% with full dependence syndrome) as is parasuicide (used acutely by 35%).

18.9.4 Neuropsychiatric consequences of alcohol abuse

The most likely neuropsychiatric consequences of alcohol abuse are Wernicke's encephalopathy and Korsakoff syndrome/psychosis. This group is also more likely to suffer seizures, head injury and dementia.

Rarer conditions associated with alcohol abuse include cerebellar degeneration, central pontine myelinosis and Marchiafava–Bignami disease (demyelination of the corpus callosum, optic tracts and cerebral peduncles).

Wernicke's encephalopathy

A disorder of acute onset featuring:

- Nystagmus
- Abducens and conjugate gaze palsies (96%)
- Ataxia of gait (87%)
- Global confusional state (90%)
- Hypothermia and hypotension

Note: the 'classic triad' (ocular signs, ataxia and confusional state) of symptoms is not always present.

It is caused by thiamine deficiency, most commonly secondary to alcoholism, but more rarely due to:

- Carcinoma of the stomach
- Toxaemia
- Pregnancy

- Persistent vomiting
- Dietary deficiency

Pathology

- **Macroscopic**: petechial haemorrhages
- **Microscopic**: dilatation and proliferation of capillaries, small haemorrhages, pale-staining parenchyma, reactive change in astrocytes and microglia, neurones relatively spared

Structures affected

- Mammillary bodies
- Walls of third ventricle
- Floor of fourth ventricle
- Periaqueductal grey matter
- Certain thalamic nuclei – medial dorsal, anteromedial, pulvinar
- Brainstem
- Cerebellum anterior lobe/vermis
- Cortical lesions rarely seen

Treatment

Parenteral thiamine. Up to 80% of sufferers go on to develop Korsakoff syndrome.

Korsakoff syndrome

A marked memory disorder with good preservation of other cognitive functions.

Clinical features

- Chronic disorder usually following Wernicke's encephalopathy
- Inability to consolidate new information
- Retrograde amnesia of days/years
- Patchy preservation of long-term memory
- Confabulation, not complaints of poor memory
- Apathy
- Lack of insight

Pathology

As for Wernicke's encephalopathy.

Treatment

Thiamine. There may be a response in only 20% of sufferers.

18.10 SLEEP DISORDERS

18.10.1 Normal sleep

In normal sleep, drowsiness first gives way to increasingly deep non-REM (rapid eye movement) sleep. The first REM period occurs after 50–90 minutes and lasts for 5–10 minutes. The cycle repeats at approximately 90-minute intervals so that there are four to six REM periods each night. In total, REM occupies 20%–25% of a night's sleep (see Figure 18.2).

Figure 18.2 Pictorial representation of the adult sleep cycle. Shaded areas indicate REM sleep

- **REM sleep**
  - Asynchronous, mixed frequency EEG
  - Bursts of rapid conjugate eye movements
  - Prominent autonomic changes – increased heart rate, blood pressure – penile tumescence
  - Decreased muscle tone
  - Extensor plantar responses may occur
- **Non-REM sleep**
  - EEG synchronous, with sleep spindles, K-complexes, generalised slowing with delta waves
  - Four stages recognised: stages 3 and 4 characterised as 'slow wave' sleep

loss of muscle tone leading to collapse); cataplexy occurs in response to an emotional stimulus (eg laughing, crying) and is pathognomic of the disease.

- Hypersomnolence   100%
- Cataplexy   90%
- HLA DR2 positive   99%
- Major affective disorder or personality problems   50%
- Sleep paralysis   40%
- Hypnagogic hallucinations (auditory hallucinations while dropping off to sleep)   30%
- Physical associations: obesity, insulin-resistant diabetes, hypotension, reduced food intake

18.10.2 Insomnia

Insomnia is seen in a wide range of psychiatric and medical disorders. Psychiatric disorders may account for up to 36% of patients with insomnia. Paradoxically, sleep deprivation may be used to treat depression and may precipitate mania.

Table 18.10 summarises the pattern of insomnia in various disorders.

18.10.3 Narcolepsy

Narcolepsy is a condition that is often undiagnosed. Typically, onset is between the ages of 10 and 20, and the increased risk in a first-degree relative is ×40. The syndrome of narcolepsy comprises **excessive daytime** somnolence and **cataplexy** (sudden

In narcolepsy, REM sleep occurs at the **onset** of nocturnal sleep. Daytime attacks also consist of periods of REM sleep occurring out of context.

18.11 TREATMENTS IN PSYCHIATRY

18.11.1 Antipsychotics

Antipsychotics are indicated in schizophrenia, mania, other paranoid psychoses and psychotic depression. 'Atypical' antipsychotics have preferable side-effect profiles and are now used as first-line treatment in schizophrenia.

Antipsychotics are most effective against the 'positive' symptoms of schizophrenia. They have an immediate sedative action but the antipsychotic action

Table 18.10. Mental disorders and sleep disturbance

Disorder	Pattern of insomnia
Major depression	Initial (early morning waking) and late insomnia in up to 80%
Mania	Globally reduced sleep
Generalised anxiety disorder	Initial and middle insomnia
Post-traumatic stress disorder	Intrusive nightmares about trauma
Acute confusional state	Disturbed sleep cycle

may be delayed for 3 weeks. They play an important role in preventing relapse.

Clozapine is effective in treatment-resistant schizophrenia and severe tardive dyskinesia. However, there is increasing evidence that the atypical antipsychotics clozapine, olanzapine and, to a lesser extent, risperidone are linked to hyperglycaemia, impaired glucose tolerance and occasionally to fatal diabetic ketoacidosis.

Table 18.11 gives examples of the different classes of antipsychotic drugs and their side-effects.

18.11.2 Antidepressants

Antidepressants are indicated in depressive illness, anxiety disorders (especially panic disorder and phobic disorders) and obsessional illness.

In depressive illness, antidepressants have a response rate of around 65%, with a delay in action of between 10 days and 6 weeks. The presence of 'biological' symptoms can help in the prediction of response. Antidepressants also play a prophylactic role in recurrent depressive disorders.

Table 18.11. Side-effects of antipsychotic drugs

Class	Example	Side-effects
Atypical antipsychotics (highly selective blockade of mesolimbic D_2 receptors and serotonin ($5HT_{2A}$) receptors)	Sulpiride/amisulpride Olanzapine Risperidone Clozapine (also α_1-receptor antagonist)	Hyperprolactinaemia Weight gain Nausea, dyspepsia Blood dyscrasias (neutropenia (3%), agranulocytosis (1%)); fatal myocarditis and cardiomyopathy Hypersalivation
Typical antipsychotics (D_2-receptor antagonists of the mesolimbic, tuberoinfundibular and nigrostriatal systems)		All of the following side-effects can be seen with each of the three classes of typical antipsychotic drugs:
Phenothiazines	Chlorpromazine, thioridazine	**Extrapyramidal**: acute dystonia, parkinsonism, akathisia, tardive dyskinesia
Butyrophenones Thioxanthenes	Haloperidol, droperidol Flupentixol, zuclopenthixol	**Anticholinergic**: dry mouth, constipation, etc **Anti-adrenergic**: postural hypotension **Antihistaminergic**: sedation **Endocrine**: hyperprolactinaemia, photosensitivity (especially phenothiazines) **Other:** Lowered seizure threshold Neuroleptic malignant syndrome Prolonged QT_C interval

Drugs which inhibit 5HT reuptake are particularly useful in obsessional illness. Most antidepressants (particularly SSRIs) are associated with hyponatraemia, which is mediated via syndrome of inappropriate ADH (SIADH); elderly women are particularly vulnerable to developing this. Abrupt cessation of paroxetine causes a discontinuation syndrome with flu-like symptoms, dizziness and insomnia.

Table 18.12 gives examples of the different classes of antidepressants and their side-effects.

The side-effects and toxicity of lithium are described in detail in Chapter 2, Clinical Pharmacology, Toxicology and Poisoning.

18.11.3 Benzodiazepines

Benzodiazepines are only indicated for the short-term relief of severe, disabling anxiety. The *British National Formulary* recommends only 2–4 weeks of use. They are not indicated for 'mild' anxiety but

Table 18.12. Examples of the different classes of antidepressants and their side-effects

Class	Example	Side-effects
SSRI*	Citalopram Fluoxetine Fluvoxamine Paroxetine Sertraline	Nausea, sexual dysfunction, headache, sleep disturbance (early), increased anxiety (early)
Tricyclic	Amitriptyline Imipramine Clomipramine	**Anticholinergic**: dry mouth, constipation, etc **Anti-adrenergic**: postural hypotension **Antihistaminergic**: sedation Weight gain Lower seizure threshold Cardiac arrhythmias
SNRI**	Venlafaxine	Nausea Hypertension
MAOI***	Phenelzine	Anticholinergic Anti-adrenergic Hypertensive reaction with tyramine-containing foods Important drug interactions
RIMA****	Moclobemide	Potential tyramine interaction
Presynaptic α_2-antagonist	Mirtazapine	Agranulocytosis

*SSRI = selective serotonin re-uptake inhibitor
**SNRI = selective noradrenaline re-uptake inhibitor
***MAOI = monoamine oxidase inhibitor
****RIMA = reversible inhibitor of monoamine oxidase A

can be used as adjunctive treatment for anxiety, agitation and behavioural disturbance in acute psychosis or mania. They are only indicated for insomnia if the condition is severe, disabling or subjecting the patient to extreme distress. Table 18.13 shows the pharmacokinetics of some benzodiazepines.

Benzodiazepine withdrawal syndrome may not develop for up to 3 weeks, but can occur within a few hours for short-acting drugs. Symptoms include insomnia, perspiration, anxiety, tinnitus, decreased appetite, decreased weight, perceptual disturbances and tremor.

The recommended withdrawal regime involves transferring the patient to an equivalent dose of diazepam, preferably taken at night. Ideally the dose should be decreased by approximately 1/8 of the daily dose every 2 weeks. If withdrawal symptoms occur, the dose is maintained until symptoms improve.

18.11.4 Electroconvulsive therapy (ECT)

ECT is indicated in severe or treatment-resistant depression or where there are psychotic symptoms, life-threatening lack of food and fluid intake, or for stupor and elderly (especially agitated) patients. 'Biological' features help predict the likely response.

It is also indicated to treat catatonia associated with schizophrenia and in treatment-resistant cases of mania.

Side-effects of ECT

- **Early**
  - Headache
  - Temporary confusion
  - Impaired short-term memory (bilateral ECT worse than unilateral)
  - (Rare) fractures, dislocation, fat embolism
- **Late (6–9 months)**
  - No memory impairment detected
  - Subjective impairment

Contraindications to ECT

Raised intracranial pressure (the only absolute contraindication), cardiac arrest less than 2 years previously, other cardiac disease, pulmonary disease, history of cerebrovascular accident.

ECT has a mortality rate of 3 deaths per 100 000 (cf general anaesthesia in healthy adults, 1 per 100 000. The mortality rate of untreated major depression is 10%, however.

Table 18.13. Pharmacokinetics of benzodiazepines

Longer half-life	Diazepam equivalent (mg)*	Half-life (hours)	Shorter half-life	Diazepam equivalent (mg)*	Half-life (hours)
Diazepam	5	20–90	Lorazepam	0.5	8–24
Chlordiazepoxide	15	20–90**	Oxazepam	15	6–28
Nitrazepam	5	16–40	Temazepam	10	6–10
Chlorazepate	–	50–100	Alprazolam	–	6–16
Flurazepam	–	50–100			

*Approximate equivalent doses to diazepam 5 mg
**Includes active metabolites

18.11.5 The psychotherapies

Table 18.14 lists the different forms of psychotherapy available, their indications and delivery.

Table 18.14. The psychotherapies

Type	Frequency	No. of sessions	Indications
Counselling	Weekly to monthly	6–12	Mild depression Anxiety Bereavement
Cognitive behavioural	Weekly	8–12	Depression Anxiety Somatoform disorder Eating disorders
Behavioural	Weekly	6–12	Phobias Anxiety Obsessional illness Sexual dysfunction Dementia
Psychoanalytic	1–5/week	50–indefinite	Neurosis Personality disorders Psychosexual
Group	Weekly	6–12	Anxiety Substance misuse Eating disorders

Chapter 19
Respiratory Medicine

CONTENTS

19.8 Miscellaneous respiratory disorders

19.8.1   Pleural effusion
19.8.2   Pneumothorax
19.8.3   Obstructive sleep apnoea/ hypopnoea syndrome (OSAHS)
19.8.4   Adult respiratory distress syndrome (ARDS)
19.8.5   Rare lung disorders

pleural effusions:

Exudate (×30g/L)

- infective.
- Connective tissue disease.
- Malignant
- pancreatitis
- P.E
- Dressler's
- yellow nail

transudate (× <30g/L) .

- ♡ failure
- ↓albumin.
- hypothyroidism
- Meig's syndrome.

Respiratory Medicine

19.1 LUNG ANATOMY AND PHYSIOLOGY

The human lung is composed of approximately 300 million alveoli each around 0.3 mm in diameter. Gas exchange takes place in the alveoli, and air is transported to these via a series of conducting airways. It is warmed and humidified in the upper airways and transported through the trachea, main bronchi, lobar and segmental bronchi to the terminal bronchioles, the smallest of the conducting tubes. These airways take no part in gas exchange and constitute the anatomical dead space (approximately 150 ml). The terminal bronchioles lead to the respiratory bronchioles, which have alveoli budding from their walls. Lung tissue distal to the terminal bronchiole forms the primary lobule.

19.1.1 Ventilation

The most important muscle of inspiration is the diaphragm, a muscular dome that moves downwards on inspiration. The external intercostal muscles assist inspiration by moving the ribs upwards and forwards in a 'bucket-handle' movement.

- The accessory muscles of respiration include the scalene muscles, which elevate the first two ribs, and the sternocleidomastoids, which elevate the sternum; these are not used during quiet breathing
- Expiration is passive during quiet breathing
- During exercise, expiration becomes active and the internal intercostal muscles and the muscles of the anterior abdominal wall are utilised
- The greatest ventilation is achieved at the lung bases and this is matched by increased perfusion in these areas

Normal lung is very compliant. **Compliance** is reduced by pulmonary venous engorgement and alveolar oedema and in areas of atelectasis. Surfac-

tant, secreted by type 2 alveolar epithelial cells, substantially lowers the surface tension of the alveolar lining fluid, increasing lung compliance and promoting alveolar stability. Lack of surfactant leads to respiratory distress syndrome.

Resistance to airflow is related to the radius of the airway, but the greatest overall resistance to flow occurs in medium-sized bronchi. Airway calibre is influenced by lung volume; at low lung volumes small airways may close completely, leading to areas of atelectasis, particularly at the lung bases.

19.1.2 Perfusion

The pulmonary vessels form a low-pressure system conducting deoxygenated blood from the pulmonary arteries to the alveoli where they form a dense capillary network. The pulmonary arteries have thin walls with very little smooth muscle; the mean pulmonary artery pressure is 15 mmHg and the upper limit of normal pressure is 30 mmHg.

- Pulmonary vascular resistance is one-tenth systemic vascular resistance
- Hypoxic vasoconstriction refers to contraction of smooth muscle in the walls of the small arterioles in a hypoxic region of lung; this helps to divert blood away from areas with poor ventilation so maintaining ventilation and perfusion matching

19.1.3 Control of respiration

The respiratory centre comprises a poorly defined collection of neurones in the pons and medulla; to a certain extent, the cortex can override the function of the respiratory centre. Chemoreceptors are crucial to the control of respiration, and these may be **central** or **peripheral**:

- **Central chemoreceptors** are located on the ventral surface of the medulla. They respond to increased hydrogen ion concentration in the cerebrospinal fluid (CSF), generated by increased pCO_2 in the blood
- **Peripheral chemoreceptors** are located in the carotid bodies (at the bifurcation of the common carotid arteries) and the aortic bodies (near the aortic arch); they respond to hypoxaemia, hypercapnia and pH changes

In people with normal respiratory function the most important factor for control of ventilation is the pCO_2, which is maintained to within 3 mmHg of baseline (normal range 35–45 mmHg). However, in patients with severe lung disease, chronic CO_2 retention develops and the hypoxic drive to ventilation becomes very important.

- Ventilation may increase by 15 times the resting level during severe exercise
- Cheyne–Stokes respiration is characterised by periods of apnoea separated by periods of hyperventilation; it occurs in severe heart failure or brain damage and at altitude

19.1.4 Pulmonary function tests (PFTs)

Peak expiratory flow rate (PEFR)

This is measured in litres per minute and is a useful guide to airways obstruction. Attention to technique is important in order to obtain accurate, repeatable readings.

- It is most useful in asthma as it reflects central airways obstruction
- It may underestimate disease severity in chronic obstructive pulmonary disease (COPD)

Spirometry

- FEV_1 refers to the volume of gas expired in the first second of a forced expiration
- FVC refers to the total volume of gas expired on forced expiration (forced vital capacity)
- The normal ratio of FEV_1/FVC is 70%–80%
- A reduction in FEV_1 with a preserved FVC occurs in airways obstruction (eg asthma or COPD). In patients with severe COPD a **slow vital capacity** is a more accurate measurement as it allows time for the lungs to empty fully and hence a true FEV_1/FVC ratio can be determined
- Restriction refers to a reduction in FVC with a preserved FEV_1/FVC ratio and occurs in conditions such as pulmonary fibrosis, neuromuscular disorders, obesity and pleural disease

Flow volume loops

A flow volume loop (Figure 19.1) is produced by plotting flow on the y axis against volume on the x axis.

If a subject inspires rapidly from residual volume (RV) to total lung capacity (TLC) and then exhales as hard as possible back to RV, a record can be made of the maximum flow volume loop. This loop shows that expiratory flow rises very rapidly to a maximum value, but then declines over the rest of expiration. During the early part of a forced expiration the maximum effort-dependent flow rate is achieved within 0.1 s, but the rise in transmural pressure leads to the airways being compressed and therefore to the flow rate being reduced. The flow rate is then said to be effort-independent.

A great deal can be learned by comparing the form of the loop to that which is normally seen ('triangle sitting on a semi-circle'). Several patterns can be

Figure 19.1 Typical flow loop

TLC - Total lung capacity
VC - Vital capacity
RV - Residual volume
PIFR - Peak inspiratory flow rate
PEFR - Peak expiratory flow rate
FEFR - Forced expiratory flow rate

recognised, reflecting various disorders (Figure 19.2).

Lung volumes

- Tidal volume, inspiratory and expiratory reserve volumes and vital capacity can all be measured by the use of a spirometer (see Figure 19.3)

- TLC, RV and functional residual capacity can be measured using a helium dilution method, nitrogen washout or body box

19.1.5 Gas transfer

Transfer of carbon monoxide is solely limited by diffusion and is used to measure gas transfer. Either a single breath-hold or a steady-state method can be used. Results are expressed both as total gas

Figure 19.2 Flow volume loops in different disorders

Pressure-dependent collapse

If intrathoracic airways collapse immediately expiration begins there is an abrupt early fall from peak flow, ie pressure-dependent collapse typical in emphysema

Volume-dependent collapse

If the airways collapse progressively with expiration, the scooping out of the expiration limb is more gradual, ie volume-dependent collapse. This is seen in chronic pulmonary disease

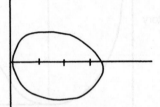

Inspiratory loop

If the lungs are abnormally stiff or springy, airway closure is delayed, as in children and young women, producing a descending portion which is convex. Inspiration is opposed slightly, producing a flatter inspiratory loop

Flattened inspiratory expiratory loops

If extrathoracic obstruction exists, both the inspiratory and expiratory loops will be flattened, eg tracheal compression by goitre, nodes

Figure 19.3 Subdivision of lung volume

TV	= Tidal volume	TLC	= Total lung capacity
VC	= Vital capacity (VC = IC + ERV)	RV	= Residua volume (RV = TLC – VC)
FEV$_1$	= Forced expiratory volume 1 s	IC	= Inspiratory capacity
FRC	= Functional residual capacity	ERV	= Expiratory reserve volume
	(FRC = ERV + RV)		(ERV = VC – IC)

transfer (DLCO) or gas transfer corrected for lung volume (KCO, ie KCO = DLCO/VA where VA is alveolar volume).

Causes of hypoxaemia

- **Hypoventilation**
  - Opiate overdose
  - Paralysis of respiratory muscles
- **$\dot{V}/\dot{Q}$ mismatch**
  - Pulmonary embolus
- **Low inspired partial pressure of oxygen**
  - High altitude
- **Breathing a hypoxic mixture**
- **Diffusion impairment**
  - Pulmonary oedema
  - Fibrosing alveolitis
- **Bronchiolar-alveolar cell carcinoma**
- **Shunt***
  - Pulmonary AV malformations
  - Cardiac right-to-left shunts

*Hypoxaemia caused by shunt cannot be abolished by administering 100% oxygen

Oxygen and carbon dioxide transport

Oxygen is transported in the blood by combination with the haemoglobin (Hb) in red cells. A tiny amount is dissolved (0.3 ml/100 ml blood, assuming pO$_2$ of 100 mmHg). The oxyhaemoglobin dissociation curve is sigmoid in shape. Once oxygen saturation falls below 90% the amount of oxygen carried to the tissues falls rapidly. The p50 (the partial pressure at which haemoglobin is 50% saturated) is 26 mmHg.

- The curve is **shifted to the right** by high temperature, acidosis, increased pCO$_2$ and increased levels of 2,3-diphosphoglycerate (2,3-DPG); this encourages offloading of oxygen to the tissues
- The curve is **shifted to the left** by changes opposite to those above, and by carboxyhaemoglobin and fetal haemoglobin

Carbon dioxide is transported in the blood as bicarbonate, in combination with proteins as carbamino compounds, and it is also dissolved in plasma. Carbon dioxide is 20 times more soluble than oxygen and about 10% of all CO_2 is dissolved. CO_2 diffuses into red blood cells where carbonic anhydrase facilitates the formation of carbonic acid, which dissociates into bicarbonate and hydrogen ions. Bicarbonate diffuses out of the cell and chloride moves in to maintain electrical neutrality.

Acid–base control

The normal pH of arterial blood is 7.35–7.45. Blood pH is closely regulated and variation outside this pH range results in compensation either by the lung or the kidney to return pH to normal. Failure to excrete CO_2 normally results in a respiratory acidosis; this is usually due to hypoventilation. Hyperventilation causes lowering of the pCO_2 and alkalosis.

pH can also be altered by metabolic disturbance. Metabolic acidosis and alkalosis are considered in Chapter 13, Metabolic Diseases. Mixed respiratory and metabolic acid–base disturbances are common.

Arterial blood gases

Normal values are:

- pH 7.35–7.45
- pO_2 >10.6 kPa (77 mmHg) whilst breathing room air
- pCO_2 4.7–6.0 kPa (35–45 mmHg)
- HCO_3 (bicarbonate) 22–28 mmol/l

When recording blood gases the percentage of inspired oxygen should always be stated. The value in kilopascal (kPa) should be multiplied by 7.6 to convert to mmHg.

19.1.6   Adaptation to high altitude

The barometric pressure decreases with altitude: at 18 000 feet it is half the normal 760 mmHg. Hyperventilation, due to hypoxic stimulation of peripheral chemoreceptors, is an early response to altitude.

The respiratory alkalosis produced is corrected by renal excretion of bicarbonate.

- Hypoxaemia stimulates the release of erythropoietin from the kidney, and the resultant polycythaemia allows increased carriage of oxygen by arterial blood
- There is an increased production of 2,3-DPG, which shifts the oxygen dissociation curve to the right, allowing better offloading of oxygen to the tissues
- Hypoxic vasoconstriction increases pulmonary artery pressure causing right ventricular hypertrophy. Pulmonary hypertension is sometimes associated with pulmonary oedema – altitude sickness

19.2   DISEASES OF LARGE AIRWAYS

19.2.1   Asthma

Asthma is a chronic inflammatory disorder of the airways. In susceptible individuals this inflammation causes symptoms that are associated with widespread but variable airflow obstruction, which is reversible either spontaneously or with treatment. There is an increase in airway sensitivity to a variety of stimuli.

The prevalence of asthma has been increasing in recent years, principally among children. Approximately 5.1 million people suffer from asthma in the UK – 1.4 million of these are children. Around 1500 asthma deaths occur annually in the UK.

The development of asthma is almost certainly due to a combination of genetic predisposition and environmental factors. Atopy is strongly associated with asthma. The most important allergens are the house dust mite (*Dermatophagoides pteronyssinus*), dog allergen (found in pelt, dander and saliva), cat allergen (predominantly in sebaceous glands), pollen, grasses and moulds.

Factors provoking asthma attacks

- Exposure to sensitising agents
- Exercise
- Infection
- Gastro-oesophageal reflux
- Drugs, including aspirin, non-steroidal anti-inflammatory agents, β-blockers
- Cigarette smoke, fumes, sprays, perfumes, etc
- Failure to comply with medication

In patients with asthma the airways are narrowed by a combination of contraction of bronchiolar smooth muscle, mucosal oedema and mucus plugging. In the early stages changes are reversible, but, in chronic asthma structural changes (including thickening of the basement membrane, goblet cell hyperplasia and hypertrophy of smooth muscle) develop and ultimately lead to irreversible fibrosis of the airways. Asthma is regarded as a complex inflammatory condition and mast cells, eosinophils, macrophages, T lymphocytes and neutrophils are all involved in the pathogenesis. A variety of inflammatory mediators are released, including histamine, leukotrienes, prostaglandins, bradykinin and platelet activating factor (PAF).

Chronic asthma

The hallmark of chronic asthma is variable and reversible airflow obstruction. This causes:

- Shortness of breath
- Chest tightness
- Wheeze
- Cough

At times the cough may be productive of sputum which may be clear, or yellow/green, due to the presence of eosinophils. The normal diurnal variation in airway calibre is accentuated in asthmatics and symptoms may be worse at night.

Physical signs of asthma

- Tachypnoea
- Wheezing, most marked in expiration
- Hyperinflation of the chest
- Nasal polyps (particularly in aspirin-sensitive asthmatics)
- Atopic eczema

Diagnosis of asthma

The diagnosis of asthma is clinical and is often confirmed by diary recordings of the peak expiratory flow rate (PEFR). The pattern of lung function tests may be very helpful (see box below). Challenge tests with histamine or methacholine, or with exercise, can be used to assess airways' responsiveness where the diagnosis is unclear. Responsiveness is expressed as the concentration of provoking agent required to decrease the FEV_1 by 20%.

Typical lung function tests in asthma

- Significant (>20% difference) diurnal peak expiratory flow rate (PEFR) variability on at least 3 days per week for a minimum of 2 weeks
- Significant improvement in PEFR (>15%) and FEV_1 (at least 400 ml) after bronchodilator or a trial of oral or inhaled steroids
- Increased lung volumes
- Reduced FEV_1
- FEV_1/FVC ratio <70%
- Gas trapping

Other clinical features that are helpful in making a diagnosis of asthma are:

- A history of asthma in childhood or of eczema or hay fever
- A family history of asthma

- Symptoms of perennial rhinitis, nasal polyps or chronic sinusitis
- History of wheezing associated with aspirin, NSAIDs or β-blockers

Skin-prick tests

Skin-prick tests can be used to assess atopy. Many asthmatic subjects make IgE in response to common allergens. A tiny quantity of allergen is introduced into the superficial layers of the dermis and tests are read at 20 minutes. The diameter of the weal is measured in millimetres, the size of the weal correlating well with bronchial challenge testing. Serum total IgE is commonly raised in asthmatics. Specific IgE may be measured by radio-allergosorbent testing (RAST).

Treatment

The aims of **prophylactic** treatment in asthmatic patients are to:

- Minimise symptoms during day and night
- Minimise the need for 'reliever' (eg bronchodilator) medication
- Avoid exacerbations
- Prevent limitation of physical activity
- Maintain normal lung function (FEV$_1$/PEFR >80%)

The mainstay of treatment is inhaled corticosteroid with short-acting β-agonists to relieve symptoms. Treatment is altered in a stepwise fashion as recommended in the BTS/SIGN National Guidelines. The dose of inhaled steroid should initially be appropriate to the severity of symptoms and is adjusted to achieve control.

- Long-acting β-agonists (eg salmeterol or eformoterol) should be added in patients who are inadequately controlled on beclometasone dipropionate (200 mg/day) or an equivalent steroid inhaler
- Oral theophylline preparations or β$_2$-agonist tablets are of benefit in some patients
- Leukotriene-receptor antagonists (*see also* Chapter 2, Clinical Pharmacology, Toxicology

and Poisoning) may be particularly useful for exercise-induced asthma, and in patients with aspirin sensitivity

- Long-term oral corticosteroids are reserved for patients with very severe asthma
- Allergen avoidance may be helpful in reducing the severity of existing disease in patients exposed and sensitised
- Smoking cessation is essential and should be advised
- Omalizumab is a possible add-on therapy for patients with severe persistent allergic asthma
- All inhalers are now required to be CFC-free

Acute severe asthma

Asthma symptoms may worsen acutely necessitating prompt treatment to relieve the attack. An immediate assessment is essential, looking for signs of severity, which include the following:

- Speech impairment
- Respiratory rate >25 breaths/min
- Tachycardia (pulse >110 beats/min)
- PEFR 33%–50% of predicted

Life-threatening asthma is associated with any one of the following:

- Hypoxaemia
- PEFR <33% of predicted
- Exhaustion
- Bradycardia (pulse <60 beats/min)
- Hypotension
- A silent chest
- A normal or raised pCO$_2$

Arterial blood gases should be performed if the patient is hypoxic on air (saturations <92%) and a chest X-ray is necessary to exclude pneumothorax.

Management consists of high-flow oxygen therapy, nebulised bronchodilators (β-agonists, ipratropium), steroids and, if infection is considered likely, antibiotics. PEFR should be measured regularly to assess the response to treatment.

- If there is no improvement with nebulisers, then intravenous infusions of either salbutamol or aminophylline should be used
- A single dose of intravenous magnesium can be given to patients who have not had a good response to bronchodilators, or to those with life-threatening asthma
- If the patient is severely ill, or not improving with treatment, **they should be promptly transferred to an Intensive Care Unit**

Allergic bronchopulmonary aspergillosis

Most patients with allergic bronchopulmonary aspergillosis are asthmatics but the condition may occur in non-asthmatics. This condition is considered in detail in Section 19.3.6.

19.2.2   Chronic obstructive pulmonary disease (COPD)

COPD is defined as a chronic, slowly progressive disease characterised by airflow obstruction that does not markedly change over several months. Most of the lung function impairment is fixed although some reversibility can be produced by bronchodilator therapy. Long-term prognosis is determined by post-bronchodilator FEV_1. COPD is an inflammatory condition that progresses even if the patient has stopped smoking.

COPD currently accounts for 6%–7% of all UK deaths. However, the incidence of COPD is increasing and it is likely to become the third commonest cause of death worldwide (it is currently fourth) by 2020. It is the only one of the 'top 10' worldwide causes of death that is increasing.

The diagnosis is made by:

- History of cough with sputum production, wheeze and shortness of breath
- History of frequent winter bronchitis and delayed recovery from viral infections
- Reduced FEV_1/FVC ratio without reversibility

Causes of COPD

- Smoking (usually a history of at least 20 pack-years)
- Air pollution
- Low birth weight and low socioeconomic status
- Dust exposure
- Alpha-1-antitrypsin deficiency

COPD is due to a combination of chronic bronchitis and emphysema.

Chronic bronchitis is defined as chronic cough and sputum production for at least 3 months of two consecutive years in the absence of other diseases recognised to cause sputum production.

Emphysema is characterised by abnormal, permanent enlargement of the air spaces distal to the terminal bronchioles, accompanied by destruction of their walls without obvious fibrosis. Emphysema may be centri-acinar (predominantly affecting the upper lobes and associated with smoking), panacinar, paraseptal or predominantly localised around scars (scar emphysema).

Signs of COPD

Many patients with COPD will have no abnormal physical signs until the disease is advanced:

- Hyperinflation
- Central cyanosis
- Weight loss
- Cor pulmonale: raised JVP, right ventricular heave, loud P2, tricuspid regurgitation, peripheral oedema, hepatomegaly
- Flapping tremor
- Pursed-lip breathing
- Wheeze
- Reduced breath sounds

Investigations

- **PFTs:** FEV_1 <80% predicted, FEV_1/FVC <70%; patients have large lung volumes and reduced

[handwritten annotations at top of page: 1st line : SABA / SAMA   2nd: FEV₁ >50% LABA/LAMA   FEV₁ <50% LABA + ICS/LAMA   3rd: oral Neophylline]

gas transfer factor (DLCO) in emphysema. COPD may be graded by the FEV_1:

- **Mild COPD**: FEV_1 50%–80% of predicted
- **Moderate COPD**: FEV_1 30%–50% of predicted
- **Severe COPD**: FEV_1 <30% of predicted
- **Chest X-ray**: may be normal or show evidence of hyperinflation, bullae or prominent vasculature due to pulmonary hypertension
- **Arterial blood gases**: may indicate type 1 or type 2 respiratory failure
- **Full blood count (FBC)**: possible polycythaemia
- **ECG**: may show P-pulmonale, right axis deviation, right bundle branch block
- **Sputum culture**: *Haemophilus influenzae*, *Streptococcus pneumoniae* or less commonly *Staphylococcus*, *Moraxella catarrhalis* or Gram-negative organisms

Treatment of COPD

Several recent clinical trials have shown no impact of inhaled steroids on disease progression in COPD although they do reduce exacerbations and improve quality of life in those patients with moderate or severe disease who have at least two exacerbations each year. Pulmonary rehabilitation is increasingly recognised as an important part of disease management.

Treatments available for COPD

- Smoking cessation
- Lung volume reduction surgery (for patients with severe emphysema) or bullectomy
- Inhaled anticholinergic drugs
- Inhaled short- or long-acting β_2-agonists
- Theophyllines
- Inhaled steroids*
- Diuretics
- Long-term oxygen therapy (LTOT)
- Pulmonary rehabilitation
- Transplantation

*Systemic steroids are reserved for very severe cases

Pulmonary rehabilitation

This plays a key role in the management of respiratory diseases causing breathlessness, particularly COPD. A multidisciplinary team, usually comprising a physiotherapist, occupational therapist, respiratory nurse, dietician and sometimes psychologist, is needed. Patients usually participate 2–3 times per week over 6–8 weeks. Aerobic exercise including specific upper and lower limb strengthening is followed by educational and relaxation sessions. Pulmonary rehabilitation has been shown to be effective for all patients with COPD regardless of severity and all motivated patients should be referred for this treatment.

Treatment of acute exacerbations

Antibiotics are indicated for acute exacerbations if two of the following are present:

- Increased breathlessness
- Increased sputum volume
- Increased sputum purulence

Regular bronchodilators (nebulised or inhaled) are given in addition to short courses of oral steroids and controlled oxygen therapy.

If initial blood gases show hypercapnia and acidosis:

- Patients should be treated along conventional lines for an hour and arterial blood gases then repeated
- If significant acidosis (pH <7.35) with hypercapnia persists, then non-invasive positive-pressure ventilation (NIPPV) should be instituted via a face mask

19.2.3   Alpha-1-antitrypsin deficiency

Many different phenotypes of α1-antitrypsin are known, the common ones being designated M, S and ZZ. MM confers 100% protease inhibitor activity while the most severe deficiency is produced by ZZ. Panlobular emphysema develops, which is most marked in the basal areas of the lungs. Emphysema is thought to result from an imbalance in the lung between neutrophil elastase (which destroys elastin) and the elastase inhibitor α1-antitrypsin (which protects against the proteolytic degradation by elastin). The decline in lung function is accelerated in smokers.

- PFTs show airflow obstruction, large lung volumes and reduced KCO
- Cirrhosis of the liver is more common, particularly in those of ZZ phenotype
- Smoking cessation is imperative
- Replacement therapy with α1-antitrypsin is not routinely given
- Lung transplantation may be an option for some patients
- Genetic counselling should be offered and siblings of index cases should be genetically tested

19.2.4 Long-term oxygen therapy (LTOT)

Two trials have established the benefit of LTOT. In the MRC trial, oxygen via nasal cannulae was given to raise the pO_2 to 8 kPa (60 mmHg) for at least 15 hours per day compared to patients with COPD receiving conventional therapy. After 3 years of treatment, survival was 50% better in the group receiving oxygen.

The NOTT trial compared 12 and 24 hours of continuous oxygen therapy and was terminated prematurely due to better survival in the group receiving 24-hour therapy. Patients are eligible for LTOT if they **exhibit all of the following**:

- pO_2 on air <7.3 kPa (55 mmHg)
- Normal or elevated pCO_2
- FEV_1 <1.5 litres
- pO_2 7.3–8 kPa (55–60 mmHg) with evidence of pulmonary hypertension, polycythaemia peripheral oedema or nocturnal hypoxaemia

Arterial blood gases must be measured when the patient is clinically stable (at least 5 weeks post-exacerbation), and on two occasions that are at least 3 weeks apart. pO_2 on oxygen should be >8 kPa (60 mmHg) without an unacceptable rise in pCO_2. Oxygen should be given via a concentrator

for at least 15 hours per day. The patient should have stopped smoking before LTOT is considered.

19.2.5 Respiratory failure

Respiratory failure is an inability to maintain adequate oxygenation and carbon dioxide excretion. There are two recognised types of respiratory failure:

- **Type 1** respiratory failure is present when there is hypoxaemia with normal or low levels of carbon dioxide
- **Type 2** respiratory failure is hypoxaemia with high pCO_2

Causes of respiratory failure

- **Reduced ventilatory drive**
  - Opiate overdosage, brainstem injury
- **Mechanical problems**
  - Chest trauma causing flail chest
  - Severe kyphoscoliosis
  - Obesity
- **Neurological conditions (affecting chest wall muscles)**
  - Guillain–Barré syndrome
  - Polio
- **Alveolar problems**
  - *Barriers to diffusion:*
    - Pulmonary oedema
    - Pulmonary fibrosis
  - *$\dot{V}/\dot{Q}$ mismatch:*
    - Pulmonary embolus
    - Shunt (cardiac or pulmonary)
  - *Reduced inspired partial pressure of oxygen:*
    - High altitude
- **Upper airway obstruction**
  - Laryngeal tumour
  - Obstructive sleep apnoea
- **Lower airway obstruction**
  - Bronchospasm
  - Sputum retention

- **Type 1 respiratory failure** may be corrected by increasing the inspired oxygen concentration

- **Type 2 respiratory failure** may require mechanical ventilatory support. Respiratory stimulants such as doxapram may be useful for those with reduced respiratory drive

19.2.6 Ventilatory support

This may be invasive or non-invasive.

Non-invasive positive-pressure ventilation (NIPPV)

This involves the use of a securely fitting nasal or full face mask. The technique has been used to provide long-term respiratory support in the community for patients with respiratory failure due to conditions such as severe chest wall deformity, neuromuscular disorders or obesity hypoventilation syndrome.

- It is used increasingly to manage episodes of acute respiratory failure due, for example, to exacerbations of COPD – as an alternative to (and often more appropriate than) ventilation on the Intensive Care Unit (ICU)
- NIPPV can be carried out on general wards using portable bi-level pressure support ventilators. Supplementary oxygen can be given via the port on the face mask. Regular monitoring of blood gases is necessary and the ventilator settings are altered in response. As the patient improves, time spent off the ventilator is lengthened until the patient is weaned
- When NIPPV treatment is instituted, a decision as to whether ICU referral would be appropriate if the patient were to deteriorate should be clearly stated in the case notes

Positive-pressure ventilation

Conventional ventilation requires access to the airway, by means of either an endotracheal tube or tracheostomy. Indications for positive pressure ventilation are:

- Type 2 respiratory failure from any cause
- Paralysis of respiratory muscles (eg Guillain–Barré syndrome)
- Multiple organ failure

- Trauma cases, including injury to the chest or cervical spine
- Inability to maintain a clear airway
- Reduced conscious level – Glasgow coma scale score <5
- During and after certain surgical procedures

Ventilation should be considered when there is failure to maintain oxygenation (pO_2 <8 kPa (60 mmHg)) despite high inspired oxygen concentrations (usually associated with hypercapnia and acidosis). It is often necessary in patients with multiple organ dysfunction associated with sepsis or trauma.

Continuous positive airways pressure (CPAP)

CPAP is delivered through a tightly fitting face mask or it may be used in conjunction with conventional ventilation. It provides a pneumatic splint to the airway and is the treatment of choice for obstructive sleep apnoea. CPAP improves oxygenation in patients requiring high concentrations of oxygen by the recruitment of collapsed airways. High levels may, however, cause hypotension, the rise in mean intrathoracic pressure inhibiting venous return and reducing cardiac output.

19.3 LUNG INFECTIONS

HIV/AIDS-associated respiratory disease is covered in Chapter 8, Genito-urinary Medicine and AIDS.

19.3.1 Pneumonia

Pneumonia is an acute inflammatory condition of the lung usually caused by bacteria, viruses or, rarely, fungi. The chest X-ray will show consolidation, the hallmark of which is an air bronchogram. Pneumonia continues to be an important cause of mortality across all age groups, with 50% of pneumonia deaths occurring in those aged 15–64 years.

Community-acquired pneumonia

The incidence is 5/1000 to 11/1000 adult population per year, and this is much more common in the elderly. Causal organisms are given in the following box.

Causes of pneumonia

- *Streptococcus* pneumoniae (60%–70%)
- Atypical organisms, including *Mycoplasma pneumoniae* (5%–15%), *Legionella pneumophila*, *Chlamydia psittaci*, *Chlamydia pneumoniae* and *Coxiella burnetii* (Q fever)
- *Haemophilus influenzae*
- *Staphylococcus aureus*
- Gram-negative organisms
- Viruses, including influenza, varicella zoster, CMV

General investigations for patients admitted to hospital with pneumonia

These include FBC, biochemical profile (including liver function tests), C-reactive protein (CRP), arterial blood gases, chest X-ray and blood and sputum cultures.

Paired serological tests for atypical organisms and viruses and urinary antigen tests for *Legionella* and *Pneumococcus* should be used in selected cases

Signs of severe pneumonia (CURB–65 criteria)

- **C**onfusion (<8/10 score on abbreviated mental test (AMT))
- **U**rea >7 mmol/l
- **R**espiratory rate >30 breaths/min
- **B**P systolic <90 mmHg and/or diastolic <60 mmHg
- Age >**65**

Patients with three or more CURB criteria are at high risk of death and are regarded as having **severe community-acquired pneumonia**.

- Hypoxaemia (pO_2 <8 kPa despite oxygen therapy) and multilobe involvement also confer a worse prognosis

- The presence of co-existing disease is a bad prognostic factor

Specific pneumonias

Streptococcus pneumoniae

There is an abrupt onset of illness, with high fever and rigors. Examination reveals crackles or bronchial breathing, and herpetic cold sores may be present in >1/3 of cases.

- Elderly patients may present with general deterioration or confusion
- Capsular polysaccharide antigen may be detected in serum, sputum, pleural fluid or urine
- Increasing incidence of penicillin resistance, particularly in countries such as Spain
- Vaccine available

Mycoplasma pneumoniae

Mycoplasma pneumoniae tends to affect young adults; it occurs in epidemics every 3–4 years. There is typically a longer prodrome, usually of 2 or more weeks, and the white cell count may be normal. Cold agglutinins occur in 50%; the mortality is low.

- Extrapulmonary complications include: peri/myocarditis, erythema multiforme, erythema nodosum, Stevens–Johnson syndrome, haemolytic anaemia, disseminated intravascular coagulation (DIC), thrombocytopenia, meningo-encephalitis, cranial and peripheral neuropathies, bullous myringitis, hepatitis and pancreatitis

Legionella pneumophila

Outbreaks are usually related to contaminated water cooling systems, showers, or air conditioning systems, but sporadic cases do occur. Legionnaire's disease usually affects the middle-aged and elderly, patients often having underlying lung disease. Males are affected more than females (3:1). Diagnosis is by direct fluorescent antibody staining or serological tests; antigen may be detected in the urine.

Clinical and laboratory features

- Gastrointestinal upset common; diarrhoea, jaundice, ileus and pancreatitis may occur
- WCC often not elevated with lymphopenia; thrombocytopenia/pancytopenia may occur
- Hyponatraemia due to syndrome of inappropriate antidiuretic hormone (SIADH)
- Headache, confusion and delirium are prominent and focal neurological signs may develop
- Abnormal liver and renal function in approximately 50%
- Acute renal failure, interstitial nephritis and glomerulonephritis may develop

Staphylococcus aureus

Staphylococcus aureus pneumonia may follow a viral illness; it has a high mortality (30%–70%). The disease is more common in intravenous drug addicts.

Specific features include:

- Toxin production with extensive tissue necrosis
- Staphylococcal skin lesions may develop
- Chest X-ray shows patchy infiltrates with abscess formation in 25% and empyema in 10%
- >25% of patients have positive blood cultures

Treatment of pneumonia

All patients should be given appropriate concentrations of oxygen and they may require intravenous fluids if circulating volume is depleted. Treatment is with oral amoxicillin and a macrolide (eg clarithromycin) for non-severe cases requiring hospitalisation. A third-generation cephalosporin given intravenously coupled with a macrolide is indicated in severe cases.

- A single antibiotic can be used for community patients or those admitted to hospital for non-medical reasons
- Newer fluoroquinolones (eg moxifloxacin) provide an alternative for patients who are allergic to penicillin or macrolides

- Intravenous treatment should be stepped down to oral treatment after 48 hours provided the patient is improving
- If a specific organism is isolated the appropriate antibiotic is given

Treatment should continue for 7–10 days depending upon response. Up to 21 days of treatment is recommended for *Legionella* pneumonia.

Nosocomial (hospital-acquired) pneumonia

This is defined as pneumonia that develops 2 days or more after admission to hospital (0.5%–5% of hospitalised patients). The organisms usually involved include:

- *S. aureus*
- Gram-negative bacteria: *Klebsiella, Pseudomonas, Escherischia coli, Proteus* spp., *Serratia* spp., *Acinetobacter* spp.
- Anaerobes
- Fungi
- *S. pneumoniae* (and other streptococci) are less common

Treatment is with broad-spectrum agents (eg third-generation cephalosporins).

Aspiration pneumonia

Aspiration pneumonia may complicate impaired consciousness and dysphagia. Particulate matter may obstruct the airway, but also chemical pneumonitis may develop from aspiration of acid gastric contents, leading to pulmonary oedema.

- Anaerobes are the principal pathogens, arising from the oropharynx
- There are typically two to three separate isolates in each case
- Multiple pulmonary abscesses or empyema may result
- Treat with metronidazole in combination with broad-spectrum agent (eg third-generation cephalosporin)

Cavitation may develop in certain lung infections (see following box).

Cavitation associated with lung infections

- *S. aureus*
- *Klebsiella pneumoniae*
- *Legionella pneumophila* (rare)
- Anaerobic infections
- *Pseudomonas aeruginosa*
- *Mycobacterium tuberculosis* and non-tuberculous mycobacterial infections

Lung abscess

This may be suspected when the patient is slow to improve from pneumonia. A chest X-ray will show single or multiple fluid-filled cavities. Prolonged courses of antibiotics are needed, sometimes with percutaneous drainage.

19.3.2 Empyema

A collection of pus in the pleural space may complicate up to 15% of community-acquired pneumonias and is more common when there is a history of excess alcohol consumption, poor dentition, aspiration or general anaesthesia.

- A diagnosis of empyema is suspected if a patient is slow to improve, has a persistent fever or elevation of the white cell count or CRP, and has radiological evidence of a pleural fluid collection. The pH of pleural fluid is <7.2
- Untreated, extensive fibrosis occurs in the pleural cavity, weight loss and clubbing develop and the mortality rate is high
- The mainstay of treatment is drainage of the pleural space combined with continuous high-dose intravenous antibiotic treatment. Daily intrapleural administration of streptokinase has been shown to liquefy the pus and to facilitate percutaneous drainage
- For those who fail to resolve with medical therapy, thoracotomy and decortication of the lung may be necessary

19.3.3 Tuberculosis

Unlike community-acquired pneumonia, the number of new cases of tuberculosis (TB) declined in the UK throughout the 20th century, mainly due to the improvement in living standards. In recent years, however, the incidence of TB has begun to increase again. Those at risk include:

- Those on low incomes
- Homeless people
- Alcoholics
- HIV-positive individuals
- Immigrants from countries with a high incidence of TB

The most commonly involved site is the lung – with lymph node, bone, renal tract and GI tract being less common. Tuberculous meningitis is the most serious complication.

Primary TB

Primary infection occurs in those without immunity. A small lung lesion known as the Ghon focus develops in the mid- or lower zones of the lung and is composed of tubercle-laden macrophages. Bacilli are transported through the lymphatics to the draining lymph nodes, which enlarge considerably and caseate. Infection is often arrested at this stage and the bacteria may remain dormant for many years. The peripheral lung lesion and the nodes heal and may calcify. The entire process is often asymptomatic. However, specific immunity begins to develop and tuberculin skin tests become positive.

Post-primary TB

Organisms disseminated by the blood at the time of primary infection may reactivate many years later. The most common site for post-primary TB is the lungs, with bone and lymph node sites being less common. Reactivation may be precipitated by a waning of host immunity, for example due to malignancy or immunosuppressive drugs (including steroids).

Clinical picture

Primary infection is often asymptomatic, but may cause mild cough and wheeze or erythema nodosum. Clinical features of reactivation or re-infection are described in the following box.

Features of TB reactivation or re-infection

- Persistent cough
- Weight loss
- Night sweats
- Haemoptysis
- Pleural effusion
- Pneumonia
- Meningitis
- Lymphadenopathy

Miliary TB

This is caused by widespread dissemination of infection via the bloodstream. It may present with non-specific symptoms of malaise, pyrexia and weight loss. Eventually hepatosplenomegaly develops and choroidal tubercles may be visible on fundoscopy. The chest X-ray shows multiple rounded shadows a few millimetres in diameter. It is universally fatal if left untreated.

Diagnosis of TB

- **Chest X-ray**
  - May show patchy shadowing in the upper zones with volume loss and cavitation, and ultimately fibrosis
- **Pleural fluid aspiration and biopsy**
- **Bronchoscopy and lavage**
  - Used for those unable to expectorate; transbronchial biopsy if miliary disease is a possibility
- **Early morning urine specimens**
  - For renal tract disease
- **Liver biopsy**
- **Lymph node biopsy**
- **Bone marrow aspirate**
- **Morning sputum collections**
  - For acid and alcohol-fast bacilli smear
- **CSF culture**

Specimens are examined for acid and alcohol-fast bacilli (AAFB) using Ziehl–Neelsen or auramine stains and then cultured on Löwenstein–Jensen medium. Cultures are continued for at least 6 weeks as the organism is slow-growing. Polymerase chain reaction (PCR) for tuberculous DNA can be used to provide a rapid diagnosis. This allows early differentiation from non-tuberculous mycobacterial infection (which would be important before embarking on an extensive screening programme of contacts) and can also be used to detect multidrug-resistant disease.

Treatment

(*See also* Section 11.6.1 in Chapter 11 Infectious Diseases.) This is with a combination of four drugs:

- Rifampicin 6 months
- Isoniazid 6
- Pyrazinamide 2
- Ethambutol 2

Short courses of treatment for 6 months are now standard. All drugs are given for 2 months and isoniazid and rifampicin are continued for a further 4 months.

- Sensitivity testing will identify drug resistance and all four drugs are continued until sensitivities are known
- If pyrazinamide has to be discontinued due to side-effects, a 9-month regime is necessary
- Second-line agents (eg ethionamide, propionamide, streptomycin, cycloserine) may be needed
- Compliance can pose major problems and directly observed therapy (DOT – larger doses of drugs administered three times per week) is used when poor compliance is anticipated

Multidrug-resistant TB (MDR-TB) signifies resistance to rifampicin and isoniazid and currently accounts for 2% of tuberculous infections. It is mainly concentrated in the London area.

Once 2 weeks of antituberculous chemotherapy has been completed, the patient is considered to be non-infectious.

Side-effects of antituberculous treatment

Side-effects are common:

- **Hepatitis**: may be caused by rifampicin, isoniazid and pyrazinamide
- **Optic neuritis**: may be caused by ethambutol; **visual acuity** should be checked before treatment is initiated
- **Peripheral neuropathy**: may be due to isoniazid; 10 mg of pyridoxine daily is given in those at particular risk of this complication (eg alcoholics, diabetics and in patients with renal failure)

Prevention

The schools' BCG programme has now been withdrawn. Babies and infants at high risk are screened opportunistically for active disease and then offered BCG vaccination. The efficacy of BCG varies greatly in different communities but usually helps prevent disseminated disease. All immigrants to the UK from high-risk countries are screened for latent disease. Mantoux testing is offered to all those without a definite BCG scar, followed by BCG vaccination if the Manotoux test is negative, or chemoprophylaxis if it is positive. **Chemoprophylaxis** comprises isoniazid for 6 months or rifampicin and isoniazid for 3 months.

- Patients with pulmonary TB (particularly those who are sputum smear-positive for AAFB) are potentially infectious and close contacts should be screened for disease. Mantoux testing is offered to those aged <35 years, and a chest X-ray performed for patients aged >35 years
- More recently selective immunological (interferon-γ) tests have been developed and are useful where Mantoux testing may be inaccurate
- The use of anti-tumour necrosis factor alpha (TNFα) therapy can be associated with reactivation of latent TB. Patients due to start such treatment should be screened for active/past TB. Those who have had adequately treated past TB should be monitored closely. Where past TB has not been treated fully a course of chemoprophylaxis is given

TB is a notifiable disease.

Opportunistic mycobacterial infections

These account for 10% of all mycobacterial infections. Causative organisms include the following:

- *Mycobacterium kansasii* (commonest)
- *Mycobacterium xenopi*
- *Mycobacterium malmoense*
- *Mycobacterium avium intracellulare*

These organisms cause disease that is clinically and radiologically identical to TB, and that is indistinguishable from TB on sputum smear. Pulmonary disease, lymphadenitis (in children) and disseminated infection are the commonest clinical problems. Most patients are middle-aged/elderly with significant underlying COPD, bronchiectasis or previous TB. A minimum of two positive cultures taken a week apart in a patient with an appropriate clinical picture is necessary to make the diagnosis. The organisms are ubiquitous in the environment and are low-grade pathogens. Opportunistic mycobacterial infections constitute a relatively higher proportion of mycobacterial infections in patients with acquired immunodeficiency syndrome (AIDS).

- The onset of symptoms is usually gradual
- Treatment programmes are generally longer than for TB, and are continued for at least 9 months and often for 2 years
- Rifampicin and ethambutol are the mainstay of treatment; clarithromycin or ciprofloxacin may be added
- Opportunistic infections do not need to be notified
- Contact tracing is unnecessary as person-to-person infection is very rare

19.3.4 Bronchiectasis

This is the permanent dilatation of subsegmental airways, which are inflamed, tortuous, flabby and partially/totally obstructed by secretions. Bronchiectasis may be cystic, cylindrical or varicose, with the cystic pattern being the most severe. The obstruction often leads to post-obstructive pneumonitis so that the lung parenchyma may be temporarily or permanently damaged.

Causes of bronchiectasis*

- Congenital
- Post-infective (eg following episodes of childhood measles, pneumonia or pertussis)
- Immune deficiency
- Post-tuberculosis
- Allergic bronchopulmonary aspergillosis (ABPA) – proximal
- Complicating sarcoidosis or pulmonary fibrosis
- Idiopathic – 60%
- Distal to an obstructed bronchus (or a bronchus severely compressed from encroaching lymph nodes)
- Secondary to bronchial damage resulting from a chemical pneumonitis (eg inhalation of caustic chemicals)
- Mucociliary clearance defects: primary ciliary dyskinesis or associated with situs inversus (Kartagener syndrome) or associated with azoospermia and sinusitis in males (Young syndrome)
- HIV/AIDS
- Alpha-1-antitrypsin deficiency

*In 60% of cases no cause is identified

Clinical features

There is a history of chronic sputum production, which is often mucopurulent and accompanied by episodes of haemoptysis. Occasionally bronchiectasis can be 'dry' with no sputum production but with episodic haemoptysis. Exertional dyspnoea and wheeze may be associated. Patients complain of malaise and fatigue; one-third have symptoms of chronic sinusitis. There may be few abnormal clinical findings other than occasional basal crackles or wheeze on chest examination; clubbing may be present. In more advanced disease weight loss and cachexia are prominent.

Investigations

- **Sputum microbiology**: most commonly shows *H. influenzae*, *S. pneumoniae* or *Pseudomonas aeruginosa*; mycobacteria and fungi may also be seen
- **Chest X-ray**: may be normal or may show thickening of bronchial walls and in *cystic* bronchiectasis, ring shadows ± fluid levels. The upper lobes are most frequently affected in ABPA, cystic fibrosis, sarcoidosis and tuberculosis
- **Pulmonary function tests**: may be normal or show an obstructed/restricted pattern (or both)
- **High-resolution CT scanning**: is diagnostic in >90% of cases
- **Immunoglobulin levels (or antibody response following vaccination, eg *H. influenzae* or pneumococcus)**: may demonstrate deficiency of humoral immunity

Conditions associated with bronchiectasis

- Rheumatoid arthritis
- Malignancy (childhood acute lymphoblastic leukaemia, adult chronic lymphocytic leukaemia)
- Sjögren syndrome
- Yellow nail syndrome and primary lymphoedema
- Inflammatory bowel disease (usually ulcerative colitis)
- Infertility

Treatment

As far as possible the aetiology of the bronchiectasis should be established in every case. If there is an underlying immune deficiency state, treatment with intravenous gamma globulin replacement therapy is beneficial. Regular physiotherapy with postural drainage and using 'the active cycle of breathing' helps to clear the airways.

- Inhaled bronchodilators are often used

- **Antibiotics** are usually given in response to an exacerbation, but some patients require continuous oral therapy; azithromycin given three times per week is one option
- Nebulised antibiotics can be used to reduce the microbial load and they are particularly useful when a patient is colonised with *Pseudomonas*
- Adequate hydration is important but mucolytics are generally not helpful
- Surgery is reserved for those with localised severe disease; lung transplantation has been successful

Complications

Infective exacerbations are the principal problem. Haemoptysis usually settles with treatment of the infection but occasionally embolisation of the bleeding vessel is required. Chest pain over an area of bronchiectatic lung is not uncommon. In the long term, systemic amyloid may result.

19.3.5 Cystic fibrosis

Cystic fibrosis is the most common fatal autosomal recessive condition in the Caucasian population, affecting 1 in 2500 live births; 1 in 25 adults are carriers of the gene. The cystic fibrosis gene has been localised to the long arm of chromosome 7 and codes for the cystic fibrosis transmembrane conductance regulator protein (CFTR), which functions as a chloride channel (*see also* Chapter 7, Genetics). Over 800 mutations have been identified, the most common being Δ508. The basic defect involves abnormal transport of chloride across the cell membrane; in the sweat gland there is a failure to reabsorb chloride and in the airway there is failure of chloride secretion. Diagnosis is made by detection of an abnormally high sweat chloride (>60 mEq/l) and by genetic analysis.

Pulmonary disease

A significant inflammatory infiltrate may be identified in the lungs at a very early age. The airways become obstructed by thick mucus due to decreased chloride secretion and increased sodium reabsorption, and so bacterial infection becomes established in early life.

Infection occurs in an age-related fashion: infants and young children become colonised with *S. aureus* and subsequently *H. influenzae*. In the teenage years infection with *Pseudomonas aeruginosa* occurs.

The other major pathogens involved are:

- *S. pneumoniae*
- *Burkholderia cepacia* complex
- *Mycobacterium tuberculosis*
- Non-tuberculous mycobacteria
- *Aspergillus fumigatus*
- Viruses

Chronic infection and inflammation cause lung damage with bronchiectasis affecting predominantly the upper lobes. Patients have breathlessness and reduced exercise tolerance, cough with chronic purulent sputum production, and occasional haemoptysis. Physical signs include clubbing, cyanosis, scattered coarse crackles and occasional wheeze. Slight haemoptysis is often associated with infection but major haemoptysis may occasionally necessitate pulmonary arterial embolisation.

- Pulmonary function tests show airflow obstruction; chest X-ray may show hyperinflation, atelectasis, visible thickened bronchial walls, fibrosis and apical bullae; pneumothorax occurs in up to 10% of patients
- In the terminal stages of disease, respiratory failure develops; 90% of deaths are attributable to respiratory failure. The average life expectancy has increased into the fourth decade of life

Gastrointestinal tract

Pancreatic insufficiency is present in over 90% of patients. Malabsorption causes bulky offensive stools, with weight loss and deficiency of fat-soluble vitamins (A, D, E and K). Babies may present with meconium ileus and adults may develop an equivalent syndrome with obstruction of the small bowel due to poorly digested intestinal contents, causing abdominal pain, distension, vomiting and severe constipation.

- Obstruction of the biliary ductules in the liver may eventually lead to cirrhosis with portal hypertension, splenomegaly and oesophageal varices
- Gallstones (in 15% of patients), peptic ulcer and reflux oesophagitis are all more prevalent
- Pancreatitis may develop in older patients

Involvement of other systems

- **Diabetes**: eventually occurs in up to a third of patients. There is a gradual loss of pancreatic islet cells with fibrosis developing. Ketoacidosis is very uncommon
- **Upper airway disease**: nasal polyps occur frequently (up to one-third of patients); chronic purulent sinusitis may develop
- **Fertility**: virtually all males are infertile due to abnormal development of the vas deferens and seminiferous tubules, but fertility in women is only slightly reduced. Although many women with cystic fibrosis have had successful pregnancies, pregnancy may lead to life-threatening respiratory complications
- **Osteoporosis** is more common with an increased risk of fractures
- **Renal disease**: renal calculi (oxalate stones) are more common in people with CF. There is also a high prevalence of urinary incontinence in females

Treatment of cystic fibrosis

Care for patients with cystic fibrosis is best given in a specialist unit, which can provide extensive multidisciplinary input.

Antibiotics and respiratory treatments

In the UK most centres give antibiotics when sputum becomes increasingly purulent, pulmonary function tests are deteriorating or the patient is generally unwell with weight loss. Most patients become chronically colonised with *Pseudomonas aeruginosa* and so two different antibiotics (eg cefta-zidime and tobramycin) are used in combination to prevent resistance developing.

- Up to 10% of patients become colonised with a group of bacteria called *Burkholderia cepacia*, some of which are highly transmissible from one individual to another and are associated with a worse prognosis. These patients are therefore segregated from other patients in the hospital, at outpatient clinics and also socially
- Most patients need continuous anti-staphylococcal treatment

Nebulised antibiotics reduce the microbial load and are useful in those who need frequent courses of intravenous antibiotics; colistin or tobramycin are used continuously in a twice-daily regimen.

- DNase helps to liquefy viscous sputum and is helpful in some patients. Bronchodilators and inhaled steroid are given to treat airflow obstruction. Physiotherapy, using the active cycle of breathing technique, should be tailored to individual needs

Pancreatic enzyme supplements

Given with main meals and snacks to those with pancreatic insufficiency. Meconium ileus equivalent is treated with vigorous rehydration and regular oral Gastrografin®. Good nutritional status is associated with improved prognosis; supplementary overnight feeding with nasogastric tube or via gastroenterostomy can help to maintain body weight.

Transplantation

Double-lung transplantation (if only single lung transplant performed the new lung would be vulnerable to infection from the remaining damaged lung) may be appropriate for some patients with terminal respiratory failure. Non-invasive positive-pressure ventilation may be utilised to support a patient before transplantation. The optimal timing of lung transplantation must be assessed in each individual case. Liver and occasionally pancreas transplants are also carried out in some patients.

Future developments in cystic fibrosis

Screening of newborns for cystic fibrosis will soon be practised throughout the UK. Extensive research is being carried out into gene therapy, although this is still a long way from having a clinical application.

19.3.6 *Aspergillus* and the lung

Aspergillus causes three distinct forms of pulmonary disease: allergic bronchopulmonary aspergillosis, colonising aspergillosis and invasive aspergillosis.

Allergic bronchopulmonary aspergillosis

Most patients with allergic bronchopulmonary aspergillosis (ABPA) are asthmatics but the condition may occur in non-asthmatics.

The disease is due to sensitivity to *A. fumigatus* spores mediated by specific IgE and IgG antibodies. The allergic response results in airways becoming obstructed by rubbery plugs of mucus containing *Aspergillus* hyphae, mucus and eosinophils; plugs may be expectorated. The following changes may be found on investigation:

- Lobar or segmental collapse of airways
- Fleeting chest X-ray shadows due to intermittent obstruction of airways
- Positive skin-prick tests and RAST to *Aspergillus*
- Positive precipitins to *A. fumigatus*
- Raised serum IgE >1000 ng/ml
- Peripheral blood and pulmonary eosinophilia
- The condition may result in proximal bronchiectasis

Treatment is with oral corticosteroids which may be required long-term; itraconazole is also useful and may allow the dose of steroid to be reduced.

Colonising aspergillosis

Fungal colonisation of cavities in the lung parenchyma, of dilated bronchi or the pleural space.

A mass or ball of fungus develops known as an aspergilloma. *A. fumigatus* is usually responsible, but occasionally *A. niger*, *A. flavus* or *A. nidulans* may be implicated. Cavities due to TB, sarcoidosis, cystic fibrosis or pulmonary neoplasms may be colonised. Cough and sputum production often occur and are features of the underlying disease. Haemoptysis is a common complication, and this may be massive.

- An aspergilloma is usually suspected by chest X-ray, which demonstrates a cystic space containing a rounded opacity. An air space is visible between the fungal mass and the cavity wall – the 'halo' sign
- Precipitating antibodies are nearly always present but response to skin testing is variable
- Sputum examination may reveal fungal hyphae

Many aspergillomas require no specific treatment. Treatment is indicated for recurrent haemoptysis, systemic symptoms and where there is evidence of fungal invasion of surrounding tissue. Intra-cavity instillation of amphotericin paste is sometimes useful, and systemic treatment with the newer azoles (eg voriconazole) may be helpful in some cases. Surgical resection of the affected area of lung may be curative but surgery can be technically difficult.

Invasive aspergillosis

Fungal infection spreads rapidly through the lung causing granulomata, necrosis of tissue and suppuration. It occurs most commonly in the immunosuppressed host and may be rapidly fatal. Progressive chest X-ray shadowing (which may cavitate), associated with fever, chest pain and haemoptysis that does not settle promptly with antibacterial agents, suggests invasive aspergillosis.

- Cough with copious sputum production, often with haemoptysis, is usual
- Examination of sputum or bronchoalveolar lavage fluid may demonstrate fungal hyphae
- High-resolution CT scanning shows pulmonary infiltrates with the 'halo' sign. Treatment is with systemic antifungal agents

19.4 OCCUPATIONAL LUNG DISEASE

19.4.1 Asbestos-related disease

Exposure to asbestos was previously commonplace in many occupations including ship builders, laggers, builders, dockers and workers in factories engaged in the manufacture of asbestos products.

Effects of asbestos on the lung

Pleural plaques

These appear 20 years or more after low-density exposure. They develop on the parietal pleura of the chest wall, diaphragm, pericardium and mediastinum, and commonly calcify. Pleural plaques are usually asymptomatic but they may cause mild restriction.

Diffuse pleural thickening

This can extend continuously over a variable proportion of the thoracic cavity, but is most marked at the lung bases. It causes exertional dyspnoea; PFTs show restriction, decreased compliance and reduced total lung capacity, but the KCO is normal.

Pleural effusions may occur in asbestos-related disease, usually within 15 years of exposure. They often resolve spontaneously, leaving thickening of the visceral pleura.

Asbestosis

The onset of asbestosis is usually >20 years after exposure (but with higher levels of exposure fibrosis occurs earlier). Fibrotic changes are more pronounced in the lower lobes; patients present with slowly worsening exertional dyspnoea and clinical examination reveals fine inspiratory crackles in the lower zones. Clubbing may occur.

- Chest X-ray shows small irregular opacities, horizontal lines and, in more advanced disease, honeycomb and ring shadows
- High-resolution CT (HRCT) confirms fibrosis associated with pleural disease
- PFTs show a restrictive defect with reduced KCO

- There is an increased risk of lung cancer (see below)
- The disease is untreatable and death is usually due to respiratory failure or malignancy

Lung cancer

Mesothelioma is the commonest malignancy associated with asbestos exposure. The risk of lung cancer is also substantially increased, particularly in smokers (see below).

Compensation claims for occupational lung disease

Patients with all of the above asbestos-related diseases (except pleural plaques) are entitled to state compensation and a disability pension. Patients can also claim against their employers for negligently exposing them to asbestos for any of the above asbestos-related conditions (including pleural plaques). They should be advised to begin legal action within 3 years of being told that they have an asbestos-related condition.

- The same applies for patients with coal workers' **pneumoconiosis** and **occupational asthma** and a small number of other industrial diseases

19.4.2 Coal workers' pneumoconiosis (CWP)

The incidence of this pneumoconiosis is related to total dust exposure. Dust particles 2–5 μm in diameter are retained in the respiratory bronchioles and alveoli. Simple CWP is characterised by small rounded opacities (<1.5 mm in diameter) on chest X-ray, and is associated with focal emphysema. The lesions are asymptomatic.

Progressive massive fibrosis (PMF)

Progressive massive fibrosis involves the development of larger opacities (>3 cm in diameter) on a background of simple CWP.

- PMF lesions are usually in the upper zones and may cavitate

- Cough, sputum production and dyspnoea occur with reduced life expectancy, deaths occurring from progressive respiratory failure
- PFTs show a mixed obstructive/restrictive pattern with reduced KCO

Coal mining is recognised as a cause of **COPD**.

Caplan syndrome is the development of multiple round pulmonary nodules in patients with rheumatoid arthritis and a background of CWP. Nodules may develop before the joint disease, and occur in crops in the periphery of the lung. They may be associated with pleural effusion and may ultimately calcify.

19.4.3 Silicosis

This is caused by inhaling silicon dioxide, a highly fibrogenic dust; those commonly affected are quarry workers, hard-rock miners and civil engineers. Silicosis was commonly associated with TB in the first half of the 20th century.

- An acute illness characterised by dry cough and breathlessness occurs within a few months of exposure to very high levels of dust
- With more chronic exposure silicotic nodules form, which are 3–5 mm in diameter and predominantly affect the upper lobes
- Eggshell calcification occurs around enlarged hilar glands
- Gradually worsening breathlessness is associated with restrictive lung physiology and a fall in gas transfer
- There is no effective treatment (other than lung transplantation in patients with respiratory failure), but the disease is compensable
- Silicosis is associated with an increased incidence of tuberculosis

19.4.4 Berylliosis

The inhalation of fumes from molten beryllium causes an acute alveolitis. However, most cases of berylliosis are due to chronic low-level exposure, causing a tissue reaction similar to sarcoidosis. Non-caseating granulomata form in the lungs and lymph nodes surrounded by fibrous tissue; the chest X-ray shows fine nodulation evenly distributed throughout the lung fields with bilateral hilar lymphadenopathy.

- A positive blood and bronchoalveolar lavage beryllium lymphocyte proliferation assay is strongly associated with the presence of chronic beryllium disease
- Interstitial fibrosis develops, with shrinking of the lungs
- Patients develop progressive breathlessness with death ultimately occurring due to respiratory and right heart failure

19.4.5 Byssinosis

This is caused by exposure to cotton dust, flax and hemp. Acute exposure causes airways narrowing in a third of affected individuals. However, chronic byssinosis develops after years of heavy exposure to cotton dust; symptoms are worse on the first day back after a break from work, and include chest tightness, cough, dyspnoea and wheeze.

- There is a progressive decline in FEV$_1$ during the working shift, most marked on the first day of the week
- Prevention is by reducing the levels of cotton dust to which employees are exposed
- Bronchodilators may provide some relief of symptoms

19.4.6 Occupational asthma

Occupational asthma is now the commonest industrial lung disease in developed countries. A large number of agents encountered at work cause asthma and are officially recognised for industrial compensation, as listed in the following box.

Causes of occupational asthma

- Isocyanates
- Acid anhydride and amine hardening agents
- Platinum salts
- Stainless steel welding
- Resin used in soldering flux
- Epoxy resins
- Proteolytic enzymes
- Azodicarbonamide (PVC, plastics)
- Pharmaceuticals
- Glutaraldehyde
- Many other chemicals
- Wood dust
- Any known sensitising agent in the workplace
- Laboratory animals and insects
- Dyes
- Flour/grains

Occupational asthma develops after a period of asymptomatic exposure to the allergen, but usually within 2 years of first exposure. Detection depends on a careful history, and PEFR monitoring both at work and at home. Once occupational asthma has developed, bronchospasm may be precipitated by other non-specific triggers such as cold air, exercise, etc. Occupational asthma may develop in workers with previously diagnosed asthma. In order to identify the substance involved, specific IgE levels may be measured or occasionally bronchial provocation testing may be performed. Early diagnosis and removal of the individual from exposure to the allergen are essential if they are to make a full recovery. Asthma symptoms may persist despite termination of exposure.

19.4.7 Reactive airways dysfunction syndrome (RADS)

This reactive airways dysfunction syndrome (RADS) refers to bronchial hyper-responsiveness following the inhalation of high concentrations of irritant gas, aerosols or particles. Asthma-like symptoms usually develop within minutes to hours after exposure and airways hyper-reactivity persists over a prolonged period of time. 'Irritant asthma' occurs following multiple exposures to lower concentrations of irritants.

19.4.8 Extrinsic allergic alveolitis (hypersensitivity pneumonitis)

This is a hypersensitivity pneumonitis caused by a specific immunological response (usually IgG-mediated) to inhaled organic dusts.

- **Farmer's lung** is due to the inhalation of thermophilic actinomycetes (usually *Micropolyspora faeni* and *Thermoactinomyces vulgaris*), when workers are exposed to mouldy hay
- **Bird fancier's lung** is caused by inhaled avian serum proteins, present in excreta, and in the bloom from feathers; it primarily affects those who keep racing pigeons and those keeping budgerigars as pets
- **Ventilation pneumonitis** occurs in inhabitants of air-conditioned buildings where thermophilic actinomycetes grow in the humidification system
- **Bagassosis** is due to exposure to *Thermoactinomyces sacchari* in sugar cane processors
- **Malt worker's lung** is due to the inhalation of *Aspergillus clavatus*
- **Mushroom worker's lung** is due to the inhalation of thermophilic actinomycetes

Clinical features of extrinsic allergic alveolitis

The clinical features depend on the pattern of exposure. An acute allergic alveolitis develops several hours after exposure to high concentrations of dust. Breathlessness and 'flu-like' symptoms occur, sometimes associated with fever, headaches and muscle pains. The symptoms are short-lived and usually resolve completely within 48 hours.

- Inspiratory crackles may be heard on chest auscultation
- The disease may present in a sub-acute or chronic form characterised by cough, breathlessness, fatigue and weight loss
- Clubbing may occur in association with irreversible pulmonary fibrosis

Investigation and treatment

The diagnosis of extrinsic allergic alveolitis is made by establishing a history of exposure to antigen and the demonstration of precipitating antibodies in the patient's serum.

- **Chest X-ray** may show a generalised haze sometimes associated with nodular shadows. In chronic cases, progressive upper zone fibrosis and loss of lung volume occurs
- **Spirometry** becomes restrictive and gas transfer is reduced
- **Histology** of lung biopsy tissue shows a mononuclear cell infiltrate with the formation of non-caseating granulomata
- Fluid obtained from bronchoalveolar lavage (**BAL**) has a high lymphocyte count
- **Precipitins**: the demonstration of specific IgG antibodies in serum against the identified antigen. Precipitins may be present in the absence of clinical disease

Once the diagnosis is established the patient should be isolated from the antigen; if this is impossible respiratory protection should be worn. Corticosteroids accelerate the rate of recovery from an acute attack but are generally not helpful once established fibrosis develops.

Pulmonary fibrosis in extrinsic allergic alveolitis

Multiple episodes of acute exposure to agents causing extrinsic allergic alveolitis, or long-term low-grade exposure, as occurs in budgerigar owners,

can lead to irreversible lung fibrosis. These chronic cases present with progressive dyspnoea, weight loss and fatigue. The chest X-ray will show lung shrinkage but calcification or cavitation does not develop. HRCT demonstrates reticular, nodular and ground-glass opacities. Prompt diagnosis of extrinsic allergic alveolitis is important as the disease is reversible when diagnosed early.

19.5 TUMOURS

19.5.1 Lung cancer

Lung cancer is the most prevalent cancer worldwide and accounts for 1 in 3 cancer deaths in men and 1 in 6.5 cancer deaths in women. Female mortality from lung cancer now exceeds that from breast cancer. Twenty per cent of smokers will develop lung cancer. The prognosis is poor, with a 1-year survival of 20%. The 5-year survival rate is only 5.5%. Lung cancer is rare under the age of 40 but the incidence rises steeply with age, peaking in the 70–74-year age group.

> **Causes of lung cancer**
>
> - **Smoking** X10
>   - Over 90% of lung cancers occur in current or ex-smokers
> - **Atmospheric pollution**
>   - Persistently higher lung cancer rates in urban populations; passive smoking
>   - Industrial exposures
>   Asbestos fibre, aluminium industry, arsenic compounds, benzoyl chloride, beryllium
>   - Increased incidence in patients with cryptogenic fibrosing alveolitis and systemic sclerosis

Smoking is the leading cause of lung cancer. Although smoking rates have declined amongst adult men and to a lesser extent among women, there is an increasing number of teenage smokers, particularly girls.

Histological types of lung cancer

- **Squamous cell** (35%): usually arises from a central airway
- **Small cell** (20%): arises in central airways and grows rapidly, producing both intrathoracic and metastatic symptoms
- **Adenocarcinoma** (30%): may be peripheral and slow-growing. Now the commonest form of lung cancer
- **Undifferentiated large cell** (10%)
- **Bronchiolar-alveolar** cell carcinoma (5%)

Clinical features of lung cancer

Patients commonly present with cough, breathlessness, haemoptysis, chest pain, hoarse voice or weight loss. Lung cancer should be suspected if a pneumonia fails to resolve radiologically. Occasionally an asymptomatic lesion will be noted on a routine chest X-ray.

Intrathoracic complications of lung cancer

- Collapse of lung distal to obstructing tumour
- Recurrent laryngeal nerve palsy causing hoarseness
- Dysphagia due to compression of the oesophagus by enlarged metastatic lymph nodes or tumour invasion
- Pericarditis with effusion
- Phrenic nerve palsy with raised hemidiaphragm
- Pleural effusion
- Superior vena caval obstruction causing headache, distension of the veins in the upper body, fixed elevation of the JVP, facial suffusion with conjunctival oedema
- Rib metastases
- Spontaneous pneumothorax

Metastases can occur throughout the body but the most commonly involved sites are:

- Supraclavicular and anterior cervical lymph nodes, adrenals, bones, liver, brain and skin

Haemoptysis is one of the common presenting symptoms of lung cancer.

Causes of haemoptysis

- **Common causes**
  - Carcinoma of the bronchus
  - Pneumonia/acute bronchitis
  - Bronchiectasis
  - Pulmonary tuberculosis
  - Pulmonary embolus
  - Mitral valve disease
  - Infective exacerbation of COPD
- **Rarer causes**
  - Vascular malformations
  - Mycetoma
  - Connective tissue disorders
  - Vasculitis
  - Goodpasture syndrome
  - Cystic fibrosis
  - Bleeding diathesis
  - Idiopathic pulmonary haemosiderosis

Paraneoplastic syndromes

- **Syndrome of inappropriate ADH (SIADH):** chiefly associated with small-cell lung cancer. May resolve with chemotherapy but recurs with tumour progression. Treatment involves fluid restriction initially and demeclocycline for resistant cases
- **Ectopic adrenocorticotrophic hormone (ACTH):** mainly associated with small-cell lung cancer
- **Hypercalcaemia:** usually associated with multiple bony metastases from squamous cell carcinoma; ectopic parathyroid hormone (PTH) secretion occurs in a few squamous cancers
- **Gynaecomastia:** associated with large-cell carcinoma and adenocarcinoma; may be painful
- **Hyperthyroidism:** rare (due to ectopic thyroid-stimulating hormone (TSH)) – squamous cell lung cancer

- **Lambert–Eaton syndrome**: almost exclusively associated with small-cell lung cancer; produces a proximal myopathy, reduced tendon reflexes and autonomic features
- **Clubbing**: occurs in 10%–30% of lung cancers; may resolve after resection (see box below)
- **Hypertrophic pulmonary osteoarthropathy (HPOA)**: produces periostitis, arthritis and gross finger clubbing. HPOA is most commonly associated with adenocarcinoma and least frequently with small-cell carcinoma. It involves the long bones (tibia/fibula, radius/ulna or femur/humerus). It is associated with subperiosteal new bone formation visible on plain X-ray and is often painful

Pulmonary causes of clubbing

- Carcinoma of the bronchus
- Asbestosis
- Lung abscess
- Cystic fibrosis
- Tuberculosis
- Cryptogenic fibrosing alveolitis
- Bronchiectasis
- Empyema
- Mesothelioma

Pancoast syndrome

This is due to a tumour of the superior sulcus. The most common presenting complaint is pain (due to involvement of the eighth cervical and first thoracic nerve roots) extending down the medial side of the upper arm to the forearm and hand. The small muscles of the hand may atrophy. Horner syndrome may develop. Chest X-ray demonstrates a shadow at the extreme apex, and there may be destruction of the first and second ribs.

Diagnosis of lung cancer

Wherever possible, the histological type of lung cancer should be confirmed and the patient should be staged, usually by computed tomography (CT) scanning. Non-small-cell lung cancers are staged using the TNM classification whilst small-cell lesions are classified as either limited stage (confined to one hemithorax) or as extensive disease. An assessment of performance status is important prognostically. Increasingly, positron emission tomography (PET) scanning is being used to assess a solitary pulmonary nodule or to complete staging prior to surgery or radical radiotherapy

Diagnosis of lung cancer

- CT thorax
- Percutaneous CT-guided biopsy of peripheral nodules
- Bronchoscopy
- Biopsy of metastatic deposit (including lymph nodes)
- Resection of peripheral nodules
- Sputum cytology is occasionally useful if the patient is unfit for bronchoscopy and the tumour is proximally situated

Treatment of lung cancer

The management of all cases of lung cancer should be discussed at a multidisciplinary team meeting. **Surgery** offers the best chance of cure. At the time of presentation only 10%–20% of patients with non-small-cell lung cancer will be operable. The 5-year survival rate depends on the clinical stage (60% for stage I tumours but only 7% for stage IIIb tumours, when disease is locally advanced). Patients whose tumour is technically operable, but who are unfit for surgery due to co-existing medical conditions or poor lung function, may be treated with **radical radiotherapy**.

- **Palliative radiotherapy** is very effective in relieving pain from bony metastases, controlling haemoptysis and cough. Dysphagia due to oesophageal compression by lymph nodes responds well to radiotherapy
- **Superior vena caval obstruction** can also be treated with radiotherapy, although stenting provides more immediate relief of symptoms
- **Chemotherapy** for unresectable non-small-cell lung cancer offers a small survival benefit but has been shown to provide effective palliation
- **Unresectable tumours** that compromise the trachea or large airways may be palliated by local techniques to maintain airway patency. These include brachytherapy (intraluminal radiotherapy), laser therapy, airways stents and/or photodynamic therapy

Small-cell lung cancer is associated with an extremely poor prognosis if left untreated, with a median survival of only 8 weeks. The tumour is, however, much more sensitive than other types of lung cancer to chemotherapeutic agents, and cycles of combination chemotherapy can result in remission in up to 80% of cases.

APUD

- Median survival is now 14–20 months for limited disease and 8–13 months for extensive disease
- Once the disease has relapsed, mean survival is 4 months

ECTOPIC →ADH, ACTH, lambert-Eaton.

19.5.2 Mesothelioma

This is most common in men between the ages of 50 and 70 years. The lesion arises from mesothelial cells of pleura, or less commonly, the peritoneum. **Asbestos exposure** is responsible for at least 85% of malignant mesotheliomas, and the risk of mesothelioma increases with the dose of asbestos received. Crocidolite (blue asbestos) is more potent than amosite (brown asbestos) and both are more potent than chrysotile (white asbestos) in causing mesothelioma.

There is usually a latent period of >30 years between asbestos exposure and development of mesothelioma. The tumour arises from the visceral or parietal pleura, and expands to encase the lung. Pleural mesothelioma presents with chest pain, weight loss and dyspnoea and may cause pleural effusion.

- Annual incidence of mesothelioma in the UK exceeds 1300 cases. Controls over asbestos exposure only came into force in the 1970s, and the incidence of mesothelioma is rising and is expected to peak around 2015. A detailed occupational history is essential
- Chest X-ray and CT thorax usually show an effusion with underlying lobulated pleural thickening and contraction of the hemithorax
- Diagnosis is made by pleural biopsy, often done as a video-assisted thoracic surgery (VATS) procedure (*see* Section 19.6.4); the main differential diagnosis is adenocarcinoma of the pleura or benign pleural thickening
- **Treatment** is unsatisfactory; radical surgical procedures should only be performed within the setting of a randomised trial. Radiotherapy is helpful for pain relief and for prevention of seeding of the biopsy track. Randomised trials of chemotherapy for mesothelioma are currently ongoing. Pleural effusions should be drained and talc pleurodesis considered once a tissue diagnosis has been made. Involvement of the palliative care team is often helpful
- Median survival from presentation is 8–14 months for pleural mesothelioma and 7 months for peritoneal mesothelioma
- Patients with mesothelioma may be eligible for industrial compensation

19.5.3 Mediastinal tumours

Mediastinal tumours are often asymptomatic and they may be an incidental finding on a routine chest X-ray. In adults, 90% are benign. Clinical presentation is with stridor, superior vena caval obstruction, dysphagia, Horner syndrome, hoarseness or pericardial effusion. The causes of mediastinal masses can be divided according to situation in the mediastinum:

- **Anterior mediastinum**: thymoma, retrosternal thyroid, lymphoma, teratoma, fibroma, lipoma, seminoma and choriocarcinoma
- **Middle mediastinum**: aortic arch aneurysm, left ventricular aneurysm and pericardial cysts
- **Posterior mediastinum**: neurogenic tumours (neurofibroma, neuroblastoma, neurolemoma, chemodectoma and phaeochromocytoma), oesophageal tumours and diaphragmatic hernia

The initial investigation is usually chest X-ray which will be followed by CT scan. Occasionally radionuclide scans are needed to confirm the presence of functioning thyroid tissue. Magnetic resonance imaging (MRI) scanning may be used to define tissue planes and operability.

19.6 GRANULOMATOUS AND DIFFUSE PARENCHYMAL LUNG DISEASE

19.6.1 Sarcoidosis

Sarcoidosis is a multisystem granulomatous disorder primarily affecting young adults. The aetiology is unknown. The prevalence varies among different populations but in the UK it is 20/100 000 to 30/100 000, being highest among West Indian and Asian immigrants. The characteristic histological lesion is the granuloma composed of macrophages, lymphocytes and epithelioid histiocytes which fuse to form multinucleate giant cells. The disease may present acutely with erythema nodosum and bilateral hilar lymphadenopathy on the chest X-ray (good prognosis with most patients showing radiological resolution within a year) or insidiously with multi-organ involvement. Ninety per cent of patients have intrathoracic involvement.

Chest X-ray changes are graded as:

- **Stage 0**: clear chest X-ray
- **Stage 1**: bilateral hilar lymphadenopathy (BHL)
- **Stage 2**: BHL and pulmonary infiltration
- **Stage 3**: diffuse pulmonary infiltration

Patients may have no respiratory symptoms or complain of dyspnoea, dry cough, fever, malaise and weight loss. Chest examination is frequently normal; finger clubbing is rare.

Diffuse parenchymal lung involvement may progress to irreversible fibrosis; the mid- and upper zones of the lungs are most frequently affected. Calcification of the hilar nodes or the lung parenchyma may occur with chronic disease. Pleural effusion is rare.

Upper airway involvement (infrequent): the nasal mucosa may become hypertrophied and cause obstruction, crusting and discharge; perforation of the nasal septum and bony erosion are rare.

Extrapulmonary disease

- **Lymphadenopathy**: painless, rubbery lymph node enlargement is more common in black patients; the cervical and scalene lymph nodes are most frequently affected
- **Splenomegaly** (25%)
- **Liver involvement**: this is common but, apart from liver enlargement, is often subclinical (derangement of liver function tests). Liver biopsy is of diagnostic value in 90% (typical sarcoid granulomata)
- **Skin**: erythema nodosum (most commonly in Caucasian females) in disease with BHL; skin plaques, subcutaneous nodules and lupus pernio (violaceous lesions on the nose, cheeks and ears) seen in chronic disease
- **Acute anterior uveitis** (25%): chronic iridocyclitis affects older patients and responds poorly to treatment
- **Heerfordt–Waldenström syndrome**: consists of parotid gland enlargement, uveitis, fever and cranial nerve palsies
- **Neurological manifestations** (uncommon): cranial nerve palsies (facial nerve most often affected), meningitis, hydrocephalus, space-occupying lesions and spinal cord involvement; granulomata infiltrating the posterior pituitary may produce diabetes insipidus, hypothalamic hypothyroidism or hypopituitarism

- **Cardiac sarcoid** may result in cardiac muscle dysfunction or involve the conducting system, producing arrhythmias, bundle-branch block or complete heart block
- **Renal involvement**: renal impairment may be associated with hypercalcaemia. Acute renal failure can be due to granulomatous interstitial nephritis. Glomerulonephritis is a rare complication (*see also* Chapter 15, Nephrology)
- **Bone cysts**: with overlying soft tissue swelling, bone cysts occur most often in the phalanges, metacarpals, metatarsals and nasal bones; arthritis is common
- **Hypercalcaemia**: this occurs in at least 5% of cases of sarcoidosis and it is due to excess production of vitamin D and gut activity (calcium reabsorption)

Diagnosis

The combination of BHL with erythema nodosum (EN) in a young adult is virtually diagnostic of acute sarcoidosis. The combination of BHL and EN in association with fever and arthralgia is known as Löfgren syndrome. The main differential diagnoses are TB and lymphoma, and every effort should be made to confirm the diagnosis of sarcoidosis histologically.

- **Thoracic CT** appearances are often characteristic, showing hilar and mediastinal lymphadenopathy, nodules along bronchi, vessels and in subpleural regions, ground-glass shadowing, parenchymal bands, cysts and fibrosis
- **Tissue biopsy** (transbronchial and endobronchial biopsy) can demonstrate non-caseating granulomata in 85%–90% of cases with respiratory involvement
- Elevated serum angiotensin-converting enzyme (ACE) and calcium are consistent with the diagnosis but are non-specific. The 24-hour urinary calcium excretion is often raised
- **The Kveim–Siltzbach test** (intradermal injection of extract of spleen from a patient with active sarcoidosis with skin biopsy at 4–6 weeks demonstrating a granulomatous response) **is no longer used**

- Anergy to Heaf testing favours a diagnosis of sarcoid but patients who are HIV-positive or who have overwhelming TB may also be anergic

Treatment of sarcoidosis

The best prognosis is associated with acute sarcoidosis which frequently undergoes complete remission without specific therapy.

- Stage 0 and 1 disease usually resolves spontaneously
- With stage 2 disease, lung function tests should be performed serially and treatment instituted if there is evidence of progressive deterioration
- Steroids are the mainstay of therapy for chronic disease but response is unpredictable

Steroid therapy is definitely indicated for hypercalcaemia and hypercalciuria which persist despite dietary calcium restriction, and also for ophthalmological and neurological complications. Other immunosuppressive agents (eg azathioprine or methotrexate) may be used as steroid-sparing agents.

19.6.2 Histiocytosis X

Three clinical entities are recognised:

- **Eosinophilic granuloma**: solitary bone lesions occurring in children and young adults. Lung disease is known as Langerhans' cell histiocytosis
- **Letterer–Siwe disease**: a diffuse multisystem disorder of infancy which is rapidly lethal
- **Hand–Schüller–Christian disease**: characterised by exophthalmos, bony defects and diabetes insipidus (in children and teenagers). Diffuse nodular shadows occur in the lung with hilar lymphadenopathy

In adults histiocytosis is often confined to the lung. It is rare and most likely in young adults.

Patients present with non-productive cough and breathlessness. The chest examination is usually normal.

- Strongly associated with smoking
- Chest X-ray shows multiple ring shadows on a background of diffuse reticulonodular opacities mainly in the upper and mid-zones; the lung bases are spared
- With disease progression larger cysts and bullae form and interstitial fibrosis develops. Spontaneous pneumothorax occurs in 25%. Lung volumes are preserved
- Diagnosis is by high-resolution CT scanning and occasionally lung biopsy
- **Treatment** includes smoking cessation and steroids; spontaneous remission occurs in 25% of patients, but in a further 25% the disease may be rapidly fatal. Patients may progress to end-stage fibrotic lung disease

19.6.3 Pulmonary fibrosis

Interstitial lung disease is associated with many conditions, including the connective tissue diseases (particularly systemic lupus erythematosus (SLE) and systemic sclerosis), rheumatoid arthritis and sarcoidosis. When pulmonary fibrosis develops without obvious cause, it is known as idiopathic pulmonary fibrosis. Extrinsic allergic alveolitis also causes diffuse interstitial fibrosis.

19.6.4 Idiopathic pulmonary fibrosis ('usual interstitial pneumonia' – UIP)

This is a specific form of lung fibrosis characterised by UIP on lung biopsy. It accounts for around 80% of patients with interstitial lung fibrosis. The prevalence is increasing (currently 20–30 per 100 000 in some areas). It is a disease of the middle-aged and elderly, more common in men, and is possibly the result of an inhaled environmental antigen; metal and wood dusts have been implicated but no causal relationship has been identified. There may be an association with Epstein–Barr virus (EBV). Patients present with a dry cough and breathlessness, and signs include cyanosis, finger clubbing and fine late inspiratory crackles.

- **Lung function tests**: small static lung volumes, with reduction in gas transfer and restrictive spirometry
- **Blood gas analysis**: typically shows type 1 respiratory failure with hypoxaemia and a normal or low pCO_2
- **Chest X-ray**: reveals small lung volumes and interstitial shadowing most marked at the bases and peripheries. HRCT is useful to determine the degree of inflammatory change and the likelihood of response to steroids
- **VATS** (video-assisted thorascopic surgery) or open lung biopsy can be used to confirm the diagnosis and histology shows variable degrees of established fibrosis and acute inflammation

Treatment of idiopathic pulmonary fibrosis

Steroids and other immunosuppressive agents are used with variable success; clinical trials are currently investigating a number of new agents. Patients with established honeycomb fibrosis on HRCT do not usually respond. Single-lung transplantation should be considered in patients below the age of 65 years. Patients may benefit from pulmonary rehabilitation, oxygen therapy and, in terminal cases, morphine/lorazepam in order to palliate symptoms.

Other forms of interstitial lung disease

The following conditions are recognised subtypes of interstitial lung disease:

- Non-specific interstitial pneumonia (NSIP)
- Desquamative interstitial pneumonia (DIP)
- Acute interstitial pneumonia (AIP)
- Respiratory bronchiolitis-associated interstitial lung disease (RBILD)
- Lymphocytic interstitial pneumonitis (LIP)

Of these, NSIP, DIP and RBILD are more steroid-responsive and carry a better prognosis. AIP carries the same poor prognosis as adult respiratory distress syndrome (ARDS).

Extrinsic allergic alveolitis (EAA or hypersensitivity pneumonitis)

(This is covered in Section 19.4, Occupational lung disease.)

Drugs causing pulmonary fibrosis

- **Amiodarone**
  - Causes an alveolitis (which may be reversible on drug cessation), progressing to diffuse fibrosis; commoner when higher doses are used
- **Sulfasalazine**
- **Methotrexate**
- **Busulfan**
- **Bleomycin**
- **Cyclophosphamide**
- **Nitrofurantoin**
- **Gold**
- **Melphalan**

Causes of reticular-nodular shadowing on chest X-ray

- **Upper zone**
  - Extrinsic allergic alveolitis
  - Sarcoidosis
  - Coal workers' pneumoconiosis
  - Silicosis
- **Basal zone**
  - Idiopathic pulmonary fibrosis
  - Lymphangitis carcinomatosis
  - Drugs
  - Connective tissue disorders

Causes of calcification on chest X-ray

- **Lymph node calcification**
  - Sarcoidosis
  - Silicosis
  - Tuberculosis
- **Parenchymal calcification**
  - Healed tuberculous lesions
  - Healed fungal infections
  - Previous varicella pneumonia
  - Mitral stenosis*
  - Chronic left ventricular failure*
  - Hyperparathyroidism
  - Chronic renal failure
  - Vitamin D intoxication
  - Benign tumours
  - Busulfan lung
  - Caplan syndrome
  - Alveolar microlithiasis
- **Pleural calcification**
  - Calcified pleural plaques following asbestos exposure, and pleural calcification due to previous haemothorax or TB

*Results in secondary pulmonary haemosiderosis

19.7 PULMONARY VASCULITIS AND EOSINOPHILIA

19.7.1 Wegener's granulomatosis

Small/medium-sized arteries, veins and capillaries are involved with a granulomatous inflammation. Ninety per cent of Wegener's cases present with upper or lower respiratory tract symptoms. Upper airway involvement includes crusting and granulation tissue on the nasal turbinates, producing nasal obstruction and a bloody discharge; collapse of the nasal bridge produces a saddle-shaped nose; cANCA is present is 90% of cases (*see also* Chapter 10, Immunology; Chapter 15, Nephrology and Chapter 20, Rheumatology).

- **Respiratory symptoms**: cough, haemoptysis, breathlessness and pleurisy. Stenosis of a main airway may cause severe breathlessness and stridor
- Large rounded shadows may be visible on the chest X-ray and these often cavitate. Pleural effusions and infiltrates may develop
- Seventy-five per cent develop glomerulonephritis and eye and joint involvement are common. Patients may have a typical vasculitic skin rash and mononeuritis multiplex may also develop
- **Prognosis**: untreated, the median survival is 5 months. Treatment with cyclophosphamide and steroids has now reduced mortality to around 10%

19.7.2 Churg–Strauss syndrome

A syndrome of necrotising vasculitis, eosinophilic infiltrates and granuloma formation, there is often a prior history of asthma and sometimes allergic rhinitis. Peripheral blood eosinophilia occurs with eosinophilic infiltrates of the lungs and often the gastrointestinal tract. Vasculitic lesions appear on the skin (purpura, erythema or nodules).

- pANCA is positive in 50%
- Chest X-ray shows nodular or confluent shadows without cavitation
- Treatment is with steroids and/or cyclophosphamide

19.7.3 Polyarteritis and Henoch–Schönlein vasculitis

- Microscopic polyangiitis (MPA) may involve the lungs to produce pulmonary haemorrhage, haemoptysis and occasionally pleurisy; granulomata are not a feature

- Lung involvement is uncommon in polyarteritis nodosa; it consists of pulmonary infiltrates (composed mainly of neutrophils) without granuloma formation
- Pulmonary involvement is a rare feature in Henoch–Schönlein purpura (HSP). The disorder can be associated with streptococcal or hepatitis B (less often with viral or fungal) infections

19.7.4 Connective tissue disorders

- **Rheumatoid disease**: has many pulmonary associations which include bronchiectasis, obliterative bronchiolitis, bronchiolitis obliterans organising pneumonia (BOOP), pulmonary fibrosis, nodules, Caplan syndrome and pleurisy with effusion
- **SLE**: pulmonary fibrosis, BOOP, pleural effusion and shrinking lung syndrome can all occur
- **Systemic sclerosis**: associated with bronchiectasis, pulmonary fibrosis, and aspiration pneumonia (due to dysphagia)

All may cause pulmonary hypertension but this occurs most frequently in systemic sclerosis patients.

Pulmonary vasculitis occurs in association with
- Ulcerative colitis
- Giant-cell arteritis
- Takayasu arteritis
- Behçet syndrome
- Multiple pulmonary emboli
- Infection

19.7.5 Pulmonary eosinophilia

This describes a group of disorders characterised by peripheral blood eosinophilia and eosinophilic infiltrates in the lungs.

Causes of pulmonary eosinophilia

- Churg–Strauss syndrome
- Löffler syndrome
- Drug-induced (eg nitrofurantoin, sulfasalazine, imipramine, phenytoin)
- Allergic bronchopulmonary aspergillosis (ABPA)
- Chronic eosinophilic pneumonia
- Hypereosinophilic syndrome
- Acute eosinophilic pneumonia
- Tropical pulmonary eosinophilia (associated with parasite infection, eg *Strongyloides stercoralis, Toxacara canis*)

Löffler syndrome (simple pulmonary eosinophilia)

Transient radiographic shadows and peripheral blood eosinophilia are seen in association with the passage of parasites (commonly *Ascaris lumbricoides*) through the lungs. The illness usually lasts less than 2 weeks and the eosinophilia is moderate. Symptoms are mild and include cough, rhinitis, night sweats and fever. The condition usually resolves spontaneously.

Chronic eosinophilic pneumonia

Peripheral blood eosinophilia and persistent pulmonary infiltrates occur without any obvious cause.

- The **chest X-ray** is often described as a 'reverse batwing', being the photo-negative appearance of pulmonary oedema
- **Lung biopsy** shows airspace consolidation with an eosinophilic inflammatory infiltrate
- **Symptoms** are more severe than in simple pulmonary eosinophilia. The condition responds to steroids

Hypereosinophilic syndrome

Characterised by very high eosinophil counts (mean 20×10^9/l), the syndrome has clinical manifestations (weight loss, fever, night sweats, hepatomegaly and lymphadenopathy) similar to chronic eosinophilic pneumonia. Cardiac involvement occurs in 60% (producing arrhythmias and cardiac failure).

- Thromboembolism occurs in two-thirds of patients
- Other organ involvement: central nervous system (intellectual deterioration and peripheral neuropathies), GI tract and the kidney (proteinuria and hypertension)
- Steroids are effective

Acute eosinophilic pneumonia

Patients present with an acute illness with fever, myalgia, pleurisy and respiratory failure. The chest X-ray shows diffuse infiltrates, but these are not usually peripheral. The blood eosinophil count is usually normal although the eosinophil count in fluid obtained from BAL is very high. Treatment is with high-dose steroids and ventilatory support.

19.8 MISCELLANEOUS RESPIRATORY DISORDERS

19.8.1 Pleural effusion

Transudates are usually clear or straw-coloured, whereas exudates are often turbid, bloody and may clot on standing. Fluid protein content should be examined: protein levels >30 g/l (or fluid to serum ratio >0.5) and lactic dehydrogenase (LDH) levels >200 IU/l (fluid to serum ratio of >0.6) are consistent with an exudate. pH <7.1 also suggests an exudate.

- Low concentrations of glucose in the pleural fluid compared to serum glucose are found in infection and with rheumatoid arthritis
- In pancreatitis the amylase level may be higher in pleural fluid than in blood
- **Cell content should be examined**. Transudates contain <1000 white cells made up of a mixture of polymorphs, lymphocytes and mesothelial cells. Exudates usually have a much higher white cell count. In bacterial infection this is usually polymorphs but in TB, lymphocytes predominate

- Malignant cells from a primary bronchial carcinoma or from metastatic disease may be found in approximately 60% of malignant pleural effusions
- Any patient with pneumonia who develops a pleural effusion should have the fluid analysed for pH. A pH of <7.2 suggests a developing empyema

Causes of pleural effusion

- **Transudates**
  - **Common**
    - LVF
    - Cirrhosis of the liver
    - Nephrotic syndrome
    - Acute glomerulonephritis
    - Other causes of hypoproteinaemia
  - **Uncommon**
    - Myxoedema
    - Pulmonary emboli
    - Sarcoidosis
    - Peritoneal dialysis
- **Exudates**
  - **Common**
    - Pulmonary embolism
    - *Infections:*
      Bacterial pneumonia
      TB
    - *Malignancy:*
      Primary carcinoma of bronchus
      Metastatic carcinoma
    - *Connective tissue disorders:*
      Rheumatoid arthritis
      Systemic lupus erythematosus
    - *Subdiaphragmatic:*
      Pancreatitis
      Subphrenic abscess
    - *Trauma:*
      Haemothorax
      Chylothorax
  - **Uncommon**
    - *Infections:*
      Fungal
      Viral
      Parasitic
    - *Malignancy:*
      Lymphoma
      Pleural tumours
    - *Connective tissue disorders:*
      Wegener's granulomatosis
      Sjögren syndrome
      Immunoblastic lymphadenopathy
    - *Subdiaphragmatic:*
      Hepatic abscesses
    - *Trauma:*
      Ruptured oesophagus

Other rare causes

- Meigs syndrome
- Asbestos exposure
- Familial Mediterranean fever
- Yellow nail syndrome
- Post-thoracotomy syndrome
- Dressler syndrome

If the cause of an exudative effusion is not apparent, the patient should have further investigation with contrast-enhanced CT thorax and pleural biopsy. Medical thoracoscopy is increasingly performed and allows direct visualisation of the pleura. Biopsies can be taken and if the appearances are of malignancy talc pleurodesis can be performed.

19.8.2 Pneumothorax

Pneumothorax may be classified as either primary or secondary, the latter complicating underlying lung disease. Presenting symptoms are of pleuritic chest pain and breathlessness and the degree of dyspnoea relates to the size of the pneumothorax.

Primary spontaneous pneumothorax usually occurs at rest and the peak age of presentation is in patients in their early twenties. Pneumothorax is much more common in smokers.

Clinical signs of pneumothorax

- Diminished breath sounds
- Decreased chest excursion on the affected side
- Hyper-resonance of percussion note
- Auscultatory 'clicks'

Signs of tension

- Severe breathlessness
- Hypotension
- Mediastinal shift
- Cardiac arrest (often electromechanical dissociation)

Diagnosis

This is made when a visceral pleural line is seen on chest X-ray. In patients with emphysema it must be differentiated from large, thin-walled bullae. In general, the pleural line is convex towards the lateral chest wall in pneumothorax, whereas a large bulla tends to be concave towards the lateral chest wall. CT scan can be used to differentiate between these two conditions.

Treatment

- In a patient who has no underlying lung disease and with no clinical distress accompanying a small pneumothorax, no specific therapy is required but follow-up chest X-ray should be arranged to ensure lung re-expansion
- In all other patients, aspiration of the pneumothorax should be attempted first, except if there are signs of a tension pneumothorax, when a drain should be inserted immediately
- If the pneumothorax recurs despite aspiration, a small-bore chest drain should be inserted. This may be removed when the lung has fully re-

expanded and no air leak (bubbling) has occurred for at least 24 hours
- If the lung fails to re-expand within a few hours then suction should be applied to the drain. Chest drains should not be clamped. Once the lung has been fully re-inflated for 24 hours, and bubbling has ceased, the suction can be discontinued. Provided that the lung remains fully inflated, the drain can then be removed. Removal of the drain too early is likely to result in recurrence of the pneumothorax
- If the lung does not re-expand with chest drain and suction then the patient should be referred for thoracic surgery
- Patients with recurrent pneumothorax on the same side will also need thoracic surgical intervention

19.8.3 Obstructive sleep apnoea/ hypopnoea syndrome (OSAHS)

It is estimated that approximately 1%–2% of adult men and 0.5%–1% of women suffer from obstructive sleep apnoea. The cardinal symptom is daytime somnolence due to the disruption of the normal sleep pattern. This leads to poor concentration, irritability and personality changes and a tendency to fall asleep during the day. Road traffic accidents are more frequent in this group of patients. The problem is exacerbated by night-time alcohol intake and sedative medication.

Pathogenesis

During sleep, muscle tone is reduced and the airway narrows so that airway obstruction develops between the level of the soft palate and the base of the tongue. Respiratory effort continues but airflow ceases due to the obstructed airway; eventually the patient arouses briefly and ventilation is resumed. The cycle is repeated several hundreds of times throughout the night.

- Over 80% of men with OSAHS are obese (BMI >30 kg/m^2). Hypothyroidism and acromegaly are also recognised causes. Retrognathia can cause OSAHS, and large tonsils may obstruct the airway. Patients with OSAHS have higher blood pressure than matched controls

- Patients (or their partners) give a history of loud snoring interrupted by episodes of apnoea. There may be a sensation of waking up due to choking. Sleep is generally unrefreshing
- Patients suspected of suffering from OSAHS have some measure of daytime somnolence made (eg using the Epworth scoring system). Mental concentration is impaired
- Diagnosis is made by demonstration of desaturation (SaO_2 below 90%) associated with a rise in heart rate and arousal from sleep, together with cessation of airflow. The frequency of apnoeic/hypopnoeic episodes per hour is used to assess disease severity. The diagnosis can be made in most patients by home pulse oximetry recordings or by limited sleep studies, but where the diagnosis is in doubt, full polysomnography (sleep studies) may be needed

Treatment of sleep apnoea

- Nocturnal continuous positive airways pressure (CPAP) administered via a nasal mask
- Tonsillectomy if enlarged tonsils are thought to be the cause
- Correction of underlying medical disorders (eg hypothyroidism)
- Weight loss for individuals who are obese
- Anterior mandibular positioning devices are useful in some patients
- Tracheostomy (only as a last resort)

Uvulopalatopharyngoplasty is not generally of benefit.

Once a patient has been diagnosed as suffering from OSAHS, and if they are suffering from excessive daytime somnolence, then the Licensing Authorities should be informed and the patient should refrain from driving. Patients may resume driving once their OSAHS has been satisfactorily treated. Holders of heavy goods vehicle (HGV) licences may also have their licence reinstated once they have been adequately treated.

19.8.4 Adult respiratory distress syndrome (ARDS)

This is a syndrome comprising:

- Arterial hypoxaemia
- Bilateral fluffy pulmonary infiltrates on chest X-ray
- Non-cardiogenic pulmonary oedema (pulmonary capillary wedge pressure <18 cmH_2O)
- Reduced lung compliance

Causes of ARDS

- Sepsis
- Burns
- DIC
- Pneumonia
- Aspiration of gastric contents
- Near-drowning
- Drug overdoses (eg diamorphine, methadone, barbiturates, paraquat)
- Trauma
- Pancreatitis, uraemia
- Cardiopulmonary bypass
- Pulmonary contusion
- Smoke inhalation
- Oxygen toxicity

Management

No specific treatment is available and management is essentially supportive. Supplemental oxygen is given and patients frequently require mechanical ventilation. Pressure-controlled inverse-ratio ventilation is used as this lowers peak airway pressure, reduces barotrauma and creates better distribution of gas in the lungs. With the addition of positive end-expiratory pressure (PEEP) there is greater alveolar recruitment, increased functional residual capacity, better lung compliance and reduced shunt. Turning the patient into the prone position intermittently allows those dependent parts of the lung which are susceptible to atelectasis to re-expand and improves blood flow to the ventilated parts of the lung.

- Inhaled nitric oxide (NO) is a potent vasodilator which causes selective vasodilatation of the ventilated areas of the lung when inhaled at low concentrations
- Use of exogenous surfactant in adult patients has no proved value
- Corticosteroids have been shown to be beneficial in the latter stages of ARDS (characterised by progressive pulmonary interstitial fibroproliferation)

19.8.5   Rare lung disorders

Lymphangioleiomyomatosis

This affects young/middle-aged women and is characterised by non-neoplastic proliferation of atypical smooth muscle resulting in airways and vascular obstruction, cyst formation and progressive decline in lung function. It may occur spontaneously or as part of the tuberous sclerosis complex. Fifty per cent of patients have renal angiomyolipomas.

- Patients present with progressive breathlessness, pneumothorax or chylous effusions
- The chest X-ray may appear normal initially but HRCT shows thin-walled cysts. The condition must be differentiated from histiocytosis X
- Pregnancy and oestrogen replacement are associated with more rapid disease progression
- The only known cure is lung transplantation. Hormonal therapy with progesterone is used to slow disease progression
- Average survival is 10–20 years

Alveolar proteinosis

A disorder characterised by the accumulation of phospholipid and proteinaceous material in the alveoli and distal airways. The male:female ratio is 3:1, with age of onset 30–50 years. Patients present with dyspnoea of effort and cough; occasionally constitutional symptoms (fever, weight loss and

malaise) develop. Haemoptysis and chest pain may occur.

- Chest X-ray shows bilateral infiltrates with air bronchograms in a butterfly pattern
- Bronchoalveolar lavage establishes the diagnosis, yielding milky fluid
- Treatment consists of interval whole lung lavage under general anaesthesia

Pulmonary amyloidosis

The lungs are frequently involved in systemic amyloidosis (most often in primary amyloidosis); either the lung parenchyma or the tracheobronchial tree may be predominantly affected. The diagnosis is usually confirmed by biopsy. (*See also* Chapter 15, Nephrology.)

- **Bronchial tree:** plaques visible on bronchoscopy; leads to breathlessness, wheezing, stridor and haemoptysis
- **Nodules:** may develop throughout the lung parenchyma or a solitary nodule may occur
- **Diffuse parenchymal amyloidosis:** may develop with amyloid deposited along the alveolar septa and around blood vessels; this form is extremely rare

Idiopathic pulmonary haemosiderosis

This condition is of unknown cause and is characterised by recurrent episodes of alveolar haemorrhage, haemoptysis and secondary iron-deficiency anaemia. It may present in childhood with chronic cough, pallor and failure to thrive. Generalised lymphadenopathy and hepatosplenomegaly may occur.

- In the early stages the chest X-ray shows transient blotchy shadows
- Eventually **pulmonary fibrosis** develops, and this is associated with chronic dyspnoea and finger clubbing. Steroids are unhelpful and patients die of cor pulmonale or of massive bleeding

Chapter 20
Rheumatology

CONTENTS

Rheumatology

20.1 RHEUMATOID FACTOR

Rheumatoid factors (RF) are antibodies to human IgG, usually reacting with the Fc portion. Routine hospital tests detect IgM rheumatoid factors, but RF may be of any immunoglobulin isotype (IgM/IgG/IgA).

- **Agglutination tests** (Latex/SCAT): detect only IgM RF
- **RIA/ELISA tests**: can detect any class of RF (IgA, IgG, IgM)

IgM RF is found in

- Normal population (4% overall; 25% of the elderly)
- Chronic infections (usually low titre)
  - Syphilis 10%
  - Leprosy 50%
  - Bacterial endocarditis 25%
  - Pulmonary tuberculosis 5%–20%
- Other 'immunological' diseases
  - Autoimmune liver disease
  - Sarcoidosis
  - Paraproteinaemias
  - Cryoglobulinaemias
  - Transplant recipients
- Connective tissue disorders (often high titre)
  - Rheumatoid arthritis 70%
  - Rheumatoid arthritis with extra-articular features 100%
  - Sjögren syndrome >75%
  - Systemic lupus erythematosus (SLE) 20%–40%
  - Scleroderma 30%
  - Polyarteritis nodosa 0%–5%
  - Dermatomyositis 0%–5%
- Miscellaneous
  - Relatives of rheumatoid arthritis patients
  - Increasing age
  - Transiently during acute infections

In rheumatoid arthritis, RF is an assessment of prognosis rather than a diagnostic test.

20.2 RHEUMATOID ARTHRITIS

Rheumatoid arthritis (RA) is a chronic, symmetric inflammatory polyarthritis. It characteristically involves small joints, and can be both erosive and deforming. Soft tissues and extra-articular structures may also be involved in the disease process. RA is the most common form of inflammatory arthritis. It affects 1%–3% of the population in all racial groups, with a female:male ratio of 3:1. It may start at any age but onset is most commonly in the 40s.

The cause is not known but both genetic and environmental factors are thought to play a part, with genetic factors accounting for 10%–30% of the risk of developing RA. There is an association with HLA DR4 and patients with DR4 tend to have more severe disease.

Prognosis is variable and difficult to predict in individual cases:

- 50% are too disabled to work 10 years after diagnosis
- 25% have relatively mild disease
- There is excess mortality

The following are associated with a worse prognosis:

- Positive rheumatoid factor
- Extra-articular features
- HLA DR4
- Female sex
- Early erosions
- Insidious onset
- Severe disability at presentation

20.2.1 Clinical features

The onset of disease may take several forms:

- Insidious (weeks/months) 55%–70%
- Intermediate 15%–20%
- Acute (days) 8%–15%

Other rare patterns of onset:

- **Palindromic**: episodic with complete resolution between attacks
- **Systemic**: presentation with systemic/extra-articular features
- **Polymyalgic**: symptoms initially similar to polymyalgia rheumatica

20.2.2 Musculoskeletal features

Joints

Symmetric metacarpophalangeal (MCP) joint and wrist arthritis is characteristic but any synovial joint can be involved. RA tends to start in the hands and feet but, in time, most joints of the upper and lower limbs become affected. The cervical spine is involved in more than 30%. Hip or distal interphalangeal (DIP) joint involvement is unusual in early disease.

Characteristic deformities

- Ulnar deviation of MCP joints
- Boutonnière deformities of fingers
- Swan-neck deformities of fingers
- Z deformity of thumbs

Soft tissue involvement in RA

- Tenosynovitis
  - Tendon rupture (extensor more frequently than flexor)
  - Carpal tunnel syndrome (common)
- Ligament laxity
  - Atlanto-axial subluxation (most are asymptomatic)
  - Sub-axial subluxation
- Lymphoedema
  - Rare

20.2.3 Extra-articular manifestations

Extra-articular features may arise in several ways:

- True extra-articular manifestations of the rheumatoid process
- Non-articular manifestations of joint/tendon disease (not specific to RA)
- Systemic effects of inflammation (not specific to RA) (eg amyloidosis)
- Adverse drug effects

True extra-articular manifestations of rheumatoid disease:

- Present in approximately 30% of patients with RA
- Rheumatoid factor is always positive
- Arthritis tends to be more severe

Rheumatoid nodules are the most characteristic extra-articular feature.

Rheumatoid nodules

- 20%–30% of cases
- Rheumatoid factor always positive
- Any site – most commonly subcutaneous at extensor surfaces and pressure points
- Mimic malignancy in the lung and may cavitate
- Associated with more severe arthritis
- Sometimes induced by methotrexate therapy
- The pathology of a rheumatoid nodule involves a central area of fibrinoid necrosis surrounded by pallisading macrophages with a fibrous capsule

Eye involvement is common: 20%–30% of patients have keratoconjunctivitis sicca (Sjögren syndrome). Episcleritis (painless reddening of the eye lasting about a week) is likely to be as common but usually goes unnoticed. Scleritis (reddening and pain) is a manifestation of vasculitis and is uncommon. Repeated attacks of scleritis produce scleromalacia (blue sclera) and the eye may perforate (scleromalacia perforans). This is very rare. In contrast to the spondyloarthropathies, iritis is not a feature.

Vasculitis is usually benign, manifesting as nail fold infarcts and mild sensory neuropathy in association with active joint disease. The much rarer systemic rheumatoid vasculitis carries a significant mortality. Its features include cutaneous ulceration, mononeuritis multiplex and involvement of the mesenteric, cerebral and coronary arteries. Renal vasculitis is unusual.

Cardiorespiratory manifestations: pleural and pericardial disease are common (30%) but asymptomatic in all but a few cases. Less common features include interstitial lung disease and the very rare, and often rapidly fatal, obliterative bronchiolitis. Caplan syndrome (massive lung fibrosis in RA patients with pneumoconiosis) is very rare.

Felty syndrome (splenomegaly, neutropenia and RA) is rare. Patients with Felty syndrome usually have a positive ANA and may have associated leg ulcers, lymphadenopathy and anaemia.

Systemic effects of inflammation

- Malaise, fever, weight loss, myalgia
- Anaemia of chronic disease
- Increased incidence of coronary heart disease
- Osteoporosis (immobility also contributes)
- Lymphadenopathy
- Amyloidosis (now rare)

Non-articular manifestations of joint/tendon disease

- Entrapment neuropathy, most commonly carpel tunnel syndrome, may occur in up to 30% of patients, but is usually mild. It may be the first symptom of RA
- Cervical myelopathy due to atlanto-axial subluxation (rare, but high mortality)
- Hoarseness and stridor due to cricoarytenoid arthritis (rare, but dangerous)

Adverse drug effects

- **Skin rashes**: may be due to non-steroidal anti-inflammatory drugs (NSAIDs) or disease-modifying drugs. Rashes occur in about 10% of patients treated with gold or penicillamine
- **Renal impairment**: due to prostaglandin inhibition, or the much rarer acute interstitial nephritis, may be due to NSAIDs. Proteinuria occurs in about 10% of patients receiving gold or penicillamine but only a few develop nephrotic syndrome. The proteinuria usually resolves after cessation of treatment
- **Gastrointestinal**: NSAIDs commonly cause peptic and intestinal ulceration. Gold may cause stomatitis (common) and enterocolitis (rare). Diarrhoea is common with leflunomide
- **Hypertension**: this can occur with NSAIDs, ciclosporin A and leflunomide
- **Respiratory**: acute pneumonitis may occur with methotrexate or leflunomide
- **Infection**: the anti tumour necrosis factor alpha (anti-TNFα) agents are associated with increased infection rates and may reactivate latent tuberculosis

Other extra-articular features/ associations of RA

- Palmar erythema (common)
- Recurrent respiratory infections
- Pyoderma gangrenosum
- Depression (30%)

20.2.4 Investigations

The diagnosis of RA is based primarily on the history and examination. Laboratory tests and X-rays may be helpful but are rarely diagnostic in early disease. In clinical studies, RA can be diagnosed when four or more of the following are present:

- Morning stiffness >1 hour for more than 6 weeks
- Arthritis of hand joints (wrist, MCP or PIP) for more than 6 weeks
- Subcutaneous nodules
- Characteristic X-ray findings
- Arthritis of three or more joint areas for more than 6 weeks

- Symmetric arthritis for more than 6 weeks
- Positive rheumatoid factor

Radiology

- Early changes
  - Soft tissue swelling
  - Juxta-articular osteoporosis
- Intermediate changes
  - Joint space narrowing (due to cartilage loss)
- Late changes
  - Bone and joint destruction
  - Subluxation
  - Ankylosis (rare nowadays)

Laboratory studies

- Rheumatoid factor is positive in 70%
- Antibodies to cyclic citrullinated peptide (anti-CCP) have a high specificity for RA and can be particularly useful in RF-negative patients
- Most laboratory abnormalities are secondary to active inflammation or drug effects and are not specific to RA. They are used to monitor disease activity and screen for adverse drug effects
- Erythrocyte sedimentation rate (ESR), C-reactive protein (CRP) and plasma viscosity reflect disease activity
- Alkaline phosphatase is often mildly raised in active disease
- Anaemia is common and may be:
  - Iron-deficient: gastric blood loss from NSAIDs
  - Normochromic: with active disease (often with thrombocytosis)
  - Aplastic: rare drug effect (eg aurothiomalate, NSAIDs)
  - Haemolytic: rare as a manifestation of RA, but mild forms common with sulfasalazine
- Immunoglobulin levels may be raised, particularly in active disease
- Complement levels are usually normal, or elevated as an acute phase response
- Ferritin may be elevated in an acute phase response and cannot be used to assess iron status
- Synovial fluid examination is rarely helpful in diagnosis but is often done to exclude other

diagnoses (eg sepsis, gout). Rheumatoid effusions, like those of most other inflammatory arthropathies, contain large numbers of polymorphs

Assessment

Patients are evaluated with regard to disease activity, joint damage and function. Disease activity can be assessed simply by counting the number of inflamed joints, but in clinical studies and when assessing patients for anti-TNFα therapies a composite score such as the DAS28 (**d**isease **a**ctivity **s**core using 28 joints) would be used. This is based on the number of swollen joints, tender joints, ESR and the patient's self assessment:

- DAS28 >5.1: high disease activity
- DAS28 3.2 – 5.1: moderate disease activity
- DAS28 <3.2: low disease activity
- DAS28 <2.6: remission

20.2.5 Drug therapy

Drugs used in the treatment of RA fall into two categories: **symptom-modifying** and **disease-modifying**. The disease-modifying drugs are also referred to as slow-acting antirheumatic drugs or second-line drugs; the newer **biologic agents** also fall into this category. **Corticosteroids** produce rapid improvement in symptoms and may have disease-modifying actions.

- **Symptom-modifying drugs**: reduce pain, stiffness and swelling (eg NSAIDs)
- **Disease-modifying antirheumatic drugs (DMARDs)** have additional actions and will:
  - Reduce pain, swelling and stiffness
  - Reduce ESR and CRP
  - Correct the anaemia of chronic disease
  - Slow disease progression

Other extra-articular features do not respond to disease-modifying drugs, though nodules may regress. Methotrexate is unusual in that it can increase the formation of rheumatoid nodules.

Methotrexate is the DMARD of choice in RA. The aim is to begin treatment with DMARDs as soon as

RA is diagnosed and achieve control of inflammation as quickly and completely as possible. Methotrexate may be used alone or in combination with other disease-modifying agents. Since DMARDs take several weeks to become effective, corticosteroids are employed during this period. Corticosteroids may be given intra-articularly, parenterally or orally.

DMARDs in common use are listed in Table 20.1, together with the necessary parameters for monitoring.

Other agents with DMARD activity include sodium aurothiomalate (gold), azathioprine, ciclosporin and D-penicillamine

Biologic disease-modifying agents

These agents are very effective at controlling the symptoms of RA and reducing joint damage. Their effectiveness is enhanced when used in combination with methotrexate.

TNFα blockers (infliximab, adalimumab, etanercept) and anti-CD20 (rituximab) are routinely used in the UK. Other agents that are effective but not in routine use are interleukin 1 (IL-1) blockers (anakinra) and CTLA4-Ig (abatacept).

The biologic agents are used in severe active rheumatoid arthritis (DAS28 >5.1) when standard disease-modifying therapy has failed. The onset of clinical effects can be rapid compared with traditional disease-modifying drugs (usually apparent within 2 weeks). A fall in DAS28 of 1.2 is regarded as a good response to treatment.

TNFα blockers

- **Infliximab**: chimeric (human/mouse) monoclonal antibody against TNFα – administered intravenously
- **Adalimumab**: human monoclonal antibody against TNFα – administered subcutaneously
- **Etanercept**: TNFα receptor fusion protein consisting of a dimer of the extracellular portion of two p75 receptors fused to the Fc portion of human IgG1 – administered subcutaneously

Adverse effects:

- Immunosuppression: severe infections (mostly respiratory but disseminated tuberculosis can occur). Live vaccines are contraindicated in patients receiving these agents
- Injection site reactions (common but rarely significant)
- Worsening of heart failure
- Antinuclear antibodies develop in about 10% of patients, but clinical lupus is rare
- Demyelination (rare)

Rituximab

- A chimeric mouse/human monoclonal antibody directed against CD20, a cell surface marker found on B lymphocytes. The effect is to deplete B lymphocytes. The time to clinical effect is slower than that for the TNFα blockers, taking up to 16 weeks to become maximal

Adverse effects:

- Infusion reactions
- Immunosuppression

Table 20.1. Disease-modifying drugs in common use

Drug	Monitoring
Methotrexate	Full blood count (FBC), liver function tests (LFTs)
Sulfasalazine	FBC, LFTs
Leflunomide	FBC, LFTs, blood pressure (BP)
Hydroxychloroquine	Ophthalmological

Infliximab and rituximab are usually given in combination with methotrexate. Adalimumab and etanercept can be used with methotrexate or as monotherapy. Biologic disease-modifying agents are also effective in psoriatic arthritis, ankylosing spondylitis and juvenile arthritis.

20.3 SPONDYLOARTHROPATHIES (HLA-B27-ASSOCIATED DISORDERS)

This group of disorders is characterised by seronegative (ie rheumatoid factor-negative) inflammatory arthritis and/or spondylitis. The peripheral arthritis is typically asymmetric, involving larger joints, especially the knees and ankles. Characteristic musculoskeletal features include enthesitis (inflammation at sites of tendon insertion), sacroiliitis and dactylitis. These arthropathies should not be confused with seronegative RA, which is a symmetric small-joint arthritis.

The spondyloarthropathies include

- Ankylosing spondylitis
- Psoriatic arthritis
- Reactive arthritis (including Reiter syndrome)
- Enteropathic arthritis
- Many cases do not fit into these categories and are referred to as undifferentiated spondyloarthritis

Associated conditions

- Anterior uveitis
- Psoriasis
- Inflammatory bowel disease
- Erythema nodosum
- Pyoderma gangrenosum

There is an association with HLA B27 and a tendency for relatives to have other conditions within the group (Table 20.2).

Table 20.2. Associations with HLA B27

Prevalence of HLA B27 in spondyloarthropathies	%
Normal Caucasian population	8
Ankylosing spondylitis	90
Reiter syndrome	70
Enteropathic spondylitis	50
Psoriatic arthritis	20
Psoriatic arthritis with sacroiliitis	50

20.3.1 Ankylosing spondylitis

Typically begins with the insidious onset of low back pain and stiffness in a young man. The age of onset is usually between 15 and 40 years and the male:female ratio is about 5:1. It is less common than RA, with a prevalence of about 0.1%. The prognosis is good.

Clinical features of ankylosing spondylitis

- **Articular**
  - Sacroiliitis is the characteristic feature, but radiological changes may not be evident for several years
  - Spondylitis (100%)
  - Peripheral arthritis (35%)
  - Intervertebral discitis (rare)
- **Extra-articular**
  - Anterior uveitis (25%)
  - Aortic incompetence (4%)
  - Apical lung fibrosis (rare)
  - Aortitis (rare)
  - Amyloidosis (rare)
  - Heart block (rare)

Diagnosis

Definitive diagnosis requires radiological evidence of sacroiliitis, inflammatory spinal pain and limited spinal movement or chest expansion. Since sacro-iliitis may take many years to become evident on X-rays, these criteria have a poor sensitivity in early disease and magnetic resonance imaging (MRI) evidence of sacroiliitis may be diagnostically useful in the early stages.

Investigations

- ESR/CRP may be elevated
- Normochromic anaemia
- Alkaline phosphatase often mildly elevated
- Radiology (see box below)

HLA B27 in diagnosis

This should not be a routine test in back pain. Although a negative result makes ankylosing spondylitis unlikely, a positive result is of little help.

Radiology

- **Sacroiliac joints**
  - Irregular/blurred joint margins
  - Subchondral erosion
  - Sclerosis
  - Fusion
- **Spine**
  - Loss of lumbar lordosis
  - Squaring of vertebrae
  - Romanus lesion (erosion at the corner of vertebral bodies)
  - Bamboo spine (calcification in anterior and posterior spinal ligaments)
  - Enthesitis (calcification at tendon/ligament insertions into bone)

Assessment

A number of indices and scores are used in the assessment of patients both in clinical practice and research. The BAS-DAI is used to identify patients suitable for treatment with anti-TNFα therapies and to assess their response to treatment.

- BAS-DAI (Bath Ankylosing Spondylitis Disease Activity Index)
  - Fatigue

- Spinal pain
- Joint pain
- Localised tenderness
- Morning stiffness
- BAS-FI (Bath Ankylosing Spondylitis Functional Index)
  - Activities of daily living
- BAS-G (Bath Ankylosing Spondylitis Patient Global Score)
  - General well-being in the last week
  - General well-being in the last 6 months
- BAS-MI (Bath Ankylosing Spondylitis Metrology Index)
  - Cervical rotation
  - Tragus to wall distance (a measure of thoracic kyphosis, measured as the distance between the tragus of the ear and the wall with the patient standing with their back to the wall)
  - Lumbar lateral flexion
  - Lumbar flexion (modified Schober's test)
  - Intermalleolar distance

Treatment

- Physiotherapy and regular home exercise
- NSAIDs
- Sulfasalazine or methotrexate help peripheral arthritis but are not effective for spinal disease
- Anti-TNFα therapy is very effective. Used when the BAS-DAI score is above 4 despite NSAIDs
- Surgery (joint replacement, spinal straightening) in end-stage disease

20.3.2 Reiter syndrome

Reiter syndrome is a form of reactive arthritis characterised by a triad of arthritis, conjunctivitis and urethritis. Reactive arthritis usually begins 1–3 weeks after an initiating infection at a distant site. Antigenic material from the infecting organism may be identified in affected joints but complete organisms cannot be identified or grown, and the arthritis does not respond to treatment with antibiotics.

Reiter syndrome is said to be 20 times more frequent in men than in women. This is likely to be an overestimate because cervicitis may go unrecognised. The true male:female ratio is more likely to be 5:1. Post-dysenteric reactive arthritis has an equal sex distribution. The age of onset is 15–40 years.

Recognised precipitating infections:

- **Post-urethritis** (*Chlamydia trachomatis* – 50%)
- **Post-dysenteric** (*Yersinia, Salmonella, Shigella, Campylobacter*)

Clinical features of Reiter syndrome

- **Classic triad**
  - Arthritis
  - Conjunctivitis
  - Urethritis
- **Rare features**
  - Heart: pericarditis, aortitis, conduction defects
  - Lung: pleurisy, pulmonary infiltrates
  - CNS: meningo-encephalitis, peripheral neuropathy
- **Other features**
  - Circinate balanitis (25%)
  - Buccal/lingual ulcers (10%)
  - Keratoderma blenorrhagica (10%)
  - Iritis (chronic cases only – 30%)
  - Plantar fasciitis/Achilles tendonitis
  - Fever/weight loss

Prognosis

- Complete resolution, no recurrence in 70%–75%
- Complete resolution, recurrent episodes in 20%–25% (usually B27 +ve)
- Chronic disease in <5% (usually B27 +ve)

Treatment

- Mild disease: NSAIDs
- Chronic disease may need disease-modifying drugs
- Prominent systemic symptoms may need corticosteroids

20.3.3 Psoriatic arthritis

Chronic synovitis occurs in about 8% of patients with psoriasis. The arthritis may precede the diagnosis of psoriasis in 1 in 6 of these patients. Males and females are equally affected.

Patterns of psoriatic arthritis

- Polyarthritis similar to RA (most common type)
- Distal interphalangeal joints (5%–10%)
- Sacroiliitis and spondylitis (20%–40%)
- Asymmetric oligoarthritis (20%–40%)
- Arthritis mutilans (<5%)

Characteristic features of psoriatic arthritis

- Nail pitting and onycholysis
- DIP joint arthritis
- Telescoping fingers in arthritis mutilans
- Paravertebral calcification
- Dactylitis

Drug treatment

The same approach is adopted as for treatment of rheumatoid arthritis:

- Symptom-modifying drugs (analgesics, NSAIDs)
- Disease-modifying drugs (eg sulfasalazine, methotrexate)
- Anti-TNFα therapy for refractory disease (either in combination with methotrexate or as monotherapy)

20.4 INFLAMMATORY CONNECTIVE TISSUE DISORDERS

20.4.1 Markers in inflammatory connective tissue disorders

Antinuclear antibodies

Antinuclear antibodies (ANAs) are directed against a variety of nuclear antigens and may be induced by certain drugs (hydralazine). Like rheumatoid factors, ANAs can be of any immunoglobulin class (remember that IgG can cross the placenta).

Indirect immunofluorescence is the routine method for detecting ANA. It is highly sensitive and the fluorescence staining pattern can give some indication of the type of ANA/disease present:

- **Homogeneous staining** suggests lupus
- **Speckled staining** suggests mixed connective tissue disease
- **Nucleolar staining** suggests scleroderma
- **Centromere staining** suggests CREST syndrome (ie **c**alcinosis, **R**aynaud' phenomenon, **o**esophageal dysmotility, **s**clerodactyly, **t**elangiectasia)

ANAs are found in

- Drug-induced lupus (100%)
- Systemic lupus erythematosus (SLE) (95%)
- Scleroderma (90%)
- Sjögren syndrome (80%)
- Mixed connective tissue disease (93%)
- Polymyositis (40%)
- Normal population (5%, titres usually below 1:320)

ANA in rheumatoid arthritis suggests Felty syndrome or Sjögren syndrome. ANA against double-stranded DNA (anti-dsDNA) in high titre is virtually diagnostic of SLE. The ANA in drug-induced lupus is usually against single-stranded DNA (anti-ssDNA).

Anti-dsDNA

High titres are specific for SLE; anti-dsDNA is present in approximately 80% of patients with SLE.

Methods of detection

- Radioimmunoassay (Farr assay)
- *Crithidia lucillae* immunofluorescence
- Enzyme-linked immunosorbent assay (ELISA)

Extractable nuclear antigens

These are specific nuclear antigens and therefore are usually associated with positive ANA tests. They are useful in defining the type of connective tissue disease present. Method of detection: counter immunoelectrophoresis or ELISA.

Extractable nuclear antigens

- **Anti-Ro** – Sjögren syndrome, congenital heart block, neonatal lupus syndrome, ANA-negative SLE
- **Anti-La** – primary Sjögren syndrome
- **Anti-Sm** – SLE (20%, very specific: conferring a high risk of renal lupus)
- **Anti-RNP** – mixed connective tissue disease (100%), SLE
- **Anti-Jo 1** – seen in a specific variant of polymyositis
- **Anti-Scl70** – progressive systemic sclerosis (20%)
- **Anti-centromere** – CREST syndrome

Antiphospholipid antibodies

Antiphospholipid antibodies are associated with arterial or venous thrombosis, transient neurological deficits, fetal loss, livido reticularis and thrombocytopenia (Hughes syndrome; see Section 20.4.2). Different antibody isotypes exist: IgG and to a lesser extent IgM isotypes of anticardiolipin antibodies (ACLA) are associated with the clinical features presented.

Antiphospholipid antibodies have activity against a variety of cell membrane phospholipids, and the most commonly measured are those against cardiolipin. Protein complexes such as β2-glycoprotein-1, which have anticoagulant properties, are found on cell membranes, and it is the interaction between antiphospholipid antibodies and these proteins that is likely to explain the development of thrombosis. About 10% of patients with anticardiolipin-associated thrombosis have antibodies to β2-glyco-protein-1 itself. Antiphospholipid antibodies are found in 2% of the normal population.

Antibody levels are measured by ELISA. The presence of antiphospholipid antibodies can also be reflected in false-positive VDRL tests and a prolonged activated partial thromboplastin time which is not corrected by the addition of normal plasma (lupus anticoagulant test). Lupus anticoagulant (LA) and ELISA show 80% concordance. LA detects some antibodies not picked up by ELISA.

20.4.2 Systemic lupus erythematosus (SLE)

A multisystem inflammatory connective tissue disorder with small-vessel vasculitis and non-organ-specific autoantibodies. It is characterised by skin rashes, arthralgia and antibodies against dsDNA. Young women are predominantly affected, with a female:male ratio of 10:1. It is more common in West Indian populations. Ten-year survival exceeds 90%.

Clinical features of SLE
<ul><li>**Common** (>80% of cases)<ul><li>Arthralgia or non-erosive arthritis</li><li>Rash (malar, discoid or photosensitive)</li><li>Fever</li></ul></li><li>**Others**<ul><li>Serositis (30%–60%): pericarditis, pleurisy, effusions</li><li>Renal: proteinuria (30%–60%), nephrotic syndrome less common, glomerulonephritis (15%–20%)</li><li>Neuropsychiatric (10%–60%): psychosis, seizures</li><li>Haematological (up to 50%): leucopenia, thrombocytopenia, haemolysis</li></ul></li></ul>

- Alopecia (up to 50%)
- Raynaud's phenomenon (10%–40%)
- Oral or nasal ulcers (10%–40%)
- Respiratory (10%): pneumonitis, shrinking lung syndrome
- Cardiac (10%): myocarditis, endocarditis (Libman–Sacks)

Investigations for SLE

The FBC may show the following abnormalities:

Abnormalities of FBC in SLE
<ul><li>Anaemia of chronic disease (normal mean cell volume (MCV))</li><li>Neutropenia</li><li>Thrombocytopenia</li><li>Haemolytic anaemia (high MCV, reticulocytosis)</li><li>Lymphopenia</li><li>Aplastic anaemia (rare)</li></ul>

ESR reflects disease activity. CRP usually rises with active disease of the joints or serositis (pericarditis, pleurisy), but in active lupus of other organ systems it may not rise. This discrepancy can be used to differentiate between a flare of SLE and intercurrent infection.

Low C3 and C4 suggest lupus nephritis.

Lupus variants

Drug-induced lupus is more common in men than in women. It is usually mild and always resolves on stopping the drug. CNS and renal disease are rare. ANA is positive but antibodies to dsDNA are not usually present. The pathogenesis is not known, and antibodies to the drug do not occur. The drugs commonly implicated (procainamide, isoniazid and hydralazine) all have active amido groups.

Antiphospholipid antibody syndrome (Hughes syndrome): recurrent venous or arterial thromboses, fetal loss and thrombocytopenia. Libman–Sacks endocarditis and focal neurological lesions (such as cerebrovascular accident (CVA) or transient ischaemic attack (TIA)) in lupus are usually due to anti-phospholipid antibodies.

Treatment of lupus depends on severity and organ involvement.

Treatment of SLE

- Cardiovascular risk reduction
  - Cardiovascular risk is markedly increased so risk factor reduction (obesity, blood pressure, lipids, smoking, exercise) is important
- Sunscreens
  - Sunburn can provoke a generalised flare in disease
- Corticosteroids and immunosuppressive drugs
  - For vital organ involvement
- Plasma exchange
  - In difficult cases with aggressive disease
- Rituximab (monoclonal antibodies against B lymphocytes)
  - Used in severe disease refractory to other treatments
- Anticoagulation
  - For thrombotic features
- NSAIDs and antimalarials
  - (eg hydroxychloroquine) used for arthritis and skin-limited disease

---

20.4.3 Dermatomyositis and polymyositis

Polymyositis is an idiopathic inflammatory disorder of skeletal muscle. When associated with cutaneous lesions it is called dermatomyositis. These condi-tions are rare (5 cases per million). Five-year survival is 80% with treatment. Myositis may also occur with other connective tissue disorders.

Clinical features of dermatomyositis and polymyositis

- **Muscle disease**
  - Proximal weakness
  - Swelling and tenderness of muscles
- **Others**
  - Pulmonary muscle weakness
  - Interstitial lung disease
  - Oesophageal dysfunction
  - Arthralgia
  - Weight loss
  - Fever
- **Skin rash**
  - Heliotrope discoloration of the eyelids
  - Gottron's papules (scaly papules over MCP/PIP joints)
  - Periungual telangiectasia
  - Erythematous macules

Juvenile dermatomyositis differs from the adult form. Vasculitis, ectopic calcification and lipody-strophy are commonly present.

Malignancy

The elderly with dermatomyositis and polymyositis have a higher prevalence of malignancy than would be expected by chance and this is most pronounced in dermatomyositis. There is no association between dermatomyositis/polymyositis and malignancy in children or adults of young and middle age.

Laboratory tests in dermatomyositis/polymyositis

- **Muscle**
  - Elevated muscle enzymes: creatine kinase (CK), aspartate transaminase (AST), lactate dehydrogenase (LDH)
  - Abnormal EMG
  - Biopsy showing inflammation, muscle fibre necrosis and regeneration
- **Autoantibodies**
  - Antinuclear antibodies may be present
  - Anti-Jo 1 is associated with a specific syndrome of: acute-onset myositis; interstitial lung disease; fever; arthritis; Raynaud's phenomenon; mechanic's hands (fissuring of the digital pads without ulceration and periungual infarcts)

Treatment

- **Corticosteroids**: CK falls rapidly but muscle power takes many weeks to improve
- **Immunosuppressives**: methotrexate or cyclophosphamide are used in resistant cases

20.4.4 Systemic sclerosis

Systemic sclerosis is a connective tissue disorder characterised by thickening and fibrosis of the skin (scleroderma) with distinctive involvement of internal organs. It is a rare condition, occurring in all racial groups, with an incidence of 4–12/million per year. It is more common in women (female:male ratio 4:1) and may start at any age.

Some cases may be due to exposure to substances such as vinyl chloride.

Clinical features of systemic sclerosis

- **Raynaud's phenomenon**
  - Initial complaint in 70%
  - Associated digital ulcers and calcinosis (very unusual in primary Raynaud's phenomenon)
- **Musculoskeletal**
  - Arthralgia
  - Erosive arthritis in about 30%
  - Myositis (usually mild, often asymptomatic with raised CK)
  - Flexion deformities of fingers due to skin fibrosis
- **Pulmonary**
  - Fibrotic interstitial lung disease
  - Pulmonary hypertension
- **Renal**
  - Scleroderma renal crisis (malignant hypertension, rapid renal impairment with 'onion skin' intrarenal vasculature)
- **Scleroderma**
  - Early oedematous phase
  - Later indurated and hidebound
  - Affected areas may become pigmented and lose hair
- **Gastrointestinal**
  - Motility can be impaired at any level (smooth muscle atrophy and fibrosis)
  - Oesophagus (reflux, dysphagia, peptic strictures)
  - Gastric dilatation
  - Intestine (bacterial overgrowth, malabsorption, steatorrhoea, pseudo-obstruction
  - Colon (constipation)

Investigations

Laboratory tests include:

- Elevated ESR or CRP
- Autoantibodies
  - Rheumatoid factor positive in 30%
  - Antinuclear factor positive in 90% (homogeneous, speckled or nucleolar staining)
  - Anti-centromere and anti-Scl70 are quite specific
  - Anti-centromere-positive in 50%–90% of limited and 10% of diffuse scleroderma
  - Anti-Scl70 (anti-topoisomerase-I) positive in 20%–40%

Disease patterns

- **Limited scleroderma with systemic involvement – CREST**
  - Scleroderma limited to the face, neck and limbs distal to the elbow and knee
  - Usually begins with Raynaud's phenomenon
  - CREST (calcinosis, Raynaud's, oesophageal dysmotility, sclerodactyly, telangiectasia)
  - Anti-centromere antibody-positive in most
  - Renal crisis rare, pulmonary hypertension more common
  - Better prognosis (70+% 10-year survival)
- **Diffuse scleroderma with limited involvement**
  - Scleroderma involving trunk and proximal limbs as well as face and distal limbs
  - Usually begins with swelling of fingers and arthritis
  - Anti-Scl70 antibodies 20%–40%
  - Pulmonary hypertension rare, renal crisis more common
  - Worse prognosis (50% 10-year survival)

- **Scleroderma without internal organ disease**
  - Plaques: morphoea
  - Linear: coup de sabre

Treatment

- **Supportive**
  - NSAIDs for arthralgia/arthritis
  - Proton-pump inhibitors for reflux
  - Intermittent antibiotics for bacterial overgrowth in the small bowel
  - Vasodilators for Raynaud's phenomenon
  - Prostacyclin or iloprost infusions for severe Raynaud's phenomenon and digital ischaemia
- **Specific**
  - D-Penicillamine can slow the progression of skin disease
  - Steroids and immunosuppressives for interstitial lung disease
  - **Steroids do not help the skin**

20.4.5 Sjögren syndrome

A connective tissue disorder characterised by lymphocytic infiltration of exocrine glands, especially the lacrimal and salivary glands. The reduced secretions lead to the dry eyes and dry mouth of the sicca syndrome. Secondary Sjögren syndrome describes the presence of sicca syndrome and either RA or a connective tissue disorder. About 30% of rheumatoid patients have secondary Sjögren syndrome.

Clinical features of Sjögren syndrome

- **Dryness from atrophy of exocrine glands**
  - Eyes (xerophthalmia), which may lead to corneal ulceration
  - Mouth (xerostomia), with increased dental caries
  - Respiratory, with hoarseness, dysphagia, respiratory infections
  - Vaginal, causing dyspareunia
- **Arthralgia or arthritis**
  - Can be erosive
- **Raynaud's phenomenon**
- **Lymphadenopathy**
- **Gland swelling**
  - In the early stages (eg parotid)
- **Vasculitic purpura**
- **Neuropathies**
- **Renal tubular acidosis** (30%)
- **Pancreatitis**

Laboratory tests

- Anaemia and leucopenia are common
- ANA frequently present
- Anti-Ro or anti-La present in primary Sjögren syndrome
- ESR and CRP reflect disease activity
- Rheumatoid factor positive in most cases
- Polyclonal hypergammaglobulinaemia

Treatment

- **Artificial tears**: plugging of lacrimal punctae in severe cases
- Moistening sprays for the mouth
- **NSAIDs** and sometimes hydroxychloroquine for arthritis

20.4.6 Mixed connective tissue disease/overlap syndromes

Some patients have features of more than one connective tissue disorder and are said to have 'overlap syndromes'. One specific overlap syndrome, mixed connective tissue disease, is associated with anti-RNP antibodies. The clinical features are Raynaud's phenomenon, swollen hands and other features from at least two connective tissue disorders (SLE, scleroderma or polymyositis).

- **Prognosis**: the 10-year survival is 80%. Patients who have features mainly of scleroderma and polymyositis fare much worse, with a 10-year survival as low as 30%

20.5 VASCULITIS

20.5.1 Overview of vasculitis

Systemic vasculitis usually presents with constitutional symptoms such as general malaise, fever and weight loss, combined with more specific signs and symptoms related to specific organ involvement. The diagnosis is based on a combination of clinical and laboratory findings, and is usually confirmed by biopsy and/or angiography.

Aetiology

Infections, malignancy and drugs may all lead to vasculitic illness but, in many cases, the trigger for endothelial injury is unknown. The following mechanisms of endothelial cell injury have been proposed in the pathogenesis of vasculitis:

- **Immune complex deposition**: hepatitis B-associated polyarteritis nodosa
- Direct endothelial cell infection: HIV
- **Anti-endothelial cell antibodies**: Kawasaki disease, Behçet syndrome
- **ANCA-mediated neutrophil activation**: Wegener's granulomatosis, microscopic polyangiitis
- T cell-dependent injury: giant-cell arteritis

Clinical features of vasculitis

- **General**
  - Constitutional (fever, weight loss, fatigue, anorexia)
  - Musculoskeletal (arthralgia, arthritis, myalgia)
- **Related to specific organ involvement**
  - Kidney (glomerulonephritis – manifest by acute renal failure, proteinuria/haematuria); *see* Nephrology, Chapter 15
  - Respiratory (alveolitis, infiltrates, haemorrhage, sinusitis)
  - Neuropathy (mononeuritis multiplex, sensory neuropathy)
  - Gastrointestinal (diarrhoea, abdominal pain, perforation, haemorrhage)
  - Cardiovascular (jaw or extremity claudication, angina, myocardial infarction)
  - Central nervous system (headache, visual loss, stroke, seizures)
  - Skin (livedo reticularis, urticaria, vasculitic lesions including purpura and erythema multiforme)

20.5.2 Classification of vasculitis

The vasculitides are classified according to the size of vessel involved and the pattern of organ involvement.

- **Large vessels**
  - Takayasu arteritis
  - Giant-cell/temporal arteritis
  - Aortitis associated with ankylosing spondylitis
- **Small/medium-sized vessels**
  - Granulomatous:
    - Wegener's granulomatosis
    - Churg–Strauss syndrome
    - Granulomatous angiitis of the CNS
  - Non-granulomatous:
    - Polyarteritis nodosa
    - Kawasaki disease
    - Arteritis/vasculitis of RA, SLE, Sjögren syndrome
    - Microscopic polyangiitis
- **Small-vessel vasculitis**
  - Leucocytoclastic vasculitis: allergic or hypersensitivity vasculitis
  - Henoch–Schönlein syndrome
  - Cryoglobulinaemia
  - Drug-induced vasculitis
  - Vasculitis of RA, SLE, Sjögren syndrome
  - Microscopic polyangiitis
- **Others**
  - Behçet syndrome (vasculitis and venulitis)

Laboratory tests

- ESR/CRP are invariably elevated in active disease
- Normochromic anaemia and leucocytosis (usually a neutrophilia) are common
- Eosinophilia is characteristic of Churg–Strauss syndrome but may occur in any vasculitis
- Assessments of renal function and urinalysis are essential if vasculitis is suspected since renal involvement is one of the most important factors affecting prognosis

Anti-neutrophil cytoplasmic antibodies (ANCA)

These antibodies are directed against constituents of the neutrophil cytoplasm, proteinase 3 (PR3) and myeloperoxidase (MPO). When neutrophils are activated PR3 and MPO move to the cell surface. Antibodies to either granule will cause activation of the respiratory burst and degranulation, particularly in the presence of TNFα, causing endothelial cell damage. ANCA may therefore play a role in the pathogenesis of its associated disorders. Titres often reflect disease activity.

- **cANCA** (cytoplasmic staining pattern, anti-PR3) is found in Wegener's granulomatosis (90% of patients) and microscopic polyangiitis (40%)
- **pANCA** (perinuclear staining pattern, anti-MPO) is found in microscopic polyangiitis (60%), Wegener's granulomatosis (20%), connective tissue disorders, other vasculitides

Other inflammatory disorders can be associated with positive ANCA in the absence of vasculitis (eg connective tissue disorders, autoimmune hepatitis and inflammatory bowel disease); in these conditions the immunofluorescence staining may be atypical or appear similar to pANCA patterns.

Treatment

- **Large-vessel group**: corticosteroids only for most cases
- **Medium/small vessels**: corticosteroids and immunosuppressives (cyclophosphamide, azathioprine, MMF)
- **Small-vessel group**: corticosteroids and immunosuppressives in some cases; certain conditions (eg leucocytoclastic vasculitis) are benign and do not require treatment

Prognosis

The size of vessel involved and presence of renal involvement are the most important factors determining prognosis. Despite treatment with immunosuppressive agents and steroids, up to 20% of patients with systemic vasculitis of the small/medium-vessel group die within one year of diagnosis. Patients with large- or small-vessel vasculitis have a much more favourable outlook.

20.5.3 Polymyalgia rheumatica, giant-cell and other large-vessel arteritides

Giant-cell arteritis is a vasculitis of large vessels, usually the cranial branches of arteries arising from the aorta. Polymyalgia rheumatica is not a vasculitis, but is found in 40%–60% of patients with giant-cell arteritis. Both are disorders of the over-50s and both are relatively common. Polymyalgia has an incidence of 52/100 000 people aged over 50, and giant cell-arteritis of 18/100 000 people over 50. Treatment is with corticosteroids.

Features of polymyalgia rheumatica and giant-cell arteritis

- **Polymyalgia rheumatica**
  - Female:male ratio 3:1
  - Age >50 years
  - Proximal muscle pain (shoulder or pelvic) *without* weakness
  - Early morning stiffness
  - Raised acute phase response (ESR/CRP)
  - Abnormal liver function tests (alkaline phosphatase/gamma glutamyl transpeptidase (GGT))
  - CK normal
  - Synovitis of knees, etc may occur
  - Response to corticosteroids is dramatic and prompt (within 24–48 hours)
- **Giant-cell arteritis**
  - General malaise, weight loss, fever
  - Temporal headache with tender, enlarged, non-pulsatile temporal arteries
  - Scalp tenderness
  - Jaw claudication
  - Visual disturbance/loss
  - Polymyalgia rheumatica
  - Positive temporal artery biopsy (patchy granulomatous necrosis with giant cells)

Takayasu arteritis (pulseless disease)

This rare condition presents with systemic illness such as malaise, weight loss and fever. The main vasculitic involvement is of the aorta and its main branches, producing arm claudication, absent pulses and bruits. Thirty per cent of patients have visual disturbance. Diagnosis is by angiography and treatment involves corticosteroids.

20.5.4 Wegener's granulomatosis

A rare disorder (incidence 0.4/100 000) characterised by a granulomatous necrotising vasculitis.

Any organ may be involved but the classic Wegener's triad includes:

- **Upper airways** (sinuses, ears, eyes): saddle nose, proptosis
- **Respiratory**: multiple pulmonary nodules
- **Renal**: focal proliferative glomerulonephritis, often with segmental necrosis (*see* Nephrology, Chapter 15).

20.5.5 Churg–Strauss syndrome (allergic angiitis and granulomatosis)

A rare systemic vasculitis with associated eosinophilia and asthma. Any organ can be involved but the lung and skin are the most commonly affected. Though corticosteroids are required, the condition of most patients can be controlled without additional immunosuppressives. In some cases, the disease is triphasic.

- **Prodromal**: allergic features of asthma, rhinitis
- **Eosinophilia**: with eosinophilic pneumonia or eosinophilic gastroenteritis
- **Systemic vasculitis**

ANCA +ve in 60% Smalls medium vessel

20.5.6 Polyarteritis nodosa *vasculitis*

Primary necrotising vasculitis of small/medium-sized vessels with formation of microaneurysms. It is uncommon, with an incidence of 5–9 per million, but it may be as much as 10 times more frequent in areas where hepatitis B is endemic. Presentation is usually with constitutional symptoms. Any organ may be involved but commonly skin, peripheral nerves, kidney, gut and joints are affected. Treatment is with corticosteroids and immunosuppressives.

- Hepatitis B surface antigen is present in 30% of cases worldwide, but <10% in the UK
- Mild eosinophilia may be present
- LFTs often abnormal
- ANCA is positive in <10%
- Renal disease is typically manifest by accelerated-phase hypertension and renal

infarcts; glomerulonephritis is less common and is seen in ANCA-positive overlap syndromes

20.5.7 Microscopic polyangiitis (microscopic polyarteritis)

Usually presents between the ages of 40 and 60 with constitutional illness and renal disease. Though classified with the medium/small-vessel disorders, microscopic angiitis tends to affect small arteries and arterioles of the kidney. Organs involved include:

- **Kidney**: glomerulonephritis (*see* Nephrology, Chapter 15) as for Wegener's granulomatosis
- **Skin**: palpable purpura
- **Lung**: infiltrates, haemoptysis, haemorrhage
- **Gut**, **eye** or **peripheral nerves** can also be involved

ANCA is positive in most cases: pANCA in 60% and cANCA in 40%.

20.5.8 Kawasaki disease

An acute febrile illness with systemic vasculitis which mainly affects children under the age of 5 years. The peak onset is at 1.5 years and it has an incidence of about 6/100 000 in the under-5s. It is more common and more severe in males. The cause is not known but its occasional occurrence in mini-epidemics suggests an infectious agent. (*Rickettsia* has been implicated.)

Clinical features of Kawasaki disease

- Fever
  - (Followed by thrombocytosis)
- Mucocutaneous
  - Rashes, red cracked lips, strawberry tongue, conjunctivitis
- Vasculitis
  - With coronary aneurysm formation
  - Myocardial infarctions in 2.5%
- Lymphadenopathy
  - (Especially cervical)

Treatment differs from most other vasculitides. Corticosteroids are contraindicated since they increase coronary aneurysms. Anti-inflammatory doses of aspirin are used during the acute febrile phase and antiplatelet doses are given once the fever resolves and thrombocytosis occurs. Intravenous immunoglobulin is also effective.

20.5.9 Behçet syndrome

Behçet syndrome is a rare condition most commonly found in Turkey and the eastern Mediterranean where there is a strong association with HLAB5. There is an equal sex ratio but the disease is more severe in males. The pathological findings are of immune-mediated occlusive vasculitis and venulitis. The diagnosis is based on clinical features.

Main clinical features

- Recurrent oral ulceration (100%)
- Recurrent painful genital ulceration (80%)
- Recurrent iritis (60%–70%)
- Skin lesions (60%–80%)

Other features

- Cutaneous vasculitis
- Thrombophlebitis
- Pathergy reaction (red papules >2 mm at sites of needle pricks after 48 hours)
- Erythema nodosum
- Arthritis (usually non-erosive, asymmetric, lower limb)
- Neurological involvement (aseptic meningitis, ataxia, pseudobulbar palsy)
- Gastrointestinal involvement

20.6 CRYSTAL ARTHROPATHIES AND OSTEOARTHRITIS

20.6.1 Gout

Hyperuricaemia is common and usually asymptomatic, but in some individuals uric acid crystals form within joints or soft tissues, leading a variety of diseases.

Clinical features of gout

- Acute crystal arthritis
  - Particularly affecting the small joints of the feet (eg first MTP, usually recurrent)
- Gouty nephropathy
  - Tubulointerstitial disease due to parenchymal crystal deposition
  - Acute intratubular precipitation resulting in acute renal failure
  - Urate stone formation (radiolucent)
- Chronic tophaceous arthritis
  - These are aggregations of urate crystals affecting articular, periarticular and non-articular cartilage (eg ears)

Aetiology

Uric acid is a breakdown product of purine nucleotides. Purines can be synthesised from precursors, but significant amounts are ingested in normal diets and released at cell death. Hyperuricaemia arises because of an imbalance in uric acid production/ingestion and excretion.

Causes of gout

- **Primary** (innate)
  - Idiopathic (90% of these are due to under-excretion of uric acid)
  - Rare enzyme deficiencies: eg hypoxanthine-guanine phosphoribosyltransferase (HGPRT) deficiency (Lesch–Nyhan syndrome)
- **Secondary hyperuricaemia**
  - *Increased uric acid production/intake*
    - Myeloproliferative and lymphoproliferative disorders
    - High purine diet, eg purines in beer (even non-alcoholic)
    - Cytolytic therapy
    - Acidosis, eg the ketosis of starvation or diabetes
    - Extreme exercise, status epilepticus
    - Psoriasis
  - *Decreased uric acid excretion*
    - Renal failure
    - Drugs (diuretics, low-dose aspirin, ciclosporin, pyrazinamide)
    - Alcohol
    - Lead intoxication (saturnine gout)
    - Down syndrome

Diagnosis

- Negatively birefringent needle-shaped crystals must be identified in joint fluid or other tissues for a definitive diagnosis
- In chronic tophaceous gout the X-ray appearances (large punched-out erosions distant from the joint margin) are characteristic and may allow diagnosis
- In clinical practice, a characteristic history with hyperuricaemia is often thought sufficient, but there are pitfalls: uric acid may fall by up to 30% during an acute attack; hyperuricaemia is common and may be coincidental

Treatment of gout

- **Acute attack**
  - NSAIDs (colchicine or steroids may be used if NSAID-intolerant)
- **Prophylaxis** (the aim is to reduce serum uric acid <360 $\mu mol/l$)
  - Allopurinol, a xanthine oxidase inhibitor, is the drug of first choice
  - Benzbromarone (a uricosuric agent) can be used if allopurinol is not tolerated
  - Probenecid and sulfinpyrazone are less effective uricosurics
  - Losartan and fenofibrate have mild uricosuric effects
  - All may precipitate acute attacks at the outset of treatment unless an NSAID or colchicine is given

Other management issues:

- Lose weight if obese
- Reduce alcohol intake
- Reduce excessive dietary purine intake
- Identify and treat associated factors (hyperlipidaemia, hypertension, hyperglycaemia)
- Withdraw drugs which cause hyperuricaemia such as diuretics

Indications for prophylaxis

- Recurrent attacks of arthritis
- Tophi
- Uric acid nephropathy
- Nephrolithiasis
- During cytolytic therapy of leukaemia
- HGPRT deficiency

20.6.2 Calcium pyrophosphate deposition disease (CPDD)

This is a spectrum of disorders ranging from asymptomatic radiological abnormalities to disabling polyarthritis. The underlying problem is the deposition of calcium pyrophosphate crystals in and around joints. This is most commonly idiopathic and age-related, but may occur in metabolic disorders, especially those with hypercalcaemia or hypomagnesaemia. Calcium pyrophosphate forms positively birefringent brick-shaped crystals.

Variants:

- **Asymptomatic**: radiological chondrocalcinosis (30% of over-80s)
- **Acute monoarthritis**: pseudogout (usually knee, elbow or shoulder)
- **Inflammatory polyarthritis**: mimicking RA (10% of CPDD)
- **Osteoarthritis**: often of hips and knees but with involvement of the index and middle MCP joints (rarely seen in primary osteoarthritis)

Causes of CPDD

- Hyperparathyroidism
- Wilson's disease
- Bartter syndrome
- Hypomagnesaemia
- Haemochromatosis
- Hypophosphatasia
- Ochronosis

Treatment of CPDD

- Chondrocalcinosis alone needs no treatment
- NSAIDs for arthritis
- Correction of metabolic disturbances (if possible)

20.6.3 Osteoarthritis

Osteoarthritis (OA) is the most common joint disease. It is characterised by softening and degradation of articular cartilage, with secondary changes in adjacent bone. The prevalence of OA on X-ray rises with age and affects 70% of 70-year-olds. Many individuals with radiological OA, however, are asymptomatic.

Common joints involved are:

- Distal interphalangeal joints (Heberden's nodes)
- Proximal interphalangeal joints (Bouchard's nodes)
- Base of thumb (first carpometacarpal joint)
- Hips
- Knees
- Spine

Metacarpophalangeal joint OA suggests a secondary cause (eg CPDD).

OA subsets

- **Primary**
  - Localised (one principal site, eg hip)
  - Generalised (eg hands, knees, spine)
- **Secondary**
  - Inherited dysplastic disorders
  - Mechanical damage (eg osteonecrosis, post-meniscectomy)
  - Metabolic (eg ochronosis, acromegaly)
  - Previous inflammation (eg sepsis, gout, RA)

Treatment

- Exercise
- Physiotherapy
- Occupational therapy
- Analgesics, including NSAIDs
- Intra-articular injection (steroid or hyaluronic acid)
- Surgery

20.7 ARTHRITIS IN CHILDREN

Classifications

- Juvenile idiopathic arthritis (previously termed 'juvenile chronic arthritis' (JCA))
- Systemic connective tissue disease
- Reactive arthritis (eg rheumatic fever)
- Other (psoriatic, viral, leukaemic)

20.7.1 Juvenile idiopathic arthritis

Juvenile idiopathic arthritis is a persistent arthritis of more than 3 months' duration in children under the age of 16. It is one of the more common chronic disorders of children and is a major cause of musculoskeletal disability and eye disease. The cause is not known. A number of distinct clinical patterns of onset are recognised (Table 20.3).

20.7.2 Systemic (classic Still's disease)

The hallmark is a high spiking fever which, with the salmon-pink evanescent rash, is virtually diagnostic. There is usually visceral involvement with hepatosplenomegaly and serositis. Initially the arthritis may be flitting as in rheumatic fever, but in 50% of cases this develops into a chronic destructive arthropathy. This is usually a disease of the under-5s, but adult cases do occur.

20.7.3 Polyarticular

Arthritis of more than four joints. This is probably two distinct disorders. Younger children with negative rheumatoid factor have a symmetric arthritis of large joints (especially the knees), though the small joints can be affected. Older children, usually teenagers, with a positive rheumatoid factor have, in fact, early-onset rheumatoid arthritis.

20.7.4 Pauci-articular

Arthritis of between one and four joints. Again there are two distinct groups: older boys with sacroiliitis and HLA B27 who probably have juvenile-onset ankylosing spondylitis; and younger girls, usually ANA-positive, who may have uveitis. Regular ophthalmological screening is required in this group.

Treatment of arthritis in children

- Physiotherapy and splintage
- Occupational therapy
- NSAIDs
- Disease-modifying agents (eg methotrexate) in persistent polyarticular disease
- Corticosteroids may be needed for systemic disease
- Anti-TNFα therapy for refractory disease

Table 20.3. Clinical patterns of onset of juvenile idiopathic arthritis

	Systemic	Polyarticular	Pauci-articular
Frequency (%)	10	30	60
Number of joints involved	Variable	five or more	four or fewer
Female:male ratio	1:1	3:1	5:1
Extra-articular features	Prominent	Moderate	Rarer
Uveitis (%)	Rare	5	20
Rheumatoid factor (%)	Rare	15	Rare
Antinuclear factor (%)	10	40	85
Prognosis	Moderate	Moderate	Good

Chapter 21
Statistics

CONTENTS

Statistics

21.1 STUDY DESIGN

21.1.1 Research questions

A research study should always be designed to answer a particular research question. The question usually relates to a specific population. For example:

- Does taking folic acid early in pregnancy prevent neural tube defects?
- Is a new inhaled steroid better than current treatment for improving lung function amongst cystic fibrosis patients?
- Are those who smoke more likely to develop cancer?

Random samples of the relevant groups are taken. For example, pregnant women, cystic fibrosis patients, those who do and do not smoke.

Based on the outcome in the samples, inferences are made about the populations from which they were randomly sampled. Statistical analysis enables us to determine what inferences can be made.

Studies are either experimental or observational.

21.1.2 Experimental studies

In experimental studies, individuals are assigned to groups by the investigator. For example, pregnant women would be assigned to take either folic acid or a placebo; cystic fibrosis patients would be assigned to either the new or current treatment. In both of these examples the second group is known as a **control group**.

Note that a control group does not necessarily consist of normal healthy individuals. In the second example the control group comprises cystic fibrosis patients on standard therapy.

Individuals should be randomised to groups to remove any potential bias. **Randomisation** means that each patient has the same chance of being assigned to either of the groups, regardless of their personal characteristics. Note that 'random' does not mean haphazard or systematic.

> **Experimental studies may be:**
>
> - **Double-blind**: neither the patient nor the researcher assessing the patients/treating clinician knows which treatment the patient has been randomised to receive
> - **Single-blind**: either the patient or the researcher/clinician does not know (usually the patient)
> - **Unblinded** (or open): both the patient and the researcher/clinician know

Clinical trials are experimental studies.

21.1.3 Crossover studies

In a crossover study, each patient receives treatment and placebo in a random order. Fewer patients are needed because many between-patient confounders may be removed. For example, even though pairs of cystic fibrosis patients may be chosen and randomised to groups on the basis of their disease severity this does not ensure that the groups will be of similar age or sex.

Crossover studies are only suitable for chronic disorders that are not cured but for which treatment may give temporary relief. There should be no carryover effect of the treatment from one treatment period to the next.

21.1.4 Observational studies

In observational studies the groups being compared are already defined (eg smokers and non-smokers) and the study merely observes what happens.

Case–control, cross-sectional and **cohort** are particular types of observational studies that, respectively, consider features of the past, the present and the future to try to identify differences between the groups.

- If we take groups of individuals with and without cancer with the aim of identifying different features in their past that might explain a causal route for the cancer, this is a **case–control** study
- If we take groups of smokers and non-smokers and follow them forward in time to see whether one group is more prone to cancer, then this is a **cohort** study

21.1.5 Confounding

Confounding may be an important source of error. A confounding factor is a background variable (ie something not of direct interest) that:

- is different between the groups being compared

and

- affects the outcome being studied

For example, in a study to compare the effect of folic acid supplementation in early pregnancy on neural tube defects, age will be a confounding factor if:

- either the folic acid or placebo group tends to consist of older women

and

- older women are more, or less, likely to have a child with a neural tube defect

When studying the effects of a new inhaled steroid against standard therapy for cystic fibrosis patients,

disease severity will be a confounder if:

- one of the groups (new steroid/standard therapy) consists of more severely affected patients

and

- disease severity affects the outcome measure (lung function)

In the comparison of cancer rates between smokers and non-smokers, diet will be a confounder if:

- smokers eat less fruit and vegetables

and

- eating more fruit and vegetables reduces the risk of contracting cancer

If a difference is found between the groups (folic acid/placebo, new steroid/standard therapy and smokers/non-smokers) we will not know whether the differences are, respectively, due to folic acid or age, to the potency of the new steroid or the severity of disease in the patient, or to smoking or diet.

Confounding may be avoided by matching individuals in the groups according to potential confounders. For example, we could age-match folic acid and placebo pairs or deliberately recruit smokers and non-smokers with similar fruit and vegetable consumption. We could find pairs of cystic fibrosis patients of similar disease severity and randomly allocate one of each pair to receive the new steroid while the other receives standard therapy.

21.2 DISTRIBUTIONS

21.2.1 Types of data

Data may be either categoric or numeric.

- With **categoric** variables each individual lies in one category
- **Numeric** data are measured on a number scale

Ranks give the order of increasing magnitude of

numeric variables. For example:

Sample of seven readings:

2.3   5.0   3.9   1.3   −2.1   1.3   4.2

In order of magnitude:

−2.1   1.3   1.3   2.3   3.9   4.2   5.0

Ranks:

1   2.5   2.5   4   5   6   7

Note that there are seven values in the sample and the largest value has rank 7. Where there are ties (for example, the two values 1.3), the ranks are averaged between the tied values.

The **mode** is the value that occurs most often. In the example above:

Mode = 1.3

The **median** is the middle value when the values are ranked. In the example above:

Median = 2.3

The **mean** is the arithmetic average. In the example above:

$$\text{Mean} = \frac{2.3 + 5.0 + 3.9 + 1.3 - 2.1 + 1.3 + 4.2}{7}$$

$$= \frac{15.9}{7} = 2.27$$

21.2.2 Skewed distributions

The distribution of a set of values may be asymmetric or skewed (Figure 21.1).

In a sample of this type the mean is 'pulled towards' the values in the outlying tail of the distribution and is unrepresentative of the bulk of the data.

Note that the skew is named according to the direction in which the tail points. In Figure 21.1a, the tail points to the left, to negative values and downwards.

If the distribution is skewed then the median is preferable as a summary of the data.

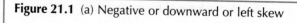
Figure 21.1 (a) Negative or downward or left skew (b) Positive or upward or right skew

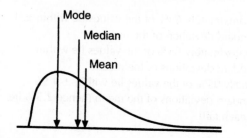

21.2.3 Normal distribution

The normal distribution is symmetric and bell-shaped (Figure 21.2). The normal distribution is sometimes called the Gaussian distribution.

Figure 21.2 Normal distribution

21.2.4 Standard deviation

The standard deviation ($= \sqrt{\text{variance}}$) gives a measure of the spread of the distribution values. The smaller the standard deviation (or variance) the more tightly grouped the values (Figure 21.3).

If the values are normally distributed, then:

- Approximately 68% of the values lie within ± 1 standard deviation of the mean
- Approximately 95% of the values lie within ± 2 standard deviations of the mean
- Exactly 95% of the values lie within ± 1.96 standard deviations of the mean (hence 2.5% lie in each tail)

21.3 CONFIDENCE INTERVALS

21.3.1 Standard error of the mean (SEM)

Often abbreviated to 'standard error' (SE), this is a measure of how precisely the sample mean approximates the population mean.

$$\text{Standard error} = \frac{\text{standard deviation}}{\sqrt{n}}$$

where n is the sample size

The standard error is smaller for larger sample sizes (ie as n increases, SEM decreases). The more observations in the sample (the bigger the value of n) the more precisely the sample mean estimates the population mean (ie the less the error).

The SEM can be used to construct **confidence intervals**:

- The interval (mean ± 1.96 SEM) is a 95% confidence interval for the population mean
- The interval (mean ± 2 SEM) is an approximate 95% confidence interval for the population mean
- The interval (mean ± 1.64 SEM) is a 90% confidence interval for the population mean

There is a 5%, or 0.05, or a 1 in 20 chance that the true mean lies outside the 95% confidence interval:

- 'We are 95% confident that the true mean lies inside the interval'

There is a 10%, or 0.1, or 1 in 10 chance that the true mean lies outside the 90% confidence

Figure 21.3 (a) Small standard deviation.   (b) Large standard deviation

interval:

- 'We are 90% confident that the true mean lies inside the interval'

Note the difference between the standard deviation and the standard error:

- **Standard deviation** (SD) gives a measure of the spread of the data values
- **Standard error** (SE) is a measure of how precisely the sample mean approximates the population mean

For example, FEV_1 is measured in 100 students. The mean value for this group is 4.5 litres with a standard deviation of 0.5 litres. If the values are normally distributed then:

approximately 95% of the values lie in the range $(4.5 \pm 2(0.5))$

$= (4.5 \pm 1 \text{ litres})$

$= (3.5, 5.5 \text{ litres})$

Standard error $= \dfrac{0.5}{\sqrt{100}} = \dfrac{0.5}{10} = 0.05$

An approximate 95% confidence interval for the population mean FEV_1 is given by:

$(4.5 \pm 2(0.05)) = (4.5 \pm 0.1) = (4.4, 4.6) \text{ litres}$

This means that we are 95% confident that the population mean FEV_1 of students lies in the range 4.4 to 4.6 litres.

Confidence intervals can similarly be constructed around other summary statistics, for example the difference between two means, a single proportion or percentage, the difference between two proportions. The standard error always gives a measure of the precision of the sample estimate and is smaller for larger sample sizes.

21.4 SIGNIFICANCE TESTS

Statistical significance tests, or hypothesis tests, use the sample data to assess how likely some specified

null hypothesis is to be correct. The measure of 'how likely' is given by a probability (p) value. Usually, the null hypothesis is that there is 'no difference' between the groups.

21.4.1 Null hypotheses and p-values

To answer the research questions in Section 21.1 we test the following null hypotheses:

- There is no difference in the incidence of fetuses with neural tube defects between the groups of pregnant women who do and do not take folic acid supplements
- Lung function is similar in cystic fibrosis patients who receive the new inhaled steroid when compared to the patients on current treatment
- Smokers and non-smokers have equal chances of contracting cancer

Even if these null hypotheses were true we would not expect the averages or proportions in our sample groups to be identical. Because of random variation there will be some difference. The **p-value** is the probability of observing a difference of that magnitude if the null hypothesis is true.

Since the p-value is a probability, it takes values between 0 and 1. Values near to zero suggest that the null hypothesis is unlikely to be true. The smaller the p-value the more significant the result:

- $p = 0.05$, the result is significant at 5%
  The sample difference had a 1 in 20 chance of occurring if the null hypothesis were true
- $p = 0.01$, the result is significant at 1%
  The sample difference had a 1 in 100 chance of occurring if the null hypothesis were true

Statistical significance is not the same as clinical significance. Although a study may show that the results from drug A are statistically significantly better than those for drug B, we have to consider the magnitude of the improvement, the costs, ease of administration and potential side-effects of the two drugs, etc before deciding that the result is clinically significant and that drug A should be introduced in preference to drug B.

21.4.2 Significance, power and sample size

The study sample may or may not be compatible with the null hypothesis. On the basis of the study results, we may decide to disbelieve (or reject) the null hypothesis. In reality, the null hypothesis either is or is not true (Table 21.1).

The study may lead to the wrong conclusions:

- A low (significant) *p*-value may lead us to disbelieve (or reject) the null hypothesis when it is actually true – (I) in Table 21.1. This is known as a **type I error**
- The *p*-value may be high (non-significant) when the null hypothesis is false – (II) in Table 21.1. This is known as a **type II error**

The **power** of a study is the probability (usually expressed as a percentage) of correctly rejecting the null hypothesis when it is false.

Larger differences between the groups can be detected with greater power. The power to identify correctly a difference of a certain size can be increased by increasing the sample size. Small samples often lead to type II errors (ie there is not sufficient power to detect differences of clinical importance).

In practice there is a grey area between accepting and rejecting the null hypothesis. The decision will be made in the light of the *p*-value obtained. We should not draw different conclusions based on a *p*-value of 0.051 compared with a value of 0.049. The *p*-value is a probability. As it gets smaller the less likely it is that the null hypothesis is true. There is no sudden changeover from 'accept' to 'reject'.

21.4.3 Parametric and non-parametric tests

Statistical hypothesis tests are either parametric or non-parametric. Choosing the appropriate statistical test depends on:

- The type of data and their distribution
- Whether the data are paired or not

Parametric tests usually assume the data are normally distributed. Examples are:

- *t*-test (sometimes called 'Student's *t*-test' or 'Student's paired *t*-test')
- Pearson's coefficient of linear correlation

An unpaired (or 2-sample) *t*-test is used to compare the average values of two independent groups (eg patients with and without disease, treated versus placebo, etc).

A paired (or 1-sample) *t*-test is used if the members of the groups are paired. For example, each individual with disease is matched with a healthy individual of the same age and sex; in a crossover trial the measurements made on two treatments are paired within individuals.

Non-parametric tests are usually based on ranks. Examples are:

- Wilcoxon tests
- Kendall tests
- Sign
- Spearman's rank correlation
- Mann–Whitney *U*
- Chi-squared (χ^2)

Table 21.1. The null hypothesis

Decision based on study results	Null hypothesis	
	True	**False**
'Accept' null hypothesis	OK	(II)
'Reject' null hypothesis	(I)	OK

Chi-squared is used to compare proportions (or percentages) between two groups.

21.5 CORRELATION AND REGRESSION

Sometimes measurements are made on two continuous variables for each study subject, eg CD4 count and age, blood pressure and weight, FRC and height. The data can be displayed in a scatterplot (Figure 21.4).

21.5.1 Correlation coefficients

The correlation coefficient (sometimes called Pearson's coefficient of linear correlation) is denoted by *r* and indicates how closely the points lie to a line.

r takes values between –1 and 1; the closer it is to zero the less the linear association between the two variables. (Note that the variables may be strongly associated but not linearly.)

Negative values of *r* indicate that one variable decreases as the other increases (eg CD4 count falls with age).

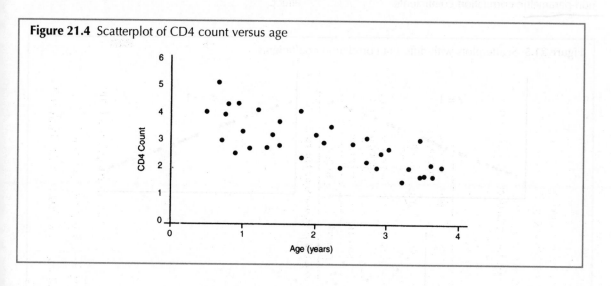

Figure 21.4 Scatterplot of CD4 count versus age

Values of −1 or +1 show that the variables are perfectly linearly related, ie the scatterplot points lie on a straight line.

Correlation coefficients (Figure 21.5):

- Show how one variable increases or decreases as the other variable increases
- Do not give information about the size of the increase or decrease
- Do not give a measure of agreement

Pearson's *r* is a parametric correlation coefficient. Spearman's rank correlation and Kendall's tests are non-parametric correlation coefficients.

- Parametric correlation coefficients quantify the extent of any linear increase or decrease
- Non-parametric correlation coefficients quantify the extent of any tendency for one variable to increase or decrease as the other increases (for example, exponential increase or decline, increasing in steps, etc)

A *p*-value attached to a correlation coefficient shows how likely it is that there is no linear association between the two variables.

A significant correlation does not imply cause and effect.

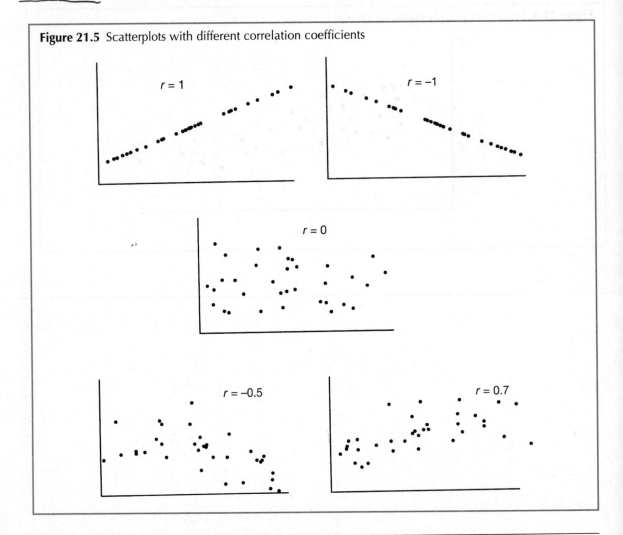

Figure 21.5 Scatterplots with different correlation coefficients

21.5.2 Linear regression

A regression equation ($Y = a + bX$) may be used to PREDICT one variable from the other (Figure 21.6).

- 'a' is the intercept – the value Y takes when X is zero
- 'b' is the slope of the line – sometimes called the **regression coefficient**. It gives the average change in Y for a unit increase in X

- If 'b' is negative then Y decreases as X increases

If the units of measurement change then so will the regression equation. For example, if age is measured in months rather than years then the value of the slope (eg the average change in CD4 for a unit increase in age) will alter accordingly (Figure 21.7).

Figure 21.6 Linear regression line

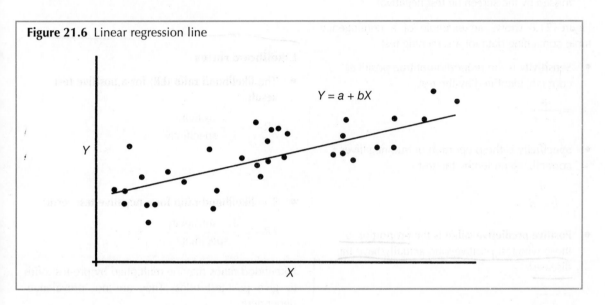

$$Y = a + bX$$

Figure 21.7 CD4 count versus age

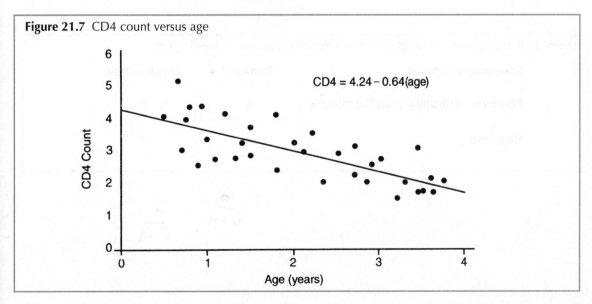

$$CD4 = 4.24 - 0.64(age)$$

21.6   SCREENING TESTS

Screening tests are often used to identify individuals at risk of disease. Individuals who are positive on screening may be investigated further to determine whether they actually have the disease.

- Some of those who screen positive will not have the disease
- Some of those who have the disease may be missed by the screen (ie test negative)

Figure 21.8 shows an example of a contingency table containing data for a screening test.

- **Sensitivity** is the proportion of true positives correctly identified by the test

$$= \frac{a}{a + c}$$

- **Specificity** is the proportion of true negatives correctly identified by the test

$$= \frac{d}{b + d}$$

- **Positive predictive value** is the proportion of those who test positive who actually have the disease

$$= \frac{a}{a + b}$$

- **Negative predictive value** is the proportion of those who test negative who do not have the disease

$$= \frac{d}{c + d}$$

Note that the positive and negative predictive values depend on the **prevalence** of the disease and may vary from population to population.

Likelihood ratios

- The **likelihood ratio (LR) for a positive test result**:

$$LR+ = \frac{\text{sensitivity}}{1 - \text{specificity}}$$

- The **likelihood ratio for a negative test result**:

$$LR- = \frac{1 - \text{sensitivity}}{\text{specificity}}$$

Likelihood ratios may be multiplied by pre-test odds to give post-test odds. They are not prevalence-dependent.

Figure 21.8 Example of a contingency table containing data for a screening test

Screening test result:	Diseased	Disease-free
Positive – indicating possible disease	a	b
Negative	c	d

$$\frac{a}{a + b}, \quad \frac{d}{c + d}.$$

Example

A screening test is applied to patients with and without disease *X*. Of 100 who have the disease, 60 test positive; of 200 without the disease, only 20 test positive.

The following table may be constructed (Table 21.2):

Table 21.2.

Screening test result	Disease X	Disease-free
Positive (indicating possible disease)	60	20
Negative	40	180

Therefore, the following are true:

- Sensitivity = 60/100 = 0.6 or 60%
- Specificity = 180/200 = 0.9 or 90%
- LR+ = 0.6/(1−0.9) = 6
- LR− = (1−0.6)/0.9 = 0.44

- The positive predictive value is 60/(60 + 20) = 0.75 or 75% (ie 75% of those who test positive actually have the disease in this sample)
- The prevalence of the disease in this sample is 100/(100 + 200) = 0.33 or 33%

If a particular patient had a prior odds of 1.5 of having the disease (meaning that he or she is 1.5 times more likely to have the disease than not to have it) then 1.5/2.5 (or 60%) of patients of this type will have the disease. The **posterior odds** of the patient having the disease will thus be determined by the result of the screening test:

- If the test is positive then the odds of having the disease will be 1.5 × 6 = 9
- If the test is negative, the odds will be 1.5 × 0.44 = 0.66

Note that, as expected, the odds of having the disease rise if the test is positive and fall if the test is negative.

A posterior odds of 9 means that the patient is nine times more likely to have the disease than not, which equates to a probability of 9/10 or 0.9 (as opposed to 0.6 before testing). A posterior odds of 0.66 equates to a probability of 0.66/1.66, or 0.4 (as opposed to 0.6 before testing).

sensitivity = 0.6

Specifity = 0.9

+ve PV 60/80

−ve. 200/220

Index

Where more than one page number appears against a heading, page numbers in bold indicate the main treatment of a subject.